Kentucky Place Names

Kentucky Place Names

Robert M. Rennick

THE UNIVERSITY PRESS OF KENTUCKY

To Betsy

Publication of this book has been assisted by a grant from the National Endowment for the Humanities.

Paperback edition published in 1987

Scholarly publisher for the Commonwealth, serving Bellarmine College, Berea College, Centre College of Kentucky, Eastern Kentucky University, The Filson Club, Georgetown College, Kentucky Historical Society, Kentucky State University, Morehead State University, Murray State University, Northern Kentucky University, Transylvania University, University of Kentucky, University of Louisville, and Western Kentucky University.

Editorial and Sales Offices: Lexington, Kentucky 40506-0024

Library of Congress Cataloging in Publication Data

Rennick, Robert M., 1932–
Kentucky place names.

Bibliography: p.
1. Names, Geographical—Kentucky—Dictionaries.
2. Kentucky—History, Local. I. Title.
F449.R46 1987 917.69'003'21 87-31617
ISBN 0-8131-0179-4

Contents

KENTUCKY COUNTIES AND COUNTY SEATS

ADAIR Columbia
ALLEN Scottsville
ANDERSON Lawrenceburg
BALLARD Wickliffe
BARREN Glasgow
BATH Owingsville
BELL Pineville
BOONE Burlington
BOURBON Paris
BOYD Catlettsburg
BOYLE Danville
BRACKEN Brooksville
BREATHITT Jackson
BRECKINRIDGE Hardinsburg
BULLITT Shepherdsville
BUTLER Morgantown
CALDWELL Princeton
CALLOWAY Murray
CAMPBELL Alexandria
CARLISLE Bardwell
CARROLL Carrollton
CARTER Grayson
CASEY Liberty
CHRISTIAN Hopkinsville
CLARK Winchester
CLAY Manchester
CLINTON Albany
CRITTENDEN Marion
CUMBERLAND Burkesville
DAVIESS Owensboro
EDMONSON Brownsville
ELLIOTT Sandy Hook
ESTILL Irvine
FAYETTE Lexington
FLEMING Flemingsburg
FLOYD Prestonsburg
FRANKLIN Frankfort
FULTON Hickman
GALLATIN Warsaw
GARRARD Lancaster
GRANT Williamstown
GRAVES Mayfield
GRAYSON Leitchfield
GREEN Greensburg
GREENUP Greenup
HANCOCK Hawesville
HARDIN Elizabethtown
HARLAN Harlan
HARRISON Cynthiana
HART Munfordville
HENDERSON Henderson
HENRY New Castle
HICKMAN Clinton
HOPKINS Madisonville
JACKSON McKee
JEFFERSON Louisville
JESSAMINE Nicholasville
JOHNSON Paintsville
KENTON Independence
KNOTT Hindman
KNOX Barbourville
LaRUE Hodgenville
LAUREL London
LAWRENCE Louisa
LEE Beattyville
LESLIE Hyden
LETCHER Whitesburg

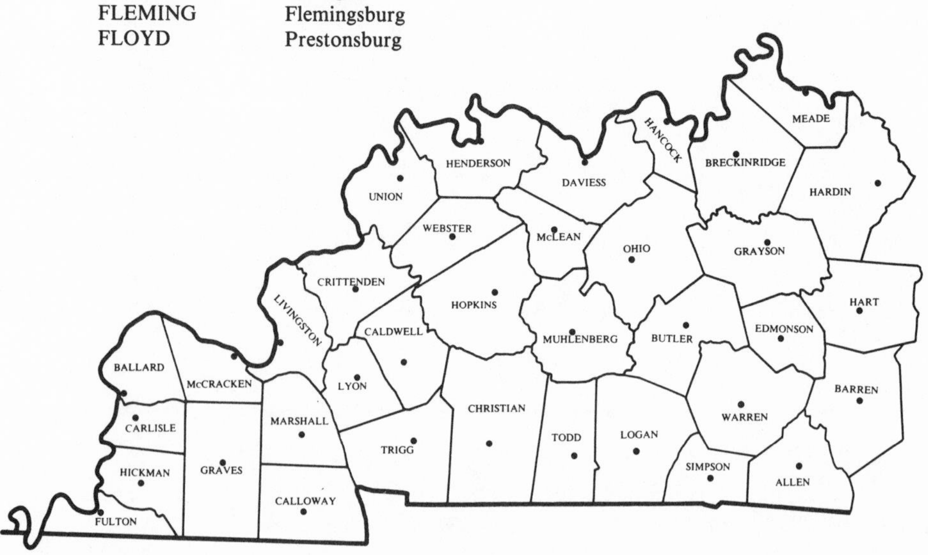

County	Seat
LEWIS	Vanceburg
LINCOLN	Stanford
LIVINGSTON	Smithland
LOGAN	Russellville
LYON	Eddyville
McCRACKEN	Paducah
McCREARY	Whitley City
McLEAN	Calhoun
MADISON	Richmond
MAGOFFIN	Salyersville
MARION	Lebanon
MARSHALL	Benton
MARTIN	Inez
MASON	Maysville
MEADE	Brandenburg
MENIFEE	Frenchburg
MERCER	Harrodsburg
METCALFE	Edmonton
MONROE	Tompkinsville
MONTGOMERY	Mount Sterling
MORGAN	West Liberty
MUHLENBERG	Greenville
NELSON	Bardstown
NICHOLAS	Carlisle
OHIO	Hartford
OLDHAM	La Grange
OWEN	Owenton
OWSLEY	Booneville
PENDLETON	Falmouth
PERRY	Hazard
PIKE	Pikeville
POWELL	Stanton
PULASKI	Somerset
ROBERTSON	Mount Olivet
ROCKCASTLE	Mount Vernon
ROWAN	Morehead
RUSSELL	Jamestown
SCOTT	Georgetown
SHELBY	Shelbyville
SIMPSON	Franklin
SPENCER	Taylorsville
TAYLOR	Campbellsville
TODD	Elkton
TRIGG	Cadiz
TRIMBLE	Bedford
UNION	Morganfield
WARREN	Bowling Green
WASHINGTON	Springfield
WAYNE	Monticello
WEBSTER	Dixon
WHITLEY	Williamsburg
WOLFE	Campton
WOODFORD	Versailles

Acknowledgments

Obviously, this project could not have been carried out without the cooperation and assistance of countless persons in each Kentucky county. To avoid slighting any of those who gave unstintingly of their time and energy to this undertaking, I risk not identifying them at all except as direct sources of information on specific places, and they are mentioned in the bibliography.

Nearly every library and archive in the state and a number of private collections were consulted, most offering useful leads and information. To the librarians and archivists I am also indebted.

I also owe my thanks to a number of newspapers and radio stations, which, following personal interviews, saw fit to publicize the survey, often requesting readers and listeners to contribute needed information to county place name coordinators or directly to me.

Introduction

Several years ago, when I became interested in the study of Kentucky's place names, I learned that the long-term interest shared by others in the subject had never led to a systematic investigation of these names—their origin or meaning, their significance to the residents of the places they identified, or their usefulness in understanding the history and culture of the people of our Commonwealth. I found that the available literature on the subject was limited to occasional passages in obscure or privately printed booklets and in county histories, newspapers, and magazine articles based largely on fragmentary and desultory gleanings from earlier literary works or the casual solicitation and acceptance of the unverified accounts of local residents. I concluded from my readings that a systematic and comprehensive investigation of all Kentucky place names—those of geographic features as well as populated places—was much needed and should be attempted.

I also learned that my interest in place names was shared by persons and groups in other states. By the late 1960s, a group of scholars in various sections of the country were setting the stage for the initiation of a comprehensive survey of all the place names of the United States. Their plans, which have since become formalized as a set of specific guidelines for a systematic national effort, called for the independent gathering and analysis of information in each state, to be funneled ultimately to some national repository of place names. I soon joined the ranks of other place names scholars as the coordinator of the Kentucky Place Name Survey, affiliated with the Place Name Survey of the United States then being organized. My task was to be the identification and location of each of the estimated 100,000 named places and geographic features that exist or have existed in Kentucky and, for each, the assembling of significant data on its geographic situation and history, and the derivation of its name.

My fellow scholars and I agree that the value to many disciplines of a systematic survey of America's place names justifies the time and energy we have dedicated to this effort. The place names of an area and especially the reasons for their application can reveal a great deal to historians, linguists, geographers, folklorists, genealogists, and others, about the people who founded, discovered, settled, or named the places, or who have identified themselves with these places through residence or some other association. Names can be a record of the events that led to the settlement of an area or the establishment of the basic institutions of its people and a reflection of the people's cultural and intellectual development. The values, interests, and experiences of a people have inspired the names they have given to their places, as have their religious beliefs, language patterns, state of economic development, political sympathies and preferences, literary tastes, and recreational interests; their popular attitudes, sentiments, and aspirations; their awareness of the local geographic setting and its significance in their lives.

Names often suggest (though they cannot confirm) the existence of extinct geographic or cultural features. Some extinct community may be recalled by the current name of a road that once extended to that place, while floral or faunal place names may indicate the prevalence or the economic importance of referents that have since vanished. Genealogists, finding in local records reference to extinct geographic features or places, could consult the directory of place names to learn the precise location of some obscure family member or record. Finally, survey efforts were promised assistance by the United States Geological Survey and the U.S. Board on Geographic Names in the hope that we would uncover conflicts or confusion in the several names applied to particular places or the misapplication of names to places on maps.

In short, the ideal once affirmed by the late Robert L. Ramsay for his seminal Missouri place name studies could be applied to our Kentucky project: that the history of a state can inhere in a complete account of its place names, including the dates of bestowal and as much information on the referents as can be determined. History teachers, he once pointed out, might well find that if all other textbooks were lost entirely, we could recover most of the state's recorded history, and much that was not recorded, by studying its place names.[1] Names are enduring monuments to the early settlers of an area or to the persons, places, or events the namers wished to commemorate; they have often outlived the very existence of the places themselves or endured long after the reasons for them have been forgotten.

The Kentucky Place Name Survey was initiated in the spring of 1971. Inspired by the success of colleagues in other states, I envisioned a cooperative effort of many persons and groups in each county of the Commonwealth under the supervision of the county's most competent historian. I recognized the value of using county residents, especially school and college students, to search available documents, county histories, old newspapers, unpublished manuscripts, and other records in local libraries and archives and, with training in oral history techniques, to carry out personal interviews. The several county efforts would be coordinated by a full-time director who would supervise the field operations to ensure some degree of uniformity and would analyze and prepare the survey findings for archiving and publication.

Though an effort was made, and in a sense is still being made, to recruit interested persons and groups in each county for the survey undertaking, no sophisticated research establishment was developed. Rather, volunteers in a number of counties were given lists of names, derived from Thomas P. Field's *Guide to Kentucky Place Names* (Kentucky Geological Survey, 1961), and a brief set of instructions. They were then left largely to their own devices to gather whatever information they could on the listed places. The relative lack of success of our efforts thus far reflects our failure to provide a permanent organizational structure to coordinate the county activities; this was due in turn to our inability to secure sufficient funds for full-time centralized leadership.

The one tangible result to date of our collective efforts to survey Kentucky's place names is this volume, which came in response to the interest of the University Press of Kentucky in publishing the preliminary findings of a study of a selective sample, numbering some two thousand community and post office names. Aside from the more obvious appeal of this opportunity, such a volume seemed the ideal way to publicize the Kentucky survey and to stimulate interest in its efforts, as well as to provide a methodology for future surveyors to ensure statewide uniformity and consistency in data gathering and analysis.

This volume includes the names of Kentucky's 120 counties and their seats, most of its incorporated communities, and a sample of its smaller, unincorporated places. Also included is a sample of post offices that serve or served rural populations without becoming identified with specific communities, and a number of places that had some economic viability in the past but are no longer in existence. Excluded of necessity are most rural neighborhoods with no concentrations of population or foci, as well as most places that, though at one time independent entities, have since become inseparable parts of larger communities.

The communities and post offices included, about one-fourth of all such places known to us, were arbitrarily selected from state and county maps and Kentucky postal records to ensure a fair representation of all counties and of all sections of the state. Generally they are the largest, best known, and/or the most important such places in each county, those that have had some county or statewide historical significance, and those with unusual or inherently interesting names.

Most of the communities included in the book are still in existence; a few are extinct but are included for their historical significance. (Though a place may no longer exist, it may linger in the memory of local oldtimers and its name may continue to be significant to them.) On the other hand, most of the post offices mentioned in the book are no longer in operation though, in most cases, the communities they served, or with which they were identified, are extant.

Most of the names in this volume will undoubtedly seem mundane to the casual reader, perhaps a disappointment to those who expect such a volume to deal largely with odd or colorful names or with humorous accounts of a name's derivation or application. From the outset, we wished to avoid the impression that this is another of those books that are designed for purely humorous effect. Rather, we sought to show how place names and the naming process reflected the characteristic cultural and historical experiences of Kentuckians. Ramsey once wrote that "sentimentalists may regret the destruction of their fondest illusions; but they will find in these and many other [accounts] that truth is not only stranger than fiction but often more interesting and even more romantic."[2]

Since our interest has been essentially historical and geographical rather than philological, the focus of this volume is on the places identified by the names rather than on the names themselves. Lexical and etymological considerations played almost no part in our investigations, for there is nothing inherent in the meanings or derivations of most American names to throw light on the reasons for their application. Such insight depends on a direct knowledge of the place itself, of its early history, and ideally of the person(s) who bestowed the name.

The naming of places in Kentucky, as elsewhere, usually reflected the desire of discoverers, developers, or pioneer settlers to locate, identify, and/or describe their whereabouts in the most appropriate way. Names were not as a rule systematically applied; in fact, "they were often given casually, as the need to identify a [place] arose or as the [place] itself suggested a name, and they often tell us more about the namer than about the [place]."[3] That is, American names, including most of those with obviously non-English origins, are either significant in terms of their meanings to the namers or in their historical association with the places they identify; or else they merely identify these places. In fact, most contemporary Americans do not seem to care why their hometowns were given their names, though the name of one's town may evoke strong feelings of loyalty or devotion or even of revulsion.

The aim of place name scholars as historians has been to trace, for each place in their sample, the namer, the source of the name, the reason for the choice of name, and the events that led to its application. We have learned, however, that researching the naming process is, at best, a difficult undertaking. The naming process is as yet imperfectly known. The namer, his memories and associations, and his language cannot be directly known to the contemporary researcher. Even the place may have changed significantly from the time it was first named. Since very few namers ever recorded their reasons for naming, let alone the events that led to the naming, and traditional accounts have always been suspect, we invariably find ourselves accepting, or even seeking, ex post facto explanations. We may read something into the meaning of a name that may not have been the intention of the namer, even going so far as to infer his motives from our own. But the reason we would have named a place *Pleasant Hill,* say, hardly tells us why he did. And although it might seem obvious that someone had found a cow on *Cow Creek,* that name could have been imported from another place. And *Lovely,* in Martin County, was, in fact, named for its first storekeeper, a Mr. S. L. Lovely, and not, as one might suspect, for some early resident's impression of the landscape.

The ultimate criterion for the selection of the places included in this volume was unquestionably the availability of sufficient information. Most of the following kinds of data had to be available and are included in each entry:

(1) the name of the place in its current approved local spelling; (2) the accepted local pronunciation of the name, recorded in an arbitrary phonetic

system using mostly conventional Roman alphabetic symbols; (3) the location of the place by county and its direction and distance in air miles from the 1980 limits of the county's seat. (Exceptions here are the county seats themselves, which are located in relation to downtown Louisville; places in Jefferson and Fayette Counties, which are located with reference to the courthouse in downtown Louisville and Lexington's New Circle Road (KY 4), respectively; and several places in Kenton and Campbell Counties, which are located from Covington and Newport, respectively.) The title of the U.S. Geological Survey topographic map on which the place appears is also given; (4) the kind of place and a brief description of it; (5) the date of establishment (if a post office or incorporated community) or, if known, the date of the settlement of the place or the earliest known use of the name; (6) other names, if any, borne by the place and a brief explanation of any changes in name; (7) changes in location of over half a mile are mentioned, but in the case of many post offices that simply moved from one store or home to another in the same identifiable community, changes were considered negligible and often are not mentioned; (8) the derivation of the name as applied to the place and, if known, an account of the naming including the identity of the namer and the reasons for the name's application. Some comments on the development of the name and its later use as derived from its association with the place are also included if historically significant.

An elaboration of this classification of data follows.

The name and the kind of place it identifies: A place name may exist alone, as usually when it specifies a populated place, or with a generic as when it designates most natural features (*Jones Creek* or *Smiths Knob*). The generic (Creek, Knob) identifies the kind of place and the specific (Jones, Smiths) distinguishes this particular place from all others. Since the same name can be borne by different kinds of places and the kind of place is not always identified by the generic (*Jones Creek* may be the name of a community or post office as well as the local stream), a designator term must be used to indicate the kind of place it is. This is certainly necessary when no generic is given. The name *Jonesville* alone would hardly indicate whether it applies to an incorporated city, village, hamlet, settlement, or post office—some of the designator terms used in this book. The specific place, of course, is identified by its current or most recent name, though it may have had other names over the years. The principal entry in this volume is the name by which the place is generally known in Kentucky. Other names, including nicknames, are cross-referenced in appropriate alphabetical positions with the principal entries.

Definitions of the principal designator terms: In Kentucky, *incorporated cities* are communities chartered by the state legislature or the respective county courts. *Villages* are concentrations of population in fairly well delineated configurations (i.e. platted or "laid out" towns), with a full complement of support services and institutions. *Hamlets* have definable areas and generally agreed upon boundaries but are focused on only one or two local institutions such as a post office, store, church, or school. *Settlements* or *residential communities* of homes scattered in more or less definable areas have no institutional bases, but their residents share a sense of community. Other designator terms: *residential suburb* or *suburban community, rail center, river* (or *shipping) port,* and *coal* or *mining town* (or *mining camp*) are self-explanatory. *Post offices* will be discussed at some length below. The designator term used in each entry is that which currently applies to the place, though the place may have had other designators in the past.

Pronunciations were recorded when possible from local informants, otherwise from natives or long-term residents of the county in which the place is or was located. The phonetic system (as given on page xxiv) represents each sound in Kentucky speech by a specific symbol. The symbols used were selected for ease of interpretation and economy in typesetting. Current variations in pronunciation are given when obvious differences occur. Historical variations obviously could not be included. The names of extinct places are pronounced according to contemporary local usage.

Dates: Although the date that a place was first settled or founded or its name was first applied would be very useful information in place name study, this is lacking for all but a few of Kentucky's most historically important places. The earliest known date of a name's use is probably available to the more thorough researchers of state and county archives, but lack of time precluded my systematic examination of these resources for each name. Such information, presented in the entries for some communities, was secured by other researchers.

Part of the difficulty in dating a community's founding lies in determining just what this means. Is "founding" the same as "settling"? Many communities grew up around someone's home or farmstead. But just when did it actually become a "community"—when the store or other local institution, upon which the community was focused, was established? We have no problem if "founding" is the filing of a formal town plat or the establishment of the local post office or the incorporation of the town; these acts are documented and the dates are thus readily available.

Given in the entry for each post office in our sample, then, is the date of its establishment and the name of the first postmaster—information derived from the *Records of Appointments of Postmasters, Kentucky*. For most currently incorporated communities, the year of incorporation is also given.

Even harder to determine than the date of the establishment of a place or the first use of its name is the date the place ceased to exist or its name ceased to be known. There is no problem, of course, in recording the date a post office was closed or a town was disincorporated, but when does a community cease to be? When all the institutions that have formed its basis—store, post office, church, school—are gone? When all the residents have moved away? (Most post offices and stores closed when improved roads made nearby towns more accessible.) Some of the places discussed in this book simply vanished, leaving no trace whatever; travelers now arriving at the site would have no idea there ever was a community there. Most of these sites are on dirt roads seldom traveled by any but local farm residents. Yet while such places may no longer physically exist their names may survive in memory.

It is harder still to determine when a name actually died out. The name may be retained in memory, if not in usage, long after the place has disappeared, perhaps by some extra-local association—an historic event or literary allusion. A name is truly obsolete only when no one recalls it or consciously uses it for any reason. Names that become obsolete are usually those never much used anyway, limited solely to maps or official records, or attached only to a local institution that has since disappeared.[4]

Other names and name changes: Some places may have or have had more than one name, even simultaneously—one official and the other a nickname. Sometimes the nickname, by usage, has come to be better known than the first. A typology of alternate names might include: (1) a name not currently in use but at least known to local persons; (2) a name currently in use by some or all local persons but admittedly not regarded by most residents as officially identifying the place (i.e. a nickname); (3) a name currently in use by outsiders but not locally; and (4) former names found on maps or other documents but not used by or even known to local persons.

As the entries in this book reveal, many communities and post offices today bear names that are not those originally given to them, and many have borne several names in their history. Some names have been shortened or corrupted, either by the natural "abrasion of common speech"[5] or in deliberate response to the recognized need for simplicity or convenience, while others have been replaced outright by more meaningful designations.

When its name no longer seemed an adequate means of locating, identifying, and/or describing a place to its residents or of commemorating some significant sentiment or experience in their lives, an attempt might be made to change it. Most likely to be changed were names derived from those of long-forgotten persons or other places known to or admired by early settlers but no longer directly associated with the place or significant to later residents. Also changed were names associated with some abandoned establishment like a railroad station, post office, or military installation. Names may also have been changed in response to a change in the character or appearance of the place; or to commemorate some important event that occurred there after the original name had been applied and gave the place a new significance; or to improve the public image of the place (local persons may have tired of jokes arising from their community's humorous or undignified sounding name); or because newcomers to a site, not knowing what it was originally called, gave it a name of their own; or to avoid confusion with other places with the same or similar names. The names of some places may also have been officially changed to resolve a conflict between the name appearing on a map or other formal document and that by which the place was locally known.

Sometime a place came to be known by more than one name—one identifying the post office and another the community in which it was located. Of the two, the post office name was usually the less important, especially if all it designated was a corner of the postmaster's store or home, or if the post office was short lived. Local persons were more likely to identify the community than the post office as their place of residence. This may explain some communities' apparent acceptance of, or acquiescence in, the names given to their post offices by the Post Office Department in Washington or the errors made in the spelling of the names submitted to the department by poorly educated prospective postmasters or others.[6]

As Cassidy reminds us, names of nineteenth-century post offices more often referred to activity than to places; or, rather, to the place where the postmaster carried out his duly authorized activities.[7] Thus the post office was an "unstable name-feature"; a postmaster's change of residence or business location within the area would lead to a change in the location of the post office, as would the replacement of one postmaster by another who operated a nearby business. Some post offices were established to serve rural households in the open country; communities later grew up around these. More often, however, the community was settled first and then the post office created to serve it.

For the record, it might be useful to review the procedure by which the residents of a nineteenth-century community secured their post office from the Post Office Department.[8] In most cases a leading citizen—the chairman of a citizens' committee to secure the post office—or the intended postmaster would write to the department requesting a formal application for the establishment of the office. The application would be filled out with the following information: the precise location of the requested office (to be accompanied by a map); its distance from other offices already in operation;[9] its location on an existing mail route, the number of the route, and its terminal points, as well as "the number of times a week the mail [was] carried over this route"; the names of the existing offices nearest the proposed one; the name of the nearest navigable waterway and/or railroad line if the new office would be close enough to them to be affected by them, as well as its distance from them; and the approximate population to be served by the new office. The information on the formal application had to be endorsed by the prospective postmaster as well as "the postmaster at the nearest office already in operation."[10]

Department officials would review the submitted information and approve or reject the application. When the application was approved (as it usually was), the proposed name for the new office would be checked against a list of all extant offices to insure against duplication.

Department policy regarding suitable post office names encouraged the adoption of the name of the community in which the new facility was to be established. Exceptions were based on a long-standing rule that no two offices in any state could have the same or similar-sounding names. This was necessary, in the days before zip codes, to avoid confusion to post office personnel.[11] The department also preferred that names already borne by an office in another state whose abbreviation was very similar (e.g. Md. and Me., or N.J. and N.Y.) be avoided, to prevent the confusion that could result from illegible handwriting. Furthermore, if possible, double names were to be avoided, along with those ending in 's. *C.H.* (for county seats) and *Town* and *City* following the name were also discouraged, as were hyphenated names. *Burg, boro,* and *center* were preferred to *burgh, borough,* and *centre.* These preferences were all in accordance with the policies and decisions of the United States Board on Geographic Names (established in 1890), although, as they were often met with considerable local resistance, they were not always enforced.

If the submitted name was rejected, the petitioner was so informed and asked to furnish a list of several other possible names, in order of preference.[12] In the event that none of these was acceptable, a clerk in the Appointment Division would select a name on his own. This, however, was less frequent than is popularly assumed.

Final authorization for the creation of the post office was made on the Order of Establishment, by the signature of the fourth assistant postmaster general followed by the signature of the postmaster general himself. The appointed postmaster was then notified of the formal establishment of his office and duly commissioned to carry out his duties.

Overall, the creation of a post office was left to the discretion of the postmaster general. It was illegal for anyone to establish or maintain a place calling itself a "post office" without his formal authorization following the above procedure.[13]

Current procedures for the establishment of a post office do not differ significantly from those prescribed in the last century. Residents of a community seeking a post office today are expected to write to the Assistant Postmaster General, Bureau of Operations, U.S. Postal Service, Washington, D.C. 20260, stipulating the population to be served and the reason for considering the existing office inadequate or unsatisfactory. There is no set population minimum for the establishment of a new office, but the size of the potential service area can be a factor in the approval of an application. A new office can be created only if existing offices are unable to provide adequate or satisfactory service. In no case can an office be established solely for the purpose of identifying or promoting the local community.[14]

A number of post offices were discontinued, some after only a brief life span, when their activities no longer justified their maintenance, or when, following the death or resignation of the postmaster, the Post Office Department was unable to secure a qualified or willing successor. Some instances of temporary discontinuance or suspension are known to have followed the patrons' boycott of an office or their interference with the appointed postmaster's performance of his duties; in each case, the office was reestablished on the assurance that its services would be used and its personnel, operations, and revenue would be safe and secure.[15]

In the nineteenth century, many a place whose founders had hoped would prosper failed to do so, while a neighboring town, more advantageously located (on a waterway, a railroad route, or a main highway) attracted the trade and population. The post office, if one had already been established, also moved to the second town, to which those persons who remained in the first community would have to journey for their mail. Though it was the usual procedure for the new post office to be given the name of the more prosperous community, instances of the transfer to the second town of the name of the first community, along with its post office, are not unknown. In such a case, the first town would often be distinguished by the prefix "Old," the second place being identified as "New." Later, some of the "Old" communities, having made an economic recovery, successfully appealed to the Post Office Department for the re-establishment of their offices. In the event that that town's original name had moved with its post office to the more prosperous community, a different name was given to the old town and its new office.[16]

On occasion, a formal request might be made by local residents for a change in the location of their post office within the community or even from their community to another. To secure the Post Office Department's permission for such a change, it was necessary to state whether the relocation would entail any additional expense for the movement of mail, whether the move had the support of the office's patrons, and the distance and direction of the proposed site from the original one.[17]

It has generally been the rule, still in effect, that the post office name should conform to that of the community in which it is located or which it serves. Discrepancies reported to the department would usually (though not always) result in a directed change of name.[18] Any request for a name change was, and still is, to be submitted to the Postmasters and Rural Carriers Division of the Bureau of Operations (of the U.S. Postal Service) for approval, subject to the endorsement of the U.S. Board on Geographic Names, our country's final authority on the proper designation of all places within our borders.[19]

The U.S. Board on Geographic Names was established in 1890 by President Benjamin Harrison for the purpose of standardizing all geographic names in the United States.[20] Composed of representatives of the several branches of the federal government concerned with identifying, mapping, and otherwise dealing with geographic sites in this country, the Board's major responsibility has been to settle disputes about the correct name or form of name of any geographic place or feature, such disputes usually being decided in favor of local established usage, with its decisions binding on all government offices, including the Post Office Department (since 1971, the U.S. Postal Service). In cases of local disagreement, preference has been for the "most appropriate and euphonious" name, based on the frequency of occurrence and such practical considerations as the need to avoid confusion with other places similarly named.

This preference for local usage, however, has not always been observed or, apparently, even acknowledged by the Post Office Department. In its first annual report (1891), the Board criticized the Post Office Department's practice of overlooking local usage in post office naming. Nevertheless, in the same report, the Board issued a series of specific recommendations regarding the avoidance of possessives, diacriticals, hyphens, "unnecessary" letters, and such additions as "City," "Town," and "Court House," and expressed preference for single words. Basing these recommendations on the need to seek a conformity in American naming patterns for convenience and expediency, the Board succeeded in exercising its influence upon the naming of new places, though it often failed to effect changes in already established place names. In 1894 the Post Office Department initiated its policy of standardizing all post office names, in compliance with the Board's principles.[21]

In 1906, the Board was given the authority to approve new names. All place names to be officially included on maps and post office lists and other federal records were to be submitted to the Board. A name considered unsuitable—that is, "distasteful" (read "obscene"), too common, or one which inappropriately identified the kind of place—was to be changed to one that would meet the standards. This has more or less been the Board's policy of official place naming ever since.

Popular conceptions to the contrary, the Board's authority to enforce its decisions has been limited to official government agencies; it has no right to dictate a name to a local community. However, as George R. Stewart pointed out, seldom has a local population protested an official decision and demanded restoration of the original name. Ordinarily they have continued the traditional usage regardless of the official designation.[22]

In some of the statements made above, we have seen that preparing a volume on Kentucky's community and post office names has required many arbitrary decisions. The end result is likely to be less than completely satisfying to all concerned. Time and cost considerations obviously limited our sample and the availability of a minimum of reasonably reliable information determined which places were selected. The unevenness of the entries and the tentative or cautious wording of some reflect the unequal amounts of authenticated data.

Some persons will undoubtedly object to our preference for location by distance and direction from the county seat over the use of geographic coordinates. This decision was based on the inordinate amount of time it would take to determine coordinates and the little value they would have in representing location to the readers of this volume. The use of primarily Roman alphabetic symbols to record pronunciation will probably be criticized by some linguistic purists.

Our reliance on oral testimony will certainly displease many. The methods of the oral historian and the folklorist have long been questioned and even discredited by many conventional historians, to whom authenticated data are those derived from written sources. However, as many of us have learned, written records most useful in a study of place names—diaries, letters, legal affidavits, property deeds, land grants, etc.—do not always contain accurate information. Many written accounts originated in oral testimony if not in the direct observations of the recorders themselves. We know that many legal documents were actually prepared from false declarations and were intended to deceive. Finally, most of what we need to know has never been written down and we have no choice but to rely on the memories of knowledgeable local persons.

Similarly, we cannot accept at face value Ramsay's assertion that "place names seldom originate in particular incidents"[23] or attach much significance to his implication that colorful stories were usually invented after the fact to account for unusual-sounding names "when reliable facts were unavailable."[24] While this was undoubtedly true in many instances, it was hardly true in all. Rather, "colorful stories" often related real incidents preserved in the oral traditions of a community's residents.

Few place name scholars (or even historians) are in a position to distinguish historical events from legends or even to rule out seemingly fabricated accounts—at least not from the texts alone and not when they are related as if they were true. Even with the discovery of similar accounts elsewhere, which might suggest a localized version of a so-called "migratory legend,"[25] one cannot always be sure that the same or similar circumstances have not occurred in several areas.

We are, of course, excluding from this discussion those folk accounts that are obviously not taken seriously by those who relate them nor expected to be accepted by others—the so-called "place name jokes"—though some students of place names, desperate to account for some names that seem to defy explanation, have accepted some of these at face value.[26]

For the record, in the Kentucky Place Name Survey equal care was taken in accepting statements from written and oral sources. And certainly a distinction was made between derivational accounts about which we were reasonably certain and those of doubtful authenticity. In no place name study, of course, can absolute guarantees of accuracy be made.

Perusers of other place name dictionaries may miss the classification of place names omitted from this volume. Such typologies, while clearly intended as merely classifications of the names themselves, are sometimes taken by readers to be classifications of name origins or derivations. But such systems are obviously heuristic or even a priori. That *Pleasant Hill,* for instance, is usually considered a "subjectively descriptive" name is hardly sufficient evidence that the namer was inspired by his impressions of the local scenery. Could not the name have been imported from another place, that from which the namer or some other early settler had come? Moreover, the name itself does not tell us why *that* name rather than some other was applied to the place. Why was it not named instead for its first settler or his place of origin, or for any other reason unrelated to the place itself? In any event, readers seeking an adequate classification of names are referred to the introduction to George R. Stewart's *American Place Names.*[27]

At this point we should also caution researchers and readers about drawing certain conclusions from collected raw data on name derivations.

Care should be taken not to infer the popularity of certain names or classes of names among the population of an area at the time of its early settlement or naming from the frequency of use of these names. This frequency may be due solely to the opportunity that a very few persons (e.g. postmasters) had to bestow them. Namers were generally a small minority, usually the better educated or at least the more articulate of the population, and naming preferences simply reflected their personal interests and proclivities.

Though names derived from literary and scriptural sources often reflected the reading interests of the namers, one cannot always assume that the use of a name made famous in literature was inspired by that literary work itself. It might have been a personal name or else one derived from that of another place named for the literary antecedent.

We should also avoid assuming the religious fervor of early settlers or namers from the comparative frequency of scriptural and other "religious-sounding" place names. It may well be that in their search for a unique name, when other, perhaps preferred, names were already in use, namers turned to their Bibles, often the only reading matter available to them. Of course, many communities also took their names from those of local churches.

In spite of Kentucky's rich and colorful history of Indian–white conflict, or even, perhaps, because of it, there are virtually no "genuine" Indian names (i.e., given to a place by Indians themselves) in the state. While bands of Shawnees, Cherokees, Chickasaws, and some other tribes passed through or hunted in Kentucky, few ever actually settled here for an extended period of time. Only one such name is given in this volume, cross referenced with the main entry name for the post office and community of Indian Old Fields. All other "Indian-sounding" names in the state were given by white settlers for a variety of reasons; some were imported from elsewhere and some were simply made up and have no intrinsic meaning at all. (Could *Elkatawa* be an example?)

Considerable time is wasted by researchers in pursuit of the elusive member of a family for which a place may have been named. In many cases the place was named for the family itself, rather than a specific member, though knowing the identity of the local progenitor might be historically useful. Similarly, there is no reason to assume that a post office bearing the family name of its first postmaster was actually named for him. It could have been named for another member of his family, perhaps the dominant family in the community at the time it was named.

More mundane difficulties in our research efforts should also be noted. In seeking written sources, I learned, as some of my Kentucky colleagues have, that county records until very recently were seldom catalogued and were randomly distributed in court houses, libraries, or local or state archives, if not neglected altogether by local officials. Moreover, some informants, who may turn out to have the only information that exists about some place or name, simply did not wish to be interviewed—by anyone. Time considerations were also obviously handicapping. We have all learned that it will take more time than any of us has to locate and examine all the records and interview all the knowledgable informants available. Data specifically on place names are usually not separated from other information on a place in written or oral histories. What is relevant to us must then be abstracted from the whole. In short, given the considerations mentioned in this paragraph, for which I acknowledge Mrs. Constance Cameron, who has pursued the elusive place names of Jefferson County,[28] not all sources that should have been examined were.

Errors occur in the entries in spite of all efforts to check the accuracy of our data. No dictionary will ever likely be error-proof. Take, as the most obvious example, the spelling of many of the names themselves. Early settlers and even literate local officials were not, as a rule, good spellers and many probably did not think that spelling accuracy or consistency in the records was especially important. Moreover, the main source of early- and mid-nineteenth-century names—the registers of each state's post offices maintained by the Post Office Department in Washington—was compiled in large notebooks by clerks with often indecipherable handwriting.

Much of the information provided by older informants with imperfect memories also likely contains many inaccuracies that, for lack of counter evidence, have escaped detection.

In spite of all the difficulties mentioned, I believe that our place name study was well worth the effort. I am confident that Kentucky now has at least a preliminary publication on its community and post office names that will be of some value to others, or at least a helpful precursor to the more systematic and comprehensive survey of all of Kentucky's place names. It is my fervent wish that this humble effort will inspire others to continue this important work.

1. Robert L. Ramsay, *Our Storehouse of Missouri Place Names.* University of Missouri Bulletin 53, no. 34, Arts & Science Series 1952, no. 7, p. 137.

2. Ibid, p. 8.

3. Lester Dingman, "Which Way to Willie's Bottom?" Paper presented at the 1974 annual meeting of the Middle Atlantic Division, Association of American Geographers, p. 2.

4. Frederic G. Cassidy, *Dane County Place-Names* (Madison: Univ. Wisconsin Press, 1968), p. xv.

5. Howard Barker, "Surnames in the United States," *American Mercury* 26 (June 1932): 223–30. According to Ramsay (*Storehouse,* p. 8), "No place name can be adequately interpreted in the light of its present-day form alone, but must always be traced back as far as possible to its earliest recorded or conjectural form." This is ideal, of course, in view of the inadequacy of records.

6. George R. Stewart, *Names on the Land* (Boston: Houghton Mifflin, 1967), pp. 325ff.

7. Cassidy, *Dane County Place-Names,* p. 212.

8. The following account is based on Marshall Cushing, *The Story of Our Post Office* (Boston, A. M. Thayer, 1893), pp. 277–86.

9. There was a rule that no two offices could be less than two miles apart, except on a railroad line where the required distance was one mile and in the case of natural obstructions like an unfordable river or an exceptionally steep hill, where no set distance was given.

10. The latter requirement could be waived at the discretion of the department if it were suspected that the neighboring postmaster had refused endorsement for personal reasons.

11. I noted elsewhere that "One of the reasons for so many odd named towns . . . is that by the time these places were founded or their post offices were established, 'the best names had already been preempted.' So, overly imaginative citizens would come up with words which could not possibly be confused with already existing names." Robert M. Rennick, "The Folklore of Place-Naming in Indiana," *Indiana Folklore* 3, no. 1 (1970): 38. Interior quotation from A. S. Isaacs, "Towns with Strange Names," *Harpers Weekly* 54 (Oct. 1, 1910): 33. Even more often will we find a particular name applying to several post offices at different times; when a particular office closed, its name would then be free for use by another office.

12. A number of applications are known to have included such a list of alternatives to begin with, Post Office officials making their own choice from among them.

13. *Postal Laws and Regulations,* 1887, Title IV, chap. 15, sec. 436.

14. *1970 Postal Manual,* Postal Laws and Regulations, Part 151.

15. Cushing, *Our Post Office,* 286.

16. Rennick, "Folklore of Place-Naming," pp. 37–38.

17. *Postal Laws and Regulations,* 1887, sec. 438.

18. *Laws,* 1970, sec. 842.13.

19. Ibid., sec. 842.11.

20. The following account is based on Stewart, *Names on the Land,* pp. 342–43.

21. Ibid., p. 426.

22. Ibid., p. 354.

23. Robert L. Ramsay, *The Place Names of Franklin Co., Missouri.* University of Missouri Studies 26, no. 3 (1954): 39.

24. Ramsay, *Storehouse,* p. 77.

25. W. F. H. Nicolaisen, "Place-Names and Their Stories," *Ortnamnssallskapets I Uppsala Arsskrift* (1977): 26.

26. Ronald L. Baker, Place Name Jokes," *Newsletter of the Indiana Place Name Survey* 4 (1976): 3.

27. George R. Stewart, *American Place Names.* (New York: Oxford U. Press, 1970).

28. Constance Cameron, "Place Names of Jefferson County, Kentucky (1750–1800)." Master's thesis, U. Louisville, July 1971, preface.

PRONUNCIATION KEY

Symbol	Pronounced as	Symbol	Pronounced as
ae	b**a**t	uh	**u**p
ā	**a**te	o͞o	b**oo**k
ah	st**o**p	ū	bl**ue**
ϵ	d**ar**e	yū	**u**se
eh	y**e**t	ɜ	**ear**n, f**ur**ther (accented syllable only)
ee	b**ee**	ə	**a**lone, system (unaccented syllable)
ih	s**i**t	gh	**g**ive
eye	m**i**le	dj	**G**eorge
oh	**o**ld	ŋ	si**ng**
ow	c**ow**	th	**th**in
aw	**aw**e	t͟h	**th**ere
âh	w**a**ter	ʒ	vi**s**ion
âw	m**o**re		
oi	t**oy**		

ABBREVIATIONS

cent	century	lb	pound(s)	rr	railroad
co	county	mi	mile(s)	ry	railway
co.	company	n	north	reest	reestablished
e	east	pm	postmaster	reinc	reincorporated
est	established	po	post office	s	south
ft	foot, feet	pop	population	sq mi	square miles
inc	incorporated	r	river	w	west
jct	junction	rd	road		

SAMPLE ENTRY

Place name

County in which located

Pronunciation (stressed syllable in italics)

7.5-minute U.S. topographic map on which place occurs

Designator and text

Adolphus (Allen): ə/*dahl*/fəs (Adolphus). This hamlet with po on US 31E, 6½ mi ssw of Scottsville, was named for Adolphus Alexander, a Scottsville attorney, who is said to have represented the Chesapeake & Nashville (now L&N) Ry when it built its line through this place to the co seat in 1886. The community may first have been called Alexander, but Elonzo P. Hinton est the local po on Mar 20, 1888, as Adolphus, since there already was an Alexander po in Kentucky. 101, 488, 1281.

References (list begins on page 329)

Place Names

Aaron (Clinton): *ɛ*/ən (Wolf Creek Dam). This po was est on Mar 11, 1908, by Adison R. Aaron, at a point 1 mi n of its present site on US 127, 7 mi nnw of Albany. Rosie Conner's store occupies the old po site, which is still identified as Aaron on current maps. 1263.

Abbotsford (Henry). See *Sulphur*

Aberdeen (Butler): *aeb*/er/deen (Flener, Morgantown). This village extends n for 1 mi along US 231 from a point just across the Green R from Morgantown. Andrew Duncan, who est the po on July 14, 1871, was a native of Ayrshire, Scotland, and probably named it for the Scottish city. 482.

Absher (Adair): *aeb*/shər (Cane Valley). This extinct po at the jct of KY 551 and Snake Creek Rd, 4½ mi nne of Columbia, was est on June 20, 1884, with Samuel M. Humble, pm, and named for a local family. 1426.

Acorn (Pulaski): *ā*/kawrn, *ā*/kern, *āk*/rən (Shopville). This po is on KY 1675, 1 mi s of KY 80 and 11 mi e of Somerset. Several accounts of its naming exist. In one, J. N. Mayfield was struck by a falling acorn while considering possible names. In another, he was feeding acorns to his hogs when the name occurred to him. In yet another, a stranger, noting the large number of acorns on the ground and the unusually large oak trees that had produced them, suggested the name. Mayfield's wife, Mary, became the first pm on Mar 20, 1896. 1008, 1410.

Adair County: ə/*dɛ*. 407 sq mi. Pop 15,123. Seat: Columbia. Adair Co was est in 1801 from part of Green Co and named for Gen. John Adair (1757–1840), who commanded Kentucky forces in the Battle of New Orleans (1815) and became Kentucky's 8th governor (1820–24).

Adair Court House PO (Adair). See *Columbia*

Adairville (Logan): ə/*dɛ*/vəl (Adairville). This 5th class city, located where US 431 crosses the South Fork of the Red R, 10½ mi s of Russellville, is on the site of one of the first settlements in the county (either Kilgore's Station or Dromgoole's Station [*druhm*/ghūlz], said to have been est in 1788 by James Dromgoole). The site was laid off on Nov 10, 1818, by Gen. Robert Ewing and Michael Traughber, and named by Ewing for Gen. John Adair (see *Adair Co*). The po was est on Apr 20, 1832, with John Farmer, pm, and the town was inc in 1833. 42, 125, 206.

Adams (Lawrence): *aed*/əmz (Adams). This po at the jct of KY 32 and 1760, on the Right Fork of Little Blaine Creek, 6 mi sw of Louisa, was est on Aug 17, 1888, and named for its first pm, James Adams, or his family. 1095.

Adams' Mill PO (Pulaski). See *Pulaski*

Adams Town (Owen). See *New Liberty*

Adamsville (Magoffin). See *Salyersville*

Addison (Breckinridge): *aed*/əs/ən (Rome). This extinct po and L&N RR station lie in the upper end of Holt's Bottom of the Ohio R, 10 mi nw of Hardinsburg. The po was est as Holt [huhlt] on June 3, 1880, with Christopher C. Monroe, pm. On Mar 6, 1889, Lloyd D. Addison, pm since 1886, had the po renamed for him. On Mar 2, 1889, William H. Boltinghouse est another Holt po 1 mi below Addison, on the grounds of the Holt mansion, the birthplace of Joseph Holt (1807–94), a member of Buchanan's cabinet and Lincoln's judge advocate general. The Holt and Addison po closed in 1958 and 1965, respectively. 214, 663.

Adele (Insko PO) (Morgan): *ā*/dehl, *ihn*/skoh (Cannel City). This hamlet with po at the jct of KY 134 and 191, 11 mi s of West Liberty, was est as a station on the Ohio & Kentucky RR and named for the daughter of the rr's first president, W. Delancey Walbridge. The po, est on Feb 18, 1903, with John H. Stricklin, pm, may have been named for a postal inspector. The community is now locally called Adele while the Insko name is applied only to the po. 1115, 1222.

Adolphus (Allen): ə/*dahl*/fəs (Adolphus). This hamlet with po on US 31E, 6½ mi ssw of Scottsville, was named for Adolphus Alexander, a Scottsville attorney, who is said to have represented the Chesapeake & Nashville (now L&N) Ry when it built its line through this place to the co seat in 1886. The community may first have been called Alexander, but Elonzo P. Hinton est the local po on Mar 20, 1888, as Adolphus, since there already was an Alexander po in Kentucky. 101, 488, 1281.

Advance (Greenup). See *Flatwoods*

Aetnaville PO (Ohio). See *Reynolds Station*

Aflex (Pike): *ā*/flehx (Delbarton). This coal town extends along KY 292 and up Cutler Hollow, on the Tug Fork of the Big Sandy R, just above Williamson, West Virginia, and 17 mi ne of Pikeville. The po was est on Mar 16, 1916, with Walter P. Beale, pm, and, like the town, was named for A. F. Leckie, president of the Leckie Collieries there. 1201.

Ages and *Brookside* (Harlan): *ādj*/əz, brook/sahd (Evarts, Harlan). Two almost contiguous coal towns are now served by a single po, on KY 38 and Clover Fork of the Cumberland R, 3½ mi e of Harlan. In Feb 1975 the separate 4th class po's of Ages and Brookside, only 1200 ft apart (the closest in the US) were combined into one called Ages-Brookside, located in the Eastover Mining Co. offices at Brookside. The Ages po had been est on June 8, 1892, with Loyd Ball, pm, and named for Ages Creek, which joins Clover Fork at this point. (The Creek is said to have been named for a Mr. Ages). In 1917 Harlan Collieries was est at what came to be called Brookside, given the name by Amme Keyes Whitfield in 1918 for its location between two brooks. To serve the co. more directly, the Brookside po was est on Mar 24, 1930. 1173.

Airdrie (Muhlenberg): *ād*/ree, *ɛ*/dree (Paradise). This abandoned village on a bluff overlooking the Green R, 10 mi ene of Greenville, has long been locally referred to as Old Airdrie. It was founded in 1855 by Sir Robert S. C. A. Alexander for the workers of his local iron furnace and named for the small city in Scotland that was home to the Alexanders. From 1856 to 1859 the po at *Paradise,* a mi up r, was relocated at Airdrie and by this name the community was inc in 1858. But the furnace failed in 1859 and most of the residents moved away. 244.

Akersville (Monroe): *āk*/erz/vihl (Fountain Run). This hamlet with extinct po is on KY 87, 13 mi wsw of Tompkinsville. According to tradition, when the postal inspector was told the local citizens were having a "slow go" selecting a name for their new po, he suggested they name if Slowgo [*sloh*/ghoh], and by this name the po was est on Oct

10, 1882, with John N. Akers, pm. In 1885, apparently because the name was embarrassing, it was changed to Akersville for the family of a nearby storekeeper. The community has also been known as Highoaka or Highoakie [hah/*oh*/kə, hah/*oh*/kee] from the local Baptist church, so named at one time for its site on a hill, in a grove of tall oaks. Oldtimers still refer to the place by this name. The po closed in 1956. 497, 1395.

Albany (Clinton): *awl*/bən/ee (Albany, Savage). This 5th class city and co seat is on US 127, 105 mi sse of downtown Louisville. When the co was organized in 1835, its seat was at Paoli, now an extinct village 2 mi s of the present courthouse. Here a po was est on July 25, 1833. When an election was held in 1837 to find a permanent location for the seat the site of Benny Dowell's tavern was chosen. While the town is now generally believed to have been named for the capital of New York, it is said that, as the voting began, some of the more mellowed citizens began shouting ''all for Benny'' which got slurred to ''All Benny'' [awl/*behn*/ee], still a variant pronunciation. The Paoli po was moved to this site on Sept 4, 1837, and renamed Albany with Preston H. Leslie, pm. The town was inc in 1838. 966. 1263.

Albrittain PO (Muhlenberg). See *Penrod*

Alcalde (Pulaski): ael/*kael*/də (Somerset). This hamlet with po on KY 769, is just n of Pitman Creek and 2 mi se of Somerset. Benjamin F. Hamilton, a Spanish-American War veteran, liked the sound of this Spanish word for mayor and applied it to the po he est on May 22, 1907. 1410.

Alexander (Allen). See *Adolphus*

Alexander (Fulton). See *Crutchfield*

Alexandria (Campbell): ael/əx/*aen*/dree/ə (Alexandria). This 5th class city and co seat, on US 27 and KY 10, is 7½ mi sse of downtown Newport and 82 mi ne of downtown Louisville. The location is said to have been settled sometime before 1793 by Frank Spilman and his family who probably came from King George Co, Virginia, and may have named it for the Virginia city. The Alexandria po was est on May 17, 1819, with William DeCoursey, pm. By Sept 1819 Spilman had laid out the town and begun selling lots. The city was inc in 1834, and was made the seat of Campbell Co by the act that est Kenton Co in 1840. 94.

Allegre (Todd): *ael*/ə/ghree (Allegre). This hamlet with po is centered at the jct of KY 106 and 178, 8 mi nnw of Elkton. Two related historical derivations and a folk etymology have been offered for its name. In 1884 when residents requested a po, William B. Brewer, then pm of nearby Fairview, was asked by postal authorities to inspect the site and name the new po. He was accompanied by a Colonel Allegree, a Fairview school teacher, and named it for him. Mrs. Ida Kranz, however, insists that the eponym was William Allegree who taught a subscription school, locally called Allegree Schoolhouse, in the vicinity of the proposed po. The folk etymology, called a joke by an older resident, relates that citizens gathered to choose a name spent all day but could not agree. Anxious to go home, one suggested that ''we all agree on something.'' This inspired another to say, ''That's it, let's all call her allegree.'' The *Allegree* po was est on Oct. 20, 1884, with J. A. Brasher, pm. Though the Post Office Department later dropped the final ''e,'' many local persons still use the original spelling. 635, 928.

Allen (Floyd): *ael*/ən (Harold). This 6th class city, inc as Allen City, lies at the confluence of Beaver Creek and the Levisa Fork of the Big Sandy R, 3½ mi s of Prestonsburg. The site was probably settled early in the 19th cent and had a short-lived po called Mouth of Beaver, est on Aug 21, 1854, with Thomas P. Johns, pm. The town developed around the C&O RR station, which opened in 1904–05, and the po, est as Allen on May 16, 1905, which may have been named for T. J. Allen, an early resident and storekeeper (ca. 1880s). The station and community were called Beaver Creek or Beaver Creek Junction until, in 1936, both adopted the po name. Soon after the highway bridge across the river was opened to traffic in 1937, the pop of Allen City, or what is now locally called Old Allen, began to spill across the river into what came to be called East Allen and is now known as New Allen. Most of the community's new businesses and homes and its po are located in New Allen. 678, 976.

Allen Court House PO (Allen). See *Scottsville*

Allen County: *ael*/ən. 338 sq mi. Pop 14,048. Seat: Scottsville. Allen Co was in 1815 from parts of Warren and Barren cos and named for Lt. Col. John Allen (1771–1813), Shelbyville lawyer and state legislator (1801–13). He was one of the 9 officers killed in the Battle of River Raisin, Jan 22, 1813, for whom Kentucky cos were named.

Allendale (Green): *ael*/ən/dāl (Summersville). The existence of this hamlet on KY 61, 8½ mi nnw of Greensburg, may be traced back to the est of the Brush Creek po on Feb 17, 1841. This was named by George Ellmore, the first pm, for its location between Little and Big Brush Creeks, the latter a tributary of the Green R. In 1846 it was moved to and/or renamed Allendale by Thomas J. Town, probably for a local family, and was discontinued in 1863. In 1865 Town moved the early *Summersville* po to the Allendale site and renamed it Allendale. This po closed in 1919.

Allen Springs (Allen): *ael*/ən *Sprihŋ*z (Allen Springs). This hamlet with extinct po on US 231, 8 mi nw of Scottsville, is all that remains of a spa whose curative sulphur waters attracted many visitors in the mid 19th cent. On Feb 18, 1837, James T. Harney est at his boardinghouse the short-lived Allen Springs po, which name the nearby Carpenters Mill po assumed when it moved to this site in 1848. 101.

Allensville (Todd): *ael*/ənz/vəl (Allensville). This important 19th cent village and rail shipping center is on the present KY 102, 1 mi from its jct with US 79, 7 mi se of Elkton. The name was applied around 1810 to a place near its present site, probably to honor a pioneer Allen family. The Allensville po was est there on Apr 26, 1819, with William B. Scott, pm. When a branch of the L&N RR was completed to the present Allensville site in 1860, the town and po were moved to it, the town becoming known colloquially as New Allensville. It was inc as Allensville in 1867. 168, 225, 1234.

Allock (Perry): *ael*/ahk (Vicco). This settlment with po is on Stacy Branch of Carr Fork Creek, just n of Vicco and 5½ mi ese of Hazard. First called simply Stacy Branch, this was for years the camp for the Carrs Fork Coal Co. and was named for its owners, J. B. Allen and H. E. Bullock. The Allock po was est on July 14, 1920, with Edward H. Griffith, pm. 1186, 1327.

Almo (Calloway): *ael*/moh (Dexter). This rail center with po, 5 mi n of Murray, was probably est and named in the early 1890s by the Nashville, Chattanooga & St. Louis (now L&N) RR. No one knows when or by whom the vicinity was first settled, or why this name was applied to a po that was called Buena when est on Feb 11, 1891, with James W. Craig, pm. The site may first have been called Buena Vista, for reasons unknown, though a beautiful view can be seen from the top of a nearby bluff. On Nov 18, 1892, the po was renamed Almo, which may have been a shortening of Alamo of Texas independence fame. 258, 972, 1401, 1441.

Alonzo (Allen): ə/*lahn*/zoh (Adolphus). This hamlet on KY 100 near the Middle Fork of Drakes Creek, 8 mi sw of Scottsville, was probably named by and for Alonzo D. Brashear, who est the po in operation from 1886 to 1905. 101, 1281.

Alpha (Clinton): *ael*/fə (Cumberland City). This po, until Dec 1975, was on old KY 90, 1000 ft s of new KY 90, and 7 mi ne of Albany. It was est on Jan 28, 1852, and named by John M. Davis, the first pm, for a member of his family. It is not known if she was the Alpha E. Davis mentioned in postal records as the second pm. In Dec 1975 the po was moved to a point in Wayne Co midway between its former location, given above, and the old *Zula* po site, but retained the Alpha name. 338, 1263.

Alpine (Pulaski): *ael*/peyen (Burnside). This settlement with extinct po is on US 27, 10½ mi sse of Somerset. About ¾ mi s, a town called Happy Hollow grew up around a coal mine. The local po of this name, est on Feb 15, 1888, with Irvin Williams, pm, was renamed Alpine in 1892, a name apparently thought more suited to the area's high rugged terrain and many pine trees. The po later moved n, and closed in 1976. 1113, 1410.

Alton (Anderson): *âhl*/tən (Lawrenceburg). This village is strung out for about 1½ mi along US 127, from just s of the Franklin Co line, to a point 2½ mi nnw of Lawrenceburg. Alton was once officially called Rough and Ready for Zachary Taylor, in whose administration the po of this name was est on Feb 6, 1850. By this name also the place was inc in 1854. In 1876 the po and town were renamed Alton but no one knows why or for what. Some think that the name refers to the town's altitude, 839 ft above sea level, somewhat higher than the rest of the valley in which it is situated. The town enjoyed considerable prosperity as a trading center until the Southern Ry built Alton Station less than a mile sw and est a po by this name on Apr 22, 1890. Alton's businesses began drifting to the new community that sprang up around the station and much of what was left was later destroyed by a series of fires. The Alton po closed in 1910. Alton Station, whose po closed in 1963, is now considered a separate community strung out along KY 512, e of its jct with the rr. 439, 711.

Altona (Marshall): ael/*tohn*/ə (Little Cypress). This virtually extinct town on the Tennessee R, lies 3 road mi nw of Calvert City and 12½ mi n of Benton. Possibly on the site of the co's first settlement (ca. 1820), the community may early have been called Covington's Ferry, the name given to the local po est on Oct 25, 1865, with William D. Covington, pm. In 1867 Anthony Birdwell, then pm, had the name changed to Birdwell. The place may also have been called Birdwell's Landing, for Anthony or another of his name had a store and steamboat landing there. Newton J. Robertson named the po Altona in 1870 but no one knows why. In 1872 the Paducah & Elizabethtown RR bypassed Altona and est its station at what came to be called *Calvert City*. The Altona po was renamed Caldwell in 1873 and closed in 1874, ostensibly because of the increasing economic importance of Calvert City. Another Altona po operated on the same site as the original from 1894 to 1905, when its papers were transferred to Calvert City. George R. Stewart believed that all the Altonas in the US ultimately derive from the name of a city in Germany. 76, 204, 806.

Alton Station (Anderson). See *Alton*

Altro (Breathitt): *ael*/troh (Canoe). This hamlet with po on the North Fork of the Kentucky R, just above the mouth of Bush Branch, 11 mi s of Jackson, was for years the home of section gangs employed to maintain the tracks of the L&N RR, which had a station, now closed, at this point. The first po to serve the area was est on Sept 5, 1892, at Bush Branch, a small settlement on the branch that had been named for the pioneer Bush family. In 1916 the po was moved 1½ mi ne to the Altro station, which the rr had est, and for an unknown reason had so named, around 1912. 1164, 1310.

Alumbaugh (Estill): *ael*/əm/bâw (Leighton). This settlement is on Station Camp Creek, just below the mouth of Sparks Branch, 6 mi sse of Irvine. Its now extinct po, est on May 14, 1891, was named for its first pm, John P. Alumbaugh. It closed in 1959. 865.

Alum City (Lewis). See *Vanceburg*

Alvaton (Warren): *ael*/və/tən (Allen Springs, Polkville). This hamlet with po lies at the jct of US 231 and KY 872, 5 mi se of Bowling Green. The po was est on June 18, 1883, with Samuel J. Witherspoon, pm, and named for Alva Dickerson Larmon, wife of John Larmon of nearby Larmon's Mill. 1191.

Alvin PO (Floyd). See *Emma*

Amanda Furnace (Greenup): ə/*maen*/də (Ironton). A settlement of this name once existed around an iron furnace on the banks of the Ohio R, just below the mouth of White Oak Creek and a little over a mi nw of the Boyd Co line (within the limits of the present city of Russell), some 8 mi ese of Greenup. The furnace was built in 1829 by James E. McDowell and the Poage brothers and named for Amanda Jane, the infant daughter of co-owner William Lindsay Poage. It ceased operation in 1861. Inexplicably, a po called Amanda was in operation somewhere within the present limits of Boyd Co between 1828 and 1862. The present-day blast furnace of Amanda, 1 mi se of the original furnace site, was built in 1963 by Armco Steel and named for the older furnace. The hill between Ashland and Russell is still locally called Amanda Hill. 128, 188, 1092, 1451.

Amanda PO (Boyd). See *Amanda Furnace*

Amanda PO (Cumberland). See *Amandaville*

Amandaville (Cumberland). (ə)/*maen*(*d*)/ə/vəl (Amandaville). This settlement with extinct po on KY 704 lies across Crocus Creek from the mouth of Puncheon Camp Creek, 7 mi nne of Burkesville. On Dec 17, 1856, Nathan Elliott est and named the po Amandaville for his wife or daughter. It was discontinued in 1872 and re-est in the same vicinity, if not on the same site, as Amanda in 1884. But 2 months later it again became Amandaville. It closed in 1957. 223.

Amba (Floyd): *aem*/bee (Harold). This hamlet, popularly known as Ambytown, extends 1 mi up KY 979 in the Mud Creek valley from a point 1 mi sw of Harold and 10½ mi se of Prestonsburg. The Amba po was named for Amba Walters, the daughter of a Harold physician who helped to est it on June 7, 1902, with Andrew J. Roberts, pm. It closed in 1959. 1394.

Ambrose PO (Jessamine). See *Sulphur Well*

Ambytown (Floyd). See *Amba*

Anchorage (Jefferson): *aeŋk*/rədj (Anchorage). This 5th class city and residential suburb is centered at the jct of Evergreen Ave and LaGrange Rd (KY 146), 12¼ mi e of the courthouse in Louisville. It was founded by Edward Dorsey Hobbs, president of the Louisville and Frankfort (now L&N) RR, when the tracks were laid through the area in the 1840s and was first called Hobbs Station. By this name the po was est on Jan 5, 1865, with William Henry Cox, pm. In 1872 the station, po, and community were renamed Anchorage, allegedly at Hobbs's suggestion, for the home to which his friend James W. Goslee, a riverboat captain, had retired in 1857. Goslee, it is said, took the anchor from his last boat and placed it on his front lawn to signify that he had come to his final anchorage. A Louisville branch po now serves the community. 91.

Anco (Knott): *aen*/koh (Vicco, Carrie). This recently closed po lies at the head of Yellow Creek, 2 mi from its confluence with Carr Fork Creek and 6 mi ssw of Hindman. The po was est on Oct 6, 1922, and named for its first pm, Anderson Combs. 1262.

Anderson County: *aen*/der/sən. 204 sq mi. Pop 12,555. Seat: Lawrenceburg. Anderson Co was est in 1827 from parts of Franklin, Mercer, and Washington co's and named for Richard Clough Anderson, Jr. (1788–1826), Kentucky legislator and congressman, appointed by Pres. Monroe the first minister from the US to Colombia.

Anglin PO (Carter). See *Hitchins*

Anneta (Grayson): ae/*neh*/tə (Nolin Reservoir (formerly Dickeys Mills)). This hamlet is on KY 259, 7 mi ese of Leitchfield. Though the vicinity was first settled by Van Meters in the early 19th cent, its po (now a rural branch of the Leitchfield po) was not est until Nov 28, 1882, when Peter Decker, the first pm, named it for his daughter. 387.

Annville (Jackson): *aen*/vəl (Tyner). This village extends for a mi along KY 30, 4 mi w of its jct. with US 421 at Tyner, and 7 mi s of McKee. The po, est as Chinquapin Rough by Franklin P. Riley on July 17, 1878, was renamed Annville in 1886 for Nancy Ann, the wife of local storekeeper, Edward W. Johnson. Numerous chinquapin or dwarf chestnut tress once grew on the banks of the Pond Creek rough at that site. 1054, 1418.

Ansel (Pulaski): *aen*/səl (Science Hill). This extinct po on the w bank of Fishing Creek, opposite the mouth of Buncombe Branch and 7 mi nw of Somerset, was est on June 18, 1886, and named for its first pm, Ansel L. Wood. 1170.

Anthoston (Henderson): *aen*/thahs/tən (Henderson). This residential settlement on KY 136, 3½ mi s of Henderson, was first called Bloomington. Since Kentucky already had a po by this name, Dr. H. H. Farmer, a local landowner, suggested a translation into the Greek, ''anthos.'' The po was est as Anthoston on June 26, 1884, with William P. Roll, pm. It closed in 1902. 12.

Antioch (Metcalfe). See *Knob Lick*

Anton (Hopkins): *aen*/tahn (Madisonville East). This settlment extends for almost a mi along KY 85, 3 mi e of Madisonville. Its po was est on Mar 5, 1900, and named for Anton Brucken, a local sawmill operator. The po closed in 1906. 159.

Apex (Christian): *ā*/pehx (Haleys Mill). This po est by Robert W. Sharber and in operation from 1902 to 1915, was originally located some 2 mi e of the hamlet now called Apex on KY 189, 16 mi nne of Hopkinsville. Its original location is not precisely known, but the name supposedly derives from its being the highest point of ne Christian Co. The store and po were probably moved sometime before 1911. 1403.

Arcadia (Madison). See *Terrill*

Argillite (Greenup). *ahrgh*/əl/eyet, *ahr*/ghyū/leyet (Argillite). This hamlet with po on the e bank of the Little Sandy R, at the jct of KY 1 and 207, 5 mi s of Greenup, was named for the first iron furnace built in the Hanging Rock region of ne Ky. and s Ohio. The word refers to a rock consisting primarily of clay minerals discovered in the bluff into which the charcoal-burning furnace was built in 1818 by Richard Deering and the brothers Thomas and David Trimble. A nearby po, est as Argylite on June 14, 1860, with James Lampton, pm, was discontinued in Oct 1861 and re-est as Argillite in 1874. 7, 23, 1092.

Argo (Pike): *ahr*/ghoh (Hurley). This hamlet with po is on KY 194 and Knox Creek, at the mouth of Camp Creek, 23 mi e of Pikeville. The po, est on July 13, 1906, with Eli Hurley, pm, is said to have been named for Argo starch. It was first located 1½ mi down Knox Creek, a tributary of the Tug Fork, of the Big Sandy R., at the mouth of Middle Elk Creek, at what was then called Middle Elk Station of the Big Sandy & Cumberland (now Norfolk & Western) RR. This station is now called Bill Siding. The po was moved to its present site in 1936. 1123.

Argylite PO (Greenup). See *Argillite*

Arjay (Bell): *ahr*/djā (Pineville). The name of this coal town extending along KY 66 and the Left Fork of Straight Creek, from a point nearly 3 mi ne of Pineville, was derived from the initials of R. J. Asher, a coal operator. Its po was est on Feb 23, 1911, with George W. Hairston, pm. 1111.

Arlington (Carlisle): *ahrl*/ihŋ/tuhn (Arlington). This 6th class city is centered at the jct of US 51 and KY 80, 5 mi s of Bardwell. This was the site of a town called Neville, laid out in 1873 on Robert Buckner Neville's land by the Mississippi Central (now Illinois Central Gulf) RR. According to some accounts, a faction in the developing community wanted to call it Holtsville for Tom Holt, co-owner of the local store. To avoid friction, rr officials sought another name and accepted the suggestion of one of their number who had noted the resemblance of a small knoll 3 mi n of town to his home in Arlington Heights, Virginia. In 1874 the Mixville po was moved to this site and renamed Arlington. With this name the town was inc on Feb 5, 1876. It was selected as the seat of newly est Carlisle Co 10 years later, but was challenged by the city of *Bardwell.* Because of the latter's proximity to the center of the new co, a commission unanimously moved the seat to Bardwell. 85, 86, 261.

Arminta Ward's Bottom (Martin). See *Inez*

Arnold (Ohio): *ahr*/nəld (Rosine). This settlment with extinct po, 13 mi ese of Hartford, was first called Havens for Ancel Havens, an early storekeeper and gristmill owner. When the po was est on July 14, 1884, it was named for William Arnold on whose land it was located. Vitula (Mrs. David) Arnold was the first pm. 560, 905.

Artemus (Knox): ahr/*teem*/əs (Artemus). This village with p.o. and L&N RR station are on the Cumberland R, opposite the mouth of Brush Creek, 2½ mi se of Barbourville. The station was named for Artemus Herndon who donated the right of way and depot site in 1888. On Sept 8, 1888, James Durham est the local po of Elon, which was renamed Brush Creek in 1889 and Artemus in 1891. 1068, 1409.

Arthurmabel (Magoffin): *ahr*/thər/*mā*/bəl (David). This extinct po was located on KY 7 and the Licking R, 12 mi se of Salyersville. It was est on Jan 5, 1925, by Burney Arnett at his home on KY 7, ½ mi above the mouth of the Molly Branch of Licking R, and named for his 2 oldest children. It was later moved 2½ mi n, where it remained until it closed in 1959. 1422.

Ashbrook (Anderson): *aesh*/brook (Ashbrook). A once prosperous, but now extinct village on KY 53, 9½ mi sw of Lawrenceburg, Ashbrook was founded by Capt. John H. McBrayer around 1878, and named for the many ash trees in the area. The po, est on June 6, 1890, by Thomas N. Calvert, a storekeeper, closed in 1913. 480, 711, 1387.

Ashbyburg (Hopkins): *aesh*/bee/bergh (Calhoun). Little remains of this early steamboat landing on KY 370, on the Green R about a mi below the mouth of Pond R and 13 mi nne of Madisonville. It was named for Stephen Ashby (1776–1841), a Virginian who had settled in the vicinity about 1808. On Jan 3, 1829, it became the first inc town of Hopkins Co. The local po operated from 1849 to 1969. 577.

Ashcamp (Pike): *aesh*/kaemp (Hellier). This hamlet with po is centered at the jct of KY 195 and 197, at the mouth of Ashcamp Branch of Elkhorn Creek, 14½ mi sse of Pikeville. The stream and the po, est as Ash Camp on Sept 13, 1870, with George Barclay, pm, were probably named for the ashes found there by early settlers who attributed them to an old Indian campsite, or possibly to a pioneer potash-producing operation at the site or to the many local ash trees which, before the turn of the century, gave rise to a fairly large-scale logging operation there. 921, 1347.

Asher (Leslie): *aesh*/ər (Hoskinston). This hamlet with po is centered at the jct of US 421 and KY 1780, at the mouth of Beech Fork of the Middle Fork of the Kentucky R, 7½ mi s of Hyden. The po was est on May 22, 1900, with Henry M. Hensley, pm, and named for the Asher family of se Kentucky, descendants of Dillion Asher (1777–1844), an English-born Revolutionary War veteran who settled on Red Bird R about 1810. 1248.

Ashers Fork (Clay): *aesh*/ərz*fawrk* (Creekville). An extended settlement with recently close po lies near the head of the Left Fork of Ashers Fork of Goose Creek, 13 mi se of Manchester. The community and the po, est on July 25, 1940, with Mrs. Daisy H. Schaffer, pm, were named for the stream. (See also *Asher*). 150, 1418.

Ashland (Boyd): *aesh*/lənd (Ashland). This 2nd class industrial city on the Ohio R just nw of Catlettsburg, is the largest community in e Kentucky. The site was part of a large tract between the Big and Little Sandy rs that was settled about 1790 by Virginia-born George Poage, Sr. (1754–1821) and his family, and was first called Poages Settlement. The Kentucky Iron, Coal and Manufacturing Co., organized in 1853, secured 1500 acres there, laid out the town, and convinced the Lexington & Big Sandy (now C&O) RR to extend its line to this point. Poages Settlement was considered an unsuitable name for a developing city, and at the suggestion of Levi Hampton, an admirer and friend of Henry Clay, it was replaced by the name of Clay's Lexington estate. The po at Pollards Mill, est on Dec 23, 1847, was renamed Ashland in 1854 and the town of Ashland was inc that year. Pollards Mill had been named for the gristmill owned by Henry B. Pollard in the nw section of the present city. 7, 128.

Ashland PO (Webster). See *Clay*

Ashlock (Cumberland): *Aesh*/lahk (Blacks Ferry). This hamlet, several hundred yards from the Monroe Co line, less than ½ mi from the Tennessee line, and 11½ mi ssw of Burkesville, may have been named for the family of Isaac Ashlock, an early settler. 1385.

Asphalt (Edmonson): *aes*/fâhlt (Brownsville). This po, in operation from 1920 to 1958, 1 mi n of the Green R and 4 mi w of Brownsville, was named for the rock asphalt extensively quarried throughout the area. 942.

Asylum PO (Jefferson). See *Lakeland*

Atchison (Taylor): *aech*/ə/sən (Campbellsville). This hamlet with extinct po on KY 372, 2½ mi se of Campbellsville, is now also known as Smith Ridge for its location on the elevation of this name. Both the po est on June 21, 1899, with Jesse C. Atchley, pm, and the ridge were named for local families. It is not known why or how Atchley was corrupted to Atchison. The po closed in 1918. 263, 1291.

Athens (Fayette): *ā*/*th*ənz (Ford). This village is located at the jct of KY 418 and 1973, 6½ mi se of Lexington's New Circle Rd. First called Cross Plains for its location at the crossing of 2 buffalo traces, the site is said to have been settled about 1783. It was laid out in 1826 by Harvey Bledsoe, who became the first pm of Athens, and was inc under that name in 1825. No one knows why it was called Athens or why the name has such an unusual local pronunciation. According to one theory, as Cross Plains the community had a reputation for lawlessness, and when the respectable citizens decided to clean it up they thought its image could be improved with a new name. Perhaps "Athens" was suggested by Lexington's nickname, "The Athens of the West," which, it is fairly certain, preceded the renaming of Cross Plains. The po closed in 1909. 175, 182, 557, 1335.

Athens Station (Fayette). See *Chilesburg*

Athertonville (LaRue): *aeth*/er/tən/vihl (New Haven). This once prosperous distillery town with extinct po is on US 31E, 1 mi from the Rolling Fork R and 8 mi ne of Hodgenville. Peter Lee Atherton brought his family to this site about 1790, and here his son, John McDougall, built a distillery in 1867 and est a town for his workers. The local po was called Medcalf for another local family when first est Apr 10, 1884, but was renamed Athertonville the following month. Opinions differ on whether the place was named for Peter or John or for the family as a whole. 383, 1319.

Athol (Lee): *aeth*/əl (Tallega). This L&N RR station and po are at the jct of KY 52 and 315, 7½ mi e of Beattyville. Bowman, the first po in the vicinity, was est in Breathitt Co on June 20, 1890, with Stephen J. Crawford, pm, and renamed Athol in 1892 by a Scotsman for his home district in Scotland. In 1927 the po was moved to its present site. 1372.

Atterson (Casey): *aed*/ə/sən (Clementsville). This extinct hamlet in a comparatively isolated area 7½ mi w of Liberty was named for and probably by Atterson Belton when he est the local po on Jan 2, 1883. The po closed in 1944. 1397.

Auburn (Logan): *aw*/bə(r)n (Auburn). This 5th class city is on US 68, 8 mi e of Russellville. Attracted by a grove of maple trees, the Hayden and Blackey families settled here in the early 19th cent and called the place Federal Grove. It may also have been called Black Lick Settlement for a local creek, a sluggish stream with a very dark appearance. By the Black Lick name the first po was est on Mar 3, 1860, by John H. Wood. According to some historians, by 1860, when the Memphis Branch of the L&N RR was being built through, the place was called Woodville for John (perhaps also called Harrison) Wood. Wood and John H. Viers (or Veirs), a plowright, are said to have vied for the site of the station. Wood lost and the station was built near Viers's foundry. Viers succeeded Wood as pm in June 1861. A year later, Harrison Woodward (the name given in the postal records) moved the po to its present site, and renamed it Auburn. By this name the town was inc in 1865. Historians agree that A. J. Carney, a surveyor who may have laid out the town, suggested it be named for his birthplace in New York, but some prefer a derivation directly from the lines in Oliver Goldsmith's *The Deserted Village,* "Sweet Auburn, loveliest village of the plain," that, in 1805, had inspired the New York community's name. 42, 204, 206, 1344.

Augusta (Bracken): âw/*ghuhs*/tə (Felicity, Higginsport). This 4th class city is on the Ohio R floodplain, 6 mi nne of Brooksville. It was part of a large Revolutionary War grant by Virginia to Capt. Philip Buckner, who laid off 600 acres for a town. He placed it on sale by public auction in 1795. The new property owners then petitioned the Kentucky legislature for the est of a town to be called Augusta, possibly for the large Virginia co which had once included all of Kentucky. The county's seat was located here from 1797 to 1800 and again from 1802 to 1839 when it was removed to Brooksville, a more centrally located place. The po was est as Augusta or Bracken Court House on Jan 1, 1801, with William Brooks, pm. 183, 345.

Ault (Elliott): âhlt (Ault). This extinct po on KY 54, at the head of Sinking Creek, 8 mi nw of Sandy Hook, was est on Dec 23, 1914, by John M. Catron and named for John Ault, a highly respected grocery salesman from Grayson. 1188, 1412.

Austerlitz (Bourbon); *aw*/ster/lihts (Austerlitz). This extinct po and rr station are at the jct of KY 57 and the L&N RR, 7½ mi s of Paris. The station is said to have been named by an early resident after he had visited the site of Napoleon's 1805 victory. The po, with James M. Whaley, pm, was est on Apr 23, 1884. 538, 1414.

Austin Barren): *âhs*/tən (Austin). This settlement and active po are centered at the jct of KY 87 and the Jeff Hicks Rd, 11 mi ssw of Glasgow. The po was est on May 23, 1887, by Hezekiah J. Kelley, who is said to have named it for Austin, Texas, and a Rev. Mr. Austin, a Baptist preacher. 791.

Auxier (Floyd): *ahk*/shər (Prestonsburg). This village with po lies across the Levisa Fork of the Big Sandy R from US 23, ¼ mi above the mouth of Johns Creek and 3 mi n of Prestonsburg. It was founded about 1900 to house the workers of the N. E. Coal Co. and named for the shortlived po est just over the Johnson Co line in 1897. The po was re-est as Auxier in its present location on Feb 18, 1902, and the C&O RR built the

Auxier station in 1903. Historians do not agree on which, if any particular, member of the pioneer Auxier family the name honors. Some allege it was John B. Auxier, then an old man, who had earlier distinguished himself as a surveyor and had been responsible for marking the southern boundary of Johnson Co when it was created in part out of Floyd Co in 1843. 89, 943.

Awe (Lewis): aw (Head of Grassy). This extinct po, 6½ mi up Straight Fork of Kinniconick Creek and 11 mi s of Vanceburg, was est on May 20, 1898, and named for and by its first pm, Anthony Wayne Everman. The unusual name once inspired newspaperman J. S. Mavity to write: "Straight Fork . . . dashes its water against the rocks and crags down a narrow valley probably 50 yards wide from hill to hill, and he who has looked upward through the tops of the tall spruce, pine, and hemlock endeavoring to see the sun at any time except noonday may feel the solemn awe which probably gave this post office its name." The po closed in 1935. 1103, 1200.

Axtel (Breckinridge): *aex*/tehl (Kingswood). This hamlet, extending 1½ mi along KY 79 from a point 8½ mi s of Hardinsburg, may first have been called St. Anthony, the name that still applies to the local Catholic church. But according to local tradition, the po was named Axtel after Billy Cannon, a local tanyard operator, had appended to his application for it these words: "We have wrote to ax yo to tel us a name fo our post office." The po opened Oct 3, 1891, with Samuel Bennett, pm, and closed in 1977. 214, 290, 1398.

Bachelors Rest (Pendleton): *baech*/əl/ərz *rehst* (Berlin). This settlement, 5 mi ese of Falmouth, was allegedly named for the bachelors who sunned themselves on benches in front of the local store. The po, est as Batchelors Rest, [*sic*] on May 16, 1870, with Robert A. Stanly, pm, was renamed Mains in 1887 when Sarah Mains became pm. It closed in 1903. 1229

Backusburg (Calloway): *baek*/əs/bergh (Kirksey). This now abandoned mill and trading village was on KY 464, 9 mi nw of Murray. A po was est in the area as Clarks River, for the nearby stream, on Apr 27, 1846, with Jonathan W. Terrell, pm, and was discontinued on July 6, 1860. It was re-est as Backusburgh, possibly at the same site, on Nov 7, 1873, with William P. Bean, pm, and named for Asa Backus, who had opened a saw- and gristmill there with Jac Thomas some 4 years before. According to tradition, a flip of a coin decided the contest between Asa and another man for naming the po. The po closed on Oct 14, 1905. 829, 1401.

Bacon Creek PO (Hart). See *Bonnieville*

Bagby PO (Kenton). See *Independence*

Bagdad (Shelby): *baegh*/daed (North Pleasureville). This village with p.o. is centered at the jct of KY 12 and 395, 8½ mi ne of Shelbyville. The po of *Christiansburg,* est on Jan 20, 1827, 2 miles nw, was moved here in 1861 and renamed Bagdad with Richard Radford as pm. No one knows why this name was applied to the po and station on the old Louisville Cincinnati & Lexington (now L&N) RR; nearly all of the traditional accounts have been challenged. According to one of these, the station was named for the pm, a favorite of the early railroad men, who had been nicknamed "Daddy's Bag." The name was reversed and shortened and the station and po came to be called Bagdad. It is more frequently said that the local miller's son had a speech impediment, so that his attempts at saying "granddad" or anything else usually came out "Bagdad." Another story is that, whenever a customer appeared at the mill with a sack of grain to be ground, the boy would call out to his father "bag, dad?" 228, 517.

Bailey Creek (Harlan): *bā*/lee *kreek* (Nolansburg, Evarts). The hamlet with extinct po is on the stream of that name, a n bank branch of Clover Fork of the Cumberland R, 7 mi e of Harlan. The creek is said to have been named for Carr Bailey, a Revolutionary War veteran, who had settled at its mouth and was one of the first settlers of Harlan Co. The local po of Smithville, est on July 28, 1857, with Hugh Smith, pm, was renamed Bayly's Creek [*sic*] in 1875 with Joseph S. Kelly, pm, and discontinued in May 1880. It was re-est as Bailey on Sept 23, 1880, with John B. Kelly, pm, and discontinued in 1900. 890.

Bailey PO (Harlan). See *Bailey*

Baileys (Knox). See *Baileys Switch*

Baileys Switch (Knox): *bā*/leez *swihch* (Heidrick). This hamlet with po at the mouth of Middle Fork of Richland Creek, just s of US 25E and 2 mi n of Barbourville, grew up around a camp occupied by Daniel Boone in 1769 and again in 1775 when he was laying out the Wilderness Rd. The po of Baileys Switch was est on Sept 15, 1890, with John R. Bailey, pm, shortly after the L&N RR erected a switch on Bailey's land. Though the po is still known as Baileys Switch, the community is now locally called merely Baileys since the switch is gone. 744, 1409.

Bairdstown (Nelson). See *Bardstown*

Baizetown (Ohio): *bāz*/town (Flener). This hamlet with extinct po lies at the jct of KY 505 and 1118, 11 mi ese of Hartford. Around 1880 a small store was started on the John Henry Baize farm here and on May 23, 1893, the Baizetown po was est by storekeeper-pm John D. Oliver, who named it for Baize or his family. 905.

Bakerton (Cumberland): *Bāk*/er/tən (Burkesville). This crossroads settlement with po is on Clay Lick Bottom, ¼ mi w of the Cumberland R and 3½ mi nne of Burkesville. The po was est on May 29, 1848, on the 1½ mi below the mouth of Crocus Creek to serve Bakerton Landing, a major tobacco shipping point for the Nashville market. The landing was named for the Baker family, whose progenitor, James Baker, with his 3 brothers pitched his first camp in 1805 in what became known as First Night Hollow, on Big Renox Creek, 2 mi w. 223, 900, 1385.

Baldwin (Madison): *bahld*/wihn (Valley View). This crossroads hamlet with extinct po is on KY 1985, 1½ mi w of Tates Creek and 7 mi wnw of Richmond. The po, in operation between 1890 and 1915, was named for a local landowning family. William E. Baldwin was the first pm. 1294.

Balkan (Bell): *bâhl*/kən (Balkan). This coal town with po, 1 mi up Toms Creek from Tejay on the Cumberland R and 8 mi e of Pineville, commemorates the fact that nearly all of the early miners were of Slavic descent. The po was est on Dec 20, 1912, with Edwin R. Roberts, pm. 740

Ballard (Anderson): *bael*/ərd (McBrayer). This virtually extinct crossroads hamlet on KY 842, 7½ mi sw of Lawrenceburg, is in the "Cut-off" section of the county, so called from its having been cut off from Mercer and Washington cos when Anderson Co was formed. The po, est on Aug 8, 1893, was named either for Thomas Ballard, who, as pm of Lawrenceburg at that time, had helped to secure the po for the community; or for William Ballard, the first of that name to be listed in a co census and whose farm was a short distance from the po site. It closed in 1904. Caldwells Store, an earlier po in the area, est by and named for Benjamin F. Caldwell and in operation from 1866 to 1883, may also have been referred to as Ballard. 712, 958, 1387.

Ballard (Floyd). See *Garrett*

Ballard County: (*bael*/ərd. 254 sq mi. Pop 9,000. Seat: Wickliffe. Ballard Co was est in 1842 from Hickman and McCracken cos and named for Bland W. Ballard (1761–

1853), Indian fighter and scout for George Rogers Clark's Ohio and Wabash campaigns, who later fought in the War of 1812 and served in the Kentucky legislature.

Ballardsville (Oldham): *bael*/ərdz/vihl (Ballardsville). This hamlet with extinct po is centered at the jct of KY 22 and 53, 2½ mi sse of LaGrange. The po was est sometime before 1829 and named for a family of early settlers. It closed in 1903. 1316.

Balls Landing (Owen). See *Perry Park*

Balltown (Breckinridge). See *Mattingly*

Balltown (Nelson) *bawl*/town (New Haven). This hamlet on KY 46, just e of US 31E, 4½ mi ssw of Bardstown, was named for James Ball who settled there just before 1800. A po was in operation here from 1884 to 1904. 1386.

Bandana (Ballard): baen/*daen*/ə (Bandana). This village lies at the jct of KY 358, 473, and 1105, 13½ mi nne of Wickliffe. The po of Bandana was est on July 14, 1880, by William Clayton to serve a community then known as Skillet. There are 2 traditional local explanations of these names: the name Bandana was inspired either by the sight of a peddler who regularly walked the 5 mi from Ogden's Landing on the Ohio R with his wares wrapped in a "bandana handkerchief poke slung over his shoulder" or by such a handkerchief left behind by a party of hunters who had prepared a meal in a skillet. The community was once inc. 38.

Banner (Floyd): *baen*/er (Harold). This po at the mouth of Prater Creek, a branch of the Levisa Fork of the Big Sandy R, 5 mi sse of Prestonsburg, was named for David Banner. He is said to have come here from Virginia to buy cattle, fallen in love with a local girl, and stayed to est the po on June 30, 1897. 1370.

Banock (Butler). See *Dexterville*

Bantatown (Henry). See *Pleasureville*

Baptist (Wolfe): *baep*/təst (Landsaw). This settlement with extinct po just off Baptist Fork of Stillwater Creek, 3 mi e of Campton, was named for the Stillwater Old Baptist Church, which was organized there in 1837 by William Lykins and Daniel Duff. The po was est on Apr 9, 1917, in Roscoe Wells's store, with Wells as pm, and closed in 1974. 1017.

Barbourmeade (Jefferson): *bahr*/bər/meed (Anchorage). This 6th class city lies between I 71 and KY 22, 9 mi ene of the court house in downtown Louisville. Inc in 1962, it was probably named for Barbour Lane, which forms its western boundary and which, in turn, was named for Thomas and Richard Barbour, pioneer settlers of the Harrods Creek area to the n. The community has always been served by the Louisville po. 719.

Barbourville (Knox): *bahr*/bər/vihl (Barbourville, Heidrick). This 4th class city and the seat of Knox Co lies at the confluence of Richland Creek and the Cumberland R, 130 mi se of downtown Louisville. It was named for James Barbour, a Virginia-born pioneer, who, in Oct 1800, offered to the first co court 38 acres for its seat from the 5000 acres he had acquired in that vicinity. The po was est on Apr 1, 1804, with Richard Henderson, pm. 398

Barcreek (Clay): *bahr* kreek (Barcreek). This extinct po, ½ mi up Bear Creek from its confluence with Redbird R and 8 mi ne of Manchester, was est on Mar 7, 1900, with Elijah Herd, pm, and closed in 1969. The name was probably a vocalized corruption of Bear Creek though today most people tend to pronounce the latter "*bɛ*/kreek." The creek, according to tradition, was named by early hunters who had killed a bear on its banks. There is also the possibility that the po was named for a large sandbar formed at or near the site. 940, 1418.

Bardo (Harlan): *bahr*/doh (Harlan). This coal-town with extinct po is on KY 72, at the mouth of Jones Branch of Catron Creek, 5½ mi s of Harlan. The name is said to have been corrupted from Bordeaux (the French city), and was suggested by James Bowling, the superintendent of a nearby mine, who had served in France in World War I. The po was est on Mar 12, 1928, with Peter H. Bean, pm. 335.

Bardstown (Nelson): *bahrdz*/town (Bardstown). This 4th class city and the seat of Nelson Co, is on US 31E, 62, and 150, 32 mi sse of downtown Louisville. According to tradition, the site had been settled by 1776 and was first called Salem or Salem Town. In 1780 William Bard (1738–1802), a Pennsylvania-born surveyor, arrived to represent his brother, David, who had been granted a 1000-acre tract here by Gov. Patrick Henry of Virginia. William soon laid off the town, which as Bardstown was made the seat of newly created Nelson Co in 1784. In early records the name was variously spelled Bards Town, Bardstown, Bairdstown, and even Beardstown partly because of confusion about the proper spelling of the family name. The Bards were the sons of Archibald Bard, an Irish immigrant, who was also known as Beard. In Scotland, years before, their family name had been spelled as Baird. To complicate matters, unrelated families of Baird and Beard had also settled in the area before 1800. The po was est as Bairdstown on Oct 1, 1794, with Benjamin Grayson, pm, and is said to have retained this spelling until around 1820 when William Bard's sons legitimized the present form. 199, 465, 1078.

Bardstown Junction (Bullitt): *Bahrdz*/town *djuhŋ*k/shən (Shepherdsville). This rr town with extinct po is located on the present KY 61, 2½ mi s of Shepherdsville. It grew up around the jct of the L&N RR and the Bardstown and Louisville RR. The latter, completed in 1860, was a 17-mi-long line built by the people of Bardstown to give them access to the main Louisville to Nashville line. The local po was est on Feb 21, 1862, as Nelson Junction. In 1866 it became Bardstown Juntion, and in the late 1880s it was briefly called Trunnelton [*truhn*/əl/tən] for a local family. The Bardstown Juntion name was restored in 1890. 1352.

Bardwell (Carlisle): *bahrd*/wehl (Arlington, Wickliffe). This 5th class city and seat of Carlisle Co, at the jct of US 51 and 62, 190 mi sw of downtown Louisville, was founded around 1874 when the Mississippi Central (now Illinois Central Gulf) RR was being built in the area. Its name may at first have been Crittenden, probably for John J. Crittenden, Kentucky governor and US senator, but because other places in the state had that name, it was changed. Some say the name came from the railroad's superintendent of construction whose name had already been given to the station and commissary just n of the town site. Others say the name derives from a corruption of either an artesian or bored well just n of the present rr station, which supplied water for the station and commissary, or a "boarded" well, one lined with boards to retain the walls while the well was being dug. The po was est as Bardwell on June 22, 1874, with Thomas S. Turk, pm, and the town was inc in 1879. In 1886 it became the seat of the new co. 85, 86, 521, 592.

Bark Camp (Whitley): *bahrk kaemp* (Sawyer). This hamlet with a recently discontinued po on KY 1277, 12 mi nnw of Williamsburg, grew up around a mid 19th cent camp for tanbark gatherers who supplied area tanneries. A local sawmill accounts for the name Bark Camp Mills, by which the po was known from its inception in 1858 to 1931 when it became just Bark Camp. 1267, 1380.

Bark Camp Mills PO (Whitley). See *Bark Camp*

Barksdale (Graves). See *Brewers*

Barlow (Ballard): *bahr*/loh (Barlow). This 6th class city on US 60 and the Illinois Central Gulf RR, 5½ mi nne of Wickliffe, is said to have been first settled in 1849 by

Thomas Jefferson Barlow from Scott Co. It is most likely his name that was applied to the town that was inc as Barlow City on Mar 6, 1872, and to the po that was est on Aug 23, 1875. The "City" was dropped from the po name in 1903. 484.

Barlow City (Ballard). See *Barlow*

Barnes Store (Caldwell). See *Fryer*

Barnsley (Hopkins): *bahrnz*/lee (Madisonville East). This residential settlement, on present US 41A, 3½ mi s of Madisonville, was founded in 1886 when the Cooperative Mining and Manufacturing Co. of Hopkins Co, est by a Knights of Labor Lodge, opened a mine at this site. Both the community and the po, est on Aug 17, 1888, by William Walton, were called Barnsley, for reasons unknown. For a time the community was also called Walton City. The po closed in 1928. 159.

Barrallton (Bullitt): *baer*/əl/tən (Valley Station). This extinct po lies in the Knob Creek Valley, on KY 1526, 5 mi wnw of Shepherdsville. The po was est on Feb 13, 1885, and probably named for the first pm, Joseph Alden Barrall, or his family.

Barren County: *baer*/ən. 482 sq mi. Pop 33,713. Seat: Glasgow. Barren was est in 1798 from parts of Green and Warren cos and named by early explorers to whom this large treeless area of se Kentucky seemed singularly infertile and not conducive to farm settlement. Most historians believe that the Indians periodically burned away the tree growth to facilitate their buffalo hunts.

Barrier (Wayne): *baer*/ee/ər (Monticello). This hamlet with recently discontinued po, at the head of Elk Spring Valley, is centered at the jct of KY 92 and 1479, 5½ mi se of Monticello. It was named for a prominent area family, the descendants of Rev. Richard Barrier (1768–1854), a pioneer preacher from South Carolina. The po was est on June 25, 1902, with Ephraim Miller, pm. 1407.

Barterville (Nicholas): *bahr*/tər/vihl, *bahr*/tərz/vihl (Piqua). This hamlet, at the jct of 5 roads at the head of Crooked Creek, 4 mi n of Carlisle, is said to have been first settled in 1820 by Jacob Meyers. Its early history as a trade or bartering center probably accounts for its name. The local po was in operation from 1879 to 1973. According to tradition, its founders preferred the name Helena, but found another po in Mason Co with this name. 47.

Barthell (McCreary): bahr/*thehl* (Barthell). Nothing remains of this, the first coal mining town built by the Stearns Coal and Lumber Co. and the first station (completed May 1903) on its Kentucky and Tennessee Ry, 3½ mi w of *Stearns*. Located 1 mi up Roaring Paunch Creek from the Big South Fork of the Cumberland R, 4 mi sw of Whitley City, it was named for Edward Barthell, a Nashville and Chicago attorney who performed much of the legal work involved in the firm's acquisition of large tracts of Kentucky and Tennessee coal and timber land. The po, also extinct, was est on May 4, 1905, with Fred A. Cain, pm. 208, 1162.

Baskett (Henderson): *baes*/kət (Spottsville). Only the po, a church and a store remain of a once-thriving coal town and railroad station 1 mi n of the present US 60 and 4 mi e of Henderson. Thw town was founded in 1888 to house the employees of the Baskett Coal Co., soon after the sinking of a mine shaft on land then owned by the sons of John Baskett (1798–1865). In 1889 the Louisville Henderson and St. Louis (now L&N) RR station was completed and named for John or Jesse Baskett, from whom the land was acquired. The Baskett po was est on May 14, 1890, with William H. Baskett, pm. Until recently the community was known as Baskett Station. 909, 1216, 1221.

Baskett Station (Henderson). See *Baskett*

Batchelors Rest PO (Pendleton). See *Bachelors Rest*

Bath Court House PO (Bath). See *Owingsville*

Bath County: baeth. 277 sq mi. Pop 9,994. Seat: Owingsville. Est in 1811 from part of Montgomery Co, Bath was named for its many medicinal springs.

Battletown (Meade): *baet*/əl/town (New Amsterdam). This crossroads hamlet with po on KY 228, 1 mi w of the Ohio R and 7½ mi nw of Brandenburg, probably preceded the est of the Battletown po on May 7, 1890. According to local tradition, Mack Bennett, the first pm, named it for an afternoon-long, inconclusive fistfight between Nathan Hubbard and Jimmy Bennett either over the location or the naming of the po, or possibly over a woman. 935, 1260.

Baughs Station PO (Logan). See *Diamond Springs*

Bayard PO (Shelby). See *Eminence*

Bayly's Creek PO (Harlan). See *Bailey Creek*

Bays (Breathitt): bāz (Seitz). This store and po are located on KY 1094, 4½ mi up Hunting Creek from its confluence with Quicksand Creek and 9 mi ne of Jackson. The po was est on Mar 30, 1898, and named for the landowning family of its first pm, Alley M. Bays. 1310.

Bear Creek (Cumberland). See *Pherba*

Bear Creek PO (Cumberland). See *Modoc*

Beard ('s Station) (Oldham). See *Crestwood*

Beardstown (Nelson). See *Bardstown*

Bearville (Knott): *bɛ*/vihl (Carrie). The po serving this hamlet on Big Branch of Balls Fork of Troublesome Creek, 4 mi nw of Hindman, was est in the early 1950s with Lucinda Combs, pm. Over the years it had been necessary to distinguish the several Combs families in that section by giving them nicknames. One family was called the "Bear Combses," perhaps for some incident in the life of an ancestor, and the po was named for them. 1288, 1391.

Bearwallow (Barren and Hart): *bɛ*/wahl/ə (Park). Though the community is now limited to several homes centered on the jct of US 31E and KY 685 and 1141, 9 mi n of Glasgow and 7½ mi s of Munfordville, its name has come to identify a fairly large area on both sides of the co line. It was allegedly applied by early hunters to a depression to which bears and other wild animals would come to wallow and drink at the local spring. The Bear Wallow po was in operation between 1850 and 1906. 863, 1331.

Bearwallow (Madison). See *Dreyfus*

Beattyville (Greenup). See *South Portsmouth*

Beattyville (Lee): *bā*/dee/vihl (Beattyville). This 5th class city and the seat of Lee Co, lies at the jct of KY 11 and 52, at the forks of the Kentucky R, 111 mi se of downtown Louisville. For reasons unknown it was first called Taylors Landing, but in 1850 it was officially est as Beattyville by an act of the KY legislature. It was named for Samuel Beatty (1793–1880) who arrived at the site in 1843 and is credited with having founded the town. In 1870 Beatty also donated the land for the new co's seat. 132, 1372.

Beauty (Martin): *byū*/tee (Kermit). This coal town with po extends e for about 1½ mi along KY 40 and Buck Creek from a point 5 mi ese of Inez. It was est in 1918 as Himlerville by Martin Himler, a Hungarian-American journalist, for his cooperatively run Himler Coal Co. and its employees, primarily Hungarian and other central European immigrants. By this name the po was est on Jan 17, 1921, with Himler as pm. The place soon came to be considered one of the cleanest and most attractive mining towns in Kentucky. In 1929 the company's holdings were sold to Arch Hewitt of Huntington and in Oct of that year the po was renamed Beauty, for the attractiveness of the area, it is said. Some say, though, that the new name was derived from "Kentucky Beauty

Coal," the name of the coal marketed by J. H. Mandt's Hysteam Coal Corp. which later took over production. 377, 502, 867.

Beaver Creek Junction (Floyd). See *Allen*

Beaver Dam (Ohio): *bee*/ver *daem* (Hartford, Horton). This 5th class city with po is on US 62 and 231, less than 1½ mi sse of Hartford. The immediate vicinity was first settled around 1795 by the family of Martin Kohlmann (Coleman), a German immigrant, who is said to have named the local stream Beaver Dam Creek for the many beaver dams he had noted along it. Within a few years the settlement of Beaver Dam had grown up around the local Baptist church, founded in 1798. It was not until Apr 10, 1852, however, that the po of Beaver Dam was est with James S. Coleman, pm. The town was inc in 1873. 75, 266.

Beaverlick (Boone): *bee*/ver/lihk (Union). This hamlet with extinct po at the jct of KY 338/1292 and Ryan or Mud Lick Rd 10 mi s of Burlington was the site to which hunters and trappers brought their catches to sell to fur co. agents in the Ohio Valley between 1780 and 1820. The po, est as Beaver Lick on Nov 28, 1853, with John W. Tucker, pm, was probably named for its location at the head of what is now called Beaver Branch of Big Bone Creek, on which beaver in profusion were observed. The name assumed its one-word spelling in 1895. 891.

Beaver Ponds (Powell). See *Stanton*

Beckham County. See *Olive Hill*

Becknerville (Clark) *behk*/nər/vihl (Ford). This hamlet on KY 1923, 4½ mi wsw of Winchester, was called Haydens Corner for much of the 19th cent since it was part of the 129 acres purchased by pioneer Samuel Hayden (or Haydon), Sr. from David McGee's 1400 acre preemption. The po, est on Sept 22, 1884, with Joel H. Powell, pm, was named for William Morgan Beckner (1841–1910), a Winchester attorney, educator, newspaperman, and county judge. The po closed in 1904. 1349.

Beckton (Barren): *behk*/tən (Lucas). This hamlet lies at the jct of KY 685 and 1297, 5 mi w of Glasgow. The po was est on Dec 18, 1883, and named for James B. Beck (1822–90), US congressman (1867–75) and senator (1877–90). The po closed in 1903. 791.

Bedford (Trimble): *behd*/fərd (Bedford). This 6th class city located on US 42 and 421, 30 mi ne of downtown Louisville, is the seat of Trimble Co. It is said to have been settled around 1808 by the family of Richard Bell who built his home on the hill above what was to become the famed antebellum resort of Bedford Springs. The town was chartered in 1816 and probably named for Bell's Virginia hometown. The po was est on Mar 23, 1818, with William E. Young, pm. In 1937, soon after the co was est, the town was made its seat. 405, 913.

Beech (Breathitt): beech (Canoe). This extinct po on KY 1388 and Bowling Creek (a branch of the Middle Fork of the Kentucky R), 11½ mi s of Jackson, was est on Aug 22, 1925, with Mrs. Mary T. Johnson, pm, and named for the abundance of beech trees in the area.

Beech Creek (Muhlenberg): *beech kreek* (Drakesboro). This village extends for over a mile in a nw direction along KY 246 from Beech Creek, for which it was named, to a point about 5½ mi e of Greenville. The creek, a wet weather branch of Pond Creek, was named for the many beech trees along its banks. The Beech Creek po was est on July 12, 1906, with Anderson D. Kirkpatrick, pm. (See *Beechmont.*) 1253.

Beech Creek Junction (Muhlenberg). See *Beechmont*

Beech Fork (Leslie). See *Helton*

Beech Grove (McLean): *beech ghrohv* (Beech Grove). This village with po is at the jct of KY 56, 136, and 147, 8½ mi nw of Calhoun. According to tradition, it was first located on the bank of Mason Creek, a Green R tributary, ½ mi n of the present site, and was called Buckhorn. It was served by the po of Mason Creek from Apr 6, 1866, till 1878 when it was relocated at its present site and renamed Beech Grove for a local grove of beech trees. 344.

Beechland (Washington). See *Litsey*

Beechmont (Muhlenberg): *beech*/mahnt (Drakesboro). This village with po extends n and w from the jct of US 432 and KY 246, 7½ mi e of Greenville. The community was first called Beech Creek Junction for the local L&N RR station at the point where the Beech Creek spur joins the Owensboro and Russellville line. The spur extends 1½ mi w to the station, po, and community of *Beech Creek* and another 1½ mi to Wright, a station that served a local coal mine. The Beechmont name, applied first to the po est at the jct on Dec 16, 1949, is said to have been suggested by Mrs. Bernice McLemore. 1253.

Beechy (Greenup): *beech*/ee (Load). This rural settlement with extinct po lies nearly 2 mi up Beechy Creek from its confluence with Tygarts Creek and 7 mi wnw of Greenup. The po was est on Mar 27, 1903, in Jackson's store with William J. Smith, pm, and named for the stream on whose banks grew many large beech trees. The po closed in 1934. 268, 1213.

Beefhide (Pike and Letcher): *beef*/hahd (Jenkins East, Jenkins West). This scattered settlement extends for nearly a mi along Beefhide Creek, for which it was named. Its citizens claim somewhat greater loyalty to Pike Co since they are now served by the Lionilli po, and access to Pikeville is easier than to Whitesburg. Though a Beefhide po was est on Apr 17, 1901, with Merdelia Potter, pm, local traditions refer to a settlement on the site before the Civil War. According to one account of the name, a Civil War patrol had camped on the creek, killed some local livestock, consumed the beef, and left the hides. Others suggest that the name derives from a 19th cent slaughterhouse in the vicinity, or possibly from one or more tanning operations maintained by local families. The most commonly heard accounts are of travelers who named the creek for the many slaughtered beeves seen hanging in local barns and farmyards. 1265, 1456.

Bee Gee PO (Harlan). See *Chevrolet*

Beelerton (Hickman): *beel*/ər/tən (Crutchfield). This settlement with extinct po on KY 1529, 7 mi se of Clinton, grew up around James A. Dodson's store and was named for Dr. George Beeler, a Clinton physician. The po, est on July 31, 1886, with John J. Kennedy, pm, closed in 1904. 919.

Bee Lick (Pulaski): *bee* lihk (Woodstock). This extinct po on KY 39, at the jct of Pulaski, Lincoln, and Rockcastle co, 15½ mi nne of Somerset, was est in Lincoln Co on Jan 29, 1861, with John Bobbitt, pm, and named for the local creek. The creek had earlier been named for the larger number of honey bees along its banks. The po was moved to its Pulaski Co site in 1887 and closed in 1910. 1170.

Bee Spring (Edmonson): *bee sprihŋ* (Bee Spring). This village with po at the jct of KY 238 and 259, 6½ mi n of Brownsville, was early located by a large spring that attracted numerous bees. The Bee Spring po was est on Aug 22, 1854, with Frederick Meredith, pm. 942.

Belcher (Pike): *behl*/chər (Elkhorn City, Hellier). This hamlet with po is centered at the jct of US 460 and KY 80, at the mouth of Ferrell Creek, a tributary of Russell Fork of the Levisa Fork of the Big Sandy R, 11½ mi se of Pikeville. The po was est on Jan 3,

1908, and named by the first pm, Elbert Belcher, for his father, George W. Belcher (ca. 1852–1924), the first storekeeper. 1085.

Belfonte (Boyd). See *Bellefonte*

Belfry (Pike): *behl*/free (Belfry, Williamson). This village with po extends for about a mi along US 119 and Pond Creek, 14 mi ne of Pikeville. In 1913 the Williamson and Pond Creek (now N&W) Ry opened a station at this point in its just completed line up the creek to McVeigh and called it Belfrey for reasons now unknown. Shortly thereafter the Semet-Solvay Co., a Belgian firm, opened a coal mine nearby, and a tract of land across the creek from the station was laid off for a town and given the Belfry name. A po est there on Feb 26, 1921, was called Ep for James Epperson ("Ep") Runyon, a local sawmill operator (and later Pike Co court clerk) and friend of some of the Semet-Solvay officials. In 1926 the po assumed the Belfry name. 1142, 1143.

Bell County: behl. 361 sq mi. Pop 32,255. Seat: Pineville. The co was est in 1867 as Josh Bell Co and named for Joshua Fry Bell (1811–70), a Danville lawyer and one-term US congressman. While in the Kentucky legislature (1864–67), he suggested the formation of a new co from parts of Harlan and Knox co's, which he felt were too large. The name was shortened by legislative act in 1872.

Bellcraft (Letcher): *behl*/kraeft (Mayking). This now defunct coal camp on Sandlick Creek, ¾ mi n of Whitesburg's nw city limits, was built around the time of World War I by a man named Craft who named it for his wife Belle. 37, 1265.

Bellefonte (Greenup): *behl*/fahnt (Ashland). This 6th class city is a residential suburb for Ashland's business and professional elite on the Boyd Co line, bordering the cities of Russell on the n and Flatwoods on the nw, and 8 mi se of Greenup. It was laid out in 1918 from the Wheatley farm and named for the charcoal-fueled Bellefonte (iron) Furnace, (meaning "beautiful furnace") which was built in 1826 by Archibald Paull, George Poage, and others, and operated until 1893. A po called Belfonte was est by Henry A. Pennington on Nov 11, 1904, at an undetermined site in Boyd Co but was discontinued after only 5 months and its papers transferred to Ashland. 689, 1177, 1451.

Belle Grove PO (Fleming). See *Plummers Landing*

Belle Grove Springs PO (Fleming). See *Plummers Landing*

Belleview (Boone): *behl*/vyū (Rising Sun). Though this Ohio R hamlet on KY 18, less than ½ mi below the mouth of Willoughby Creek and 6 mi wsw of Burlington, has since pioneer days been known as Belleview, its recently closed po had always been Grant. The Belleview name (if this is its original spelling—an 1880 map gives the name as Bell Vue) probably referred to the attractive view of the r from this point. Yet at least one co historian has suggested a derivation from the warning bells said to have been used by lookouts on the hill to signal approaching Indians. The po was est on July 15, 1869, with Jesse Hewitt, pm, and named for John Grant, a local landowner, to avoid confusion with other Belleviews (variously spelled) in Kentucky. 239, 891.

Bellevue (Campbell): *behl*/vyū (Newport). This 4th class city lies across the Ohio R from Cincinnati and between the cities of Newport on the w and s, Woodlawn on the s, and Dayton on the e and n. It was laid off into town lots in 1866 and named by A. S. Berry for its location on the site of the hilltop estate of Gen. James Taylor, large landowner, businessman, and cofounder of the city of Newport. From the estate, which may originally have been called Belleview, one could get a fine view of the Ohio and Licking r's and points beyond. The town was inc by the Kentucky legislature in 1870. It has always been served by a branch of the Newport post office. 327, 1300.

Bell Farm (McCreary): *behl* fahrm (Barthell). This hamlet with recently closed po

(1975) on Rock Creek, a branch of the South Fork of the Cumberland R, 11½ mi wsw of Whitley City, was one of the coal towns est by the Stearns Coal and Lumber Co. and the w terminus of its Kentucky and Tennessee Ry, which extended for 20 mi from *Stearns*. The Bell Farm po was est on Feb 17, 1925, with James C. Anderson, pm, and named for the large farm there long owned by the Bell family. 208, 1162.

Belmont (Bullitt): *behl*/mahnt (Shepherdsville). This hamlet with an extinct L&N RR station and po is on KY 251, ¾ mi w of I 65 and 5½ mi s of Shepherdsville. It was named for the Belmont Furnace, a steam-powered furnace built for the Belmont family in 1844 at a site 1½ mi e for the smelting of low grade iron ore mined in the co. The po, which was est at the furnace site on Mar 8, 1847, as Crooked Creek Furnace for the local stream, became Belmont in 1854 and was later moved to the present site of the hamlet where a station on the L&N's main line was soon est. 119, 742.

Belton (Muhlenberg): *behl*/tən (Drakesboro). This hamlet with po on US 431, just w of the L&N RR and 8 mi ese of Greenville, was named for Tom Bell, a local landowner. It is not known how long this name has been applied to the place, but it appears along with Yost PO on a 1917 topographic map. That po, est on Mar 6, 1883, with Thomas J. Leigh, pm, is said to have been named for the Cincinnati postal official who approved it. In 1926 it was renamed, presumably to conform to the community name. 320.

Benevola PO (Henry). See *Campbellsburg*

Benge (Clay): bihndj (Portersburg). This hamlet with extinct po on KY 472, at the mouth of Alderson Branch of Mill Creek, 9½ mi wnw of Manchester, was probably named by and for its first pm, Elmira Jane Benge, when on Aug 1, 1881, she est the po in her store. She was a descendant of "King" David Benge (1760–1854), a Revolutionary War veteran from Albemarle Co, Virginia, who first settled in Madison Co, Ky. in 1790 and then moved to Clay Co to seek a better range for his cattle. 150, 1329, 1418.

Benham (Harlan): *behn*/əm (Benham). This 5th class city with po extends e for 2 mi along KY 160, in the narrow Looney Creek Valley, from a point 20½ mi ene of Harlan. It was founded in 1911 to house the workers of the newly developed coal operations of the Wisconsin Steel Corp., a subsidiary of International Harvester, and was named for the Benham Spur, a long ridge bordering Looney Creek to the s. According to tradition, the spur bore the name of a hunter or, perhaps, a Civil War deserter whose body had been found there torn to pieces by wild animals. The po est as Yowell in 1900 with Henry M. Blair, pm, became Benham on July 23, 1911. The town was inc in Mar 1961. 804, 889, 1124, 1173.

Bennettstown (Christian); *behn*/əts/town (Herndon). This rural settlement is located by the jct of KY 107 and 287, 11 mi ssw of Hopkinsville. Its po, est on Feb 15, 1867, was named for Stephen Bennett, a local merchant and extensive landowner who had settled there about 1850. The po closed in 1916. 116, 1403.

Bennettsville (Knox). See *Trosper*

Bennettsville (Muhlenberg). See *Bremen*

Benson (Franklin): *behn*/sən (Frankfort West). A small settlement is all that remains at the site of Benson (Flag) Station or Benson Depot and Benson PO, located just below the confluence of North Benson and Main (or Big) Benson Creeks, 4 mi w of Frankfort. The po was est on June 6, 1854, with Aaron B. Dooley, pm, and discontinued in 1920. The station and po were named for the creeks, which were first explored by Richard Benson, a scout for James Harrod's party on its initial trip up the Kentucky R (of which Main Benson Creek is a tributary) in 1774. In 1775, Benson returned to this area from Harrodsburg and built a cabin on Little (or South) Benson Creek, and in 1780 received a 1400-acre tract for preemption and settlement. His name identified the streams on all early land grants, deeds, and maps. 514, 1290.

Benton (Marshall Co.): *behn*/tən (Hardin, Oak Level). This 4th class city and the seat of Marshall Co, is on US 641, just e of the Purchase Parkway, a mi w of Clarks R, and 160 mi sw of downtown Louisville. It was founded as the new co's seat in 1842 on land owned by Francis Clayton and named for then US Senator Thomas Hart Benton (1782–1858) from Missouri. The po was est on July 8, 1842, with John H. Beardin, pm, and the town was inc on Jan 11, 1845. 133.

Benton's Ferry (Ohio). See *Rockport*

Berea (Madison): bə/*ree*/ə (Berea). This 4th class city with po lies mostly on a 2-mi-long rocky ridge, just e of I 75 and 9 mi s of Richmond. A community by this name had been est by 1854 on land then owned by Cassius M. Clay, the antislavery politician, who envisioned here a place where people could live and produce without slaves. On July 20, 1854, William B. Wright, to whom Clay had sold some land on the ridge, est the po he or Clay named Berea for the Biblical city in Macedonia where Paul once preached to open-minded listeners (Acts 17:11). Wright's po closed in 1860 but in 1867 a second Berea po was opened by William N. Embree. This was a transfer of the po that had been est several mi n as Menelos in 1850 and later renamed Johnson's Shop. Berea was inc in 1890. 163.

Bergen PO (Mercer). See *Burgin*

Berlin (Bracken): *bɜ*/lən (Berlin). Only some homes on KY 10, 4½ m w of Brooksville, remain of this once busy rural trade center named for the capital of the country of origin of many of its early residents. The po has had a curious history. Est as Pleasant Ridge on Feb 23, 1844, with Owen T. McClenahan, pm, it was either moved to or renamed Berlin on Feb 11, 1859, by Samuel B. Lennex (or Lennix or Lenox). In Oct of that year, Lennex renamed it Hagensville for a local family of Hagens. In 2 months it was again Berlin; less than 2 years later the Hagensville name was reapplied; in 1865, it was Berlin once again; 6 months later it was Hagensville; then finally it became Berlin in Sept 1868, and kept that name until it closed in 1913. On Mar 15, 1869, Berlin was inc by the Kentucky legislature. The name Berlin is used exclusively today; many co residents to not recall the Hagensville name at all and Pleasant Ridge identifies only a Methodist church 1½ mi n. 30, 1240.

Bernard PO (Livingston). See *Grand Rivers*

Bernice (Clay): bɜn/*ees* (Manchester). This extinct po on Jacks Branch of Goose Creek, some 3½ mi n of Manchester, was est on Nov 15, 1907, by Elisha B. Treadway. He named it for his 8-year-old daughter, Bernice, who recalls that her father submitted several names to the Post Office Department including those of her older sister, Ethel, and her aunt Myrtle. Bernice's name was chosen. Her mother, Sophia Jones Treadway, became the first pm. The po closed in 1955. 1042.

Bernstadt (Laurel): *bɜn*/staed, *bɜn*/stehd, *bɜn*/stəd (Bernstadt). This village with po is located along KY 80 4 mi w of London. This vicinity was settled by German-speaking Swiss immigrants in what has been described as Kentucky's first mass migration from a foreign country, the largest of several foreign "colonies" encouraged by the Kentucky Bureau of Immigration est by the legislature to settle Europeans in sparsely occupied rural areas. A company run by Paul Schenck bought 39,000 acres of Laurel Co farmland around 1880 and resold it, over a period from 1881 to 1886, to 336 families. Since most or all of them came from Canton Bern they named their new home *Die Kolony Bernstadt* or, popularly, the Swiss Colony. The Bernstadt po was in operation from 1881 to 1964. Four mi ne at the jct. of KY 30 and 490, 2½ mi n of

London, is the village of East Bernstadt, a coal town with its own L&N station and po. The latter was est on June 15, 1881, as Mullins, with David R. Dishon, pm, and changed to East Bernstadt on June 21, 1882 for its proximity to Bernstadt. 260, 539, 751.

Berry (Harrison): *behr*/ee (Berry). This 6th class city with po lies at the jct of KY 1032 and the South Fork of the Licking R, 9½ mi nw of Cynthiana. First called Berry's Station, it was laid out as a village in the mid-1850s on land donated to the Covington and Lexington (later Kentucky Central and now L&N) RR. by George W. Berry. Berry, a Virginian, built his home there in 1836 and later opened a store and est the po as Berry's Station on Apr 10, 1856. The town was inc in 1867. In 1880 the po name was shortened to Berry. 167, 472.

Berrys Lick (Butler): *behr*/eez *Lihk* (Quality). This hamlet with po is located on KY 626 and Flatrock Branch of Muddy Creek, a tributary of the Green R, 11½ mi ssw of Morgantown. It has been known as Berrys Lick since the po was est on Jan 1, 1810, with John McReynolds, pm, but is often called Turnertown [*tɜn*/er/town]. Both names came from pioneer families. Berrys Lick referred to a local salt lick owned by the Berrys from which salt was later mined. The Turner family's progenitor is said to have been a Virginian named Thomas Turner who arrived there in the early 19th cent. 28, 788, 1341.

Berry's Station (Harrison). See *Berry*

Bethel (Bath): *behth*/əl (Owingsville). This village extending along a 1 mi stretch of KY 11 is 8 mi nw of Owingsville. According to tradition the village, first laid out in 1817, was named for an early log church located in the present Longview Cemetery just n of town. The cemetery if said to date back to 1780. The po was est by George North on Dec 2, 1843. The ubiquitous name Bethel for churches in the US refers to the place in the Holy Land that Jacob dedicated as the "House of God." It is the second (after Jerusalem) most frequently mentioned place in the Bible. 15, 186.

Bethel (Butler). See *South Hill*

Bethel (Grayson). See *South*

Bethel Cross Roads PO (Laurel). See *Mershons*

Bethelridge (Casey): *Behth*/əl *rihdj* (Mintonville). This hamlet with po is on KY 70, 10 air miles se of Liberty. The po was est on May 14, 1890, with storekeeper Silas Wesley as pm, and named for the local Bethel Church and its location on the w end of Bethel Ridge. It has always been spelled as one word. 220

Bethlehem (Henry): *behth*/lee/hehm (Franklinton). This hamlet with po is at the jct of KY 22 and 573, 5½ mi ese of New Castle. No one knows why the name was applied. Before 1854, the place was known as Mobley Stand, probably for a pioneer family. The po, est as Henrico on Aug 20, 1853, with John Kephart, pm, assumed the Bethlehem name the following Feb. 59, 627, 869.

Betsey (Wayne): *beht*/see (Frazer). This hamlet with po on KY 1619, 6½ mi ne of Monticello, was once called the Meadow Creek Community for the nearby stream which joins Lake Cumberland at Mill Springs, some 3 mi nw. The community and its po, est on Nov. 21, 1907, with Willie T. Correll, pm, are said to have been named for either Betsey Barnes (Mrs. Thomas Copenhaver) or Betsey Dodson (Mrs. Matthew Denney), highly respected local residents. 1298, 1328, 1381.

Betsy Layne (Floyd): *beht*/see *lān* (Harold). This village with po lies on both sides of the Levisa Fork of the Big Sandy R, 9 mi se of Prestonsburg. The community is said to have been founded around 1875 on the Betsy Layne Branch of the Levisa at the site of that section of the present community known as Justell [*djuhst*/əl]. It was named for Betsy Layne (nee Elizabeth Johns), the wife of Tandy Middleton Layne. The Betsy Layne po was not est, however, until May 1, 1908, with Clayton L. Hitchins, pm. Justell was founded in the early 1920s as a separate community by Clyde Layne and named for Messrs. Justice and Elliott, the owners of a local coal co. The Justell po was est on Oct 27, 1922, with Clyde's wife, Ella, as pm, and closed in 1959. 131, 976, 1370.

Betty (Knott): *beht*/ee (Wayland). This extinct po on KY 80, at the mouth of Triplett Branch of Jones Fork of Right Beaver Creek, 10 mi ne of Hindman, was in operation from Feb 1, 1950, to May 5, 1956. It was named for the granddaughter of Hattie (Mrs. George) Cox, the first pm, and served the community of Porter. Porter was named for the owner of the Porter Mining Co., who, in the 1920s, est there a way station at the end of a spur line he had built from what became known as Porter Junction, just n of Lackey on the main C&O RR line. 1028, 1238.

Beulah (Hopkins): *byū*/luh (Coiltown). This hamlet at the jct of KY 70 and 109, 9 mi wsw of Madisonville, was first called Pulltite [*pool*/teyet] for the first church est there. When the present Beulah Church building was erected, the name was changed to Beulah. The community has never had a po. 498.

Beverly (Bell): *Behv*/er/lee (Beverly). This po at KY 2011 and the mouth of Cow Fork of Red Bird R, 14 mi ne of Pineville, serves the Red Bird Settlement School and Hospital. The po was est on Oct 24, 1876, as Red Bird with Wilkerson Asher, pm. In 1887 his daughter, Amanda Jane Knuckles, who succeeded him, had the name changed to Knuckles, but it was spelled Nuckles in the postal records. Confusion with the po of Nuckols in McLean Co, eventually led the Post Office Department to request another name. John Beverly Knuckles, who had by that time become pm, suggested his own middle name, by which the po has been known since 1911. 241.

Beverly (Christian): *behv*/er/lee (Church Hill). This extinct po was on KY 345, 5 mi s of Hopkinsville. On Mar 1, 1854, John J. Caldwell moved the Genoa [*dj*ən/*oh*/uh] po, which had been est in 1846 on Winston Davie's farm, 3 mi n and renamed it for Beverly Caldwell, the local storekeeper. After some discontinuity the po closed for good in 1902. 1403.

Bevier (Muhlenberg): *b*ə/*veer* (Drakesboro). This hamlet with extinct po is on the L&N RR, just e of US 431 (KY 70), and 4½ mi ene of Greenville. The po was est on Mar 29, 1882, with Robert Wickliffe, pm, about the time that the Owensboro & Nashville Branch of the L&N was extended to this site. The po and station were named for R. S. Bevier of Russellville, the first president of the Owensboro & Nashville, which line had been acquired by the L&N in 1880. 320.

Bewleyville (Breckinridge): *byū*/lee/vihl (Big Spring). This hamlet lies at the jct of KY 333 and 1238, 11½ mi ene of Hardinsburg. The po was est on July 14, 1846, with William H. Seaton, pm, and named for the Bewley family, who had settled in the vicinity before 1800. The po closed in 1907. 532, 1398.

Big Boiling Spring (Logan). See *Russellville*

Big Boiling Springs (Russell). See *Russell Springs*

Big Bone (Boone): *bihgh* bohn (Union, Rising Sun). This hamlet with extinct po lies across KY 338 from Big Bone Lick State Park, 1½ mi from the Ohio R and 9½ mi s of Burlington. It was named for the nearby salt lick discovered by the French explorer Charles Lemoyne de Longueuil in 1729 and described by later visitors as a spring-fed plantless bog of some 10 acres in which for centuries countless large mammals had become mired, leaving their bones scattered over the area. A short-lived po called Big Bone Lick was est here on June 7, 1820, with Thomas Edmonson, pm. Another po, called Bigbone, was opened on Jan 21, 1890, but has since closed. 239, 768.

Big Bone Lick (Boone). See *Big Bone*

Big Buffalo Crossing (Hart). See *Woodsonville, Munfordville*

Big Clifty (Grayson): *bihgh klihf*/tee (Big Clifty). This village with po is on US 62, 1 mile s of the Hardin Co. line and 7 mi ne of Leitchfield. The Big Clifty po, named for the stream 1½ mi to the sw, was in operation from June 7, 1843, to Oct 23, 1845. In Dec 1850 the Southland po, which had been est on Apr 6, 1846, just over the Hardin Co line and named for its first pm, William South, was renamed Big Clifty and moved to the Grayson Co site. 1117, 1307.

Big Creek (Clay): *bihgh* kreek (Big Creek). This village with po extends along US 421 (KY 80) from about ½ mi w of the Leslie Co line for over a mi to the mouth of the creek of the same name, a branch of Redbird R. It is 9½ mi e of Manchester. The creek, not really long as Redbird branches go, has a fairly high water level and its frequent flooding probably accounts for its name. Though serving one of the earliest settled areas of Clay Co, the po itself was not est until Jan 10, 1871, with James Marcum, pm. 1329.

Bighill (Madison): *bihgh*/*hihl* (Bighill). This hamlet with po at the jct of US 421 and KY 21, 12½ mi sse of Richmond, was named for the Bighill Mountain, about a mi to the s. The hill was an obstacle for pioneers and a landmark to aim for as they traveled over the old pioneer road (now US 421) into the Bluegrass area. The Bighill po was est on May 22, 1843, on the Rockcastle Co line some 3 mi s (that is, on the other side of the mountain from its present site). It was discontinued after 4 months and reest at its present location on June 8, 1846, with William W. Smith, pm. 459, 1294.

Big Laurel (Harlan): *bihgh lahr*/əl (Nolansburg). This hamlet with po was named for its location at the mouth of Big Laurel Creek, a branch of Greasy Creek, 9½ mi ne of Harlan. The po was est on May 25, 1925, with Alice E. Boggs, pm.

Big Muddy (Butler). See *Dunbar*

Big Rock (Leslie): *bihgh* rahk (Leatherwood). This po est in 1931 on Cutshin Creek, opposite the mouth of Low Gap Branch, 11½ mi se of Hyden, was named for a huge bald rock within 100 yards of it. 1248.

Big Spring (Breckinridge): *bihgh* sprihŋ (Big Spring). This small village lies at the jct of Breckinridge, Hardin, and Meade cos, 15½ air miles east of Hardinsburg. The name refers to an all-weather spring, that rises in Hardin Co and flows for about 50 feet, passing the jct of the 3 cos, then sinks and reappears several times and finally flows underground for 3 more mi to emerge in the Sinking Creek, a Breckinridge Co tributary of the Ohio R. A po est in 1826 still operates in Breckinridge Co. 653, 1398.

Big Spring Station (Woodford). See *Spring Station*

Bill Siding (Pike). See *Argo*

Bimble (Knox): *bihm*/bəl (Artemus, Fount). This village with po is centered at the jct of old US 25E and KY 1304. On Jan 24, 1898, Will Payne est the po 1 mi from this site and, according to local tradition,named it for a pair of his prize oxen, Bim and Bill. Around 1940 the po was moved to Loss R. Yeager's store at the present site. For some years this location was also called Yeager [*yā*/ghər] until confusion with a Yeager Station near Pikeville led to a 1966 Board on Geographic Names decision in favor of the exclusive use of Bimble. 1071.

Birdsville (Livington): *bɜdz*/vəl (Smithland). A settlement with some 70 residents and extinct po is all that is left of this once-thriving village, set on a high rocky hill overlooking the Ohio R, 5½ mi nnw of Smithland. The po was est on Apr 17, 1860, with Richard M. Nelson, pm, and named for Byrd Jameson, local storekeeper and ferryman. The difference in spelling is not accounted for. 117, 1182, 1382.

Birdwell PO (Marshall). See *Altona*

Birdwell's Landing (Marshall). See *Altona*

Birk City (Daviess): *bɜk siht*/ee (Reed). Little remains of this once thriving Green R port, located some 22 mi above the Green's confluence with the Ohio R and 7 mi w of Owensboro. The community was named by and for its enterprising founder, Jonas Adam Birk (1814–77), a German immigrant who settled there in 1857 and laid out the town the following year. On April 20, 1864, he est the Birk's City po which closed in 1903. 694, 1348.

Birk's City PO (Daviess). See *Birk City*

Birmingham (Marshall): *bɜm*/ihŋ/haem (Birmingham Point). One of the two towns completely inundated by the flooding of Kentucky Lake in the early 1940s, Birmingham was on the Tennessee R at the mouth of Bear Creek, about 9 mi ene of Benton. Its history begins in 1849 when Thomas Love, a Scotsman, arrived from Eddyville. Apparently attracted by the economic potential of the virgin forested area, he est a store and, on Oct 3, 1851, a po, with Laben S. Locker, pm, which he named for Birmingham, England. He laid out the town in 1853 and it was inc in 1860. 76, 133, 583.

Bivinsville (Todd). See *Clifty*

Blackey (Letcher): *blaek*/ee (Blackey). This village with po on KY 7, at the confluence of Rockhouse Fork and the North Fork of the Kentucky R, 7½ mi w of Whitesburg, was once a rail shipping point for area coal mines. It is believed that this is the site of one of the co's earliest settlements, called Indian Bottom for the many Indian relics once found in the long bottom strip along the r. On Sept 10, 1908, the Blackey po was est with James H. Brown, pm, presumably named for Blackey Brown, a respected local citizen whose nickname denoted his dark complexion. It closed in 1913. Some 63 years before, however, Stephen Hogg had est the po of Indian Bottom ½ mi above the mouth of Rockhouse Fork. This had a noncontinuous existence until, on Nov 12, 1919, it moved to the Blackey site and assumed that name. There is nothing left of a community called Indian Bottom though the name has been preserved in two nearby churches. 623, 1265.

Blackford (Webster): *blaek*/fawrd (Blackford). This hamlet with po and on KY 413, across the Tradewater R from Crittenden Co and 13½ mi wsw of Dixon, was first called Blacksford for a r crossing on the farm owned by Rich Black. In 1887 a station on the just-completed Ohio Valley (now Illinois Central Gulf) RR was est here as Blackford, as was the po opened on Aug 29, 1887, with James M. Clement, pm. 1088, 1117.

Blackford PO (Hancock). See *Pellville*

Black Gnat (Taylor): *blaek* naet (Greensburg). This hamlet is on US 68 (KY 70), on the Green Co line, 4½ mi wsw of Campbellsville. According to tradition, some time in the late 19th cent the local schoolhouse was being painted white, but by the time the job was done, it was covered with black gnats and someone remarked, "There sure are a lot of black gnats here." The school and, later, the community were called Black Gnat. The hamlet has never had its own po. 1339.

Black Gold (Edmonson): *blaek ghohld* (Bee Spring). This rural settlement, 5 mi nw of Brownsville, is named for the rock asphalt or "black gold" long mined in that area. It never had a po by that name. 942.

Black Hawk PO (Nicholas). See *Myers*

Blackjack (Simpson): *blaek*/djaek (Woodburn). This hamlet with extinct po on KY 1171, 3½ mi ne of Franklin, was named for the black jack or scrubby oak saplings allegedly used to erect the local schoolhouse. The po was est on Aug 4, 1902, and Perry T. Stamps, the storekeeper, was the only pm. It closed in 1906. The name has been spelled as both one word and two. 18.

Black Lick PO (Logan). See *Auburn*

Black Lick Settlement (Logan). See *Auburn*

Black Rock (Grayson): *blaek* rahk (Leitchfield). This stop on the Illinois Central RR at US 62, 2½ mi sw of Leitchfield, was named for the tar-filled rock nearby. The po est here on June 30, 1891, by Charles F. Heyser is closed. 1307.

Blacks Ferry (Cumberland): *blaex fehr*/ee (Blacks Ferry). This hamlet with extinct po on KY 953 and the se bottom of the Cumberland R lies just below the mouth of Judio Creek, 8½ mi sw of Burkesville. The po, transferred from nearby Judio on Mar 18, 1884, was renamed for a pioneer Cumberland R family. It was closed in 1960. 1385.

Blacksford (Webster). See *Blackford*

Blackwater (Laurel): *blaek*/wâht/ər (Blackwater). This recently discontinued po was on Blackwater Creek, 10 mi se of London. The creek was named either for the fallen leaves that gave its water a darkish appearance or for a place in Virginia, or both. The po, est on Nov 1, 1893, with John S. Gilbert, pm, was named for the stream. 542.

Blackwater PO (Morgan). See *Maytown*

Blaine (Lawrence): blān (Blaine). This 6th class city with po is centered at the jct of KY 32 and 201, on Hood Creek, just above its confluence with Blaine Creek for which it was named, and is 13 mi sw of Louisa. The creek, one of the major branches on the Big Sandy R, was named for Ephraim Blaine, a Pennsylvania-born Marylander who arrived in the area in 1783 to survey lands he had been granted for Revolutionary War service. The community site may have been settled before 1800 and a trade center for area farm families had already been est there by 1822. The Blaine po has been in operation at least since May 10, 1828, and Neri Swetnam may have been the first pm. Though inc as Blaine in 1886, the community was also known for much of the 19th cent as Blainetown and Mouth of Hood. 234, 815, 1175.

Blaine Trace (Elliott). See *Edsel*

Blairs Mills (Morgan): *Blɛz mihlz* (Wrigley). This po is located in Perry's Grocery on KY 711, 10½ mi n of West Liberty. It was est on Elam Branch of Devils Fork (of the North Fork of the Licking R) on Aug 18, 1876, with Cyrus Perry, Jr., pm, and named for the Blair family's waterpowered gristmill on Devils Fork. In 1949 the po was moved ½ mi w to its present location. 1125.

Blair Town (Pike): *blɛ* town (Broadbottom). This hamlet on US 23/460 and the Levisa Fork of the Big Sandy R, less than 3½ mi nw of Pikeville, was named for Rev. Whetzel Blair who owned the site in the early 20th cent. It has never had its own po. 1371.

Blandville (Ballard): *blaend*/vihl (Blandville). This hamlet with po is a recently disincorporated town, located at the jct of KY 802 and 1837, 6½ mi e of Wickliffe. It was est in 1842 as the first seat of Ballard Co. Like the co it was named for Capt. Bland Ballard (1761–1853), famed Indian fighter and state legislator. John H. Stovall, on whose land the town was laid out, became the first pm on Nov 11, 1842. The town was inc on Jan 14, 1845. After a courthouse fire in 1880 in which all records were destroyed, the seat was removed in 1882 to *Wickliffe*, a new town on the Mississippi R. 169, 444.

Blaze (Morgan). See *Yocum*

Blevins (Lawrence): *blehv*/ənz (Mazie). This extinct po was first est in Elliott Co on Mar 14, 1899, and named for its first pm, Thomas W. Blevins. In 1929 Lonnie E. Boggs moved it to the Right Fork of Cains Creek, at the mouth of Coalbank Branch, 15½ mi w of Louisa, where it remained until it closed in 1956. 1097.

Bliss (Adair): *blihs* (Columbia). An extinct po on KY 80, ½ mi n of the Cumberland Parkway and 3 mi w of Columbia, Bliss was est on Mar 9, 1900, and named for a respected local school teacher who had recently come from Louisville. This vicinity has also been referred to as the Turk community for a local landowning family and, indeed, a Turk po was in operation in the area for about 6 weeks in the winter of 1891–92. 878, 1426.

Bloomfield (Bath). See *Sharpsburg*

Bloomfield (Nelson): *blūm*/feeld (Bloomfield). This 5th class city with po is on US 62 and KY 55 and 48, 9 mi ne of Bardstown. At or near this site, on the e fork of Simpson Creek, the po of Middleburg was est on July 1, 1803, with Hadin (?) Edwards, pm. In 1807 Edwards was succeeded by John Bemiss, M.D., who had arrived in Kentucky from New York State a few years before. In 1817 Bemiss is said to have founded the town and named it Bloomfield for his wife, the former Miss Bloomer, and his son-in-law, a Mr. Merrifield. The po was renamed Bloomfield in 1818 and the town was inc in 1819. 199, 884.

Bloomington (Henderson). See *Anthoston*

Bluebanks PO (Estill). See *Wisemantown*

Blue Diamond (Perry): blū *dah*/mənd (Hazard North). A settlement with po is all that remains of this once important coal town on First Creek and KY 267, 2½ mi nnw of Hazard. It was named for the Blue Diamond Coal Co., which est mines in that area around the time of World War I. The po has been in operation since June 28, 1916, when Hiram H. Braden was appointed its first pm. 1327.

Blue Heron (McCreary): blū *hehr*/ən (Barthell). This abandoned coal town on the Big South Fork of the Cumberland R, 5½ mi sw of Whitley City, was built in 1937 by the Stearns Coal and Lumber Co. of Stearns, Ky. for the employees of its No. 18 mine. It was customary for the firm to identify its brands of coal by the names of birds (e.g. "Golden Eagle" and "Scarlet Tanager") and the coal from this mine was "Blue Heron." Yet, according to a local tradition, the place was also named for the "raucous long necked, long legged birds the miners saw when they first came to the Big South Fork . . . to dig the riversides for coal." In either case, while this name officially designated the community, most of its residents referred to it simply as Mine 18. By 1962 coal production had ceased; the mines and po, est in 1937, closed and the town died. 364, 1162, 1163, 1384.

Blue Hole (Clay): *blū* hohl (Hima). This hamlet with po is on KY 11, 2 mi up Collins Fork from its confluence with Goose Creek, and 3 mi s of Manchester. The po, est on Aug 4, 1916, by Charles S. Townsley, was named for a large and deep pocket of unusually clear water that, as local people are wont to describe it, "always looked so blue." About this time the Cumberland & Manchester (now L&N) RR named its local station Rodonnel [roh/*dahn*/əl] for reasons now unknown. Coal and timber are still shipped from this station but the Blue Hole name is used almost exclusively by local people to identify their community. 1329.

Blue Lick Springs PO (Nicholas). See *Blue Licks*

Blue Licks (Nicholas): *blū lihx* (Cowan). This settlement with extinct po is on the Licking R, just w of US 68, and 7 mi n of Carlisle. In 1773 Major John Finley and a party of Pennsylvania surveyors discovered the salt licks at what has since been called the Upper Blue Licks near the present community of Milltown. Several days later the party went down the r and discovered what they then called the Lower Blue Licks for the salt springs and licks on the low fossiliferous beds of blue-gray limestone. Here the buffalo would come to drink and lick the salt, and it was in this vicinity that the last battle of the American Revolution, known as the Battle of Blue Licks, was fought on Aug 19, 1782. The first settlement in what became Nicholas Co was made here by David Tanner, who arrived before 1784 to develop the salt works that attracted pioneer settlers from miles around. The co's first po was est here before 1805 as Lower Blue Licks though it bore the name Blue Lick Springs from 1850 until it closed in 1919. Sometime before 1850 the medicinal properties of the springs were discovered, and from 1860 to around 1900 an important health resort was located here. Local people have variously referred to this vicinity as Down at the Licks, Blue licks, the Spring, the Salt Works, the Lower Blue Lick Springs, and Lower Blue Licks. 47, 907, 1374.

Blue Moon (Floyd): *blū mūn* (Harold). This extinct po was on KY 2030, at the head of Trace Fork of Little Mud Creek, 11 mi sse of Prestonburg. The po was est in Dec 1936 by Alex L. Meade, a local school teacher, and named by his daughter, Alice, for a brand of perfume, a bottle of which she had just received as a Christmas present. The po closed in 1957. 1112.

Blue Spring (Trigg): *blū sprihŋz, blū sprihŋ* (Canton). This settlement is located on the ridge across Blue Spring Creek from Lake Barkley State Park, 5½ mi wsw of Cadiz. Both stream and settlement were named for the spring with the bluish water that feeds into the creek ¾ mi above the settlement. It has never had its own po. Some local people refer to both spring and settlement in the plural, but it is properly written in the singular only. 999, 1325.

Blue Spring Grove PO (Barren). see *Hiseville*

Bluestone (Rowan): *blū*/stohn (Farmers). This residential settlement with extinct po is just n of the C&O RR tracks, ¼ mi n of US 60, and 3 mi wsw of Morehead. The po was est as Freestone, about a mi w of the present site, on Apr 16, 1883, with Henry F. Martin, pm. It was moved and renamed Bluestone in 1920. Both places were named for a fine-grained and even-textured sandstone of medium hardness, gray to bluish in color and comparatively easy to cut in all directions without splitting. Popular as a building material in the late 19th and early 20th cents, it was quarried and milled at both locations by a group of New Yorkers. 697, 841, 952, 1273.

Bluff Boom (Green): *bluhf būm* (Greensburg). A residential settlement is all that remains of this sawmill community. Around 1885 the Whitney Brothers built a large sawmill here on some bottom land between a bluff and the bank of the Green R, 2 mi ene of Greensburg. It was supplied by timber rafted down the river and stopped and diverted by a chain of logs erected across the river to a man-made island. This was the boom at the base of the bluff or, simply, the "bluff boom." The po, since closed, was est on Jan 8, 1908 by Isaac Henson. 518, 1339.

Bluff City (Henderson): *bluhf siht*/ee (Spottsville). This hamlet, 9 mi e of Henderson, was settled sometime before its now extinct po was est on July 10, 1872. It was named for its location on a high bluff overlooking the Green R. 12, 1216.

Blythe (Monroe): bleyeth (Vernon). This extinct Cumberland R shipping port and po lies across from Turkey Neck Bend and is 7 mi ese of Tompkinsville. The po was est on Oct 22, 1910, and named for its first pm, Leslie C. Blythe, or his family. For years it was better known as Dogtown [*dawgh*/town]. According to Stanton Taylor, this name was applied by his father, Charley Taylor, the owner of a local ax handle factory, for the many wild dogs in a 2 to 3 mi section around the po. Lenneth Jones, in a WPA manuscript, recalled that the community had first been called Little Skillet and that the Dog Town name had been suggested by Dr. W. K. Richardson, a physician, for "the unusual number of dogs in the town and great number of fights had by the natives." 923, 1396.

Blythe PO (Marshall). See *Little Cypress*

Boaz (Graves): bohz (Melber). A hamlet with po was until recently located at the jct of KY 849 and the Illinois Central Gulf RR tracks, just yards e of Mayfield Creek and 9 mi n of Mayfield. The po, est on Sept 20, 1869, with William J. Adams, pm, was named for Joshua Boaz, one of the largest property owners in the co, who in 1854 gave the New Orleans and Ohio (now Illinois Central Gulf) RR passage through his plantation. The station became an important shipping point on the rr and the community that developed around it was inc in 1888. In the past few years, the community has begun to shift to the Viola-Boaz Rd, over ¼ mi to the e, where the po was relocated. 1031, 1228.

Bobtown (Madison): *bahb*/town (Bighill). This hamlet at the jct of US 421 and KY 1016, 8 mi sse of Richmond, is said to have been named, sometime before 1872, by Whitfield Moody, apparently the community's most influential citizen. When he was asked what he was going to name the place, Bob Fitch, a longtime Negro resident, happened to walk by with a sack on his back, which prompted Moody to reply "I'm going to name it after Uncle Bob—Bobtown." The local po may have been called Motte, for reasons unknown, and was in operation from 1899 to 1911. 373, 962.

Boggy (Bogey) (Graves). See *Pryorsburg*

Bohon (Mercer): bə/*hahn, boh*/hahn (Cornishville). This hamlet with extinct po on KY 390, 4 mi nw of Harrodsburg, was founded about 1851 around Jimmy Wilson's crossroads store. That and the po, which was est there on Apr 25, 1854, with Wilson as pm, were named for the largest family of local landowners, descendants of Walter Bohon (1762–1825), a Virginian who had arrived sometime after 1791. Though officially known as Bohon, the community was locally referred to for much of the 19th cent as Bohontown. 1264.

Bolton PO (Boyd). See *Boltsfork*

Boltsfork (Boyd): *buhlts*/*fawrk* (Boltsfork). This hamlet with extinct po lies at the jct of KY 3 and 773 and the confluence of Bolts Fork and the East Fork of the Little Sandy R, 10½ mi ssw of Catlettsburg. The stream and community are said to have been named for pioneer settler Isaac Bolt, an English immigrant who arrived in the 1810s. A son, Montraville Bolt (1816–99) was the first pm when the po was est as Bolts Fork on Jan 11, 1867. In the 1890s it became Boltsfork, and it closed in 1914. Montraville's brother, Greenville Bolt, est the po of Bolton, somewhere in the vicinity, in 1858. 227.

Bon (Whitley). See *Bon Jellico*

Bonanza (Floyd): bə/*naen*/zə (Prestonsburg). This hamlet with extinct po lies at the forks of Abbott Creek (a tributary of the Levisa Fork of the Big Sandy R) and the jct of KY 1427 and 1750, 4½ mi w of Prestonsburg. The name is alleged to have originated with the local remark that it would be a bonanza if they ever got a po. They did, on Jan 31, 1881, named it Bonanza, and chose James Hill as the first pm. The po closed in 1969. According to George R. Stewart, the name, which in Spanish means "prosperity," described rich ore strikes in a number of western mining areas and thus had a commendatory significance, suggesting the wealth or potential wealth of a place. 204, 976, 1370.

Bond (Jackson): bahnd (Tyner). This village with po is on KY 30, 7½ miles s of McKee. The po was est as Isaacs on May 5, 1899, and named for its first pm, Andrew Isaacs, or his family. In 1914 it was changed to Bond soon after the inc of the Bond-Foley Lumber Co. by N. U. Bond, a New Jersey native who had arrived there 2 years before and opened a large lumber mill. 1418, 1425.

Bon Harbor (Daviess): *bahn hahr*/bər (Owensboro West). Some 2 mi below Owensboro is the site of a projected manufacturing city and Ohio R shipping port that never materialized and is now devoid of any sign that it was once even a village. The plans for this community and landing were initiated by Robert Triplett, a Virginian who arrived in the 1820s to open several coal mines in what later became the Bon Harbor Hills about a mi sw of his projected site. At the landing, in 1842, he founded a town he called Bon Harbor for the natural harbor there and built several textile factories and homes for the workers. A po called Bonharbor was est here on Apr 17, 1848, but lasted only 2 years. By 1860 Triplett's efforts to develop his industrial metropolis had failed. In the 1890s, however, coal mining was re-est in the Bon Harbor Hills and a small miners' settlement also called Bon Harbor Hills was founded between the hills and Owensboro. 81, 99, 104, 1348.

Bon Jellico (Whitley): bahn *djehl*/ə/koh, *bahn* Djehl/ə/koh (Williamsburg). A virtually extinct coal town on Brier Creek and KY 92, 1 mi wsw of Williamsburg, is identified simply as Bon on current maps. It was est by and named for the Bon Jellico Coal Co., which perhaps had high aspirations for the quality of the coal it would find in the vicinity. It never had its own po. (See *Jellico*). 1208, 1380.

Bonnieville (Hart): *bahn*/ee/vihl (Upton, Munfordville). This 6th class city with po lies at the jct of US 31W and Bacon Creek, ½ mi w of I 65 and 5½ mi n of Munfordville. The community and po (est on Mar 16, 1843) were first called Bacon Creek, which name is said to have been inspired by the local tale of the "man who stole some bacon and was about to be caught . . . when he threw it into the stream." Neither Judge Kendrick Jameson, who gave the right of way through his farm to the L&N RR in the 1850s, nor his son, William Kendrick Jameson, who had ambitious plans for the place, regarded Bacon Creek as a suitable name, and in 1880 the po was renamed Bonnieville for Scottish folk heroine "Bonnie Annie Laurie." 863

Bonnyman (Perry): *bahn*/ə/mən (Hazard North). This residential community with po, lies at the jct of KY 15 and 267, 2½ mi nw of Hazard. It was named for Alex Bonnyman of Knoxville, Tennessee, the president of the Blue Diamond Coal Co., which est mines in that area around World War I. The Bonnyman po has been in operation since July 12, 1918, when Leonard J. Hammel was appointed its first pm. 1327.

Booker PO (Washington). See *Booker Station*

Booker Station (Washington): *b͞o͞ok*/ə *stā*/shən (Maud). This extinct po and station were on the L&N RR's Bardstown Branch 1 mi from Beech Fork which forms the Nelson Co line and 6½ mi nw of Springfield. A settlement may have existed there prior to the est of the Booker po on May 21, 1890, with Charles T. Berry, pm. It was named for a local landowning family. The po closed in 1914. 1314.

Boone (Rockcastle): būn (Berea). Boone Gap in the hills less than a mi n probably accounts for the name of this community on US 25, 11 mi n of Mount Vernon, its recently discontinued po (est on Feb 27, 1901), and its Central Kentucky (now L&N) RR station called Gap.

Boone County: būn. 246 sq mi. Pop 41,800. Seat: Burlington. Boone Co was est in 1798 from part of Campbell Co and named for Daniel Boone, the famed frontiersman and pioneer settler (1735–1820).

Boone Court House PO (Boone). See *Burlington*

Boone Furnace (Carter): *būn fɜn*/əs (Wesleyville, Tygarts Valley). This settlement is on Grassy Creek, some 4 mi w of its confluence with Tygarts Creek, and 12½ mi nw of Grayson, where a stone blast iron furnace was built in 1856 by Sebastian Eifort and others and presumably named for Daniel Boone whom Eifort is said to have much admired. Here on Sept 29, 1857, Oliver P. Kibbee est a po, which he had expected to call Crossing but instead named Mt. Pleasant. In 1860 Eifort renamed it for the furnace and the community that he had developed around it. This po closed in 1884, some 13 years after the last blast. On july 27, 1922, the Hike po was est by the site of the furnace, then as now in ruins, and named for George Hike, a Syrian pack peddler who had opened a store in this vicinity. This po closed in 1942 and the community, though still officially called Boone Furnace, is locally referred to only as "on Grassy." 1177, 1250.

Boonesborough (Madison): *būnz*/buhr/ə (Ford). Nothing remains of the first chartered town in Kentucky—est and laid out as a town in Oct 1779 on 640 acres, which included all the land along the s bank of the Kentucky R from the site of Lock 10 down to the Memorial Bridge and US 27, s to the top of the hill where Boone's fort was later located. It centered on Daniel Boone's original settlement of 1775. Though by 1790 it had nearly 120 homes, had become an important river shipping port, and was even suggested for the state's capital in 1792, it never really materialized as a town and by the 1820s there was little left to mark it as a town. Yet from 1828 to 1866 it had a po, Boonesboro, later spelled Boonesborough, which was in operation again in 1914 for less than a year. Today the site, 9½ air miles n of Richmond, is occupied by the Boonesborough State Park. 57, 1294,1373.

Booneville (Owsley): *būn*/vihl, būn/vəl (Booneville). This 6th class city and seat of Owsley Co (the smallest co seat in the state) is on KY 11 and 30 and the South Fork of the Kentucky R, and is 116 mi se of downtown Louisville. The first permanent settlers were James Moore and his family in the 1790s and thus, for years, the settlement was called Moores Station. Elias Moore donated an acre to locate the new co's seat there in 1843 and his brother, James, Jr., est the Owsley Court House po on May 20, 1844. The po was officially renamed Booneville on Dec 8, 1846, because Daniel Boone, while on a surveying trip for some land companies in 1780–81, is said to have camped by a spring near the site of the present courthouse. The town was inc as Booneville on Mar 1, 1847. 229, 1287.

Boons Camp (Johnson): *būnz* kaemp (Offutt). This hamlet with po is on the site of a camp on Greasy Creek and KY 40, 5½ mi ene of Paintsville, said to have been used by Daniel Boone on one or more occasions in the 1790s while hunting with the settlers of Blockhouse Bottom. According to tradition, Boone was returning from a hunt with a large amount of game when he carelessly "left marks of fat upon the trailside trees" bordering the creek, hence Greasy Creek [*ghree*/zee *kreek*]. The Boons Camp po was est May 16, 1876, with James Mollett, pm. No one can account for the unusual spelling. 193.

Bordley (Union): *bawrd*/lee (Bordley). A small settlement is all that remains of a thriving 19th cent trade center at the jct of KY 758 and the Boxville Rd, 8½ mi s of Morganfield. The po was est on Feb 21, 1828, about a mile away by William J. Ross, the first pm, who named it for a friend in England. In 1858 James P. Woodring and Jacob Strouse built a store at the present Bordley site to which they then moved the po. The po closed in 1911. 157, 238.

Boreing (Laurel): *bawr*/ihŋ (Lily). This hamlet with recently discontinued po on KY 229, 6 mi se of London, was first called Camp Ground for the religious meetingplace there long ago. The po was est on Apr 8, 1884, with Daniel Vinsant, pm, and named for Vincent Boreing, a Laurel Co newspaperman, school superintendent (1868–72), county judge (1886) and US congressman from that district of Kentucky (1899–1903). The *Camp Ground* name still applies to the local elementary school. 1282

Bosco (Floyd). See *Hueysville*

Boston (Daviess). See *Whitesville*

Boston (Pendleton): *bahs*/tən (Butler). A settlement called Boston on US 27, nearly ½ mi w of the L&N RR and 5½ mi n of Falmouth, is all that remains of the once incorporated sawmill town of Boston Station. The mill was built by the Licking River Lumber and Mining Co. sometime before 1860 on the Covington and Lexington (now L&N) RR. The Meridian po (est on Feb 14, 1855) was moved 1 mi s to this site in 1860 and renamed Boston Station for the Massachusetts home town of most of the co's stockholders. The station itself was later known as Lynn or Lynn Station. The po closed in 1922. 846.

Boston (Whitley). See *Lot*

Boston Station (Pendleton). See *Boston*

Boswell's Crossroads (Harrison). See *Leesburg*

Bottom Fork (Letcher). See *Mayking*

Bourbon County: *bɜ*/bən. 292 sq mi. Pop 19,700. Seat: Paris. Kentucky's 5th co was est in 1786 from part of Fayette Co and was thus one of the 9 co's formed while Kentucky was still a part of Virginia. It was named to honor the French royal family for their help in America's war for independence.

Bourbontown (Bourbonton) PO (Bourbon). See *Paris*

Bourne (Garrard): bawrn (Buckeye). Little but the Mt. Hebron Church remains to mark a once prosperous village called Mt. Hebron [mownt *hee*/brən] on KY 1355, 6 mi n of Lancaster. Today the place is known by the name applied to its po when it was est on Apr 1, 1891, in John B. Bourne's store. The po closed in 1949. 1428.

Bow (Cumberland): boh (Burkesville). This hamlet, locally known as Cedar Creek, is strung out along the lower ends of Bear and Cedar Creeks, branches of the Cumberland R. It is still served by the Bow po on old KY 90, 1½ mi s of Burkesville. The po was est on June 7, 1901, with William Glidewell, pm, and named for the large and prominent Bow family whose progenitor, Nathaniel Bow, had arrived in the co from Pittsylvania Co, Virginia, before 1810. 1385.

Bowling Green (Warren): *boh*/lihŋ ghreen (Bowling Green North, Bowling Green South). This 2nd class city, and seat of Warren Co, is on US 31W, 68, and 231, just w of I 65, and 88 mi ssw of downtown Louisville. The town was est in 1798 as Bolin Green on 2 acres donated the year before by Robert Moore for the seat of the newly created co. The po of Bowling Green was est on Apr 1, 1802, with Robert's brother George as pm, and the town inc with this name in 1810. It was most likely named for Bowling Green, the seat of Caroline Co, Virginia which in turn had been named for the nearby estate of Col. John Hoomes as a condition for his donation of the site for the public buildings. The estate boasted a large lawn where the game of bowls was played by country gentlemen. This derivation seems plausible because many pioneer Warren Co families had come from this section of Virginia. Some local historians, however, think the name referred to Robert Moore's "ball alley" near his home, which is mentioned in old records as a source of local recreation. For years this industrial, commercial, and cultural capital of south central Kentucky has been called "The Park City" for its downtown Fountain Square Park in which a fountain was erected in 1881. 291, 961, 977.

Bowman PO (Breathitt). See *Athol*

Boxer PO (Breathitt). See *Wilhurst*

Boxville (Union): *bahx*/vihl (Waverly). A hamlet consiting of a store and a half dozen homes marks the site of this once-thriving tobacco processing and farm trade center at the jct of KY 56 and 141, 5½ mi se of Morganfield. In 1851 Lincoln Agin, a shoemaker, moved to this site and opened a shop in a little box-shaped house and the area about it soon came to be called, derisively, Boxville. By 1865 Agin and David Springer, a blacksmith, had acquired the site, attracting other businesses around which the town was est as Boxville. On July 14, 1868, the po, since discontinued, was est and Agin became the first pm. 157.

Boyd (Harrison): boid (Berry). This settlement is on KY 1054 and the South Fork of Licking R, 11½ mi nnw of Cynthiana. On Dec 8, 1854, on the site of a watermill built by Whitehead Coleman in 1810, Thomas Boyd est a po, which he named Boyd's Station for Andrew Boyd, Sr., an early settler. Within a short time it became a coal and water supply station on the Covington and Lexington (later Kentucky Central and now L&N) RR and the village grew up around the station. In 1880 the po became simply Boyd, which name it bore until it closed. 167.

Boyd County: boid. 160 sq mi. Pop 55,451. Seat: Catlettsburg. Boyd Co was est in 1860 from parts of Greenup, Carter, and Lawrence cos and named for Linn Boyd (1800–1859), for 18 years a congressman from Kentucky. From 1855 to 1859 he served as speaker of the US House of Representatives and died before assuming office as lieutenant governor of Kentucky.

Boyds Crossing (Graves). See *Boydsville*

Boyds Landing PO (Trigg). See *Canton*

Boyd's Station (Harrison). See *Boyd*

Boyds Store (Graves). See *Boydsville*

Boydsville (Graves): *boidz*/vəl (Lynnville). This crossroads hamlet is on the Tennessee state line, 16 mi sse of Mayfield. The po was est as Boyds Store on Aug 31, 1831, which probably explains its name. It was discontinued in 1834 and reest as Boydsville on July 17, 1866, with John W. Maxwell, pm. This po has been discontinued. The community may also have been known, in antebellum times, as Boyds Crossing. 169, 1228.

Boyle County: boil, *baw*/əl. 182 sq mi. Pop 24,977. Seat: Danville. Boyle Co was est in 1842 from parts of Mercer and Lincoln co's and named for John Boyle (1774–1834), congressman, chief justice of the Kentucky Court of Appeals (1810– 26), and US district judge for Kentucky (1826–34).

Bracken County: *braek*/ən. 203 sq mi. Pop 7,743. Seat: Brooksville. Est in 1796 from parts of Campbell and Mason cos, Bracken is said to be named for 2 creeks, Big and Little Bracken, which had been named for William Bracken, a pioneer hunter and Indian fighter who had settled on one of them and may have been killed there by Indians.

Bracken Court House PO (Bracken). See *Augusta*

Bracktown (Fayette): *braek*/town (Lexington West). This predominantly black settlement extends for about a mi between US 421 and the Old Leestown Pike, just s and w of the Federal Correctional Institute and 2 mi nw of Lexington's New Circle Rd. In 1887 Robert Stone subdivided 21 acres of the northern section of the present Bracktown into lots, which he sold to blacks for $100 an acre. He called this section Stonetown for himself. At that time part of the land s of Stonetown was owned by the Rev. Frederick Braxton, a black preacher of Lexington, whose efforts on behalf of the est of a viable black settlement led the residents to name the entire community Bracktown for him. 33.

Bradford (Bracken): *braed*/fərd (Moscow). Now the site of Lenox Lumber Co. and little else, this former Ohio R landing at the jct of KY 8 and 1109, 8 mi nnw of Brooksville, was first called Metcalfes Landing for a local family. By this name a po was est on Apr 22, 1863, with John T. Sullivan, pm. It was renamed Bradford on Apr 2, 1866, with Silas W. Norton, pm, and the landing became known as Bradford's Landing for Laban J. Bradford who, with his brother, owned the land and most of the businesses. 27.

Bradford's Mill (Marion). See *Bradfordsville*

Bradfordsville (Marion): *braed*/fərdz/vihl (Bradfordsville). This 6th class city with po lies just e of the forks of the Rolling Fork of Salt R, 6½ mi se of Lebanon. Peter Bradford, for whom it was named, is known to have hunted in this vicinity around 1780 and later to have est and operated a large grist- and sawmill near the ford on the r, at the w end of the present town. An early settlement at that site was called Centerville for its alleged location at the center of the state. It soon went by the name of Bradford's Mill, and the po est on Mar 10, 1834, with John Scanland, pm, was called Bradfordsville, by which name the town was formally est in 1836. 849.

Bradley (Magoffin): *braed*/lee (Salyersville South). This hamlet with recently discontinued po is on KY 1888 and Burning Fork of the Licking R, 3 mi se of Salyersville. The po was est on Sept 13, 1895, with Elliott Howard, pm, and named for Kentucky's Gov. William O. Bradley (1895–99). 1180.

Bradley Springs (Monroe). See *Hestand*

Bramblett (Nicholas). See *East Union*

Bramlett (Green): *braem*/lət (Gresham). This hamlet with extinct po is on KY 487 and Snake Branch of Russell Creek, 6 mi sse of Greensburg. According to local tradition, the name for the po, est on July 16, 1925, in Les Pickett's store, was drawn from a hat. The winning entry was that of Bramlett Squires, local landowner. 901.

Bramlette PO (Carroll). See *Sanders*

Brandenburg (Meade): *braen*/dən/bergh (Mauckport, Guston). This 5th class city and the seat of Meade Co is on the Ohio R, 27 m sw of downtown Louisville. In 1825 the Kentucky legislature authorized the transfer of the co's seat from Claysville to a site offered by Solomon Brandenburg by his landing and ferry. The town was laid out and the po was est in 1826 and named for him. 187, 650.

Brandy Keg (Floyd): *braend*/ee kehgh (Lancer). This residential settlement extends along and is named for the 4-mile-long Brandykeg Creek, which joins the Levisa Fork of the Big Sandy R just above the Lancer section of Prestonsburg. A Brandy Keg po was in operation there from 1905 to 1915. According to tradition, some early traveler lost a keg of brandy somewhere in the vicinity. The name was recorded on old maps as "Cag," suggestive of the old pronunciation. The Brandy Keg name also applies to the boat dock a mile n on Dewey Lake in the Jenny Wiley State Resort Park. 1370.

Brassfield (Madison): *braes*/feeld (Moberly). This extinct po and station on the long-defunct Richmond Nicholasville Irvine & Beattyville (later L&N) RR was on KY 499, 8 mi ese of Richmond. The po was est on Aug 31, 1893, by David G. Martin, first pm and station agent, who named it for his grandfather, James Eli Brasfield (1782–64), a Virginia-born pioneer settler. 135.

Breathitt (Breathitt). See *Jackson*

Breathitt County: *brehth*/ət. 495 sq mi. Pop 16,945. Seat: Jackson. Breathitt Co was est in 1839 from parts of Estill, Clay, and Perry co's and named for John Breathitt (1786–1834), Kentucky's 11th governor (1832–34).

Breathitt Court House PO (Breathitt). See *Jackson*

Breckinridge (Harrison). See *Trickum*

Breckinridge County: *brehk*/ən/rihdj. 565 sq mi. Pop. 16,000. Seat: Hardinsburg. Breckinridge Co was est in 1799 from part of Hardin Co and named for John Breckinridge (1760–1806), a Kentucky attorney general (1793–97) and legislator (1797–1801) who later served in the US Senate (1801–5) and as US attorney general (1805 till his death).

Breckinridge Court House PO (Breckinridge). See *Hardinsburg*

Breckville (Madison). See *Union City.*

Breeding (Adair): *breed*/ihŋ (Breeding). This village with po is at the head of Casey Fork (of Harrods Fork of Crocus Creek) on KY 61, 11 mi sw of Columbia. The vicinity was first settled around 1802 by George Breeding (1772–1857), a Virginian, whose son James, later a noted preacher, was born there in 1803. The po was est as Breeding's on Mar 30, 1830, and probably named for George. It was discontinued in 1892. Another po called Elroy, est nearby in 1885, was moved to and renamed Breeding in 1894. 9.

Bremen (Muhlenberg): *bree*/mən (Central City West). This coal town with po extends for about a mi along KY 81, 1 mile from the McLean Co. line, and 9 mi n of Greenville. For years referred to as "the Dutch Settlement," this area was settled by German immigrants, and when the po was est on Feb 9, 1832, by Peter Shaver, it was named for the birthplace of his father, Andrew Shaver (or Schaber). The po moved several times between Muhlenberg and McLean cos before returning to the former to stay in 1866. For some time in the late 19th cent the community was also called Bennettsville, for the po was then located in Andrew Bennett's store and blacksmith shop. It was inc in 1869. 189.

Brewers (Marshall): *brū*/ərz (Oak Level). This hamlet with extinct po at the jct of KY 80 and 1836, over a mi e of the West Fork of Clarks R and 6 mi sw of Benton, was named for Peter Brewer who had built a water-powered gristmill and store on the West Fork sometime before 1840. The po of Barksdale, est in Graves Co on Feb 22, 1859, by Rolly Sutherland, was presumably moved to the mill site in 1861 and renamed Brewers Mills. In 1896 the po was renamed Brewers. Sometime after the mill ceased operation, the river shifted its course, drying up the mill pond, and the site is "now on a high and dry bottom." 76.

Brewersburg (Green). See *Pierce*

Brewers Mills (Marshall). See *Brewers*

Briar Thicket (Boone). See *Hebron*

Briartown (Boyle). See *Junction City*

Bridgeport (Franklin): *brihdj*/pawrt (Frankfort West). This village lies just s of US 60, ½ mi n of I 64, and 2 mi wsw of Frankfort. The first home within its present limits was built in 1797 by Sherman Nunnery. By 1826 the site had come into the possession of Frederick Robb who est the town and named it in 1835 for the local covered bridge that had been built over South Benson Creek in 1811 on the original route between Lexington and Louisville. (According to Jillson, however, it may have been named for 2 such bridges, the second having been erected in 1824 over Armstrong's Branch.) A po was in operation from 1837 to 1904 and the town was inc in 1848. 52, 514.

Bridgeport (Metcalfe). See *East Fork*

Briensburg (Marshall): *breye*/ənz/bergh (Briensburg). This hamlet with extinct po extends along US 68 and KY 58 from their jct at a point 2½ mi nne of Benton. It was named for its founder, James Brien, a blacksmith, who arrived in the vicinity in 1819–20. A state legislator, he secured passage of a bill for the creation of Marshall Co in 1842 and the town he founded was a candidate for the co's seat. Its po was est on May 1, 1856, with William M. Yancey, pm, and after an intermittent existence it closed for good in 1905. Inc in 1861, Briensburg became a prosperous commercial town but later declined. 76, 133.

Briggs Mills PO (Ohio). See *Olaton*

Brightshade (Clay): *braht*/shād (Ogle). This hamlet with po is now located at the confluence of Mill and Goose Creeks, 10 mi se of Manchester. The po was originally est some 4 mi n, at the mouth of Otter Creek, where a southern Clay Co pioneer named Bright Short is said to have built his home and store. In his front yard stood 3 large hemlock trees which, with their shade, served as a natural stopping place for travelers up and down Goose Creek. They came to refer to it as Bright's Shade and it was suggested that this name be applied to the po est there in 1883. Postal officials apparently accepted this but dropped the 's and combined the 2 words to make Brightshade. 796, 1329.

Bristow (Rowan). See *Elliottville*

Bristow (Warren): *brihs*/toh (Bristow). Now identifying the homes and businesses along US 31W/68, just ne of its jct with Moorman Rd. and 2½ mi n of Bowling Green, this name was first applied to the L&N RR station and now extinct po ¼ mi s. John Ewing, who donated 2 acres for the depot, is said to have named the station, probably for Francis M. Bristow who then represented that district in the US Congress. The po, est as Bristow Station on June 22, 1860, with Zachariah G. Taylor, pm, became simply Bristow in 1880. 644.

Bristow Station (Warren). See *Bristow*

Broad Bottom (Pike): *brâhd baht*/əm (Broad Bottom). This hamlet with po, slightly over 1 mi e of the Floyd Co line and 3½ mi nw of Pikeville, was named for its location in a low-lying area across the Levisa Fork of the Big Sandy R from US 23/460. The po was est as Broadbottom (*sic*) on Jan 26, 1924, with Henry H. Funk, pm.

Broadhead PO (Rockcastle). See *Brodhead*

Brock's Station (Gallatin and Owen). See *Sparta*

Brodhead (Rockcastle): *brahd*/hehd (Brodhead). This 6th class city with po is on US 150, at the head of Dicks R, and 4 mi nw of Mount Vernon. Until the Lebanon Branch of the L&N RR reached this point in Feb 1868, it was the site of a drovers' stable and stagecoach stop called Stigalls Station [*stihgh*/âwlz *sta*/shən]. The station and po, est on May 14, 1868, with Elsworth O. Farris, pm, were renamed for the contractor responsible for building the line up to this point or, perhaps, for Richard Brodhead (1811–63), a US senator from Pennsylvania (1851–57). The po name was at first mistakenly spelled Broadhead but corrected by 1890, and a Board on Geographic Names decision in 1897 guaranteed that it would thenceforth be Brodhead. The town was inc in 1880. 458.

Bromley (Kenton); *brahm*/lee (Covington). This 5th class city is 2½ mi from downtown Covington of which is it a westside suburb. Laid out in 1848 by a local pharmacist, Charles Collins, and named for his birthplace, the city of Bromley in England, it was inc in 1890. It has never had its own po. 683.

Bromley (Owen): *brahm*/lee (Glencoe). This hamlet is located on KY 35, just n of its jct with US 127, 6½ mi n of Owenton. The community and its po, in operation from 1881 to 1906, are said to have been named for the brothers Al and Robert Bromley, residents. 625.

Bronston (Pulaski): *brahn*/stən (Frazer, Burnside). This residential community with po extending along KY 790 e to Lake Cumberland, is across the lake from Burnside, and 5 mi s of Somerset. It was named for Nicholas Brown in whose store the po was est on Feb 6, 1882, with Thomas C. Brown, pm. The name is a contraction of "Brown's Town." 215

Brookies Crossroads (Brookie Town) (Woodford). See *Clifton*

Brooklyn (Campbell). See *Dayton*

Brooklyn (Mercer): *brōōk*/lən (Wilmore). This now extinct Kentucky R port was located ½ mi e of the jct of Woodford, Jessamine, and Mercer cos and 9 mi ne of Harrodsburg. Only the Brooklyn Bridge that takes US 68 traffic between Mercer and Jessamine cos now marks its existence. To this site a Virginian named Brook and his 2 nephews are said to have paddled down the Kentucky R in a canoe hewed out of a linden tree. Fellow citizens would often borrow their canoe, which came to be known as "Brook's Lin," and the place where it docked, formerly known as Todd's Ferry, was soon called Brook's Lin Landing. Later it was shortened to simply Brooklin and Brooklyn, the latter undoubtedly influenced by the name of the city near New York. No evidence has been found to support this legend. The Brooklyn Bridge, completed in 1871, was named for the town but was probably also suggestive of the bridge then being constructed between Brooklyn and New York City. It collapsed in 1953 and the present bridge was completed and opened in 1954. 40, 844, 1264.

Brooks (Bullitt): brōōx (Brooks). This hamlet with po lies at the jct of KY 1020 and 1526, ½ mi w of I 65, and 3 mi n of Shepherdsville. The community grew up around Brooks Station, est on the L&N RR's main line between Louisville and Nashville in 1857 and probably named for the local family of Joseph Brooks. (An L&N historian, however, claimed that it was named for Joshua W. Brooks who built the line between 1853 and 1859). The po, est as Brooks Station on Jan 26, 1858, with Thomas S. Hougland, pm, became Mt. Vitio in 1867 and Brooks in 1885. 31, 637.

Brookside (Harlan). See *Ages*

Brooks Station PO (Bullitt). See *Brooks*

Brooksville (Bracken): *brōōx*/vihl (Brooksville). This fifth class city and seat of Bracken Co is located at the jct of KY 10 and 19, about 87 mi ene of downtown Louisville. This site was known as Woodwards Crossroads when the co government was moved here from Augusta in 1833. William and Joel Woodward were the first settlers, having arrived from Germantown before 1800. They were soon joined by others and the little village named for them appealed to many persons seeking a more central location for the co's seat. On Feb 16, 1839, the Kentucky legislature authorized the relocation in a bill submitted by Rep. David Brooks and on this day the crossroads was renamed for him. The first po to serve this vicinity was est as *Brookville Court House* (*sic*) on Oct 15, 1842, with Joseph C. Linn, pm. It was only after 1900 that the spelling was officially changed to its present form. 27.

Brookville Court House PO (Bracken). See *Brooksville*

Browder (Muhlenberg): *brow*/der (Drakesboro). This village with po at the jct of US 431 and KY 70, 7 mi e of Greenville, is a former coal town and rr station. It was named for W. F. Browder, a Russellville lawyer and official of the Owensboro & Nashville (now L&N) RR. The po was est on June 15, 1905, with James E. Reynolds, pm. 1253.

Browning (Warren): *brown*/ihŋ (Rockfield). This hamlet with extinct po on KY 1083, 7 mi w of Bowling Green, was named for Quinton and Daniel B. Browning, the sons of

George Strother Browning of Logan Co, who settled early on adjoining farms in this vicinity. The po, in operation from 1902 to 1906, had only one pm, Melvin E. Porter. 209.

Browning Corner (Pendleton): *brown*/ihŋz *kâhr*/ner (*sic*) (Claysville). This crossroads settlement, 6½ mi se of Falmouth, was once a thriving community named for a local family. There is no record of its ever having a po. 1379.

Browningtown (Bullitt): *brown*/ihŋ/town (Samuels). This settlement on KY 1604, 6 mi ese of Shepherdsville, was named for the Browning family, which had settled there before the Civil War. Its identification as Brownington on current maps is an error. 860.

Brownsboro (Oldham): *brownz*/buhr/ə (Crestwood, Anchorage). Now but a crossroads hamlet ½ mi n of I 71 and 6 mi sw of LaGrange, this was once the co's principal industrial and commercial town. It developed around a trading post and Callahan's Tavern, a stage stop, at the jct of 2 pioneer rds. The name, possibly honoring Kentucky's first senator, John Brown (1757–1837) was first applied to the po est on Mar 26, 1827, with Jacob Oglesby, pm, and was bestowed on the town when it was chartered by the Kentucky legislature in 1830. The po was discontinued in 1908. 200, 555.

Brownsboro Station PO (Oldham). See *Glenarm*

Brownsboro Village (Jefferson): *brownz*/buhr/ə *vihl*/ədj (Jeffersonville). This 6th class city lies between the Louisville city limits (on the w), the cities of Bellewood (on the s) and Druid Hills (on the e), and the Brownsboro Rd (on the n). It was probably named, when est in 1955, for the thoroughfare, named in turn for the town of *Brownsboro,* 11 mi ne. The city does not have its own po. 1296.

Browns Crossroads (Clinton) *brownz kraws*/rohdz (Albany). This recently closed po was originally located at the jct of the old Burkesville Rd and the present KY 639, 2 mi wnw of Albany. Francis M. Brown est it in his store there on July 15, 1869. Later both store and po were moved 1 mi nw up the Burkesville Rd. Now only homes and farms mark both locations. 1263.

Browns Grove (Calloway): *brownz ghrohv* (Lynn Grove). This small settlement with extinct po is on KY 893 near the head of Mayfield Creek, and 8 mi e of Murray. It grew up around the store that James A. Brown started there sometime before 1893. He est the Browns Grove po in his store on July 21, 1893. 1401.

Brown's Landing (McLean). See *Livermore*

Brown's Lock (Warren). See *Greencastle*

Browns Valley (Daviess): *brownz vael*/ee (Sutherland). This store, rr spur, and extinct po are named for the broad valley through which US 431 and the L&N RR run between Owensboro, 6 miles n, and the McLean Co line. Before the est of the Browns Valley po on June 9, 1887, by its eponym, Orville O. Brown, this place was identified as Crow Hickman Station on the old Owensboro & Russellville (now L&N) RR. The po closed in 1933. 930.

Brownsville (Edmonson): *brownz*/vihl (Brownsville). This fifth class city on KY 70/259, 73 mi ssw of downtown Louisville, is the seat of Edmonson Co. The po, est on May 23, 1826, with Jesse Crump, pm, and the town, created by an act of the Kentucky legislature on Jan 30, 1828, were probably named for Jacob Brown (1775–1828), the commanding general of the US Army from 1821 to 1828. 44.

Brownsville (Fulton): *brownz*/vihl (Hickman). This hamlet on KY 925, 2 mi sw of Hickman, was named for Shadrack Brown who settled there around 1845 and donated the land for the local cemetery. No po of this name ever existed in the co. 190.

Bruin (Elliott): *brū*/ən (Bruin). This po is at Dickerson's garage and store at the jct of KY 7 and 409, 7 mi ne of Sandy Hook. Samuel Mobley est the po on Dec 28, 1869, on Bruin Creek, which joins the Little Sandy R at the Carter Co line, 2½ mi n. The creek is said to have been named either for a bear killed there by an early settler or for Johnny Mullins's dog, Bruin, who had treed the bear, the only one the early settlers had ever seen on that creek. 926, 1412.

Bruner's Town (Jefferson). See *Jeffersontown*

Brush Creek PO (Green). See *Allendale*

Brush Creek PO (Knox). See *Artemus*

Bryants Station (Christian). See *Gracey*

Bryants Store (Knox): *braents stawr* (Barbourville). This hamlet with po on KY 1809 and Little Poplar Creek, 5½ mi ssw of Barbourville, was named for a pioneer family that maintained an early store there (and still does). Though in opeation intermittently, the po was est by Minor Bryant on Sept 6, 1873. 1350.

Bryantsville (Garrard): *braents*/vihl (Bryantsville). This village with po just off US 27, 7 mi nw of Lancaster, is said to have been on the site of Smiths Station, est by Rev. James Smith in 1779. This later became Smithtown and was, by an act of the Kentucky legislature in 1836, renamed Bryantsville for the local family of John Bryant, a Revolutionary War veteran. On Mar 17, 1818, Smith's son Edmund est the local po as Burnt Tavern at the famed travelers' rest between Lexington and Nashville, opened by Edmund around 1800 and named for its having been burned and rebuilt twice. In 1845 the po was renamed Bryantsville for the village. 130, 333, 1225.

Buchanan (Lawrence): buhk/*aen*/ən (Prichard). This hamlet is centered at the jct of old US 23 and KY 707, at the mouth of Bear Creek, a tributary of the Big Sandy R. The community was first called Canterbury for the family of Reuben Canterbury who est the local po on Jan 14, 1830, and named it for himself. In 1838, when Benjamin Turman, a ferryman, became pm, the po was renamed Turman's Ferry. The po was moved to a site in the vicinity of the present Prichard, West Virginia in 1853 and until 1861, when it was returned to Lawrence Co, it was known as Round Bottom. On its return to the Kentucky side of the r it assumed the name Buchanan, presumably for George Buchanan who had been appointed pm. In 1880 when the Chatteroi (now C&O) RR reached this section, the local station was est as Rockville for some big rocks just below the depot. Around 1900 the station and the community itself assumed the name of the po. The po closed in 1963. 234, 1249.

Buckeye (Garrard): *buhk*/eye (Buckeye). Little remains of a once-flourishing farm trade center on KY 39, 7 mi nne of Lancaster. It was named for the large buckeye tree, an early landmark in the area, that stood near the Liberty Baptist Church upon which the village was centered. The Buckeye po, est on July 11, 1844, by James H. Letcher, Jr., closed in 1915. 1041.

Buckhorn (McLean). See *Beech Grove*

Buckhorn (Perry): *buhk*/hawrn (Buckhorn). This hamlet with po is located on KY 28 and Squabble Creek, ½ mi above its confluence with Middle Fork of the Kentucky R, and 16 mi wnw of Hazard. The po was est on June 12, 1902, with Laura York, pm. According to tradition, the first settler in the vicinity was Jerry Smith, allegedly from Tennessee. He is said to have named the local Buckhorn Spring for a foursnag buck he had killed there and whose antlers he had hung over the spring. He is also supposed to have named the creek for a fight between his brother and others over the division of game. 114.

Buckner (Oldham): *buhk*/nər (LaGrange). This village with po extends over a mi along the L&N RR and KY 146 w from a point 1½ mi wsw of LaGrange. It was founded as Buckner's Station on the old Louisville and Frankfort (now L&N) RR sometime before Jan 1867, when the po of Buckner's Station was est with William A. Campbell, pm. This became Buckner in 1880. The Buckners were a family of early settlers. 1316.

Buckner's Station (Oldham). See *Buckner*

Bucks Branch PO (Floyd). See *Martin*

Bucksnort (Hancock). See *Pellville*

Bucksnort (Hardin). See *Sonora*

Buechel (Jefferson): *byū*/chəl (Louisville East). This unincorporated residential suburb of Louisville is centered at the intersection of the Southern Ry and the Bardstown Rd, 7 mi se of the courthouse in Louisville. Within the community's unofficial limits was the co's first pioneer settlement, Sullivan's Old Station, est in 1779 in the vicinity of the present Goldsmith Lane and Bardstown Rd jct. The area along Bardstown Rd may first have been called Two Mile Town for its location in Two Mile Precinct. On Apr 25, 1883, John Buechel, a Swiss immigrant, est a po in his name at the White Cottage, a tavern he had acquired in 1880, which soon became known throughout the co as Buechel Tavern. In 1907 the Southern Ry built a depot just below the tavern that was called first Stine's Station and then Buechel. A section of Buechel was inc in 1951 as West Buechel. 714, 802.

Buena PO (Calloway). See *Almo*

Buena Vista (Calloway). See *Almo*

Buena Vista (Taylor). See *Mannsville*

Buffalo (LaRue): *buhf*/ə/loh (Hodgenville). Until it was recently disincorporated, this 19th cent mill town and trade center at the jct of KY 61 and 470, 3½ mi sse of Hodgenville, was one of Kentucky's smallest 6th class cities. According to one tradition, the community was settled around 1850 by the Creal family and named to commemorate the discovery of a buffalo's rib lying along the bank of a local stream. It is more probable that the name merely recalls that buffaloes had wallowed in the vicinity in early pioneer times. The po, est on Sept 16, 1856, by William L. Creal, local storekeeper, is still in operation. 68.

Buffalo (Perry). See *Fourseam*

Buffalo City (Union). See *Sturgis*

Buffalo Lick (Union). See *Sturgis*

Bugtussle (Monroe): *buhgh*/tuhs/əl (Fountain Run, Gamaliel). This hamlet on KY 87, virtually on the Tennessee state line, and 10½ mi sw of Tompkinsville, was named in jest for the profusion of local doodlebugs. Ralph B. Marshall gave this account in his report to the Board of Geographic Names: "According to the oldest residents in this community, the name was acquired during the time the wheat thrashers toured the county thrashing the farmers' wheat. The thrashers slept in beds of hay in the barns and stayed so long that it was said the bugs got so large they would tussle in the hay, thereby giving the name of Bugtussle to the community." It has never had it own po. 1003, 1395.

Bullitt County: *b͞ool*/ət. 300 sq mi. Pop 43,150. Seat: Shepherdsville. Kentucky's fastest growing co since 1960, it was est in 1796 from parts of Jefferson and Nelson cos and named for Alexander Scott Bullitt (1762–1816), who helped draft Kentucky's first constitution in 1791, and was the first president of the Kentucky Senate (1792–99) and the first lieutenant governor of Kentucky (1800–4).

Bullittsburg (Boone). See *Bullittsville*

Bullitts Lick (Bullitt): *bool*/əts *lihk* (Valley Station). This is the site of Kentucky's first industry and the first commercial salt works w of the Alleghenies, near the present Bullitts Lick Church on KY 44, just w of Shepherdsville. The lick was discovered by and named for Virginia surveyor Capt. Thomas Bullitt in 1773. The operation of the salt works began in 1779, and the community which grew up around it to house and support the workers was known as Saltsburg. Production ended in 1830 and today all trace of the works is gone. 31, 562, 1352.

Bullittsville (Boone): *bool*/əts/vihl (Burlington). This hamlet with extinct po on KY 20 and Woolper Creek, 3 mi n of Burlington, may have been named for Capt. Thomas Bullitt who, in 1773, led a surveying party for Virginia's Governor Dunmore down the Ohio R as far as present-day Louisville. He is said to have surveyed a section of the shore of the r that came to be known as Bullitts Bottom (now North Bend) and may even have visited the Bullittsville site. The latter, however, is not to be confused with Bullittsburg, a community some 3 mi w which centers on a Baptist church organized in 1794. The Bullittsville po was est as Corneliusville on Jan 22, 1827, and probably named for Robert Cornelius, the first pm. In 1848 it was moved and renamed Mitchellsville for then pm Benjamin Mitchell, and was given the name Bullittsville when, in 1853, it was moved to that site where it remained until it closed in 1918. The precise locations of these earlier pos are not known. 1284.

Bullseye (Carter). See *Gregoryville*

Buncombe (Allen). See *Maynard*

Buradell's Landing (Marshall). See *Altona*

Burdick (Taylor). See *Ireland*

Burdine (Letcher): *b3*/dahn (Jenkins East). This coal town, located on US 23/119 and Elkhorn Creek, 12½ mi ene of Whitesburg, is a part of *Jenkins*. Local people, however, consider it a separate town, and it does have its own po, which was est on Jan 25, 1898, 13 years earlier than Jenkins'. General consensus is that it was named for Burdine Webb, who carried the mail from Whitesburg. 1218, 1254, 1265.

Burg (McCracken and Graves). See *Melber*

Burg (Morgan). See *Wheelrim*

Burgess Station (Burnaugh). See *Burnaugh*

Burgin (Mercer): *b3gh*/ən (Harrodsburg, Danville). This 5th class commercial and manufacturing city with PO lies at the head of Cane Run (a branch of Dicks R), on the site of the pioneer Cane Run Settlement, 2½ mi east of Harrodsburg. In 1874 Temple Burgin, landowner and stockdealer, deeded the right of way to the Cincinnati Southern (now Southern) Ry and a station was est which the rr company named Burgin Station. Around this the town of Burgin was laid out in 1877 and inc in 1878. Its po was est as Bergen on July 24, 1877, with B. Frank Taylor, pm, and the misspelling was not corrected until 1886. 606, 1264.

Burgin Station (Mercer). See *Burgin*

Burkesville (Cumberland): *b3x*/vəl (Burkesville, Waterview). This 5th class city and seat of Cumberland Co is centered at the jct of Ky 90 and 61 and is 95 mi s of downtown Louisville. According to early records, the site was first called Cumberland Crossing, aptly denoting its location on the Cumberland river. A town was laid out in 1798 on land owned by Samuel Burks, a Virginia settler, and undoubtedly named for him at that time. Francis Emmerson, as sole proprietor of the land by 1810, succeeded in having the city of Burksville inc by the Kentucky legislature. Contemporary historians largely discount the popular tradition that the town was named by a 10-to-7 vote in a special election to decide between Burksville and Thurmantown, the latter for an early ferryman. Though the po was est on Jan 1, 1807, as Burkesville or Cumberland Court House, with Christopher Brooks, pm, the town's name continued to be spelled Burksville until the 1870s when the "e" that the Post Office Department had always seen fit to retain was officially inserted. 223, 307, 1385.

Burkhart (Wolfe): *bзk/hahrt* (Lee City). This po is located on KY 1094, at the mouth of Poor Branch of Red R, 14½ mi e of Campton. It was est on July 16, 1909, and named for the family of John L. Burkhart, its first pm. 1236.

Burk Hollow (Whitley). See *Fairview*

Burlington (Boone): *bзl*/ihŋ/tən (Burlington). The seat of Boone Co—one of the 2 unincorporated Kentucky Co seats (the other is Whitley City)—is on KY 18 and 338, 71 mi ne of downtown Louisville. In 1799, as Craigs Camp [*krehghz kaemp*], 74 acres of this land were donated for the seat of the new co by John H. Craig and Robert Johnson and it was officially called Wilmington. The po was est as Boon(e) Court House on July 1, 1807, with John Love, pm. In 1816 the town was renamed Burlington and the po assumed this name in 1821. The town was inc in 1824 and reinc in 1910, but this status has been allowed to lapse. No one knows why the Wilmington or Burlington names were applied. 26, 109.

Burna (Livingston): *bзn*/ə (Burna). This hamlet with po is centered on the jct of US 60 and KY 135, 7 mi nne of Smithland. The community is said to have been founded around 1890 by John Steele and may first have been called Tail Holt. According to tradition, residents seeking a more respectable name for their new po arranged a contest in which the names of local girls were nominated and the winning entries submitted to the postal authorities. Chosen was that of Burna Phillips, the daughter of Grant Phillips. In a variant of this account, a number of names were placed in a hat and Miss Phillips's was drawn. The po was est as Burna on Dec 13, 1906, with William G. Fort, pm. *Tail Holt,* says Prof. Kathy Wood, an area folklorist, referred in a humorous way to the hardships of early settlers in earning a living from the soil there: they "felt they had only a tail holt on earning a living." 138, 1182.

Burnaugh (Boyd): *bзn*/aw (Burnaugh). This hamlet is on US 23 and the C&O RR, in the w bank bottom of the Big Sandy R, 9 mi s of Catlettsburg. The name was probably a combination of the nearby Burgess Station on the old Chatteroi (now C&O) RR—named for George R. Burgess (1813–1900), landowner and justice of the peace—and the Kavanaugh po, in operation between 1901 and 1910, which may have been named for the old Kavanaugh Chapel. 1091, 1249, 1311.

Burnett Spring PO (Trigg). See *Roaring Spring*

Burning Fork (Magoffin): *bзn*/ihŋ *fawrk* (Salyersville South). This po at the jct of KY 114 and 1888, 2 mi e of Salyersville serves the area drained by the Burning Fork Creek, which joins the Licking River just above downtown Salyersville. The creek was named for the nearby Burning Spring from which natural gas, said to have been ignited by the Indians, burned continuously until about 1900 when a gas well was drilled nearby and the gas drained off. The po was est on Jan 4, 1928, with Roy M. Cain, the local storekeeper, as the first pm. Other pos called Burning Spring had also been in operation in the vicinity from 1829 to 1839 and from 1854 to 1859. 868, 1370.

Burning Spring PO (Magoffin). See *Burning Fork, Salyersville*

Burning Springs (Clay): *bзn*/ən *Sprihŋz* (Maulden, Manchester). This village with extinct po is on US 421 and the Burning Springs Fork of Bray Creek (a tributary of Sextons Creek), 6½ mi nnw of Manchester. A very early settlement, it was named for the ignitable springs of natural gas, in seemingly inexhaustible supply, discovered before 1800 at several sites in the area. One local spring is said to have furnished gas for 75 years. On Jan 17, 1888, Lafayette M. Rawlings moved the old Napier po (est Sept 25, 1884, by John C. Napier) a few mi to the Burning Springs site and renamed it for the community. The po closed in 1965. 44, 1259, 1329.

Burnside (Pulaski): *b3n*/sahd (Burnside, Somerset). This 5th class city with po is on US 27 (KY 90) and the Cumberland R, 3½ mi s of Somerset. On a high point of land, ½ mi above the mouth of the South Fork of the Cumberland, the site was first called Point Isabel or The Point, referring to the local legend of the maiden who, disappointed in love, jumped off a bluff to her death; or to a man named Isobel who allegedly ran a ferry at this site in pioneer days. During the Civil War a detachment of Gen. Ambrose E. Burnside's Union Army was stationed here and the place was called Camp Burnside. The po, est as Point Isabel on June 5, 1877, with Henry Beaty, pm, was discontinued the following year and reest as Burnside in 1880, by which name the town was inc in 1890. Prior to the impounding of Lake Cumberland in 1950, the federal government relocated almost the entire town to the adjacent highlands. 442, 624, 1410.

Burnt Tavern PO (Garrard). See *Bryantsville*

Burton PO (Lewis). See *Burtonville*

Burtonsville PO (Daviess). See *Whitesville*

Burtonville (Lewis): *b3t*/ən/vihl (Burtonville). This hamlet with extinct po at the jct of KY 989 and 1237, 14 mi sw of Vanceburg, is said to have been called Equalization before the Civil War. According to the late J. S. Mavity, this name was applied "because four citizens built their homes exactly alike along the roadside. They claimed that the Declaration said that all men were born free and equal, and it was their endeavor to keep the citizens of their town in that condition. Not many years after this building of the original houses, their owners moved away and the other oldest inhabitant, Mr. Burton, added 'ville' to his name and christened the town anew." Others claim, though admittedly with no foundation, that it was named for a Burton Price. The Burtonville po was est on Feb 18, 1878, with William B. Burriss, pm, and closed in 1958. A Burton po, perhaps at the same site, had been in operation in 1873–74. 1200, 1209.

Bush (Laurel): Bo͞osh (Hima). This po on KY 80, 10½ mi e of London, was est as Bush's Store on Feb 18, 1840, and named for George A. Bush, the first pm and storekeeper. It was renamed Bush in 1894. 1282.

Bush Branch PO (Breathitt). See *Altro*

Bush's Store (Laurel). See *Bush*

Buskirk (also called **Salem**) (Morgan): *buhs*/kerk, *sa*/ləm (Cannel City). A hamlet with po at the jct of KY 205 and 844 and the forks of Salem Fork of Grassy Creek, 8 mi ssw of West Liberty. While the po, est on Mar 9, 1925, has always been called Buskirk for the first pm, Thomas J. Buskirk, both this name and Salem have long been used interchangeably to identify the community. Salem refers to the creek and to the local Christian church est around 1884. Richard Phipps is said to have founded the community and given it the Salem name. 112.

Buskirk (Johnson). See *Thelma*

Butler (Fleming). See *Plummers Landing*

Butler (Pendleton): *buht*/lər (Butler, DeMossville). This 5th class city with po is on KY 177 and the Licking R, about a mi w of US 27, and 7 mi n of Falmouth. The community was first called Fourth Lock for the lock and dam whose construction had begun in 1837 in an unsuccessful effort to make the Licking R navigable. It was later called Clayton, for reasons unknown. The town was est about 1852–53 when the Covington and Lexington (now L&N) RR was built through and may early have been called Butler Station, possibly at the suggestion of Joel Ham, a local contractor on the earlier dam project, for William O. Butler, US congressman from that district (1839–43). The po, est on Mar 10, 1857, as Clayton with Richard M. J. Wheeler, pm, was renamed Butler in 1860. The town was inc in 1868. 397, 1230.

Butler County: *buht*/lər. 431 sq mi. Pop 11,032. Seat: Morgantown. Butler Co was est in 1810 from parts of Logan and Ohio co's and named for Gen. Richard Butler (1743–91), Revolutionary War officer and later superintendent of Indian affairs for the Northern District who, with George Rogers Clark, arranged the treaty of 1786 with the Shawnee and Delaware Indians. He was killed in General St. Clair's military campaign against the Ohio Indians.

Butler Court House PO (Butler). See *Morgantown*

Butler Station (Pendleton). See *Butler*

Butterfly (Perry): *buht*/ər/fleye (Krypton). This hamlet with po lies on the North Fork of the Kentucky R, just below the mouth of Lower Second Creek, and 4 mi nw of Hazard. The po was est on Mar 4, 1920, with Mose C. Feltner, pm, and allegedly named for the large number of butterflies observed there. The local L&N Railroad station, since closed, was called *Sonia,* as was a local school, but it is not known why. 1114, 1272

Butter Pint (Adair). See *Gadberry*

Buttonsberry (McLean): *buht*/ənz/behr/ee (Livermore). This is now a hamlet on KY 85, 1 rd mi w of the town of Island, and 7½ air miles se of Calhoun. Sometime before 1900 Alva Karnes opened a slope coal mine in the vicinity from which he built a mi-long tram that connected with the Owensboro and Nashville Branch of the L&N RR at Karnes Junction, just south of Island. The settlement that grew up around the mine is said to have been named Buttonsberry after Karnes had spied a button in a local berry patch. It has never had its own po. 932.

Buzzard Roost (Nicholas). See *Sprout*

Bybee (Madison): *beye*/bee (Moberly, Panola). This crossroads hamlet with po on old KY 52, 8 mi e of Richmond, grew up around the Bybee Pottery and was named for it. According to legend the pottery was est in the first decade of the 19th cent, but recorded history traces it back to 1845 when Eli Cornelison shaped the first earthenware from the clay deposits 3 mi away and started the family business that is now in its 6th generation. The po was est on July 7, 1902, with Matt T. Bybee, pm. 312.

Bypro (Floyd): *beye*/proh (Wheelwright). This coal town with po lies at the mouth of Otter Creek, a branch of Left (Fork of) Beaver Creek, and the jct of KY 122 and 306, 21½ mi s of Prestonsburg. The site may have been called Briar Bottom in the last quarter of the 19th cent. The po was est as Bypro on May 19, 1926, with Roy E. Webb, pm, and named for the Byproduct Coal Co. there. The local C&O RR station is called Wheelwright Junction, for it serves the mining town of *Wheelwright* a short distance to the s. 1429.

Caceys Station (Fulton). See *Cayce*

Cadentown (Fayette): *ka*/dən/town (Lexington East). This suburban community centers at the jct of Liberty and Todds Rds, about 1½ mi e of Lexington's New Circle Rd and se of downtown Lexington. On land he had purchased in 1867 from the farmstead of Capt. John Starks, a Revolutionary War veteran, Owen Caden, for whom it was named, est the community to house freed slaves. 33.

Cadiz (Trigg): *kād*/ihz, kād/eez (Cadiz, Cobb). This 5th class city and the seat of Trigg Co, is on Little R and US 68 (KY 80), 139 mi sw of downtown Louisville. It was laid off in 1820 on 52 acres deeded by Robert Baker for the new co's seat to be called Cadiz. The po was est on Jan 5, 1821, with James H. Haden, pm, and the town was inc in 1822. The origin of the name has never been determined. One oft-heard explanation is that a Spaniard in an early surveying party had suggested that it be named for his hometown. It definitely was not named for the city in Ohio. 166, 1325.

Cains Store (Pulaski): *kānz* stawr (Mintonville). A hamlet with recently discontinued po at the jct of KY 80 and 837, 12 mi w of Somerset. The po had 3 locations. It was est on Mar 30, 1863, with Christopher C. Gossett, pm, and named for Smith Cain (1822–92), a local landowner in whose store the po was located. In the mid 1930s, following the completion of KY 80, the po and store were moved about 3 mi to a point on the highway just w of the head of Wolf Creek. Around 1960 the po was moved to its present site about a mi w on KY 80, to be closer to its patrons. The community served by the po at its 2 most recent locations has been locally called Caintown. 1410.

Cairo (Henderson): *kā*/roh (Poole). This hamlet with extinct po extends for almost a mi along US 41A, 6½ mi ssw of Henderson. The first name proposed by Albert G. Walker for the po he est there on Aug 1, 1840, was rejected by the postal authorities. Why he then suggested Cairo has never been determined; there is no evidence that he named it for the town in southern Illinois. Kentucky's Cairo was inc in 1873. Its po closed in 1903. 12.

Calaboose, Callaboose (Wolfe): *kael*/ə/būs (Pomeroyton). This extinct po was on the ridge w of Big Calaboose Creek (a branch of the Red R), 3 mi n of Campton. The name is said to have been applied early in the 19th cent to the then inaccessible and inhospitable creek, whose steep-sided ravine was virtually impossible to get out of when the creek level was high. This apparently reminded some early travelers of the Spanish word *calabozo* meaning a "place of detention." The local po was est on June 19, 1909, as Hardeman, probably for its first pm, George W. Hardeman, but in Apr 1911 it assumed the name Callaboose. No one seems to agree, even now, on the proper spelling of the name. Occasionally one still comes across the folk etymological account of the female moonshiner named Calla who somehow got the po named for her. 423, 1236.

Caldwell County: kaw/*wehl,* koh/*wehl,* kâhld/*wehl,* kə/*wehl, kahl*(*d*)/wehl. 347 sq mi. Pop 13,200. Seat: Princeton. Caldwell Co was est in 1809 from part of Livingston Co and named for Gen. John Caldwell who, after service in George Rogers Clark's Indian campaign of 1786, participated in the 1787–88 Danville Conventions considering Kentucky statehood. He went on to serve in the Kentucky senate (1792–96) and was for several months, until his death in 1804, Kentucky's second lieutenant governor.

Caldwell PO (Marshall). See *Altona*

Caldwells Store (Anderson). See *Ballard*

Caleast (Madison): *kael*/*eest* (Richmond South). This extinct po and crossroads store were on KY 52, 1 mi w of the present I 75 and 3 mi s of Richmond. The po, probably named for its first pm, Calvin East, was in operation from 1894 to 1905. 1294.

Caledonia (Boone). See *Petersburg*

Calhoun (McLean): *kael*/hūn (Calhoun). This 5th class city and seat of McLean Co is on the n bank of Green R, 90 mi sw of downtown Louisville. Henry Rhoads (1739–1809), a German-born Pennsylvanian, is reported to have laid out a town at the Long Falls of Green R in 1784–85 and called it Rhoadsville. In 1785 his brother

Solomon is said to have built a fort on the hill overlooking the r. The community was renamed Fort Vienna, ostensibly by John Hanley who had acquired Rhoads's land by suit in 1787. A po was est there as Calhoun on Feb 23, 1849, with William H. Williams, pm, named for John Calhoon (*sic*) (1797–1852), lawyer, circuit judge, and US congressman (1835–39). The town was laid off and chartered in 1852 and contended successfully with *Rumsey*, across the r, for the seat of the new co which was est in 1854. 567, 932.

California (Campbell): kael/ə/*fawrn*/yə (New Richmond). This 6th class city with po is on the Ohio R, 5 mi se of Alexandria. It is likely that sometime before 1813 a settlement was founded at this site around James Kennedy's ferry, for a po of that name was est on June 6 of that year, with John Reed, pm. In 1817 this po was moved about 1½ mi sw and renamed Flagg Spring [*flaegh sprihŋ*], ostensibly for a local spring around which some wild iris or flagg may have grown. On Dec 10, 1852, the po of California was est at the Kennedy's Ferry site with John H. Nelson, pm, and probably named for the western state. (Curiously, it has been suggested that Campbell Co's California may first have been called Oregon, or at least a community of that name may have preceded the est of the California po at that site). After this po was closed in 1863, the Flagg Spring po was returned to this site and renamed California. Then another Flagg Spring po was opened at the Flagg Spring site in 1870 and operated there until Jan 1907. The town of California was inc in 1874. A residential community at the jct of KY 10 and 735, less than 1 mi se of the Flagg Spring po site, still bears the Flagg Spring name. 464, 985, 1300.

Callaway (Bell): *kael*/ə/wā (Balkan). This village with po is on the Cumberland R and US 119, 6½ mi e of Pineville. The local po was est as Letcher on Jan 14, 1831, with Lewis Green, pm, and named for then Kentucky Congressman (and later Governor) Robert P. Letcher (1788–1861). In 1855 the name was changed to Callaway, probably for Charles J. Callaway who served as pm from 1838 to 1875.

Callis Grove (Trimble). See *Hisle*

Callis PO (Trimble). See *Hisle*

Calloway County: *kael*/ə/wā. 386 sq mi. Pop 28,900. Seat: Murray. Est in 1822 from part of Hickman Co, this co was named for Col. Richard Calloway, one of the founders, with Daniel Boone, of the Boonsborough settlement. He represented Kentucky Co in the Virginia General Assembly and was killed by Indians at Boonesborough in 1780.

Calvert (Marshall). See *Calvert City*

Calvert City (Marshall): *kael*/vərt *siht*/ee (Calvert City). This 4th class industrial city with po lies at the jct of KY 95 and the Illinois Central Gulf RR, 2 mi s of the Tennessee R and 9½ mi n of Benton. Around 1870 the Paducah & Elizabethtown (now ICG) RR was offered a right-of-way by P[otilla] W[illis] Calvert if it would build a station on his land and name it for him. This was done and the town built up around it was inc as Calvert City on Mar 18, 1871. The Calvert City po was est on Aug 27, 1872, with Wilson H. Calvert, pm. In 1957 the Board on Geographic Names reversed its 1924 decision which had favored Calvert, the name applied to the local rr station. 76, 133, 987, 992.

Calvin (Bell): *kael*/vən (Varilla, Middlesboro North). This hamlet with po and a station on the Kentucky & Virginia (L&N) RR, is located on the Cumberland R just below the mouth of Hances Creek, 4 mi ese of Pineville. While the station has always been known as Page, the po was est as Calvin on Apr 3, 1908, with Belle Pursifull, pm, and named for the local magistrate, Henry Calvin Miracle. Until 1966 when the Board of

Geographic Names decided in favor of Calvin, the community had also been identified as Page on topographic maps. 993, 1058.

Camargo (Montgomery): kə/*mahr*/goh (Levee). This 6th class city with extinct po, on US 460, 4 mi se of Mt. Sterling, is generally believed to have been named for a town in Mexico by veterans of Zachary Taylor's army in the Mexican War (1846–48). But according to one account, it may have honored a Mexican entertainer named Camargo who "delighted" American servicemen during their stay in his country. Yet references to an early 19th cent church of this name in the co have also been found. The po was est on Nov 22, 1848, with J. M. Ricketts, pm, and closed in 1963. 1032, 1237.

Camdensville (Anderson). See *Glensboro*

Campbell *County: kaem*/(b)əl. 152 sq mi. Pop 83,800. Seat: Alexandria. This co was est in 1794 from parts of Mason, Scott, and Harrison co's and named for Col. John Campbell, Irish-born Revolutionary War officer and Jefferson Co pioneer landowner, who may have helped to lay out the forerunner of Louisville. He represented Campbell Co in Kentucky's first constitutional convention and the state senate.

Campbell Court House PO (Campbell). See *Newport*

Campbellsburg (Henry): *kaem(b)*/əlz/bergh (Campbellsburg). This 6th class city with po extends for 1 mi w along US 421 from its jct with KY 55 and 574, 1½ mi e of I 71 and 6 mi n of New Castle. What may first have been called Campbellsville for a local family was est on Jan 29, 1840, by legislative act as Chiltonsville and named for the family of Charles J. Chilton, a trustee. Three weeks later, another act changed its name to Campbellsburg and the po, which had been est in the vicinity as Benevola on Feb 25, 1830, was also renamed Campbellsburg in Sept 1840. The arrival of the Louisville Cincinnati & Lexington (or Short Line, now L&N) RR at a point ½ mi e and the construction of a depot in 1869 led to a population shift and soon to the distinction between Old and New Campbellsburg. The po and other businesses were moved to the vicinity of the depot, and New Campbellsburg was inc in 1876. Over the years the corporate boundaries of the latter have extended to include most of Old Campbellsburg and the town is now known simply as Campbellsburg. 59, 1256.

Campbellsburg (Russell). See *Creelsboro*

Campbellsville (Henry). See *Campbellsburg*

Campbellsville (Taylor): *kaem*/bəlz/vihl (Campbellsville). This 3rd class city and seat of Taylor Co is on US 68 (KY 55), 62 mi sse of downtown Louisville. It was est by the Kentucky legislature on Jan 3, 1817, and named for Andrew Campbell who had founded and laid it out on land he had acquired and settled as early as 1808. The po dates from Jan 2, 1817, and the town, inc in 1838, became the seat of newly est Taylor Co in 1848. 1291.

Camp Dix (Lewis): *kaemp dihx* (Head of Grassy). The late Dick Howard's fishing camp on Kinniconick Creek and the present KY 59, 7 mi sse of Vanceburg, was a very popular vacation spot. Dick's Camp became Camp Dix when the Mouth of Laurel po, 2 mi below, was moved to the campsite on July 1, 1935. Mouth of Laurel po was est on June 17, 1864, and named for its location at the mouth of this fork of Kinniconick. The Camp Dix po still serves that vicinity. 1103.

Camp Ground (Laurel). See *Boreing*

Camp Knox (Green). See *Haskinsville*

Camp Knox (Hardin). See *Ft. Knox, Stithton*

Camp Nelson (Jessamine and Garrard): kaemp *nehl*/sən (Little Hickman). This hamlet of indistinct boundaries lies on both sides of the Kentucky R in the area just below the mouth of Hickman Creek, at least 6 mi s of Nicholasville and 9 mi n of Lancaster. On the site of a natural ford and antebellum community on the Jessamine Co side of the r, the first Union Army recruiting station in Kentucky was est in 1863 and named for Gen. William Nelson, who had been killed in a duel with a fellow officer in 1862. The first po to serve the area was est as Jessamine on Oct 17, 1853. It moved across the river to Garrard Co in 1861 but returned to Jessamine Co as Camp Nelson on Aug 21, 1863. Its intermittent existence on both sides of the r ended in 1920 by which time it had come to occupy a site by the old US 27 bridge on the Garrard Co side. The area was recently developed as a tourist attraction with stores, a motel, craft and specialty shops. About 1½ miles n of the river is the *Camp Nelson National Cemetery* with the graves of over 5000 Union dead. 130, 1390.

Campton (Wofe): *kaem(p)*/tən (Campton). This 6th class city and the seat of Wolfe Co, is located on KY 191 (old KY 15), just s of the Mountain Parkway and 116 mi ese of downtown Louisville. According to tradition, when Nim Wills arrived at the present site of the courthouse, he saw the remains of an old camp that he assumed had been made by Jonathan Swift on one of his famed silver mine adventures. Soon a settlement grew up around the site and was called first Camp Town and then Campton, while the local stream still bears the name Swift Camp Creek. The po was est as Campton on Jan 16, 1867, with Francis M. Vaughn, pm, and the town was inc in 1870. 67.

Campton Junction (Powell). See *Natural Bridge*

Canada (Pike): *kaen*/ə/də (Belfry). This hamlet with po on US 119 at the forks of Big Creek, 12 mi ne of Pikeville, was named for one or more local families of Canada or Kennedy. The po was est on May 3, 1876, with Lewis Runyon, pm. 1143.

Candy (Perry). See *Fourseam*

Cane Run Settlement (Mercer). See *Burgin*

Cane Valley (Adair): *kān vael*/ee (Cane Valley). This village with po is on old KY 55, 4½ mi n of Columbia. At the head of Caney Fork of Russell Creek, Patrick Henry Bridgewater opened a store, started a steam-powered saw- and flour mill, and, on Aug 6, 1855, est a po he named for the thick cane brakes in the valley. 9, 388.

Caney (Morgan): *kān*/ee (Cannel City). This hamlet with po, centered at the jct of KY 191 and 1000, 7 mi s of West Liberty, was once a thriving trade center. The community grew up around the Walnut Grove Church which had been organized by pioneer Baptist preacher Daniel Williams at the mouth of Brushy Fork of Caney Creek and named for the local grove of walnut trees. It may have been known early as the Walnut Grove Community and as Pinhook for the bent pins residents often used for fishing. The po, est on Aug 2, 1854, by David Isaac Lykins, was named Caney, it is said, for one Elcaney Lykins, a highly respected local resident, and the community also assumed this name. 271.

Caney (Creek) (Knott). See *Pippa Passes*

Caney Fork (Barren). See *Etoile*

Caneyville (Grayson): *kā*/nee/vihl (Caneyville). This 6th class city with po on US 62, 10 mi wsw of Leitchfield, probably began as a pioneer trading post just below the forks of Caney Creek, for whose cane bottoms it was named. Its po was est on Feb 25, 1837; the town was founded 3 years later, and chartered by the Kentucky legislature on Apr 9, 1880. 313, 572.

Cannel City (Morgan): *kaen*/əl *siht*/ee (Cannel City). This is now a hamlet with po, extending about 1½ mi along KY 191, on Stone Coal Fork of Caney Creek, and 8½ mi s of West Liberty. It developed around and was named for the cannel coal mines est there around 1900, and until the mines closed in the mid-1930s was a prosperous community of some 1500 residents. The local po has been in operation since Jan 27, 1902. 506, 603.

Cannon (Knox): *kaen*/ən (Fount). This po on KY 11 and Little Richland Creek, 2½ mi ne of Barbourville, was est on May 29, 1901, by Henry L. Cannon and named for his family. Yet one occasionally hears the name attributed to the cannon set up during the Civil War by pro-Union militia to halt Gen. Felix Zollicoffer's approach to a local salt works during his march on Barbourville. 1409.

Cannonsburg (Boyd): *kaen*/ənz/bergh (Ashland). This suburban community with extinct po is just se of the jct of US 60 and KY 180, ¾ mi n of I 64, and 4½ mi ssw of Ashland. Popular accounts tying the name to Civil War artillery must be discounted since the name was applied as early as 1840. In 1836 Jeremiah M. Cannon bought a 100-acre tract on the Marsh Run branch of East Fork of Little Sandy R from Jacob Vanbibber. The local po was est as East Fork on Aug 7, 1839, with John Colvin as pm, and the name was changed in 1850 to Cannonsburg. The po was discontinued in 1932. 1091, 1177.

Canoe (Breathitt): kə/*nū*, *kū*/nū (Canoe). This settlement with po is on KY 1877, ½ mi up Canoe Creek from its confluence with the Middle Fork of the Kentucky R and 7½ mi ssw of Jackson. The po est as Canoe Fork on Aug 14, 1891, with William Little, pm, became simply Canoe in 1894. According to tradition, the creek waters got so low that someone's canoe could not be floated out and had to be abandoned. 1310.

Canoe Fork (Breathitt). See *Canoe*

Canterbury PO (Lawrence). See *Buchanan*

Canton (Trigg): *kaent*/ən (Canton). This village with po is on US 68 (KY 80) and the e bank of Lake Barkley of the Cumberland R, 7½ mi sw of Cadiz. The site was first settled in 1799 by a party led by Abraham Boyd, a North Carolinian, whose horse-powered mill, cotton gin, and warehouse became the nucleus of a thriving shipping center known as Boyds Landing. With this name the po was est on Oct 15, 1820, with George A. Gordon, pm. In 1823 Boyd laid out the town he called Canton, and the po was renamed accordingly in Aug of that year. No one knows why the Canton name was applied. The place may have been named for one or more of the American cities that then bore this name or, reflecting Boyd's aspirations, for the seaport in China with which American ships were by then engaged in considerable trade. 98.

Canyon Falls (Lee): *kaen*/yən *fawlz* (Tallega). The site of a church and mission school and an extinct po on KY 708 and Bear Creek, a tributary of the Middle Fork of the Kentucky R, 6½ mi e of Beattyville, was first called Carters Chapel for a local church. On Oct 14, 1909, Andrew J. Bowman est the now defunct po, which was named for the local canyon and falls. The falls were later dynamited into nonexistence for the construction of a new road. 132, 1372.

Carbon Glow (Letcher): *kahr*/bən *ghloh* (Blackey). This community with extinct po lies at the head of Caudills Branch, 2 mi from its confluence with Rockhouse Creek and 7 mi nw of Whitesburg. Once a large coal camp, it was built in the 1920s by, and named for, the Carbon Glow Coal Co. On Feb 16, 1926, the po of David (which had been est on Dec 26, 1908, by William Caudill and named for David Caudill) was moved ¾ mi up the branch and renamed for the new coal camp. It has been suggested that, in seeking a name to connote the superior quality of its product, the co. modified "glowing coal"—which had that connotation—with "carbon" as a fancier rendering of coal, reversed the words for a catchier name, and came up with Carbon Glow. Or the co. may have wished to trade on the success of the Welsh mining towns called Glo thus-and-so, as did a firm in neighboring Perry Co, which had founded and named a camp *Glomawr* a decade before. In any case, the slate dumps are now the only evidence of the mining that characterized the vicinity in the past. 1218, 1265.

Carcassonne (Letcher): *kahr*/kə/zohn (Blackey). This small settlement with po is on Elk Creek (or Gent) Mt., 9 mi wnw of Whitesburg. The po was est as Gander [*ghaen*/dər] on Mar 27, 1907, with Harrison Banks, pm, and was named, it is believed, for the many wild geese found there at the time. In the early 1920s, a settlement school was opened there by Hendrix D. Caudill. The large cliffs surrounding the school are said to have so reminded one young teacher of the walled city of Carcassonne in southern France that she succeeded in getting it named the Carcassonne Community Center. In 1937 the po was renamed Carcassonne. 1265.

Carlisle (Nicholas): kahr/*lah*/əl (Carlisle). This 4th class city and seat of Nicholas Co is on KY 32 and 36, 87 mi e of downtown Louisville. It was founded in 1816 on land donated by John Kincart for the relocation of the co's seat from *Ellisville*, 5 mi n, and probably named by him for his late father Samuel's hometown, Carlisle, Pennsylvania. The po was est on Jan 28, 1817, with Jesse Bouldin, pm. 1374.

Carlisle County: *kahr*/lah/əl. 191 sq mi. Pop 6,300. Seat: Bardwell. Est in 1886 from part of Ballard Co, Carlisle Co was named for John Griffin Carlisle (1835–1910). He served Kentucky in the US Congress from 1877 to 1891, the last 6 years as Speaker, and in the US Senate from 1890 to 1893 when he was appointed Secretary of the Treasury in Cleveland's second administration.

Carlsbad (Grant). See *Dry Ridge*

Carlton PO (Boone). See *Rabbit Hash*

Carmack (Lyon): *kahr*/maek (Eddyville). Little remains of this settlement, on what had been KY 522, 2½ mi sw of Old Eddyville. First called Pottertown for a pottery and store est there in the late 1880s by J. Frank Bonner, it was renamed for its location ½ mi ne of the forks of Carmack Creek, a branch of the Cumberland R. Since this stream is so identified on early surveys, it is doubtful that it was named for Edward W. Carmack (1858–1908), US senator from Tennessee (1901–7), as has been suggested. The Carmack post office, also est by Bonner, was in operation from 1890 to 1912, the Pottertown name, having already been applied to a po in Calloway Co. 96, 1025.

Carmen PO (Pike). See *Venters*

Carntown (Pendleton): *kahrn*/town (Moscow). This settlement with extinct po is on KY 154, between KY 8 and the Ohio R, just below the mouth of Stepstone Creek, 11½ mi nne of Falmouth. This site may first have been called Barker's Landing and Stepstone but the po was est on July 5, 1839, as Motier [*mawt*/ə/yər] with Francis Chalfant, pm. It was discontinued in 1872 and re-est the following year with Hiram J. Carnes as pm. Jacob Carnes, who had become pm in 1884, had the name changed to Carntown in 1891. The po was discontinued in 1920. Stepstone Creek was named by surveyors in 1793 for the resemblance of its bed to a series of stone steps. The derivation of the other names is unknown. 847.

Carpenter (Whitley): *kahr*/pən/tər (Frakes). This hamlet with po is on KY 92, 10½ mi e of Williamsburg. The po was est on Aug 1, 1882, and named for its first pm, E. A. Carpenter, or his family.

Carpenters Mill PO (Allen). See *Allen Springs*

Carr Creek (Knott Co.): *kahr kreek* (Blackey). This hamlet with recently discontinued po is on the new Carr Fork Lake, ¾ mi up KY 160 from its jct with KY 15, and 6 mi s of Hindman. For many years the community centered on a boarding school founded in 1920 by 2 Massachusetts women, Olive V. Marsh and Ruth E. Watson. The po of

Dirk, est on Dec 22, 1905, to serve this area, was renamed Carr Creek in 1928 to honor the school, which had just sent its basketball team to compete in the national high school tournament in Chicago. The school had been named for the Carr Fork of the North Fork of the Kentucky R, which in turn had been named for a pioneer settler, historically identified only as "Old Man Carr," who was said to have been scalped by the Indians on nearby Defeated Creek. Or perhaps, as Harry Caudill recently suggested, Carr Fork was named for Willie Carr, a mulatto who had "accompanied a band of North Carolinian" hunters to that area around 1794. Pursued by Indians, he jumped from a high ledge into "the rock-strewn creek." The origin of Dirk is unknown. 321, 1262, 1370.

Carrington PO (Menifee). See *Sudith*

Carroll County: *kaer*/əl. 130 sq mi. Pop 9,287. Seat: Carrollton. Est in 1838 from part of Gallatin Co, Carroll Co. was named for Charles Carroll of Carrollton, Maryland (1737–1832), one of the signers of the Declaration of Independence.

Carrollton (Carroll): *kaer*/əl/tən (Carrollton). The seat of Carroll Co, this 4th class city on the Ohio R and US 42, 39 mi ne of downtown Louisville, was first called Port William, probably for William Porter, an early settler. A town was laid out at this site in 1792 by Benjamin Craig and James Hawkins on part of 613 acres they had purchased from the 2000-acre French and Indian War grant of Col. William Peachy, and was formally est as Port William by an act of the Kentucky legislature on Dec 13, 1794. According to a descendant, Porter, the son of John and Elizabeth Porter of Somerset Co., Maryland, arrived with his family in 1790, bought up considerable land in the vicinity of the future town, and became prominent in its early affairs. Port William became the seat of newly organized Gallatin Co in 1798, and a po of this name was est there in 1807 with Robert Plummer, pm. When *Carroll Co* was formed in 1838, both town and po were renamed Carrollton for the Maryland home of Charles Carroll (1737–1832), the last surviving signer of the Declaration of Independence, for whom the co itself was named. 143, 412, 896, 1330.

Carrollton PO (Fayette). See *Donerail*

Carrs (Lewis): Kahrz (Concord). This settlement with extinct po in the Ohio R bottom, 6 mi nw of Vanceburg, may first have been called Stouts Landing for a pioneer family. The po was est as Station Landing on June 4, 1867, with Ritcherson M. Stout, pm. In less than a year it had been renamed Carrs for Frederick M. Carr, then pm and storekeeper. The po closed in 1953. 1200.

Carrsville (Livingston): *kahrz*/vəl (Rosiclair, Shetlerville). Now a hamlet with po, Carrsville, until recently one of the state's smallest cities, is located on the Ohio R, 17 mi n of Smithland. It was probably first settled by a family of Lusks before 1803. By 1840 Billy Karr, for whose family the village was named, is known to have est there a landing and a trading post which early steamboat men may have referred to as Karrs (or Carrs) Landing. (No one seems to know why the name was corrupted.) In 1840 Billy divided his extensive local land holdings into lots for sale, and the town that he then laid out was inc in 1860. On Aug 15, 1854, the Carrsville po was est with Leander Berry, pm. 1151, 1189, 1439.

Carsons Landing (Butler). See *Logansport*

Carter City (Carter) *kahr*/tər (Tygarts Valley, Wesleyville). This village with po lies at the confluence of Smith and Buffalo Creeks, the latter a tributary of Tygarts Creek, and at the jct of KY 2 and 474, 11 mi nw of Grayson. In 1893 the Kinniconick & Freestone (C&O) RR was completed from Garrison on the Ohio R to this point to haul area livestock, farm, and forest products. On Jan 24, 1895, the Goble po, which had been est in 1886 at a site some 2 mi e, was moved by its pm, James M. Zornes, to the tracks, and M. K. Ratliff, a large landowner, laid out a town. It was called Carter, the name that had come to be applied to the station by passengers on the first train runs, and by this name it was inc in 1906. Though the po has always been called Carter, the town itself has been known as both Carter and Carter City. 36, 317, 1250.

Carter County: *kahr*/tər. 407 sq mi. Pop 25,029. Seat: Grayson. Carter Co was est in 1838 from parts of Greenup and Lawrence co's and named for Col. William Grayson Carter, then a state senator from the district that included the new co.

Carter PO (Carter). See *Carter City*

Carters Chapel (Lee). See *Canyon Falls*

Cartersville (Garrard): *kahr*/tərz/vihl (Paint Lick). This hamlet with extinct po is on KY 954, 10 mi se of Lancaster. According to one account, it was at first called Linchburg, until Byham Carter est a gristmill and blacksmith shop there and it was renamed for him or his family. It may also have been named for John B. Carter who opened the local po on Apr 29, 1890. No one seems to know the origin of the Linchburg name, or the reason for its curious spelling. Some have even questioned whether these identify the same place. The po closed in 1925. 130, 918, 1225.

Casey (Butler): *kā*/zee (Welches Creek). A settlement with extinct po on KY 340, 8 mi nne of Morgantown, Casey was named for the family of George W. Casey who became the first pm on Oct 2, 1919. 1341.

Casey County: *kā*/see. 445 sq mi. Pop 14,761. Seat: Liberty. Casey Co was est in 1806 from part of Lincoln Co and named for Col. William Casey, Virginia-born pioneer settler of the upper Green R Area.

Caseys Landing (Union). See *Caseyville*

Caseyville (Meade). See *Paynesville*

Caseyville (Union): *kā*/see/vihl (Dekoven). This settlement with extinct po, once a prosperous Ohio R port, lies 2 mi above the mouth of Tradewater R and, 12½ mi sw of Morganfield. It was founded in 1826–27 by Nicholas Casey (1790–1863), the Harrodsburg-born son of pioneer surveyor Peter Casey whose Revolutionary War military grant included extensive acreage in Union Co. First called Caseys Landing for Nicholas's woodyard, ferry, and steamboat supply depot, it was renamed Caseyville when, through Nicholas's influence as a state legislator, it was inc in 1837. The po was est on Aug 6, 1838, with John Casey, pm. 157, 238, 1229.

Casky (Christian): *kaes*/kee (Hopkinsville). Now a small settlement, this once prosperous shipping point is on the L&N RR, 2 mi se of Hopkinsville. It is generally believed that the station and po were named for James Casky who donated the land for the depot. James was the son of Joseph Casky, a Virginian who had arrived in Christian Co in the 1830s and acquired extensive land holdings in the area se of Hopkinsville. On May 18, 1868, James est the po as Casky Station but this was changed to Casky in Dec 1880. The po closed in 1933. 1403.

Casky Station (Christian). See *Casky*

Castle PO (Morgan). See *Stacy Fork*

Cat Creek PO (Powell). See *Rosslyn*

Catherine (Russell); *kaeth*/rən (Eli). This extinct po, about 2 mi s of the jct of Casey, Russell, and Pulaski co's and 10 mi ne of Jamestown, was est by John Wesley Eads, local storekeeper and first pm, on Dec 23, 1908, and named for his wife, Polly Catherine Eads. 1110, 1144.

Catlettsburg (Boyd): *kaet*/ləts/bergh (Catlettsburg). This 4th class city and the seat of Boyd Co is located at the confluence of the Big Sandy and Ohio rs, just se of the city of

Ashland and 159 mi e of downtown Louisville. The first permanent settlers were Virginians Alexander Catlett and his son Horatio, who had arrived about 1798, and for whom the po, est by Horatio on Dec 5, 1810, was named. The community grew up around Horatio's tavern which, from 1808 to 1833, catered to Ohio R travelers. By the mid 19th cent it had become an important steamboat landing called the Mouth of Sandy or Big Sandy Landing. The town was laid out in 1849 by James Wilson Fry to whose grandfather, James Wilson, Horatio had sold his property in 1833. It was inc in 1858 and became the seat of newly organized Boyd Co in 1860. The section of the present city s of Division St. was annexed in 1893. Until then it was a separate town called Hampton City, which had been laid out by and named for Rev. William Hampton in 1852 and chartered in 1870. Catlettsburg reached its peak of prosperity before 1900 as one of the largest hardwood timber markets in the world. Its strategic location also made it the principal "port for the trans-shipment of goods between Ohio and Big Sandy steamboats." 221, 548, 561, 820.

Cato (Harlan). See *Cawood*

Cato PO (Pulaski). See *Eubank*

Causey (Leslie): *kâhs*/ee (Cutshin). This hamelt with recently closed po is 1 mi up Baker Fork of Wolf Creek, 8 mi se of Hyden, in the Cutshin Creek watershed. The po, est on June 7, 1906, with John M. Baker, pm, was named for a local family. 1248.

Cave City (Barren): *kav sih*/tee (Horse Cave). This 5th class city with po is centered at the jct of US 31W and KY 70, 7 mi n of Glasgow. In 1853 the Knob City Land Co. of Louisville acquired the site from Thomas T. Duke with plans for a resort to trade on its proximity to Mammoth Cave. The tract was surveyed and laid off into town lots. On June 12, 1860, the aptly named po of Woodland, which had been est in 1850 not far n, was moved to the Knob City site by Beverly Curd, the storekeeper, and renamed for either the many caves of varying size in the area or for one large cave within the future city's limits. The town was inc in 1866. 378, 655.

Caverna PO (Hart). See *Horse Cave*

Cawood (Harlan): *kā*/wo͞od (Evarts). This village with po is on US 421, at the mouth of Crummies Creek, a branch of Martins Fork of the Cumberland R, and 5½ mi se of Harlan. The po was est on Apr 4, 1890, with Wilson S. Hensley, pm, and named for the family whose progenitor is said to have been Berry Cawood (1758–1848), a Revolutionary War veteran. Berry's son John may have been the site's first settler, about 1814. The local L&N RR station is called Cato. 890, 1044.

Cayce (Fulton): *kā*/see (Cayce). This village with extinct po on KY 94 and 239 and the Illinois Central Gulf RR, 7½ mi e of Hickman, was probably named for a local merchant, James Hardie Cayce, who was also the first pm of the po est on July 20, 1860, as Caceys Station. This error was officially corrected in 1874 and "Station" was dropped from the po name in 1880. The po closed in 1965. Contrary to popular belief, this was not the birthplace of famed rr engineer John Luther (Casey) Jones (1864–1900) but the town to which he and his family moved from their native Missouri when he was 13. His nickname—always "Cayce" in his lifetime—was derived from his hometown to avoid confusion with the numerous other Joneses then employed by the Illinois Central RR. The corrupted "Casey" spelling came only with the developing legend after his death. 48, 103, 251.

Cebb (Caldwell). See *Cobb*

Cecilia (Hardin): *sə*/*sihl*/yə (Cecilia). This village with po is at the jct of 2 branches of the present Illinois Central Gulf RR and KY 86, 1 mi nw of US 62 and 3½ mi wsw of Elizabethtown. It is not known how early the Cecilia name or some form of it was first applied to the site but it is known to have derived from the family of Col. Charles Cecil, a prominent early Hardin Co citizen whose 3 sons, Henry, Thomas, and Ambrose D., had founded Cecilian College there in 1860. With the coming of the rr (later made part of the Illinois Central System) in 1870, a station was est called Cecilian Junction, and the town was known as Cecilian, the name by which its po was est on Jan 13, 1871. In 1912, po, station, and community alike assumed the shortened spelling Cecilia for reasons that are not known. 757, 800.

Cecilian (Hardin). See *Cecilia*

Cecilian Junction (Hardon). See *Cecilia*

Cedar Creek (Cumberland). See *Bow*

Cedar Creek PO (Owen). See *Monterey*

Cedar Flats (Breckinridge). See *Chenaultt*

Cedar Spring (Edmonson): *seed*/ər *sprihŋ* (Smith Grove, Rhoda). This rural settlement on KY 259 at the southern edge of Mammoth Cave National Park, 7 mi se of Brownsville, was named for the grove of cedar trees around one of a number of area springs that furnished water for early settlers. The community does not have its own po. 942.

Center (Metcalfe): *sehn*/tər (Center). This village with po extends for ½ mi along KY 314, 11 mi nnw of Edmonton. According to most co historians, it was first settled around 1800 by Joseph Philpott from Frederick, Maryland, and may first have been called Frederick. It was definitely known as Lafayette [lā/fee/*eht*] after the visit of the famous Frenchman to America in 1825. The po was est as Centre (later Center) on Nov 14, 1838, with Samuel W. Thompson, pm, because the Lafayette name was already in use in Christian Co. Centre or Center referred to its location equally distant from Glasgow, Edmonton, Greensburg, and Munfordville, the 4 area co seats. For some reason, however, an act of the Kentucky legislature, approved on Feb 6, 1839, officially named the community Frederick. It was finally inc as Centre in 1871. While it has generally been assumed that Frederick was named for Philpott's hometown, Judge Joseph Martin has suggested the possibility of its having been named for a Major Frederick Smith, a Revolutionary War veteran. 142, 192.

Centerpoint (LaRue). See *Magnolia*

Center Point (Monroe): *sehn*/ter point (Vernon). This hamlet with extinct po is on KY 212, at the edge of the Cumberland R's n bottom, ¾ mi e of the confluence of Meshack Creek and the r, 8½ mi e of Tompkinsville. On land believed to have been first settled in the 1790s, the po was est as Centre Point on Aug 27, 1835, with William J. Dixon, pm, and named for its location midway between Burkesville, Tompkinsville, and Celina. By the early 20th cent, the name was being spelled in the modern way, Center Point. The po was discontinued in 1939. 1395.

Centertown (Ohio): *sehn*/(t)ər/town (Hartford). This 6th class city with po on KY 85 and 69, 4½ mi sw of Hartford, is in the midst of what has been an important coal producing area. It may have been called Centerville as early as 1860 for its location midway between Hartford and the Green R shipping port of Point Pleasant, but the po was est as Centre Town on Feb 1, 1866, with Charles H. Dillingham, pm, and later became Centertown. The town was inc in 1890. 905, 1245, 1400.

Centerville (Bourbon): *sehn*/ter/vihl (Centerville). This hamlet is centered at the jct of US 460 and KY 353, 1 mi ne of the confluence of Bourbon, Scott, and Fayette co's and 6 mi w of Paris. A po est as Centreville on July 1, 1812, with Ayers Stewart, pm, was named for its location between Lexington, Paris, Georgetown, and Cynthiana. The town was inc on Feb 20, 1850. The po has since closed. 167, 538.

Centerville (Crittenden). See *Crayne, Salem*
Centerville (Madison). See *Kirksville*
Centerville (Marion). See *Bradfordsville*
Centerville (Ohio). See *Centertown*

Central City (Muhlenberg): *sihn*/trəl *siht*/ee (Central City East, Central City West). This 4th class industrial city, the largest in the co, is on US 62 and 431, just n of the Western Kentucky Parkway, and 3½ mi nne of Greenville. The town, est around 1870 when the Elizabethtown & Paducah (now Illinois Central Gulf) RR was built through, was earlier a settlement called Moreheads Horse Mill for a steam-powered gristmill run by Charles S. Morehead, a local farmer. In 1873 the town was inc as Stroud City [*strowd siht*/ee] for John Stroud who had by then come into possession of Morehead's property. In 1882 it was re-inc as Central City for the Central Coal and Iron Co., which had begun developing its holdings there in 1873. The po, est by George Shaver on Aug 7, 1871, was first called Owensborough Junction in anticipation of the completion of the Owensboro & Russellville (now L&N) RR to this site by the summer of 1872 when it would cross the E&P and provide service for *Owensboro*, some 30 mi n. In 1880 the po was renamed Stroud and, in 1882, Central City. 189, 866.

Ceralvo (Ohio): sər/*ael*/voh (Central City East). This small settlement is all that remains of a thriving 19th cent Green R shipping port, 8½ mi sw of Hartford, which was nearly altogether destroyed by the 1937 flood. The town was laid out in 1851 by H. D. Taylor and inc in 1870. The po was est on Feb 22, 1855, with Aaron W. Davis, pm, and discontinued in 1944. The name's origin has long mystified co historians. Some have suggested a derivation from the Spanish words *cera* (wax) and *albo* (white), or the Spanish and Portuguese *cerro* (a small craggy hill) and *albo* or *alvo* (white). According to one account, with no elucidation, the town may have been named by an early settler whose wife came from a lovely Scottish village high on a cliff overlooking a r, for a large section of Ceralvo was built on a high bank above the Green. A nearby highway marker suggests that the name was taken from the Spanish word for deer, "ciervo," for legend has it that "a large herd of deer once watered and crossed the river" at this point. If, as is generally believed, the name was brought it by early settlers, its origin may never really be known. 634, 1067.

Cerulean (Trigg): sə/*rūl*/yən (Gracey). This small community, a recently disincorporated city, is on Muddy Fork of Little R, at the jct of KY 124, 126, and 624, 8 mi ne of Cadiz. The famed 19th cent health resort of Cerulean Springs had its beginnings in 1817 and after 1835 achieved prominence as a major resort of the Upper South. The local po was established as Cerulean Springs in 1824; it was discontinued in 1843 and re-est in 1870. In 1894 it became simply Cerulean, by which name the community is still generally known though it was inc as Cerulean Springs in 1888. It is not known when either name was first applied to the place. According to legend, the springs' original black sulphur content was changed by the New Madrid earthquake of 1811 to that of chloride of magnesia with its characteristic sky blue cast. The po has recently closed. 98, 166, 756.

Cerulean Springs (Trigg). See *Cerulean*

Chad (Harlan): chaed (Louellen). This hamlet with extinct po and a station on the L&N RR's Cumberland Valley Division is on US 119 and the Poor Fork of Cumberland R, 17½ mi ene of Harlan. The po of Creech, est on June 15, 1881, with John W. Creech, pm, was moved 1 mi e in 1924 and renamed Chad for the station which had been named for Chadwell Nolen, an L&N agent there, or for Chad Buford, the hero of John Fox, Jr.'s famous novel *The Little Shepherd of Kingdom Come*. 740, 1173.

Chalybeate (Edmonson): kə/*lihb*/ee/ət (Rhoda, Smith Grove). This hamlet with extinct po lies at the jct of the present KY 101 and 1659, 4 mi sse of Brownsville. To exploit the number of mineral springs in the area, a late 19th cent health resort was located in the vicinity. The po of Chalybeate Springs was est here on Oct 12, 1888, with William T. Dunn, pm, but the "Springs" was dropped from the name in 1895, and the po was discontinued in 1931. 942.

Chalybeate Springs PO (Edmonson). See *Chalybeate*

Chapeze (Bullitt). See *Limestone Springs*

Chaplin (Nelson): *chaep*/lən (Chaplin). This prosperous village with po is centered at the jct of US 62 and KY 458, 1 mi from Chaplin R, for which it was undoubtedly named, and 13 mi ne of Bardstown. The po was est on Jan 4, 1832, with Asher Bodine, pm, and the town was first inc in 1850. Capt. Abraham Chapline (1754–1824), one of James Harrod's party which settled Harrodsburg in 1774, discovered this branch of Salt R that bears his name. The name of the stream and community is no longer spelled with the terminal "e." 339.

Chaplinton (Chaplaintown) (Barren). See *Pageville*

Chappell (Leslie): *chaep*/əl (Cutshin). This po at the mouth of Robin Branch of Greasy Creek, 10 mi s of Hyden, was est on Dec 17, 1895, and named by and for its first pm, Henry M. Chappell, the first of his family to settle in that vicinity. 1248.

Charleston (Hopkins): *chahrl*/stən (Dawson Springs). This hamlet with extinct po extends for over a mi along KY 109, 10 mi sw of Madisonville. According to old-timers, it should be Charles' Town for it was named for "Free Charles" (last name unknown), a Negro freedman who ran a local tavern. The po, in operation from 1855 to 1909, and coal loading station on the Illinois Central RR served a major western coal-producing area. 432.

Charlotte Furnace (Carter). See *Iron Hill*

Charlotte Station (Harlan). See *Grays Knob*

Charters (Lewis): *chahr*/tərz (Charters). This settlement with extinct po is at the jct of KY 10 and 989, 5½ mi w of Vanceburg. The po was est on Nov 13, 1871, as Salt Lick Valley for its location in the valley just below the forks of Salt Lick Creek. It was renamed Valley in 1875 and Charters in 1915, the latter change to avoid confusion with Valley Station in Jefferson Co. It has been suggested that Charters was named for Anna Charters Redden but the Valley name has also remained in local usage. The po closed in 1952. 1200, 1359.

Chatham (Bracken) *chaed*/əm (Brooksville). This rural settlement with extinct po is centered at the jct of KY 19 and 606, 3 mi ne of Brooksville. Little is known of its early history, but the po, est on Dec 4, 1871, by William S. McKibben, was supposedly named by him for a town in New York. 27

Cheap (Greenup). See *Flatwoods*

Chenaultt (Breckinridge): shən/*awlt* (Derby). This extinct rural settlement lately centered on an abandoned school on KY 259, ¾ mi east of the Ohio R, 15½ mi n of Hardinsburg. It was first located on the r as Little Dixie Landing, presumably for the large number of Negroes who worked on the wharf, and was later called Cedar Flats for the many such trees surrounding it. On June 30, 1890, the po was est as Chenault (*sic*) for John Chenaultt, pioneer owner of the large tract along the r from the mouth of Yellowbank Creek to Flint Island, which included this site. It is not known when the move inland occurred. 935.

Chenoa (Bell): chə/*noh*/ə, shə/*noh*/ee (Kayjay). Only a po remains at the site of this coal town and station on Clear Creek and KY 190, 10 mi sw of Pineville. To this point a

12-mi-long branch of the Cumberland River and Tennessee (later L&N) RR was completed in Oct 1893. And here W. A. Chenoa opened a cannel coal mine and est a po, on Mar 13, 1894, to serve the camp that grew up around it. 949.

Cherry (Calloway). See *Cherry Corner*

Cherry Corner (Calloway) *cheh*/ree *kawr*/nər (New Concord). This rural settlement, strung out along KY 121 and the Carty Rd, and centered at the jct of KY 121 and 893, 3 mi ese of Murray, was an alternate stop on the old stage and mail route between Paris, Tennessee, and Aurora Kentucky in the 1840s. It is said to have been named for a Mr. Cherry, a local storekeeper. However, it was not until Feb 14, 1889, that a po called Cherry was est in the vicinity with John C. Hicks, pm, and by this shortened name the place is identified on many current maps. The po closed in 1908. 1401, 1441.

Cherry Hill PO (Cumberland). See *Modoc*

Chesnutburg (Clay): *chehs*/nət/bergh (Maulden). This hamlet with po is located at the mouth of Chesnut Branch of Sexton Creek, 9 mi n of Manchester. Both the branch and the po, est on Jan 12, 1904, with Susan Chesnut, pm, were named for the local Chestnut family, the first of whom may have been Billy Chesnut, who arrived from North Carolina in the mid 19th cent. The Chestnut spelling on current maps is in error. 150, 1259.

Chestnut Grove (Shelby): *chehs*/nuht *ghrohv* (Ballardsville). This hamlet is on KY 53 and Bullskin Creek. Its extinct po, est on Jan 26, 1837, with Caleb Guthrie, pm, was named for a local grove of chestnut trees. A mi s is the site of the Gleneyrie School [*ghlihn*/ɛ/ee whose curious name may have been derived from the two words: "glen" for a sheltered place and "eyrie," a nest for a bird of prey, suggesting, perhaps, somebody's home on a high spot. Nothing seems to be known of the name or the reason for its application. Also nearby, possibly centered at the jct of KY 53 and 362, just n of the school, was a section called Egypt, said to have been settled around 1884 during a time of severe drought. Its never failing spring-fed pond attracted farmers from miles around. 902, 1378.

Chevrolet (Harlan): *shehv*/roh/lā (Harlan). This coal town and L&N RR station with po is at the mouth of Enoch Branch of Martins Fork of the Cumberland R and US 421, 2½ mi se of Harlan. The first local mine was opened in 1918 by the Wiliams ByProduct Coal Co., owned by John and Dover Williams of Knoxville, Tennessee, which soon sold out to the larger Blue Diamond Coal Co. The local po of Bee Gee, est on June 5, 1918, with Frank C. Eaton, pm, was renamed Chevrolet in Dec of that year for the car driven by either an early mail carrier or the foreman of the construction gang building a coal tipple, whose model 490 Chevrolet car is said to have been the first to drive over the local rd. 1173.

Chicago (Marion). See *St. Francis*

Chicken Bristle (Metcalfe). See *Savoyard*

Chicken City (Letcher). See *Ulvah*

Childers PO (Pike). See *Hellier*

Chilesburg (Fayette): *cheyelz*/bergh (Clintonville). Little remains of a village with extinct po and a station at the jct of the C&O RR and KY 1973, 1½ mi s of US 60 and 5 mi e of Lexington's New Circle Rd. This was Chilesburg's second location. It was originally located on the old Winchester Pike (now US 60), and grew up around a tavern and stage stop maintained by Richard Chiles (1785–1853), a Virginian, who is said to have had a po there from a very early date until at least 1829, about which time it was discontinued. This po was re-est on May 16, 1863, with Mrs. Alice McGrady, pm. Shortly after the completion of the Lexington and Big Sandy (now the C&O) RR in 1872, the Chilesburg po and village were moved to the new site, where William E. Christian had just built a depot and est Athens Station to serve the town of *Athens,* 4 mi s. The po there closed in 1954. 175.

Chiltonsville (Henry). See *Campbellsburg*

Chinnville (Greenup). See *Raceland*

Chinquapin Rough PO (Jackson). See *Annville*

Chip PO (Letcher). See *Neon*

Christian County: *krihs*/djən. 722 sq mi. Pop 67,600. Seat: Hopkinsville. This co was est in 1796 from part of Logan Co and named for Col. William Christian (1743–86), a pioneer leader who had secured a Virginia land grant to 9000 acres in Jefferson Co. for Revolutionary War service and was killed while leading a raid against a band of marauding Indians.

Christian Court House (Christian). See *Hopkinsville*

Christiansburg (Shelby): *krihs*/chənz/bergh (North Pleasureville). This hamlet with extinct po at the jct of 2 branches of the L&N RR, 7 mi ne of Shelbyville, was formerly called Hinesville, for reasons unknown, or Christiansburg Depot. About a mi ne, at what is now known as Old Christiansburg, the community of Christiansburg was founded in 1819. No one is sure why it was so named though many accept the story of the stranger who, befriended by the residents, suggested the name because there were so many good people living there. It was inc in 1824 and again in 1850. The po, est at the original site on Jan 20, 1827, with Walker Daniel, pm, was later moved to *Bagdad.* On June 29, 1865, it was re-est at the Hinesville–Depot site and again named Christiansburg. 902, 1378.

Christiansburg Depot (Shelby). See *Christiansburg*

Christiansburg PO (Shelby). See *Bagdad*

Christopher (Perry): *krihs*/təf/ər (Hazard South). This residential community with extinct po lies directly across the North Fork of the Kentucky R from Hazard Community College and KY 15, and just s of the Hazard city limits. The po, est as Douglas on Jan 9, 1914, with Stephen A. D. Jones, pm, was aptly renamed Christopher in 1918 for the local Columbus Mining Co. The firm, though, is said to have been named for the Ohio city whence its founders had come. 1186, 1434.

Church Hill (Christian): *chɜch hihl* (Church Hill). This rural settlement with extinct po is on KY 695, 1 mi n of I 24 and 4 mi sw of Hopkinsville. The store and po, est there on Nov 12, 1849, with William T. Whitlock, pm, was named for the extant South Union Baptist Church, which had probably been organized in the early 1840s. The "Hill" part of the name is curious for, though the church sits on a slight rise, the vicinity is but gently rolling farmland and not hilly in the conventional sense. The po was closed in 1902. 1403.

Cicero PO (Woodford). See *Clifton*

Cisco (Magoffin): *sihs*/koh (White Oak). This po is on KY 1869, at the mouth of Bend Branch of the Licking R, across from Carpenter Bend, and 6 mi nnw of Salyersville. It was est on May 26, 1902, and may have been named by and for its first pm, Hatler Cisco, or for his family. Until recently the po was located on Pricy Creek at the Morgan Co line.

Clark County: klahrk. 255 sq mi. Pop 28,334. Seat: Winchester. Clark Co was est in 1792 from parts of Bourbon and Fayette co's and named for Kentucky's military hero, Gen. George Rogers Clark (1752–1818).

Clarksburg (Lewis): *klahrx*/bergh (Vanceburg). This settlement on KY 10 and the Salt Lick Creek bottom, 1½ mi w of Vanceburg, was the co's 2nd seat, from 1809 to 1864.

As the co was named for Meriwether Lewis of the famed Lewis and Clark exploration team, its seat was named for William Clark, the other half of the team. The po, est as Lewis County Court House on Jan 7, 1811, was renamed Clarksburg in 1820. It closed in 1932. 179.

Clarkson (Grayson): *klahrk*/sən (Clarkson). This 6th class city with po is on US 62 just n of the Western Kentucky Parkway, 2½ mi e of Leitchfield. In 1870–71 the Elizabethtown & Paducah (now Illinois Central Gulf) RR was built to this site and the Grayson Springs Station was est to serve the famed resort 2 mi s. This name also identified the po opened there on Jan 24, 1871, with Isaac H. Pirtle, pm. In 1882 the po was renamed Clarkson for Manoah P. Clarkson, the proprietor of the resort. The town was inc as Clarkson on May 1, 1888, but it was not until the late 1930s that the station finally adopted this name for conformity's sake. 489.

Clarks River PO (Calloway). See *Backusburg*

Clarksville (Ballard). See *Ft. Jefferson*

Clay (Webster): klā (Providence). This 5th class city with po is on KY 130, 132, and 270, 6½ mi wsw of Dixon. The po, est on July 6, 1837, with Thomas W. Powell, pm, was first called Ashland, probably for Henry Clay's Lexington home. After an intermittent existence it was renamed Clay in 1854. It was discontinued in 1865 and re-est for a brief time the following year as Winstead with Bush D. Winstead (1837–67), a local merchant and Webster Co's first circuit court clerk, as pm. The Clay name was restored 3 months later. The town was inc as Claysville in 1860 and as Clay in 1872. 1088, 1174.

Clay City (Powell): klā *siht*/ee (Clay City). This 5th class city with po is on the Red R and KY 11/15, just n and e of the Mountain Parkway and less than 2 mi w of Stanton. In 1786 Stephen Collins and his brother from Lexington discovered deposits of iron pyrite near here and shortly thereafter built the first iron forge w of the Alleghenies. The settlement that grew up around it was called Collins Forge. The Collins holdings were later sold to Clark and Smith who est a furnace there in 1805, the forerunner of the Red River Iron Works by which name the community and its po were known for most of the 19th cent. The po, which had been est at least by the early 1820s, was moved across the r sometime in the 1880s to a settlement between the present Clay City and the Mountain Parkway interchange and renamed Waltersville [*wahl*/tərz/vihl] for a local family. The name still identifies this section just outside the Clay City limits. The large forge around which the Iron Works community had been built was located in the middle of the present day Clay City. By 1883 the town had come to be known as Clay City—perhaps officially when the po of that name was est on Aug 13, 1883, with Arthur M. Robertson, pm. It was inc as Clay City in 1890. While some have alleged that it was named for Henry Clay, this is locally doubted since reference is often made to an old brickyard on the n side and the area clay deposits that supplied it. Also, a Clay Lick was mentioned on the old Collins land grant of 1786. 1334.

Clay County: klā. 471 sq mi. Pop 22, 659. Seat: Manchester. Est in 1806 from parts of Madison, Floyd, and Knox co's, Clay Co was named for General Green Clay (1757–1826), prominent pioneer surveyor and military leader in the War of 1812, who represented Kentucky in the Virginia legislature (1788–89) and served in the Kentucky General Assembly (1793–1808). He was a cousin of Henry Clay.

Clay County Court House PO (Clay). See *Manchester*

Clay Lick PO (Owen). See *Gratz*

Claymour (Todd): *klā*/mawr (Sharon Grove). This settlement with extinct po at the jct of KY 106 and 178, 5 mi ssw of Elkton, was once a thriving village. It was early called both Crossroads and Shakerag. John C. Wright offers 2 accounts of the latter name. According to one, "fastidious housekeepers of the frontier made frequent trips to the front door to shake the dust from their cleaning rags. The incessant shaking of rags caused those who passed through the area to think of the community as one whose ladies literally 'shook rags.' According to the other . . . the . . . name was derived from poorly-dressed men who shook their rags as they stood outside in cold weather with nothing to do." In 1889 2 local merchants, John Kennedy and Will Adams, having been asked to name the new po, suggested Clay for the abundance of yellow clay subsoil so characteristic of the area. When they learned that this name was already in use, and noting that there was more of this clay here than in most other places, they offered Clay More instead. The 2 words were then run together and, for some reason, deliberately misspelled, and what emerged, Claymour, was accepted by the postal authorities. Thus, on Aug 22, 1889, the Claymour post office was est and James H. Heltsley became pm. It closed in 1922. 225, 1184.

Claypool (Warren): *klā*/pūl (Meador). This crossroads settlement with extinct po is at the jct of KY 234 and 961, less than ½ mi w of Bays Fork of Barren R and 9½ mi ese of Bowling Green. The po was est on Jan 29, 1856, with John S. Saunders, pm, and named for the family of Warren Co pioneer Stephen Claypool (1788–1862). His son, Col. Elijah Claypool, served for years in the Kentucky militia and represented the co in the state legislature (1849–50). 170, 209.

Claysville (Webster). See *Clay*

Clayton PO (Pendleton). See *Butler*

Clayvillage (Shelby): *klā vihl*/ədj (Waddy). This hamlet with extinct po on US 60, 5 mi e of Shelbyville, was first called Shytown until the po was est on Feb 27, 1829, with William L. Perry, pm, as Clay Village. It was named for Henry Clay who, it is said, once visited the place on a campaign trip, admired it, and suggested that it be named for him. It was laid off as a town in 1830 and inc in 1839. The po was closed in 1908. Over the years the 2 words of the name have locally been combined though on current maps it continues to be spelled Clay Village. 902.

Clear Creek (Floyd). See *Ligon*

Clear Creek (Rockcastle). See *Disputanta*

Clear Creek Juntion (Floyd). See *Hi Hat*

Clear Creek PO (Bell). See *Clear Creek Springs*

Clear Creek Springs (Bell): *kleer* kreek *sprihŋz* (Middlesboro North). This famed summer resort is in Pine Mt. State Park, on Clear Creek and KY 1491, 2 mi sw of Pineville. Dr. Thomas Walker, the pre-Revolutionary War explorer of much of se Kentucky, is said to have named this stream Clover Creek for the profusion of wild clover growing on its banks. It was renamed later for the clarity of the spring waters which discharge into the creek at that point and which, in the early days, were believed to have curative powers. J. M. C. Davis is credited with having est the resort in the mid 19th cent. A po called Clear Creek was in operation here from 1855 to 1867. On a 1927 topographical map the community is identified as Clear Springs Camp. 79, 1299.

Clearfield (Rowan): *kleer*/feeld, *klihr*/feeld (Morehead). This village with po is located on KY 519, just s of the confluence of Dry and Triplett Creeks, and just sw of Morehead. In 1905, near the site of Dixon Clark's early 19th cent water-powered sawmill and store on Dry Creek, the Clearfield Lumber Co. of Clearfield, Pennsylvania, est its sawmill and the dispatch point and northern terminus of its Morehead & North Fork RR. to receive timber shipments from its extensive Licking Valley holdings. Blaine Fulton became the first pm on Aug 4, 1908. 208, 952.

Clear Point (Clear Pint) (Hart). See *Uno*

Clear Pond PO (Marshall). See *Gilbertsville*

Clear Springs Camp (Bell). See *Clear Creek Springs*

Cleaton (Muhlenberg): *klee*/tən (Central City East, Drakesboro). This coal town with po is on the Owensboro & Nashville Branch of the L&N RR, just e of US 431 and 4 mi ne of Greenville. The po was est on Aug 3, 1901, by William R. Walls who named it and the community for his wife, Heskey Cleaton Walls. 320.

Clementsville (Casey): *klehm*/ənts/vihl (Clementsville). This hamlet with extinct po is located at the jct of KY 70 and 551, 8 mi wsw of Liberty. In 1802 Henry Clements and a group of Catholics from St. Ann Parish in Washington Co settled on Casey Creek, some 4 mi above the present Clementsville. Here in 1810 St. Bernard's Church was built to become the nucleus of a community of Catholic farmers which was named for Henry or his son, Philip. In 1857, for reasons unknown, the community was moved to the present Clementsville site where a new St. Bernard's Church was built. Nothing but open farmland marks the original site now generally known as Old Clementsville. While it is likely that a po existed at that site, there is no evidence of one and it was certainly not called Clementsville, the only po of this name having been est by Albert Clements at the community's present site on May 11, 1891. It closed in 1967. 212, 1397.

Cleveland (Owen). See *Perry Park*

Cliffside (Elliott). See *Green*

Clifton (Woodford): *klihf*/tən (Tyrone). This once-thriving r port, now a settlement on the e side of the Kentucky R, 4½ mi wnw of Versailles, was laid off as a town in 1841 by John Berryman for the employees of his large hemp factory. It may then have been called Woodford City, but in 1848 it was inc as Clifton for the name that pioneer Thomas Railey, in 1790, had given his new home on the cliff above the future townsite. A po called Clifton was in operation from May 1848 to Sept 1849. In the 1860s the village may have been called Cicero, for reasons unknown, while its landing was called Woodford Landing and, perhaps, Clifton Ferry as well. The po was re-est on Sept 20, 1880, as Cicero with William Lane, pm. In 1895 the po was moved 2 mi e to Brookies Crossroads (at the jct of the present KY 1964 and Steele Pike) where Tipton Shryock ran a grocery. (An old map identifies this site as Brookie Town named for a pioneer family of distillers.) With the closing of the po in 1903, the Cicero name was replaced by Clifton by which name the community is now exclusively known. 180, 1457–59.

Clifty (Todd): *klihf*/tee (Allegre). This hamlet with po is on KY 107/181, 12 mi n of Elkton. It was once called Bivinsville for an early family and nicknamed Lickskillet for reasons unknown. It is in a section of the co known as "The Cliffs," a rather impressive formation in the northern end of the co which rises 300 to 500 ft on both sides of a valley, itself varying 300 to 600 ft in width. This area and possibly the community itself was settled before 1830 and the Clifty po was est on July 24, 1838, with John Higgins, pm. 225, 1234.

Clinton (Hickman): *klihnt*/ən (Clinton, Oakton). This 5th class city and the seat of Hickman Co, is on US 51, 198 mi sw of downtown Louisville. It was founded in 1828 on land acquired from Stephen Ray for a proposed shift of the co's seat from Columbus to a more central location. Though the po was est on Dec 18, 1829, with Allen Caldwell, pm, and the town was inc in 1831, there was little development until its status as the co's seat was resolved in 1845. It has been said, though never confirmed, that the name honored a Captain Clinton who had been stationed there in 1826. 162, 169.

Clinton County: *klihn*/(t)ən. 196 sq mi. Pop 9,058. Seat: Albany. Est in 1835 from parts of Cumberland and Wayne cos, Clinton Co is generally believed to have been named for DeWitt Clinton (1769–1828), Governor of New York (1817–21, 1825–28) and projector of the Erie Canal. There is little credibility to the popular tradition that it was named for Clinton Winfrey, the 12-year-old son of State Representative Francis H. Winfrey who had sponsored the act creating the new co.

Clinton Station (Hickman). See *Oakton*

Clintonville (Bourbon): *klihnt*/ən/vihl (Clintonville). This hamlet with extinct po is at the jct of KY 57 and 1678, 7 mi s of Paris. The site was settled around 1800 by the brothers George and John Stipp and first called Stipps Crossroads. When the po was est by Walter Jones on Aug 29, 1831, the community was renamed Clintonville for the local Masonic Lodge which had been so named in 1825 or 1826 for DeWitt Clinton, New York's governor who had just completed the Erie Canal. By this name it was inc for a brief time in 1850. 167. 1414.

Clintwood PO (Pike). See *Virgie*

Clio PO (Pulaski). See *Waitsboro*

Closplint (Harlan): *klohz*/plihnt (Louellen). This coal town with L&N RR station and po, on KY 38 and the Clover Fork of Cumberland R, 13½ mi ene of Harlan, was named for and by the Clover Splint Coal Co. which opened its local mine in 1926. The po was est on Feb 16, 1928, with James Roy Parsons, pm. 1173.

Closplint No. 2 (Harlan). See *Louellen*

Clover Bottom (Jackson): *kloh*/vər *baht*/əm (Johnetta). This po is at the jct of US 421 and KY 1955, on Clover Bottom Creek, 9 mi nw of McKee. Green V. Holland est the po on July 11, 1862, and named it for the creek which flows through a rich limestone bottom with a heavy growth of clover. 1418.

Clover Fork (Harlan): *klohv*/ər *fawrk* (Benham). This has been a coal town since 1912, located on KY 38 21½ mi e of Harlan. It was named for its location near the head of one of the 3 forks of the Cumberland R. The aptly named stream flows w to join Martin and Poor Forks in the vicinity of Harlan. The local po, since closed, was one of the oldest in the co, having been est as Clover Fork on July 28, 1857, with Isaac W. Huff, pm. 1173.

Cloverport (Breckinridge): *kloh*/vər/pawrt (Cloverport, Mattingly). This 5th class city with po is on the Ohio R at the mouth of Clover Creek, 9 mi wnw of Hardinsburg. The settlement is said to have been est just e of the mouth of Clover Creek around 1798 and was first called Joesville for its proprietor Joseph Huston or, perhaps, for him and his brother-in-law Joseph Allen, another early landowner in that area, or even for Joseph Plumblet, who had leased 21 acres from Huston and is considered the first permanent settler. On Jan 28, 1828, the Kentucky legislature est a town on this site which was named for the creek, which in turn had been named for the profusion of wild clover on its lower banks. On Oct 16 of that year, George LaHeist started the Cloverport po. On Feb 11, 1860, the original town was combined with a growing section below the mouth of Clover Creek and inc as Cloverport. 214, 937.

Clyde (Russell): *klahd* (Jabez). This extinct po lies ½ mi beyond the end of KY 92, 6 mi sse of Jamestown, in that section of the now uninhabited part of Russell Co that lies s of Lake Cumberland. The po was est on Mar 30, 1887, with Isaac Frealy, pm, and named for Clyde Decker, a local resident. It was discontinued in 1913. 1375.

Coalgood (Harlan). See *Mary Helen*

Coalton (Boyd): *kohl*/tən (Rush). This former coaltown and now factory community is centered at the jct of US 60 and KY 966, just ne of an I 64 interchange, 8½ mi wsw of Catlettsburg. In 1864 the Ashland Coal Co. acquired 9000 acres in what came to be called the Coalton and Rush tracts, and on Mar 30, 1865, the po, which had been est as Metcalfe Furnace in 1848 and later called Star Furnace (see *Star*), was moved here with Benjamine (*sic*) F. Waite, pm, and called Coalton. The po closed in 1928. 7.

Coalville (Harlan). See *Three Point*

Cobb (Caldwell): kahb (Cobb). Now a hamlet with extinct po on KY 672, less than ¼ mi n of KY 128, 8½ mi se of Princeton, this is the site of a one-time station on the Ohio Valley (now Illinois Central Gulf) RR, built between Princeton and Clarksville, Tennessee, in the late 1880s. It was named either for the superintendent of the rr or a prosperous and influential family in neighboring Lyon Co. The local po was est on Dec 12, 1887, by Lawrence B. Sims and called Glen Allen, probably for a local family. In Feb 1888 the name was changed to Cebb, an obvious error which was corrected the following Apr. The station and po are gone. 1196, 1278.

Cobb's Mill (Owēn). See *Lusbys Mill*

Cobhill (Estill) *kahb*/*hihl* (Cobhill). This hamlet with po is located on top the hill on KY 1182, 3 mi ne of its jct with KY 52, and 7 mi e of Irvine. It was named for early settlers Henry and Samuel Cobb, the sons of a Caswell, North Carolina migrant, Jesse Cobb (1769–1836). The brothers, known to have been born in Estill Co (Henry, the older, on July 11, 1802), became large landowners, farmers, and loggers in the Cobhill area. It was not until Mar 30, 1898, long after they had passed from the scene, that Achilles D. Howell est the Cobhill po. It is not known if this name was applied to the place before this time or why it was spelled with one "b." 865.

Coburg (Adair): *koh*/bergh (Cane Valley). This hamlet with extinct po lies at the jct of KY 55 and 1913, 6 mi n of Columbia. This is said to have been a settlement made about 1875 of German-speaking people who most likely named their new community for their home in North Bavaria. The po of Tampico, which had been est in Taylor Co as Subletts Store in 1855 with James A. Sublett, pm, and renamed in 1857, became Coburg in 1903. 325.

Cody (Knott): *koh*/dee (Blackey). One of several communities completely inundated by the recent flooding of Carr Fork Lake, Cody was centered at the jct of KY 15 and 160, at the mouth of Breeding and Defeated Creeks, branches of Carr Fork (of the North Fork of the Kentucky R), 6½ mi s of Hindman. Its po, est on Nov 18, 1897, with Shade Smith, pm, was named for a local family. 1288.

Coffey's Mill (Casey). See *Middleburg*

Coiltown (Hopkins): *koy*/əl/town (Coiltown). This coal town at the jct of KY 502 and 1034, 6 mi w of Madisonville, was probably named for W. D. Coil, the president and general manager of the local Rose Creek Coal Co. It never had a po of its own. Coiltown Junction, where spur lines of the Illinois Central & Gulf and L&N rrs meet, is 1½ m se of Coiltown; and near the end of the L&N tracks, 1½ mi w of the jct, is Coiltown Station with tipple and coal mines. 159.

Coke PO (Anderson). See *Tyrone*

Colby Hills (Clark). See *Colbyville*

Colby Station (Clark): *kûhl*/bee/vihl (Ford). This abandoned station and extinct po on the C&O RR, 3½ mi w of Winchester, is identified merely as Colby on contemporary maps. It was named for the old Colbyville Tavern, owned by and named for Colby Taylor, which was one of the 2 pioneer wayside inns between Winchester and Lexington (its rival was the Chilesburg Tavern in Fayette Co). Colby's tavern, at the jct of the present Colby (KY 1927) and Becknerville Rds, ¼ mi e of the station, housed the Colbyville po, which Taylor est on Dec 11, 1826. In 1852 this was moved to and/or renamed Fishback, probably for its new pm, George T. Fishback, and was discontinued in 1856. A Colby Station po at the station was in service from 1890 to 1894. A post-World War II residential suburb called Colby Hills, just w of the Winchester city limits, was named for the Colby Road which forms it southern boundary. 975, 1349.

Coldiron (Harlan): *kohl*/ahrn (Wallins Creek). This village lies between US 119 and the Cumberland R, 7 mi w of Harlan. Its po was est on Nov 16, 1928, with Mary E. Coldiron, pm, and probably named for Elihu Coldiron, an early settler. 335.

Cold Spring (Campbell): *kohld sprihŋ* (Newport). This 5th class city on US 27, 4½ mi sse of downtown Newport and 2 mi nw of Alexandria, may date from the pioneer Reese's Settlement, named for the family of Thomas Reese. The Cold Spring name, which may have been applied to the community before 1800, referred to a perennial spring of clear cold water, which still exists and which was for years the local water supply. The Cold Spring po was est by Oliver M. DeCoursey on June 13, 1832, and was combined with the nearby Highland Heights office in 1955 to form the Cold Spring–Highland Heights po, which is now a branch of the Newport po. The city of Cold Spring was inc in 1940. 754, 985.

Coldwater (Calloway): *kohld*/wâht/ər (Kirksey). This hamlet with extinct po., 7 mi w of Murray, has had several sites since its po was est on Dec 9, 1856, near the jct of present KY 121 and 229. Just n of the original site was a cold flowing spring developed by Byrd Ezell before 1845. In 1856 he sold the spring and surrounding land to Asa Scarborough, who opened a store and the po he called Coldwater. Sometime later these were moved w to the vicinity of the West Fork of Clarks R, and in 1868 to their present location, where the po remained until it closed in 1907. According to historian Brown Tucker, there were actually 2 cold water springs about 1 mi apart. The owners of each, disputing which was the colder, requested an impartial comparison test. Apparently Mr. Scarborough's was the colder. Another local legend tells of 2 men who opened stores in the vicinity. One sold whiskey which local people dubbed "hot water" while the other served only cold water. 829, 1401, 1441.

Colemansville (Harrison): *kohl*/mənz/vihl (Berry). This hamlet with extinct po is on KY 1032, 10½ mi nw of Cynthiana. It was est as a town by legislative act in 1831 on land then owned by Robert S. Coleman and probably named for him (or for Whitehead Coleman, said to have had a mill in that vicinity earlier in the cent). The first po between Lexington and Covington was est by John Smith in 1829 as Mouth of Raven for its location in Smith's home at the mouth of this tributary of the South Fork of the Licking R, just above and across from the present city of Berry. On Feb 1, 1834, this po was moved 1 mi nw to Colemansville and so renamed. It closed in 1878. 158, 822.

Colesburg (Hardin): kohlz/bergh (Colesburg). This hamlet and L&N RR station with extinct po lies between Ky 434 and I 65, 5½ mi ne of Elizabethtown. The area is said to have been settled at least by 1800, and was named for pioneer William Cole. It is not known when the name was first applied to the settlement but it was in use for the station on the L&N RR's main line by 1858–59. The first po to serve this vicinity was est on Aug 19, 1856, as Robertsville or Robertsonville with Querry Florence, pm. It was renamed Colesburg in 1893. 136.

Coles PO (Woodford). See *Nugents Crossroads*

Coletown (Fayette): *kohl*/town (Coletown). This settlement along Walnut Hill Rd, is centered on its jct with Shelby Lane in southern Fayette Co, 4½ mi sse of Lexington's New Circle Rd. It was named for a freed slave, Milly or Millie Cole, who in 1843 had inherited 10 acres from Sarah Johnson, sister to her former master. On Milly's death in 1868, the property was subdivided for her 3 children who were joined by other families to form the settlement. 33.

College Hill (Madison): *kahl*/ədj *hihl* (Palmer). This hamlet with po on KY 977, 1 mi w of the Kentucky R and 8½ mi ene of Richmond, was once called Texas. According to the popular account given by J. T. Dorris, "(Abner) Oldham, a commissioner appointed to divide Nathan Lipscomb's 2700 acre estate in 1843, while riding over the land, was pulled from his horse by a large growth of briers. When he got up he exclaimed: 'I wouldnt have all this damned Texas country as a gift.' " Local people started calling the community that developed in this vicinity Texas and the name came to be generally accepted. Still according to tradition, Walter K. Norris's application for a Texas po in 1874 was at first rejected as another Texas po was already in operation in Washington Co. But later that year the postal authorities accepted his second petition, which suggested that the po be called College Hill for the Texas Seminary, a private secondary school founded there in 1868. Thus the po of College Hill was est on Jan 15, 1875, and shortly thereafter the school was renamed College Hill Seminary. The community was inc by the Kentucky legislature as College Hill on Mar 22, 1873. 56, 460.

Collins Forge (Powell). See *Clay City*

Collinsworth PO (Jackson). See *Sand Gap*

Colson (Letcher): *kohl*/sən (Mayking). This coal town with extinct po is scattered along Rockhouse Creek and KY 7 from Indian Creek to Camp Branch. The po, most recently located on Trace Fork of Rockhouse, 7½ mi nnw of Whitesburg, was est on May 26, 1897, and named for David G. Colson (1861–1904), then US congressman for that district. It closed in 1977. 1218.

Colton (Harlan). See *Totz*

Columbia (Adair): *kə*/*luhm*/byə (Columbia). This 4th class and the seat of Adair Co, is on KY 55 and 80 and Russell Creek, 77 mi sse of downtown Louisville. A settlement by this name is said to have existed here by 1802, when it became the seat of the newly est co. The town was laid off in the fall of 1802 by Daniel Trabue and others on land acquired from Blackmore Hughes 2 years before. John Field, who had opened the first store here in 1800, became the first pm of what was est as Adair Court House on Apr 1, 1806, and which later became Columbia Court House or Columbia. No one knows how it got its name but it is thought to have been named by those who felt that Christopher Columbus "had been robbed of an honor to which he was justly entitled when the Western Hemisphere took the name of 'America.' " Whether the name Columbia was actually coined or merely first recorded by the poet Philip Freneau in 1775 as an alternative name for the incipient country, its early appeal was also a reflection of current disdain for England's assumption of the Cabots' discovery of America. 32, 205, 564, 848.

Columbia (Columbiatown) (Fayette). See *Columbus*

Columbia Court House PO (Adair). See *Columbia*

Columbus (Fayette): *kə*/*luhm*/bəs (Clintonville). This all-black settlement is located just off Royster Rd and n of US 60, 5 mi e of Lexington's New Circle Rd. In 1893 Clarence H. Crimm divided his farm and sold it off in individual lots to freed slaves. He named the development Columbia or Columbiatown—in preference to Crimmtown—for the Columbian Exposition which had just closed in Chicago. For some reason it is now called Columbus. 33.

Columbus (Hickman): kə/*luhm*/bəs (Arlington). This 5th class city, with po lies on KY 80, 58, and 123, ½ mi e of the Mississippi R and 7½ mi nw of Clinton. The oldest town in the *Jackson Purchase*, it was first settled in 1804 on the Mississippi floodplain and known as Iron Banks, a translation of *les rivages de fer*, allegedly applied by early French travelers for "the towering rusty looking bluffs" overlooking the r at that point. A po was est here on Oct 26, 1820, with Henry L. Edrington, pm, and was called Columbus, probably for the discoverer of America who was then being similarly honored in several other states. The town was created by the Kentucky legislature in Dec 1820, laid out in 1821, and made the first seat of Hickman Co in Dec of that year. The seat was later moved to the more centrally located Clinton. After the disastrous 1927 floods, the town was relocated on the 140-foot bluff above and ½ mi e of the floodplain. Nothing remains of the town on its original site. Unfounded is the deep-rooted local tradition that Thomas Jefferson had planned the location or else the removal of the US capital to this more centrally located site; there is no mention of any such plan in any known writings by or about him. Nor is there any record that the town was ever called Columbia; that name appearing on an old map was most likely an error. 161, 242, 504, 665, 960, 1118.

Combs (Perry): kohmz (Hazard North). This coal town and L&N RR station with po is on the North Fork of the Kentucky R and KY 80 just sw of its jct with KY 15, and ½ mi nw of Hazard. The town superseded several area coal camps including those operated by the Domino and Lennut Coal Co.'s, and was first called Dolen for them. The nearby Domino and Lennut po's, which had opened in 1914, were the first to serve the vicinity. The Combs po was est on July 17, 1922, with Dewey Colwell, pm, and named for Abijah Benjamin Combs (1882–1955), a livestock and real estate dealer and onetime sheriff of Perry Co, who had subdivided and sold most of the site as home and business lots. In 1932 the community was renamed Combs for the po. 45, 476, 780.

Commercial Point (Union). See *Sturgis*

Commercial Summit PO (Whitley). See *Pine Knot*

Concord (Calloway). See *New Concord*

Concord (Lewis): *kahn*/kawrd (Concord). This village is located at the jct of KY 8 and 57, on the Ohio R, just below the mouth of Sycamore Creek, and 10½ mi wnw of Vanceburg. It was founded in 1830 by Edward and John Stevenson (or Stephenson) on land that had been in their family since the turn of the cent, and was named for either the town in New Hampshire or its famed Revolutionary War precedent, the town in Massachusetts. The first storekeeper, Samuel Stevenson, est the po on Jan 3, 1834. 179, 1103.

Confederate (Lyon): kən/*fehd*/ər/ət (Lamasco). This extinct po was est on Aug 19, 1885, by Linn Gresham, at his store on the present KY 274, just n of the mouth of Confederate Branch of McNabb Creek, and near the Bethany Baptist Church. Confederate was named ostensibly for the Confederate veterans who lived in the area. Across the rd from the store was Confederate Springs, which made the store a favorite stopping place for travelers and a meeting place for local farmers. The po closed in 1914. 230, 580, 1025.

Confederate City (Rowan). See *Farmers*

Confederate Cross Roads (Rowan). See *Farmers*

Confluence (Leslie): *kahn*/flū/əns (Buckhorn). This hamlet is on KY 257, 7 mi n of Hyden. Its po was est on Dec 1, 1890, with George B. Huff, pm, and named for its location at the mouth of Wilder Branch of Middle Fork of the Kentucky R. 1248.

Congleton (Lee): *kahŋ*/əl/tən (Beattyville). This settlement extending along KY 11, about 1½ mi s of Beattyville and the Kentucky R, was named for a prominent landowning family in the vicinity. Its po, est on June 18, 1925, with Algin Cecil, pm, has since closed. 1372.

Conner's PO (Gallatin). See *Napoleon*

Connersville (Boone). See *Florence*
Connorsville (Shelby). See *Harrisonburg*
Conrard (Pulaski): *kahn*/ərd (Billows). This extinct po on the Line Creek Rd, 13 mi ene of Somerset, was est on Sept 16, 1899, with William R. Burdine, pm, and named for Charles A. Conrard (1866–1918), then secretary to the 4th assistant postmaster general and later (1901–09) chief clerk of the Post Office Department. The po was discontinued in 1975. 1039, 1050.
Consolation (Christian): kahn/sə/*lā*/shən (Dawson Springs SE). This hamlet on KY 109, 10½ air miles nnw of Hopkinsville was settled in the early 1830s by Joab Clark, a Universalist preacher who, according to tradition, so firmly believed that it was God's consolation that he settle there and build his church that he called the place Consolation. Variations of this explanation include his having stated, after receiving many promises but little cash for the erection of his church, "well, that's some consolation." The settlement has never had its own po. 386, 1403.
Constantine PO (Breckinridge). See *Hudson*
Conway (Rockcastle): *kahn*/wā (Wildie). This village, L&N RR station, and po are on US 25, just e of Roundstone Creek and I 75, and 7½ mi n of Mount Vernon. The po, which was est as Conwayton on Feb 29, 1884, with William Hart, pm, and became simply Conway several months later, was named for a Mr. Conway, a surveyor and partner in Conway and Taylor, late 19th cent land owners and developers. 1243.
Conwayton (Rockcastle). See *Conway*
Cookseyville PO (Crittenden). See *Tolu*
Cooks Spring PO (Greenup). See *South Portsmouth*
Cook's Station (Logan). See *Russellville*
Cook's Valley PO (Calloway). See *Harris Grove*
Coolidge PO (McCreary). See *Whitley City*
Coolidge (Perry). See *Fusonia*
Cool Spring PO (Warren). See *Smiths Grove*
Coonskin (Carroll). See *Worthville*
Cooper (Wayne): *kōōp*/ər (Monticello). This hamlet with extinct po on KY 167, 3¼ mi s of Monticello, was settled early in the 19th cent and for years was known as the Pleasant Bend community for the nearly complete loop made by Beaver Creek, just se of the po. The po was est on May 2, 1892, in the Miller Brothers' store and is said to have been named by the store's owners for their nephews, Fount(ain Fox) and Clem Cooper. Fount (1870–1955) was the first pm. The po was closed in late 1975. 861.
Co-operative (McCreary): koh/*ahp*/ər/ət/əv, koh/*ahp*/ər/*ā*/tihv (Barthell). Only a few homes and the po remain, along KY 1363 and White Oak Creek, 7½ mi wsw of Whitley City, of the 2nd largest of the mining towns est by the Stearns Coal and Lumber Co. of Stearns, Ky. The community and its po, est on Sept 8, 1922, were named for the local mine opened in 1921 as a cooperative effort of a number of employees to whom co. stock had been sold. The Cooperative Mine ceased production in 1950, and in 1963 the po was moved to a store on KY 1363, almost a mi w of the original town site. 208, 1162, 1163, 1384.
Coopersville (Wayne): *kōōp*/ərz/vihl (Coopersville). This hamlet with po is on KY 92 and Kennedy (or Canada) Creek (a branch of the Little South Fork of the South Fork of the Cumberland R), 7 mi se of Monticello. The po was est on May 25, 1875, with William H. Parker, pm, and named for the large number of Coopers in the area. They may have been the descendants of Jacob Cooper (1807–93) who, sometime after 1832, had a farm on the ridge 1½ mi n of the present po site. 80.

Copland (Breathitt). See *Saldee*

Coral Hill (Barren): *kahr*/əl *hihl* (Hiseville). This extinct po on KY 740, ½ mi n of Beaver Creek and 3 mi nne of Glasgow, was in operation from 1858 to 1907 and named for the large "outcrop of coralline formation which is found there in great quantities." 791.

Coral Ridge (Jefferson). See *Fairdale*

Corbin (Whitley and Knox): *kawr*/bən (Corbin, Vox). This 3rd class industrial city with po and L&N RR station is on US 25W, just w of I 75 and s of US 25E, 11½ mi n of Williamsburg, and 11 mi ese of Barbourville. For years small farmsteads in the area were collectively called Lynn Camp for the creek which here separates Whitley and Knox co's. The creek was named for the camp of pioneer William Lynn who arrived at this site around 1800 with a party of hunters from Bowling Green, Virginia. He or his party is said to have gotten lost and the remains of the old campsite on the ne bank of the creek were noted 2 years later by a search party, which then named the creek. When the L&N RR reached this vicinity in 1882 it named its station Lynn Camp. The po, est on July 24, 1883, by storekeeper James Eaton, was called Cummins for the town's propietor and founder, Nelson Cummins, who was instrumental in getting the rr station located here. On Jan 2, 1885, the po was renamed by Eaton for Rev. James Corbin Floyd, a minister of the local Christian Church, whom he held in high regard. Since Eaton was also the L&N's local agent, the station was also renamed Corbin. The town was inc in 1902. 391, 420, 1267.

Cordell (Lawrence); kawr/*dehl* (Blaine). This recently discontinued po at the mouth of Steel Branch of Brushy Creek, 12 mi sw of Louisa, was est on Dec 29, 1898, with Bascom Sturgell, pm, and named for a local family.

Corinth (Grant): *kahr*/ihnth (Sadieville). This 6th class city with po is centered at the jct of US 25 and KY 330, 1½ mi e of I 75, and 9 mi s of Williamstown. It is said to have been an early stage stop on the old Covington to Lexington Pike but did not develop as a town until the coming of the Cincinnati & Southern Ry in 1876. It is not known when the name was applied to the community but its po was est as Corinth on Oct 22, 1868, with David W. Williams, pm, and in this name it was inc in 1878. It was undoubtedly named for the Corinth Christian Church which, in turn, was named for the ancient city in Greece to whose early Christians St. Paul wrote two memorable letters. At some time the Grant Co Corinth was also known as Mullanixville. At least one historian has suggested that this was the first name given to the rr station and was that of the station agent. 531, 1342.

Corn Creek PO (Trimble). See *Wises Landing*

Corneliusville PO (Boone). See *Bullittsville*

Cornersville PO (Graves). See *Farmington*

Cornettsville (Perry): *kawr*/nəts/vihl (Vicco). This hamlet with po and an L&N RR station is on KY 7 and the North Fork of the Kentucky R, 9 mi se of Hazard. The po was est as Salt Creek on June 8, 1868, with Anderson Cornett, pm, and named for the early 19th cent salt works at the mouth of Leatherwood Creek, ½ mi sw. It was renamed in 1896 by then pm and storekeeper, John B. Cornett, for the fact that nearly all of the residents were descendants of his pioneer grandfather, William Cornett (1761–1836), a Virginia-born Revolutionary War veteran who had settled at the mouth of Bull Creek, ½ mi above the post office and store site in 1796–97. 49, 1327.

Cornishville (Mercer): *kawr*/nihsh/vihl (Cornishville). This village with po lies at the jct of KY 1989 and the Chaplin R, 7 mi wnw of Harrodsburg. The po office was est in the vicinity of a gristmill on Oct 9, 1846, with Garland Symmes, pm. It may have been named for George Doggett Cornish, member of a prominent pioneer family there which produced Samuel Cornish, the builder of many of Kentucky's early covered bridges. 1264.

Cornwell (Menifee): *kawrn*/wehl (Frenchburg). This hamlet with extinct po on US 460, 3½ mi west of Frenchburg was named for William Cornwell who built the first home there around 1870. The Cornwell po, est on Jan 3, 1878, with Arnold Ingraham, pm, was moved in 1889 1 mi e to Rothwell, then the terminus of the Kentucky and South Atlantic RR. 341.

Corydon (Henderson): *kahr*/ə/dən (Poole). This 5th class city with po on US 60/641 and the Illinois Central Gulf RR, 4 mi sw of Henderson, was settled in 1848 by Dr. John N. Dorsey who opened the first store there with his brother, William L. On Sept 1, 1849, John became the first pm, and William laid out the town in 1850. It was inc in 1867. John's wife, Patsy Atcherson Dorsey, is credited with having named the town for the shepherd hero in "Pastoral Elegy," a popular song of the day. The name had first been applied to the lovesick swain in Virgil's *Eclogues*. 874.

Cottle (Morgan): *kahd*/əl (Lenox). This hamlet with po is just n of the jct of US 460 (KY 7) and KY 364 and just e of the Licking R, 3 mi se of West Liberty. The po was est on Mar 11, 1931, with Herbert Hammonds, pm, and named for pioneer settler Joseph Cottle. 1346.

Cottonburg. (Madison): *kaht*/ən/bergh (Kirksville). This recently discontinued po was on KY 595, 1½ mi e of Paint Lick Creek, and 7½ mi w of Richmond. The po was est on May 21, 1886, with Benjamin F. Cotton, pm, and named for a large family of landowners, perhaps specifically for Jerome Cotton. 1041.

Cottongim (Clay): *kaht*/ən/ghihm (Hima). This extinct po on KY 11 and Collins Fork of Goose Creek, just below the mouth of Whites Branch and 6 mi ssw of Manchester, was est on July 3, 1918, by Sallie Cottingim (Mrs. Luther) Hacker and named for her family. Pierce Cottengim (original spelling), born in South Carolina in 1792, was the Clay Co progenitor of that family in the early 19th cent. Near the site of the old po is the site of the Jonsee Station [*Djahn*/*see*] of the Cumberland & Manchester Branch of the L&N RR. This station was named for John C. White from whom the rr had secured its right-of-way and depot site in 1916. The po was discontinued in 1963. 739, 1266.

Counter PO (Mercer). See *Stringtown*

Counts Cross Roads (Carter). See *Pleasant Valley*

Covington (Kenton): *kuhv*/ihŋ/tən (Covington, Newport). This 2nd class industrial city with po is at the mouth of the Licking R, directly across the Ohio R from Cincinnati and 80 mi ne of downtown Louisville. The city grew from a tract of 200 acres between the Licking and the Ohio called The Point from which military activities against the trans-Ohio Indians were staged. By 1794 a settlement that may also have been called *Kennedys Ferry* had been est here around Thomas Kennedy's tavern, landing, and ferry. In 1815 the brothers John S. and Richard Gano and Thomas D. Carneal, who had acquired some 150 acres of Kennedy's property, founded a town which they named for Gen. Leonard Covington of Maryland (1768–1813) who had been mortally wounded at the Battle of Chrysler's Field in the War of 1812. The Covington po was est on Oct 3, 1815, with Henry M. Buckner, pm, and the town was granted a city charter in 1834. 195, 474.

Covington's Ferry (Marshall). See *Altona*

Cowan (Fleming): *kow*/ən (Cowan). This hamlet with extinct po extends sw along KY 32 for about 1½ mi from KY 560, 7½ mi w of Flemingsburg, to a point about a mi from the Nicholas Co line. The L&N RR station and the po, est as Cowan by Frank M. Allan on June 13, 1872, were named for John Cowan, a highly respected farmer on whose land the station was located. The po closed in 1958. 381, 1369.

Cowcreek (Owsley): *kow/kreek* (Cowcreek). This extinct po on KY 28, at the forks of Cow Creek, 4 mi se of Booneville, was est on Aug 10, 1900, with Alfred Eversole, pm. The creek, an 8-mi-long branch of South Fork of the Kentucky R, was named for the buffalo cow said to have been killed on its banks by Richard Reynolds in 1815. 229.

Coxs Creek (Nelson): *kahx*/əz kreek (Fairfield). This settlement with po on US 31E/150, 4½ mi n of Bardstown, and the nearby creek, a branch of Salt R, were named for Col. Isaac Cox, Jr. (1756–87), a Pennsylvania-born Revolutionary War veteran. Cox arrived in the vicinity in April 1775 to settle on a 1000 acre pre-emption and est the nearby Cox's Station, said to have been the first pioneer station in the co. The crossroads settlement of Cox's Creek was founded at the jct of the present US 31E and KY 509 where the po was est on Nov 28, 1856, with John C. Cox, pm. In the early 1960s the Kentucky Highway Department ordered the removal of the local store and po, which obstructed the view of oncoming traffic at the intersection and had been responsible for a number of serious accidents. The po is now about ½ mi s of the intersection. 43, 199, 1386.

Crab Orchard (Lincoln): *kraeb* awr/chərd (Crab Orchard, Brodhead). This 6th class city with po is centered at the jct of US 150 and KY 39 and 643, 8½ mi se of Stanford. It is generally assumed that this pioneer station on the Old Wilderness Rd was named for the large forest of crabapple trees there, a most impressive sight to travelers from Virginia. (Another explanation offered though not necessarily accepted by the late Will N. Craig is that it was named for Isaac Crabtree, a long hunter, "who later acquired a pre-emption which included a large section of this orchard. For the sake of euphony the names were correlated, the tree of his name giving to Orchard (*sic*), thus forming the name *Crab Orchard*.") The Crab Orchard po was est on Feb 23, 1815, with Archibald Shanks, pm. A variety of mineral springs made this an attractive resort area and one of the most popular watering places in the south for over a century. The famed Crab Orchard Springs Hotel, built around 1827 by Isaac Shelby III, was considered, before the Civil War, the "Saratoga of the South". 50, 1241, 1448.

Crackers Neck (Elliott). See *Newfoundland*

Crackers Neck (Wolfe). See *Flat*

Craftsville PO (Letcher). See *Millstone*

Craigs Camp (Boone). See *Burlington*

Crailhope (Green): *krāl/hohp* (Center). The second site of this settlement with extinct po, of which little remains, is at the jct of KY 218 and 1048, 10½ mi sw of Greensburg. At a place, perhaps on the Little Barren R, that may also have been called New York, D. D. Higgason and William Daniel Myers opened the Crailhope store in which, on Sept 12, 1883, Myers est the Crailhope po. The name recalls the pioneer James Crail and his family who arrived on the Little Barren around 1800. Three theories have been offered for the second part of the name: local people hoped they would survive a smallpox outbreak, or they hoped they would be able to make it up the difficult Crails Hill during the winter, or it was early considered such a "trifling" place that it was hoped it would fare better in time. In any event, the po moved up KY 218 to more level terrain, and later closed. 1315.

Crane Creek PO (Fleming). See *Plummers Landing*

Cranes Nest (Knox): *krānz nehst* (Heidrick). This settlement with po is on KY 1803, at the mouth of Hubbard Branch of Richland Creek, and 7½ mi n of Barbourville. Though residents have always spelled this name with the terminal "s," the Post Office Department, since the est of the po on July 13, 1874, has spelled it without one. According to tradition, someone is supposed to have found a crane's nest in the vicinity and this must then have been considered unusual. 1350, 1409.

Cranks (Harlan): kraeŋx (Evarts). This hamlet with po just w of the jct of US 421 and KY 568, 9 mi se of Harlan, was named for its location on Cranks Creek, a branch of Martins Fork of the Cumberland R. The name of the creek and nearby Cranks Ridge and Gap is said to have been corrupted from Thranks, that of a pioneer surveyor. Yet it could have been named for one or more families of Crank known to have lived in Knox, Bell, and Clay co's in the early 19th cent. The Cranks po was est on Apr 9, 1908, with Harvey L. Ledford, pm. An earlier po on the creek—in fact, one of the oldest in the co—was Cranks Creek, in operation from May 27, 1848, to Sept 8, 1849, and again, though perhaps at another site, from Oct 25, 1871, to Jan 8, 1874. 46, 119.

Cranks Creek PO (Harlan). See *Cranks*

Crayne (Crittenden): krān (Marion). This village with po is on US 641 (KY 91) and the Illinois Central Gulf RR, 3 mi s of Marion. There was very likely a settlement at this site prior to the est there of the Crayneville po on Jan 12, 1888. The po and rr station were named for a local family whose progenitor may have been a pioneer settler, George Crayne. In 1907 the po was renamed Crayne to avoid confusion with Caneyville in Grayson Co to which mail had been frequently missent. About a mi s of Crayne was the site of Centerville, founded in 1799 by South Carolinian James Armstrong which from 1804 to 1809 served as the centrally located seat of the original Livingston Co from which Crittenden and adjacent Caldwell co's were formed. With the creation of Caldwell Co in 1809, the Livingston Co seat was removed to Salem. Nothing remains to mark the site of Centerville but a few foundation stones. 1009, 1324.

Crayneville (Crittenden). See *Crayne*

Creal (Green): kreel (Magnolia). This hamlet with po is on KY 61 and the Tom Bill Branch of Brush Creek, 13½ mi nw of Greensburg. Though the community has always been Creal, named for a very prominent early Green and Russell co's family (see *Creelsboro*), its po, in operation from 1883 to 1919, was called Dezarn [də/*zahrn*] for the family of its first pm, Elisha Dezarn. 1339.

Creech PO (Harlan). See *Chad*

Creekmore (McCreary): *kreek*/mawr (Ketchen). This hamlet is on KY 1470 near the head of Hayes Creek, 9 mi se of Whitley City. The recently discontinued po was est on Jan 3, 1893, and named for and by its first pm, Embry K. Creekmore. 1367.

Creelsboro (Russell): *kreelz*/buhr/oh (Creelsboro). This hamlet with extinct po is located on Long Bottom of the Cumberland R, now at the jct of KY 379 and 1058, 9 mi sw of Jamestown. One of the oldest communities in the co, it was est by legislative act as Creelsburgh in 1819 at or near the site of William Campbell's ferry, and may first have been known as Campbellsburg. The po, est as Creelsburgh on Jan 17, 1828, with Thomas C. Graves, pm, became Creelsboro (or Creelsborough) in 1864. It had been named for Elijah and Elsey (Elza) Creel, early proprietors of the site, and the progenitors of a family of distinguished diplomats. Their son, Reuben, served as US Consul in Mexico during the Civil War while his son, Enrique, was governor of Chihuahua, 1903 and Mexican ambassador to the US, 1906–9. 120, 759.

Creelburgh (Russell). See *Creelsboro*

Cremona PO (Letcher). See *Haymond*

Crescent Springs (Kenton): *krehs*/ənt *sprihŋz* (Covington). This 5th class suburban city with extinct po centering on KY 371 just n of I 75, and 4 mi wsw of downtown Covington, is part of the 3000-acre military grant first settled by the family of Robert McKay (McCoy) from Frederick Co, Virginia, in 1785. The name was applied to the vicinity with the arrival of the Cincinnati Southern (now Southern) RR in 1877. According to one account, the "Crescent" referred to the shape of the tracks passing through the settlement; according to another it designated the "Queen and Crescent Railroad," a nickname of the Cincinnati Southern. The 3 area springs furnished an abundant supply of water to community and rr alike. The Crescent Springs po was est on Sept 25, 1891, and closed in 1918. 879.

Crestwood (Oldham): *krehst*/wood (Crestwood). This 6th class city with po is on KY 22 and 146, contiguous on the sw to the city of Pewee Valley, and 6 mi sw of LaGrange. The po was est on July 2, 1857, as Beard's Station for Joseph Beard who had donated the land for the local Louisville & Frankfort (now L&N) RR station. After the name was shortened to Beard in 1880, rr men got to calling the station "Whiskers," and while old-line residents good-naturedly accepted this, newcomers from Louisville would not. Fearing ridicule, they succeeded in getting the name of the po, station, and community changed to Crestwood in 1909. No one knows why this inapt name was chosen, for the place is "hardly at the crest of the gradual ascent of the wooded country round about." 963.

Crews Creek PO (Kenton). See *Independence*

Crider (Caldwell): *krah*/dər (Crider). This hamlet with extinct po on the now Illinois Central Gulf RR and KY 91, 4½ mi nw of Princeton, has borne this name since the 1830s when it was settled by several related families of Criders who had come to Crittenden Co from Pittsylvania Co, Virginia, in the first decade of the 19th cent. While this vicinity may have been served by the Walnut Grove po from 1841 to 1874, the Crider po itself was est on Jan 20, 1888, with Simpson M. Welden, pm. It was discontinued in 1954. 1278.

Crittenden (Ballard). See *Bardwell*

Crittenden (Grant): *kriht*/ən/dən (Walton). This 6th class city with po is on US 25 and I 75, 8 mi n of Williamstown. The community, which may be on the site of a travelers' rest est there in 1812 by Lewis Myers, was first called Pin Hook until 1834, when Mary A. (Mrs. John) Fenley renamed it for John J. Crittenden (1787–1863), the popular Kentucky statesman who was later to serve as its 15th governor. The local po, which John Fenley had est as Sanders on Apr 14, 1831, was also renamed Crittenden in 1834. The town was inc in 1839. 69, 84.

Crittenden County: *kriht*/ən/dən. 360 sq mi. Pop 9,200. Seat: Marion. Crittenden Co was est in 1842 from the eastern part of Livingston Co, and named for John J. Crittenden (1787–1863), sometime US attorney general and senator and 15th governor of Kentucky (1848–50).

Crockett (Morgan): *krahk*/ət (Dingus). This hamlet with po is on KY 172 and Fannin Fork of Elkhorn Creek, 9½ mi ne of West Liberty. First settled by Fannins, Hutchinsons, and Barkers, it was for many years called Wheeler Town for the many Wheelers who also lived in the vicinity. The po was est on Apr 19, 1900, and named by the first pm, Peter Fannin, for his son, David Crockett Fannin. 112.

Crocus (Adair): *kroh*/kəs (Creelsboro). This extinct po is on KY 1313, just short of the Russell Co. line, 8½ mi se of Columbia. In 1840 a community in this vicinity was founded by legislative act and named Millersville, probably for John Miller, local landowner. The po of this name, est on June 3, 1845, with Archelaus A. Strange, pm, moved to Russell Co in the early 1860s and closed in 1879. Another po, est Aug 10, 1885, with James P. Miller, pm, was named Crocus for the creek 1½ mi s, which had probably been named for the wild crocuses growing on its banks. However, according to Judge Wells' history of Cumberland Co, through which it flows to join the Cumberland River above Burkesville, the creek was named by early surveyors for the local Indians who seemed to resemble a tribe called the Crocus. 223, 305.

Crofton (Christian): *krahf*/tən (Crofton). This 5th class city with po is located at the jct of US 41 and KY 800, 1 mi w of the Pennyrile Parkway and 10½ mi n of Hopkinsville. James E. Croft, the owner of this site, agreed in 1870 to deed land for a depot to the Evansville Henderson & Nashville (now Evansville & Nashville Division of the L&N) RR if the station would be named for him. On Dec 12, 1871, the Wooldridges Store po, which had been est in 1850 at a point 2½ mi s, was moved to the station site and renamed Crofton. The community that grew up around station and po was inc on Feb 6, 1873. 1403.

Cromona PO (Letcher). See *Haymond*

Cromwell (Ohio): *krahm*/wehl (Cromwell). This village with po is on US 231, ½ mi n of the Green R and 9 mi se of Hartford. Before the arrival of the rr's in Ohio Co in 1871, the community was located on the r, around Porter's Landing, and was one of the more important Green River towns. The po, established as Porter's Landing on May 28, 1846, with Felix J. King, pm, was renamed Cromwell in 1852 for Oliver Cromwell Porter, said to have built the first home there in 1835. As elsewhere, the rr's drew trade away from the r, and the community immediately around Porter's Landing, now called Old Cromwell, has since been nearly altogether abandoned. 75, 170.

Crooked Creek Furnace PO (Bullitt). See *Belmont*

Crooks PO (Bath). See *Preston*

Cropper (Shelby): *krahp*/ər (North Pleasureville). This hamlet with po centered at the jct of KY 43 and the L&N RR and 8 mi ne of Shelbyville, was in an area first settled by the Dutch Tract families (see *Pleasureville*). One of their number, James Cropper, is said to have been the first to build a home and store at this site and the community was named for him. The po, est as *Croppers Depot* on Sept 29, 1851, with James H. Cropper, pm, becamse simply Cropper in 1882. It was inc as a town in 1890. Though the town was certainly not named for being the rail shipping point for area sharecroppers or tenant farmers, as some over the years have contended, it did provide this service on the old Louisville Cincinnati & Lexington which became the Lexington Branch of the L&N RR. 1378.

Croppers Depot PO (Shelby). See *Cropper*

Crossland (Calloway): *kraws*/lənd (Lynn Grove). This crossroads hamlet with extinct po is on the Tennessee state line, 6½ mi ssw of Murray. The po est by Boswell Harding on Mar 24, 1868, was named for Judge Edward Crossland (1827–81) of the Common Pleas Court, who later served this district in the US Congress (1871–75). The po was discontinued in 1925. 146, 169, 1401.

Cross Plains (Fayette). See *Athens*

Cross Plains (Henderson). See *Niagara*

Cross Plains (Metcalfe). See *Savoyard*

Cross Roads (Boone). See *Florence*

Crossroads (Breckinridge). See *Custer*

Crossroads (Bullitt). See *Mt. Washington*

Cross Roads (Daviess). See *Whitesville*

Crossroads (Grayson). See *Yeaman*
Crossroads (Hart). See *Cub Run*
Cross Roads (Lincoln). See *Hustonville*
Crossroads (Livingston). See *Joy*
Crossroads (McLean). See *Sacramento*
Crossroads (Todd). See *Claymour*
Crossroads (Union). See *Sturgis*
Crossroads (Wayne). See *Touristville*
Cross Roads PO (Jefferson). See *Okolona*
Crow Hickman Station (Daviess). See *Browns Valley*

Crowtown (Caldwell): *kroh*/town (Princeton West, Crider) This strictly residential extension of Princeton, the co seat, stretches nw for about ½ mi along KY 91 just n of the Princeton interchange on the Western Kentucky Parkway. It was named for several families of Crows that had settled in the vicinity early in this cent. Several years ago a local womans' club was unsuccessful in its efforts to adopt Lakeview as a more pleasant-sounding name for the community; the Board on Geographic Names in 1967 decided in favor of Crowtown for its historic precedence. Today both names are used locally. The community has never had its own po. 1000, 1278, 1351.

Cruise (Laurel): krūz (Parrot). This extinct po at the end of KY 1228, about 1¼ mi s of the forks of Rockcastle R and 11½ mi n of London, was named for an old settler who may have owned and operated a nearby ferry and tavern. Another tavern keeper, Welcom Mullins, est the po on June 21, 1899. 545.

Crum (Lewis): kruhm (Stricklett). No one really knows how this settlement on KY 344, at the mouth of Lee Branch of Kinniconick Creek, 10½ mi sw of Vanceburg, got its name. Though Crum is a family name in ne Kentucky, there are no known Crum families in this area. It is possible, though, that one or more had lived there in years past, or early settlers may have wished to honor friends or relatives from another place. J. S. Mavity once offered this folk etymological explanation: "The country store in that section had gathered up everything worth grabbing and then came a cyclone along and blowed the store away. Several years after that, E. G. Clark, a native thereabout, discovered that calves and chickens had again taken root in that vicinity and he thought there might be a crum of comfort there, so he started another store and got a post office established called Crum." The po, est on May 2, 1882, with Thomas B. Clark, pm, was discontinued in 1924. 1103, 1200.

Crummies (Harlan): *kruhm*/eez (Evarts). This hamlet with po and an L&N RR station is on US 421 and Long Branch of Crummies Creek, 7 mi se of Harlan. It was undoubtedly named for the stream, a tributary of Martins Fork of the Cumberland R, along which, it is said, someone had once observed a large herd of buffalo (or deer) with crumpled horns. A cow with crooked horns is still called a crummie or crummy. The po was est on Aug 11, 1928, with Thurman C. Chappell, pm. 10, 46, 899.

Crutchfield (Fulton): *kruhch*/feeld (Crutchfield). Only 2 churches and a po remain of this once-prosperous sawmill town and trade center on the Illinois Central Gulf RR, just w of US 51 and 13 mi e of Hickman. Though the town is said to have once borne the name Alexander for one of the railroad's station agents and even the nickname Slap Out for reasons now unknown, it has generally been identified by the name applied to its po when est on Mar 9, 1874, to honor an early resident. 1126.

Cuba (Graves): *kyū*/bə (Cuba). This hamlet with extinct po is now located on KY 303, 9½ mi s of Mayfield. The po, est on Feb 12, 1858, was undoubtedly named for the Caribbean island whose acquisition from Spain was then a popular cause in the slaveholding states. After an intermittent existence, the po closed for good in 1905.

When the construction of KY 303 bypassed the original business district, new businesses were est on the highway and a distinction is now locally made between New and Old Cuba. 1228.

Cubage (Bell): *kuhb*/ədj (Varilla). This po on KY 987 and Brownies Creek, a tributary of the Cumberland R, was est on May 17, 1879, with Andrew Wilder, pm, and named for Cubage Creek, a branch of Brownies nearly 2 mi below (w of) the present po site, some 10 mi ese of Pineville. According to tradition, the first settlers found the words "cub bear killed here" carved on a beech tree on the creek and thus Cubage may have been a corruption of Cub Beech, a possible early name for that stream. Bell Co's late historian, H. H. Fuson, reported but tended to discount the contention that it was named for a Mr. Cubage (Cubbage?), one of a party of pioneer hunters, who remained on the creek until he could overcome a case of frostbitten feet. 79, 1051.

Cub Run (Hart): *kuhb ruhn* (Cub Run). This village with po at the jct of KY 88 and 728, 8 mi w of Munfordville, was named for its location above the head of Cub Run, a tributary of the Green R. One story is that a group of hunters was sitting around when a bear cub happened to run past. This prompted one to remark "Look at the cub run." That may be how the stream got its name. Or else a Mr. Craddock, on a hunting trip, found a mother bear and her cub. He killed only the mother, and when later asked why he had not also killed her cub, he replied "the cub run." The community was first called Crossroads and was a popular meeting and camping spot in pioneer days. The existence of another po of this name led to the consideration of an alternative. The name of the creek proved an acceptable one and on Jan 7, 1874, Aaron Reams became the first pm of Cub Run. A third account of the naming has to do with its application to the po: While considering its name, the village elders spotted a bear cub. When one raised his gun to shoot it, the others shouted "Run, cub, run!" and that suggested the name. 546, 863, 1331.

Cullen (Union): *kuhl*/ən (Sturgis). This extinct po at the jct of KY 758 and 950, 6 mi s of Morganfield, was est on Feb 11, 1885, and named for its first pm, Joseph Cullen, or his family. It served a community known until then as Weaver City for Gen. James B. Weaver of Iowa, the Greenback Party's candidate for president in 1880, later to poll over a million votes as the Populist candidate for that office in 1892. The Cullen po was discontinued in 1906. 157.

Cumberland (Harlan): *kuhm*/ber/lənd (Benham, Louellen). This 4th class city with po and the largest town in the co, it centered at the jct of US 119 and KY 160, 19 mi ene of Harlan. Until 1926 the town was called Poor Fork for its location on one of the 3 forks of the Cumberland R. The stream, which is said to have been named for the relative unproductivity of its soil, flows wsw to join the Cumberland R at Baxter, just below Harlan. The po, one of the oldest in the co, was est as Poor Fork on Feb 11, 1837, with Hezekiah Brunson, pm. After an intermittent existence it, like the town, was renamed Cumberland on June 1, 1926 by local businessmen who sought a more significant and propitious name for their growing community. 553, 889.

Cumberland City (Clinton): *kuhm*/bər/lənd *siht*/ee (Cumberland City). This hamlet with extinct po at the jct of KY 588 and 829, 8 mi nne of Albany, was once a Poplar Mt. Coal Co. town. The po was est on Apr 26, 1867, with Samuel M. Dick, pm, and probably named for the Cumberland R, some 4 mi n. The po closed in 1940. 1263.

Cumberland County: *kuhm*/bər/lən(d). 304 sq mi. Pop 7,234. Seat: Burkesville. Est in 1798 from part of Green Co, Cumberland Co was named for the r that flows through it, which in turn is said to have been named by the explorer Dr. Thomas Walker for the Duke of Cumberland.

Cumberland Court House PO (Cumberland). See *Burkesville*

Cumberland Falls Station (McCreary). See *Parkers Lake*
Cumberland Ford (Bell). See *Pineville*
Cumberland Valley (Livingston). See *Tiline*
Cummins PO (Whitley). See *Corbin*
Cundiff (Adair): *kuhn*/dəf (Amandaville, Creelsboro). This hamlet whose po, 1 mi e of Crocus Creek and 10 mi sse of Columbia, was est on Jan 29, 1925, was probably named for the first pm, Rester C. Cundiff. Prior to this, the community was called Melson Ridge for the local elevation that had been named for several local families.
Cunningham (Carlisle): *kuhn*/ihŋ/haem (Blandville). This village with po is centered at the jct of US 62 and KY 1820, 6 mi ene of Bardwell. It was founded around 1880 on a site that may first have been settled in 1822 by George Reeves. The po on Aug 4, 1882, by Jesse W. Moss, local storekeeper, and named for a temporary resident. 86.
Curdsville (Daviess): *k3dz*/vihl (Curdsville). This settlement with po and, once a busy 19th cent shipping port and manufacturing town, is on the Green R, just above the mouth of Panther Creek and 10 mi w of Owensboro. It was first settled around 1842 by Aquilla Spray. According to tradition, when Spray est the po in his store on Feb 19, 1855, he named it for a Green R steamboat captain, H. T. Curd, who had promised him a barrell of whiskey to do this. 99, 104, 930.
Curdsville (Mercer). See *Burgin*
Curlew (Union): *k3*/lū (Dekoven). This abandoned coal town and extinct po is located at the jct of the present KY 667 and Martin Rd, ½ mi wnw of DeKoven, and 11 mi sw of Morganfield. The po of Curlew, est on Sept 3, 1858, and named for the owner of the local mines, became Curlew Mines in 1860. Now the Curlew name identifies only several homes. 1129.
Curlew Mines (Union). See *Curlew*
Curreys (Jefferson). See *Fisherville*
Curt (Breathitt): K3t (Canoe). This recently closed po on Cane Creek and KY 397, 2 mi s of KY 30 and 3½ mi s of Jackson, was est on April 28, 1928, with John Hall, pm, and named for Curt Turner, a respected local farmer. 1222.
Curtis (Metcalfe): *k3t*/əs (Edmonton). Little remains of a once-thriving sawmill town on the South Fork of the Little Barren R, 1 mi s of KY 496 and 2½ mi se of Edmonton. It was first locally known as the Mann community for the local school, 1 mi n of the creek, which had been built on land donated by James Harvey Mann. The po was est on May 29, 1901, by James Breeding and Curtis Everett and named for the latter, a native of Summer Shade. The po was closed in 1929. 232.
Custer (Breckinridge): *kuhs*/tər (Custer). This hamlet with po lies at the jct of KY 86 and 690, 10 mi ese of Hardinsburg. To serve a community then called Crossroads, this po was est on Aug 8, 1876, with Felix Loeb, pm, and named for Gen. George Armstrong Custer (1839–76), for on the day the application for the office was sent, word had reached Washington of Custer's defeat at the Little Big Horn. 290, 1398.
Cutshin (Leslie): *kuht*/shən (Cutshin). This hamlet with po is on KY 699 and the creek for which it was named, 7½ mi se of Hyden. The po was est on Aug 21, 1860, with James C. Brewer as the first pm. The creek heads almost at the Harlan Co line and flows in a generally nw direction to the Middle Fork of the Kentucky R at Smilax, 5 mi below the po. The several traditional accounts of the name seem to refer either to some unidentified early traveler or hunter who fell while crossing the turbulent waters of the stream in flood, cutting his shin on a jagged rock, or to an early settler on the stream bottom who cut his shin with an ax while felling timber for his new home. More likely the name merely suggests a stream that is difficult to cross. 855, 1223.

Cyclone (Monroe): *sah*/klohn (Sulphur Lick). This hamlet with extinct po is on KY 163, 8½ mi n of Tompkinsville. The po, est on Nov 28, 1891, with Samuel M. Billingsley, pm, was named for a cyclone that had struck the vicinity in the late 19th cent and killed several persons. 1297.

Cynthiana (Harrison): sihn/thee/*aen*/ə (Cynthiana). This 4th class industrial city and seat of Harrison Co is centered at the jct of US 27 and 62 and KY 32 and 36, 73 mi e of downtown Louisville. On Dec 10, 1793, the year the co was created, a log settlement on the South Fork of the Licking R was chartered as a town and made the co seat. It was named for Cynthia and Anna, the daughters of Robert Harrison who donated the land on which it was est. The po has been in continuous operation since Apr 1, 1801. 167.

Dabolt (Jackson):*dā*/bohlt (Parrot). This po on KY 2003, 6½ mi s of McKee, was est on May 18, 1928, and named for Frederick P. Dabolt, the superintendent of the Bond-Foley Lumber Co., the principal employer in this section of the co at that time. 1425.

Daisy (Perry): *dā*/zee (Tilford). This po on KY 699 and Lower Hicks Branch, originally lay across Leatherwood Creek from its present location, 9½ mi sse of Hazard. It was est on July 21, 1905, with Lizzie Cornett, pm, and may have been named for Daisy Cornett. 1272, 1327.

Dallasburg (Owen). See *Wheatley*

Dallo PO (Russell). See *Salem*

Dalna (Letcher). See *Hot Spot*

Danleyton (Greenup): *daen*/əl/tən (Argillite). This once thriving village is now but a rural settlement on KY 747, ½ mi s of its jct with KY 207, less than ½ mi e of the East Fork of the Little Sandy R, and 5½ mi sse of Greenup. A po was est here on Apr 16, 1883, with George W. Callihan, pm, and named for Daniel Callihan, a local resident. It was discontinued in 1917. 23, 368, 1213.

Danville (Boyle): *daen*/vəl (Danville, Junction City, Bryantsville). This 3rd class city, generally considered "the first capital of Kentucky," is the seat of Boyle Co, on US 150 and 127, 62 mi se of downtown Louisville. The town was founded by and named for Walker Daniel in 1783–84 on the site of John Crow's Station which Daniel, as an officer of the newly est Kentucky District Court, had just acquired for its seat. Here on Aug 20, 1792, Kentucky's first po was est, with Thomas Barbee, pm. Danville became the seat of Boyle Co when it was est in 1842. 70, 1224.

Danville Junction (Boyle). See *Junction City*

Danville Station (Boyle). See *Junction City*

Datha (Jackson): *dā*/thə (Tyner). This extinct po lay on the Clay Co line, near the head of Terrell Creek, a tributary of the South Fork of Rockcastle R, 12 mi sse of McKee. The po, in operation from 1905 to 1917, was named by local storekeeper William S. Bowling for his sweetheart and future wife, Emma Datha Langdon, who was the first pm of record. 1428.

Daugherty PO (Butler). See *Dexterville*

Davella (Martin); də/*vehl*/ə (Inez). This po on KY 3 and the Middle Fork of Rockcastle Creek, 5 mi ssw of Inez, was est on July 14, 1902, by Dave Delong who named it for his wife, Ella, and himself. 1360.

David (Floyd): *dā*/vəd (David). Once a model coal town and now a residential settlement with po, David lies at the end of KY 404 and Lick Fork of the Left Fork of Middle Creek (a branch of the Levisa Fork of the Big Sandy R), 7 mi sw of Prestonsburg. The Princess Elkhorn Coal Co. purchased the nearly inaccessible Lick Fork property of

Jake Shepherd and, in 1941, est a coal camp and po, which it named for David L. Francis, general manager and later president. 176, 194, 579.

David PO (Letcher). See *Carbon Glow*

Daviess County: *dā*/vəs. 463 sq mi. Pop. 85,947. Seat: Owensboro. Est in 1815 from part of Ohio Co, Daviess Co was named for Col. Joseph Hamilton Daveiss (1774–1811), the pioneer lawyer who, as US attorney for Kentucky, prosecuted Aaron Burr for treason in 1806. He was killed at the Battle of Tippecanoe. His name was misspelled in the act that created the co and was never corrected.

Davisburg PO (Christian). See *Fairview*

Davistown (Garrard): *dāv*/əs/town (Bryantsville). This Negro settlement across Dix R and the present Lake Herrington from Boyle Co, 7½ mi nw of Lancaster, was named for the late W. M. Davis, the owner of a large tract of land in that vicinity. The community has never had its own po. 918, 1225.

Davys Run (Carter): *dā*/veez *Ruhn* (Willard). Though the po was est as Gollihue [*ghahl*/ə/hyū or *ghahl*/ee/hyū] on Mar 28, 1923, and named for a local family, this settlement with extinct po, 2.3 mi up Davy Run from its confluence with Little Fork of the Little Sandy R, and 6 mi sse of Grayson, is now locally known almost exclusively as Davys Run. Little is known of its early history or for how long it bore either name. The Gollihue name is generally believed to predate its application to the po and a community is said to have existed there even before the old narrow gauge rr was constructed to haul coal to Denton. It is assumed that the current name honors Davy Lunsford who ran the train between this point and Denton, about 1½ mi ne. Some have questioned this, however, believing that the name may have been in use before rail service was initiated there. The po closed in 1937. 36, 827, 1326.

Dawson City (Hopkins). See *Dawson Springs*

Dawson PO (Hopkins). See *Dawson Springs*

Dawson Springs (Hopkins): *daw*/sən *sprihŋz* (Dawson Springs). This 4th class industrial and commercial city on the Tradewater R extends s from the Western Kentucky Parkway to the Christian Co line, 12 mi sw of Madisonville. In 1872 the Elizabethtown and Paducah (now Illinois Central Gulf) RR est its station on land donated by Bryant N. Dawson and called it first Tradewater Station and then, in 1874, Dawson. On May 15, 1872, Dawson became the first pm of the Dawson po. In 1881 and again in 1893, while digging wells, Washington I. Hamby discovered the mineral waters that led to the development of the town as one of the principal health resorts in the upper South. In 1882 the town was inc as Dawson City but renamed Dawson Springs in 1898 in preference to Dawson Wells, a more accurate name since the water was not spring-derived but came from shallow wells. By 1950 it had become the strip mining capital of western Kentucky. 382.

Dayhoit (Harlan): *dā*/hoit (Wallins Creek, Harlan). This village with po lies on the Cumberland R just below the mouth of Ewing Creek, 2½ mi w of Harlan. The po was est on Aug 7, 1897, as Day for a local family. In 1913 the name was changed to Wilhoit for Roy Wilhoit, the founder of a local coal co. In 1915 the po was moved to the site of the White Star Coal Co. mines, 1 mi up Ewing Creek, and renamed White Star. When it closed in 1930 its papers were transferred to the Dayhoit po, which had been est on Apr 22, 1921, at or close to the Wilhoit site where the Wilhoit station of the Kentucky & Virginia (now L&N) RR had been located several years before. Dayhoit was undoubtedly a combination of the names of Day and Wilhoit, its predecessors. 1173.

Day PO (Harlan). See *Dayhoit*

Daysboro (Wolfe): *dāz*/buhr/ə (Hazel Green, Cannel City). This hamlet with recently closed po lies on the Red R at the jct of KY 191 and 1953, 9½ mi ene of Campton. The po was est as Daysborough in Morgan Co on Mar 5, 1878, with Nathan H. Salley, pm, and named for Floyd Day, a merchant and later timber producer who, in 1889, was to build the Mountain Central RR. This po was discontinued in 1880 and reest at its Wolfe Co location in 1886. The spelling was simplified to its present form in 1893. 289, 1372.

Daysville (Todd): dāz/vəl (Olmstead). This hamlet on US 68, 4 mi e of Elkton, was founded around 1833 and probably named for George H. Day, a local storekeeper. On Apr 17, 1844, the po was est, probably by Day (though Benjamin T. Perkins was the first pm). It was discontinued in 1910. 225.

Dayton (Campbell): *dā*/(t)ən (Newport). This 4th class city is located across the Ohio R from Cincinnati, e and n of Bellevue, n of Ft. Thomas, and a little over 1 mi ne of the Newport po. Dayton was the product of a merger in 1867 of the 2 adjacent but separate communities of Jamestown and Brooklyn, which had been chartered in 1848 and 1849, respectively. The local po, which was est on Nov 12, 1849, as Brooklyn with Samuel Bassett, pm, was discontinued in 1856 and reest as Dayton in 1868. In 1896 it became a branch of the Newport po. No one really knows why any of these names was applied. It is thought that some of Brooklyn's early settlers had come from New York; Jamestown might refer to the Virginia colony since nearby *Newport* was named for the English sea captain who had brought the first settlers to Virginia. It is no longer accepted that Dayton was named for the Ohio city, nor is there any evidence that the name refers to the early Dayton Mill here, which is said to have been est by a pioneer family of Daytons. In 1866 a Cincinnati newspaper reported a list of names that had been suggested for the new town: Crescent, Stanberry, Bendville, Berryville, North Point, Hallam, Lookout, Campbleton (*sic*), Buchanan, and Skillbeck. But by July 4, 1866, the Dayton name had been applied and accepted by the residents. 326, 1300.

Deanefield (Ohio). See *Reynolds Station*

Deanwood (Crittenden): *deen*/wood (Shady Grove). Little remains of this hamlet on KY 120, 8 mi e of Marion, which was once called Iron Hill [*ahrn hihl*]. This name, recalling the local iron industry, which is said to have peaked and declined before 1850, was given to the po est at this site on Apr 29, 1873, with James W. Woolf, pm. On Oct 16, 1914, Joseph N. Dean, who had been pm since 1900, succeeded in effecting a name change to Deanwood for his family. By 1917 the po had closed. 1324.

Deatsville (Nelson): *deets*/vihl (Samuels). This hamlet with po is located by the jct of KY 523 and the Bardstown Branch of the L&N RR, 7 mi nw of Bardstown. A po est as Deatsville on Oct 30, 1850, with Leander P. Bradshaw, pm, was moved in 1860 to the site of the hamlet of *Samuels*, over 1½ mi se, and renamed Samuels Depot. On Mar 13, 1866, a po called Sayers Depot was opened by William Samuels at a short-lived train stop on the Sayers farm midway between Deatsville and Samuels. Richard W. Deats, who became its pm in 1869, had the po moved to and renamed Deatsville on Aug 24, 1870. It is not known when the Deatsville name was first applied to that site but it probably honored R. W. Deats, a veterinarian, pioneer settler, and his family's progenitor in that area. 199.

Decatur (Russell): dee/*kat*/ər (Phil, Eli). This extinct po on Goose Creek, less than ¾ mi from the Casey Co line and 9½ mi nne of Jamestown, was est on Oct 1, 1900, and named by its first pm, Cyrenius Wade, for his son, Decatur Wade. 1233.

DeCoursey (Kenton): də/*kawr*/see (Newport). This settlement and the largest of the L&N RR yards are located along KY 177, just e of the city of Taylor Mills and n of Fairview, 6 mi above downtown Covington at the confluence of the Licking and Ohio rs. William DeCoursey, Sr. (1756–1841), was a Maryland-born Revolutionary War veteran who arrived in northern Kentucky as early as 1794 and lived for a while in the area that bears his name. A station on the L&N RR named for the DeCoursey family was in existence before 1868. The yard was built in 1913–14. 94, 1252.

Decoy (Knott and Breathitt): *dee*/koi, *dee/koi* (Vest, Tiptop). This hamlet with po 12 mi nnw of Hindman and 15½ mi e of Jackson straddles the co line. Though the area was first settled around 1809, the po was not est until Nov 14, 1904, with Henry C. Shepherd, pm. Shepherd was the hero of a most unusual place naming account: Henry's goal of intellectual self-improvement included systematic study of a mail order dictionary. One day therein he came across the word "decoy," to entrap, and was shortly able to apply this concept when he successfully set a trap for his unfaithful wife and her man. He was later to say to his neighbors that he had decoyed them. When it came time to est a po in the community, Henry was asked to be the pm, and he requested it be named Decoy, for this word had much significance to him. 1275.

Dehart (Morgan): *dee/hahrt* (West Liberty). This hamlet with extinct po is on KY 722, 1 mi up Greasy Creek from its confluence with the Licking R, and 4 mi nw of West Liberty. The po was est on Oct 5, 1909, and named for its first pm, David Boone Dehart, or his family. It closed in 1963. 112.

Dekoven (Union): dee/*kohv*/ən (Dekoven). This hamlet with extinct po, once a large coal mining town, is centered on the jct of KY 667 and 1508, 1½ mi from the Ohio R and 10½ mi sw of Morganfield. It is said that in 1843 John Willworth, a native of Flanders, began the operation of a mine in this vicinity. The camp he est there, and later the town that grew up around it, was called DeKoven meaning roughly, in Flemish, a "camp or village among the hills." This, according to tradition, was how he described a local Indian settlement he had earlier visited. The DeKoven po was est on June 13, 1871, with Warren Howell, pm, and the town was inc in 1886. In that year, with the coming of the Ohio Valley (now Illinois Central Gulf) RR, the community and po were moved ½ mi to the rr. In 1938 the rr closed its local station and the po was discontinued shortly thereafter. 351, 957.

Delaware (Daviess): *dehl*/ə/wɛ (Delaware). Now a settlement of weekend residents in the sw corner of the co, 15 mi wsw of Owensboro, this was once a busy 19th cent Green R port. It was laid out in 1864 by Andrew M. Allen from part of his Green R farm and named for Delaware Creek, which joins the r just above the townsite. The po, which Allen est in his store on Dec 1, 1860, operated intermittently until it closed for good in 1966. 99, 104.

Della PO (Leslie). See *Lewis Creek*

Delmer (Pulaski): *dehl*/mər (Delmer). A settlement on KY 235, 6½ mi sw of Somerset, Delmer's extinct po was est on June 23, 1903, and named by the first pm, William Sherman Burton, for his 1-year-old son Delmer. 1410.

Delphton PO (Scott). See *Donerail*

Delta (Wayne): *dehl*/tə (Coopersville). This hamlet with po is on KY 790, 5 mi up Big Sinking Creek, at the mouth of Turkey Hollow, and 10 mi ene of Monticello. The po was est on June 27, 1906, and named by the first pm, J. W. H. Hammond, for his daughter-in-law Delta Casada Hammond. 1034.

Delvinta (Lee): dehl/*vihn(t)*/ee (Heidelberg). This settlement with extinct po is on KY 587, 6½ mi sw of Beattyville. The community and its po, est on Nov 11, 1898, with Florence H. Treadway, pm, were named by her husband, Capt. Morgan J. Treadway, a Booneville lawyer, who had retired to this site in 1897 to grow grapes. The name refers to "a place of vines." 622.

Democrat (Letcher): *dehm*/oh/kraet (Mayking). This hamlet with po is now located on KY 7 at the mouth of Lower Appletree on Rockhouse Creek and 8 mi n of Whitesburg. According to Arthur Dixon, a former co judge, it was first called Razorblade, which may refer to its original location on Razorblade Branch of Rockhouse Creek, 1 mi above the present site. A po called Stick was est in this vicinity on Feb 12, 1889, with Elhanan King, pm, though the exact location is uncertain. The po was renamed Democrat on Oct 31, 1902. In 1915 it was located at the mouth of Big Branch of Rockhouse, but was later moved to its present site. Though no one seems to know why the Razorblade and Stick names were applied, everyone agrees that Democrat was named for the one lone Democrat in a staunchly Republican precinct, the pm himself. 272.

DeMossville (Pendleton): də/*mâhs*/vəl, də/*mâhs*/vihl (DeMossville). This hamlet with po extends ½ mi from KY 177 to the mouth of Grassy Creek, across the Licking R from Campbell Co and is 9 mi nnw of Falmouth. The first po to serve this area was Grassy Creek, est on Dec 30, 1820, with Roswell Kittridge, pm, probably at the forks of Grassy, 1 mi sw of its confluence with the Licking R. In 1854 the po moved to the confluence to be on the new Covington and Lexington (now L&N) RR. It was renamed DeMossville, by which name a settlement may already have been est to honor the DeMoss family, descendants of Peter DeMoss, said to have come to America with General LaFayette. The new town was chartered as DeMossville in 1860. 845, 847, 1230.

Demplytown (Oldham): *dehmp*/lee/town (LaGrange). This residential settlement along KY 1817 between the Cedar Point and Halls Hill rds, 4 mi wsw of LaGrange, was named for the local Demply family sometime before 1900. It has never had its own po. 990.

Denney (Wayne): *dehn*/ee (Coopersville). This hamlet with extinct po is on KY 776, near the head of Turkey Creek, 10 mi e of Monticello. The po was est on Apr 8, 1891, and named by its first pm, Dupuy Denney, for himself or his family, the descendants of pioneer Matthew Denney (1782–1875). Charles Denney, Matthew's uncle, is said to have secured the first patent on the large area encompassing the po site in 1804. The po closed in 1975. 1274.

Denniston (Menifee): *dehn*/əs/tən (Scranton). A hamlet on US 460, 5 mi ese of Frenchburg, Denniston's po was named by and for its first pm, Joseph C. Denniston, when est on Mar 9, 1900, on Betty Gap Ridge. The po was later moved s to the highway. 970.

Dent (Perry). See *Leatherwood*

Denton (Carter): *dehn*/(t)ən (Rush). This hamlet with po lies at the mouth of Glancy Fork of Straight Creek and the jct of KY 1512 and 773, 5 mi se of Grayson. Frank J. Wood est the po on Dec 14, 1881, and named it Heflin for an old Carter Co family. On Feb 1, 1883, it was changed to Denton for Fanny Denton, the Tennessee-born wife of local landowner Charley Stewart, who ran the local hotel after his death. 36.

Deposit PO (Jefferson). See *Fairdale*

Depot PO (Graves). See *Pryorsburg*

Depoy (Muhlenberg): də/*poy* (Greenville). This village with po on US 62 and the Illinois Central Gulf RR, 2½ mi w of Greenville, was first called Gordon's Station. It was renamed, when the po was est on Aug. 9, 1887, for Elmer Depoyster, an early Illinois Central agent there. 320.

Devils Fork (Elliott). See *Lytten*

Dewey (Floyd): *dyū*/ee (Lancer). Nothing marks the site of a po in operation from 1904 to 1938 on Johns Creek, 3½ mi nne of Prestonsburg, which was named for either Admiral George Dewey (1837–1917) of the Battle of Manila Bay or Dewey Wells, a local resident. The Johns Creek flood control dam, 1 mi n of the po site, was named for it as was the lake, created in 1950, that covers the po site. 194, 1370.

Dewitt (Knox): *dee/wiht* (Scalf). This hamlet with po on Stinking Creek, just above the mouth of Road Fork Creek, and 8 mi e of Barbourville, was named for an old man who lived in that vicinity in the mid 19th cent. Nothing else is known about him. Jesse Campbell est the po on Apr 26, 1894. 1409.

Dexter (Calloway): *dehx*/tər (Dexter). This former 6th class city and rail shipping point on the Nashville Chattanooga and St. Louis (now L&N) RR, is now but a hamlet with po on US 641, 7½ mi n of Murray. Though this area was settled earlier in the 19th cent, it was not until 1890, when the then Paducah Tennessee & Alabama RR was being built through, that plans for a village there materialized on the site of the rr construction camp. Sam M. Jones, the landowner, donated the right of way and the site for the station on condition that he be allowed to name it. He chose the name of a thriving rr town in Missouri, which at that time was giving employment to several of Jones's former Calloway Co neighbors. The po was est near the depot on Dec 19, 1890, with General Buford Williams, pm. 1199.

Dexterville (Butler): *dehx*/ter/vihl (Flener). This settlement and extinct po about a mi n of KY 79 and 5½ mi n of Morgantown, was named for 2 brothers, Isaac B. and Joe Dexter, who arrived here in 1885 from Centertown in Ohio Co, bought a big farm, and opened a general store and steam-powered gristmill. On Feb 3, 1886, the Daughterty [*dahr*/tee] po, est in 1884 at the site of what became Banock, 2.7 mi n, was moved to the Dexter store and reest as Dexterville with Isaac as the first pm. 486.

Dezarn PO (Green). See *Creal*

Diablock (Perry): *dah*/ə/blahk (Hazard South). This residential suburb, a former coal town, lies on the North Fork of the Kentucky R, just above Hazard's southern city limits. It was founded by and named for the Diamond Block Coal Co. there. Its now extinct po was est on Nov 15, 1916, with William B. Haynes, pm. 110.

Diamond Springs (Logan): *dah*/muhn(d) *sprihŋz* (Dunmore, Rosewood). This name was applied to both a defunct po on the L&N RR, 12 mi nnw of Russellville, and a rustic resort on Rawhide Creek, 2½ mi w, which the po served and for which it was named. The springs site itself was developed in 1893 by James C. Sneed, a Tennessee veteran of John Hunt Morgan's Civil War campaigns, in an isolated but picturesque timbered area fed by 4 or 5 springs of "iron water." Two accounts have been offered for the unusual name. According to co historian May Belle Morton, tiny quartz- or mica-inlaid rocks sprinkled around the bed of the stream seemed to glisten like diamonds. Margaret Barnes Stratton described the sun shining through the leaves of giant beech trees, in contrast with the shadows of the trees themselves, showing a glittering effect on the ground and the walls of the adjacent cliffs. Two mi e, on the present US 431, a po called Baughs Station [*bâhz stā*/shən], probably a stage coach stop, was est on Mar 23, 1858, by George N. Baugh. By 1880, when the "Station" was dropped from the name, it had moved to the tracks of the Owensboro & Nashville (now L&N) RR, and in 1901 was renamed Diamond Springs. 42, 206, 1344.

Dingus (Morgan): *dihŋ*/əs (Dingus). This hamlet with po is on KY 437, at the mouth of Burks Creek (given on current maps as Birch Fork of Williams Creek), 8½ mi e of West Liberty. The po is said to have been est at the mouth of Grays Branch of Burks on Apr 4, 1883, and named for its first pm, Charles B. Dingus, or his family. It later moved 1½ mi down Burks to its present location. 112.

Dirk PO (Knott). See *Carr Creek*

Disputanta (Rockcastle): dihs/pə/*taent*/ə (Wildie). This extinct po was on KY 1787, at the mouth of Davis Branch of Clear Creek, and 10 mi nne of Mount Vernon. D. N. Williams is said to have suggested the name when 2 local factions could not agree on what to call their new po. It was est on June 25, 1886, with Henry H. Wood, pm, to replace the Reidsville po in operation from 1878 to 1884, probably at the site of the Reids' tannery ¾ mi s. The Disputanta po, which closed in Dec 1977, served the larger community long known locally as Clear Creek. 835, 1243.

Dixie (Carroll). See *Sanders*

Dixie (Henderson): *dihx*/ee (Poole). This hamlet on KY 145, 9½ mi ssw of Henderson, was first settled before 1841, probably by William Q. Dixon and William S. Sutton. Dixon's son George W. est the po on Sept 15, 1879, and named it Dixie when its proximity to Dixon in adjacent Webster Co precluded the use of his family's name. The po closed in 1907. 12, 1221.

Dixon (Webster): *dihx*/ən (Dixon). This 6th class city and seat of Webster Co is on US 41A, 109 mi wsw of downtown Louisville. On this site in 1794, William Jenkins, a Virginian said to have been the first settler of the co, est the famed Halfway House, a stagecoach inn. The new co's seat was laid out in 1860 on land then owned by Ambrose Mooney, and named for Archibald Dixon of nearby Henderson (1802–76), who had been appointed to complete Henry Clay's term in the US Senate, 1852–55. The po was est as Dixon's Court House on July 24, 1860, with William Herrin, pm, and the town was inc in 1861. 842, 1174.

Dixon's Court House PO (Webster). See *Dixon*

Dizney (Harlan): *dihz*/nee (Pennington Gap). This hamlet with po is on KY 215 and Yocum Creek, at the mouth of Bills Creek, 10½ mi e of Harlan. The po was est about ½ mi w on Yocum Creek on Jan 15, 1898, with John G. Farley, pm. In 1921 pm Roscoe F. Weaver removed it 2 mi w to the present site of *Kenvir* and renamed it for that developing coal town. The Dizney po was reest in 1922 by Henry Surgener. Dizney was probably named for E[lijah] Frank[lin] Dizney, the first principal of Black Mt. Academy, which had been est by the Congregational Church at nearby Evarts in 1893. The Dizney community is now also locally referred to as Punkin Center [*puhŋ*/kən *sehn(t)*/ər]. 46, 1052.

Dogtown (Monroe). See *Blythe*

Dog Trot (Crittenden). See *Sheridan*

Dolen (Perry). See *Combs*

Domino PO (Perry). See *Combs*

Donansburg (Green): də/*naenz*/bergh (Center, Exie). This crossroads hamlet is on KY 88, 6½ mi w of Greensburg. The area was settled before 1800 by Virginians but the po, since closed, was not est until June 1, 1888, with William T. Chewning, pm. It was named for Dr. Dave Donan who had surveyed the vicinity for a rr that never went beyond Greensburg. 774.

Donerail (Fayette): *dahn*/ə/rāl (Georgetown). Nothing remains of a hamlet with rr station and po at the jct of the Ironworks R and the Southern Ry, ¼ mi w of the Present I 75 and 5½ mi n of Lexington's New Circle Rd. A po called Donoraile (later Donnerail) had been est as early as 1826, probably in the tavern opened in 1807 by Archibald Hutchison at the jct of the Georgetown Pike (now US 25) and the Ironworks Pike, ½ mi nw of the future Donerail Station. Hutchison is said to have called his tavern Doneraile, but it is not known when or why. In 1835 the po was moved to Scott Co by Jeremiah (or Jerry) Delph; by 1838 he had returned it to Fayette Co as Carrollton, and several months later renamed it Delphton. Under this name it was discontinued in 1851. In 1879 it was reest as Donerail at the newly opened Cincinnati Southern RR depot with Squire C. Gaines, pm. Two accounts of the name have little historical likelihood. According to a tale attributed to Charles Staples, the Lexington historian, "an Irish peddler stayed overnight at the tavern at Delphton in the early days, and awoke to discover his watch and chain were missing. . . . He loudly proclaimed that he had never been robbed before except at Doneraile, in the old country, and thereafter the village was called Doneraile." In the other account, Irish rr workers, when laying the tracks of the Cincinnati Southern in the late 1870s, applied the name Donneraille to their camp. The po closed in 1958. 393, 511, 1055, 1335.

Donnellys Store (Union). See *Waverly*

Dorton (Pike): *dawr*/tən (Dorton). This village with po is centered at the confluence of Dorton and Shelby Creeks and the jct of US 23 and KY 610, 13 mi s of Pikeville. Named for William P. Dorton (ca. 1842–1934), the po was est on July 2, 1873, with John Bumgardner, pm. 1085.

Douglas PO (Casey). See *Walltown*

Douglas PO (Perry). See *Christopher*

Dover (Mason): *doh*/vər (Higginsport). This 6th class city with po lies in the Ohio R bottom n of KY 8, 8½ mi nw of Maysville. From his father, a Virginia surveyor sent to Kentucky by George Washington to handle the land concerns of Virginians there. Arthur Fox, Jr., acquired 2200 acres of Ohio R bottom land, on which he built his home. In 1818 he helped lay out a town, which he may have named for Dover, England, from which his father is alleged to have emigrated. The Dover po was est on Jan 2, 1823, with Stephen Thomas, pm, and the town was chartered in 1836. 858.

Dowagiac PO (Hart). See *Pike View*

Doylesville (Madison): *doi*/əlz/vihl, *daw*/yəlz/vihl (Union City). This hamlet on KY 1986, 1 mi s of the Kentucky R and 9 mi ne of Richmond, was named for Pat Doyle, the first storekeeper. A po was in operation from 1847 to 1930. 57, 1294.

Draffenville (Marshall): *draef*/ən/vihl (Briensburg). This accumulation of businesses extends for nearly 2 mi along US 68 and is centered at its jct with US 641 and the Purchase Parkway. There was nothing in this vicinity before 1938 when construction of the Kentucky Dam, 7 mi ne, and the access rd to it (US 641) began. At that time Charley Draffen, apparently with an eye to the future, divided his farm into lots for sale. Stores were built on them and after a while local people began calling the area Draffenville informally. It has no po. 1337.

Drake PO (Warren). See *Whites Chapel*

Drakesboro (Muhlenberg): *drāx*/buh/rə (Drakesboro). This 5th class city with po on US 431, 5 mi e of Greenville, began as a lumber camp called Ricedale. Frank M. Rice, the local storekeeper, est the po with this name on Oct 2, 1882. In 1888 the town was inc as Drakesboro for one of its first settlers, a William Drake who had died there in 1868, and the po was so renamed in 1889. 189.

Drennon Springs (Henry): *drehn*/ən *sprihŋz* (Worthville). This abandoned site of a fashionable 19th cent spa is located 2 mi up Drennon Creek from its confluence with the Kentucky R and 8 mi ne of New Castle. The 7 springs around which the resort developed in the 1830s and 1840s had been discovered in 1773 by Matthew Bracken and Jacob Drennon and named for the latter. A Drennon Springs po, in operation from 1885 to 1915, was replaced in 1922 by a transfer of one from Glenmary, a now extinct port at the mouth of the creek. This too has since closed. 394, 1256.

Dreyfus (Madison): *drā*/fəs (Bighill). This hamlet with po in the se section of the co, just above the head of Drowning Creek and 9½ mi se of Richmond, has also been known locally as Bearwallow [bɛ /*wahl*/ə]. The Dreyfus name was probably applied first to the po, est on Jan 28, 1899, with John S. Ogg, pm, and undoubtedly honored the French officer whose treason trial had been much in the news in the late 1890s.

Drift (Floyd): drihft (Wayland, McDowell). This coal town with po is on KY 122 and the Left Fork of Beaver Creek, 12 mi s of Prestonsburg. The Drift po, est on Apr 23, 1909, with Hasadore Martin, pm is said by some to have been named for the first mine in the vicinity, a drift (rather than shaft or slope) mine. This has been disputed by others who cannot recall any coal mining on Left Beaver until after the rr was completed from Martin in 1917. Perhaps there is something to one local tale of the discovery of driftwood on the creek. No other historically valid explanations of the name have been offered. 986, 1135.

Dripping Spring PO (Edmonson). See *Rocky Hill*

Drip Rock (Estill): *drihp* Rahk (Leighton). This hamlet with recently closed po is on KY 89, just n of the Jackson Co line, less than 7 mi s of Irvine. The po, est on Dec 13, 1880, in Jackson Co, was named for the steady dripping of spring water from a ledge of limestone rocks near the old Drip Rock School just s. The po was moved to its most recent site on Mar 4, 1939, when Mrs. Ethel Harrison became pm. 865.

Dry Fork (Barren): *dreye fawrk* (Tracy). This settlement with extinct po on KY 921, 10½ mi s of Glasgow, was named for a nearby wet weather branch of Peter Creek. The po was est on July 31, 1848, with Alfred P. Maury, pm. 791.

Dry Ridge (Grant): *drah*/*rihdj* (Williamstown). This 5th class city extends for over 3 mi along KY 22 from the Williamstown city limits n and w to a point over a mi w of I 75. In the vicinity of Campbell's (pioneer) Station (ca. 1790), it was named for the north-side ridge that divides the Kentucky and Licking R watersheds between Williamstown and Crittenden, but which itself is not drained by any natural waterways. The lack of water on this direct route from Lexington to Cincinnati forced early travelers to stop at inns before they reached the ridge. At one of these inns, James Kinlear's, a po called Dry Ridge was est on July 1, 1815. The discovery of mineral springs here in 1908 led to a tourist boom when hotels like the Carlsbad (obviously named for the famed resort city in the Sudetenland) were built. An official change of name to Carlsbad in 1911 was short-lived as the Post Office Department would not accept this name for the local po. 400, 910.

Dubre (Cumberland): *dū*/bree (Dubre). This hamlet with po on KY 90 lies at the mouth of Pittman Creek, a branch of Marrowbone Creek, 10 mi wnw of Burkesville. The po was est on July 1, 1937, with Mrs. Delie B. Jeffrey, pm, and named for a local family. 1385.

Dukedom (Graves): *dyūgh*/dəm (Cuba). This village lies on the Tennessee state line, roughly half in Kentucky (on KY 129, 15 mi s of Mayfield) and half in Tennessee's Weakley Co. It, was probably named for Duke A. Beadles who est the po on the Tennessee side on July 30, 1833. The po was moved to the Kentucky side in 1846 and returned to Tennessee in 1852 where it has been ever since.

Dukes (Hancock): dyūx (Cloverport). This settlement is located at the jct of KY 144 and 1265, 5 mi se of Hawesville. Although the po was est by John L. Duke on June 7, 1893, it is believed that he or other members of his family had founded a community here by 1870. The po closed in 1907. 871, 1332.

Dulaney (Caldwell): də/*lā*/nee, dū/*lā*/nee (Princeton West). Little remains of this once incorporated community less than 1 mi s of the Western Kentucky Parkway and 3½ mi w of Princeton. On Dec 2, 1872, about the time the Illinois Central RR was built through to Princeton and a passenger and freight depot was constructed here, James W. McKinney est the Dulaney po. This was probably named for Henry F. Delany (the family's spelling), a pioneer Livingston and Caldwell Co lawyer, Presbyterian minister, and state legislator, who was born in Virginia in 1784 or 1785 and had come to western Kentucky before 1805. The po closed in 1935. 461, 1278.

Dunbar (Butler): *duhn*/bahr (South Hill). This hamlet with po is on KY 70, nearly a mi e of Muddy Creek, a tributary of the Green R, and 4 mi sw of Morgantown. The community may first have been called Big Muddy for the creek and the Big Muddy Baptist Church, organized in 1875. On Apr 19, 1898, the po was est as Dunbar and named for 2 local families, the Dunns and the Barrows. 1035, 1106.

Duncan (Mercer): *duhnk*/ən (Cornishville). This crossroads hamlet with extinct po is on KY 390, 8½ mi nw of Harrodsburg. The po, est on Feb 23, 1847, with Abraham B. Voorhies, pm, was probably named for John Ray Duncan, prominent in early Mercer Co affairs and the grandson of pioneer Ft. Harrod settler Gen. James B. Ray. It was inc as Duncansville in 1851. 1264.

Duncansville (Mercer). See *Duncan*

Dundee (Ohio): *duhn*/dee (Dundee). This hamlet on KY 69, just s of the Rough R, and 9½ mi ne of Hartford, was an early mill town. The community was settled sometime before 1846 and first called Hines Mill for the water-powered mill believed to have been built there by William R. Lowry and Warren W. Hines. On May 28, 1846, the local po was est as Hines Mills with Hines as pm. In 1872 the po was moved 1½ mi s to *Sulphur Springs*. The mill was destroyed by fire in 1892 but 2 years later was rebuilt by the Renfrows, a local family. In 1898 Andrew R. Renfrow reest the local po as Dundee, a name said to have been suggested, for reasons now unknown, by J. S. Fitzhugh. 390, 490, 631, 632, 1400.

Dunham (Letcher): *duhn*/əm (Jenkins East). This coal town at the head of Elkhorn Creek, 10 mi ne of Whitesburg, is now part of inc Jenkins whose downtown area lies 2 mi s. The now defunct po of Dunham was est on June 24, 1913, with Joel H. Roache, pm, to serve a camp set up by the Consolidation Coal Co. It was named for A. S. Dunham, the co.'s auditor. 1265.

Dunmor (Muhlenberg): *duhn*/mawr (Dunmor). This village, L&N RR station, and po are on US 431, 12½ mi se of Greenville. The po was est on May 14, 1884, with James W. Clark, pm, soon after the station on the Owensboro & Nashville line was opened, and was possibly named for Virginia's colonial Gov. Lord John Dunmore. Yet the presence of local families of Dunns suggests that their name may have been the source. The town was inc in 1886. 320.

Dunnville (Casey): *duhn*/vəl (Dunnville). This village with po is on US 127 just s of the confluence of Goose Creek and the Green R, 7½ mi ssw of Liberty. On Mar 30, 1878, the town was inc and named for James Richard Dunn, a Virginian who had settled there sometime after 1840, built a water-powered multipurpose mill, and acquired much land along the r. On July 3, 1879, the local po, which had been est on July 11, 1862, in Addison Williams's store as Williams Store, was renamed Dunnville. 212, 438, 1397.

Durbin (Boyd): *dɜb*/ən (Burnaugh). This extinct po was on KY 752 at the forks of Durbin Creek, a tributary of the Big Sandy R, 1 mi w of US 23 and 10 mi s of Catlettsburg. The po was est on Mar 5, 1900, with Robert Struther, pm, and named, as was the creek, for Amos Durbin, an early settler. 1091.

Durhamtown (Taylor): *dɜ*/əm/town (Saloma). This very old rural settlement on KY 744, 4½ mi nw of Campbellsville, was probably named for Samuel Durham (1752–

1837 or 1838), Virginia-born progenitor of the Durham families of central Kentucky. A po was in operation there from Sept 21, 1883, to Jan 7, 1884. 1291.

Duvalls Landing PO (Greenup). See *Limeville*

Dwale (Floyd): dwāl (Harold, Lancer). This village with po lies between the new US 23/460 and the Levisa Fork of the Big Sandy R, just n of Allen and 3 mi s of Prestonsburg. The po was first est as Haws Ford on Mar 10, 1868, with John M. Layne, pm, and named for pioneer settler Robert Haws's ford over the r at or near this site. This po was discontinued in 1870 and reest for a brief period as Hawes Ford in 1874. It was reest again on Sept 15, 1890, by Scottish-born Capt. John Finlayson, the local superintendent of the Yellow Poplar Lumber Co. of Chicago, who is said to have named it for a town in Wales. However, authorities on Welsh place names are not familiar with any such place. 1020, 1370.

Dwarf (Perry): dwâhrf (Hazard North, Carrie). This hamlet with po on Troublesome Creek is centered at the jct of KY 80 and 476, 5½ mi nne of Hazard. The local po, est on July 24, 1878, was named Tunnel Mill, for the tunnel which Sam and Felix Combs, using hand drills and gunpowder, had recently cut through 172 ft of solid rock for the purpose of carrying water to their mill. The po closed in 1881 but was reest on July 13, 1883, as Dwarf, honoring the Combs brothers' brother Jeremiah, called "Short Jerry" for his stature. 45, 114, 1327.

Dycusburg (Crittenden): *dai*/kəs/bergh (Dycusburg). This hamlet with po at the jct of the present KY 70, 295, and 902, 11½ mi ssw of Marion, was a thriving 19th cent shipping port on the Cumberland R. The town was laid out by William E. Dycus on land then owned by G. B. Dycus, pioneer settler, and named for the Dycus family. It was inc on Feb 3, 1847, and the po was est as Dycusburgh on Nov 7, 1848, with George S. Atkins, pm. It was recently disincorporated. 870, 1324.

Dyer (Breckinridge): *deye*/ər (Constantine). This hamlet with recently closed po lies at the jct of KY 86 and 401, 12 mi ese of Hardinsburg. The po was est on May 8, 1914, by James H. Harrington and named for a local family whose progenitor was Tom Dyer, a pioneer hunter from Tennessee. According to family legend, Tom, while hunting with some companions late one fall, broke his leg and was left under a cliff with some provisions while the others returned to Tennessee. After several days, he was found and brought to the cabin of Abitha Alice Turpin who nursed him back to health. He later married her and sired the Dyer family of this co. 1398.

Eadston PO (Rowan). See *Hays Crossing*

Eadsville (Wayne): *eedz*/vihl, *eedz*/vəl (Jabez). This extinct po was on KY 789, .3 mi s of jct with KY 1720 and less than 4 mi nnw of Monticello. On June 27, 1890, James E. Eads, a local merchant, est the po on the hill overlooking Eads Landing on the Cumberland R and named it for himself or his family. Around 1926 his son, Joel S. Eads, moved it to his store, ¾ mi s, where it remained until he retired in 1950 and it was discontinued. 1244, 1357, 1402.

Earlington (Hopkins): *ɜl*/ihŋ/tən (Madisonville East, Madisonville West). This 4th class city with po on US 41A, 1½ mi s of Madisonville, was founded by the St. Bernard Mining Co. in 1870 and named for John Baylis Earl (1823?–1906), a Madisonville attorney, and one of the pioneer developers of the coal industry in western Kentucky. The first po to serve this vicinity was Hall, from 1852 to 1863, named for an early 19th cent landowner, Caleb Hall, while the Earlington po itself was est on Apr 26, 1871, with Thomas J. McEuen, pm. 62, 159.

East Allen (Floyd). See *Allen*

East Bernstadt (Laurel). See *Bernstadt*

East Fork (Boyd). See *Cannonsburg*

East Fork (or **Bridgeport**) (Metcalfe): *eest fawrk, brihdj*/pawrt (East Fork). This hamlet with extinct po lies where KY 544 crosses the East Fork of the Little Barren R, 5 mi ne of Edmonton. Though the po was est as East Fork on Aug 4, 1853, and the community is identified on all maps by this name, the latter has always been locally referred to as Bridgeport. By this name the town was officially created by legislative act in 1870 and named for the covered bridge that spanned the r at this point. 295, 1261.

East Hickman (Fayette and Jessamine): *eest hihk*/mən (Coletown). This hamlet with extinct po is on KY 1974 and East Hickman Creek, for which it was named, 5 mi s of Lexington's New Circle Rd and the same distance ne of Nicholasville. East Hickman Creek, which joins West Hickman Creek at Union Mills, 3 mi e of Nicholasville, to form an important Kentucky R tributary, was named for Rev. William Hickman, a pioneer Baptist preacher. The East Hickman po was in operation between 1876 and 1906. 175.

East McDowell (Floyd). See *McDowell*

Easton (Hancock): *eest*/ən (Fordsville). This hamlet at the jct of KY 1700 and 2124, 13 mi sse of Hawesville, was once a prosperous trade center named for Samuel Easton who, on Mar 3, 1893, est the Easton po in his store. This po was discontinued in 1913. 684.

East Pineville (Bell): *eest pahn*/vihl (Middlesboro North). This hamlet with extinct po is on US 119, across the Cumberland R from and 1½ mi se of Pineville. The local po was est on Dec 3, 1925, as Jayem [*djā*/*ehm*], named for J[ohn] M[arshall] Robsion, Sr. (1873–1948), of Barbourville who represented Kentucky's 9th District in the US Congress from 1919 to 1930 and 1935 to 1948. 1416.

East Point (Johnson): *eest* pawnt (Prestonsburg). This hamlet with po is now located on KY 1428, just w of the confluence of Little Paint Creek and Levisa Fork of the Big Sandy R, and 3½ mi s of Paintsville. It was first located at the mouth of the creek, just across the r from Blockhouse Bottom, one of the pioneer Big Sandy settlements, and was settled by Auxiers and Greers after their abandonment of the Bottom. The po, est in Floyd Co on Feb 6, 1871, with William T. Hager, pm, is said to have been built on a high point and faced e. It was moved to Johnson Co in 1877. 89.

East Union (Nicholas): *eest yūn*/yən (Sharpsburg). This settlement on KY 57, 5 mi sse of Carlisle, was founded around 1800 and named by a congregation of Dunkards or German Baptists from Rowan Co, North Carolina, possibly for its site just e of the union of the forks of Somerset Creek, a tributary of Hinkston Creek. An East Union po was in operation from 1854 to 1857. In 1889 Will Bramblett secured another po in his store there and it was called Bramblett though the village has remained East Union. The Bramblett po closed in 1904. 47, 886, 1374.

Eastwood (Jefferson): *eest*/wōōd (Fisherville). This village with po is on US 60/460, 1 mi n of I 64 and 17 mi e of the court house in Louisville. The name may have been applied to the community as early as 1851, for there was an Eastwood Methodist Church there by that time. It could refer to the family of John Eastwood, a member of William Harrod's co militia in 1779–80. A station on the Shelby RR (later a branch of the L&N), located on Taylor family land was called Taylor Station, and a po of this name was est on July 15, 1872, with Edward G. Taylor, pm. By 1881 both were known as Eastwood. 97, 715.

Echols (Ohio): *ehk*/əlz (Paradise). This coal co. town is on the Illinois Central Gulf RR, 1¼ mi e of Rockport on the Green R, just n of the present Western Kentucky Parkway, and 8½ mi ssw of Hartford. The town was est in 1874 when a Mr. Echols from Illinois opened the local mine. The po was est on Nov 2, 1881, with Andrew Duncan, pm. Little remains at the original town site. The Echols community is now centered at its present po on Tunnel Hill, ¾ mi ne of the original town site. 401, 1086.

Eddy Grove (Caldwell). See *Princeton*

Eddyville (Lyon): *ehd*/ə/vihl (Eddyville). This 5th class city and the seat of Lyon Co, is on US 62/641, 138 mi sw of downtown Louisville. David Walker, who had acquired a patent for its original site on the bank of the Cumberland R sometime after 1790, is said to have laid it out as a town and named it for the large eddies in the r at that point. In 1800 Matthew Lyon (for whose son the co was named in 1854) brought his Vermont-born fellow pioneers to settle here. They purchased lots from Walker and secured the town's inc in 1810. It was, in succession, the seat of Livingston Co on its formation in 1799, of the newly est Caldwell Co in 1809, and finally of Lyon Co. The Eddyville po was est on Apr 1, 1801. The city was moved to its present location in 1959–62, after half the old town site was secured for the Barkley Lake impoundment. 230, 633.

Eden (Martin). See *Inez*

Edgoten (Christian): *ehdj*/oh/tən (Oak Grove). This extinct po and stop on the Tennessee Central (now Illinois Central Gulf) RR are ½ mi e of US Alt. 41 and 13 mi s of Hopkinsville. The po was est on Mar 13, 1906, with James A. McKenzie, pm, and named for its location by the state line, at the very "edge of Tennessee." In fact, the store in which it was located may have been called Edge-of-Tenn which was slurred to Edgoten. The po closed in 1922 and the store and station are gone. 1403.

Edmonton (Metcalfe): *ehd*/mən/tən (Edmonton). This 5th class city and seat of Metcalfe Co is on US 68, KY 163 and 496, less than 1 mi s of the Cumberland Parkway, and 82 mi s of downtown Louisville. It was named for Edmund P. Rogers (1762–1843), a Virginia-born Revolutionary War officer who surveyed and laid off the town on his own land in 1800. Though est by legislative act in 1836, it was little more than a trading post with po until it was inc as the new co's seat in 1860. The curious spelling may be an error in recording the name of the po, est on Feb 17, 1830, which was never corrected. 232, 590.

Edmonson County: *ehd*/mən/sən. 302 sq mi. Seat: Brownsville. Est in 1825 from parts of Grayson, Hart, and Warren cos, the co was named for Capt. John Edmonson (1764–1813), one of the 9 officers killed at the Battle of River Raisin on Jan 22, 1813, for whom Kentucky cos were named.

Edna (Magoffin): *ehd*/nə (White Oak). This hamlet with po is at the jct of US 460 and KY 1081, 5 mi nw of Salyersville. The po was est on Nov 21, 1900, at the mouth of Johnson Creek 1 mi s, and named by Kate Patton for her daughter Edna Patton Amyx. 1422.

Edsel (Elliott): *ehd*/səl (Mazie). This extinct po and hamlet were on KY 856 and Blaine Trace (a branch of the Little Fork of Little Sandy R), 11½ mi e of Sandy Hook. When Wade Blevins est his po there in 1929 he wished to name it Jewell for his daughter, but the name was already in use in Kentucky. Instead he submitted Edsel, that of a nephew, a local resident. Some people have long contended that it was named for the son of Henry Ford, who had succeeded his father as president of the Ford Motor Co. in 1919. Though this is unlikely, an attempt was initiated in 1957, with the production of the ill-fated Edsel car, to capitalize on the identity of the names. A plan to launch an extensive advertising campaign at this hamlet never materialized, as it was found that the rds were too bad to allow an Edsel car to be driven there. Local people now generally refer to the vicinity as Blaine Trace, though the Edsel name is still sometimes used. The po closed in 1960. 1412.

Edwards (Logan): *ehd*/wo͞odz (Lewisburg). This now defunct hamlet and station on the Owensboro & Nashville (now L&N) RR, 7 mi nnw of Russellville, was est around 1872 on land owned by George B. Edwards, a Russellville banker, for whom it was named. The Edwards po, also extinct, was est on Oct 21, 1885, with Marion L. Pitt, pm. The hamlet was also called Edwards Station. 206.

Edwards Station (Logan). See *Edwards*

Egypt (Elliott). See *Stark*

Egypt (Jackson): *ee*/djihpt (Tyner). This po is on US 421, 10 mi se of McKee. The po, est on Nov 9, 1876, with Adam Rader, pm, may have been named by the Amyx family who settled here shortly after the Civil War. "They felt it was a fur piece from nowhere when they moved up here [from Hawkins Co, Tennessee]. . . . They were homesick and felt like they were exiled into Egypt—harking back to the Biblical Egypt." 1418.

Egypt (Shelby). See *Chestnut Grove*

Eighty Eight (Barren): *ā*/tee *āt* (Temple Hill). This hamlet centers on a po on KY 90, 7½ mi se of Glasgow, which was est Sept 20, 1869, by Dabney L. Nunnally, the local storekeeper. According to tradition, Nunnally "wrote a very poor hand, and when the time came to name the post office, he said 'call it 88. I can write that so anybody can read it.'" Others prefer to believe that the po was then 8.8 mi from Glasgow. In either case, the Post Office Department stipulated that the name be spelled out. 895.

E. K. Junction (Carter). See *Hitchins*

Ekron (Meade): *ehk*/rən (Guston). This 6th class city with po lies at the jct of KY 144 and the L&N RR, 3½ mi s of Brandenberg. The town was founded on land donated by a Dr. Roberts, local physician and farmer, and its name, that of a Biblical city, was suggested by his wife. It was adopted over Loneoak (for a lone oak tree that once stood by a large pond and offered shade for resting slaves). A po was est here on Jan 14, 1889, with Charles E. Anderson, pm. 1046, 1070.

Elamton (Morgan): *ee*/ləm/tən (Lenox). This po is now on Williams Creek and KY 487, ¾ mi above the mouth of Pelfrey Branch and 5 mi e of West Liberty. The po was est at the head of War Creek on Aug 29, 1883, and probably named for its first pm, James S. Elam, or his family. J. W. Pelfrey later moved the po to his store at the mouth of Pelfrey Branch, whence it was moved to its present site. 112.

Eldorado (Mercer). See *McAfee*

Elihu (Pulaski): ehl/*ah*/hyū (Somerset). This hamlet with po is located where KY 1247 and the Southern Ry cross Pitman Creek, 1¼ mi s of Somerset. Soon after the completion of the Cincinnati Southern (now Southern) RR through this vicinity, storekeeper Elihu Taylor petitioned for a po. After the postal officials had rejected several names in turn as already in use in Kentucky, they are said to have selected his given name for the po, which was est on May 7, 1883. Taylor insisted on the unusual pronunciation of his name. 215.

Elizabeth (Christian). See *Hopkinsville*

Elizabethtown (Hardin): ə/*lihz*/ə/bəth/town (Elizabethtown, Cecilia). This 4th class industrial city and seat of Hardin Co is at the jct of the Bluegrass and Western Kentucky Parkways, I 65, and US 62, 36 mi s of downtown Louisville. In 1793, at what was first called Severns Valley Station (for John Severns, a surveyor from Fort Harrod), Col. Andrew Hynes had 30 acres of his land surveyed and laid out for the new co's seat. He named it Elizabethtown for his wife (nee Warford, from Maryland). This name first appears in the Hardin Co court records in May 1795 and by this name the town was officially est in 1797. The po may have begun operation as Hardin Court House or Elizabethtown in Jan 1804 with George Helm, pm. The city is now generally called Etown. 568, 1420.

Eliza PO (Johnson). See *Williamsport*

Elizaville (Fleming): ə/*lahz*/ə/vihl (Elizaville). This hamlet with po at the jct of KY 32 and 170, 4 mi w of Flemingsburg, was settled early—for its po existed by at least 1819 when John St. Clair was pm—and named for the daughter of pioneer settler John Cochran. It was chartered as a town on Feb 27, 1835. 491.

Elizaville Station (Fleming). See *Nepton*

Elkatawa (Breathitt): *ehl*/kə/tâh, *ehl*/kə/toi (Jackson). This hamlet with po is on KY 52 and Lindon Fork of Cane Creek (a tributary of the North Fork of the Kentucky R), 1½ mi w of Jackson. It is popularly believed that the community and its po, est on Apr 21, 1891, with Eli C. Jones, pm, were named by the Kentucky Union (later Lexington & Eastern and now L&N) RR, which had reached this point in Dec 1890. For some reason they chose to honor Tenskwautawa, the so-called "Prophet," the brother of the Shawnee chief Tecumseh. Elkatawa is said to be an obvious corruption of Ellskwatawa which, in turn, is supposed to have been corrupted from Tenskwautawa. This contention is highly suspect but no one has yet come up with a better explanation. 97, 744.

Elk Creek (Spencer): *ehlk kreek* (Taylorsville). This hamlet with extinct po extends along KY 55 for ½ mi between KY 155 and 1169, 4 mi n of Taylorsville. It was named for its location on Elk Creek, a branch of Salt R where many elk had been observed in pioneer times. The po was est on May 1, 1856. 1239.

Elk Horn (Taylor): *ehlk* hawrn (Campbellsville). This hamlet with po lies some 6 mi up Robinson Creek from its confluence with the Green R and 2½ mi ese of Campbellsville. The po was est on May 10, 1876, with William O. Robinson, pm. According to one tradition, sometime in the 19th cent a hunter brought a 12 lb set of elk's horns to John Dearen's mill where it was placed on display, soon to become a landmark for the community which assumed this name. County historians, however, think the name was in use before Dearen owned his mill. Most likely someone had found a pair of well-preserved antlers in the vicinity. In 1965 the site of Old Elk Horn was largely abandoned for the impoundment behind the new Upper Green River Dam. A New Elk Horn has since been relocated 100 yards s. 522, 1127, 1291.

Elkhorn City (Pike): *ehlk*/hawrn *siht*/ee (Elkhorn City). This 4th class city with p.o. lies at the confluence of Elkhorn Creek and Russell Fork of the Levisa Fork of the Big Sandy R, 14 mi se of Pikeville. The community is said to have been founded or at least first settled by William Ramey, a native North Carolinian, around 1810 and early called Elkhorn, after an elk's horn allegedly found somewhere on the creek's banks. Since that name had already been applied to a po in Taylor Co, the local po, est on Oct 16, 1882, with James G. Bentley, pm, was called Praise [prāz] for "Camp Praise-the-Lord," a tent colony that the evangelist George O. Barnes had set up for a revival there in Aug 1881. When the C&O RR was completed to this point in 1907 the local station was called Elkhorn City. On Sept 1, 1952, in response to local pressure for a uniform name, the Post Office Department agreed to rename its local po Elkhorn City. The name Praise is still applied to a small stream, the Praise Fork of Russell, over a mile nw of town. 194, 402, 413, 888, 1354.

Elkton (Todd): *ehlk*/tən (Elkton). This 4th class city and seat of Todd Co lies at the jct of US 68 and KY 181, 117 mi sw of downtown Louisville. At its original location on the Elk Fork of Red R, which in presettlement times was a watering place for large elk herds, the Elkton po was est on June 10, 1817, with William Greenfield, pm, and the town was laid out in 1819 by Thomas Garvin and Thomas Jameson. This site became Old Elkton when on May 8, 1820, Maj. John Gray succeeded in attracting the new co's seat to his land, which forms the main section of the present town, ½ mi w of the creek. The town at this location was chartered on Dec 9, 1821. 168, 225.

Elk Valley (Muhlenberg). See *Nonnel*

Ellen (Lawrence): *ehl*/ən (Adams). This extinct po on Berry Branch of Rich Creek, a tributary of Blaine Creek, .9 mi s of KY 32 and 8 mi sw of Louisa, was named for the young daughter of Arthur Hughes, who was instrumental in having the po est on Feb 24, 1906, with Greenville T. Berry, pm. The po was discontinued in 1960. 1094.

Ellington (Cumberland): *ehl*/ihŋ/tən (Waterview). Little remains of this settlement with extinct po on present KY 485 and the ridge edge of Whites Bottom of the Cumberland R, 3 mi sw of Burkesville. The po, est on Apr 19, 1898, was originally up on the ridge, and was named for James Ellington, who donated the land. 223, 1385.

Elliott County *ehl*/yət. 234 sq mi. Seat: Sandy Hook. Est in 1869 from parts of Lawrence, Carter, and Morgan cos. Elliott Co was probably named for John Milton Elliott (1820–79), member of the US Congress (1853–59) and the Congress of Confederate States (1862–65) and later justice of the Kentucky Court of Appeals (1876–79). However, some countians prefer to think that his father, John Lisle Elliott, a Kentucky legislator, was the source of the name.

Elliottville (Rowan): *ehl*/yət/vihl (Haldeman). This village extends for about ½ mi on KY 32, at the head of Christy Creek and 7 mi e of Morehead. It was first called Hoggetown [*hâhgh*/town] for Squire and James Hogge who settled there in 1870 and opened the first store. The po was est as Elliottville on Sept 12, 1876, though nothing is known of the Elliott for whom it was named. In 1878 Charley Ward, a local storekeeper and judge, had the town inc as Bristow, also for reasons unknown, but the Elliottville name has continued to identify both po and community. 411.

Ellisburg (Casey): *ehl*/əs/bergh (Ellisburg). This hamlet and extinct po on KY 78 and the Big South Fork of the Rolling Fork R, 9 mi n of Liberty, were named for Richard Ellis, a pioneer settler from Norfolk, Virginia. The po was est by Frank Ellis, a descendant, on Apr 30, 1879, and closed in 1949. 212.

Elliston (Grant): *ehl*/əs/tən (Elliston). This hamlet on Ten Mile Creek and KY 1942, 9½ mi nw of Williamstown, was est in 1868 as Elliston Station by the Louisville Cincinnati and Lexington (now L&N) RR and named for the descendants of Benjamin Elliston. Elliston (1770–1846), the Virginia-born son of Robert Elliston, settled on Ten Mile Creek in 1813. The po, est on May 31, 1870, with William Southward, pm, closed in June 1976. 530, 1232.

Elliston PO (Madison). See *Waco*

Elliston Station (Grant). See *Elliston*

Ellisville (Nicholas): *ehl*/əs/vihl (Piqua). This settlement with extinct po is on US 68 and Stony Creek, a tributary of the Licking R, 5 mi n of Carlisle. Sometime before 1782, James Ellis, a Revolutionary War veteran, est Ellis's Station on this site and built a log stagecoach station and tavern. The town was laid out in 1805 for the co seat and named Ellisville for James's station, but in 1816 the seat was moved to Carlisle to be more accessible to the co's pop of that time. An Ellisville po was in operation from 1809 to some time after 1820 and again from 1879 to 1906. 1374.

Elmrock (Knott): *ehlm*/rahk, *ehl*/əm/rahk (Vest). This hamlet with po is on KY 1098 and Laurel Fork of Quicksand Creek, just above the mouth of Baker Branch, 7½ mi nnw of Hindman. The po was est on Aug 9, 1911, with Rachel Ritchie, pm, and named for its location by a big elm tree and a large rock. 1391.

Eloise (Lawrence): *ehl*/oh/eez (Louisa). This residential community and extinct station are on the Chatteroi (now C&O) RR, ½ mi s of the Louisa city limits. The station was est around 1890 and named for the daughter of Col. Jay H. Northup, its general manager and the owner-developer of considerable coal and timber land in Lawrence Co. The area has never had its own po. 1120.

Elon PO (Knox). See *Artemus*

Elroy PO (Adair). See *Breeding*

Elsie (Magoffin): *ehl*/see (White Oak). This po is on the Licking R and US 460 1.2 mi s of its jct with KY 134, and 4 mi nw of Salyersville. The po was est on Apr 14, 1911, and named for the daughter of Esther M. Vanover, the first pm. 1421, 1422.

Elsiecoal (Letcher). See *Hot Spot*

Elsinore (Franklin). See *Forks of Elkhorn*

Elsmere (Kenton): *ehlz*/meer (Covington). This 4th class city and Covington suburb is bounded on the w by Boone Co and on the n and ne by Erlanger and the Dixie Highway, its main business st. In 1885 George C. Bloss and others from Cincinnati purchased what was then called the South Erlanger subdivision, little more than scattered farm sites. In 1896 the community was inc as Elsmere, named by a Mr. Nolan for a st in his hometown of Norwood, Ohio. It has never had its own po. 154, 282.

Eminence (Henry): *ehm*/ən/əns (Eminence, New Castle). This 4th class industrial city, with po—the largest in the co,—is centered at the jct of KY 22 and 55, 3½ mi s of New Castle. The first po to serve this area was est on Mar 2, 1836, as Bayard and was just over the Shelby Co line. In 1850 it was moved and renamed Eminence, allegedly for being at the highest point on the rr (later L&N) linking Louisville and Lexington. The town was inc in 1851. 1256.

Emlyn (Whitley): *ehm*/lən (Williamsburg). This settlement with po on US 25W, between I 75 and the Clear Fork of the Cumberland R, is suburban to Williamsburg, 1½ mi nnw. The po est on May 29, 1902, with Isaac C. Sproule, pm, and the L&N RR station are said to have been named by the operator of a small local coal mine for his daughter. 1380.

Emma (Floyd): *ehm*/ə (Lancer). This village with po lies on both banks of the Levisa Fork of the Big Sandy R, 3 mi se of Prestonsburg. The section on the e side of the r, at the mouth of Cow Creek, has been called Alvin and had its own po from 1914 to 1930. The main section of the community around the Emma po and the C&O RR station grew up on the site of the home and store of pioneer surveyor and first settler John Graham (ca. 1805). The po, est on Aug 26, 1908, with William H. Weddington, pm, is said by retired pm Bertha Weddington to have been named by the late Congressman John W. Langley for his wife Emma, though others claim it honored Emma (Mrs. Ruben) Taylor, the wife of a prominent real estate dealer. The rr station was originally known as Woods Station, probably for a Cow Creek family, and was at one time nicknamed Wild Hog Station as a resident is alleged to have been accused of stealing hogs from his neighbors. 699, 1006, 1171.

Emmalena (Knott): ehm/ə/*lee*/nə (Carrie). This hamlet with po is on KY 80 and Troublesome Creek, 4 mi w of Hindman. The po, est on Oct 5, 1894, was named for Emma Thurman, the wife of the local school teacher who had petitioned for it, and Orlena Combs Morgan, the storekeeper and first pm. 1288.

Emma PO (Lawrence). See *Fallsburg*

Endicott (Floyd): *ehn*/də/kət (Dewey Lake). This po lies at the mouth of Toms Branch of Buffalo Creek (a tributary of Johns Creek), ½ mi from KY 194 and 5 mi e of Prestonsburg. It was est on Aug 7, 1909, and named for the family of its first pm, John W. Endicott. 1370.

English (Carroll): *ihŋ*/lihsh (Carrollton). This village and former station on the L&N RR, 1½ mi up Mill Creek from the Kentucky R, ½ mi from I 71, and 3½ mi s of Carrollton, was named for its owner, Capt. James Whorton English, a veteran of the War of 1812. The local po, now closed, was est on Aug 2, 1876, with William L. Miles, pm. 646.

Ep (Owen): ehp (Monterey). This extinct po was on the old Monterey Rd, 1 mi e of US 127 and 5 mi s of Owenton. In operation from 1881 to 1903, it served the neighborhood now loosely known as Greenup Fork. It was named for Penelope Sullivan, born 1832, the daughter of Cyrus Wingate, a longtime state legislator. It is said that children, finding her name hard to pronounce, took to calling her "Aunt Ep" and by this name she came to be known to all her neighbors. 102, 1292.

Ep (Pike). See *Belfry*

Epley PO (Logan). See *Epley Station*

Epley Station (Logan): *ehp*/lee *stā*/shən (Lewisburg). This now defunct station on the Owensboro and Nashville (now L&N) RR and US 431, 4 mi nnw of Russellville, was on the site of an older rural settlement whose name is now unknown. The station was built around 1872 in anticipation of the rr and named for a pioneer family whose progenitor, Fritz Epley, a German, was the first settler. An Epley po was est on May 23, 1887, with B. F. Rust, pm, and discontinued in Nov 1888. It was reest as Epley Station on Mar 25, 1891, with Edward Schader, pm, and closed for good in 1921. 206, 1344.

Epperson PO (McCracken). See *Reidland*

Epworth (Lewis): *ehp*/werth (Tollesboro). This crossroads hamlet with extinct po, 15 mi wsw of Vanceburg, is ¼ mi n of Ruggles Camp, a meeting ground owned by the Methodist Church on a site donated for this purpose by William Ruggles in 1872. It has been said that local people named the nearby community for the Epworth League and that the po, est on Feb 10, 1898, was named for the community. According to Robert Ramsay, "Epworth is almost synonymous with Methodism because its founder, John Wesley was born at the little village of Epworth in England." 181, 1200.

Equalization (Lewis). See *Burtonville*

Era (Christian Co.): Ih/rə (Dawson Springs SE). According to tradition, this extinct po on KY 109, 9½ mi nw of Hopkinsville, was named for Hopkinsville's daily newspaper, *Kentucky's New Era,* which had been founded in 1869. The po was in operation from 1880 to 1913. 1403.

Eriline (Clay): ɜ/leyen (Big Creek). This po is now on the Redbird R bottom, just above the mouth of Jacks Creek, 9 mi ene of Manchester. The po was to have been named for Eveline (Mrs. Van) Britton, but the postal officials misread the name on the petition (some say it was submitted by Mrs. Britton herself and that the officials could not decipher her handwriting). It proved simpler to accept the error than to correct it. The po was est on Dec 19, 19O2, at the mouth of Hectors Creek. Van Britton became the first pm. 1301, 1329.

Erlanger (Kenton): ɜl/əŋ/ər (Covington). This 3rd class city and suburb of Covington and Cincinnati lies roughly between the Boone Co line, I 275, and the Dixie Highway (US 25), 5 mi wsw of downtown Cincinnati. It began as the crossroads community of Timberlake, named for Maj. Thornton Timberlake, pioneer settler and owner of much land on the s side of the present Dixie Highway. In 1876–77 a station on the Cincinnati

have been est before the Civil War and may first have been called Mortonsville for an early storekeeper, Morton Pieratt. It became Ezel on or before Mar 18, 1875, when the po was est by Eli (or Elie) Pieratt who is said to have named it, for reasons now unknown, for a rock in the Bible, a refuge for David (1 Sam. 20:19). It was inc as a town in 1882. On some late 19th cent maps, the name was spelled Ezell and even Ecell. 202.

Factory (Butler): *faek*/tər/ee (Morgantown). Nothing remains at the site of this po a short distance w of KY 79, ½ mi w of the head of Sandy Creek, and about 7 mi ssw of Morgantown. David Hall Pendley est the po on Jan 20, 1886, in his store at Fuqua Spring and named it for a local ax handle factory. The location of spring, factory, and po is only known approximately. 526.

Fain PO (Madison). See *Million*

Fairdale (Jefferson): *fɛ*/dāl (Valley Station, Brooks). This name is popularly applied to a sprawling area whose boundaries are roughly the Outer Loop on the n, the L&N RR tracks or the South Park Rd on the e, the Bullitt Co line on the s, and New Cut, Manslick, Keys Ferry, Jefferson Hill, and Top Hill rds on the w, and which includes the communities of Coral Ridge and South Park and the 6th class city of Hollyvilla. The Fairdale name also refers to an unincorporated community with po centering at the jct of Fairdale, Mitchell Hill, and Mt. Holly rds, almost 11 mi s of the court house in Louisville. In the mid 1850s when the L&N RR's main line to Nashville reached the present site of South Park, it est a station called Old Deposit, and on Jan 13, 1857, a po called Deposit was opened at the station. Dallas P. Farmer, the pm and local storekeeper, had the name changed to South Park in 1889. In 1927 Joseph W. Sanders moved the po over a mi s and called it Coral Ridge [*kâhr*/əl *rihdj*]. Fairdale proper is said to have grown up around a store opened in 1881 by the brothers John and Si Morgan. In 1910, at a meeting to decide on a name for the community, Oscar Reed's suggestion of Fairdale, a commendatory name, was adopted. In 1949, at the request of local residents, the Coral Ridge po was moved to, and renamed, Fairdale, and in 1955 was moved again, to its present site. The city of Hollyvilla was est in 1958 and probably named for the 19th cent community of Mt. Holly. 692, 718, 1083.

Fairdealing (Marshall): fɛ/*deel*/ihŋ, faer/*deel*/ihŋ (Fairdealing). This redeveloping hamlet with extinct po extends along US 68 from its jct with KY 962, 5 mi e of Benton. The po was est as Fair Dealing (*sic*) on Sept 7, 1838, with Thomas R. Travis, pm, and is said to have been named for a storekeeper who offered "fair deals" to his customers. After an intermittent existence, the po closed for good in 1908. 666, 1337.

Fairthorn (Hart): *fɛ*/thawrn (Magnolia). This extinct po and store was less than ¼ mi from the site of the Aetna Iron Furnace, and about 11½ mi ne of Mundfordville. Three names were submitted for the po—Rattlesnake, Smoky Hollow, and Fairthorn—and the third was accepted by the postal authorities. According to Judge Roy A. Cann, "the fact that the day was bright and sunshiny, the ground covered with snow and a large thorn tree was in view, gave the name Fairthorn." It was est on Aug 16, 1887, with William F. Scott, pm, and closed in 1913. 863.

Fairview (Bath). See *Pebble*

Fairview (Bracken). See *Johnsville*

Fairview (Christian and Todd): *fɛ*/vyū (Pembroke). This intercounty village with po extends along US 68, 8 mi e of Hopkinsville and 7 mi w of Elkton. It was probably first settled by Samuel Davis, a Revolutionary War veteran from Georgia, in 1793; he est a po in Todd Co as Davisburg on Oct 1, 1802. It was here that his son, Jefferson Davis, the future president of the Confederate States of America, was born in 1808. Later the vicinity was called Georgetown for George Nichols, a local tavernkeeper. A town at this site was inc as Fairview on Feb 6, 1846, and on June 8 the Fairview po was est on the Christian Co side. After moving between the two cos several times, the po is now back in Christian Co. 168, 225.

Fairview (Greenup). See *Maloneton*

Fairview (Harrison). See *Kelat*

Fairview (Whitley): *fɛ*/vyū (Jellico East). This aptly named residential suburb of Jellico extends along and s of KY 1804 and the L&N tracks, just w of I 75 and 9 mi s of Williamsburg. It grew up "like Topsy," according to an informant, in the 1920s in the upper half of Burk Hollow [*bɜk hahl*/ər], an extinct coal camp and L&N station est sometime after 1900 by a Mr. Burk. It does not have its own po. 1380.

Falling Springs (Woodford). See *Versailles*

Fall Rock (Clay): *fawl rahk* (Manchester). This po on US 421 and Morgan Branch of Laurel Creek, 4 mi n of Manchester, is near a 10-ft-high falls for which it was undoubtedly named. The po was est on May 22, 1924, with John Campbell, pm. The name Pinhook may also have identified the community. 1042, 1329.

Fallsburg (Lawrence): *fawlz*/bergh (Fallsburg). Now but a hamlet with po on Blaine Creek and KY 3, 5 mi nw of Louisa, this was a thriving 19th cent mill town and trade center, which was first called the Falls of Blaine. A po of this name operated there from 1842 to 1871. On Aug 6, 1883, the po was reest as Emma by Vent Hutchinson who named it for his daughter, a local school teacher. John H. Ferguson was pm. It was renamed Fallsburg on May 28, 1890, to conform to the name by which the town had been inc the preceding month. 234, 973.

Falls of Blaine PO (Lawrence). See *Fallsburg*

Falls of Rough (Grayson): *fahlz* uhv *ruhf* (Falls of Rough). This virtually extinct village with po lies on the s side of the falls of Rough R, for which it was named, 7 river mi below the present Rough R dam and 15 mi nw of Leitchfield. It developed around the Green Mill built in 1823 on a site purchased from Judge Benjamin Sebastian by Willis Green, who served his district in the US Congress, 1839–45. A po called Green's was est by Nathan Raite on Feb 10, 1830, and was renamed Falls of Rough on Jan 7, 1850. 121, 385, 447, 513, 693, 1307.

Falmouth (Pendleton): *fael*/məth (Falmouth). This 4th class city and seat of Pendleton Co is on US 27 at the Forks of the Licking R, 75 mi ene of downtown Louisville. According to an unconfirmed tradition there was a settlement there as early as 1780 that was later called Forks of Licking by the Virginia Land Office. The town was chartered in 1793 on 100 acres owned by John Waller and others and named for Waller's hometown in Virginia. The po was est on Apr 1, 1801, as Falmouth or Pendleton Ct. House with James Lanier, pm. 847.

Fancy Farm (Graves): *faen*/see/farhm (Fancy Farm). This village with po on KY 80, 8 mi nw of Mayfield, is said to have been founded by the descendants of Maryland Catholics. The first settlers may have been the Samuel Willetts, from Washington Co, in 1830. The town grew up around St. Jerome Church, built in 1836, which still serves as the community's center. The po was est on Mar 15, 1843, with John Peebles, pm. According to tradition, the name was applied by an early visitor who had been impressed with the well-maintained Willetts farm (or, some say, John Peebles's place). The town was inc from 1880 to 1950. 14, 276, 284, 466.

Faris PO (Laurel). See *Faristown*

Fariston (Laurel): *faer*/əs/tən (Lily). This hamlet with extinct po and L&N RR station is on old US 25, 3 mi s of London. The po was est as Esomton (*ees*/əm/tən] on Sept 24, 1883, with Esom Faris, pm, and probably named for him or an earlier Esom in his family. In 1887 it was renamed Faris. Faris, whose family owned much land in the area, descended from one of 4 pioneer brothers, the sons of Isham Farris (*sic*) (1747–1842) of Virginia. 1282.

Farler (Perry): *fahr*/lər (Hazard South). This po just below the forks of Right Fork of Maces Creek, 5 mi s of Hazard, was est on Oct 5, 1905, and named by local storekeeper and first pm, William B. Farler, for his family. The Farler progenitor was Virginia-born pioneer, Forrest Farler, Sr., who died here in 1870. 55.

Farmers (Rowan): *fahrm*/ərz (Farmers). This village with po is on US 60 and the C&O RR, ½ mi e of the Licking R and 5½ mi wsw of Morehead. Said to have been first settled by Maj. Jim Brain who ran a hotel at the jct of 2 principal rds, it may first have been called Farmer's Cross Roads or simply The Cross Roads. The po was est as Farmer's on Aug 28, 1849, with John B. Zimmerman, pm. No one knows why it was called Farmer's. It was also called Confederate Cross Roads and was even first inc, on Apr 23, 1873, as Confederate City though in 1882 this was officially changed to Farmers. 688, 851.

Farmer's Cross Roads (Rowan). See *Farmers*

Farmersville (Caldwell): *fahr*/marz/vihl (Crider). This crossroads hamlet on KY 139, 5½ mi n of Princeton, was founded around 1848 by Dr. William W. Throgmorton (or Throckmorton) who also est the local po on May 1, 1850. He named it for Frederick Farmer, perhaps the first settler of that vicinity (by 1810). The po operated intermittently until it closed for good in 1910. 569, 1278.

Farmington (Graves): *fahrm*/ihŋ/tuhn (Farmington). This prosperous village with po at the jct of KY 121 and 564, 6½ mi se of Mayfield, was undoubtedly named for its location on highly productive farmland and for the rural economy and life-style of its earliest residents. Though the community was founded as Farmington in Feb 1836, its po was called Cornersville *kâhrn*/ərz/vihl, possibly for its situation at the corner of some property. It is not known whether the po's change from Cornersville to Farmington on Mar 24, 1838, was a change in name only or also involved a shift in location. 1228.

Farmington (Lincoln). See *Hustonville*

Faubush (Pulaski): *faw*/boosh (Faubush). This hamlet with po on KY 196, 10½ mi w of Somerset, is said to have been named for an Indian word meaning "falling waters" referring to the several small waterfalls in the area. It is less likely to have been named for a Mr. Forbes, as some have suggested, or to be a corruption of Fallbush for a fallen bush said to have guided pioneers to a crossroads. The po was est on May 6, 1879, with Hugh F. McBeath, pm. 215, 1410.

Faye (Elliott): fā (Sandy Hook). This extinct po was on KY 7, just above the mouth of Doctors Branch of the Little Sandy R, 2 mi sw of Sandy Hook. The po was est on Nov 23, 1922, and named for its first pm, Faye G. Redwine, the daughter of John Will Green, a prominent Sandy Hook businessman. It was discontinued in 1947. 1061, 1412.

Fayette County: *fā*/ət, *fā*/*eht* 285 sq mi. Pop. 204,165. Seat: Lexington, though in Jan 1974 the co and its seat were combined into a single entity with an "urban-county government." Kentucky's 2nd most populous co, it was one of the 3 into which the Virginia legislature divided its Kentucky Co in 1780. It was named for the Marquis de LaFayette. From its original territory all or part of 42 other cos were created.

Faywood (Woodford): *fā*/wo͞od (Versailles). Once a mill town and farm trade center, this residential settlement lies where KY 1681 crosses South Elkhorn Creek, ½ mi from the Fayette Co line—which explains its name—and 5 mi ne of Versailles. The po, est on Apr 10, 1886, with John C. Hopkins, pm, closed in 1903. 1269.

Fearsville (Christian): *feerz*/vəl (Honey Grove). This hamlet lies at the jct of KY 107, 178, and 189, 9½ mi ne of Hopkinsville. The community, named for the local Fears family, has never had its own po. 1403.

Fed PO (Floyd). See *Hi Hat*

Federal Grove (Logan). See *Auburn*

Fedscreek (Pike): *fehdz*/kreek (Jamboree). This hamlet with po is on KY 366, just e of its jct with KY 1499, and 15 mi e of Pikeville. The po was est as Fedscreek on Oct 5, 1921, with Isaac C. Justice, pm, and named for Feds Creek which joins the Levisa Fork of the Big Sandy R a few hundred yards w of the po. The creek is said to have been named for a man named Fed of whom nothing else seems to be known. 1077.

Feliciana (Graves): fə/lih/see/*aen*/ə (Water Valley). Little remains of this once prosperous town just s of the jct of KY 94 and the Kingston Rd, 14 mi sw of Mayfield, which was probably settled in the early 1820s. Its po was est as Feliciana on May 20, 1829, with Levi Calvert, pm, and with this name it was formally created a town by the legislature in 1834 and inc in 1837. The po moved to what became Water Valley, 2 mi nw, in 1869–70. Graves Countians still refer to the original site as Old Feliciann. The true origin of this name will probably never be known. The popular account of the fight between 2 slave women, Felicia and Anna, is an obvious folk etymology, as is the suggestion that a New Orleans man, perhaps the first settler, combined the names of his daughters. It is most likely that it was named for the Louisiana parishes est while the area was still under Spanish rule, named in turn for Félicité, the wife of Bernardo de Gálvez, then viceroy of New Spain. 204, 818, 1228.

Ferguson (Logan): *f3*/ghəs/ən (Russellville). This now defunct station and extinct po were on the L&N RR where the tracks cross Whippoorwill Creek, 4 mi sw of Russellville. Before the est of the station in 1860, a settlement called Whippoorwill may have existed at that site. Both the station itself and the po, est on Dec 24, 1860, as Ferguson Station, were named for the first pm and station agent, Luke H. Ferguson. In 1882 the po name was shortened to Ferguson. 206.

Ferguson (Pulaski): *f3gh*/əs/ən (Somerset). This 6th class city with po adjacent to the southern limits of Somerset was est just n of the Cincinnati Southern RR shops (built in 1906) as a residential community for the workers. It was probably named for Edward A. Ferguson, the Cincinnati attorney who helped est the rr in 1869. On Feb 23, 1911, the local po was named Luretha for the infant daughter of George A Wynn, the first pm, for the name Ferguson was already in use in Logan Co. In 1950, following the closing of that po, the Board on Geographic Names approved a local request to rename the Pulaski Co po Ferguson to conform to the corporate name of the town. 215, 606, 1410.

Ferguson Station PO (Logan). See *Ferguson*

Fern Creek (Jefferson): *f3n* kreek (Jeffersontown). This unincorporated suburban community with extinct po extends for at least 1 mi in either direction along US 31E/150 from its jct with Fern Creek Rd, 11½ mi se of the court house in Louisville. It was named for the local stream along which wild ferns once grew in abundance. The area was first settled shortly after the Revolution and was, until the Civil War, noted for its orchard. The Fern Creek po was in operation from 1851 to 1902. Because of its "strung out location" the community was once called Stringtown on the Pike. 71, 716.

Field PO (Letcher). See *Uz*

Fillmore PO (Daviess). See *Masonville*

Finch Station (Shelby). See *Finchville*

Finchtown (Campbell). See *Wilder*

Finchville (Shelby): *fihnch*/vihl (Simpsonville). This hamlet with po extends for ¾ mi along KY 55 from its jct with KY 148 ne to a point 5 mi sw of Shelbyville. Here in 1841, 1 mi e of the pioneer Buck Creek Station (est ca. 1780), Ludwell Finch (1806–79) bought a farm and opened a blacksmith shop. On July 9, 1857, the Finchville po was est there. The community that grew up around it was inc in 1878. As a station on the Louisville Cincinnati & Lexington (now L&N) RR, it was also known as Finch (or Finchville) Station. 61, 902.

Finney (Barren): *fihn*/ee (Lucas). This hamlet with extinct po is on KY 252, ½ mi n of the Barren River Reservoir, 9½ mi sw of Glasgow. The community is said earlier to have been called Grangetown for the Patrons of Husbandry and was renamed Finney for the family of the wife of a prominent area resident, probably when the po was est as Finney on Apr 13, 1898, with Peter C. Henderson, pm. It is known that a Henry Finney, who died in 1864, had a saw- and grist-mill in that vicinity by 1842. 101, 791.

Firebrick (Lewis): *fah*/ər/brihk (Friendship). This village with po is on Indian Run in the ne corner of the co, just s of KY 10, and 15 mi ne of Vanceburg. Once a co. town, it was named for the local firebrick plant, no longer in operation. The po was est on Apr 19, 1892, with William G. Beyerly, pm. 1103.

Fireclay PO (Carter). See *Grahn*

Fishback PO (Clark). See *Colbyville*

Fisherville (Jefferson): *fihsh*/ər/vihl (Fisherville). This hamlet with po is on Floyds Fork of Salt R and the old Taylorsville Rd, just s of the present KY 155, 17 mi ese of the Court House in Louisville. The po that had been est in 1833 as Curreys with Edward Currey, pm, was moved to and/or renamed Fisherville in 1847 for its location by Robert Fisher's mill. In the late 19 cent, the community was a popular summer watering place for Louisville society. 715.

Fish Point PO (Rockcastle). See *Livingston*

Fishtrap (Pike): *fihsh*/traep (Millard). This po, now 2½ mi up Jonican Branch of Levisa Fork of the Big Sandy r, 6 mi e of Pikeville, has occupied several sites in the Levisa Valley between Millard and the mouth of Grapevine Creek. It was est on Feb 19, 1873, with William H. Hamilton, pm. It is thought to have been named for the local method of catching fish by setting traps in the r in the vicinity of the present Fishtrap Dam. Before the dam was built in 1962, the po lay just below the mouth of the Jonican Branch. 934, 1137.

Fisty (Knott): *fahs*/tee (Carrie). This hamlet with po lies where Clear Creek joins Troublesome Creek at the jct of KY 80 and 721, 5½ mi w of Hindman. There were so many Combses in this area that they had to be distinguished by nicknames. One was called "Fisty Sam," and according to local tradition he suggested that the new po be named for him. Margaret Ritchie became the first pm on Aug 18, 1906. 1288.

Fitch (Carter): fihch (Soldier). This extinct po on the Carter and Lewis Co line, about 300 yards from the meeting point of these 2 cos and Rowan Co and 20½ mi w of Grayson, was est on Mar 9, 1906, and named by and for its first pm, Charles H. Fitch. It closed in 1976. 1366.

Fitchburg (Estill): *fihch*/bergh (Cobhill). This extinct iron furnace town lay at the head of Furnace Fork of Millers Creek, a tributary of the Kentucky R, 3 mi n of the jct of KY 52 and 975, and 6 mi ne of Irvine. It was the site of the famed Fitchburg or Red River

Iron Furnace, a steam-powered, air blast, charcoal-burning furnace, now listed in the National Register of Historic Places, which was built in 1868 as a single structure with twin stacks, the unique design of Fred Fitch, and named for him and his brother, Frank, who managed the furnace for the Red River Iron Manufacturing Co. The Fitchburg po operated from 1870 to 1955. 116, 336, 865.

Fixer (Lee): *fihx*/ər (Zachariah). This nearly deserted and almost inaccessible community with extinct po is on Big Sinking Creek, 6½ mi n of Beattyville. According to tradition, Simpson Crabtree was unsuccessful in getting several suggested names accepted by the postal authorities. Each name he submitted was already in use, and he was repeatedly told to suggest another. Finally he wrote that he had sent in all the names he was going to and demanded that the postal authorities ''fix 'er'' themselves. The po was thus est as Fixer on July 26, 1917, with Crabtree's son-in-law, George W. Booth, Jr., as the first pm. The po closed in 1970. 1372.

Flagg Spring PO (Campbell). See *California*

Flaherty (Meade): *flaer*/ə(r)t/ee, *flaer*ə(r)d/ee (Flaherty). This village with extinct po extends along KY 144 and 1600 from their jct 11½ mi se of Brandenburg. It was founded by and named by and for Michael W. Flaherty who had arrived in the early 1880s and opened a blacksmith shop. On May 14, 1883, he est the po, which closed in 1906. 856.

Flanagan (Clark): *flaen*/ə/ghən (Winchester). This station and po on the L&N RR and KY 1923, 3 mi s of Winchester, were named for the Circuit Court Judge James Flanagan of Winchester (1810–1906), who had been appointed to this position by Governor Blackburn in 1883. The Flanagan po was in operation from Apr 16, 1888, to July 31, 1906. 1349.

Flat (Wolfe): flaet (Campton). This settlement with po lies at the head of Cave Branch of the North Fork of the Kentucky R, 5 mi s of Campton. Part of Stephen Campbell's 7000-acre Revolutionary War military patent, it may first have been called Crackers Neck [*kraek*/ərz nehk], probably for ''a neck of land that runs down in a bend in the river.'' Until the po of Flat was est on Mar 1, 1892, with Squire P. Kash, pm, the community was aptly known as Flatwoods. Some years ago Kentucky newspaperman Nevyle Shackelford recorded the unfounded tale of the Hessian soldier named Dompflecraeker whose services in the American Revolution after deserting the British were rewarded with a large tract of land in this area. One day while picking haws on his new land a sharp thorn pierced his neck and killed him. As the story goes, the place was called Crackers Neck ''not because the unfortunate man died from a wound in the neck, but because it was Cracker's neck of the woods.'' 709, 1236, 1372.

Flat Fork (Magoffin): *flaet fawrk* (Salyersville North). This po on KY 1081, 5½ mi n of Salyersville, is 1 mi up the stream for which it was named, a branch of Big Mine Fork of Little Paint Creek. The stream was named for its low bottoms. The po was est in 1934. 1421.

Flatgap (Johnson): *flaet ghaep* (Redbush). This hamlet with po lies at the jct of KY 689 and 1092, 8 mi nnw of Paintsville. The po was est as Flat Gap on Feb 26, 1873, with Henry Jayne,pm, and named for the flat and low lying gap at the divide between Mudlick and Lower Laurel Creeks in the Big Sandy R watershed. By 1894 the name of the community and its po was being spelled as one word. 89.

Flat Lick (Knox): *flaet lihk* (Artemus). This dispersed village with po extends for about 2 mi along US 25 n from the Cumberland R and the L&N RR tracks to a point 5½ mi ese of Barbourville. The oldest community in the co, it is identified by name in pioneer journals and on John Filson's 1784 map of Kentucky. It is said that a party of hunters headed by Elisha Walden of Henry Co, Virginia, est a camp here where they observed many animals attracted to a flat rock from whose crevices salt water exuded. A po called Rome, for reasons unknown, may have provided the first mail service to this vicinity when it was est by Owen R. Moyers on Sept 24, 1840. It was moved to and/or renamed Flat Lick by Ambrose Arthur on Apr 5, 1848. Yet most co historians today claim never to have heard of a Rome po in that area. Since the Civil War a distinction has been made between Old Flat Lick, the original town site through which the Cumberland R flowed until, in 1862, a flood caused the stream to alter its course, and Flat Lick. 376, 739, 1409.

Flat Lick PO (Christian). See *Lafayette*

Flat Rock (Caldwell): *flaet* rahk (Crider). This hamlet on KY 70, 8½ mi nnw of Princeton, was named for the rock outcropping around a beautiful village green. It has never had a po. 1278.

Flat Rock PO (Bourbon). See *Plum*

Flatwoods (Greenup): *flaet*/wo͞odz (Ironton). This 3rd class city with po is on the plateau overlooking the C&O tracks and the Ohio R, joining the cities of Russell to the e and Raceland to the nw, 5 mi se of Greenup. It grew out of the sparsely settled community of Advance [*aed*/*vans*] in the late 1920s. The Advance po was est on May 21, 1892, with Pleasant Craft, pm. It was discontinued in 1915 and reest on Jan 3, 1918, at some unknown location as Cheap, for John Cheap, a blind Methodist preacher. In 1938 the po was renamed Flatwoods and the town was inc under that name. The name may have described the area's original topography but it could also have derived from the "Flatwoods District," a name that had been applied before 1890 to the rolling plateau that is now the hill section of nearby Ashland. 7, 22, 1213, 1447.

Flatwoods (Wolfe). See *Flat*

Fleming (Letcher) *flehm*/ihŋ (Jenkins West). This coal-mining town with po was reclassified as a 5th class city by the Kentucky legislature in 1978, after merging with *Neon,* its near neighbor. It extends about a mi along Wright Fork of Boone Fork of North Fork of the Kentucky R, 7 mi ne of Whitesburg. The town was built in 1913–14 by the Elkhorn Coal Corp. and named for the corp.'s first president, George W. Fleming. The po was est on Mar 16, 1914, with John D. Hartman, pm. 74, 524, 1254, 1265.

Fleming County: *flehm*/ihŋ. 351 sq mi. Seat: Flemingsburg. Fleming Co was est in 1798 from part of Mason Co and named for Col. John Fleming, pioneer settler and Indian fighter.

Fleming Court House PO (Fleming). See *Flemingsburg*

Flemingsburg (Fleming): *flehm*/ihŋz/bergh (Flemingsburg). This 4th class city and seat of Fleming Co is centered at the jct of KY 11, 32, and 57, 102 mi e of downtown Louisville. It was founded in 1797 by George S. Stockton, a Virginian, ½ mi e of Stockton's Station, which he had est some 10 years before. Stockton is believed to have named both the town and the co for his half brother, Col. John Fleming (1760–94), who had built his own station about 5 mi w in 1790. On July 1, 1801, John Faris was appointed the first pm of what was then called Fleming Court House, for it had been made the seat of the new co organized in 1798. 429, 1369.

Flingsville (Grant): *flihŋz*/vihl (Walton). This hamlet with extinct po on KY 491, 8 mi n of Williamstown, was named for a local family one of whose members, George Fling, became its first pm on June 2, 1876. The po closed in 1907. 1232.

Flippin (Monroe): *flihp*/ən (Gamaliel, Fountain Run). This hamlet with extinct po at the jct of KY 249 and 678, on the South Fork of Indian Creek (a tributary of the Barren R),

9½ mi w of Tompkinsville, was the home of the pioneer Flippin family. Their progenitor, Thomas, a Virginia-born veteran of the Revolutionary War, arrived in Kentucky around 1787 and settled on Indian Creek in 1790. Some say the community, whose po was est on July 13, 1858, with William C. Brockett, pm, was named for Thomas. Others insist that it was named for his son, James, a militia colonel in the War of 1812 and the Indian campaigns, who later became a large landholder, stockraiser, and co sheriff. Still others trace the name to Colonel Flippin's son, James M., who inherited his father's land and gave the building for the po. It has even been suggested that the community was first called Johnstonville for another local family. The po closed in 1964. 148, 171, 426, 1395.

Florence (Boone): *flahr*/əns (Covington, Independence, Union, Burlington). This 3rd class industrial and commercial city, the largest in Boone Co, is on US 25 and the Kenton Co line, 3½ mi ese of Burlington. On the site of a settlement first called Cross Roads, the town was laid out in 1821 by Thomas Madden, a local property owner, and others, and named Maddensville. In 1828 after Madden had moved away and Jacob Conner, another early settler, had assumed responsibility for the town, its name was changed to Connersville. A po known to have been est before 1828 was in operation in that year as Connersville with Pitman Clondas, pm. On Apr 27, 1830, the po became known as Florence, possibly for a local or area family, though historians have no idea why this name was applied. The town was inc as Florence on Jan 27, 1830. 418, 831, 1284.

Florida Heights (Jefferson). See *Goose Creek*

Floyd County: floid. 393 sq mi. Pop. 48,764. Seat: Prestonsburg. Floyd Co was est in 1799 from parts of Fleming, Montgomery, and Mason cos and named for Col. John Floyd (1750–83), pioneer surveyor and military leader of Jefferson Co, who was ambushed by Indians near the present Louisville.

Floyd County Court House PO (Floyd). See *Prestonsburg*

Floyd PO (Owsley). See *Ricetown*

Floydsburg (Oldham): *floidz*/bergh (Crestwood). This is now a hamlet with extinct po on KY 1408, 7 mi sw of LaGrange. The po in operation from 1822 to 1861, was named for its location at or near Col. John Floyd's Ford Station. Virginia-born Floyd (1750–83) was a surveyor and Indian fighter. The town of Floydsburg was chartered by the Kentucky legislature in 1830. 1316.

Fogertown (Clay): *fahgh*/ər/town (Portersburg). This rural settlement with po is on KY 472 and Mill Creek, below the mouth of Bray Creek, and 8 mi nw of Manchester. Several accounts have been offered for the naming of the po est on May 23, 1906, with James C. York, pm. According to one, the place is on a high elevation and it would often be covered with dense fog leaving travelers to remark that this was the foggiest place they had ever seen. But there are 2 other possible explanations as well. "In this community there was an old man who smoked a large homemade pipe, and rode up and down the road many times on an old mare; as he rode along he pupped [*sic*] continuously on this big old pipe. People following him later would know that he was in the community because they'd say 'Mr. Fogger has passed by and we smell his pipe, and see his smoke; he has fogged up the town.' [or] An old lady walked up and down the road many time who never took time to comb her hair. The neighbors spoke of her as Sal Fogger because of her bushy hair. When the post office was established and a name was being selected it was suggested that they name it Fogertown." It is not known why the name has always been spelled with only one "g." 1329.

Folsom (Grant): *fâhl*/səm (Elliston). This hamlet with extinct po at the jct of KY 467 and 1132, 10 mi nw of Williamstown, was first called Lawrenceburg for a large family that lived there before the Civil War. Since this name was already in use, the po, est on Nov 15, 1893, was named for Frances Folsom (1864–1947), the wife of then President Cleveland. The po was discontinued in 1916. 1342.

Folsomdale (Graves): *fâhl*/səm/dāl (Melber). This village with extinct po is centered at the jct of US 45 and KY 849, 8½ mi n of Mayfield. The po was est by James M. Conner on June 25, 1886, and named for President Cleveland's recent bride, Frances Folsom. The po closed in 1910. 1228.

Fontana PO (Carter). See *Gregorysville*

Ford (Clark): fawrd (Ford). This once prosperous lumber town with po lies where the L&N RR crosses the Kentucky R 7 mi ssw of Winchester. The po, est on Oct 4, 1883, and the town, inc in 1888, were named for Mitchell Ford who had once owned the land. 354, 691.

Fords Branch (Pike): fawrdz *brănch* (Pikeville). This hamlet with po is centered at the mouth of Fords Branch of the Levisa Fork of the Big Sandy R, across the r from US 23/460/119, 2 mi s of Pikeville. The po was est on Jan 14, 1916, with L. Grant Adkins, pm, and named for the many Fords who still live in that section. 1354.

Fordsville (Ohio): *fawrdz*/vihl (Fordsville). This 6th class city with po is centered at the jct of KY 54 and 69, 15½ mi ne of Hartford. It is believed to have been first settled by a family of Huffs around the early 1830s and later named for Elisha Ford, its first merchant and probable founder. The po of Haynesville, est in 1837 some 4 mi nw, was moved to this site in 1846 and renamed Fordsville with Haden Wells as pm. 430.

Forkland (Boyle): *fawrk*/lənd (Parksville). This settlement with extinct po is on KY 37, 11½ mi sw of Danville. An old community, said to have been settled shortly after the Revolutionary War, it was named for its location on the North Rolling Fork R. A po was in operation between 1891 and 1905. 1224.

Forks of Big Sandy PO (Lawrence). See *Louisa*

Forks of Elkhorn (Franklin): *fawrx* of *ehlk*/hawrn (Frankfort East). This village with po on US 460, ¾ mile e of Frankfort, was named for the fact that at this point the North and South Forks of Elkhorn Creek come together to form the main Elkhorn Creek. It has always been called locally The Forks. This settlement is believed to have been est as early as 1784. When the Frankfort & Cincinnati Ry was built through, a station was est about ½ mi up North Elkhorn and first called Forks of Elkhorn. It was later changed to Elsinore, for reasons unknown. The Forks of Elkhorn po, est on Jan 13, 1848, with I. S. Hodson, pm, ran intermittently until it closed in 1965. A delightful literary legend has been offered to "account" for the site and its name: ". . . a runaway couple pursued by an angry father fled on the back of a friendly elk. As they reached a luxuriant valley in Kentucky the elk was struck by an arrow, but in dying he turned his face toward the enemy and his horns formed an impassable barrier. The pursuer turned back, and where the elk's horns sank into the ground there appeared a beautiful stream which the grateful couple, in memory of their faithful friend, called 'Elkhorn.' " 109, 370, 408, 1290.

Forks of Licking (Pendleton). See *Falmouth*

Fortbranch PO (Perry). See *Fusonia*

Fort Jefferson (Ballard):fawrt *djehf*/ər/sən (Wickliffe). This extinct hamlet and po were on a bluff overlooking the Mississippi R, nearly 1 mi s of *Wickliffe*. The site is at or very near that of a fort erected by George Rogers Clark in 1780 to protect American claims for the r as its western boundary, and from which further exploration of the region could be initiated. A settlement called Clarksville soon followed the construction of the fort but after a siege by the Chickasaws it was abandoned in Aug 1781. To this site Thomas Dupoyster brought his family in 1858. His son Joseph laid out the town of Fort Jefferson and became its first pm on June 14, 1860. In 1879 the po moved to the new town of Wickliffe. Another Fort Jefferson po was in operation for only a few mos in 1891–92 but the town soon virtually ceased to exist when its citizens also moved to Wickliffe. The site is now occupied by the Westvaco paper factory. 141, 1011.

Fort Knox (Hardin): *fawrt nahx* (Fort Knox). This unincorporated community with po, the built up section of the Fort Knox Military Reservation, is between US 31W and Mill Creek, a branch of Salt R, 11 mi nnw of Elizabethtown, while the reservation itself covers 110,300 acres in Hardin, Bullitt, and Meade cos. This land was first used by the US Army for maneuvers in 1903, became a permanent installation in 1916, and was transferred to federal government ownership in 1918. It was first called Camp Knox for Maj. Gen. Henry T. Knox (1750–1806) who organized the Artillery Corps in the American Revolution and was Washington's first secretary of war. The po of *Stithton*, est on Aug 19, 1874, served the camp, and was renamed Camp Knox on May 15, 1925. In 1932, probably to reflect its increase in size and scope, the installation and its po were renamed Fort Knox. 407, 1420.

Fort Mitchell (Kenton): fawrt *mihch/əl* (Covington). This 4th class city, a residential suburb of Covington and Cincinnati, 2½ mi sw of downtown Covington, is the site of one of the 7 fortifications defending Cincinnati, which were built in 1862 on the hills around Covington from Bromley e to Fort Thomas. It was named for Maj. Gen. Ormsby McKnight Mitchel (1809–62), a professor of mathematics, astronomy, and philosophy at Cincinnati College, who designed these installations. The city was chartered in 1909. It has never had its own po. 279, 771.

Fort Spring (Fayette): fawrt *sprihŋ* (Versailles, Lexington West). This predominantly black hamlet with extinct po is midway between Lexington and Versailles, just s of US 60 and some 3 mi w of Lexington's New Circle Rd. It used to be known as Slickaway and, before that, Reform. Several traditional accounts of these names have been offered. In one, a Maj. Thomas Streshly is said to have given 3 of his freed slaves land in the vicinity of John Parker's gristmill in 1826, on which they est a settlement called Reform. A po of this name was in operation from 1854 to 1857 with Charles W. Castleman, pm. (A variant refers to the freed slaves of a Joshua Worley who were located on this land soon after Parker's mill was built in 1794.) To this site, in antebellum times, slaves would slip away for nighttime gatherings and it thus came to be called Slipaway and eventually Slickaway. According to a less accepted account, the place was first called Slipperyway (corrupted to Slipaway and later to Slickaway) after a horse lost its footing on the icy rd and fell into the South Fork of Elkhorn Creek, killing its rider. Neither account has ever been authenticated. But the po of Slickaway was actually est there on Mar 8, 1872, with Levi Rice, pm. On Jan 29, 1886, some of the patrons, embarrassed by this ludicrous name, had it changed to Fort Spring, the name of the home of a local landowner, Harvey Worley. According to some historians, this was probably Lewis O'Neal's old stone tavern, built in 1826 over a large spring, which had become a fort or headquarters for Union troops during the Civil War. The po closed in 1903. Residents still variously refer to their home as Fort Spring, Fort Springs, and even occasionally Slickaway. The second name is clearly a misnomer, reflecting the continuing tendency in Kentucky to place an "s" on names where it does not belong. 134, 175, 292, 393, 1335.

Fort Thomas (Campbell): fawrt *tahm*/əs (Newport). This 4th class residential suburb of Cincinnati is located between the cities of Highland Heights on the s, Southgate on the s and w, Newport on the w, and Dayton on the w and n, with the Ohio R on the e, and is less than 1 mi from downtown Newport. The area in which the town was est was, for most of the 2nd half of the 19th cent, aptly called the Highlands District. In 1887 the US Congress est an army post here, which in 1890 was named for Gen. George Henry Thomas (1816–70), a ranking Union Army officer. About this time a po was opened nearby as a branch of the Newport po, which it remains. The community that grew up around the fort was inc in 1914 but without a name, there being at first some controversy over what to call it. Some wanted to preserve the Highlands name; others preferred to promote the connection with the military post. 127, 931.

Fort Vienna (McLean). See *Calhoun*

Fort Wright (Kenton): *fawrt reyet* (Covington). Now a 4th class city, this residential suburb without po is in the Cincinnati-Covington area, with Park Hills and Kenton Vale on the e, Covington and Edgewood on the s, Fort Mitchell on the w, and downtown Covington 2 mi ne. Created in 1941, it was merged with neighboring South Hills in 1960, Lookout Heights in 1967, and Lakeview in 1978. It occupies the site of one of the larger fortifications that defended Cincinnati from Confederate invasion, and was named for Maj. Gen. Horatio Gouverneur Wright (1820–99), a Union Army engineer. 441, 706.

Foster (Bracken): *fahs*/tər (Moscow). Among the smallest 6th class cities in Kentucky, this former Ohio R port is at the mouth of Holts Creek, 10½ mi nw of Brooksville. It was first called Fosters Landing for Israel Foster, an early settler and large landowner, and a po of this name was est by Richard T. Lindsay on Aug 19, 1847. In Jan 1850 the po was renamed Foster and the town was inc under this name. 27, 30.

Fosters Landing (Bracken). See *Foster*

Foudraysville (Fleming). See *Hillsboro*

Fount (Knox): fownt (Fount). This settlement with recently discontinued po about 300 yards e of KY 11, 7½ mi nne of Barbourville, was named for Fountain F. Rowland, the local storekeeper and first station agent for the Cumberland & Manchester (now L&N) RR, through whose farm the rr was extended in 1916. The first po to serve this area was Payne's, est by Dutton Jones in 1874. Lewis Henderson Jarvis moved it to *Girdler* in 1888. It was then moved to the Fount site as Hopper in 1895 and Rowland, who had become pm in 1907, renamed it for himself on June 21, 1916. 743.

Fountain Powder Mills PO (Hart). See *Powder Mills*

Fountain Run (Monroe): *fown*/tən *ruhn* (Fountain Run). This 6th class city with po is on KY 82, 14 mi w of Tompkinsville. Since its first name, Jimtown—said to have been for Jim Barlow, local storekeeper—was not acceptable to the Post Office Department, it was renamed for 7 bubbling springs in the vicinity when the po was est on Jan 29, 1847. As residents observed, these springs seemed to bubble up like fountains. 1395.

Fourmile (Bell): *fawr*/mahl (Pineville). This coal town and L&N RR station with po are on the Cumberland R, less than ½ mi from the Knox Co line and 2 mi nw of Pineville. The po was est on Dec 16, 1899, with Edward L. Shell, pm. According to some, it was named for its location 4 mi down the r from Pineville; others are sure it was named for the length of Fourmile Creek, which joins the Cumberland just above the po. Perhaps it was both. 1416, 1417.

Four Oaks (Pendleton): *fawr* ohx (Falmouth). This extinct po was on US 27, just n of Blanket Creek, and 2 mi s of Falmouth. The po, est on Feb 26, 1891, with Sallie Parker, pm, was named for the 4 oak trees there at the time. Only one of them is still standing. The po closed in 1903. 1230.

Fourseam (Perry): *fawr*/seem (Hazard South). This mining camp is .4 mi up Buffalo Creek, a branch of the North Fork of the Kentucky R, and 1 mi s of Hazard. It was named by the Fourseam Coal Co. for the 4 seams of coal in the local mine that was opened just before World War I. The place has also been called Buffalo and the station on the L&N RR's Buffalo Creek Spur is now known as Candy. The community has never had its own po. 1327.

Fourth Lock (Pendleton). See *Butler*

Fox Creek (Anderson): *fahx kreek* (McBrayer). This hamlet with extinct po extends for ½ mi along US 62 from its jct with KY 513, just s of Salt R and 3½ mi sw of Lawrenceburg. It was probably founded in the 1840s or 1850s and named for the small tributary of Salt R on which it is located. The stream, in turn, was named for the many foxes there. On Mar 23, 1886, Ezekiel Rice est the local po as Horace, for reasons unknown. Within 5 weeks he renamed it Hawkins, for a local family, and 3 weeks later changed it again to Fox Creek, to conform to the community's name. The po closed in 1913. 140, 1387.

Foxport (Fleming): *fahx*/pawrt (Burtonville). This hamlet with extinct po lies at the jct of KY 344 and 1902, just w of the North Fork of the Licking R, 8 mi ene of Flemingsburg. The 19th cent port itself and its po, in operation between 1880 and 1915, were named for the pioneer Fox family. This family also gave its name to Fox Creek which drains much of the southern end of Fleming Co. 1369.

Frakes (Bell): frāx (Frakes). This po serving the community traditionally known as South America [sowth ə/*mehr*/ə/kə] is on KY 190 and Pine Creek, 14½ mi sw of Pineville. This area, first settled in the 1850s, early received its nickname for its remoteness and relative inaccessibility. In 1925, Indiana-born Rev. Hiram Milo Frakes, pastor of a small Methodist church in Pineville, came into the area and persuaded its natural leader, Bill Henderson, to donate land for a school, from which grew the Henderson Settlement School. The local po, est as Linda on Apr 10, 1908, with James H. Hamblin, pm, was renamed on June 1, 1936, for Frakes. 735, 811.

Francisburg (Union). See *Uniontown*

Frankfort (Franklin): *fraeŋk*/fərt (Frankfort East & West). This 2nd class city, Kentucky's capital and seat of Franklin Co, is on US 60, 127, 421, and 460, 44 mi e of downtown Louisville. The site was acquired in the late 18th cent by James Wilkinson who, envisioning it as a major Kentucky R shipping port, laid out the town and gave it its name. Stephen Frank was one of a party of men from Bryan's Station who, on their way to the salt deposits at Mann's Lick in southern Jefferson Co in 1780, camped for the night nearly opposite the entrance to Devils Hollow, then one of the natural fording places on the r, or at the site of the present Lock 4 (there seems to be some disagreement as to precisely where this happened); they were attacked by Indians and Frank was killed. Soon the ford became a common crossing point on the r and came to be known as Frank's Ford. In 1786 Wilkinson succeeded in having his town officially registered by the Virginia General Assembly as Frankfort. On Nov 1, 1793, the Kentucky legislature convened here for the first time, and on Oct 1, 1794, Daniel Weisiger became Frankfort's first pm. 108, 115, 1290.

Franklin (Simpson): *fraeŋk*/lihn (Franklin). This 4th class city and seat of Simpson Co is on US 31W, 3 mi w of I 65, and 108 mi ssw of downtown Louisville. It was founded in 1819/20 as the co's seat on 62 acres purchased from William Hudspeth and probably named for Benjamin Franklin. There is no evidence to support an often-encountered local contention that it was named for a local physician. The po was est on Sept 29, 1822, with Robert W. Simpson, pm. 18.

Franklin County: *fraeŋk*/lihn 212 sq mi. Seat: Frankfort. est in 1794 from parts of Woodford, Mercer, and Shelby cos, Franklin Co was named for Benjamin Franklin (1706–90), American statesman, diplomat, and scientist. Frankfort is the state capital.

Franklins Cross Roads (Hardin): *fraeŋk*/lihnz *kraws*/rohdz (Howe Valley). This hamlet with extinct po lies at the jct of KY 86 and 1375, 6½ mi w of Elizabethtown. The po was est on Nov 17, 1857, and named for Samuel Franklin, its first pm, or his family. After an intermittent existence it closed for good in 1905.

Frazer (Wayne): *frā*/ʒər (Frazer). This hamlet with po lies at the jct of KY 90 and 1568, 11 mi ne of Monticello. The po was est on Feb 10, 1880, with Samuel H. Frazer, pm, and named for James K. Polk Frazer, a Monticello attorney and progenitor of an important local family. 1406.

Frederick (Metcalfe). See *Center*

Fredericksburg (Gallatin). See *Warsaw*

Fredericksburg (Washington). See *Fredericktown*

Fredericktown (Washington): *frehd*/rihk/town (Maud). This hamlet with extinct po lies at the confluence of Cartwright Creek and the Beech Fork R, just s of US 150 and 7 mi nw of Springfield. It evolved from the activities at Parkers Landing, one of the principal flatboat shipping ports in the Salt R system, and was a part of the 1000-acre survey recorded about 1785 by Richard Parker, its proprietor. The town was est by legislative act as Fredericksburg on Jan 17, 1818, and named for Frederick Hill who managed the local warehouse for Parker. The po, however, was called Fredericktown when it opened on Dec 15, 1828, with Edward G. Overton, pm, and this name has identified the community ever since. The po closed in 1911. 434, 1314.

Fredonia (Caldwell): frə/*dohn*/yə (Fredonia). This 6th class city with po is on US 641 and KY 70, 91, and 902, 10 mi nw of Princeton. According to tradition, the town was laid out in 1836 by Harvey W. Bigham and named for his infant daughter. On July 8 of that year, the Fredonia po was est with Samuel Rorer, a local storekeeper, as pm. When the Ohio Valley RR was being built through the area in 1887, a neighboring community, possibly then known as South Fredonia, was laid out by S. H. Cassidy. Another Cassidy in Kentucky prevented the adoption of this name and it was called Kelsey instead for Capt. P. G. Kelsey, the rr's president. A po was est at that site on Dec 9, 1889, and called Fredonia Depot, but it was renamed Kelsey the following Feb. For 16 years the Kelsey and Fredonia pos operated less than ½ mi apart until the postal authorities closed Fredonia in 1906 and applied its name to the Kelsey po. The 2 communities are now one and few residents even recall the Kelsey name. Fredonia was once a popular place name, used in at least 18 states; it had been offered around 1800 by Samuel Latham Mitchell of New York as a name for the United States. Mitchell apparently combined "freedom" with the Latin ending of such names as Caledonia to suggest something like "Land of Freedom." At least one folk etymological explanation has been offered for the name Fredonia. When the Kentucky town's fathers were considering the name, a Negro slave was heard to mention that he had a new baby at home named Donia and that someday she would be a "free donia." 181, 278, 466, 495, 1278.

Fredonia Depot PO (Caldwell). See *Fredonia*

Fredville (Magoffin): *frehd*/vihl (David). This po is on KY 7 and the Licking R, 10½ mi se of Salyersville. It was est on Nov 20, 1916, at the mouth of Buck Creek, 1½ mi below its present site, and named for the son of its first pm, Cynthia Ann Carpenter. Fred (1894–1946) was later a co judge and served his district in the Kentucky legislature. In 1946 the present pm, Mae Arnett, moved the po to its present location. 1422.

Freeburn (Pike): *free*/bern (Matewan). This once inc coal town with po is on KY 194, at the mouth of Peter Creek, a tributary of Tug Fork of the Big Sandy R, 19½ mi ene of Pikeville. The local po was est on Apr 24, 1911, with Henry C. Cline, pm, and first called Liss for Liss Hatfield. In 1932 it was renamed Freeburn, allegedly for a free-burning coal mined in the area. 1198.

Freestone PO (Rowan). See *Bluestone*

Freetown (Monroe): *free*/town (Gamaliel). Little remains of this settlement between KY 100 and the East Fork of Barren R, 5 mi wsw of Tompkinsville. In the 1840s William Howard, a large landowner, freed his slaves and settled them at this site. The community has no po. 1395.

Frenchburg (Menifee): *frehnch*/bergh (Frenchburg, Scranton). This 6th class city and seat of Menifee Co is on US 460 and KY 36, 109 mi ese of downtown Louisville. The town was laid out and est as the seat when the co was created in 1869. It was named for Judge Richard French (1792–1854) of Mt. Sterling, who had lost to Richard H. Menifee, Jr., in the 1837 race for a Congressional seat in Kentucky's 11th District. The town was inc in 1871 and its po was est on Feb 24 of that year with Samuel Greenwade, pm. The once popular contention that it was named for some local families of French descent is hardly taken seriously anymore. 169.

Frew PO (Johnson). See *Staffordsville*

Fritz (Magoffin): frihts (Seitz). This hamlet with po is on KY 1094 and the Right Fork of the Licking R, 5 mi sw of Salyersville. The po was est as Jondun [*djahn*/*duhn*] on Aug 3, 1912, and named for its first pm, John M. Dunn. Adam D. Stephens who succeeded him had the name changed to Nola in 1913 and then to Fritz in 1916. The latter honored Fritz Arnett who had filed the original petition for the po. The po closed in 1921 but was reest on June 10, 1947, by Eulah Back. 1180.

Frog Level (Todd). See *Sharon Grove*

Frost (Greenup): frawst (Portsmouth). This community with extinct po is at what is now the jct of US 23 and KY 1215, about a mi e of the mouth of Tygarts Branch and 11 mi nnw of Greenup. The community was settled before 1820 as Mt. Zion, named for the Mt. Zion Methodist Episcopal Church on Mt. Zion (now Sand) Hill. When Benjamin F. King, Jr., est the po on Dec 18, 1888, the existence of a Mt. Zion in Kentucky and instructions to select a short name led him to suggest the names Rain, Hail, Snow, and Frost. Only the Frost name was still unused, and so it was applied to the community and po, while the rr station was called Kings Station; only the church retained the original name. 22, 1447.

Frozen Creek (Breathitt): *froh*/zən kreek (Jackson). This po is on the North Fork of the Kentucky R, a short distance above and across the r from the mouth of the creek for which it was named, and 3 mi nw of Jackson. The po was est somewhere in that vicinity on Apr 9, 1850, with Benjamin F. Sewell, pm. For a time in the late 19th and early 20th cent it was called Hargis for an influential Breathitt Co family. The creek was most likely named by early settlers for the frozen water at its mouth during the winter. They often had to sand the slick ice before crossing the creek at that point. The account of Daniel Boone's refuge in the hollow sycamore tree is probably apochryphal. According to this tradition, the giant tree which stood near the mouth of the creek sheltered Boone and several companions one night in a heavy snowstorm. The next morning, nearly frozen to death, they named the creek Frozen. 236, 639.

Fruit Hill (Christian): frūt *hihl* (Haleys Mill). This hamlet with extinct po lies at the jct of KY 189 and 800, 10 mi ne of Hopkinsville. In 1831 or earlier, a Fruit Hill po was est by Moses H. Allen, said to have been named for the orchards on a hill near the site. It was discontinued in Jan 1865. On July 10, 1871, Thomas J. Powers est a po called White Plains at a settlement that may have dated back to 1819 but had been all but destroyed by occupying forces of both sides during the Civil War. In 1874 Powers moved his po to a site ¾ mi away and renamed it Fruit Hill, after which, we are told, White Plains disappeared completely as a community. It is not known if the 2 Fruit Hill po were at the same site. Curiously, the day after Powers' move, the po of Little Prairie, 12 mi n in Hopkins Co, officially took the name of *White Plains*. A recent description of the area suggests the derivation of the Christian Co White Plains name: ". . . white dogwood bloomed in abundance. You could look over the area from a hill and the country looked like a big cotton field, a white plain. . . ." The Fruit Hill po closed in 1918. 273, 1403.

Fryer (Caldwell): *frah*/yər (Dalton). This hamlet at the jct of KY 70 and 293, a little over a mi from the Hopkins Co line, has often mistakenly been referred to as Barnes Store for the local store that Edward L. Barnes acquired in 1908. Though the community was at one time called (The) Hall for a local Grange hall, it is officially and locally Fryer, honoring a large landowner who lived across the rd from the later store site. The area was served by the Quinn po est by, and probably named for James B. Quinn on July 8, 1893, at a site some 2 mi nnw of Fryer. In 1909 Barnes moved the po to his store, continuing to call it Quinn until it closed in 1913. 843, 1022.

Fulgham (Hickman): *fuhldj*/əm (Dublin). This crossroads hamlet with extinct po at the jct of KY 58 and 307, 6 mi e of Clinton, was founded in the late 1880s around a store owned by a Mr. Fulgham, likely a descendant of pioneer Anthony Fulgham. The po was est on Mar 26, 1900, with Robert S. Bazzell, pm, but closed in 1904. 162.

Fullerton (Greenup). See *South Shore*

Fulton (Fulton): *fo͞ol*/tən (Crutchfield, Water Valley). This 4th class city is on the Tennessee state line and is 15½ mi ese of Hickman. It is the largest community in Fulton Co, for which it was named. On Apr 15, 1847, pioneer settler Benjamin F. Carr est the local po as Pontotoc, a Muskogean word for "cattail prairie," which had already been applied to a po in Mississippi. Discontinued in 1854, it was reest by Carr in 1861 as Fulton. It was discontinued again in Dec 1862, yielding to the just est po at nearby Fulton Station, the recently completed jct on the Illinois Central RR. The town there was inc as Fulton in 1872 and the po assumed this name in 1880. 78, 204, 680.

Fulton County: *fo͞ol*/tən. 211 sq mi. Pop 8,971. Seat: Hickman. Fulton Co was est in 1845 from part of Hickman Co and named for Robert Fulton (1765–1815), an artist and inventor whose Clermont, on its maiden trip up the Hudson R in 1807, was the first commercially successful steamboat on American waters.

Fulton's Forge (Greenup). See *Wurtland*

Fulton Station PO (Fulton). See *Fulton*

Fultz (Carter): fuhlts (Grahn). This po and store are at the mouth of Big Run on Little Sinking Creek, 4½ mi sw of Grayson. The po was est on Feb 6, 1901, with George W. Littleton, pm, and named for one or more local families. 1326.

Fungo (Trigg). See *Golden Pond*

Furnace (Estill): *fɜn*/əs (Stanton). Little remains of a once thriving community that grew up around the Estill Steam Furnace on KY 213, 6 mi n of its jct with KY 52. This charcoal-burning, steam-powered furnace was built in 1830 by Thomas Deye Owings and for years supplied pig iron to the Red River Iron Works at Clay City. An Estill Furnace po was est on Mar 26, 1857, with Jesse Jones, pm, but was closed on Mar 4, 1864. On June 21, 1882, Charles W. Russell became the first pm of a reest po called Furnace, 8 mi ne of Irvine, which was recently discontinued. 122, 865.

Fusonia (Perry): fyū/*sohn*/yə, fyū/*sohn*/ee (Vicco). This community with extinct po lies at the mouth of Big Branch of North Fork of the Kentucky R, 6½ mi se of Hazard. The first po to serve this area was Fortbranch, est on Nov 17, 1905, at the mouth of this stream, which was named for Benge's fort near its head. In 1913 it was moved to Fusonia's present location, where an L&N RR station called Hombre [*hahm*/bree] (later Coolidge, presumably for the president) had been est the year before. The po closed in 1925. In early 1919 a po was est as Fusonia at the Fuson Mining Co.'s camp 1 mi s, with Robert E. Potter, the mine superintendent, as pm. When the mine closed in the early 1930s the po was moved to the Coolidge station but retained the Fusonia name until it closed in 1967. 1021, 1226.

Gadberry (Adair): *ghaed*/bər/ee (Columbia). All that remains of this hamlet on KY 704, less than 3 mi s of Columbia, is the Smith Chapel Church. Before the Civil War a community here is said to have been called Butter Pint. Joe Creason relates the tale of a small boy who "had been sent to a neighbor's house to get butter. 'How much do you want?' he was asked. 'Oh,' the boy replied, 'I guess about a pint.' " The po was est as Gadberry on Sept 24, 1884, with Finus Hurt, pm, and named for pioneer settler James Gadberry. It closed in 1958. 352.

Gad PO (Leslie). See *Thousandsticks*

Gaines' Cross Roads (Boone). See *Walton*

Gaines PO (Boone). See *Walton*

Gainesville (Allen): *ghānz*/vihl (Scottsville). This hamlet with extinct po is on Big Difficult Creek, 4 mi s of its union with the Barren R and 5½ mi n of Scottsville. In 1846 Samuel B. Gaines, a Virginian, arrived in the vicinity from nearby Port Oliver where he had a store, On July 1 of the following year, he est a po and founded the Gainesville community, which he named for himself. 101, 248.

Galdie (Magoffin): *ghael*/dee (Ivyton). This extinct po on KY 7 and the Licking R, 8 mi se of Salyersville, was est on Nov 20, 1916, by Telia Brown. She named it for her younger sister Goldia (1912–60) but the postal officials misread the name and it was recorded as Galdie. In 1918 Telia's father, Andy J. Brown, was appointed pm and served for 5 years after which his daughter resumed this position, which she held till 1963 when she retired and the po was discontinued. 1179, 1422.

Gallatin County: *ghael*/ə/tən. 99 sq mi. Pop 4,842. Seat: Warsaw. Est in 1798 from parts of Franklin and Shelby cos, Gallatin Co was named for Albert Gallatin (1761–1849), Swiss-born secretary of the Treasury under Presidents Jefferson and Madison (1802–14) and minister to France and England (1816–23, 1826–27).

Gallup (Lawrence): *ghael*/əp (Louisa). This extinct po and C&O RR station lay on the Levisa Fork of the Big Sandy R, 6½ mi s of Louisa. The po was est on Aug 1, 1881, with George C. Chapman, pm, and named for the family of George W. Gallup (ca 1829–81), a New York-born Louisa attorney and businessman who was also a contractor in the construction of the C&O RR through that section. The po closed in 1966. 128.

Galveston (Floyd): *ghael*/vəs/tən, ghael/*vehs*/tən (McDowell). This po on Branham Creek, a branch of Mud Creek 16½ mi sse of Prestonsburg, was est on Dec 23, 1891, with Lafayette Clark, pm, and named for the city in Texas. 1197.

Gamaliel (Monroe): ghə/*mal*/yəl (Gamaliel). This 6th class city with po centers at the jct of KY 63, 87, and 100, 6 mi sw of Tompkinsville. It was inc in 1956. Though the vicinity was probably settled before 1800, the name may have been first applied to the local school when it was est by legislative act in 1840. The name of the Biblical teacher of the Apostle Paul, it may have been suggested by a Dr. Bobo, an English physician then practicing in that area or, more likely, by Samuel Dewitt, a local school teacher and preacher. The twon grew up around the school, and a po was est as Gamaliel on Aug 29, 1870, with John E. Dotson, pm. 779, 1395.

Game PO (Barren). See *Rocky Hill*

Gander PO (Letcher). See *Carcassonne*

Gap (Rockcastle). See *Boone*

Gap Creek (Wayne). See *Windy*

Gapville (Magoffin): *ghaep*/vihl (Ivyton). This po on KY 1734, 1.8 mi e of KY 7 and 9 mi se of Salyersville, now serves the upper section of Salt Lick Branch of the Licking R. It was est on Apr 10, 1888, at the head of Puncheon Camp Creek, 2½ mi ne of its present site, and named for the nearby gap in the mountains through which travelers used to pass between the Licking R and Big Sandy R watersheds. 1422.

Garden Cottage PO (Pulaski). See *Pisgah*

Garden Village (Pike): *ghahr*/dən *vihl*/ədj (Millard). This subdivision without po lies between US 460/KY 80 and the Levisa Fork of the Big Sandy R, below the mouth of Peyton Branch and 4 mi se of Pikeville. The community was est in 1945 by William E. Justice on the site of Liberty, the proposed first seat of Pike Co. Public disapproval of this site had led to the decision of a court-appointed commission in 1823 to est the seat at Pikeville. Justice is said to have recalled a place by this name he had once visited in New York. 1138, 1437, 1438.

Gardnersville (Pendleton): *ghahrd*/nərz/vihl (Walton). This hamlet with extinct po on KY 491, 10½ mi nw of Falmouth, was named for the local Gardner family. The po, est on Feb 16, 1858, with Stephen T. Price, pm, closed in 1908. 1379.

Garfield (Breckinridge): *ghahr*/feeld (Garfield). This hamlet with po is centered at the jct of US 60 and KY 86, 4½ mi e of Hardinsburg. The po was est on June 28, 1880, and named for the recently nominated Republican candidate for US president, James A. Garfield. 478, 1398.

Garlin (Adair): *ghahr*/lən (Columbia, Montpelier). This recently discontinued po on KY 206, 2 mi e of Columbia, was est on Jan 9, 1903, and probably named for Garlin Leach, the first pm.

Garrard (Clay): *ghaer*/ə(r)d (Barcreek, Manchester, Ogle). This prosperous village with po lies on Goose Creek at the jct of US 421/KY 80 and KY 11, about a mi s of Manchester. This was the site of the famed salt works at the Buffalo Lick est in 1806 by Col. Daniel Garrard (1780–1866), son of James Garrard, Kentucky's 2nd governor who had acquired the land some years before. The Garrard name was not applied to the place, however, until the Cumberland & Manchester (now L&N) RR was completed through it in 1917, and the po was est on Apr 28 of that year by James H. Brashear. It was named for the Garrard family or, more specifically perhaps, for William T. and Edward G. Garrard, grandsons of Daniel, who then owned the right-of-way. 744, 1259, 1329.

Garrard County: *ghaer*/əd. 232 sq mi. Pop 10,853. Seat: Lancaster. Garrard Co was est in 1797 from parts of Lincoln, Madison, and Mercer cos and named for James Garrard (1749–1822), Kentucky's 2nd governor (1796–1804).

Garrett (Floyd): *ghɛ*/ət (Wayland). This coal town with po is on KY 7/80 and the Right Fork of Beaver Creek, 13 mi s of Prestonsburg. It was founded around 1914 as an Elk Horn Coal Co. town named for the brothers John and Robert Garrett, Baltimore bankers and coal co. financiers. The po est as Ballard on June 2, 1910, with Nathaniel Estepp, pm, became Garrett in 1914.

Garrettsburg (Christian): *ghaer*/əts/bergh (Herndon). Nothing remains of a once thriving village at the jct of KY 345 and the present Boddie Rd, 11½ mi s of Hopkinsville. It is believed to have been first settled by and named for Garrett Minor Quarles, a Virginian, who arrived in the 1820s and est the Garrettsburgh (*sic*) po on Sept 12, 1827. The po closed in 1908. 166, 1403.

Garrison (Lewis): *ghaer*/əs/ən (Garrison). This thriving village with po is on KY 10 at the confluence of Kinniconick Creek and the Ohio R, 6½ mi e of Vanceburg. Once called Stone City for the many quarries in the area that provided stone for shipment down the r from the local landing, it was renamed, perhaps in the 1880s, for the prominent Garrison family. Some say it was named for Sam Garrison, a pioneer settler; others, for J. H. Garrison who owned much of the land there after the Civil War. Stephen R. Garrison est the Garrison po on Feb 26, 1886. The local Masonic Lodge still bears the Stone City name. 770, 1200.

Gasper Butcher's Station (Logan). See *Russellville*

Gates (Rowan). See *Hays Crossing*

Gatliff (Whitley): *ghaet*/ləf, *ghaet*/lihf (Saxton). This once thriving coal town with extinct po extends for over 1 mi along KY 904, on Bennetts Branch of Patterson Creek, 8 mi ese of Williamsburg. It was named for and probably by Dr. Ancil Gatliff, M.D. (1850–1918), a coal developer who opened the local mines in 1906. The po, est on Mar 28, 1908, with David W. Davies, pm, has since closed. The Gatliffs, still a prominent Whitley Co family, are descended from Capt. Charles Gatliff (1745–1838), a Virginia-born Indian fighter, who came to Kentucky in 1779–80 and settled at the confluence of Maple Creek and the Cumberland R in 1786. 516, 882, 1380.

Gays Creek (Perry): *ghāz* kreek (Buckhorn). This po is now on KY 28, above the head of the creek for which it was named and 12 mi nw of Hazard. At several locations since it was est on Dec 26, 1888, the po has served the residents of this branch of the Middle Fork of the Kentucky R (now Buckhorn Reservoir), said to have been first settled by, and named for, Henry Gay, a Revolutionary War veteran, who died there around 1830. His descendants are still an important family in that section. 510.

Gearheart (Floyd). See *Price*

Geigerville (Boyd). See *Rush*

Geneva (Lincoln): djə/*nee*/və (Halls Gap). This upper Green R Valley hamlet is on KY 698, 7 mi sw of Stanford. An unnamed community until around 1910, it is said to have been named in that year at the suggestion of a Mr. Willimon, the mail carrier from Hustonville, for Geneva Newall, a friendly child with whom he was much taken. There is no record of a po of this name. 60, 1448.

Genoa PO (Christian). See *Beverly*

Georgetown (Fayette). See *Little Georgetown*

Georgetown (Scott): *djawrdj*/town (Georgetown). This 4th class city and seat of Scott Co is on US 25, 62, and 460, and just w of I 75, 60 mi e of downtown Louisville. In 1782 the Rev. Elijah Craig is said to have founded a community near where, 6 years before, the McClelland brothers and Col. Robert Patterson had est the short-lived McClellands Station. Craig named his settlement Lebanon or Lebanon Station, for reasons unknown, and by this name a town was inc there by the Virginia legislature in 1784. In 1790 it was renamed George Town for George Washington at the request of a delegation led by Col. Robert Johnson. Until 1846 the name was officially spelled as 2 words, though according to postal records the name of the po, est on Jan 1, 1801, with Thomas Lewis, pm, was always spelled as one word. There is no basis to the local legend that the place was named by the daughter of the town's wealthiest citizen for her boyfriend. 13.

Georgetown (Todd). See *Fairview*

Germantown (Mason and Bracken): *djɜm*/ən/town (Germantown). This 6th class city with po lies at the jct of KY 10, 165, and 596, just above the head of Bracken Creek, 10 mi w of Maysville and 5 mi ese of Brooksville. Settled by Pennsylvania Germans around 1788 near Buchan's (pioneer) Station, the town was laid out in 1794–95 by Whitfield Craig and others on 320 acres then owned by Philemon Thomas and was inc in Dec 1795 as Germantown. The po was est in Mason Co on Dec 8, 1817, but for the rest of the cent shifted back and forth across the co line and is now in Bracken Co. During World War I an effort to rename it *Maytown* was unsuccessful. 27, 134a, 1246.

Ghent (Carroll): djehnt (Vevay South). This 6th class city with po lies on the Ohio R, 6 mi above Carrollton and directly across from Vevay, Indiana. The site was first settled in 1795 by members of the Reverend Mr. Craig's "Traveling Church." Among them were a Mr. McCool whose name was applied to nearby McCool's Creek and the community was first called McCool's Creek Settlement. Another pioneer was John Sanders whose son, Samuel, opened a tavern on the present site of Ghent, and sometime before 1814 laid out a town there from a survey by Rev. John Scott. Seeking a more fitting name for his town, Samuel asked his friend Henry Clay, who is said to have suggested the name of the Belgian city in which he had participated in the concluding of a treaty ending the War of 1812. This was apparently acceptable for a po of this name was est on June 7, 1816, and the city was inc on Jan 18, 1824. 87, 143, 412, 446, 646.

Gilbertsville (Marshall): *ghil*/bərts/vihl (Calvert City, Briensburg). This village, from 1953 to 1976 a 6th class city, is on KY 282, just w and n of I 24, and 10½ mi n of Benton. Horatio Jones opened a store near this site in 1870 and, on Feb 15, 1871, est a po he called Clear Pond. Discontinued in 1873, the po was reopened on May 3, 1876, and renamed for State Senator Jesse C. Gilbert who had arranged for the town's first inc in 1874. The original town site was cleared when the Kentucky Dam, TVA's largest, was built (1938–44) and the town was relocated just w. *Gilbertsville* is now considered the "headquarters" of the Dam, which is the northern border of Kentucky Lake. The Gilbertsville po is now 1½ mi s of the town. 76, 1337.

Gilman's Point (Jefferson). See *St. Matthews*

Gilpin (Casey): *ghil*/pən (Liberty). This hamlet with extinct po, is on Trace Fork of the Green R, less than 5 mi se of Liberty. The *Shackelford* po was est there on July 15, 1881, and probably named for the family of Revolutionary War veteran Zachariah Shackelford, which owned much of the land there. In 1887 the first pm, William Gilpin, renamed the po for his parents, Eli and Rebecca Gilpin, who had arrived in that vicinity in 1851. The po closed in 1965. 212, 1397.

Gilstrap (Butler): *ghihl*/straep (Flener). This extinct po on KY 1118, 6 mi n of Morgantown, was est on May 13, 1893, and named for the first pm, Preston W. Gilstrap, or his family. The name has been spelled with both one "l" and 2. 1341.

Gimlet (Elliott): *ghihm*/lət (Ault). This hamlet with extinct po is on KY 504, at the head of Big Gimlet Creek, a tributary of the Little Sandy R and 8 mi n of Sandy Hook. The community was settled before the Civil War by the family of Peter Mauk, a surveyor. The narrow, winding creek resembles the tool for which it was named. Though on an old deed it was spelled Gimblet, the correct spelling is generally believed to be Gimlet. The po, est a mi w on Aug 1O, 1880, with John W. Sparks, pm, closed in 1961. 1412.

Ginseng (LaRue): *djihn*/sehŋ (Howardstown). This extinct community and po lay near the mouth of the West Fork of Otter Creek, 2½ mi above Otter's confluence with the Rolling Fork R and 9 mi se of Hodgenville. The po was est on Dec 29, 1898, with Charles S. Ferrill, pm, and named for the plant that is still being dug by local residents for a market in Elizabethtown. 1313.

Girdler (Knox): *gɜd*/lər (Fount). This rapidly growing hamlet with po at the jct of KY 11 and 1304, 4 mi nne of Barbourville, was named for a local family. The community may have preexisted its first po, est on Jan 7, 1888, with Lewis Henderson Jarvis, pm. This po was moved to or very near the present site of *Fount* in 1895, when Tyre Marcum became pm, and was called Hopper. The present Girdler po was est on Apr 28, 1899, with Millard F. Hibberd, pm. 1409.

Glades PO Pulaski). See *Walnut Grove*

Gladys (Lawrence): *ghlaed*/əs (Blaine). This extinct po lay on the ridge between Cooksey Fork of Cat Fork of Blaine Creek and the head of Daniels Creek, 9 mi w of Louisa. The story is told that when the po was to be est with William M. Crabtree, pm, on July 13, 1909, someone came to the local school and asked all the girls their names. The name of Gladys Sophie Pennington was chosen for the po. It closed in 1950. 1094.

Glasgow (Barren): *ghlaes*/ghoh (Glasgow North and South). This 3rd class industrial city and seat of Barren Co is on US 31E and 68, just n of the Cumberland Parkway and 82 mi s of downtown Louisville. Its central location, the presence of a large spring, and especially the donation of 50 acres by proprietor John Gorin led to the choice of this site for the new co's seat in 1799. The town was probably named for the city in Scotland since the father of William Logan, one of the 2 commissioners who located the seat, had come from there. The town in Virginia, which some historians claim was the source of its name, was not est until 1890. The Glasgow, Kentucky, po was est on July 1, 1803, with Gorin as pm, and the town itself was chartered in 1809. 83, 664, 1160.

Glasgow Junction (Barren). See *Park City*

Gleanings (LaRue): *ghleen*/ihŋz (Howardstown). Little remains of this once thriving trade center on KY 462 and the Rolling Fork R, 10½ mi e of Hodgenville. It was early settled but not developed until the late 1870s. The now extinct po was est on June 17, 1886, with William D. Ford, pm, and named for the gleaners of the Bible. 68, 1436.

Glen Allen (Caldwell). See *Cobb*

Glenarm (Oldham): *ghlehn*/ahrm (Crestwood). This settlement with extinct po and L&N RR station lies at the jct of the present KY 146 and Glenarm Rd, ½ mi s of I 71 and 5 mi sw of LaGrange. The po was est as Brownsboro Station on Feb 26, 1862, with James Campbell, pm, for the station on the old Louisville and Frankfort RR designed to serve the town of Brownsboro, 2 mi w. Within 10 weeks, for reasons unknown, the name had been changed to Peru though the station continued to be known as Brownsboro Station. In 1906 both station and po adopted the name Glenarm, said to be the suggestion of a Mr. Telford, he or family having come from Glenarm in Co Antrim, Ireland. The po closed in 1920. 1316.

Glencoe (Gallatin): *ghlehn*/koh (Glencoe). This 6th class city with po lies at the jct of US 127 and KY 467, just n of Eagle Creek and 6 mi se of Warsaw. The village is said to have been est in the early 1860s though the Glencoe po had been in intermittent operation since Mar 16, 1848. It was named for the Glencoe Valley in Scotland. 87.

Glendale (Hardin): *ghlehn*/dāl, *ghlehn/dāl* (Sonora). This village with po is centered at the jct of KY 222 and the L&N RR, 5 mi s of Elizabethtown. The town grew up around Lewis B. Walker's country store and was first called Walker's Station. The po that Walker est on Mar 2, 1859, was named for the Glendale station, which the L&N had just located there and which they are said to have named for the hometown of one of the line's engineers. 136.

Glen Dean (Breckinridge): *ghlehn deen* (Glen Dean). Now but a hamlet with po, this once prosperous industrial and rr town 9 mi ssw of Hardinsburg was named for the pioneer Dean family and the glen or small valley formed by Daniels Creek, on which it was located in 1890. On June 19 of that year, William C. Moorman est the po of Glendeane in a box car on the newly laid tracks of the "Fordsville Spur" of the Louisville Henderson & St. Louis (later L&N) RR. Within a few months, William Johnson Dean had laid out a town on part of his family's 2700 acres. It was inc in 1901. By 1910, at the suggestion of postal officials, the name was changed to Glen Dean to end the obvious confusion with Glendale in Hardin Co. Historian Burnett Powell recently observed that since the family name Dean refers to a valley and a "glen" is but a narrow, secluded valley, the name Glen Dean is clearly tautological. Historians like Powell tend to discount the once popular notion that the rr had named its station for Mary Glen Dean, Johnson's niece. 178, 214, 1398.

Glendeane PO (Breckinridge). See *Glen Dean*

Glenmary (Henry). See *Drennon Springs*

Glennsville (Adair). See *Glens Fork*

Glensboro (Anderson): *ghlehnz*/bər/ə (Glensboro). Now a hamlet with extinct po, this was once a thriving factory and farm trade center on the Salt R at the jct of KY 44 and 53, 7½ mi w of Lawrenceburg. It may have been first settled in the late 1830s and a short-lived po called Salt River may have been est at or near this site in 1839. On Feb 7, 1848, the Camdenville po was est in Elijah Orr's store and he became pm. It was closed in 1864 and reest as Orr on Feb 24, 1881, with Thomas D. Brown, pm. The name was changed again on Sept 12, 1904, to Glensboro, for its location in a narrow secluded spot between 2 hills. Formally laid out in 1860 by W. E. Bell and inc as Camdenville, the community was officially renamed Orr by legislative act in 1885 and became Glensborough (*sic*) the year the po assumed this name. The po closed in 1913. 710, 711.

Glens Fork (Adair): *ghlehnz* fawrk, *ghlehnz fawrk* (Montpelier, Columbia). This once thriving town at the jct of KY 55 and 768, 6½ mi se of Columbia, is now a mere hamlet with po. It was named for its location on Glens Fork of Russell Creek which was probably named for David Glenn's hunting party, which camped in the vicinity while securing provisions for George Rogers Clark's Illinois campaigns. While the po was est as Glens Fork on Sept 2, 1857, with Robert Garnett, pm, the community itself was probably first called Glennsville [*ghlehnz*/vəl] and was inc under this name on Mar 25, 1872. It also suffered through the nickname of Hardscratch, perhaps reflecting the difficulties in making a living there. 1289, 1426.

Glenview (Jefferson): *ghlehn*/vyū (Jeffersonville). This wealthy suburb with po lies along exclusive Glenview Ave which extends between River Rd (overlooking the Ohio R) and I 71 and is about 7 mi ene of downtown Louisville. The site was settled around 1793 with the building of an estate by James S. Bate who called it Berry Hill for his old Virginia home. In the mid 19th cent part of his 5000-acre estate was acquired by James

McFerrin who named it Glenview Farm, probably for the attractive view of the surrounding hills and valleys. The community of Glenview was an outgrowth of the old Fincastle Club, a kind of country club, founded in the 1880s. The po was est on May 11, 1893, with John W. Owen, pm. 726.

Glenville (McLean): *ghlehn*/vihl (Glenville). This hamlet with extinct po lies at the jct of KY 81 and 140, 4½ mi ne of Calhoun. The first po to serve this area was est by John Moseley on June 12, 1825, as Long Falls Creek for the stream ¾ mi s. In 1859 the po was moved to and/or renamed Glenville with William S. Givens, pm; it again became Long Falls Creek in 1864 but resumed the Glenville name in 1884, and was discontinued in 1905. It was named for the many Glenn families in the area. It may have borne the nickname Lick Skillet for the scarcity of food in the area at one time. 932.

Glenville (Washington). See *Maud*

Glidden (Harlan). See *Lenarue*

Glo (Floyd). See *Wayland*

Glomawr (Perry): *ghloh*/mahr (Hazard South). This residential suburb, formerly a coal town with extinct po, lies on Raccoon Creek, a tributary of the North Fork of the Kentucky R, 1 mi ese of Hazard. The mine was opened in 1914 by the East Tennessee Coal Co. and its camp is said to have been named by W. E. Davis for the old Welsh word for high coal. The po was est on Nov 15, 1915, with Henderson Monhollen, pm. 74, 1186.

Glovers Creek (Metcalfe). See *Summer Shade*

Goble PO (Carter). See *Carter City*

Goddard (Fleming): *ghahd*/ərd (Plummers Landing). This settlement with extinct po across Sand Lick Creek from KY 32, 6½ mi se of Flemingsburg, grew up around and was named for Goddards Church, the local Methodist church, which had been organized by 1810 and honored pioneer settler and Revolutionary War veteran Joseph Goddard. For some reason the local po was est on Oct 27, 1881, as Sandford, for another local family, but was renamed Goddard in 1902 and bore this name until it closed in 1958. For a time in the late 19th cent the place was also called Hamburg, for reasons unknown, and it briefly bore the nickname Tuffy before World War I for the "rough and tough" character of some of its citizens. 1369.

Godman PO (Muhlenberg). See *Moorman*

Godwin PO (Caldwell). See *Otter Pond*

Goff PO (Grayson). See *Steff*

Goffs Corner (Clark): *ghahfs kawr*/nər (Hedges). This hamlet at the jct of KY 15 and 974, 9½ mi ese of Winchester, was probably named for the family of John Hedges Goff. The community has never had its own po. 1349.

Goffs Crossing (Grayson). See *Steff*

Goins (Whitley): *ghoh*/ənz (Frakes). This extinct po on Harpes Creek, 1½ mi e of its confluence with Poplar Creek at Siler, and 12 mi e of Williamsburg, was est on Apr 30, 1901, and named for its first pm, Eli Goins, or his family. 1267.

Goldbug (Whitley): *ghohld*/buhgh (Wofford). This extinct po, just w of the jct of I 75 and US 25W, 2½ mi n of Williamsburg, is said to have been est on Aug 11, 1896, by "Goldbugs," the supporters of the gold standard in the presidential election of that year. 1380.

Gold City (Simpson): *ghohld siht*/ee (Drake). This hamlet with extinct po lies at the jct of KY 265 and 622, 6½ mi e of Franklin. While digging a well, several residents uncovered rocks thought to be gold-bearing but found, in fact, to be valueless. Yet for a while people were excited about the find, thinking they had come upon a major gold area. On Feb 8, 1886, the Temperance po was moved to this site and named Gold City. It was discontinued in 1909. 1024, 1363.

Golden Pond (Trigg): *ghohl*/dən *pahnd* (Fenton). This extinct village extended for nearly a mi along US 68 from a point 2½ mi w of the Cumberland R and 11 mi wsw of Cadiz. Its early history is enshrouded in legend though it is known that the name was applied to the po est on Dec 28, 1848, with E. C. Spiceland, pm. The precise location of this po is unknown, though some believe it may have been at or near the pond for which it was allegedly named. This pond is 2¼ mi w of the village site. According to the most frequently heard account, the late afternoon sun shining on the surface of the pond gave the appearance of molten gold. There is probably no credence to the tale of the man who "salted the area around the pond with gold dust or nuggets in an effort to start a real estate boom" and then gave this name to the settlement he est there. In the early 1900s the name Golden Pond was associated with the moonshine produced there, reported to be of high quality. It has been said that the village of Golden Pond was also known for a time as Fungo [*fuhn*/ghoh, *fuhŋ*/oh], allegedly for the Saturday night attractions of the local saloon for 19th cent iron and timber workers of the area. Others claim that Fungo, if such a name was ever applied to anything, referred to a one room school in se Lyon Co whose trustees were trying to attract prospective pupils. Its full name was "Fun to Go to School." Still others recall the Fungo settlement on US 68 in the vicinity of Fenton. 96, 98, 776, 805, 1325, 1403.

Gollihue (Carter). See *Davys Run*

Goodnight (Barren): *ghood*/neyet (Glasgow North). This hamlet with extinct po, just off US 31E, 5 mi n of Glasgow, was named for Isaac Herschel Goodnight (1849–1901), a member of the US Congress at the time the po was est on Jan 9, 1891, and later judge of the 7th Kentucky Circuit Court. The po closed in 1902. 791.

Goodson PO (Clinton). See *Seventy Six*

Goose Creek (Jefferson): *ghūs* kreek (Jeffersonville). This 6th class city with extinct po, 8 mi ne of downtown Louisville, is on the Ohio R bottom w of River Rd, centered at the mouth of the stream for which it was named. This stream, which heads in Anchorage and flows for 13 miles, may have been named for the wild geese said to have inhabited its banks in pioneer times or, possibly, for William Goose, a wagon-maker who arrived in nearby Jeffersontown before 1800. The Goose Creek po was est on Oct 5, 1892, with Emma Frederick, pm, and discontinued in 1902. On a 1912 topographic map this place was identified as Florida Heights, which surprises local people who have always known it as Goose Creek. Yet by 1881 the Florida Heights name had been applied to a station on the Louisville Harrods Creek and Westport RR, a few hundred yards below Goose Creek. Goose Creek was inc in 1969. 100, 643, 989.

Goosehorn (Barren). See *Hiseville*

Goose Rock (Clay): *ghūs* rahk (Ogle). This hamlet with po, one of the oldest in the co, is on US 421/KY 80, 5½ mi se of Manchester. It is said to have been named for a big rock in the middle of Goose Creek on which a wild goose supposedly built her nest, laid her eggs, and raised her young. However, some historians think the goose, if she existed at all, made her nest on the bluff above the creek, for no particular rock is known for which the community could have been named. The po was est on Aug 11, 1891, as Goose Rock but its name was officially respelled as one word in 1895. A Board on Geographic Names decision in 1978, however, returned it to 2 words to conform to the official name of the consolidated school ½ mi up the creek. The Goose Creek name appeared on the pre-1800 Boone Survey, applying, as it does now, to a tributary of the South Fork of the Kentucky R. 994, 1329, 1418.

Gordon's Station (Muhlenberg). See *Depoy*

Gordonsville (Logan): *gâhr*/dənz/vəl (Olmstead). Little remains of this once prosperous village where the present KY 1151 crosses Whippoorwill Creek, 2.3 mi n of the rd's jct with US 68, and 5½ mi w of Russellville. The site was settled in 1825 by John Gordon, a Virginian, and named by his son Samuel when he est the local po, now closed, on Dec 13, 1848. 206, 1344.

Gore PO (Boyle). See *Junction City*

Goresburg (Boyle). See *Junction City*

Gorham PO (Daviess). See *Knottsville*

Goshen (Calloway). See *Stella*

Goshen (Oldham): *ghoh*/shən (Owen). This hamlet with po on US 42, 9½ mi w of LaGrange, grew up around and was named for a Presbyterian church est there in 1825 by the Rev. Gideon Blackburn. The community was founded in 1849 and first called Saltillo [sahl/*tihl*/oh] for the city in northern Mexico near which the Mexican War battle of Buena Vista was fought in 1847. The po est in 1833 at Harmony Landing, 2½ mi e on the Ohio R, was relocated here in 1851 as Goshen. George R. Stewart has written of the Biblical antecedent: "The land which the Israelites inhabited in Egypt is described in the Bible chiefly as a country for sheep though other products are also implied. On this scanty evidence, early Americans began to apply the name for commendatory reasons to places which they believed to have rich soil, or so wished others to believe. . . ." 204, 963, 1090, 1316.

Gouge's PO (Grant). See *Mason*

Gouge's Station (Grant). See *Mason*

Gourd PO (Letcher). See *Ulvah*

Grab (Green): ghraeb (Exie). A store between KY 88 and 1464, 5½ mi sse of Greensburg, is now identified as Grab. About a mi e, Daniel K. Cramer ran another country store. According to one account, he sold chocolate drops from a large barrel for a penny a handful. As he would merely reach in and grab a handful, the store came to be known as the "Grab Store." When he est the po in his store on Dec 26, 1906, he named it Grab. In another, less plausible, account, the store had 2 rooms, each with an outside door and a door between them. When the proprietor was in one room people would enter the other, grab a handful of merchandise, and skedaddle. The po has since closed. 355, 1339.

Graball (Todd). See *Kirkmansville*

Grace (Clay): ghrās (Manchester). This settlement with po is on KY 638 and Grays Fork of Little Goose Creek, 6 mi nw of Manchester. According to Shelby Lee Nicholson, US Congressman John E. White hired Grace Kelly, the teenage daughter of George Kelly of Goose Rock, as his housekeeper. He so admired her work that when a name was sought for a new po he suggested hers. On Mar 9, 1898, the Grace po was est with Dr. Iredell C. Wyatt, as pm. 1116, 1329.

Gracey (Christian): *ghrā*/see (Gracey). This village with po lies at the jct of US 68 and the Illinois Central Gulf RR, 7½ mi w of Hopkinsville. It was founded in 1887, the year the L&N RR acquired the short-lived Indiana Alabama & Texas RR whose president then was Capt. Frank P. Gracey, a Clarksville businessman. For a very brief period the local station was first called Bryants Station for Henry H. Bryant on whose land it was located. On July 7, 1887, Bryant est the Gracey po, which, with the station, was named for Captain Gracey. 145, 1403.

Gradyville (Adair): *ghrā*/də/vəl (Gradyville). This hamlet with po is on KY 80, just n of the Cumberland Parkway, 6 mi wsw of Columbia. The po was est on Apr 17, 1848, by William F. Grady (1804–63), a local farmer and horse breeder, and named for his pioneer forebears. 1426.

Graham (Muhlenberg): *ghrā*/əm, *ghrae*/yəm (Graham, Millport). This village with po extends for 1 mi along KY 175 and on intersecting rds, 5½ mi wnw of Greenville. It was est as a coal town by the W. G. Duncan Coal Co. and named for its founder and president, William Graham Duncan (1851–1929), the oldest son of Andrew Duncan, a Scotsman who brought his family from Ayrshire, Scotland, to Muhlenberg Co around 1855 to produce coal for the furnace at *Airdrie*. William Graham was later in charge of the mining operations at *McHenry* and *Echols* in Ohio Co, and in 1900 developed coal lands in the vicinity of *Luzerne* and est the coal town of that name. Graham was founded in 1903–4 in the co.'s anticipation of the need to expand its Luzerne operations, 5 mi se. The po was est on Jan 30, 1904, with William Williamson, pm. 389.

Grahamton (Meade): ghrā/*haem*/tən (Rock Haven). This extinct village and po where US 60 crosses Otter Creek, now lie within the Fort Knox Military Reservation, 2½ road mi w of US 31W and 9½ mi se of Brandenburg. In 1837 Robert Graham moved from Louisville to newly acquired land at the falls of Otter Creek, built a large stone mill, and est a village he called Grahamton. The po was est as Grahampton (an obvious spelling error that was later corrected) on Jan 2, 1880, but closed in 1907. The village site was acquired by Ft. Knox just prior to World War II. 294.

Grahamville (McCracken): *ghrā*/əm/vihl (Heath). This hamlet with extinct po is centered at the jct of KY 358 and 996, 6 mi w of Paducah. The po, in operation from May 18, 1888, to May 15, 1909, was named for its only pm, Zelotes Clinton Graham, who opened a store at this site in 1877. 146.

Grahn (Carter): ghrahn (Grahn). This village with po on KY 182 and the C&O RR, 7 mi sw of Grayson, is famed for its fire brick plant. Karl Bernhard Grahn (1845–1922) arrived in the US from his native Hanover, Germany, in 1866, and acquired some land in this vicinity on which in 1886 he discovered large deposits of marketable flint and the plastic fire clay used to manufacture fire bricks. These he shipped to outside plants until he erected the plant in Grahn in 1913. A po est here on July 30, 1888, as Fireclay was renamed Grahn in 1909. 450, 971.

Graingertown (Union). See *Grangertown*

Grand Rivers (Livingston): *ghraend rihv*/ərz (Grand Rivers, Birmingham Point). This 5th class city with po occupies the narrow ridge between the lower reaches of Lakes Barkley and Kentucky 11½ mi se of Smithland. Around 1889 Thomas W. Lawson arrived from Boston, Massachusetts, and, with short-lived plans to revive the iron industry in the land between the Cumberland and Tennessee rs, purchased several thousand acres there and built 2 large furnaces. On the site of an older community that may have been called Narrows, he laid out a city he named Grand Rivers for its location within sight of both rs. The po was est as Otisville on Mar 14, 1879. In 1882 Henry M. Ross renamed it Bernard and, a year later, Nickells, for the station that had meanwhile been located there by the Illinois Central RR. Finally, on Dec 19, 1889, it was named Grand Rivers with William G. Dycus, pm. 138, 584, 922, 1189.

Granger PO (Union). See *Grangertown*

Grangertown (Union): *ghrāndj*/ər/town (Dekoven). This village, a former coal town with extinct po on KY 109, 9½ mi ssw of Morganfield, was first called Graingertown for Andrew M. Grainger who moved there in 1880. A po called Granger was in operation from 1900 to 1908 with William L. Sullivan as its only pm. 238.

Grangetown (Barren). See *Finney*

Grant County: ghraent 259 sq mi. Pop. 13,308. Seat: Williamstown. Est in 1820 from part of Pendleton Co, Grant Co was named for either Col. John Grant (1754–1826), pioneer salt producer in the Licking Valley (see *Grants Lick*); his brother Samuel (1762–89), a surveyor who was killed by the Indians; or another brother, Squire (1764–1833), a surveyor and large landowner in Campbell Co, which he served in the State Senate (1801–6) and as sheriff (1810); or perhaps for all 3. An oft-repeated 19th cent story with no validity whatever refers to William Littell's "repeated efforts" to get the Kentucky legislature to grant him a hearing on his bill to create the new co: "the word 'Grant' became in connection therewith quite a stereotyped phrase or saying, and hence when the bill was finally called up, out of a facetious spirit some member had 'Grant' inserted for its name." 69.

Grant PO (Boone). See *Belleview*

Grants Lick (Campbell): *ghraents lihk* (DeMossville). A 19th cent industrial town, this is now but a settlement with extinct po centered at the jct of Clay Ridge Rd and KY 1926, just w of US 27 and 5½ mi s of Alexandria. It was founded around 1800, following the discovery of salt several years before by Samuel Bryan who entered into an arrangement with Col. John Grant and Charles Morgan to supply salt to bluegrass communities. It was named for Grant (1754–1826), a native of Rowan Co, North Carolina, who had acquired ownership of the site. Bryan est the po on Jan 1, 1806. 732.

Grapevine (Pike). See *Phyllis*

Grassland (Edmonson): ghraes/lənd (Brownsville). This rural settlement and extinct po on KY 1365, 3½ mi nw of Brownsville, are said to have been named for the abundance of grass and dearth of other vegetation in the area. The po was est on Mar 12, 1895, with Charles A. Alexander, pm. 942.

Grassy Creek (Morgan): *ghraes*/ee *kreek* (Cannel City). This crossroads hamlet with po lies at the jct of US 460 and KY 205, 5 mi sw of West Liberty. The community was first settled by Thomas Goodwin, a Methodist preacher, who named it and the Licking R tributary which flows through it for his home in North Carolina. Goodwin est the Grassy Creek po on Feb 19, 1858, and the local church, which for years was referred to as Goodwin's Chapel. Though the church is now gone, oldtimers still call the place The Chapel. 202, 1346.

Grassy Creek (Pendleton). See *DeMossville*

Grassy Lick (Montgomery): *ghraes*/ee *lihk* (Sideview). This crossroads hamlet with extinct po lies on Grassy Lick Creek, for which it was named, at the jct of Grassy Lick, Pruitt, and Donaldson Rds, midway between US 460 and I 64, and 3½ mi wnw of Mt. Sterling. The creek is said to have been named by pioneer hunters for the gathering place of large herds of buffalo and deer at a salt spring at the forks of the creek in an open grassy meadow, alleged to be where bluegrass was first planted in Kentucky. The po, which was est as Grassy Lick on May 14, 1886, with John W. Pharis, pm, became Grassy in 1895 and closed in 1902. The community has always been called Grassy Lick. 1032, 1237.

Grassy PO (Montgomery). See *Grassy Lick*

Grassy Pond PO (Jefferson). See *Kosmosdale*

Gratz (Owen): ghraets (Gratz). This 6th class city with po lies 6 mi sw of Owenton where KY 22 and 355 join on the Kentucky R. It was laid out as a town in 1847 on land said to have been owned by the heirs of John Brown, Kentucky's first senator, and probably named for his grandson Benjamin Gratz Brown (1826–85), who was later to become a US senator from Missouri (1863–67), governor of that state (1871), and unsuccessful running mate of presidential hopeful Horace Greeley (1872). The po was est on Nov 21, 1844, as Clay Lick for its location just above the mouth of Clay Lick Creek, but in 1851 it was renamed Gratz. It is not known if the creek had been named for an early owner or if "Clay" was descriptive. The town was inc in 1861. 1242, 1449.

Gravel Switch (Marion): *ghraev*/əl swihch (Gravel Switch). This village with po lies at the jct of KY 243 and the L&N RR tracks, 10 mi e of Lebanon. Sometime around 1870, a spur line was extended from this site on the Lebanon Branch of the L&N to a large gravel deposit tapped by the rr to supply its rail beds. The small village that grew up at this site was thus called Gravel Switch, as was the po that was moved here on Dec 2, 1870, from Rileys Station. 358.

Graves County: ghrāvz. 557 sq mi. Pop. 34,049. Seat: Mayfield. Graves Co was est in 1823 from part of Hickman Co and named for Major Benjamin Franklin Graves (1771–1813), one of the 9 officers killed in the Battle of River Raisin, Jan 22, 1813, for whom Kentucky cos were named.

Gray Hawk (Jackson): *ghrā* hâwk (McKee). This village with po extends for 1 mi along US 421, 3½ mi se of McKee. The po, est on Oct 18, 1853, with John L. Hamilton, pm, is said by some to have been named for the many gray hawks found in that area. Others, however, believe that it was named for Messrs. Gray and Hawk who owned the land there at the time it was est. While no record has ever been found of such ownership, Gray and Hawk families are known to have lived in that vicinity in the 19th cent. 1418.

Graymoor (Jefferson): *ghrā*/mawr (Jeffersonville). This 6th class city lies between Herr Lane and I 264, and US 42 and KY 1447, 7½ mi e of the courthouse in downtown Louisville. This suburban community was inc on Nov 28, 1959, to include the subdivisions of Graymoor and Woodstock. The former had been developed from part of the O.A. Winkler farm by John A. Walser, who named it for the monastery of the Friars of the Atonement in Garrison, New York, a place "noted for its hospitality for homeless and derelict men." The community has never had its own po. 452, 1167.

Grays (Knox): ghrāz (Corbin). This village with po is on KY 1232, just s of new US 25E, 7 mi nw of Barbourville. While some co historians believe this name identified a small crossroads settlement there before the L&N RR arrived in 1887, others trace it to the est of the po on Jan 25, 1888, and station and attribute it to Calvin C. Gray, a local farmer and merchant, who gave the rr its right-of-way through his farm. He was the first pm and station agent. There is also the unconfirmed tradition of an interracial marriage in Virginia of a Negro Mr. Gray who, to avoid the inevitable repercussions of such a union, brought his bride to Knox Co when it was still a wilderness. Their descendants intermarried with whites and over time the color line completely disappeared. For some reason the po name was spelled without the terminal "s" and this spelling has been preserved on all maps and records since. The "s," however, is included in local pronunciation. 742, 1409, 1267.

Graysbranch (Greenup): *grāz*/*braench* (Portsmouth, Wheelersburg). This hamlet with extinct po is on US 23, w of the mouth of Grays Branch of the Ohio R, and 5 mi nnw of Greenup. It was named for the stream, which in turn was named for the family of Thomas Lloyd Gray, a native of Prince Georges Co, Maryland, who arrived in Greenup Co around 1808 to take up a 200-acre warrant for his services in the Revolutionary War. Ten years later, his son, John Lloyd Gray, bought an additional 800-acre tract of Ohio R bottom land extending n to a point below the later village of Limeville and operated a wood yard at what he was to call Grays Landing. Over a period of time so many Lawson families had settled in this vicinity that the place was sometimes called the Lawson Settlement. On Oct 22, 1888, James B. Mackoy est a po there, which he named Mackoy for himself. This was discontinued in 1925 and reest as Graysbranch on Aug 9, 1926, to conform to the name the rr station had borne since 1889. The po was discontinued in 1958. The unusual spelling of the Graysbranch name is due to the Post Office Department's preference for one word names. 23.

Grays Knob (Harlan): *ghrāz nahb* (Harlan). This coal town with po lies on Martins Fork of the Cumberland R, 2 mi s of Harlan. The po was est on Jan 13, 1916, with Paul Berger, pm, and named for a nearby elevation. The community has also been identified as Charlotte Station, a now extinct loading station for a local mine, and was named for the second wife of the mine owner, C. R. Bennett. It has also been called Wilsonberger Station for C. E. Wilson and T. C. Berger, who founded the local Wilsonberger Coal Co. in 1917. 335, 1149, 1173.

Grayson (Carter): *ghrā*/sən (Grayson). This 4th class city and seat of Carter Co lies at the jct of US 60 and KY 1 and 7, just s of I 64 and 140 mi e of downtown Louisville. It was probably named for Col. William Grayson, aide-de-camp to Gen. George Washington, for it was located on the 70,000-acre patent issued to his family by Governor Shelby in 1795. Or, as some local historians believe, it may have been named for the colonel's only daughter, Hebe, the wife of State Sen. William G. Carter for whom the co had been named in 1838. It is said that Carter, who acquired part of the site from his wife's heirs, and William L. Ward, who owned the rest of it, were responsible for the town's est around 1840. The first po in the co, Little Sandy Salt Works, was est about a mi n on or before Feb 23, 1811, with Amos Kibbey, pm. In 1821 the po was renamed Little Sandy for the nearby stream, and it was moved to the Grayson site and given that name on May 22, 1840. Grayson was inc as a city in 1844. 36, 422, 1326.

Grayson County: *ghrā*/sən. 493 sq mi. Pop 20,854. Seat: Leitchfield. This co was est in 1810 from parts of Hardin and Ohio cos and named for Col. William Grayson (1740–90), Revolutionary War aide to General Washington and later delegate to the Virginia General Assembly and the Continental Congress, who died soon after his election as first US senator from Virginia.

Grayson Court House PO (Grayson). See *Leitchfield*

Grayson Springs (Grayson): *ghrā*/sən *sprihŋz* (Clarkson). This once celebrated spa lies on Bear Creek, 2 mi below its head, and 3½ mi ese of Leitchfield. These numerous mineral springs had been known to white settlers as the Sulphur Springs for some time before 1836 when Virginia-born James Fielding Clarkson purchased 500 acres including the springs from W. R. Hines and built a hotel. The po of Grayson Springs, est on July 28, 1841, by Manoah P. Clarkson, James Fielding's son, has since closed. 366, 619, 1307.

Grayson Springs Station PO (Grayson). See *Clarkson*

Great Buffalo Crossing (Scott). See *Great Crossing*

Great Crossing (Scott): *ghrāt krâhs*/ihŋ (Georgetown). This hamlet with extinct po is on the present KY 227, just n of US 460 and 1½ mi w of Georgetown. It grew up around a pioneer station called (The) Great Crossing or Johnson's Station, built by Virginia-born Robert Johnson in the winter of 1783–84 at the point where the great buffalo path between the Bluegrass and Ohio R crossed North Elkhorn Creek. It was also early called Great Buffalo Crossing, and, for most of the 19th cent, Great Crossings, by which name the po, in operation from 1811 to 1905, was known. Since the turn of the present century it has been Great Crossing and now is locally called simply The Crossing. 13, 109, 1293.

Great Landing (Gallatin). See *Warsaw*

Greear (Morgan): ghreer (West Liberty). This hamlet with extinct po is on US 460, at the mouth of Gose Branch of Little Caney Creek, 3 mi ssw of West Liberty. The po was est on Apr 2, 1915, and probably named for its first pm, William B. Greear, or his family.

Green (Elliott): ghreen (Bruin). This hamlet with extinct po lies at the jct of KY 7 and 504, 3 mi ne of Sandy Hook. It may early have been called Cliffside, a descriptive name, until the po was est on Feb 11, 1899, and named for the family of Robert Kilgore Green, an early settler from Virginia. Nearby KY 706 is still called the Cliffside Rd. Before 1919, when the po moved to White's Store, it was located across Hog Camp Creek, an early layover for hog drovers. It closed in 1958. 1412.

Greencastle (Warren): *ghreen*/kaes/əl (Bowling Green North) Almost nothing remains of a once prosperous Barren R port and mill town at the mouth of Swan Creek (now Taylor Branch), ½ mi s of the present KY 263 and 5½ mi n of Bowling Green. The town developed around the lock and dam built about 1845 by James Ford and Thomas Stephens, Sr., and later acquired by Capt. William Brown. The po est as Swan Creek on Apr 15, 1850, with John P. Smith, pm, became Green Castle (*sic*) in 1856, allegedly named at Brown's suggestion for the town in Pennsylvania. For a time the community was called Brown's Lock but was inc as Greencastle in 1869. The po has since closed. 209, 525, 1191.

Green County: ghreen. 289 sq mi. Pop 11,043. Seat: Greensburg. Est in 1792 from parts of Lincoln and Nelson cos, Green Co was named for General Nathaniel Greene of Revolutionary War fame. This was the 7th and last co organized in Kentucky's first legislative session. No one has ever determined what happened to the final "e."

Green Hall (Owsley): *ghreen* hawl (Sturgeon). This po is on KY 30 and the Jackson Co line, 8½ mi sw of Booneville. Est on Jan 2, 1855, it is believed to have been named for the green painted open hallway of pm James D. Foster's home, which may have been its first location. 1419.

Green River PO (Hart). See *Hardyville*

Greensburg (Green): *ghreenz*/bergh (Greensburg, Summersville). This 5th class city and seat of Green Co is on US 68, 65 mi s of downtown Louisville. Greensburg was est by the Kentucky legislature in 1794 as the seat of Green Co and inc in 1795. It was named either for the co, for the Green R on which it is located, or directly for Revolutionary War General Nathaniel Greene. The city is on the site of Glover's Station [*ghluhv*/ərz *stā*/shən] est in 1780 by John Glover on his 193-acre military grant. The po was est as Greensburg, also called Greensburg Court House, on Jan 1, 1807, with John Barnett, pm. 109, 912.

Greensburg Court House PO (Green). See *Greensburg*

Green's PO (Grayson). See *Falls of Rough*

Greenup (Greenup): *ghreen*/uhp (Greenup). This 5th class city and seat of Greenup Co lies just above the confluence of tbe Little Sandy and Ohio rs, midway between Portsmouth and Ashland, and 150 mi e of downtown Louisville. The town was laid off in 1803–4 by Robert Johnson, the proprietor, who named it Greenupsburg when it was made the seat of newly created Greenup Co. Both the co and its seat honored Christopher Greenup who was shortly to become Kentucky's 3rd governor. The po was est as Greenup Court House on July 1, 1811, with Joshua Bartlett, pm, and the town was chartered as Greenupsburg on Feb 4, 1818. In 1872 it was renamed to avoid confusion with Greensburg, in Green Co, but continued to be called Greenupsburg locally for some time. 1, 22.

Greenup County: *ghreen*/əp. 347 sq mis. Pop 39,132. Seat: Greenup. This co was est in 1803 from part of Mason Co and named for Christopher Greenup (1750–1818), one of Kentucky's first 2 congressmen (1793–97) and its 3rd governor (1804–8). He was clerk of the Kentucky Senate when the co was formed.

Greenup Court House PO (Greenup). See *Greenup*

Greenup Fork (Owen). See *Ep*

Greenup Furnace (Greenup). See *Hunnewell*

Greenup Lime Works PO (Greenup). See *Limeville*

Greenupsburg (Greenup). See *Greenup*

Greenville (Clay). See *Manchester*

Greenville (Muhlenberg): *ghreen*/vəl (Greenville). This 4th class city and seat of Muhlenberg Co is on US 62 and KY 171 and 181, 100 mi sw of downtown Louisville. It was founded in 1799 over 1 mi se of the pioneer Caney Station on 50 acres offered by William Campbell for the seat of the new co. However, it was not officially est as a town until legislative action was taken in 1812. Two accounts have been given for its name. Some have said it was suggested by Mrs. Tabitha A. R. Campbell for the "expanse of green treetops" as viewed in every direction from the hill on which the town would be located. More likely, though, it honored Revolutionary War Gen. Nathaniel Greene (1742–86). The po was est on Apr 1, 1801, with Samuel Russell, pm. 189, 319.

Greenwood Lake PO (Kenton). See *Erlanger*

Greenwood Station PO (Kenton). See *Erlanger*

Gregoryville (Carter): *ghrehgh*/ə/rə/vihl, *ghrihgh*/ree/vihl (Grahn). Little remains of this village on I 64 and Barrett Creek, between Davis Fork and Smiths Branch, 4 mi w of Grayson. A village called Bullseye grew up here around a shipping point for timber and later limestone and iron ore developed on holdings acquired in 1858 by H. B. Smith and John B. Gregory. On May 28, 1890, Smith or a namesake est the Fontana po, which in 1920 was renamed for Gregory. This po closed in 1954. 455, 1250.

Grethel (Floyd): *ghrehth*/əl (McDowell). This po is on KY 979 and Mud Creek, ¾ mi above the mouth of Branham Creek, and 13 mi sse of Prestonsburg. It was est on June 27, 1921, and named by the first pm, Frank Parsons, for his daughter. 1081.

Greys Bend (Lee). See *Primrose*

Gubers Mill PO (Campbell). See *Gubser Mill*

Gubser Mill (Campbell): *ghōōb*/sər mihl (New Richmond). This hamlet with extinct po lies at the jct of KY 1121 and Twelvemile Creek, 5 mi se of Alexandria. The po was est as Guber's Mill (an obvious error) on May 16, 1870, with John M. Chalk, pm, and named for the local gristmill begun or acquired by John Gubser, a Swiss immigrant, said to have arrived there in 1844. The po closed in 1872 and was reest by Chalk in 1881 as Gubser. It closed for good in 1906. Chalk was its only pm. 1300.

Gubser PO (Campbell). See *Gubser Mill*

Guerrant (Breathitt): ghə/*raent* (Jackson). This po serves a settlement long known as Highland on Puncheon Camp Creek, ½ mi e of its confluence with the Middle Fork of the Kentucky R and 6½ mi wsw of Jackson. The po was est as Herald on Nov 30, 1895, and named for the first pm, Breckinridge H. Herald, or his family. In 1911 it was renamed for the famed Presbyterian missionary-educator, Dr. E. O. Guerrant, who had est the Highland Institute there in the 1890s. 1310.

Gulnare (Pike): *ghuhl*/*nε* (Thomas). This hamlet with po lies on Johns Creek at the mouth of Sycamore Creek, 9 mi n of Pikeville. In 1790 William Robert Leslie made the first permanent settlement in the Big Sandy Valley at or near this site. The po, est on Oct 26, 1882, with Benjamin Alley, pm, is said to have been named for a character in a Sir Walter Scott poem. 1371.

Gum Grove (Butler). See *Huntsville*

Gunlock (Magoffin): *ghuhn*/lahk (David). This hamlet with po is on KY 7 and the Licking R, 15 mi sse of Salyersville. The po was est in 1936 by Roy Shepherd to replace the Mid po that had earlier served the people of the upper Licking watershed. It is said that Shepherd spotted the name in a newspaper article he had been reading on a western ranch called Gunlock. The Mid po, est by Jesse J. Hale on Dec 3, 1915, on the Left Fork of Brushy Creek, another Licking R tributary below Gunlock, had been named for its location between 2 other pos. After several changes in location by subsequent pms, Mid closed in 1932. 1181, 1422.

Gunn PO (Breathitt). See *Wolverine*

Gus (Muhlenberg): ghuhs (Dunmor). This extinct po on KY 949, ½ mi from Mud R and 15 mi ese of Greenville, was named for its first pm, Gusta L. Waggoner, who also ran the local store. Est on June 17, 1907, the po once served the smallest community in Kentucky to have its own po. 320.

Guston (Meade): *ghuhs*/tən (Guston). This village with po is on KY 428 and the L&N RR, ¾ mi n of US 60 and 7 mi ssw of Brandenburg. The po, est on Jan 19, 1889, with Albert J. Thompson, pm, was named for Gus[tavia] W. Richardson, a local farmer and civil servant, who had succeeded in attracting the Louisville St. Louis & Texas (now L&N) RR through this site in the 1880s. 1260.

Guthrie (Todd); *ghuhth*/ree (Guthrie). This 5th class city with po and L&N RR jct lies where US 41 crosses the Tennessee state line, less than ½ mi se of US 79 and 9½ mi s of Elkton. At this site in the 1840s was a stage stop called Pondy Woods, which later may have been called State Line. Still later, J. C. Kendall, the landowner, laid out a town there and named it for US Senator James A. Guthrie, who was the rr co.'s president from 1860 to 1868. Guthrie, a Bardstown native and one of the founders of the rr co., had also served as Franklin Pierce's secretary of the Treasury from 1853 to 1857. A po was moved here from a site across the Tennessee line on or before July 14, 1868, and named Guthrie, with William G. Spalding, pm, and the town was inc under this name on Nov 11, 1876. 97, 225, 1252, 1318.

Guthries Chapel (Cumberland). See *Tanbark*

Guy (Warren): gheye (Hadley). This settlement with extinct po lies at the jct of the present KY 1435 and Thomas Rd, 1 mi w of the Barren R and 11 mi nw of Bowling Green. The po was est on May 2, 1912, at the store run by Hugh A. and William Guy Thomas. The names of 12 local residents were submitted to the Post Office Department and that of William Guy Thomas was chosen. Hugh was named pm. 645.

Gypsy (Magoffin): *djihp*/see (Ivyton). This po on KY 1766, 2 mi up Jake Fork of Puncheon Camp Creek and 7½ mi se of Salyersville, was formerly located on Puncheon Camp above the mouth of Jake Fork. It was est on Jan 4, 1883, with Joseph Allen, pm, and named for the daughter of Branch Higgins, a school teacher, who had submitted the petition. 1084.

Habit (Daviess): *haeb*/ət (Philpot). This settlement with extinct po lies at the jct of KY 142 and 762, 5½ mi se of Owensboro. Its po was est on July 30, 1884, and named for Frederick Habitt, an English-born blacksmith who had arrived in Daviess Co in 1870. The office closed in 1906. 885.

Haddix (Breathitt): *haed*/əx (Haddix). This coal town with po lies on the North Fork of the Kentucky R, just opposite the mouth of Troublesome Creek, 3½ mi s of Jackson.

At or near this site was a settlement made before 1800 by Samuel Haddix of Clinch River, Virginia, and the first mines in the area are said to have opened here around 1852. It was not until 1911 that the Haddix name was applied to it in honor of the, by then, large extended family. The Haddix po was est on July 8, 1916, with Floyd Russell, pm. 236, 1222, 1432.

Hadley (Warren). See *Rockland*

Hagensville PO (Bracken). See *Berlin*

Hagerhill (Johnson): *hăgh*/ər/hihl (Paintsville). This village with po extends for about a mi along KY 1428, centering at its jct with US 23/460, less than 1 mi s of Paintsville. Its po was est on Jan 15, 1903, with George B. Rice, pm. It was probably named for Daniel Mart Hager (1846–1931), a local farmer and Methodist preacher, or for Sam Hager who built a large red brick house on top of a small hill in the vicinity. The local station on the old Big Sandy & Kentucky River (now C&O) RR was early called Johnson Station and is now Hager Hill. 90, 1205, 1411.

Hail (Pulaski): hāl (Hail). This extinct po on KY 1097, ½ mi s of Buck Creek and 8½ mi se of Somerset, was est on June 19, 1890, with George G. Gregory, pm, and probably named for the family of Stephen Hail, pioneer settler from Virginia. In 1914, when James M. Hail became pm, the po was moved 1 mi e of its original site, and here it remained until it recently closed. 1410.

Hailewell (Hickman): *hāl*/wehl (Oakton). This extinct settlement lay at the jct of KY 123 and Cole Rd, 5½ mi w of Clinton. It was named for a large well owned by Benjamin L. Haile, the local storekeeper who est the po there on Dec 12, 1898. The po closed in 1915. 162, 919.

Haldeman (Rowan): *hahl*/də/mən (Haldeman). Only the po, school, and some homes remain of this once prosperous village extending along KY 174, 1¼ mi e of its jct with US 60, 5½ mi ne of Morehead. Sometime before 1907, L. P. Haldeman from Columbus, Ohio, founded the town named for him to accommodate the workers of his Kentucky Firebrick Co., newly est to produce bricks from area clay deposits. The po was opened on Feb 12, 1907, with David Leadbetter, pm. 556, 1273.

Halfway (Allen): *haef*/wā (Allen Springs). This po on US 231, 6 mi nw of Scottsville, was est as Half Way on June 20, 1877, by Levi J. Spann. It was probably named for its location midway along a mail route between Bowling Green and some point near the Tennessee state line, where carriers are said to have rested and fed their horses, often staying the night. The present spelling of the name was effected on July 20, 1895. 101, 314.

Hall PO (Hopkins). See *Earlington*

Halls Gap (Lincoln): *hawlz ghaep* (Halls Gap). This hamlet with extinct po on Muldraugh's Hill is centered at the jct of KY 643 and 1247 (old US 27), 4 mi s of Stanford. The first Halls Gap po, its precise site unknown, was est on Aug 15, 1857, with Abraham Dawes, pm, and named for John Hall, pioneer settler, whose 1781 preemption included this site. It was discontinued in 1859 and reest on Jan 5, 1864, with Henderson P. Young, pm. From 1868 until it closed the following year, Young ran his po as Young's Mill. Contemporary historians, however, claim never to have heard this community called by that name. From 1890 to 1905 the community was served by the Ewell po [*yū*/əl] in J. D. Bastin's store on new US 27, a short distance w. The 2nd Halls Gap po, in operation from 1940 to 1959, was on top of the hill in Hodges' store on old US 27, a winding rd that goes through the gap itself. 876, 1276, 1448.

Hallsville PO (Perry). See *Viper*

Hamden (Perry). See *Jeff*

Hamburg (Fleming). See *Goddard*

Hamelton (Ohio). See *McHenry*

Hamlin (Calloway): *haem*/lihn (Hamlin).This po is in Aleen Claxton's grocery overlooking Kentucky Lake, at the end of KY 444 and 12 mi e of Murray. It was est on Feb 9, 1885, and named for its first pm, Robert Macon Hamlin, son of Charles S. Hamlin. 467, 593.

Hammond (Knox): *haem*/ənd (Scalf). This hamlet with recently closed po is on KY 223, 6½ mi up Road Fork Creek, a branch of Stinking Creek, and 10 mi ne of Barbourville. The po was est as Hammons on Jan 10, 1890, and named for a large local family. Inexplicably, the Post Office Department saw fit to respell it Hammond in 1892, and this name has been perpetuated on all maps and records since. 1409.

Hammons PO (Knox). See *Hammond*

Hammonsville (Hart): *haem*/ənz/vihl (Hammonsville). The oldest extant community in the co is this hamlet with extinct po, on KY 357, 10 mi nne of Munfordville. It was named for a Dr. Hammon, its first settler, who arrived around 1780. The po was est on Mar 2, 1848, with Robert H. Compton, pm, and the town was inc in 1860. 299, 863.

Hampton (Livingston): *haemp*/tən (Lola). This village with po on KY 135, 9 mi n of Smithland, is said to have grown up around a supply station located there during the Civil War, allegedly est by Confederate Gen. Wade Hampton for whom it was later named. Biographies of General Hampton and several histories of Confederate activities in Kentucky, however, make no mention of Hampton having served in Kentucky. The local po was est on Jan 14, 1878, by James H. Cameron, storekeeper. 1182, 1440.

Hampton City (Boyd). See *Catlettsburg*

Hancock County: *haen*/kahk. 189 sq mi. Pop 7,742. Seat: Hawesville. Est in 1829 from parts of Breckinridge, Daviess, and Ohio cos, this co was named for John Hancock (1737–93), president of the Continental Congress, 1775–77, and initial signer of the Declaration of Independence.

Hanging Fork PO (Lincoln). See *Hustonville*

Hanley (Jessamine): *haen*/lee (Little Hickman). This rural settlement with extinct post office is on US 27, over 1½ mi s of Nicholasville. It was named for John Hays Hanley (1788–1867), an Irishman, who came from Pennsylvania first to Nicholasville in 1813 and then to the site which bears his name in the 1830s. The owner of a large farm in the southern half of tbe co, he may also have been involved in the operation of the nearby vineyard (see *Vineyard*). The po was in operation from 1858 to 1917. The Hanly spelling on current maps is believed to be in error. 1390.

Hannah (Lawrence): *haen*/ə (Blaine). This extinct po on Cains Creek, just below the mouth of Deans Branch, 14 mi wsw of Louisa, was est on Nov 6, 1911, and named for its first pm, Hannah E. Boggs, nee Gambill. It was discontinued in 1954. 1095, 1098.

Hansbrough (Hardin): *haenz*/broh (Cecilia). This widely scattered farming settlement, locally called Hansbrough Valley, is centered at the jct of KY 1375 and the Illinois Central Gulf RR, 6½ mi sw of Elizabethtown. It was named for a local family and has never had its own po. 1420.

Hansbrough Valley (Hardin). See *Hansbrough*

Hansford (Rockcastle): *haens*/fərd (Mt. Vernon). This extinct po on KY 1152, ½ mi w of its jct with KY 1249 and 5½ mi s of Mt. Vernon, was est on Aug 7, 1871, and may have been named for its first pm, Will F. Hansford, or his family. 1251.

Hanson (Hopkins): *haen*/sən (Hanson). This 6th class city with po is on US 41A, just w of the Pennyrile Parkway, and 2½ mi n of Madisonville. The town was founded in

1869 on a 50-acre tract donated by Judge Robert Eastwood and Rev. Roland Gooch, and laid out by and named for Henry B. Hanson (1825–1905), a Saratoga Springs, New York, civil engineer for the Evansville Henderson & Nashville (now L&N) RR, which had been completed to this site in the same year. The local po was est on Dec 7, 1869, with William A. Anderson, pm, and the town was inc in 1873. 301, 396.

Happy Hollow (Pulaski). See *Alpine*

Hardburly (Perry): *hahrd*/ber/lee (Hazard North, Carrie). This coal town with po lies at the head of Jake Branch of Trace Fork of Lotts Creek, 3½ mi nw of Hazard. It was founded by and named for the Hardy Burlington Mining Co. The po was est on Apr 17, 1918, with Albert Kirk, pm. 1186, 1327.

Hardeman PO (Wolfe). See *Calaboose*

Hardin (Marshall): *hahr*/dən (Hardin). This 5th class city with po is centered at a point just s and e of the jct of US 641 and KY 80, 1 mi w of Clarks R and 4½ mi sse of Benton. In 1890 the Paducah Tennessee & Alabama (now L&N) RR secured property owned by Hardin D. Irvan of nearby Wadesborough for its depot here. A town was soon laid out around the station and named for Irvan. The po was est on Oct 31, 1891, and Irvan's son, John T., became the first pm. 76, 1337.

Hardin County: *hahr*/dən 629 sq mi. Pop 88,917. Seat: Elizabethtown. Hardin Co was est in 1792 from part of Nelson Co and named for Col. John Hardin (1753–92), Revolutionary War veteran and surveyor, who later served with George Rogers Clark in his trans-Ohio campaigns and was killed by Ohio Indians to whom he had gone on a peace mission. The co, was one of the 7 organized in Kentucky's first legislative session.

Hardin Court House PO (Hardin). See *Elizabethtown*

Hardinsburg (Breckinridge): *hahr*/dihnz/bergh (Hardinsburg). This 5th class city and seat of Breckinridge Co lies at the jct of US 6O and KY 259 and 261, 48 mi sw of downtown Louisville. It is on the site of the first settlement in the co, the pioneer Hardin's Station, which was est by Capt. William Hardin (1747–1821) in 1780. Captain Hardin was the grandson of Martin Hardin, a Huguenot colonist who came to Virginia from Canada and later resettled in Pennsylvania, and the brother of John Hardin, another Indian fighter, for whom Hardin Co was named. Hardinsburg was laid out as a town, named for William, and inc in 1800, the year after the formation of the co. Its po was est on Jan 1, 1803, as Breckinridge Court House or Hardinburg (*sic*). 214, 898.

Hardinsburg Station (Breckinridge). See *Harned*

Hardmoney (McCracken): *hahrd*/muhn/ee (Symsonia). This hamlet with extinct po lies at the jct of KY 1232 and 1684, 7½ mi s of Paducah. The po est by John H. Ballance on May 27, 1880, is said to have been named for the political controversy of the time over the use of gold backing for paper money. It is not known how this issue affected or was reflected by Ballance, who undoubtedly named the po. A local tale is that at the time he was asked to select the name Ballance was mounting his first dollar, which, he said, was the hardest money he had ever earned. The po closed in 1900. 881.

Hardscratch (Adair). See *Glens Fork*

Hardshell (Breathitt): *hahrd*/shehl (Haddix). This hamlet is on KY 476 at the mouth of Caney Creek of Troublesome Creek, 8 mi se of Jackson. The Hardshell po, now defunct, was est on Aug 11, 1917, with Garvey Noble, pm, and named for the Hardshell Baptist church there. 1310.

Hardyville (Hart): *hahr*/dee/vihl (Canmer). This village with po lies at the jct of US 31E and KY 88, 5 mi e of Munfordville. The community was est in 1861 on the site of

William Renfroe's 1820s tavern and stage relay station and probably named for James G. Hardy (died 1856), the speaker of the Kentucky House and lieutenant governor from 1855 to 1856, who was the son of Isham Hardy, a pioneer settler. According to Cyrus Edwards, "the town . . . was named for him in remembrance of a great victory he gained there in a political argument with some of the famous Whig speakers of the state." Another branch of the Hardy family has disputed this. The Hardyville po, est on Apr 7, 1868, with Thomas A. Conyer, pm, was a transfer of an earlier po called Green River, est in 1847. 66, 863, 1331.

Harg (Estill). See *Hargett*

Hargett (Estill): *hahr*/ghət (Palmer). This hamlet with extinct po lies at the jct of KY 82 and 89, 5 mi nnw of Irvine. Leroy Sams est the Woodwards Creek po here on July 28, 1879, and named it for a Red R tributary that heads nearby. On May 6, 1886, John Sams had the name changed to Sams, and under this name the po served the area until it closed in 1914. It moved briefly from Sams' store to the nearby L&N station, named Harg for Harg Allen. When Edith Patrick est another po here on Sept 23, 1915, it was called Hargett, probably for Allen or the nearby rr station. But co historian Kathryn Carter has suggested that it was named for Hargett Withers, a young boy who happened to enter the store at the time a postal inspector was seeking a name for the new po. The po was discontinued on Sept 30, 1943. 865.

Hargis PO (Breathitt). See *Frozen Creek*

Hariba (Menifee). See *Mariba*

Harlan (Harlan): *hahr*/lən (Harlan). This 4th class city and seat of Harlan Co is on US 421 and the forks of the Cumberland R, 153 mi se of downtown Louisville. By 1819, when the settlement became the new co's seat, it was already called Mt. Pleasant, for reasons unknown. The po was est on Sept 19, 1828, as Harlan Court House with John N. Martin, pm, since the Mt. Pleasant name had been preempted by another Kentucky po. In the 1860s the po was called Spurlock, probably for the pm then, one Josiah B. Spurlock, but in 1865 it adopted the name Harlan, which it has borne ever since. Though inc as Mt. Pleasant in 1884, the town was locally called Harlan Town or Harlan Court House. It was reinc as Harlan in 1912. The name honored Maj. Silas Harlan (1752–82) who fought with Gen. George Rogers Clark and was killed at the Battle of Blue Licks. 46, 128, 283.

Harlan County: *hahr*/lən. 468 sq mi. Pop 41,889. Seat: Harlan. Est in 1819 from parts of Floyd and Knox cos, this co was named for Maj. Silas Harlan (1752–82), pioneer Salt R settler, who served with George Rogers Clark in his Illinois campaign and fell at the Battle of Blue Licks.

Harlan Court House (Harlan). See *Harlan*

Harlan Town (Harlan). See *Harlan*

Harmony Landing PO (Oldham). See *Goshen*

Harned (Breckinridge): *hahrn*/əd (Hardinsburg, Kingswood). This village with po is on US 60, 1½ mi se of Hardinsburg. The site is believed to have been settled by Mose Payne before 1800 and first called Hardinsburg Station. A po called Layman, for a local family, was est on June 6, 1890, by William B. Hardin, but 6 months later it was renamed for Henry Harned, a Virginian who had moved to this place from nearby Custer shortly after the Civil War, and who donated the site of the depot and right-of-way to the Louisville Hardinsburg & Western (later Louisville Henderson & St. Louis) RR in 1890. 214, 290, 1398.

Harold (Floyd): *haer*/əld (Harold). This village with po lies on the Levisa Fork of the Big Sandy R, just above the mouth of Mud Creek and 10 mi se of Prestonsburg. At least through the 1930s the section e of the r was considered a separate community, known as Laynesville for the family of pioneer settler James Shannon Layne (1781–1871) (see *Betsy Layne*). The first po to serve the vicinity was est as Lanesville on Jan 23, 1828, with James L. Layne, pm. The spelling was corrected to Laynesville in 1878 and the po was closed in 1917. On Sept 11, 1905, the po of Harold was est on the w side of the r with Joseph D. Morell, pm, and named for Harold Hatcher, a local merchant and descendant of James H. Hatcher who settled at the mouth of Mud Creek in 1830. The po is now on the e side of the r. 976, 1370.

Harper (Magoffin): *hahr*/pər (White Oak). This po is on KY 1081 and the Left Fork of White Oak Creek, at the mouth of Round Mountain Branch, 7½ mi nw of Salyersville. The po was est on Mar 7, 1915 and named for the family of its first pm, Nannie Harper Arnett. 1421, 1422.

Harrahs Mills PO (Powell). See *Rosslyn*

Harris (Lewis): *haer*/əs (Head of Grassy). Almost nothing is left to identify this community and extinct po on the Tar Fork Rd, ½ mi w of Laurel Fork of Kinniconick Creek and 14 mi s of Vanceburg. It was named for and by its first pm and storekeeper, Joseph Harris, when the po was est on Dec 12, 1898. It closed in 1955. 1200.

Harrisburg Academy PO (Owen). See *Long Ridge*

Harrisburgh PO (Calloway). See *Harris Grove*

Harrisburg PO (Calloway). See *Harris Grove*

Harrisburg PO (Owen). See *Long Ridge*

Harris Grove (Calloway): *haer*/əs *ghrohv* (Lynn Grove). This settlement with extinct po lies at the jct of KY 893 and 1550, 5 mi wsw of Murray. It was first called Cooks Valley when its po was est with this name by Henry W. Cook on July 13, 1852. In 1858 David C. Harris became pm, but the po was discontinued in Nov of that year. An attempt to reest the po in Dec 1860 was unsuccessful, but on Nov 16, 1872, a new po called Harrisburgh was started at or near the same site by James C. Harris and named for David C. Harris or his family. On Jan 29, 1875, James renamed the po Harris Grove. It closed on Feb 15, 1908. 1401.

Harrison (Pulaski). See *Faubush*

Harrison County: *haer*/ə/sən. 310 sq mi. Pop 15,166. Seat: Cynthiana. This co was est in 1793 from parts of Bourbon and Scott cos and named for Col. Benjamin Harrison, Revolutionary War veteran from Pennsylvania and early pioneer settler of Ruddles Station. He served as member of the conventions to consider Kentucky's separation from Virginia (1787–88) and to frame its first constitution (1792), and represented the local district in the state legislature when the co was organized.

Harrisonville (Shelby): *haer*/əs/ən/vihl (Glensboro). This hamlet with extinct po is on KY 395, 11 mi se of Shelbyville. It was laid off as Connorsville in 1825 and probably renamed for Gen. William Henry Harrison when the po was est on May 9, 1839, with Robert J. R. Baker, pm. It was inc in 1847. The po closed in 1908. 44, 228.

Harrodsburg (Mercer): *hɛ*/ədz/bergh (Harrodsburg, Danville). This 4th class city and seat of Mercer Co is on US 68 and 127, 55 mi se of downtown Louisville. Laid off as Harrodstown by James Harrod on June 16, 1774, it is said to be Kentucky's oldest town. It was named the co seat when Kentucky Co was est by the Virginia legislature in 1776, then became the seat of Lincoln Co, Virginia, in 1780, and finally of the newly formed Mercer Co, Virginia, in 1785. In that year it was officially renamed Harrodsburg when chartered as a city by the Virginia legislature, though it had also been referred to by this name since its settlement. The po was est on June 11, 1794, with

Philip Bush, pm. Harrodsburg was reinc by the Kentucky General Assembly in 1838. 39.

Harrods Creek (Jefferson): *hɛ*/ədz kreek (Jeffersonville). This village with po is on the River Rd and Harrods Creek, less than ¾ mi from its confluence with the Ohio R and 8½ mi ne of the court house in downtown Louisville. The creek was early named for Capt. William Harrod, older brother of James Harrod of Harrodsburg, who commanded the militia at the Falls of the Ohio (Louisville). The village of Transylvania is said to have been laid out as a r landing at the mouth of the creek sometime before 1800. The Harrods Creek po was est on Mar 16, 1875, with James Hutchison, pm. 719.

Harrodstown (Mercer). See *Harrodsburg*

Hart County: hahrt 412 sq mi. Pop 15,402. Seat: Munfordville. Est in 1819 from parts of Hardin and Barren cos, Hart Co was named for Capt. Nathaniel G. T. Hart (1784–1813), a Lexington lawyer and merchant who, as an officer in the War of 1812, was brutally murdered by Indians after being wounded at the Battle of the River Raisin.

Hartford (Ohio): *hahrt*/fərd (Hartford). This 5th class city and seat of Ohio Co is on US 231 and KY 69, just w of the Green River Parkway, and 78 mi sw of downtown Louisville. Here on the bluff on the s side of Rough R, overlooking a ford where deer and other animals were accustomed to cross in large numbers, the pioneer settlement of Hartford Station may have been est as early as 1782, certainly by 1790. In 1799 Gabriel Madison donated the land, part of his 4000-acre Virginia patent, to the new co for its seat. The po was est as Hartford Court House on Apr 1, 1801, with Wesley Pigman, pm, and the town was inc in 1808. It is extremely doubtful that, as some have suggested, the ford was once owned by a Mr. Hart. 75, 210, 905.

Hartford Court House PO (Ohio). See Hartford

Harvey (Marshall): *hahr*/vee (Oak Level). This hamlet with extinct po centers on the jct of KY 58 and 1949, 3 mi sw of Benton. In 1857 James Harvey Ivey arrived from Nashville, Tennessee, and acquired a 600-acre farm. In 1880 he opened a crossroads store there and on Apr 13, 1881, est the Harvey po to which he gave his mother's maiden name. The Post Office Department erred in misspelling it Harvy. The po closed in 1907. 1337.

Harveyton (Perry): *hahr*/və/tən (Hazard North). This former coal town, now a residential community with extinct po, lies at the head of First Creek, a branch of the North Fork of the Kentucky R, 3 mi n of Hazard. It was founded by and named for the Harvey Coal Co., which had a mine there. The po est as Staub [stâhb] on Feb 15, 1916, with Gilbert P. Foley, pm, adopted the Harveyton name in 1923.

Harvieland (Franklin): *hahr*/vee/laend (Polsgrove). This settlement with extinct po lies on the Davis Branch of Stony Creek, a tributary of the Kentucky R, 3 mi nnw of Frankfort. It was named for John Harvie, the Virginia-born first registrar of the Kentucky Land Office, and was on the 5000-acre tract that he surveyed in 1796. He later represented the co in the Kentucky legislature, and died in Frankfort in 1838. The po of Harvieland was in operation between 1883 and 1909. 108, 115, 864.

Haskinsville (Green): *haes*/kihnz/vihl (Gresham). This extinct settlement was on KY 1913 and Caney Fork of Russell Creek, 6½ mi se of Greensburg. It was settled around 1823 by Creed Haskins, the Frederick Co, Virginia-born son of Col. Robert Haskins, on William Spiller's 1000-acre military grant. He soon built a watermill and opened a store in which he est the Haskinsville po on Feb 4, 1836. In 1872 Thomas R. Mitchell, then pm, moved the po about 1½ mi sse to the site of Col. James Knox's station and renamed it Camp Knox [*kaemp nahx*]. The po was discontinued in 1918. 599, 1339.

Hatfield (Pike): *haet*/feeld (Williamson). This settlement and Norfolk & Western RR station with extinct po lie at the mouth of Low Gap Fork of Bent Branch of Big Creek, 17 mi nne of Pikeville. The local po, est on Dec 19, 1903, and named for the family of James F. Hatfield, the first pm, was discontinued in 1925.

Havens (Ohio). See *Arnold*

Havilandsville (Harrison): *haev*/əl/ənz/vihl (Claysville). This almost extinct 19th cent industrial town is on the Licking R and the Pendleton Co line, 12½ mi n of Cynthiana. It is not identified on any current maps. The first po to serve this vicinity was Travellers Rest, est on Feb 9, 1835, on Richland Creek in Pendleton Co. In 1832 New York City-born Robert S. Haviland (1796–1858) opened the first store in the area and in 1838 built a woolen factory. On Apr 8, 1842, he became pm and renamed the po Havilandsville. 167, 475, 594.

Hawesville (Hancock): *hawz*/vihl (Tell City, Cannelton). This 5th class city and seat of Hancock Co is on US 60 and the Ohio R, 55 mi wsw of downtown Louisville. The act that created the co in Jan 1829 also located its seat on land that Richard Hawes (1772–1829), a Caroline Co, Virginia, native, had recently divided into free lots for all who would homestead on them. The Hawesville po was est on Oct 24, 1829, with Samuel C. Jennings, pm, and the town was inc in 1836. 329, 871, 939.

Hawkins PO (Anderson). See *Fox Creek*

Haws Ford PO (Floyd). See *Dwale*

Haydens Corner (Clark). See *Becknerville*

Hayes (Rowan). See *Hays Crossing*

Haymond (Letcher): *hā*/mən(d) (Jenkins West). This coal town with po extends for nearly 2 mi along Potters Fork of Boone Fork of the North Fork of Kentucky R, and up its several branching hollows, from a point about a mi e of Neon Junction to the mouth of Ramey Fork, about 8 mi ne of Whitesburg. Though the town is officially identified by its po name Cromona [krə/*moh*/nə], the Haymond name is preferred locally, and has been associated with the place since it was first applied to the coal camp begun there about 1916 by the Elkhorn Coal Corp. It was named for Thomas S. Haymond, a general manager and later vice president of the co., who had been instrumental in the development of nearby *Fleming* 2 years before. The po was est as Cromona on Dec 14, 1916, with Samuel N. Hall, pm, for reasons unknown. Curiously, another po called Cremona was in operation from 1902 to 1906 somewhere in the vicinity of Roxana, to which its papers were transferred when the Cremona po closed. 1265.

Haynesville PO (Ohio). See *Fordsville*

Hays Crossing (Rowan): *hāz kraws*/ihŋ (Haldeman). This hamlet centered at the jct of US 60 and KY 174, 4 mi ne of Morehead, was named for the families of the brothers Andrew and Orthaneal Hays who had settled in that vicinity by 1878. The local po, in operation from 1882 to 1949, was called Eadston for reasons unknown. A 1935 topographic map locates the community of *Hayes* (*sic*) on the present KY 174, ½ mi e of the jct, and places the Eadston po in the vicinity of the C&O RR station and stringtown community of Gates, w of the jct. The derivation of Gates is also unknown. 1273.

Hays PO (Breathitt). See *Wolverine*

Hazard (Perry): *haez*/ərd (Hazard North, Hazard South). This 3rd class city and seat of Perry Co is on KY 15 and 80 and the North Fork of the Kentucky R, 146 mi se of downtown Louisville. It was founded in 1821 by Elijah Combs, Sr., its first settler and proprietor, as the seat of the newly est Perry Co, and like the co was named for Oliver

Hazard Perry (1785–1819), the hero of the Battle of Lake Erie (1813). The po was est as Perry Court House on Apr 22, 1824, with Combs's son, Elijah, Jr., as pm. It was renamed Hazard in 1854. The town was inc in 1884. 1327.

Hazel (Calloway): *hā*/zəl (Murray). This 6th class city with po is on US 461, 5½ mi s of Murray. It was est in 1890 by, and on what became, the Nashville Chattanooga & St. Louis (now L&N) RR, and named for either the thick hazel groves there, the daughter of the conductor of the first through train, or the daughter of Samuel H. Dees who est the Hazel po on Dec 31, 1890. 1401, 1441.

Hazel Green (Wolfe): *hā*/zəl ghreen, *hā*/zəl *ghreen* (Hazel Green). This recently disincorporated village with po is on the Red R, centered at the jct of KY 191, 203, and 1010, and 7½ mi ne of Campton. An early settled community, its po was est on Jan 28, 1829, as Hazle Green and named for the lush green meadows dotted with hazel shrubs. It was inc as Hazel Green in 1856 and the po name was changed to this spelling in 1889. 67, 707, 1236.

Hazel Patch (Laurel): *hāz*/əl paech (Bernstadt). This settlement with po lies on Hazel Patch Creek, just above its confluence with Little Rockcastle R, and the L&N RR, ½ mi e of US 25, and 7 mi nw of London. It is several mi w of the original Hazel Patch, historically referred to as The Hazel Patch, which was the jct of 2 pioneer routes. Named for the large number of hazel bushes in the vicinity, it was a major stopping place on the Wilderness Rd for the earliest Kentucky settlers. Here a po was est on July 1, 1805, as Hazlepatch or Rice's with James Rice, pm. The present Hazel Patch was est on Feb 1, 1867, as Hazle Patch with John Hay, pm. This spelling error was corrected in 1961 when the Board on Geographic Names, conforming to local usage, reversed an 1897 decision. 139, 259, 334, 996, 1282.

Headquarters (Nicholas): *hehd*/kawr/terz (Carlisle). Now but a hamlet with extinct po, this former trade and distillery center is on KY 32/36, 4 mi nw of Carlisle. Nobody really knows how it got its name though a number of theories have been offered. The name may refer to its role as an early trade center, or may be a translation of whatever the Indians called it. It is said to have been used as a meeting place by Indians from southern Ohio after their hunting trips into Kentucky, and earlier was a gathering place for buffalo. The name may also refer to its location at the head of Wilbur Run, a branch of Brushy Creek, and thus be a corruption of "headwaters." A village was located there by 1810. It was called Headquarters when the po was est on June 12, 1848, with A. G. Stitt, pm, though it was spelled as 2 words in early postal records. The po closed in 1906. 47, 428, 1374.

Hearts Delight (Daviess). See *Knottsville*

Heath (McCracken): heeth (Heath). This crossroads hamlet with extinct po lies at the jct of KY 725 and 996, 6½ mi w of Paducah. Frank Kelly est the po on Oct 3, 1898, in his store and named it for State Senator Heath who had helped him secure it from the Post Office Department. William R. Hopson was the first pm. The po closed in 1911. 1014.

Hebbardsville (Henderson): *hihb*/ərdz/vihl (Spottsville, Reed). This hamlet with extinct po lies at the jct of KY 54 and 416, 10 mi e of Henderson. The po, est on Feb 25, 1840, with Abram Hatchitt, pm, was named for Charles Hebbard, an early settler and blacksmith. It closed in 1973. 12.

Hebron (Boone): *hee*/brən (Burlington). This village with po is centered at the jct of KY 20 and 237, 2 mi nne of Burlington. The po was est on Feb 23, 1858, with Francis L. Gordon, pm, and named for the local Hebron Lutheran Church, which had been built and dedicated in 1854. In turn, the church had been named for a church in Virginia that had donated funds for its erection. About this time the community, which had been called Briar Thicket, was given the name of the po. It is said that in earlier times the place was called Tailholt. The origin of these names is not known. 877.

Hecla (Hopkins): *hehk*/lə (Madisonville East). This residential community, just nw of the Earlington city limits and 1½ mi s of Madisonville, began as a co. town for the workers of the nearby mine of the Hecla Coal and Mining Co. This shaft mine was opened in 1873 by Jo F. Foard, a Virginian, and possibly named for one of the other Heclas in Ohio, Michigan, or Indiana. The name had earlier been applied to a mine in Michigan, which is said to have been named for the volcano in Iceland famed in the 19th cent for its "frequent and violent eruptions." The Kentucky Hecla was inc in 1882. It has never had a po of its own. 159, 204.

Hector (Clay): *hehk*/tər (Barcreek). This po is on KY 149 and Hector Creek, at the mouth of Davidson Branch, about 5 mi from the creek's jct with the Redbird R and 5½ mi e of Manchester. It was est on Dec 28, 1900, with Arazona Davidson, pm, and named for the creek, which in turn is said to have been named by Abijah Gilbert, the first settler on Redbird, for a hunting dog who was killed by a bear. 1418.

Hedges (Clark): *hehdj*/əz (Hedges). This hamlet with extinct po on KY 1960, and a station on the C&O RR, 6 mi e of Winchester, were named either for Preston Hedges, who owned the site when the rr arrived, or for the family of residents John and Jonas Hedges. The Hedges po operated from July 26, 1875, to June 14, 1930. 975, 1349.

Heenon (Pike): *hee*/nən (Varney). This hamlet with extinct po lies on Brushy Fork of Johns Creek, 12 mi n of Pikeville. The first po to serve this area was est on Apr 7, 1904, as Jarad at or below the forks of Brushy, and named for Jarad Maynard, a descendant of Christopher Columbus Maynard who had arrived on Brushy before 1800. This po closed in 1924 and was reest as Heenon a short distance down Brushy on Aug 21, 1926, with Rollin B. Maynard, pm, and named for Jarad's son. 1108.

Heflin (Carter). See *Denton*

Heflin (Ohio): *hehf*/lən (Utica). This settlement with extinct po is on KY 136, 6 mi nw of Hartford. The po was est on Aug 25, 1892, and named for the first pm, Willis M. Heflin, in whose store it was located. It closed in 1909. 1400.

Heidelberg (Lee): *hahd*/əl/bergh (Heidelberg). This hamlet with po, once an important sawmill and rr town, is on KY 399 and the Kentucky R, nearly opposite the mouth of Sturgeon Creek, and 2½ mi sw of Beattyville. According to tradition, the site of this station on the L&N RR was settled in 1799 by Joseph Brandenberg, a native Virginian, and named for his ancestral home in Germany. The po was est on Mar 3, 1904, with Lucien Treadway, pm. 252.

Heidrick (Knox): *hahd*/rihk (Heidrick). This village with po lies on Little Richland Creek, between US 25E and KY 11, adjacent to Barbourville's ne limits. In 1916 Charles C. Heidrick of Brooksville, Pennsylvania, completed his 23-mi-long Cumberland and Manchester RR to join the L&N at its station, then called J. R. Allen, in a community called Highland Park. Here he located his roundhouse and switchtrack and renamed the station Heidrick. Ben Herndon est the Heidrick po on Mar 4, 1920. 738, 1350.

Helechawa (Wolfe): heh/*lee*/chə/wah, hə/*lihch*/ə/wah, heh/*lehch*/ə/wah (Cannel City). This hamlet with po is on KY 191, just e of its jct with KY 205 and just off the Mountain Parkway, 11 mi e of Campton. It was est around 1900 as a station on the long-defunct Ohio and Kentucky RR and named for a daughter of its first president, W. Delancy Walbridge of New York. For reasons probably known only to him, he coined the name by combining parts of her name, *Hele*n *Cha*se *Wa*lbridge. The po was est on

Sept 18, 1900, as Neola (derivation unknown) with James T. Wilson, pm, and changed in 1922 by the then pm and long-term station agent, Charley B. Moore, to conform to the station's name. Over the years people have seen fit to supply other explanations for this unusual name. It has been suggested that the station was named for either an Indian maiden or Tecumseh's brother, "The Prophet"; or for someone's 3 children, Helen, Charles, and Walter; or for Walbridge's 2 daughters, Helen and Charlotte. (He did have another daughter whose name was applied to another station, *Adele*.) According to another popular account, in pioneer times the one rd to that place was a dirt rd so bad that people would say it was hell-each-a-way. In a related tradition, 2 travelers got lost in that vicinity. One, spotting 2 rds branching off from the one they had been following, asked the other which way to go. I don't know, said the other, it seems to be hell each way. 233.

Hellier (Pike): *hehl*/yər (Hellier). This hamlet with po, once an inc town and trade center for area coal camps, centered at the mouth of Brushy Branch of Marrowbone Creek, 12 mi s of Pikeville. It was named for Ralph Augustus Hellier (1871–1906), a native of Bangor, Maine, who arrived in Pike Co around 1894 to become general manager of the Elkhorn Coal and Coke Co. and, later, the Big Sandy Co. The nearby Childers po, est by Adam Childers on Jan 24, 1906, moved to and became Hellier before the end of that year. 88, 679.

Helton (Leslie): *hehl*/tən (Helton). This hamlet with extinct po is on US 421, at the mouth of Simms Branch of Beech Fork of the Middle Fork of the Kentucky R, 13 mi s of Hyden. The po was est on Feb 5, 1885, and named for the first pm, James J. Helton, or his family. A 1919 topographic map located the community nearly 1½ mi up Big Branch, another tributary of Beech. It was apparently moved later to its present site where it came to be known also as Beech Fork.

Hemlock (McCreary). See *Stearns*

Hemphill (Letcher): *hehmp*/*hihl* (Jenkins West). This coal town with po, 1 mi n of Neon and 8½ mi ne of Whitesburg, lies at the mouth of Quillen Fork of Yonts Fork. Though officially known as Jackhorn [*djaek*/hawrn] since the po was est with this name on Nov 17, 1916, it is now locally called Hemphill. It is not known why it was first called Jackhorn or why the po continues to bear this name. The Hemphill name was applied to the camp built by the Elkhorn Coal Corp. around 1920 and honors Alexander Julian Hemphill (1856–1920) of Hemphill and Associates, a Wall Street firm that financed the Elkhorn operations. 1254, 1265.

Hempridge (Shelby): *hehmp*/rihdj (Waddy). This settlement is centered on KY 714, 1 mi s of the present I 64 and 6 mi se of Shelbyville. According to tradition, one of the largest stalks of hemp ever seen was given to Henry Clay by Will Waddy, and Clay suggested that the place where it was grown be called Hempridge. A Hempridge po was in operation between 1889 and 1911. 783.

Henderson (Henderson): *hehn*/dər/sən (Henderson, Evansville South). This 3rd class industrial city and seat of Henderson Co is on the Ohio R, less than 5 mi s of Evansville, Indiana, and 95 mi wsw of downtown Louisville. In Dec 1778 the Virginia House of Delegates granted 200,000 acres between the Green and Ohio rs to Col. Richard Henderson's Transylvania Co. In the 1790s, the co.'s heirs est a town there on the site of a small stockade long known as Red Banks for the high red-colored bluffs overlooking the Ohio R. Gen. Samuel Hopkins and Col. Thomas Allen laid out the town in 1797 and named it for Colonel Henderson. The po was est on Oct 1, 1801, with George Holloway, pm, and the town was inc in 1810. 983.

Henderson County: *hehn*/dər/sən. 438 sq mi. Pop 40,849. Seat: Henderson. This co was est in 1798 from part of Christian Co and named for Col. Richard Henderson, land speculator from North Carolina, whose Transylvania Co., in Mar 1775, negotiated the purchase from the Cherokees at Sycamore Shoals much of what was to become Kentucky. This purchase was later abrogated by the Virginia legislature and the company was compensated by a grant of 200,000 acres of what is now Henderson Co.

Hendron (McCracken): *hehn*/drən (Paducah West). This hamlet on KY 994, just n of I 24 and less than 1 mi s of the Paducah city limits, was named for a local family. It has never had its own po.

Henrico (Henry). See *Bethlehem*

Henry County: *hehn*/ree. 291 sq mi. Pop 12,740. Seat: New Castle. This co was est in 1798 from part of Shelby Co and named for Patrick Henry (1736–99), Revolutionary War statesman and patriot, member of the Continental Congress (1774–76), and governor of Virginia (1776–79 and 1784–86).

Henry Court House PO (Henry). See *New Castle*

Henry PO (Morgan). See *Woodsbend*

Henrysville PO (Logan). See *Lewisburg*

Henshaw (Union): *hihn*/shaw (Dekoven). This hamlet with extinct po on KY 130, between the Illinois Central Gulf RR and Cypress Creek and 8 mi sw of Morganfield, was named for William Henshaw, who built the first home on the site and was one of the biggest farmers in the co. The po was est on Mar 18, 1887, with William H. Henshaw, pm. 238.

Hensleytown (Christian). See *Oak Grove*

Herald PO (Breathitt). See *Guerrant*

Herndon (Christian): *H3n*/dən (Herndon). This hamlet with po lies at the jct of KY 107 and 117, 7 mi ssw of Hopkinsville. The community grew up around a country store and home on nearby Knockum Hill [*nahk*/əm *hihl*], by which name it was first called. This refers to a local tradition that an early white settler had killed an Indian there with a knock on the head. The po was est on June 12, 1882, as Organette [âhr/ghən/*eht*] for the local Organ family. In 1886 it was renamed for North Carolina-born Capt. Thomas Herndon, a Clarksville, Tennessee, businessman. 1403.

Herndonsville PO (Scott). See *Stamping Ground*

Hesler (Owen): *hehs*/lər (Monterey). This hamlet with extinct po lies at the jct of KY 227 and 845, 5 mi se of Owenton. The co's first seat was located here on land sold by Jacob Hesler to Daniel McCarty Payne who laid out the town as Heslersville. A po with this name was in operation from 1820 to 1821. When a section of Gallatin Co was added to Owen in 1821, the seat was removed to the more centrally located Owenton. The po of Hesler was est on Sept 13, 1880, with William H. Sanders, pm, and closed in 1904. 647.

Heslersville (Owen). See *Hesler*

Hestand (Monroe): *hehs*/tən (Tompkinsville). This hamlet and po on KY 163, 4½ mi se of Tompkinsville, are on or near the site of what may earlier have been called Bradley Springs for a pioneer family. The po was est on July 10, 1888, and named for the family of its first pm, Joshua K. Hestand, whose father Daniel (1775–1858), a Virginian of German descent, arrived in Monroe Co in 1799. 171, 1395.

Hickman (Fulton): *hihk*/mən (Hickman). This 4th class city and seat of Fulton Co rests on a series of levels above the Mississippi R, just s of the mouth of Bayou de Chien, and 207 mi sw of downtown Louisville. In 1819 James Mills built a log home on the bluff. He was soon joined by others and a po called Mills Pt. was est on Feb 18, 1830.

In or about 1834, G.W.F. Marr (some historians give his initials as G. W. L.) acquired most of the site and laid off a town to which he gave the name Hickman, his wife's maiden name. Under this name the town was inc in 1841 and became the seat of the new co in 1845, when the name of the po was also changed to Hickman. 686.

Hickman County: *hihk*/mən. 245 sq. mi. Pop 6,065. Seat: Clinton. Est in 1821 from parts of Caldwell and Livingston cos, Hickman Co comprised the whole of the Kentucky portion of what had been purchased from the Chickasaw Indians in 1818, thereafter called the Jackson Purchase. It was named for Capt. Paschal Hickman, one of the 9 officers killed in or soon after the Battle of River Raisin, Jan 22, 1813, for whom Kentucky cos were named.

Hickory (Graves): *hihk*/ə/ree (Hickory). This recently disinc 6th class city with po is located between the Illinois Central Gulf RR tracks and US 45, 4½ mi n of Mayfield. It was est as a rr stop around 1856 on land owned by John Johns, J. W. Kemble, and R. K. Williams, and named for the huge hickory trees in the area. Johns became the first pm of Hickory Grove on Mar 9, 1858. The po name was reduced to one word in 1896 and then simply to Hickory in 1914 to avoid confusion with other similarly named pos in Kentucky, but Hickory Grove has remained the official name since the community's inc in 1873. 169, 1228.

Hickory Flat (Simpson): *hihk*/ree *flaet* (Hickory Flat). Almost nothing remains of this once prosperous crossroads hamlet at the jct of KY 100 and 622, 5½ mi e of Franklin which was named for its location in a grove of young hickory trees. The po was est on Mar 7, 1836 by the storekeeper, Samuel Hatfield, who became the first pm. It was discontinued in 1939. 18.

Hickory Grove (Graves). See *Hickory*

Hidalgo (Wayne): heye/*dael*/ghoh (Powersburg). This hamlet with extinct po is on KY 200, .2 mi w of its jct with KY 834 and 7 mi sw of Monticello. The po was est on Feb 2, 1895, by John H. Dalton, local storekeeper, who, seeking a unique name, spotted this word meaning a Spanish nobleman in a dictionary. The po was discontinued in 1975. 1376.

High Bridge (Jessamine): *heye brihdj* (Wilmore). This hamlet with extinct po, 7 mi sw of Nicholasville, is just below and across the Kentucky R from the mouth of Dix R in Mercer Co. Here the Cincinnati based Queen and Crescent (now Southern) RR built a bridge over the Kentucky R. Designed by John A. Roebling of Brooklyn Bridge fame and opened for use in 1877, it was the first cantilevered bridge in North America and the highest rr bridge over a navigable stream in the US. A po called North Tower was est here by James M. Dorman in or before 1878 and renamed for the bridge in 1888. It closed in 1977. 551, 563.

High Grove (Nelson): *heye ghrohv* (Fairfield). This hamlet with extinct po, where US 31E/150 crosses the East Fork of Coxs Creek and is joined by KY 48, is 10 mi n of Bardstown. The name is derived from the original location of the po, est on Jan 8, 1830, with Samuel Cassell, pm, in a grove of trees on a high elevation about 2 mi s of its present site. The po retained its name when it moved sometime in the 1890s; it closed in 1906. The name is given as one word on contemporary maps. 1386.

High Knob (Jackson): *heye nahb* (Tyner). This settlement with extinct po is on Sexton Creek and KY 577, 10½ mi sse of McKee. The po was est about a mi e on Oct 24, 1876, with Jesse H. McWhorter, pm, and named for a nearby high knob at the head of Huckleberry Creek. In 1897 the po was moved to where it remained until it closed. 1418.

Highland (Breathitt). See *Guerrant*

Highland (Lincoln): *heye*/lənd (Halls Gap). This hamlet is on KY 1247, 6 mi s of Stanford. Estes Marsh est the po on Sept 30, 1869, and is said to have named it either for its location on a ridge or for the Scottish Highlands whence his family had emigrated to America, or both. The po closed in 1907. 1276, 1448.

Highland Heights (Campbell): *heye*/lənd *heyets* (Newport). This 5th class city lies between the cities of Southgate on the n, Wilder on the w, and Cold Spring on the s, less than 3 mi sse of the Newport po. It was inc in 1927 as a developing suburb s of Cincinnati and aptly named for its situation on the relatively high elevation that, for much of the 19th cent, was called The Highlands. 463, 1300.

Highland Heights PO (Campbell). See *Cold Spring*

Highland Park (Knox). See *Heidrick*

Highoaka (Highoakie) (Monroe). See *Akersville*

High Plains (Breckinridge): *heye plānz* (Big Spring). An extinct po, est (in error) as Highplains on Aug 15, 1921, with Herman Blair, pm, and discontinued in 1927, served the farms in the middle of a high ridge between Custer and Big Spring, 12 mi e of Hardinsburg. Two mi e of the po site are a few homes now collectively known as High Plains Corner. 1398.

High Plains Corner (Breckinridge). See *High Plains*

Highsplint (Harlan): *heye*/*splihnt* (Louellen, Nolansburg). This coal town and station are on the L&N RR's Cumberland Valley Division, at the mouth of Seagraves Creek, a branch of Clover Fork of the Cumberland R, and 10½ mi ene of Harlan. The community and its recently discontinued po, est on Feb 7, 1918, with John D. Casey, pm, were named for the High Splint Coal Co., which had opened a mine in that vicinity. The rr was completed to this point in June 1919 and the station est there was first called Seagrave. 97, 1173.

Highway (Clinton): *heye*/wā (Albany). This settlement with extinct po is on KY 1351, 4 mi nw of Albany. According to tradition, when the residents of this community could not decide what to name their new po, the local preacher opened his Bible to Isa. 35:8 and suggested the "highway" in Christ's kingdom. The po was est on July 28, 1892, with Bro. John S. Keen, the cofounder with his wife of the local Bible Mission School, as pm. It closed in 1963. 566, 1263.

Hi Hat (Floyd): *heye* haet (McDowell). This coal town with po lies at the jct of KY 122 and 979 and the confluence of Clear Creek and the Left Fork of Beaver Creek, 19 mi s of Prestonsburg. The local po was est as Fed on Aug 17, 1881, with Jerry Caudill, pm, and may have been named for Fed Akers, a resident. Later the station located where the C&O RR's Clear Creek Spur leaves the main Left Beaver Branch line was called Clear Creek Junction. In 1943 both names were changed to Hi Hat for the Hi Hat Elkhorn Mining Co., which opened its local mine in 1936. The co., whose trade mark was a big top hat, claimed it produced a high or top grade of coal. The co. requested the name changes in part to avoid confusion with the Pike Co po of Fedscreek and to insure uniformity in the names of po, station, and community. 995, 1370, 1431.

Hike PO (Carter). See *Boone Furnace*

Hilda (Rowan): *hihl*/duh, *hihl*/dee (Farmers). This hamlet with extinct po lies at the jct of KY 32 and the Bull Fork Rd, 3½ mi nw of Morehead. Its po was est on June 30, 1897, in the home of the local mail carrier, James Thompson. The name of his daughter, Alice, was at first suggested for the po, but she preferred Hilda for a character in a book she was then reading and this name was submitted instead. The po closed in 1943. 1105.

Hillsboro (Fleming): *hihlz*/buh/roh (Hillsboro). This village with po lies at the jct of KY 111 and 158, 9 mi sse of Flemingsburg. It was first settled by the Foudray family and early bore the name Foudraysville [*fū*/dreez/vihl]. Later residents changed the name to Hillsboro for its location, and the po of this name was est on Sept 19, 1833. It was founded as a town in 1839, inc in 1846, and disincorporated in 1960. 492.

Hillside (Muhlenberg): *hihl*/seyed (Greenville, Central City West). This coal town with extinct po is on the Illinois Central Gulf RR, just n of Powderly, less than 1 mi s of the Western Kentucky Parkway, and 1¼ mi n of Greenville. The nearby po of Mercer Station, est on June 3, 1873, with William Mercer, pm, was moved to the Hillside site in 1904 and renamed for its location on the side of a hill. 1253.

Hillsville PO (Livingston). See *Tiline*

Hill Top (McCreary): *hihl*/tahp (Barthell). This po is in Bill Winchester's store on KY 92, 3 mi w of Whitley City. It was est on Feb 18, 1925, with John H. Bryant, pm, and named for its location on the ridge overlooking the now extinct mining town of *Yamacraw* on the Big South Fork R. 1384.

Hillview (Bullitt): *hihl*/vyū (Brooks). This 4th class residential city without po extends from the Jefferson Co line s for a little over 1 mi, and is less than ½ mi e of I 65 and 4½ mi n of Shepherdsville. It was inc in 1974 from parts of Maryville and 2 other subdivisions. Scrupulously avoiding existing names, the city fathers chose "the neutral and idyllic Hillview (several knobs are visible in the distance)." Or perhaps someone recalled the old Hill View po, which had served a section of the co from 1872 to 1874. The Maryville [*maer*/ee/vihl] subdivision was developed in 1960 by John A. Walser who named it for his mother and daughter and the Blessed Virgin. 303, 1166.

Hiltonian (Perry): hihl/*tohn*/ə/yən (Hazard North). This coal town with extinct po on KY 1440 and the North Fork of the Kentucky R, just n of Hazard's city limits, was named for J. B. Hilton of Chicago, an official of the co. that operated the local mine. The po was est on May 21, 1927, with Radford Stickler, pm. 1217.

Himlerville (Martin). See *Beauty*

Himyar (Knox): *hihm*/yər (Artemus). This hamlet with po and L&N RR station on the Cumberland R, 4½ mi se of Barbourville, is said to have been founded around 1898 by Stephen Watt on land he had acquired from one Sam Witt. In a public meeting to choose its name, James J. Purcifull "suggested that the fastest growing town in Kentucky be named after the Commonwealth's fastest race horse and this suggestion was enthusiastically adopted," although Himyar was upset by Day Star in the 4th Kentucky Derby on May 21, 1878. An obvious folk etymology was offered by Joe Creason: a local resident had lost a promising stallion colt. A search was begun and the man who found him shouted "him yar!" The horse's stable was later adapted for use as a po and "the welcome words of the colt's finder became its name." The po was est on May 28, 1906, with Joseph Liford, pm. 306, 356, 738.

Hindman (Knott): *hahn(d)*/mən (Hindman). This 5th class city and seat of Knott Co is on KY 80, at the forks of Troublesome Creek, 153 mi ese of downtown Louisville. In April 1884, 3 commissioners appointed to locate a site for the new co's seat est it here. The McPherson po est here on Feb 17, 1874, with Peyton M. Duke, pm was renamed on Oct 7, 1884 for then Lt. Gov. James P. Hindman. Duke gave the land for the town of Hindman, which was inc in 1886.194, 456, 944.

Hines Mills PO (Ohio). See *Sulphur Spring, Dundee*

Hinesville (Shelby). See *Christiansburg*

Hinsleyton PO (Christian). *Oak Grove*

Hippo (Floyd): *hihp*/oh (Martin). This po and store are on KY 805, 2½ mi up Brush

Creek from its confluence with the Right Fork of Beaver Creek, 10 mi ssw of Prestonsburg. The po was first est on Mar 21, 1902, on Salt Creek, 4 mi s, and named for a local resident, Bee Madison Craft, who was called "Hippo" because he complained all the time. His wife Rhoda was the first pm. The po moved at least one time and then closed in 1919. It was reest in 1926 at its present location with Ruben M. Hicks, pm. The nicknam "Hippo" for a hypochondriac or chronic complainer has been reported in other states of the upper South. 253, 1391.

Hiram (Harlan): *hahr*/əm (Louellen). This hamlet and station on the L&N RR's Cumberland Valley Division are on US 119 and the Poor Fork of Cumberland R, 16 mi ene of Harlan. The station, est around 1920, was named for landowner Hiram Lewis. The area does not have its own po. 880.

Hiseville (Barren): *heyes*/vihl (Hiseville). This 6th class city with po is centered at the jct of KY 70 and 740, 7 mi nne of Glasgow. The po of Blue Spring Grove, est on Apr 25, 1828, in a 3000-acre grove on Blue Spring Creek, 1½ miles n, was moved here in 1849. Several names were suggested for what was to become Hiseville, then a mere crossroads settlement—Amity, Social Point, and others were rejected—until Harve Jameson, a resident, proposed in fun that it be called Goosehorn. Curiously, this seemed to satisfy his neighbors, for it remained the more or less official name until Hiseville was adopted for the po on Feb 6, 1867. It honored Elijah Hise (1802–1867), then US congressman from that district. The town was chartered in 1868 and reinc in 1969. The name Goosehorn is generally thought to have been a derogation; yet there is one popular account of a dispute that early arose between 2 local factions or families regarding the geese that one or both of them raised. 66, 895.

Hisle (also called **Callis Grove**) (Trimble): *heyes*/əl, *kael*/əs *ghrohv* (Madison East). Almost nothing remains of this hamlet and po, now generally referred to as Callis Grove, on US 421, 3 mi n of Bedford. The first po to serve this vicinity was the short-lived Callis, from June 1893 to Sept 1894, with Robert E. Callis, pm. On June 4, 1909, Callis reest the po in his store as Hisle for a Trimble Co family, and was its only pm before it closed in 1913. A Methodist Church group built a large open-air tabernacle in a nearby grove and is said to have applied the name Callis Grove to it and thus to the community. 913, 1089.

Hislope (Pulaski): *heye*/slohp (Delmer). This extinct po on KY 235, 6½ mi sw of Somerset, was est on July 30, 1924, with Ethus Burton, pm, and named for a local family. 1410.

Hispanola (Madison). See *Panola*

Hitchins (Carter): *hihch*/ənz (Grayson). This village with po centers on the intersection of KY 1 and 773, 2½ mi s of Grayson. By 1873 the E.K. RR had been built to this point, to be joined in Dec 1881 by the Elizabethtown Lexington and Big Sandy (now C&O) RR. The town that developed at this site was then called E.K. Junction. A po est there on Oct 16, 1882, was named Anglin for the first telegraph operator at the Junction. These 2 names identified the place until May 1912, when both po and community were renamed for E. S. Hitchins, the manager of General Refractories, the fire brick plant just completed there. 36, 494, 1322.

Hobbs Station (Jefferson). See *Anchorage*

Hode (Martin): hohd (Webb). This hamlet with po is on KY 292, just below the confluence of Little Elk Creek and the Tug Fork R, 5½ mi e of Inez. The po was est on June 3, 1921, with Bertha Hensley, pm, and named for her brother, the late Hodeviah [*hoh*/dee/veye] Hensley, son of Rev. William Henry Hensley, a local Baptist preacher and early settler of the area. 1169, 1360.

Hodgensville PO (LaRue). See *Hodgenville*

Hodgenville (LaRue): *hahdj*/ən/vihl (Hodgenville). This 4th class city and seat of LaRue Co on US 31E, 43 mi s of downtown Louisville, is on the site of Robert Hodgen's mill. Hodgen (1742–1810), an English-born Virginian, acquired a 10,000-acre tract on the North Fork of the Nolin R, where in 1789 he built his mill. This soon became the social center of a settlement that, in 1818, by petition of his widow and sons, officially became Hodgenville. When this section of Hardin Co became LaRue in 1843, the town became its co seat. While the town has always been Hodgenville, the po was Hodgensville from its inception on Dec 7, 1826, till Mar 2, 1904. Now the names agree. 144.

Hoggetown (Rowan). See *Elliottsville*

Hogue (Pulaski): hohgh (Science Hill). This po on Fishing Creek, at the jct of KY 1246 and 1676 and 6 mi nw of Somerset, was est on Jan 31, 1908, with Hugh Frank Taylor, pm. After several names had been rejected by the Post Office Department, Taylor submitted that of a recent arrival in the community, one Pete Hogue, and this was accepted. 1410.

Holland (Allen): *hahl*/ən[d] (Holland). This hamlet with po lies at the jct of KY 99 and 100, 7 mi ese of Scottsville. The po was est on Sept 20, 1881, with John H. Francis, pm, and named for the community that had grown up around the house built by William Holland in 1810. 101, 1281.

Hollyvilla (Jefferson). See *Fairdale*

Holt PO (Breckinridge). See *Addison*

Hombre (Perry). See *Fusonia*

Homer (Logan): *hoh*/mə(r) (Homer). The remains of a once thriving rural trade center are on KY 915, 5.8 mi n of its jct with KY 79 and 7 mi n of Russellville. The community grew up around a large spring-powered multipurpose mill owned by Gray B. Dunn, who also est the po on Mar 8, 1878, which he named for Homer Felts (1870–1967), the son of a local storekeeper. 206, 1344.

Home Valley (Muhlenberg). See *Penrod*

Honeybee (McCreary): *huhn*/ee/bee (Cumberland Falls, Wiborg). This po on KY 90, 9½ mi ne of Whitley City, was est on Sept 21, 1905, with Jasper M. Harp, pm, and named for the swarms of honey bees that were then observed to fly wild in the nearby woods.

Hoodoo (Grayson). See *Pine Knob*

Hope (Montgomery): hohp (Preston). This hamlet with po lies at the jct of KY 713 and 965, 8½ mi ese of Mt. Sterling. When the Post Office Department rejected Marion B. Chester's petition for a po to be named for the prominent Magowan family, he suggested Slate, for the nearby creek. This too was turned down and, instructed to select a short name, he submitted Hope. Perhaps he hoped this would be sufficient. The po was est on Aug 9, 1890, with Chester as pm, and the community was named for the po. 507.

Hopewell (Bourbon). See *Paris*

Hopewell (Greenup): *hohp*/wehl (Oldtown). This rural settlement is on KY 1, at the mouth of Crane Creek, a tributary of the Little Sandy R and 12 mi ssw of Greenup. It was named for an iron furnace converted in 1833 by William Ward from an old bloomery forge he had built in 1824. The furnace was named in turn for a famous Pennsylvania furnace in hopes that it would prove as successful as its name source. Some, however, say the furnace, which ceased operations in 1844, was built by Richard Deering and named for the Hopewell family. Contrary to some opinions, the furnace was probably never called Camp Branch for there is no record of any such stream in the area. The old Eastern Kentucky RR station built there in 1871 housed the Hopewell po, which was est by Samuel M. Jackson on Nov 17, 1874. The po was discontinued in 1957. 1092, 1177, 1277, 1447.

Hopkins County: *hahp*/kənz. 552 sq mi. Pop 46,174. Seat: Madisonville. Est in 1806 from part of Henderson Co, Hopkins Co was named for Gen. Samuel Hopkins (1753–1819), officer in the American Revolution and War of 1812, member of the Kentucky legislature (1800–06 and 1809–13), and US congressman from Kentucky (1813–15).

Hopkins Court House PO (Hopkins). See *Madisonville*

Hopkinsville (Christian): *hahp*/kihnz/vihl (Hopkinsville, Church Hill, Kelly). This 3rd class city and seat of Christian Co is centered at the jct of US 41 and 68, 125 mi sw of downtown Louisville. It was est as the seat of the newly created co in Nov 1797 and named Christian Court House. By 1798 the co order books had begun to refer to the town as Elizabeth, probably for the wife of the first settler, Bartholomew T. Wood, a North Carolinian who may have arrived in 1794 and deeded the land for the new town. On Dec 12, 1804, by an act of the General Assembly, the name was officially changed to Hopkinsville to avoid confusion with Elizabethtown in Hardin Co. The new name honored Gen. Samuel Hopkins (1753–1819), a Revolutionary War officer who, in 1799, had become judge of the first Henderson Co Court and later served in the Kentucky legislature and US Congress. The po was est on Apr 9, 1804, as Christian Court House but a short while later was renamed for the town. This explanation has been given for the nickname Hoptown: "Back in the 1890s, Hopkinsville and Christian Co were the only legally voted wet city and county on the L&N Railroad between Evansville and Nashville. Tradition has it that as the railway coaches would approach Hopkinsville the passengers would encounter of the conductor 'How soon would we be to Hopkinsville? I want to hop off and get a drink.'" 1403.

Hopper PO (Knox). See *Fount, Girdler*

Hoppers Tan Yard PO (Todd). See *Kirkmansville*

Hopson (Caldwell): *hahp*/sən (Cobb). This crossroads hamlet with extinct po lies at the jct of KY 139 and 514, 7 mi s of Princeton. The po was est on Feb 12, 1885, by Louis A. Hopson and named for his pioneer family, probably for its progenitor, John Addison Hopson, who was born in North Carolina about 1810. The po closed in 1907. 1196, 1278.

Hoptown (Christian). See *Hopkinsville*

Horace PO (Anderson). See *Fox Creek*

Horse Branch (Ohio): *hawrs brănch* (Rosine). This village with po is on the Illinois Central Gulf RR and Horse Branch of Caney Creek, 11 mi e of Hartford. There was a stop here in antebellum times for a change of horses on the Owensboro-Morgantown stage run. According to one account, it was customary, after a long trip, to take the horses to the branch for a dip. On one occasion a horse got stuck in the mud and local people ran about excitedly crying "horse in the branch!" The Elizabethtown and Paducah (Illinois Central) RR was built through in 1871 and a station was built on land deeded by William M. Miller and Job Arnold. The po was est on Mar 8, 1871, with Miller as the first pm. Over the past few decades the community has shifted ½ mi n to US 62. 255, 703, 1400.

Horse Cave (Hart): *hawrs kāv* (Horse Cave). This 5th class industrial city lies at the jct of US 31W and KY 218, 5 mi s of Munfordville. The town was est in the 1840s by Maj. Albert Anderson of Barren Co, who in 1858 donated land for the L&N depot on condition that the station would always be called Horse Cave. Several accounts have been offered for the name of the large cave (also called Hidden River Cave) in the center of town for which the town and station were named. The Indians or a gang of horse thieves are said to have used the cave to hide their horses; or a frightened horse fell off the cliff into a sink leading down into the cave; or the cave's large entrance suggested the adjective, for anything unusually large in those days was called "horse." The po of Horse Cave was est on Mar 1, 1860, with William J. Burd, pm, and the town was inc under this name in 1864. In 1869 local residents changed the name to Caverna, but the confusion that arose from the inability to change the station's name led, in 1879, to the restoration of Horse Cave. *Caverna* has been preserved in the name of the independent school district shared with neighboring Cave City. 582, 863.

Horse Shoe Bottom (Russell): *hawrs* shū *baht*/əm (Jamestown). This extinct po about 3½ mi sse of Jamestown, was est on June 6, 1822, with William Green, pm. It served the area contained within the horseshoe-shaped bend of the Cumberland R, an area extending some 2 mi along the s side of the r, from a point opposite the mouth of Greasy Creek to a point across from and slightly above the mouth of Wolf Creek. In 1950 it was inundated by the waters of Lake Cumberland. 1233.

Hoskinston (Leslie): *hahs*/kənz/tən (Hoskinston). This hamlet with po is on US 421 and the Middle Fork of the Kentucky R, opposite the mouth of Greasy Creek, 5 mi s of Hyden. It was named for Carlo Hoskins who had settled in this vicinity shortly before he est the po on Feb 5, 1887, about 1½ mi s of the present site. 1248.

Hot Spot (Letcher): *haht*/spaht (Blackey, Roxana). This residential settlement with po, a former coal camp, is on KY 160, about ½ mi up Smoot Creek from the North Fork of the Kentucky R, and 4 mi w of Whitesburg. At or near the site of a community that may have been aptly called simply The Mouth of Smoot Creek [smūt], with a po called Smoot Creek in operation from 1890 to 1914, a Tennessee man arrived to develop a local coal seam. According to tradition, he named his camp Dalna [dael/nə] for his girl friend, Dalna Hayes. Here the Dalna po was est on July 1, 1918, with William B. Price, pm. When his ardor for Dalna had cooled and a new flame named Elsie had come to replace her in his affections, the young developer renamed his co., camp, and, in 1923, the po Elsiecoal [*ehl*/see/*kohl*]. Shortly after this camp closed, John A. Webb and David Hayes's Hot Spot Coal Co. began operations about ½ mi up Smoot Creek. In 1932 the po moved to the new camp site and was renamed Hot Spot. Ten years later it became Premium [*preem*/yuhm], though the Hot Spot name survives in local usage for the community. Why the Smoot Creek and Premium names were applied remains a mystery. 37, 737, 1218, 1265.

Houckville (Lawrence): *howk*/vihl (Blaine). This extinct po on KY 201, at the head of Cherokee Creek, and 12½ mi w of Louisa, was est on Sept 20, 1920, and probably named by and for its first pm, John H. Houck. 1095.

Howards Mill (Montgomery): *hahr*/ədz *mihl* (Preston). This 19th cent mill village and farm trade center, now only a hamlet on the KY 1331 and Slate Creek, 4½ mi e of Mt. Sterling, was named for James Howard's watermill, built there in 1845. The po was est on June 20, 1851, as Howard's Mills (there were actually 2 mills there by that time), and after an intermittent existence and a name change to Howard Mills in 1897, closed in 1903. 1237.

Howardstown (Nelson): *how*/ərdz/*town* (Howardstown). This hamlet with po lies at the jct of KY 84 and 247, ¾ mi e of the Rolling Fork R and 16½ mi ssw of Bardstown. It was named for the Howard family whose progenitor, William, an Englishman, settled on the Rolling Fork R around 1811. The po was est as Lunar on Mar 10, 1884, named for the nearby creek. Francis M. Howard, the first pm, was in this position when the po was renamed Howardstown in 1893. Around 1900, the store and po were moved to the present site to escape the flooding potential of the r. 199.

Howardsville PO (Daviess). See *Panther*

Howel (Christian): *how*/əl (Herndon). This hamlet with extinct po at the jct of KY 345 and 1483, 9 mi s of Hopkinsville was also a station on the defunct Clarksville & Princeton Branch of the L&N RR. Both the po, est on Mar 31, 1886, and the station, were named for Archer Howell, then cashier of the Clarksville National Bank and mayor of that city as well as stockholder of the Indiana Alabama & Texas RR, which became the Clarksville & Princeton Branch in 1887. A local effort to name the station and po Whitfield for (William) Whitfield Radford, a prosperous area landowner, was not successful. The Post Office Department's spelling error was apparently never corrected. 1403.

Howe's Valley PO (Hardin). See *Howe Valley*

Howe Valley (Hardin): *how vael*/ee (Howe Valley). This hamlet extends for about a mi along KY 86, which cuts through the valley of this name, 10 mi w of Elizabethtown. The po, est as Howe's Valley on Sept 8, 1852, with George W. Tate, pm, was named for the valley, which honored the pioneer family of John Howe (died 1830), a Revolutionary War veteran from Red Stone, Pennsylvania. In 1894, noting the resemblance of the name to Hawes Valley and Hawesville, the Post Office Department changed it to Howevalley and by this spelling it was known until it closed in 1908. 823, 1420.

Huddy (Pike): *huhd*/ee (Belfry). This village with po is centered at the jct of US 119 and KY 199, at the mouth of Coburn Branch of Pond Creek, 13½ mi ne of Pikeville. It was named for Thomas H. Huddy of Williamson, West Virginia, the general superintendent of the Sudduth Fuel Co., which operated a coal mine in the vicinity in the early 1920s. Its po was est on Dec 12, 1924, with Roy Charles Runyon, pm. 1145.

Hudson (Breckinridge): *huhd*/sən (Custer). This hamlet with po on KY 401, 12 mi se of Hardinsburg, was probably named for its first settler, Joseph Hudson, who may have arrived in the vicinity around 1810. A po called Hudsonville, presumably for him or his family, is said to have been in existence at this site by 1840 when Ralph E. Cox became pm, though it may have been est as early as 1828. On Jan 2, 1880 this po was moved to a point 2.7 mi ne and renamed Constantine by which name it is still in operation. On Mar 16, 1880, the present po of Hudson was est with Will G. Holbrook, pm. 1398.

Hudsonville (Breckinridge). See *Hudson*

Hueysville (also called **Bosco**) (Floyd): *hyū*/eez/vihl, *bahs*/koh (Wayland). This village is centered at the jct of KY 7 and 80 and the confluence of Saltlick Creek and the Right Fork of Beaver Creek, 12½ mi ssw of Prestonsburg. While both names now identify the village, its po, except for 2 years in the late 1880s, has been known as Hueysville since John Morris est it on July 13, 1858. It was named for a Mr. Huey (perhaps Robert S. Huey, a Pennsylvania-born clerk who is listed in the 1850 Census of Floyd Co). From 1887 to 1889, when Mike Staley was pm, the po was known as Mike. A short distance away, another po called Bosco, for reasons now unknown, operated from 1902 to 1916 when its papers were transferred to Hueysville. To this point in 1914 the Elkhorn & Beaver Valley (now C&O) Ry extended its line and est the Bosco Station. 213, 1047.

Huff (Edmonson): huhf (Brownsville). This hamlet with po lies at the jct of KY 70 and 187, 6 mi nw of Brownsville. The po est on Mar 26, 1889, by James C. Hampton, was named for a local family. 942.

Humble (Russell): *uhm*/bəl (Russell Springs). This extinct po at the jct of US 127 and KY 1545, 6 mi n of Jamestown, was est on Dec 13, 1906, with William L. Simmons, pm, and named for Miss Pearl Humble or her family. 1220, 1233.

Humility (Calloway). See *New Concord*

Hummel (Rockcastle): *huhm*/əl (Wildie). Almost nothing remains of this co. town ½ mi e of the L&N RR's Langford Station, 3½ mi ne of Mount Vernon. The town was built up in the early 20th cent around the freestone quarry and mill acquired in 1896 by the Cincinnati-based David Hummel Building Co. for which it was named. The po was est on June 11, 1923, with James A. Franklin, pm, and has since closed. The vicinity is now better known as Langford Station, probably named for the earlier Langford community founded by the pioneer Langford family. 841, 1243.

Humphrey PO (Casey). See *Mt. Olive*

Huntertown (Woodford): *huhnt*/ər/town (Versailles). This black settlement is on the Huntertown Rd between the Bluegrass Parkway and US 60, 1 mi se of Versailles. It was named for Ab. C. Hunter who sold residential lots on this site to blacks. It has never had its own po. 1269.

Hunnewell (Greenup): *huhn*/ee/wehl (Argillite). This rural settlement with extinct po on KY 207, 10½ mi s of Greenup, was the site of an important 19th cent iron furnace. In 1845 the Greenup Furnace, named for the co, was built by John Campbell and others on the site of a small farming settlement. The vicinity was known by this name until the Eastern Kentucky Ry extended its tracks to it in 1868 and est a station which was named Hunnewell for Walter Hunnewell, a Boston merchant and co-owner of the rr co. In 1869 Hunnewell and his colleagues bought the old furnace, rebuilt it, and changed its name to Hunnewell to conform to that of the station. The po was est on June 24, 1874, with Lewis Beiter, pm, and closed in 1950. 23, 188, 1092, 1447.

Hunt PO (Clark). See *Pinchem*

Huntsville (Butler): *huhnts*/vihl (Rochester). This hamlet with po on KY 106, less than 1½ mi from Mud R and 11 mi wsw of Morgantown, was settled around 1857 by Daniel Hunt, a farmer and merchant, and first called Gum Grove for the many gum trees there. On Oct 23, 1878, the local po was est as Huntsville for Daniel, and in 1888 the town of Huntsville was inc by the legislature. 574.

Hurricane PO (Crittenden). See *Tolu*

Hurst (Breathitt): h3st (Campton). This extinct po lay ¼ mi up Lower Crooked Shoal Branch of the North Fork of the Kentucky R, and 8 mi nw of Jackson. The po was named by and for Leslie Hurst who est it in his store on Jan 14, 1925. 1236.

Hustonville (Lincoln): *hyū*/stən/vihl (Hustonville). This 5th class city with po lies at the jct of US 127 and KY 78, 8 mi wsw of Stanford. In pioneer times the community was called The Cross Roads for its location at the jct of trails between the Kentucky and Green rs and between Stanford and the Falls of the Ohio (or Louisville). It was later known as Farmington. The po was est as Hanging Fork, for the creek which flows through it to Dix R, on May 30, 1818, with John Murrell, pm. For 3 months in 1826 the po was called New Store, and then Hanging Fork again until, on Apr 1, 1837, it formally adopted the Hustonville name under which the town had been chartered the year before. This name honored the 2 landowning Huston brothers, descendants of Stephenson Huston, a Revolutionary War veteran. The late Will N. Craig, a co historian, gave this account of the naming of Hanging Fork: "It is said that two desperadoes who had escaped from the authorities in Virginia were recaptured in the vicinity. After their apprehension, when enroute to Virginia where they would be hung for their depredations, they gave the officers much trouble, and the officers, being weary of the watch, decided to hang the culprits at once and thus relieve themselves of an onerous duty and at the same time carry out the mandate of the court. The hanging took place at the forks of the stream in the edge of the settlement, and thereafter both the stream and the village were called *Hanging Fork*.'' 876.

Hyattsville (Garrard): *hah*/yəts/vihl (Lancaster). This extinct po and rr station were at the jct of the present KY 52 and 1295, 2½ mi e of Lancaster. The station on the L&N RR's Richmond Branch, completed in 1868, was located on part of the 2000 acres owned by Allen Hiatt (*sic*) for whom it was named. The po was est there on July 15, 1869, with John W. East, pm. No one has been able to account for the discrepancy in the spelling of the 2 names. The po was discontinued in 1917 and the station was closed by 1934. 918, 1225.

Hyden (Leslie): *hah*/dən (Hyden East and Hyden West) This 6th class city and seat of Leslie Co is on US 421 and at the mouth of Rockhouse Creek, a branch of the Middle Fork of the Kentucky R, 139 mi se of downtown Louisville. It was founded on John Lewis's farm in 1878 as the seat of the newly est co and named for John Hyden (1814–83), then state senator from Clay Co and one of the commissioners appointed to est Leslie Co. The po began operation in Mar 1879 with Leander Crawford, pm, and the town was inc in 1882. 1248.

Hylton (Pike): *hihl*/tən (Jenkins East). This hamlet with extinct po is on KY 197 and Elkhorn Creek, 16 mi s of Pikeville. The po, est on Sept 16, 1914, with Alexander Moore, pm, was named for Robert Hylton. 1456.

Ibex (Elliott): *ah*/behx (Bruin). This extinct po was about ¼ mi w of the Little Sandy R and 5½ mi nne of Sandy Hook. The po was est on Aug 19, 1890, and named by Martin W. Green, its first pm, for the wild mountain goat that inhabits much of Alpine Europe; no one knows why. The po was discontinued in 1963. 1412.

Ice (Letcher): ahs (Whitesburg). This extinct po and coal camp lay at the jct of KY 588 and 931 and the confluence of Cowan Creek and the North Fork of the Kentucky R, 1½ mi sw of Whitesburg. When the po was est on Dec 23, 1897, the r at that point was so jammed with ice that the visiting postal inspector had little difficulty coming up with an appropriate name. A modest coal camp was est at that site sometime around World War I. 745, 1265.

Independence (Kenton): ihn/də/*pehn*/dəns (Independence). This 5th class city and seat of Kenton Co was est in 1840 at what is now the jct of KY 17 and 2045, 10 mi s of downtown Covington, as the seat of the new co, and was presumably named to mark its independence from Campbell Co. The crossroads site was donated by pioneer John McCollum. The first po to serve this area was est on Nov 20, 1837, as Everetts Creek by Isaac Everett. A month later Everett renamed it Crews Creek, which may suggest its location on what is now Cruises Creek, 4½ mi s. The following July it was changed to Bagby, site unknown, by Thomas H. Hordern, who then moved it to or renamed it Independence on Oct 7, 1840. The town was inc in 1842. The city's limits now extend from the Boone Co line e past the Taylor Mill Rd, making it n Kentucky's largest city in area. 541, 941.

Indian Bottom (Letcher). See *Blackey*

Indian Creek (Owsley). See *Ricetown*

Indian Fields PO (Clark). See *Indian Old Fields*

Indian Old Fields (Clark): *ihn*/dyən *ohl(d)* feeldz (Levee, Hedges). This settlement with extinct po on the plain drained by the Lulbegrud and Upper Howard Creeks, ¼ mi n of the Mountain Parkway and 9½ mi ese of Winchester, is on the site of what has long been considered the only genuine Indian settlement in Kentucky. The village of Eskippakithiki [ehs/*kih*/pə/kə/*thee*/kə] (Shawnee for "place of blue licks," referring to the salt deposits on Lulbegrud Creek) may have been est as early as 1718–19 by a band of Shawnee who had separated from their neighbors on the Savannah R. In 1752 John Finley built a pioneer station there, but both it and the village were abandoned the following year after an attack by hostile Indians. By 1775 other white settlers were arriving. They called the part of the plain cultivated by the Indians (the) Indian Old Corn Fields, later shortened to Indian Old Fields or simply Indian Fields, by which it is now generally known. Early pioneers, used to only small clearings in forested areas, generally designated such areas as "Indian old fields." Some historians, however, have suggested that the name referred to a place once cleared for cultivation and then returned to its natural state. On Aug 27, 1878, Levi Goff est the Indian Fields po at the se corner of the Indian Old Fields. It later served a village and station on the Lexington & Eastern (later L&N) Ry. The po recently closed. 205, 267, 873, 1349.

Inez (Martin): *ah*/*nehz*, *ah*/nehz, *ah*/neez, ah/*nehz* (Inez). This unincorporated seat of Martin Co is on KY 40, at the forks of Rockcastle Creek, 165 mi e of downtown Louisville. The vicinity, said to have been settled around 1810 by James Ward and first called Arminta Ward's Bottom, was selected in 1873 as the permanent site of the co's seat, which, for 3 years, had been located at *Warfield*. According to tradition, J. M. Stepp, commenting on the view at this place, likened it to the biblical Eden, and this name was given to the town that soon developed there. The existence of another Eden po in Kentucky, however, led to the selection of the name Inez for the po est on June 23, 1874. It was allegedly named by Leo Frank, pm of Louisa in neighboring Lawrence Co, for his daughter. Some time later, to avoid confusion, the town adopted the po name. 194, 1069.

Ingle (Pulaski): *ihŋ*/əl (Faubush). This po on KY 837, ½ mi s of Cumberland Parkway and 12½ mi w of Somerset, was est on Aug 4, 1905, and named by and for Rev. James W. Ingle, the first pm. 1410.

Insko PO (Morgan). See *Adele*

Ireland (also called **Burdick**) (Taylor): *eye*/ər/lənd, *bɜ*/dihk (Greensburg). This hamlet with extinct po lies at the jct of KY 55 and 1701, 4 mi ssw of Campbellsville. According to local tradition, a group of Presbyterians from Augusta Co, Virginia, arrived in the area around 1799 and, in 1803, founded the Ireland Seminary from which the community that grew up around it took its name. No one knows why the school was so named. The po was est as Burdick on July 10, 1882, with Alexander G. McCorkle, pm, and named for a local family. The names are used interchangeably to identify the community. 1291.

Irma (Crittenden): ɜ/mə (Cave in Rock). This extinct community was centered at the jct of the present KY 297 and 723, 9 mi wnw of Marion. On July 25, 1890, Samuel S. Sullenger est its po, which he named for his young daughter. It closed in 1913. This vicinity may also be referred to as Whites Chapel, for a church just w of the jct. 1336.

Iron Banks (Hickman). See *Columbus*

Iron Hill (Carter): *ahrn hihl*, *ah*/rən *hihl* (Tygarts Valley). Little remains of this settlement with extinct po on KY 7 and Tygarts Creek, 6½ mi nw of Grayson. The short-lived Iron Hill Furnace, built here by the Riverton Iron and Manufacturing Co. on the Lambert Ore Banks in 1873, was reorganized and renamed Charlotte Furnace [shər/*laht*/ee, shahr/*laht*/ee *fɜn*/əs] in late 1875 for the daughter of the new owner. A community grew up here and on Oct 21, 1875, the Charlotte Furnace po was est with Augustus C. Van Dyke, pm. The po closed in 1951. Since 1940 the settlement has locally been called only Iron Hill. 188, 1326.

Iron Hill (Crittenden). See *Deanwood*

Irvine (Estill): ɜ/vən, ɜ/veen (Irvine). This 4th class city and seat of Estill Co lies on the Kentucky R, opposite the mouth of Station Camp Creek, 96 mi se of downtown Louisville. It was founded in 1812 on 20½ acres owned by Gen. Green Clay and named for Col. William Irvine, both pioneer settlers of Madison Co, from which part of Estill Co was formed in 1808. Seriously wounded in the Battle of Estills Defeat in 1782, Colonel Irvine later served as clerk of Madison's co and circuit courts, was a member of the Virginia legislature and of the statehood conventions of 1787 and 1788, and died in 1820. The po was est as Irvine or Estill Court House on Mar 10, 1813, with Elijah Broaddus, pm. 782, 865.

Irvington (Breckinridge): *ɜv*/ihŋ/tuhn (Irvington, Garfield). This 5th class city with po lies at the jct of US 60 and KY 79, 10½ mi ne of Hardinsburg. R. M. Jolly and Edgar L. Bennett, 2 area businessmen, anticipating the route of the Louisville St. Louis & Texas RR, purchased 315 acres of farmland at this site. With the help of rr co. surveyors they laid off a town in 1888–89, which the co.'s chief engineer, Eugene Cornwall, called Irvington for his home in New York. On Dec 26, 1888, the local po, which storekeeper Peter P. Roberts had est as Merino on Feb 16, 1885, was renamed Irvington. Merino [mə/*ree*/noh] had been named for the nearby Mt. Merino Seminary, in operation from 1838 to 1843. 25, 736.

Irvins Store (Russell): *ɜv*/ənz *stawr* (Eli). This extinct po on KY 910, 8½ mi ne of Jamestown, was est on Jan 27, 1876, and named for its first pm, local storekeeper John D. Irvin. 1211.

Isaacs PO (Jackson). See *Bond*

Island (McLean): ah/lənd (Livermore). This 6th class city with po lies at the jct of US 431 and KY 85, 8 mi se of Calhoun. In the early 19th cent, Judge William Worthington owned a large acreage on what was known for many years as "The Island," an area of 8 sq mi surrounded during high tide by backwater from Green R and other local waterways. On Jan 15, 1829, the judge est the Worthington po in his home, ½ mi n of the present site of Island. It was discontinued in 1860. When the Owensboro and Nashville (now L&N) RR was completed in 1872, Island Station was est near Worthington's home site and a new po was organized as Island Station on May 20, 1873. Both po and town were renamed Island in 1882. 189, 435, 932.

Island Station (McLean). See *Island*

Isom (Letcher): *ahs*/əm (Blackey). This po now lies at the jct of KY 7 and 15, at the mouth of Stampers Branch of Rockhouse Creek, a branch of the North Fork of the Kentucky R, 5½ mi nw of Whitesburg. It was est on Feb 10, 1898, with Isom Sergent, pm, and prior to 1915 may have been located at the mouth of Little Colly Creek. The po and community that grew up around it were named for the local descendants of George Gideon Isom, a pioneer settler of the North Fork region, who are believed to have arrived at this site after the Civil War. The name is now limited mostly to the po, while the community is known locally as The Stock Sale; it has been a market for area livestock since the 1930s. 1265.

Isonville (Elliott): *ahs*/ən/vihl (Isonville). This hamlet with po lies at the jct of KY 32 and 706, 4 mi ese of Sandy Hook. The po was est on May 13, 1886, and named for Archibald Ison (1780–1871), a Virginian who was the first settler of the forks of Newcombe Creek. 1412.

Iuka (Livingston): ah/*yū*/kə (Grand Rivers). This hamlet with po lies at the jct of KY 93 and 917, just w of the Cumberland R and less than 10 mi ese of Smithland. Will C. Lowery est the po on July 7, 1879, as Livingston, presumably for the co, and then renamed it Iuka on Apr 27, 1882, for reasons unknown. Some say it was named for an Indian girl who was supposed to have lived with her tribe on the Cumberland R. Others say it was an Indian word meaning "welcome." According to George R. Stewart, Iuka was an early 19th cent Chickasaw chief whose people may have camped in the area, for there is some evidence there of Indian occupation. 204, 1189, 1445.

Ivel (Floyd): *ahv*/əl (Harold). This hamlet with po and rr flag stop is on US 23/460 and the Levisa Fork of the Big Sandy R, 6½ mi se of Prestonsburg. The po, at the mouth of Ivy Creek for which it was named, was est by J[ohn] K[elly] Stratton on Dec 11, 1905, with Dollie Setser, pm. 976, 1370.

Ivyton (Magoffin): *ah*/və/tən, *ah*/vihŋ/tən (Ivyton). This hamlet with po is centered at the jct of KY 867 and 1888, just sw of KY 114, and 5 mi ese of Salyersville. It was named for the profusion of ivy in that vicinity. The po was est on Sept 24, 1883, with Robert A. Patrick, pm.

Jabez (Russell): *dhā*/*behz* (Jabez). This hamlet with po is centered at the jct of KY 196 and the Cave Springs Rd, 8½ mi e of Jamestown. According to tradition, the name, derived perhaps from that of the biblical town of Jabesh-Gilead, was suggested by a traveling salesman on a visit to the small store where John S. Johnson was to est the po on July 14, 1881. 681, 1233.

Jackeysburg (Breckinridge). See *Union Star*

Jackhorn PO (Letcher). See *Hemphill*

Jacks Creek (Clay): *jaex* kreek (Big Creek). This rural settlement with extinct po lies some 2½ mi up Jacks Creek from its confluence with the Red Bird R and 11 mi ene of Manchester. It was named for the creek, which was ostensibly named by early white settlers for a friendly Indian, a cripple who served as housekeeper and companion of the famed Chief Red Bird. Legend has it that the 2 were murdered by whites and their bodies disposed of in the larger stream. The po, est on Feb 26, 1932, with Mrs. Marion Hensley, pm, closed in 1954. 956, 1259, 1418.

Jackson (Breathitt): *djaex*/ən (Jackson, Quicksand). This 4th class city and seat of Breathitt Co is on KY 15 and 30 and the North Fork of the Kentucky R, 127 mi ese of downtown Louisville. The seat of the newly est co was founded in 1839 on 10 acres donated by Simon Cockrell, Sr. The town was known as Breathitt until 1845 when its name was changed to honor the former president, Andrew Jackson. The po was est as Breathitt Court House on Oct 15, 1839, with Jeremiah W. South, pm, and changed to Jackson on Mar 25, 1845. The town was inc in 1854. 911.

Jackson County: *djaex*/ən. 346 sq mi. Pop 11,932. Seat: McKee. This co was est in 1858 from parts of Madison, Estill, Owsley, Clay, Laurel, and Rockcastle cos and named for Andrew Jackson.

Jackson Purchase, The: *djaex*/ən *pɜch*/əs. This 8500-sq-mi area comprises Kentucky's 8 and Tennessee's 20 westernmost cos, between the Mississippi, Ohio, and Tennessee rs. In 1818, Gen. Andrew Jackson paid the Chickasaw Indians $300,000 for this territory, of which 2400 sq mi is in Kentucky. *Paducah* is the largest city in the area and its principal trade and industrial center.

Jacksonville (Bourbon): *jaex*/ən/vihl (Shawhan). This hamlet is on KY 353, 6½ mi nw of Paris. The po may have been est on May 15, 1828, by William Simpson but it has since closed. Historians think it was named by the followers of Andrew Jackson. 167, 538.

Jacksonville (Russell). See *Jamestown*

Jacksonville (Shelby): *djaex*/ən/vihl (North Pleasureville). This hamlet with extinct po lies at the jct of KY 12 and 1922, 11 mi ene of Shelbyville. The po was first est as Jacksonville on Jan 3, 1870, with James Kesler, pm, and probably named for Andrew Jackson. It closed in 1875 but was reest on May 12, 1881, as Zilpah with Enoch Pinkston, pm. It closed for good in 1902. 902.

Jacobs (Carter): *djā*/kuhps, *djā*/kəbz (Ault). This po on KY 955, at the mouth of Greenbrier Branch of Jacobs Fork of Soldiers Fork of Tygarts Creek, is 16½ mi sw of Grayson. It was est on June 2, 1888, by local storekeeper Lorenzo D. O'Roark and named for Ira Jacobs, a respected pioneer landowner, the grandson of William Wood Jacobs, a Revolutionary War veteran from Frederick Co, Virginia. 36.

Jamestown (Campbell). See *Dayton*

Jamestown (Russell): *djāmz*/town (Jamestown). This 5th class city and seat of Russell Co is on US 127, 89 mi sse of downtown Louisville. It was est as the seat of the new co in 1826 and briefly called Jacksonville for Gen. Andrew Jackson until it was renamed for James Wooldridge, who with his brother John had donated 110 acres for the town. The po was est as Jamestown on Nov 4, 1826, with James G. Patterson, pm, and the town was inc on Dec 23, 1827. 758.

Jarad PO (Pike). See *Heenon*

Jayem PO (Bell). See *East Pineville*

Jeff (Perry): djehf (Hazard South). This village with po is now mostly centered at the jct of KY 7 and 15, on the North Fork of the Kentucky R, across from the mouth of Carr Fork, and 2½ mi se of Hazard. The po, est on Apr 1, 1902, with Columbus C. Hall, pm, was named for Jefferson Combs who settled there in the late 19th cent. In 1914 the L&N RR named its local station, ¼ mi s, Hamden, for a railroad inspector, it is said. This name is now but a memory. 1079.

Jefferson (Jefferson). See *Jeffersontown*

Jefferson County: *djehf*/ər/sən. 386 sq mi. Pop 678,200. Seat: Louisville. Kentucky's most populous co, this was one of the 3 into which the Virginia legislature divided its Kentucky Co in 1780, and was named for Thomas Jefferson, then Virginia's governor. From its original territory all or part of 28 other cos were created.

Jeffersontown (Jefferson): *djehf*/er/sən/town (Jeffersontown). This 4th class city and residential suburb is centered at the jct of Watterson Trail and KY 155, 11 ½ mi ese of downtown Louisville. In May 1797 Abraham Bruner successfully petitioned the Jefferson Co Fiscal Court to est the town of Jefferson on part of the 122-acre tract he had acquired 3 years before. It later became Jefferson Town and finally Jeffersontown, and for a while its residents even refered to it as Bruner's Town [*brū*/nerz/town]. The po, est on Feb 9, 1816, with Peter Funk, pm, is now a branch of the Louisville po. 107, 111, 722.

Jeffersonville (Montgomery): *djehf*/ər/sən/vihl (Means). This 6th class city with po is strung out for nearly 4 mi along US 460, ese from a point 6 mi se of Mt. Sterling, and along KY 213, 519, and 1050, which extend n and s from the main highway. By the mid 19th cent it was an important market center for eastern Kentucky cattle and was given the perhaps derogatory nickname of Ticktown, either for the tick grass grown in the area or for the fact that cattle in the local pens collected ticks. It is not known when the Jeffersonville name was applied to the place, but the po of this name was est on Mar

9, 1866, with James H. Scholl, pm, and probably named for Thomas Jefferson. The town was inc in 1876 and reinc in 1967. 1018.

Jeffrey (Monroe): *djehf*/ree (Freedom). This hamlet lies on Peter Creek, 8 mi wnw of Tompkinsville. Its po, est on Mar 10, 1903, was named for the family of its first pm, Payton J. Jeffrey. It was closed in 1937. 1395.

Jellico (Whitley): *djehl*/ə/koh (Jellico West, Jellico East). This rail center on the Tennessee state line, 9 mi s of Williamsburg, is generally identified with Tennessee though a section of it is clearly in Kentucky. This town, the nearby stream and community of Jellico Creek, the ex-coal town of *Bon Jellico,* the Jellico and Bon Jellico Mountains—all in Whitley Co—may have been named for a mountain in McCreary Co called Angelica Mountain by the early pioneers. The mountain, in turn, is said to have been named for the angelica root found locally and supposed to have some medicinal value. This name was locally corrupted to "*djihl*/ə/kee" and later to "*djehl*/ə/koh." Jellico Creek is said to have been so identified before 1818. Yet it has also been said that the town, which was settled before 1800 and may first have been called Smithburg for the large number of Smiths among its early settlers, was inc as Jerrico, and that Jellico derived from a typographical error in the charter. 211, 1380.

Jellico Creek (Whitley). See *Jellico*

Jenkins (Letcher): *djihŋk*/ənz (Jenkins East, Jenkins West). This 4th class city is centered on the original town of Jenkins near the head of the Elkhorn Creek Valley, just below Pound Gap, 10½ mi ene of Whitesburg. The Consolidation Coal Co. started this coal town in 1911 and named it for George C. Jenkins, a Baltimore financier who was bankrolling the enterprise. The po was est on Apr 25, 1911. In the late 1940s a number of coal camps from *Burdine* to *Dunham* were inc into the one 7½-mi-long city of Jenkins. 194, 350, 1265.

Jenson (Bell): *djihn*/sən (Pineville). This hamlet with recently discontinued po is on Straight Creek and KY 221, less than 3 mi ene of Pineville. When the Straight Creek Branch of the L&N RR's Cumberland Valley Division was extended from Pineville to Kettle Island in 1911, a station was est here and named for a highly respected construction foreman. The Jenson po opened on Jan 20, 1927, and closed in 1975. 1183.

Jeremiah (Letcher): *djehr*/ə/mahr, *djehr*/ə/mah/ə, djehr/*mah*/yə (Blackey). This settlement is stretched along KY 7, 6 mi nw of Whitesburg. It is centered on a po est on May 27, 1884, and named for its first pm, Jeremiah P. Dixon. Dixon was called "The Prophet" by his neighbors; his middle initial stood for "Prophet," for he was named for the biblical prophet Jeremiah. 6, 1265.

Jerrico (Whitley). See *Jellico*

Jessamine County: *djehs*/mən, *djehs*/əm/ən, *djehz*/mən. 174 sq mi. Pop 24,300. Seat: Nicholasville. This co was est in 1798 from part of Fayette Co and named by Col. John Price, a state legislator, for the jessamine (jasmine) flower, widely grown in that area, and a spring-fed creek of that name that joins the Kentucky R 3 mi s of Wilmore. The popular legend that it was named for the daughter of a Scottish-born pioneer surveyor, James Douglass, is without foundation. It is doubtful that Douglass or his daughter ever lived in the vicinity of that stream and even less likely that she was tomahawked by an Indian on its banks.

Jessamine PO (Jessamine). See *Camp Nelson*

Jetson (Butler): *djeht*/sən (Riverside, Welchs Creek). This hamlet with po is now on KY 70, 8½ mi ene of Mogantown, at a site inexplicably identified on current maps, but not in local usage, as Whittinghill. The po, est on Apr 21, 1919, with Emsley L.

Taylor, pm, was first located on Millshed Rd, some 6 mi away, and named for J. E. Taylor and Son, co-owners of a local business. 1102.

Jett (Franklin): djeht (Frankfort East). This suburban community on US 60, just n of its jct with I 64 and just s of the Frankfort city limits, was part of the farmstead acquired in 1822 by Thomas Jett (1787–1858). In 1882 Thomas's heirs donated land for an L&N RR station which was named for him. The po, est on Feb 26, 1883, with Lee A. Owen, pm, closed in 1971. 793, 1290.

Jetts Creek (Breathitt): *djehts* kreek (Tallega). This extinct po lay at the mouth of Jetts Creek on the Middle Fork of the Kentucky R, 9 mi wsw of Jackson. The creek and the po, est on Oct 20, 1857, with Newton Jett, pm, were named for the family of Stephen Jett (died 1864), pioneer settler from Virginia, who in 1820 purchased some 20,000 acres in the area, including the site of the po. 852.

Jewell PO (Pike). See *Shelby Gap*

Jim's Town PO (Carter). See *Wesleyville*

Jimtown (Fayette): *djihm*/town (Centerville). This all-black settlement is just off KY 1876, 9½ mi ne of Lexington's New Circle Rd. It was named for James Sidener, who in 1888 divided a share of his pioneer family's 1400-acre farm into lots, which he sold to freed slaves. It never had its own po. 33.

Jimtown (Monroe). See *Fountain Run*

Joes Lick PO (Madison). See *Kingston*

Joesville (Breckinridge). See *Cloverport*

Johnson County: *djahn*/sən. 264 sq mi. Pop 24,317. Seat: Paintsville. This co was est in 1843 from parts of Floyd, Lawrence, and Morgan cos and named for Gen. Richard M. Johnson (1780–1850), hero of the War of 1812, who later served in the US House of Representatives (1807–19 and 1829–37) and Senate (1819–29) and as vice president under Martin Van Buren (1837–41).

Johnson's Landing (Gallatin). See *Warsaw*

Johnson's Shop PO (Madison). See *Berea*

Johnson Station (Johnson). See *Hagerhill*

Johnsonville (Anderson): *djahn*/sənz/vihl (Ashbrook). This hamlet with extinct po on US 62, 11½ mi sw of Lawrenceburg, was first settled around 1835 by David Johnson, for whom the po, est by John F. Bean on July 20, 1854, was named. The po was discontinued in 1863. Note that though the name has no medial "s," it is generally pronounced as if it had. 604, 1387.

Johnstonville (Monroe). See *Flippin*

Johnsville (Bracken): *djahnz*/vihl (Berlin, Moscow). This settlement is strung out for about a mi along KY 1109, on Little Snag Creek, 2½ mi from its confluence with the Ohio R and 6 mi nw of Brooksville. This vicinity, settled around 1800 by William Pepper, a Virginian, was soon called Fairview by William A. Yelton, who "is said to have looked out on the surrounding hills from his home and thought it was a wondrous fair view." Since there was already a Fairview po in Kentucky, John H. Riley est the local po in 1879 as Johnsville, probably for himself and 2 other Johns, John Jackson and Johnson Yelton, who ran the store in which it was located. The po and store have since closed. The Fairview name is today preserved only in the local church. 27, 30.

Jolly Station (Breckinridge). See *McQuady*

Jonancy (Pike): joh/*naen*/see, joh/*nān*/see, *joh*/naen/see (Dorton). This coal town extends for about a mi along US 23/119 but is centered at its po just below the mouth of Elswick Branch of Shelby Creek, 10½ mi s of Pikeville. It was founded just after

World War I by the Kentucky Block Fuel Co. and, with its po, est on Nov 7, 1919, with Walter G. Andrews, pm, was named for 2 employees, Joe Hudson, a bookkeeper, and Nancy Ratliff, a timekeeper. 1023.

Jondun PO (Magoffin). See *Fritz*

Jonesboro (Fayette). See *Jonestown*

Jones Subdivision (Fayette). See *Jonestown*

Jonestown (Fayette): *djohnz*/town (Coletown). This all-black settlement is on the Tates Creek Rd, just n of West Hickman Creek and 1 mi s of Lexington's New Circle Rd. In 1893 Thomas Jones subdivided the 50-acre farm he had acquired 10 years before from the Samuel L. Wilson estate and est a village whose plot was then recorded as the Jones Subdivision. It was later called Jonesboro and is now Jonestown. It never had its own po. 33, 393.

Jonesville (Grant and Owen): *djohnz*/vihl (Glencoe). This village is on KY 36, 7 mi nne of Owenton and 10 mi w of Williamstown. It may early have been called Nonsuch, perhaps before 7 families of Joneses moved into the area. The Jonesville po was est on Aug 7, 1877. 625, 1232, 1292.

Jonsee Station (Clay). See *Cottingim*

Jordan (Fulton): *djɜd*/ən (Cayce). Little remains of a prosperous 19th cent village on KY 116, the old Mobile and Ohio (now Illinois Central Gulf) RR, and the Tennessee state line, 8½ mi se of Hickman. The first po to serve the area, Bulah, in Obion Co, Tennessee was moved to or near the Jordan site on or before Mar 29, 1859, and became known as State Line. In 1869 it was renamed Jordan Station, probably for William and George Jordan, prominent area businessmen. It was renamed Miles in 1880 for the pioneer family of Dr. Guy Simpson Miles, who had arrived from Shelby Co in 1832. It became Jordan in 1884 and closed in 1941. 729, 819.

Jordan Station PO (Fulton). See *Jordan*

Josh Bell County. See *Bell County*

Josephine (Scott): *djoh*/sə/feen (New Columbus). This extinct po was on Lytles Fork of Eagle Creek and KY 32, 12½ mi nnw of Georgetown. It was est on Sept 23, 1880, with James J. Jackson, pm, and named for Mrs. Nancy Josephine Murrell, the wife of a Union Army officer. It closed in 1913. 1293.

Joy (Livingston): djoi (Golconda). This hamlet with extinct po lies at the jct of KY 133 and 135, at the head of Buck Creek, and 14 mi n of Smithland. It was probably settled by Jim Lawless, a blacksmith, and his neighbors at first simply referred to it as Lawless's Blacksmith Shop. Later it may have been called Crossroads for its location. The name Joy is said to have been first applied to the po that Lawless est there on May 1, 1896, and may refer to the "good feelings" engendered by the product of a distillery on the forks of Buck Creek, which brought local people out on a Saturday night to "get a little joy." The po closed in 1957. 117, 1182, 1189.

J.R. Allen (Knox). See *Heidrick*

Juan (Breathitt): wahn, djū/*aen* (Canoe, Jackson). This settlement with a recently discontinued rural branch of the Jackson po lies on Shoulderblade Creek, a tributary of the Middle Fork of the Kentucky R, just ne of the jct of KY 30 and 315 and 5½ mi sw of Jackson. The po was est as Shoulder Blade on Aug 11, 1891, with James T. Chadwick, pm, and closed in 1914. It was named for the creek, which, according to tradition, was named by early hunters for what seemed to be the shoulderbone of a very large animal found near their camp. On Mar 9, 1910, at the mouth of Shoulderblade, another po was est by Matthew J. Long, a Spanish-American War veteran, and named Juan, for the

Battle of San Juan Hill, it is said. Some years later the Juan po was moved to the original Shoulderblade site. The community is now locally known as Juan with the name Shoulderblade applied only to the creek. 709, 1222.

Judio PO (Cumberland). See *Blacks Ferry*

Judy (Montgomery): *djū*/dee (Sharpsburg). This crossroads hamlet with extinct po lies at the jct of KY 11 and 537, 3½ mi n of Mt. Sterling. The po, est as Judys on Mar 12, 1887, with Hiram C. Wilson, pm, became Judy in 1892 and closed in 1903. It was named for a pioneer family whose progenitor, John Judy, was one of the 4 owners of the original site of Mt. Sterling. 1237.

Jugornot (Pulaski): *djuhgh*/ər/naht (Somerset, Burnside). This is a hollow extending about 3 mi between a point just s of Meece po and the Cumberland R, 7 mi se of Somerset. From its est on Sept 15, 1909, until it closed, the local po was called Northfield. It was first located at the head of Pumpkin Hollow but was later moved 1½ mi se. At one time, according to one tradition, local people did a thriving business producing and selling moonshine whiskey. They would charge one price if customers brought their own containers but a little more if they did not. So when someone came to buy he would be asked "Jug or not?" Another tradition refers to the common practice of rewarding voters with whiskey. You would be asked if you wanted a jug or not, and if you voted the right way you'd get your jug and not otherwise. Over time the area came to be known as Jugornot. Joe Creason once reported a variant, about a problem that arose when no one thought to bring the whiskey to the local voting place. When someone stated that the election could not be held since there was no jug, the sheriff ruled, "we'll have the election jug or not!" 1008, 1410, 1450.

Julian (Christian): *djū*/lyən (Caledonia). This hamlet with extinct po and station on the defunct Clarksville & Princeton Branch of the L&N RR lay at the jct of KY 117 and 272, 6 mi w of Hopkinsville. Both the station and the po, est on Apr 17, 1888, were named for Julien (*sic*) Gracey, longtime superintendent of the rr and son of Capt. Frank P. Gracey, a Clarksville, Tennessee, businessman for whom Gracey, 3 mi n, was named. 775, 1403.

Julip (Whitley): *djū*/ləp (Saxton). This po on KY 92, at the mouth of Deep Branch of Cumberland R, 4½ mi e of Williamsburg, was est on Oct 17, 1917, with Mrs. Nora Sullivan, pm. At this time, according to one account, "If You Wore a Tulip" was a popular song and Rosa Sullivan fancied the rhyming reference to "julip" in the last line and submitted that word to the Post Office Department. However, J. W. Sullivan, local historian and longtime storekeeper, recalled that the Julip name had been applied to the community long before the po was est. 1267, 1380.

Junction City (Boyle): *djuhŋk*/shən *siht*/ee (Junction City). This 5th class city with po is contiguous with the Lincoln Co line and less than 2 mi s of Danville. The town is said to have been founded when the L&N RR's Lebanon Branch reached this site in 1866, and was first called Goresburg for the 2 Gore brothers who ran the local hotel. The po was est as Gore on Oct 4, 1880, with Thomas W. Gore, pm, and became Goresburgh on Apr 17, 1882, and then Junction City a month later after the Cincinnati Southern (now Southern) RR made connection here with the L&N. By 1880, however, the L&N was calling its local station Danville Junction. Recently Junction City annexed the adjacent village of Shelby City [*shehl*/bee *siht*/ee]. This early settlement was named for Kentucky's first governor, Isaac Shelby, whose home was nearby. Its po est as South Danville on Apr 26, 1866, became Shelby City the following year, and closed in 1926. The town was inc as Shelby City in 1867, though the L&N station there was called Danville Station by 1870 and the community may have been nicknamed Briartown. The latter is said to have been applied by a resident, former Confederate officer W. E. Grubbs, for the heavy growth of wild briars in the area. In 1953 the Board on Geographic Names approved a local request to rescind its former approval of Shelby on the basis of continued local usage of Shelby City, which usage continues even now. 564, 929, 1224, 1279.

June PO (Pulaski). See *Ruth*

Justell (Floyd). See *Betsy Lane*

Justiceville (Pike): *djuhs*/tihs/vihl (Millard). This subdivision without po, between US 460/KY 80 and the Levisa Fork of the Big Sandy R and 5 mi se of Pikeville, was developed in 1946 by William E. Justice and named for McClelland Justice, from whom he purchased the land. 1138.

Kaler (Graves): *kā*/lər (Symsonia). This hamlet with extinct po on KY 131, 10 mi nne of Mayfield, was named for a local family. Its po, est on Apr 4, 1883, by James H. Carter, operated until 1905. 1228.

Kaliopi (Leslie): *Kael*/ee/*oh*/pee (Hyden West). This po lies at the mouth of Devils Jump Branch of Hell for Certain Creek, 2½ mi from the confluence of the latter with the Middle Fork of the Kentucky R and 5 mi nnw of Hyden. The local po, est on Feb 27, 1929, about a mi below the present site, was first called Omarsville [*oh*/mahrz-/vihl]. The first pm, Lilbern W. Woods, is said to have named it for the son of Elmer Huff, a Republican Party official at that time. After several brief changes in location to sites on nearby Big Fork, Sam Pilatos (Palatous) moved the po to his store at the present site, then known as Mouth of Devils Jump Branch, and at his request it was renamed Kaliopi on Mar 1, 1945, for his mother back in their native Greece. The name of the Hell for Certain Creek [*hehl* fər *s3t*/ən] is as old as the co itself. Among the numerous accounts of this name is this: After a heavy rain 2 travelers are said to have found the swollen stream difficult to maneuver. When one exclaimed to the other, "This is Hell," the other replied, "For certain." 1059, 1223.

Karr's Landing (Livingston). See *Carrsville*

Kaufman's Station (Anderson). See *Lawrenceburg*

Kavanaugh PO (Boyd). See *Burnaugh*

Kayjay (Knox); *kā*/*djā* (Kayjay). This po on KY 225 at the mouth of Tye Fork of Brush Creek, 8 mi s of Barbourville, was first est by Nimrod Lunsford on Nov 2, 1892, as Lunsford [*luhnz*/fərd]. It was discontinued in 1908. On Apr 9, 1931, the po was reest as Kayjay, a name derived from the initials of the Kentucky-Jellico Coal Co., which had opened a mine there the year before. It is now a rural branch of the Barbourville po. 1068.

Keaton (Johnson): *kee*/tən (Redbush). This hamlet with po is on KY 469 and Keaton Fork of Blaine Creek at the mouth ot Noisy Branch, and 13½ mi nw of Paintsville. The po was est on May 17, 1900, with Sarah A. Holbrook, pm, and named for a local family. 1411.

Keavy (Laurel): *kee*/vee (London Southwest, Vox). This hamlet with po is on KY 312, 9 mi ssw of London. According to local tradition, when the residents learned they were to be given their own po, they decided that each should have a chance to suggest a name and the best among them would be sent to Washington. Add Karr, sitting in the local store, happened to spot the word "Keavy" on a box, the name of a brand of shoes or of the co. that made them. The name somehow attracted him and he proposed it, and it was the name submitted to the postal authorities. The po was est on July 17, 1888, with Isaac R. Storm, pm. 544, 903.

Keefer (Grant): *keef*/ər (Lawrenceville). This settlement with extinct po, 1¼ mi from the Owen Co line and 7 mi ssw of Williamstown, was settled before 1820 and first called Priceburg for John Price, the pioneer storekeeper. It is not known when the name Keefer was first applied to the place, but it did identify the po in operation from 1889 to 1903, and derived from the many kieffer pear trees that still grow around the local church and cemetery. It has been said that at least part of the community was once nicknamed Strutsville, for on Sunday afternoons well-dressed young men would strut with their girl friends up and down the dusty rd. 84, 887, 1342.

Keene (Jessamine): keen (Keene). This village with po lies at the jct of KY 169 and 1267, 4½ mi nw of Nicholasville. It grew up around a stone mill built in 1794 and was laid out in 1813 as North Liberty. Its po was est on July 14, 1830, and named Keene by Ephraim Carter, the first pm, and Harvey Huggins, the storekeeper, for their hometown in New Hampshire. Under this name it was inc in 1844. 240, 817.

Kelat (Harrison): *kee*/laet (Kelat). This hamlet at the jct of KY 1032 and 1744, 8½ mi n of Cynthiana, was called Fairview when James R. Brannock arrived at the site in 1873 and opened his store. When he applied for a po with that name in 1884 he learned that it was already in use. A local teacher, T. J. Smith, asked to submit a unique name, chose Kelat, a city in the obscure Asian country of Baluchistan. With this name the po opened on Mar 20, 1884, with Zeb M. Kenady as pm. It closed in 1905. The Fairview Baptist Church preserves the community's original name. 859, 1227.

Kellacey (Morgan): kehl/*ā*/see (Ezel). This settlement with extinct po is ¾ mi up Tarkiln Branch of the Licking R and 6½ mi wnw of West Liberty. The po was est on May 22, 1922, with Ada Cox, pm, and named for the brothers Kelly and Asa Cox. 980.

Kelsey PO (Caldwell). See *Fredonia*

Kennedy (Christian): *kihn*/ə/dee (Oak Grove). This short-lived po and depot on the defunct Clarksville & Princeton branch of the L&N RR were on KY 115, 13 mi sse of Hopkinsville. Both the station and the po, est on Jan 2, 1889, were named for David Newton Kennedy of Clarksville, Tennessee, the president of the Northern Bank of Tennessee and the Clarksville Board of Trade and a stockholder of the Indiana Alabama & Texas RR, which by 1887 had become the L&N's Clarksville & Princeton branch. 1403.

Kennedys Ferry (Kenton). See *Covington*

Kennedy's Ferry PO (Campbell). See *California*

Kensee (Whitley): *kehn*/see, *kehn*/zee (Jellico West). This extinct po and coal camp on Pigeon Roost Creek, a branch of Clear Fork of the Cumberland R, ¼ mi w of US 25W and 8 mi s of Williamsburg, were probably named for their location 1½ mi from the Tennessee state line. The po, est on June 26, 1884, with James W. Fox, pm, closed in 1917. 1380.

Kenton County: *kihn*/tən. 163 sq mi. Pop 132,000. Seat: Independence. This co was est in 1840 from part of Campbell Co and named for Simon Kenton (1755–1836), Kentucky pioneer, scout, and Indian fighter.

Kenton Furnace (Greenup). See *York*

Kentontown (Robertson): *kihn*/tən/town (Piqua). This hamlet with extinct po at the jct of US 62 and KY 1521, 4½ mi sw of Mt. Olivet, was chartered in 1795 as Newtown. Since it had been laid out by John Kenton, brother to famed frontiersman Simon Kenton, it was later renamed in John's honor. The po was in operation as Kentontown by 1830, and closed in 1918. 1365.

Kenvir (Harlan): *kehn*/vər (Evarts). This coal town with po is on KY 215, 3 mi up

Yocum Creek from its confluence with Clover Fork of the Cumberland R and 8 mi e of Harlan. It was founded in 1919 by the Black Mt. Coal Corp. and its name probably refers to its proximity to the Kentucky-Virginia state line. The po was moved from Dizney, 2 mi e, to this site on Jan 3, 1921, with Roscoe F. Weaver, pm. 1173.

Kessinger (Hart): *kā*/sihŋ/ər (Munfordville). This hamlet with extinct po extends for about ½ mi along KY 88, 3 mi nw of Munfordville. Its po, est on July 12, 1887, was named for its first pm, Jacob Kessinger, or his family. The po closed in 1963. 863.

Kettle (Cumberland): *kehd*/əl (Frogue). This po is at the jct of KY 449 and 485, 5 mi s of Burkesville. It was est on July 22, 1881, with John M. Bridgefarmer, pm, probably at a point further w, above the head of the creek for which it was named. The co's late historian, J. W. Wells, offered this account of the naming of the creek in the late 18th cent: "A number of prospectors had come to that part of the county and, night overtaking them, they pitched their tent on the banks of the new creek, spread down their bedding, stacked their cooking vessels close to their place of rest, and reclined for the night. One of the men . . . awoke from a horrible dream of having spent the night with their kettle under his head. . . . He arose on the next morning and related his [dream] to his comrades. After a jovial catechizing by the members of the party, they fell on the name for the camp. Hence the name of the creek." 223, 1385.

Kettle Island (Bell): *kehd*/əl *ah*/lənd (Balkan). This coal town with po is ½ mi up Kettle Island Branch of Straight Creek, 4½ mi ene of Pineville, and a station of the same name on the Straight Creek Branch of the Cumberland Valley Division of the L&N RR is 6 rail mi ene of Pineville. The po was est on Mar 15, 1912, with Thomas B. Hail, pm. According to one tradition, local women used to do the family wash with a community kettle on a small island in the creek where water and brushwood were plentiful. A more likely explanation is that some early hunters used an old iron kettle found buried on the island as a landmark to guide their friends to good places to hunt or settle. In either case, the name was applied in pioneer days, long before the coal town, rr station, and po were est. 736, 1416.

Kevil (Ballard): *kehv*/əl (LaCenter). This 6th class city with po is on the Illinois Central Gulf RR and US 60, 13 mi ne of Wickliffe. The po was est on Sept 4, 1903, with Robert A. Russell, pm, and named for R. U. Kevil, local landowner. 445.

Keysburg (Logan): *keez*/bergh (Allensville). This hamlet with extinct po lies at the jct of KY 96 and 102, 12½ mi ssw of Russellville. It was settled around 1802 and named for Capt. John Keys, an early resident. The po was est as Keysburgh on June 14, 1834, with Samuel P. V. Gillespie, pm, and operated with several intermissions until 1906. 42, 206.

Kidds Store (Casey); *kihdz stawr* (Hustonville). This rural settlement, now all but extinct, lies at the jct of US 127 and KY 906, 6½ mi nne of Liberty. The po, est on Mar 30, 1887, was named by and for its first pm, storekeeper, and gristmill operator, Elias H. Kidd. It closed in 1954. 1397.

Kiddville (Clark): *kihd*/vəl (Levee). This once thriving village with extinct po lies at the jct of KY 974 and 1960, 9½ mi e of Winchester. It was named for the family of William Burgess Kidd, whose widow and 5 children left Middlesex Co, Virginia, in 1818 and eventually settled in this vicinity. A po was est here on July 16, 1842, and closed in 1906. 328, 1349.

Kildav (Harlan): *kihl*/*dāv* (Evarts). This coal town with extinct po on Clover Fork of the Cumberland R, 5½ mi e of Harlan, was named for Messrs. Killebrew and Davis of Nashville, Tennessee, who opened the King Harlan Coal Co. mines there in 1916. The po, since closed, was est on May 17, 1916, with Squire M. Wheeler, pm. 1173.

Kill Time (Butler). See *Welchs Creek*
Kimble PO (Russell). See *Russell Springs*
Kincheloes Bluff (Muhlenberg). See *South Carrollton*
Kings Mountain (Lincoln): *kihŋz mown(t)*/ən (Eubank, Halls Gap). This trade center with po and rr station lies at the jct of KY 501 and the Southern Ry, 10 mi s of Stanford. Though little of its early history is known, it is believed that the village of Kingsville, named for several local King families, preceded the building of the famed Kings Mountain Tunnel, completed for the then Cincinnati Southern Ry in 1876. The po of Kings Mountain Station, est on Oct 29, 1877, with Samuel Carey, pm, was renamed Kingsville in 1887 and then became Kings Mountain in 1909. Meanwhile, another Kings Mountain po had been est in the vicinity by Estes Marsh on June 19, 1874. In 1884 this was moved and/or renamed Pleasant Point and was discontinued in 1906. 1448.
Kings Mountain Station PO (Lincoln). See *Kings Mountain*
Kings Station (Greenup). See *Frost*
Kingston (Madison): *kihŋ*/stən (Moberly). This hamlet with extinct po extends for about ¼ mi along US 421, 6 mi sse of Richmond. The po of Joes Lick, named for the stream several mi s, was moved to this site in 1846 and renamed either for Theodore King, the first storekeeper, or for Kingston-upon-Hull, England, by an early settler who may have been a native of that city. The town was inc in 1872. The Kingston po closed in 1929. 57, 373.
Kingston (Trimble). See *Milton*
Kingsville (Lincoln). See *Kings Mountain*
Kingswood (Breckinridge): *kihŋz*/wo͞od (Kingswood). This village with extinct po extends along KY 79 and 232, e and s of their jct 3 mi sse of Hardinsburg. In Jan 1906 John Wesley Hughes, the founder of Wilmore College in Jessamine Co, purchased 1000 acres at this site on which he est another college he called Kingswood for the school in England that the first John Wesley, the founder of Methodism, had est in 1748. On Aug 29, 1907, storekeeper George L. Medler opened the Kingswood po. In 1919 the college was sold to the Pilgrim Holiness Church and became the site of its orphanage and senior college. Both were closed in the 1930s and the site is now a commercial orchard. 214, 1398.
Kinniconick (Lewis): *kihn*/ee/kə/*nihk* (Vanceburg). This settlement with extinct po lies 6 mi up the Kinniconick Creek from the Ohio R, at the mouth of Grassy Branch, at the jct of KY 59 and 334, 4 mi s of Vanceburg. For years locally referred to as "Kinney," the 90 mi long stream was settled by the late 1790s. At or near the site of the present Kinniconick community was Randville, named for either Col. W. S. Rand or Jacob W. Rand, the latter having taught school there in the 1860s and maintained a po called Kinny Mills (*sic*) from 1864 to 1865. On an intermittent basis, a Kinniconick po was in existence at various locations in the area from at least the 1820s until it closed in 1955. Randville also had a po from 1884 to 1914. According to historian William M. Talley, the name Kinniconick may have been derived from a Shawnee word meaning "willow bark," a reasonable assumption since the area abounds in willow trees. The spelling "Connoconoque" appears on old French maps of the Ohio Valley, which suggests that English and French explorers adapted an Indian name to their own usage. Yet George R. Stewart in his *American Place Names* writes that the name refers to "a substitute for tobacco, or the plant producing it, used by various Indians and by frontiersmen, the actual plants differing in various parts of the country. It was applied

to features, usually places where the plant was abundantly found. . . . Though originally an Algonquian word, it got into English and French, and was distributed by speakers of those languages more than by Indians." 204, 770, 1103, 1200.

Kinny Mills PO (Lewis). See *Kinniconick*

Kino (Barren): *kee*/noh, *kihn*/oh (Temple Hill). This hamlet with extinct po is on KY 1330, 7 mi ese of Glasgow. The po, in operation from 1898 to 1910, is said to have been named by Al Shirley, an employee of the Lewis Ganter Drug Store in Glasgow, for a jar of powdered kino he spotted on a store shelf. Kino, prepared from the dark reddish gum of certain tropical trees, was used in medicines and for the tanning of leather. 448.

Kirkmansville (Todd); *kɜk*/mənz/vihl (Kirkmansville). This village with extinct po lies at the jct of KY 106, 107, and 171, 13½ mi nnw of Elkton. William Kirkman, a Virginian, is said to have arrived around 18OO in this area where, on Mar 5, 1828, he est the po of Hoppers Tan Yard. This was discontinued in 1842, 8 years before his death. His son Peter, for whom Kirkmansville is said to have been named, was a partner in a local store with Lafayette Bennett, who had earlier bought out Ephraim McLean. McLean, who also owned a mill there, est a po called McLean's Mill on Feb 12, 1856. Bennett succeeded him as pm and later renamed the po Pleasant View; a month after this Peter Kirkman became pm. The po closed in Dec 1864. These are believed to have been forerunners of the Kirkmansville po, est on Feb 23, 1867, with Micajah W. Grissam, pm. The po was discontinued on Mar 10, 1967. Oldtimers still refer to the community by its long-standing nickname Graball [*ghraeb*/awl], for the tendency of all early merchants to "grab all you had when you went in there to trade with them." 225, 1304.

Kirksey (Calloway): *kɜx*/ee (Kirksey). This village now lies at the jct of KY 299 and 464, 6 mi nw of Murray. The po called Kirksey was originally located about ¾ mi nw, in the same building that had housed the earlier Radford po, est on May 14, 1857, by Joseph N. Radford. The Radford po closed in 1860. Stephen Franklin Kirksey reest it on July 14, 1871, but apparently submitted his own name to the Post Office Department instead of the names Rosedale and Reedville preferred by local factions. Jesse R. Wrather, who succeeded him on Aug 11, 1873, moved the po to its present site but kept the Kirksey name. 1401.

Kirksville (Madison): *kɜx*/vəl (Kirksville). This village with recently closed po lies at the jct of KY 595 and 1295, 7 mi sw of Richmond. Originally called Centerville, it was renamed when the po was moved from Silver Creek on July 31, 1845. The name change honored Samuel Kirkendall who had opened a store there in 1832. 57.

Kirkwood (Mercer); *kɜk*/wood (McBrayer). This hamlet lies at the jct of KY 1987 and the Kirkwood and Gash rds, 10 mi nnw of Harrodsburg. The name denotes a "church in the woods;" the hamlet was named for the local Presbyterian church ½ mi s, set amid giant oaks, poplars, and elms. The po was est on Feb 18, 1889, with John J. G. Bond, pm, and closed in 1906. This vicinity is now popularly called Tattletown [*taet*/əl/town], which is said to have characterized the gossiping that was carried on at the local blacksmith shop. 964, 1264.

Kirkwood Springs (Hopkins): *kɜk*/wood *sprihŋz* (Dalton). Virtually nothing remains of this community, just over 1 mi e of the Tradewater R and 13½ mi wsw of Madisonville. It was named for James L. Kirkwood, who in the late 19th cent developed a health resort around the curative waters of a mineral spring. The now extinct po was est on Feb 17, 1908. 159.

Kissinger Station (Franklin). See *Switzer*

Kitts (Harlan): kihts (Harlan). This coal town with po is on KY 38, just above the mouth of Kitts Creek, a branch of Clover Fork of the Cumberland R, 1 mi e of Harlan. Some say the town and its po, est on Jan 4, 1913, were named for the Kitts family, but others say they were named for a mule. 1173.

Knifley (Adair): *nihf*/lee (Knifley, Mannsville). Until recently this village was centered at the jct of KY 76 and 551, just w of Casey Creek and about 4½ mi from its confluence with the Green R, and 10½ mi ne of Columbia. It was named for a local landowning family whose progenitor, Pennsylvania-born Philip Knifley (1777–1862) arrived from the present Taylor Co. around 1814. The po was est on May 23, 1887 with Thomas R. Stults, pm. In 1965–67 many families were forced to vacate their homes for the impoundment of the Green River Reservoir leaving only a few businesses n of the jct and moving the po 2 mi n on KY 76 to a point less than ¼ mi from the Taylor Co. line. 172, 522, 748, 1289.

Knights (Henderson). See *Spottsville*

Knob Creek PO (Metcalfe). See *Knob Lick*

Knob Lick (Metcalfe): *nahb lihk* (Sulphur Well). This hamlet with po is centered at the jct of KY 70 and 1243, 7 mi nw of Edmonton. The place was settled by the 1790s as a part of a large tract granted Austin Allen for Revolutionary War service. Antioch, the name of the extant local church built about 1838, is said to have also been the first name of the community that developed around it. The po est on June 10, 1848, as Knob Creek was renamed Antioch in 1851. It closed in 1857 but was reest as Knob Lick on July 23, 1867, with Frank S. Ewing, pm, since by then the Antioch name had been preempted by a po in Washington Co. It was named for a knob about a mi n of the po site and a slash or lick s of the knob. 232, 1193.

Knockum Hill (Christian). See *Herndon*

Knott County: naht. 352 sq mi. Pop 17,871. Seat: Hindman. This co was est in 1884 from parts of Floyd, Perry, Breathitt, and Letcher cos and named for J. Proctor Knott (1830–1911), governor of Kentucky from 1883 to 1887.

Knottsville (Davies): *nahts*/vihl (Maceo). This village is centered at the jct of KY 144 and 1513, 9 mi e of Owensboro. It may first have been called Hearts Delight, and was renamed Knottsville for Leonard Knott, a Nelson Co native who built the first house on the site in 1827. In that year Thomas Gore, another Nelson Countian, est the Gorham (*sic*) po about 1½ mi e. In 1833 storekeeper James Millay moved the po and renamed it Nottsville (at least it was spelled this way in postal records). Discontinued in 1834, it was reest as Knottsville on June 29, 1837, by William Higdon. The village of Knottsville was laid out by Millay and William R. Griffith in 1836 and inc in 1868. After an intermittent existence, the po closed for good in 1915. 99.

Knox County: nahx. 388 sq mi. Pop 29,946. Seat: Barbourville. Knox Co was est in 1799 from part of Lincoln Co and named for Gen. Henry Knox (1750–1806), officer in the Continental Army and Washington's secretary of war (1785–95).

Kona (Letcher): *kohn*/ə (Jenkins West). This deteriorating coal town with po lies at the mouth of Boone Fork of the North Fork of the Kentucky R, 4½ mi ne of Whitesburg. According to S. A. Mory, Sr., of the Elkhorn Coal Corp. at Kona, the name was applied by either the L&N RR or a member of the Potter family, owners of much of the local land. On May 24, 1913, W. H. Potter est a po at the mouth of Boone and named it Mater, as suggested by his children who were studying Latin at the time. Martha Jane Potter was its first pm. By the Mater name it continued to be known until Nov 1, 1925, when William H. Potter, then pm, had it changed to Kona. Sometime after 1913,

Potter agreed to deed the right-of-way to the L&N if their station would be built near his home. The Mater name was rejected by the rr and Lula, for one of Potter's daughters, was suggested instead. This name lasted only until someone learned of another Lula, in Russell Co, when the station was renamed Kona. The name may have been derived, for some unknown reason, from the Norwegian expression "Kona Mi," meaning "that old lady of mine." Yet Charles Hewatt, an officer of the Clinchfield RR Co. of Erwin, Tennessee, some 30 years ago, felt that Kona could have been named for a station on his rr in North Carolina, whose name may have been an acronym of the symbols for potassium and sodium (K) and (Na), the major components of feldspar, a local product. 74, 740, 1265.

Kosmosdale (Jefferson): *kahz*/məs/dāl (Kosmosdale). This hamlet with extinct po is in the vicinity of the Kosmos-Portland Cement Co. plant between US 31W/60 and the Illinois Central Gulf RR, near the Ohio R, and 18 mi ssw of the courthouse in Louisville. The po was est on July 20, 1854, as Grassy Pond for a local feature. It became River View in 1860 and finally Kosmosdale for the plant in 1905. 1296.

Kragon (Breathitt): *krā*/ghən (Quicksand). This extinct po on KY 15, at the mouth of Big Branch of the North Fork of the Kentucky R, 3 mi se of Jackson, was est on Dec 28, 1914, with Fern Ragon, pm. It was named for K. Ragon, president of the Kentucky Wood Products Co., which had est a plant there in 1913. 742.

Kuttawa (Lyon): kə/*tâh*/wə (Eddyville, Grand Rivers). This relocated 5th class city with po on US 60/641 is just sw of the relocated Eddyville. It was founded and named at its original site, 1½ mi w of Old Eddyville, by Charles Anderson, Ohio's Civil War governor, on land he acquired in 1866. Historians do not agree on the meaning of the name. Some suggest it is an Indian word for "beautiful" to describe the area that had attracted Governor Anderson; or that it denotes a "city in the woods," which it also was. It may be derived from the Delaware or Shawnee word "Kuttaawaa" meaning "great wilderness," as suggested by John Mason Brown; and it may have been the Indian name for the Kentucky R. It may have first been spelled "Cuttawa" or even "Kittawa," allegedly the name of a Cherokee village in that area that had disappeared by 1755. The Kuttawa po was est on Sept 20, 1872, by Andrew P. Conant, the first storekeeper, and the town was inc in that year. 230, 527.

Kyrock (Edmonson): *kah*/rahk (Bee Spring). Little remains of this once thriving village on the Nolin R, 4½ mi n of Brownsville. The town was est by the Kentucky Rock Asphalt Co. in the early 20th cent, to maintain a labor supply imported by the Louisville-based firm which produced "Kyrock," a natural asphaltic paving material. The Kyrock po, which began operation on June 21, 1920, closed in 1955. 8, 349.

Labascus (Casey): lə/*baes*/kəs (Phil). This extinct po on KY 501, 6 mi s of Liberty, was named for its first pm, Labascus J. Minton. The po was in service intermittently from Nov 7, 1882, until it closed in 1954. 1397.

La Center (Ballard): lah/*sihn*/tər (La Center). This 5th class city with po on the Illinois Central Gulf RR is centered at the jct of US 60 and KY 358, 9 mi ne of Wickliffe. It was laid out in 1903 on part of Margaret Davis's 300-acre farm and first called Maryville for her daughter. That year Percy A. Jones requested a po to be named LaCentre since Maryville was already in use, but had to settle for an anglicized form of the name that denoted the town's location in the approximate center of the co. The po opened on Oct 21, 1903, with Jones as its first pm. Some historians believe that the name LaCentre had been suggested by Stokes T. Payne, a local land developer, in anticipation of another shift in the co's seat. 285, 685.

Lackey (Floyd and Knott): *laek*/ee (Wayland). This recently disincorporated city, with po and C&O RR station, lies at the jct of KY 7 and 80 and the mouth of Jones Fork of Right Beaver Creek, 10½ mi nw of Hindman and 13½ mi s of Prestonsburg. The po was est on Mar 2, 1880, with Adam Martin, pm, and was named for the family of a prominent Floyd Co businessman and public official, Alexander Lackey, a Virginia-born pioneer who settled at the forks of the Beaver (now Martin) around 1808. 128, 1288.

Lacona PO (Jefferson). See *Pleasure Ridge Park*

Lafayette (Christian): lə/*fā*/ət (Roaring Spring). This 6th class city with po is on KY 107, 14 mi ssw of Hopkinsville. On Feb 27, 1835, Robert C. Dunlap moved his Flat Lick po, est on Mar 24, 1826, by Lipscomb Norvell, from some point n of the town site to what then may have been a settlement already called Lafayette, for the general whose visit to America in 1824–25 was still fondly remembered. A town grew up at the new site and was inc as Lafayette on Mar 1, 1836. The Flat Lick name was derived from that of a large basin in sw Christian Co where animals came to lick the salt deposits. For many years there was confusion about the proper spelling of the town's name. Sometime before the Civil War the name came to be spelled La Fayette. Before 1900 the Board on Geographic Names officially approved Lafayette, but the Post Office Department continued the La Fayette spelling, which still seems to be favored by local residents. The curious pronunciation may be noted too, but among older persons, and especially blacks, it has often been pronounced "*lā*/fā/ət." 166, 1187, 1403.

Lafayette (Metcalfe). See *Center*

LaGrange (Oldham): lə/*ghrāndj* (LaGrange, Smithfield). This 4th class city and seat of Oldham Co is on I 71, KY 53 and 146, and the L&N RR, 20 mi ene of downtown Louisville. In 1827 Maj. William Berry Taylor's offer of this crossroads site for the relocation of the co's seat from Westport was accepted. A town was then created and named by Taylor for the country estate in France of General LaFayette, with whom he had been impressed on the Frenchman's visit to the area in 1824. In Mar 1828, for some reason, the seat was returned to Westport where it remained until 1838 when LaGrange was again, this time permanently, made the co's seat. The LaGrange po was est on Dec 1, 1828, with Thomas Berry, pm. 82, 156.

Lair (Harrison): lɛ (Shawhan). This hamlet with extinct po is on KY 675, between US 27 and the South Fork of the Licking R, 2½ mi s of Cynthiana. Hinkston's Station was est here by John Hinkston in 1775 and reest by Isaac Ruddle as Ruddle's Station in 1779. In 1791 the 3 Lair brothers from Virginia built their homes near the ruins of the station. Here a station on the then Covington & Lexington (later Kentucky Central and now L&N) RR was built and called Lairs Station. A po of the same name was est on Mar 14, 1860, but the name was shortened to Lair in 1882. It has since closed. 822.

Lairs Station PO (Harrison). See *Lair*

Lairsville (Russell). See *Rowena*

Lake (Laurel): lāk (Blackwater). This extinct po on KY 80, 10 mi e of London, was named for a large pond on first postmaster-storekeeper John Petree's farm. The name was submitted to the Post Office Department by Petree's daughter, and the po was est on Apr 27, 1900. 1282.

Lake City (Livingston): *lāk siht*/ee (Grand Rivers). This village is on US 62/641, 11 mi se of Smithland. It grew up around a store after the creation of Kentucky Lake and was named for the lake and its commercial and tourist ambitions. It has no po of its own. 1382.

Lake Dreamland (Jefferson): lāk *dreem*/lənd (Louisville West). This unincorporated suburban community without po was est by Edward Hartlage around a lake that he created in 1931 when he dammed up Bramers Run just e of the Ohio R and 6½ mi sw of downtown Louisville. He is said to have applied the name after a critic pointed out that his ambitious plans for a development there were just a dream and would never amount to anything. To some extent he was right. 727, 1296.

Lakeland (Jefferson): *lāk*/lənd (Anchorage). Little remains of this suburban community just s and e of Central State Hospital and n of LaGrange Rd and the L&N RR tracks, and 11 mi e of downtown Louisville. It was named for the spring-fed lake created after 1852 by S. L. Garr, a nurseryman of nearby Anchorage. The po was est as Asylum on Nov 4, 1887, with Mary E. Whips, pm. An attempt several months later to change its name to Anchorage Asylum for the city just s ane e failed, and in Mar 1888 the po became Lakeland. It has since closed. 91, 916.

Lakeview (Caldwell). See *Crowtown*

Lakeview (Kenton). See *Fort Wright*

Lakeville (Magoffin): *lāk*/vəl (Salyersville South). This settlement on the Licking R and KY 1090 is at the site of the extinct po at the mouth of Flynt Branch, 1½ mi s of Salyersville. The po was est as Power on Mar 31, 1898, with Kearney S. Hoskins, pm, and named for a local family. In June 1898 it was renamed for a natural lake created when the river changed its course but since filled in. 840, 1422.

Lamasco (Lyon): lə/*maes*/koh (Lamasco). This hamlet with extinct po lies at the jct of KY 93 and 903, ¼ mi s of I 24 and 8 mi se of Eddyville. It was first called Parkersville for Thomas Parker, a prominent landowner, and a po of this name was in operation from July 14, 1864, till Nov of the following year. On Mar 4, 1878, the po was reest as Lamasco with Simon J. Howard, pm. This name is said to have been suggested by a traveling salesman from Evansville, Indiana, who undoubtedly recalled the once independent town of Lamasco, an early rival of Evansville that had merged with that city in 1857. The name was derived from those of its founders, John and William Law, James B. McCall, and Lucius H. Scott. 152, 230, 1278.

Lamero (Rockcastle): *laem*/ə/roh (Livingston). This po is now on KY 490 and Trace Branch of Rockcastle R, 9 mi ese of Mt. Vernon. It was est by Clarence and Charlotte Lamoreaux at their store and restaurant at the mouth of Parker Branch in Laurel Co in 1925, with Charlotte as pm. They named it for themselves, though the name was simplified by the postal authorities. The po was moved to Rockcastle during World War II and again, in 1957, to its present site. 1073.

Lancaster (Garrard): *laeŋk*/ə/stər (Lancaster, Buckeye). This 5th class city and seat of Garrard Co is on US 27, 72 mi se of downtown Louisville. In 1797 Capt. William Buford donated land for the seat of the new co and petitioned its court for the est of a town at Wallace Crossroads, the home of Maj. Andrew Wallace. Buford's town was surveyed and platted in 1798 by Joseph Bledsoe, Jr., and named Lancaster, allegedly because one of the early settlers had come from that city in Pennsylvania and/or the Kentucky town had been planned in the design of the older city. The theory that Kentucky's Lancaster was named for a local resident is improbable. Its po was est as Lancaster Court House on Jan 1, 1801, with James G. Whelan, pm, and shortened to Lancaster around 1811. 35, 126.

Lancaster Court House PO (Garrard). See *Lancaster*

Lancer (Floyd): *laen*/sər (Lancer). This residential suburb recently inc into Prestonsburg is e of the main part of that city, between KY 1428 and the Levisa Fork of the Big Sandy R, just below the mouth of Brandykeg Creek. The po, est on Jan 31, 1917, with Magga A. Martin, pm, and named for Lancer Harris, was originally located over ½ mi n. In the mid 1930s it was moved to serve a larger pop. It closed in 1968. 194, 1370.

Landsaw (Wolfe): *laend*/sâw (Landsaw). This residential settlement with extinct po extends along KY 15 and Stillwater Creek, a branch of Red R, se from a point opposite the mouth of Murphy Fork, 4½ mi e of Campton. The community which predated the est of the po, in operation from 1898 to 1957, was named for the prominent local family whose Wolfe Co progenitor was William Landsaw (ca 1774–1826), a native of Greenbrier, now in West Virginia, who brought his family to this vicinity in 1809. 233, 1236.

Lanesville PO (Floyd). See *Harold*

Langford (Rockcastle). See *Hummel*

Langford Station (Rockcastle). See *Hummel*

Langley PO (Floyd). See *Maytown*

Langnau (Laurel): *laeŋ*/noh (Portersburg). This hamlet with recently closed po is on Ky 472, near the South Fork of Rockcastle R, and 6 mi ene of London. It was one of several "colonies" settled in the early 1880s by Swiss immigrants attracted to the co by the then recently est Kentucky Bureau of Immigration (see *Bernstadt*). The place is said to have been named for a Swiss village, 15 mi e of Bern, whence some of the colonists had come. The po was est on Mar 24, 1884, with William McCarty, pm. 544, 1195.

Larkslane (Knott); *lahrx*/lān (Handshoe). This hamlet is on KY 80 and Jones Fork of Right Beaver Creek, 5½ mi ne of Hindman. Its po was est and named by its first pm, Elizabeth Slone, for her husband, Lark Slone, and the lane that went past his home. That section of KY 80 has also been locally called Stringtown for the arrangement of the houses along the highway. 1391, 1433.

LaRue County: lə/*ru*. 263 sq mi. Pop 11,844. Seat: Hodgenville. LaRue Co was est in 1843 from part of Hardin Co and allegedly named at the request of John LaRue Helm, then speaker of the Kentucky House and later governor, for his maternal grandfather, pioneer settler John LaRue. It is said that those who had petitioned for the formation of the new co had wanted it called Lynn for Benjamin Lynn, pioneer Indian fighter and later preacher, but agreed to Helm's suggestion. Before its est, the the area was known as the Nolin Section of Hardin Co for the major stream that had also been named for Lynn (see *Nolin*). Yet a highway marker at the co seat records that "an act to create Helm Co. honoring John LaRue Helm . . . was amended by [the Kentucky] Senate to give the honor instead to Gabriel Slaughter [Kentucky's 7th governor, 1816–20]. A compromise resulted in naming it Larue [*sic*] for those of that family who were among the early explorers and settlers of the area." 68, 144.

Latonia Lakes (Kenton): lə/*tohn*/yə *lāx* (Alexandria, Independence). This 6th class city and suburb of Cincinnati and Covington is centered on KY 16 just s of the city of Taylor Mill and 7½ mi s of downtown Covington. Formerly a community of resort cottages on 3 lakes, it was inc as a city in 1953. It was named for the older community of Latonia, now part of Covington, and for the famed race track, which in turn had been named for Latonia Springs, a 19th cent summer resort. The springs, also now within the Covington city limits, were named for Leto or Latona, the Greco-Roman goddess and mother of Apollo. 245, 280.

Latonia Springs (Kenton). See *Latonia Lakes*

Laura (Martin): *lâhr*/ə, *lâhr*/ee (Varney). This po 4 mi up Pigeonroost Fork of Wolf

Creek, 10½ mi sse of Inez, was est on July 26, 1909, and named for the oldest daughter of the first pm, Gabriel Frederic. 1155.

Laurel County: *lâhr*/əl. 434 sq mi. Pop 38,402. Seat: London. Laurel Co was est in 1825 from parts of Clay, Rockcastle, Whitley, and Knox cos and named for the Laurel R on whose banks early settlers had found a thick growth of mountain laurel or rhododendron shrubs.

Laurel Creek (Clay): *lahr*/əl kreek (Barcreek). This hamlet is centered at a point about midway up Laurel Creek from its confluence with Goose Creek, a branch of the Redbird R. The Laurel Creek po on Collins Fork, 6 mi n of Manchester, was est on Apr 21, 1865, with Joseph Hubbard, pm, and named for the creek along whose banks grew an abundance of mountain laurel. It was discontinued in 1966. 1329.

Laurel Furnace (Greenup): *lahr*/əl *f3n*/əs (Oldtown). This disbanded settlement and extinct po were on Laurel Creek, 4 mi w of its confluence with the Little Sandy R and 10 mi ssw of Greenup. A charcoal-fired, cold blast iron furnace was built here in 1849 by the brothers George and Samuel Wurts and named for the famed iron works near the Delaware R in southeastern Pennsylvania whence they had come. The short-lived po was est by Benjamin Kling on Oct 12, 1854. 188, 1092, 1415.

Lawless's Blacksmith Shop (Livingston). See *Joy*

Lawrence (Anderson). See *Lawrenceburg*

Lawrenceburg (Anderson): *lahr*/əns/bergh (Lawrenceburg). This 4th class industrial city and seat of Anderson Co is centered at the jct of US 62 and 127, 45 mi ese of downtown Louisville. It was first called Kaufman's Station for its first settler, Jacob Kaufman, a German immigrant who arrived around 1780. The settlement was inc in 1820 as Lawrence. Meanwhile, the po had been est as Lawrenceburgh on Jan 22, 1817, with Jeremiah A. Matthews, pm, and named for William Lawrence, a local tavern owner and prominent citizen who had been instrumental in the town's early development. When it became the seat of Anderson Co in 1827, the legislature adopted Lawrenceburg as its official name. In its simplification efforts, the Post Office Department dropped the "h" from the po name in 1893. 1453.

Lawrenceburg (Grant). See *Folsom*

Lawrence County: *lahr*/əns. 420 sq mi. Pop 14,134. Seat: Louisa. This co was est in 1821 from parts of Greenup and Floyd cos and named for Capt. James Lawrence (1781–1813) of the USS Chesapeake whose last words, "Don't give up the ship," spoken as he lay dying of wounds received in the battle with the HMS Shannon off the Boston coast, have inspired generations of American sailors.

Lawson PO (Greenup). See *South Portsmouth*

Lawson Settlement (Greenup). See *Graysbranch*

Lawton (Carter): *laht*/ən (Olive Hill). This village with po is on KY 174 and Soldiers Creek, a tributary of Tygarts Creek, and 14½ mi wsw of Grayson. The po was est on Aug 23, 1881, and named for its first pm, Warren L. Lawton, who had arrived a short time before. 36.

Layman PO (Breckinridge). See *Harned*

Laynesville (Floyd). See *Harold*

Leatherwood (Perry): *lehth*/ər/wōōd (Leatherwood). This coal town with po lies at the head of Clover Fork of Leatherwood Creek, 13½ mi s of Hazard. In 1944 the Blue Diamond Coal Co. opened a mine at this site and named it and the town that grew up around it for the stream that joins the North Fork of the Kentucky R opposite the old L&N RR station of Dent. The local po was est in 1944 as Toner since the Leatherwood name was already in use by an office in nearby Breathitt Co. When the latter was changed to Watts in 1949, the Toner po was renamed Leatherwood, effective July 1, 1949. The creek was named in pioneer times for the many leatherwood trees that early settlers had observed along its banks. 114, 1203.

Lebanon (Marion): *lehb*/ən/ən (Lebanon East, Lebanon West). This 4th class city and seat of Marion Co lies at the head of Hardins Creek and is centered at the jct of US 68 and KY 55, 50 mi sse of downtown Louisville. Historians credit Benedict Spalding with having petitioned the Kentucky legislature for the est of the town in 1814 and John Handley with having laid it out in 1815. The town grew up around the Hardins Creek Meeting House built in 1798 by a group of Virginia Presbyterians led by James McElroy. Historians, however, do not agree which of these men named the town for the abundance of cedars on the nearby hills, reminiscent of the biblical Cedars of Lebanon. The po was est on Feb 1, 1816, with Robert S. Fogle, pm, and the town became the seat of the newly created co in 1834. 201, 367.

Lebanon Junction (Bullitt): *lehb*/ən/ən *djuhŋk*/shən (Lebanon Junction). This 5th class city with po is just w of I 65 and 8½ mi s of Shepherdsville. In 1857, when the L&N RR's branch line to Lebanon was completed from this point on the projected main line to Nashville, a station was est and named Lebanon Junction. The town grew up around the station and the local po was est on Feb 21, 1862. 31, 1252.

Lebanon (Station) (Scott). See *Georgetown*

Ledbetter (Livingston): *lehd*/beht/ər (Little Cypress). This hamlet with po is on US 60, 6½ mi ssw of Smithland. The po was est on Mar 31, 1900, and named for its first pm, the local storekeeper, Wiley K. Ledbetter. It served what was then a thinly populated area called Panhandle, which name survives in the voting precinct. 1442.

Ledocio (Lawrence): lə/*doh*/shee/oh (Adams). This extinct po on KY 1760 and the Right Fork of Little Blaine Creek, 7½ mi sw of Louisa, was est on Jan 7, 1909, and named for Ledocio Moore, the mother of the first pm, Anderson L. Moore. It was discontinued in 1935. 1094, 1098.

Lee City (Wolfe): *lee siht*/ee (Lee City). This recently disincorporated town, now but a hamlet with po, is on the Red R, and KY 1094, just e of its jct with KY 205, 11 mi e of Campton. The po was est as Red River on July 23, 1879, with Robert G. Rose, pm, and renamed Lee City in 1887, by which name the town was inc in 1888. The derivation of its name is not known. The possibility of its having been named for Lee Co is limited by the 12 mi that separate it from that co line. It is even less likely to have been named, as has been popularly assumed, for Leeborn Allen, a prominent Wolfe Co attorney, born in 1887. 1236.

Leeco (Lee): *lee*/koh (Zachariah). This oil co. town with po is on KY 1036, and the Wolfe Co. line, 9 mi n of Beattyville. The Petroleum Exploration Co.'s discovery of oil led to its est of this village in 1919 to house its workers. It was named for the co. The po was est on Oct 6, 1920, with Flossie A. Kimble, pm. 132.

Lee County: lee. 211 sq mi. Pop 7,760. Seat: Beattyville. Est in 1870 from parts of Owsley, Estill, Wolfe, and Breathitt cos, Lee Co is traditionally believed to have been named for Gen. Robert E. Lee (1807–70), commander of the armies of the Confederacy. This notion, originated or perpetuated in Collins's *History of Kentucky* (1874), has been challenged by the late J. W. F. Williams and others who have found no documentary evidence for it. They suggest it was named for Lee Co, Virginia, whence many of its earliest residents had come. The Virginia co was named for Lighthorse Harry Lee, Revolutionary War officer and later Virginia governor. 471.

Leesburg (Harrison): *leez*/bergh (Leesburg). This hamlet is on the present US 62, 8½ mi sw of Cynthiana. The first settler of that vicinity may have been Col. W. E. Boswell of Leesburg, Virginia, who est a settlement in the 1790s he called Boswell's Crossroads but renamed Leesburg when the po was est on Feb 22, 1817. The first pm was William Cogswell, Boswell's son-in-law, who was also the first storekeeper. The po closed in 1917. 167, 472.

Leesburg (Woodford). See *Nugents Crossroads*

Lee's Mills PO (Owen). See *Natlee*

Leestown (Franklin): *leez*/town (Frankfort East). This section of Frankfort, along Wilkinson St on the Kentucky R, 1 mi below the Old Capitol Building, was the first settlement n of the r and already in existence before the est of Frankfort itself. It was probably named by and for Hancock Lee, who est it as town in the summer of 1775 on land he had recently acquired and which had first been visited by his cousin, Hancock Taylor and the McAfee brothers in 1773. It was later inc by its faster growing neighbor. The area is no longer locally identified as Leestown though this name still appears on maps. 108, 115, 1290.

Leesville PO (Hart). See *Upton*

LeGrande (Hart): *lee*/ghraend (Park). This hamlet with extinct po lies at the jct of KY 218, 436, and 570, 8½ mi se of Munfordville. The po of Legrand (*sic*), in operation from 1904 to 1908, may have been named for Legrand McGee, a local farmer, but with the est of the local school, now closed, the name of both school and community was spelled LeGrande. 863, 1331.

Leitchfield (Grayson): *lihch*/feeld (Leitchfield). This 4th class city and seat of Grayson Co is on the Illinois Central Gulf RR and US 62, just n of the Western Kentucky Parkway and 60 mi ssw of downtown Louisville. According to Barker's 1795 map, the pioneer Shaw's Station was located here before the town was founded about the time of the co's organization in 1810. The town was named for Maj. David Leitch (1753–94), of Leitch's Station in Campbell Co, on one of several large tracts he is said to have owned in the future Grayson Co. After his death, his widow married Gen. James Taylor, a Campbell Co neighbor who had founded Newport, and as executors of Leitch's estate they donated the site for the new co's seat on the condition it be named for her late husband. Though the major's name is pronounced "Leech," the town's may have been corrupted to conform to that of Litchfield in Connecticut. In fact, the co's first po was est as Litchfield or Grayson Court House on Apr 10, 1813, with William Cunningham, pm, and it was not until Dec 13, 1877, that it officially assumed its present spelling. 109, 607, 1307.

Lejunior (Harlan): lee/*djūn*/yər (Nolansburg). This coal town with po and station on the L&N RR's Clover Fork Branch is 13 mi up that fork of the Cumberland R and 9½ mi ene of Harlan. The po was est as Lejunior on Dec 14, 1918, with Kenes Bowling, pm, and named for Lee Bowling, Jr., whose father had just developed the local Bowling Coal Co. Two months before, the L&N had est its station there as Shields. 1173.

Lenarue (Harlan): *lee*/nə/rū (Harlan). This coal town with extinct po extends for ½ mi along KY 990 and Turtle Creek from its confluence with Martins Fork of the Cumberland R, 3 mi se of Harlan. It was named for the Lenarue Coal Co., which had been named for the daughter of F. F. Cawood, who opened the local mine in 1920–21. The po was est on May 29, 1929, with Frank F. Cawood, pm. The local station on the L&N RR's Martins Fork Branch is called Glidden. 1173.

Lennut (Perry): *lehn*/uht (Hazard North). This coal town with L&N RR station and extinct po was named for its location at the n entrance of the rr tunnel just nw of

Hazard's present city limits and s of KY 15. It has been said that the po, est on July 10, 1914, with Kelly E. Watts, pm, was to have been called Tunnel but the prior use of this name led to its adopting the reversed spelling. 1186, 1327.

Lenox (Morgan): *lehn*/əx (Lenox). This po is now on KY 172 and the Elk Fork of the Licking R, 3 mi ne of West Liberty. The name once referred to a prosperous though short-lived sawmill town about a mi up the Fork. At or near the site of the original Lenox po, est on Sept 16, 1899, with William T. Caskey, pm, the Lenox Saw Mill Co., a subsidiary of the American Lumber and Manufacturing Co. of Pittsburgh, Pennsylvania, operated an electrically-powered bandsaw mill from 1916–17 till 1923 when the firm went bankrupt. The po is said to have been named by its petitioner, an Elliott Co storekeeper, David Davis, for a box of Lenox Laundry Soap that lay on his store shelf. 202.

Lenoxburg (Bracken): *lehn*/əx/bergh (Berlin). This hamlet with extinct po, on KY 10, 9 mi wnw of Brooksville, is said to have been named for Samuel B. Lenox who kept a store there around 1850. The Lenoxburg po, however, was not est until July 14, 1874, with William H. Landry, pm, and was discontinued on 1906. 30, 1240.

Leonville PO (Calloway). See *Lynn Grove*

Lerose (Owsley): *lee*/rohz (Cowcreek). This hamlet with po lies at the forks of Meadow Creek and the jct of KY 30 and 1717, 3 mi e of Booneville. The po, est on July 1, 1905, with William Napier, pm, was named for Lee C. Rose, local landowner. 1287.

Leslie County: *lehs*/lee. 402 sq mi. Pop 14,821. Seat: Hyden. This co was est in 1878 from parts of Clay, Harlan, and Perry cos and named for Preston H. Leslie (1819–1907), governor of Kentucky (1871–75) and territorial governor of Montana (1887–89).

Letcher (Harlan). See *Callaway*

Letcher (Letcher): *lehch*/ər (Blackey). This hamlet centers on its po on KY 7 and Rockhouse Creek, ¾ mi above its confluence with the North Fork of Kentucky R and 7 mi wnw of Whitesburg. It was est on Nov 6, 1926, with Robert F. Cooper, pm, and named for the co.

Letcher County: *lehch*/ər. 339 sq mi. Pop 30,253. Seat: Whitesburg. This co was est in 1842 from parts of Perry and Harlan cos and named for Robert P. Letcher (1788–1861), US congressman (1823–35) and governor of Kentucky (1840–44), who later served as minister to Mexico (1849–52).

Letter Box (Jackson). See *Parrot*

Levi (Owsley): *lee*/veye (Booneville). This extinct po at the jct of KY 11, 30, and 847, 1½ mi w of Booneville, was named for Levi Ross, who is said to have been a whiskey taster for the federal government. According to tradition, he erected a building there in 1848 to store the whiskey that was brought in from local distillers. The po was est on June 30, 1902, with Mary C. Treadway, pm. 229, 1287.

Levias PO (Crittenden). See *Midway*

Lewisburg (Logan): *lū*/əs/bergh (Lewisburg). This 6th class city with po on US 431, 8 mi n of Russellville, was named for Eugene C. Lewis, the chief engineer of the Owensborough & Nashville (now L&N) RR who surveyed and planned the town in 1872 when construction of the line began. The first po to serve this area was est on May 7, 1852, at the site of an old stage stop about a mi s, and named Henrysville for the family of the first pm, William F. Henry. In 1877 it was moved to and renamed Lewisburg. The town was inc the following year. 42, 206.

Lewisburg (McCracken and Graves). See *Melber*

Lewisburg (Mason): *lu*/əs/bergh (Mayslick). This hamlet with extinct po at the jct of

KY 11 and the North Fork of the Licking R, 6 mi s of Maysville, is said to occupy the site of George Clark's Station, est by Clark in 1787. In 1789 George Lewis reest the station, which was organized as the town of Lewisburg in 1795 on 70 acres of Lewis's land. However the local po, est on Apr 11, 1828, with Samuel Dobyns, pm, was always named North Fork. 858, 893.

Lewisburg (Muhlenberg). See *South Carrollton*

Lewisburg (Todd). See *Trenton*

Lewis County: *lū*/əs. 484 sq mi. Pop 14,518. Seat: Vanceburg. Lewis Co was est in 1806 from part of Mason Co and named for Meriwether Lewis (1774–1809), the coleader of the famed Lewis and Clark Expedition (1804–5), and territorial governor of Louisiana (1807–9).

Lewis County Court House PO (Lewis). See *Clarksburg*

Lewis Creek (Leslie): *lū*/əs *kreek* (Bledsoe). This po now lies on Greasy Creek, a branch of the Middle Fork of the Kentucky R, 11½ mi sse of Hyden. It was est ¼ mi below in 1936 by John Jackson, who named it Della for his daughter-in-law (Mrs. Bill Jackson). The next year it was moved to a site near Lewis Creek and renamed for the stream, which was early named for the descendants of the pioneer Lewis. The po moved several times with successive pms before reaching its present site. 1099.

Lewis PO (Barren). See *Port Oliver*

Lewisport (Hancock): *lū*/əs/pawrt (Lewisport). This 5th class city with po lies on the Ohio R floodplain, 7 mi w of Hawesville. Before 1839, when the town was chartered as Lewisport, it was a flatboat landing known as Little Yellow Banks in obvious allusion to nearby Owensboro's early identity as Yellow Banks. An effort to name it Prentisport for James Prentis, the first settler, was unsuccessful because of his insistence that it be named for his close friend Dr. John Lewis, another early settler. The Lewisport po was est on Mar 7, 1844, with William B. Schoolfield, pm. 481, 536.

Lewisport PO (Muhlenberg). See *South Carrollton*

Lexington (Fayette): *lehx*/ihŋ/tən (Lexington West, Lexington East, Nicholasville). Kentucky's 2nd largest city and seat of Fayette Co is 63 mi ese of downtown Louisville. Two closely related theories have been offered for the naming of Lexington. According to one, in June 1775 a hunting party from Harrodsburg, seated about a spring near the present center of town planning the est of a settlement and considering possible names, heard from a traveler of the recent events in Massachusetts. Then and there they chose the name of the place whose citizens had turned back the British army. The other account appeared in the *Kentucky Observer and Reporter*, published in Lexington in July 1809, and is alleged to have been based on an interview with John Maxwell, one of the men involved. In 1775 several Harrodsburg men, while assisting William McConnell in building his cabin and raising his corn crop, received the news of the Battle of Lexington and named the place for it. In 1779, at the very center of the present city, Ft. Lexington was erected, and formed the basis of the future city. In 1780 John Todd and others owning property on the site conveyed part of their holdings to the trustees of the new town, which was formally created by the Virginia legislature on May 5, 1782. It had already become the seat of Fayette Co, est in 1780; and Kentucky's first capital was est here on June 4, 1792, though it was to move to Frankfort the following year. The Lexington po was est on Oct 1, 1794, with Innes B. Brent, pm. In Jan 1974, this city merged with its co to form an "urban-county government." 203, 237.

Liberty (Casey): *lihb*/ər/tee (Liberty). This 5th class city and seat of Casey Co lies at the jct of US 27 and KY 49 and 70, 70 mi se of downtown Louisville. It is said that the town was founded shortly before 1806 by some Revolutionary War veterans on land they had been granted for military service, and that the name was bestowed for its patriotic sentiment. On Jan 1, 1808, the site was selected for the new co's seat because of its central location. The po was est on Feb 12, 1814, with David M. Rice, pm, and the town was first inc in 1830. 1397, 1452.

Liberty (Greenup). See *Lynn*

Liberty (Oldham). See *Westport*

Liberty (Pike). See *Garden Village*

Liberty Station (Carroll). See *Sanders*

Lick Branch (Bath). See *Pebble*

Lick Creek (Pike): *lihk kreek* (Lick Creek). This hamlet with po is now on KY 1373, just n of its jct with US 460, 2½ mi up the creek for which it was named, and 13½ mi ese of Pikeville. The po, est on June 10, 1908, with Valey Belcher, pm, was first located at the mouth of the creek, a branch of the Levisa Fork of the Big Sandy R, which site is now under Fishtrap Lake. It was later moved about 1 mi up the creek, and after the creation of the lake was moved to its present spot. The creek was named for a salt lick at its head. On the n bank of Fishtrap Lake is the Lick Creek Station of the Norfolk and Western RR. 1354.

Licking Station (Magoffin). See *Salyersville*

Lickskillet (Logan): *lihk*/skihl/ət (Dot). This settlement on Whippoorwill Creek, 7 mi sw of Russellville, was being referred to as Lickskillet in or about 1810. At the edge of the creek, across from a pioneer dam, was a rock that looked for all the world like a skillet, having been "worn into that shape" by the action of spring water and by deer and other wild animals that may have used it as a lick. Apparently there has never been any derogation implied in the use of this name, and it is the only name the place has ever had. The community has no po. 206, 1344.

Lick Skillet (McLean). See *Glenville*

Lick Skillet (Owen). See *Perry Park*

Lickskillet (Todd). See *Clifty*

Lida (Laurel): *leye*/də (Blackwater). This recently closed po at the jct of KY 80 and 1305, 6½ mi ese of London, was est on May 24, 1905, with Ellen Russell, pm, and named for Lida Hodge Edwards (1881–1967) whose family lived in that vicinity. According to family tradition, local people wished to name the po for her husband, US Congressman Don C. Edwards (1905–11), but for some now unknown reason chose his wife's name instead. 1152.

Liggett (Harlan): *lihgh*/ət (Harlan, Rose Hill). This coal town with extinct po is on the Catron's Creek Branch of the L&N RR's Cumberland Valley Division, on KY 72, at the mouth of the Double Branches of Catron, and 6 mi s of Harlan. It was founded around 1920 and named by the first pm, Floran D. Perkins, for his wife's family. The po, was est on Feb. 16, 1920. 335.

Ligon (Floyd): *lihgh*/ən, *lee*/ghən (McDowell, Wheelwright). This coal town with po is on KY 979, near the head of Clear Creek, tributary of the Left Fork of Beaver Creek, 20 mi s of Prestonsburg. Though the community was first called Clear Creek and some oldtimers still refer to it as such, it officially bears the name of Charles Yancey Ligon, a civil engineer with the C&O RR, who, in partnership with G. P. Salisbury, J. W. Dykstra, and Harry Ayers of Detroit, Michigan, opened a local coal mine in 1918. The Ligon po was est on Mar 2, 1920, with Hattie J. Bingham, pm. 1048, 1305.

Liletown (Green): *lahl*/town (Exie). This hamlet with extinct po lies where KY 792 crosses Greasy Creek, 8 mi sw of Greensburg. It may have been settled before 1840 and named for the pioneer Lile family. Its po was est on July 24, 1877, by John W. Neville. 1339.

Lilleys Station PO (Bourbon). See *Shawhan*

Lily (Laurel): *lihl*/ee (Lily). This village with po is on US 25 and the Laurel R, 6 mi s of London. The po was est as White Lilly (*sic*) on Sept 6, 1855, with Samuel L. Benjey, pm, which has suggested to some that it was named for a popular brand of flour processed by the J. Allen Smith Co. of Knoxville, Tennessee. This is hardly the case since the flour was not being produced that early. The po is more likely to have been named for the wild lilies that grew in abundance there. Perhaps the name reminded the more religious of the early settlers of the biblical "lilies of the field." The po was discontinued in 1880 and reest as Lily on June 15, 1881, with Fleming T. Hodge, pm. 543, 1136, 1282.

Limestone (Carter): *lahm*/stohn (Olive Hill). Little remains of a rural settlement on KY 174 and Soldiers Creek, a branch of Tygarts Creek, 14 mi wsw of Grayson. This was the site of a keg factory started by Dwight A. Leffingwell and a limestone quarry which gave its name to the po Leffingwell est there on Feb 28, 1883, The po closed in 1936. 924, 1250, 1322.

Limestone (Mason). See *Maysville*

Limestone Springs (Bullitt): *lahm*/stohn sprihŋz (Shepherdsville). Little remains of this distillery town and rr station at the head of Long Lick Creek, 4 mi s of Shepherdsville. It was est as Chapeze [shə/*peez*], a station on the Bardstown Branch of the L&N RR, sometime in the early 1880s, and probably named for Adam and Ben Chapeze, sons of pioneer lawyer Ben Chapeze (1787–1839), whose father, a French immigrant, had moved to Bardstown after Revolutionary War service. The po of Chapeze was est on May 23, 1893, with James O. Hagan, pm. In the late 1930s the community, station, and po, since closed, were renamed Limestone Springs for a local distillery, also defunct. 31, 967, 1352.

Limeville (Greenup): *leyem*/vihl (Portsmouth). This rural settlement with extinct po lies at the mouth of Limeville Branch of the Ohio R at its jct with US 23, 8½ mi nnw of Greenup. It was named for a lime-producing operation there in the 1840s by a family of Duvalls and expanded by William W. Tong. In 1871 William Cameron opened the po of Duvalls Landing somewhere in this vicinity, but this was renamed Greenup Lime Works in 1879. On Aug 2, 1888, the po became Limeville, after the local C&O RR station, but was renamed Tongs [tahŋz] on June 20, 1894. This profusion of names led to a 1968 Board on Geographic Names decision for Limeville, since the Tongs po had closed in 1958 and the Limeville name still appeared on rr signs and was borne by the local Methodist church. 23, 1001.

Linchburg (Garrard). See *Cartersville*

Lincoln County: *lihŋk*/ən. 337 sq mi. Pop 18,973. Seat: Stanford. This co was est in 1780 as one of the 3 cos into which the Virginia legislature divided its Kentucky Co. It was named for Gen. Benjamin Lincoln (1733–1810), Massachusetts-born Revolutionary War officer and secretary of war for the Continental Congress (1781–84). From its original territory all or part of 55 other cos were created.

Lincolnville PO (Pulaski). See *Nancy*

Linda PO (Bell). See *Frakes*

Lindseyville (Edmonson): *lihn*/zee/vihl (Brownsville). This hamlet with po is on KY 259, 3 mi n of Brownsville or about midway between Bee Spring and Brownsville, which gave it its original name of Midway. Since this name was already in use by a Kentucky po, Gilbert Webb named the new po he est here on Aug 22, 1935, for the largest of the 3 local families. 942, 1150.

Linefork (Letcher): *lahn/fawrk* (Roxana). This hamlet with po is on Line Fork, 9½ mi sw of Whitesburg. The po of Line Fork (*sic*) was est on May 5, 1879, with Oliver G. Holcomb, pm, probably at the mouth of Cornetts Branch. It was discontinued in 1889 and its papers were transferred to the Kings Creek po at the head of Kings Creek, nearly 3 mi e. On Nov 28, 1890, Lewis Sumpter reest the po as Linefork; it has since moved about a mi up the fork. The po was named for the creek which joins the North Fork of the Kentucky R at Ulvah. According to Harry Caudill, the stream's name was applied by pioneers Gideon Ison, Gudgeon Ingram, and William Cornett, who on arriving there in 1790 spotted a "long line of marked trees" that had allegedly been hacked by land agents for Revolutionary War veterans to mark out a boundary. 1254.

Linn Grove PO (Calloway). See *Lynn Grove*

Linnie (Casey): *lihn*/ee (Liberty). The precise location of this extinct community is not known but it is believed to have been in the vicinity of the fish hatchery on Kettle Creek, some 3 mi sw of Liberty. The local po was est on Oct 5, 1892, and named for the first pm Linnie (Mrs. Frank) Bell. It was discontinued in 1911. According to tradition, the community was once called Pluckum, for reasons unknown. 1040, 1397.

Linton (Trigg): *lihn(t)*/ən (Linton). This hamlet with extinct po is at the mouth of the Dry Creek Embayment of Lake Barkley, 12 mi ssw of Cadiz. It began as Olive's Landing, a stopping place for Cumberland R steamboats, est around 1820 by Abel Olive. By 1830 it had come to be known as Shipsport for it was then the shipping and distributing point for a large section e of the r. In 1845 John Stacker and a Mr. Ewing from Tennessee built the Stacker Furnace here, around which a village grew. About 1856 the town was laid out by S. A. Lindsay and the Whitlock brothers, and was inc in 1861 as Linton, possibly named for Lindsay; no other explanation has been offered. The Linton po was est on May 20, 1864, with William G. Carr, pm. Most of the original townsite is now under Lake Barkley, but the name is applied to a new community developing just n of the embayment. 98, 166.

Lionilli (Pike): leye/ən/*ihl*/ee (Dorton). This recently discontinued po lies 2½ mi up Beefhide Creek from its confluence with Shelby Creek, 14½ mi s of Pikeville. The po was est on Dec 3, 1921, with Benjamin F. Wright, pm, and was to have been named, at the request of an Illinois-based co., for its state name, spelled backwards. According to local accounts, the name was inadvertently misrecorded by a Post Office Department clerk. 1354.

Lisbon (Harlan). See *Louellen*

Lisman (Webster): *lihs*/mən (Nebo). This hamlet with extinct po at the jct of KY 270 and 874, 3½ mi ssw of Dixon, was once a prosperous village. It was first called Shiloh, but the po est on Apr 13, 1888, with Lynn B. Nichols, pm, was named for William Lisman, an early settler. 1088, 1174.

Liss PO (Pike). See *Freeburn*

Litsey (also called **Poortown**) (Washington): *liht*/see, *pawr*/town (Brush Grove). Little remains of a once thriving mill town where KY 438 crosses (Little) Beech Fork of the Rolling Fork R, 5 mi nne of Springfield. The community, variously known as Ryans Mill, Beechland, Litsey, and Poortown was settled before 1800 around 2 mills, about a mi apart. At or near one of these, built by James Ryan, a po was est on July 25, 1848, as Ryans Mills (*sic*) with William S. Logan, pm. In 1852 it was renamed Beechland [*beech*/lən(d)], Probably for the Beech Fork, or else for an avenue of beech trees leading to one of the area's large homes. It closed in 1904. The other mill was run by a family of Berrys and was thus first called Berry's Mill. From 1892 to 1903, the Litsey po, named for the family of pioneer Randall Litsey, operated here. Since around 1900 Beechland has been locally known as Poortown, either for a local family of Poors or, more likely, for the state of the local economy that never quite recovered from the 1893 depression. Washington Co's noted historian, Orval W. Baylor, once offered this account of the Poortown name: A stranger arriving at a crude assemblage of temporary shelters observed a party of surveyors laying off the lots for a new town. When told what they were doing he replied scornfully, "It'll be a damn poor town." Current maps show only the community of Litsey. 16, 17, 1314.

Littcarr (Knott): *liht*/kahr (Blackey). This hamlet with po at the mouth of Little Carr Fork of Carr Fork of the North Fork of the Kentucky R, is centered at the jct of KY 140 and 160, 5½ mi s of Hindman. The po was est on June 23, 1922, by Burnard Smith, whose request to name it Little Carr for its location was accepted by the postal authorities on condition that it be shortened to its present form. 1262, 1288.

Little Creek PO (Pike). See *Robinson Creek*

Little Cypress (Marshall): *liht*/əl *sah*/prəs (Little Cypress). This hamlet with extinct po on the Illinois Central Gulf RR, 11 mi nnw of Benton, was named for its location on Little Cypress Creek, about 1½ mi from its confluence with Cypress Creek, just above the point where the latter joins the Tennessee R. The creeks in turn were named for the many cypress trees upon their banks. The first Little Cypress po was in operation from 1876 to 1879. Then, on Nov 9, 1881, James A. McDonald est a po in his store about a mi w, which he called Blythe [bleyeth], probably for a local family. In 1883 William F. Story, then pm, moved his po to Little Cypress and readopted that name. 76.

Little Dixie Landing (Breckinridge). See *Chenaultt*

Little Georgetown (Fayette): *liht*/əl *djawrdj*/town (Lexington West). This almost exclusively black settlement is on Parkers Mill Rd, just e of South Elkhorn Creek and 2 mi w of Lexington's New Circle Rd. George Waltz developed some of the 200 acres he inherited from the Daniel Waltz antebellum estate as homesites for freed slaves, and they called the place Georgetown. It was later qualified to distinguish it from the seat of Scott Co. 33, 318.

Little Hickman (Jessamine): *liht*/əl *hick*/mən (Little Hickman). This hamlet is centered on a store and extinct po on KY 1268 and Little Hickman Creek, 6 mi s of Nicholasville. The po, in operation from 1867 to 1917, was named for the creek which, with neighboring (Big) Hickman Creek, also a branch of the Kentucky R, was probably named for Rev. William Hickman (1747–1830). This Virginia-born Baptist preacher arrived in Kentucky in 1779 and is said to have preached the first sermon in the Bluegrass and helped to est many area churches. Now a part of the extended Little Hickman community, in the vicinity of the Little Hickman Church, 1½ mi ne, was the store and po of Pink [pihŋk] (1887–1904), named for storekeeper John Pink Overstreet. This area has also been called Pluckemine [pluhk/ə/mihn], the name of the voting district. Some claim this name is a corruption of Plaquemine, which is alleged to have derived from that of some Indian tribe, the Piakemines, about which nothing is known. Robert M. Suell, a co historian, recalls that a Thomas Wade had received a Revolutionary War grant in this vicinity and moved here sometime before the co was est. It is possible that he brought the name with him. Could there be some connection with the New Jersey Pluckemin or the Louisiana Plaquemine, the latter referring to the persimmon tree? 207, 1390.

Little Mount (Spencer): *liht*/əl mownt (Taylorsville, Mt. Eden). This hamlet with extinct po at the jct of KY 44 and 1795, 5 mi ene of Taylorsville, was named for a Baptist church founded in 1801 some 2 mi away. The church is believed to have been named for its location on a slight rise. The possibility of calling the place Walnut Grove for the local trees was considered and turned down. The po was est in the Marattay store on Feb 14, 1868, with Jonathan J. Marattay, pm, and closed in 1906. 1239.

Little Mountain Town (Montgomery). See *Mt. Sterling*

Little PO (Greenup). See *Siloam*

Little Prairie PO (Hopkins). See *White Plains*

Little Rock (Bourbon). See *Plum*

Little Sandy PO (Carter). See *Grayson*

Little Sandy Salt Works PO (Carter). See *Grayson*

Little Skillet (Monroe). See *Blythe*

Livermore (McLean): *lihv*/ər/mawr (Livermore). This 5th class city with po lies at the confluence of the Rough and Green rs, 6½ mi ese of Calhoun. Founded in 1837 by William A. Brown, it was first called Brown's Landing, but was renamed Livermore when Brown est the po on May 15, 1838. Some historians say the name honored James Henry Livermore, allegedly the first settler and/or storekeeper, about which nothing else is known; others claim it was for Alonzo Livermore (1801–88), a civil engineer from Pennsylvania, who supervised the construction of Green R's Lock and Dam No. 2 at Rumsey. The town was inc in 1850. 189, 270, 573.

Livingston (Rockcastle): *lihv*/ihŋ/stən (Livingston). This 6th class city with po is on US 25 and the Rockcastle R, 7 mi se of Mt. Vernon. A po called Fish Point, for reasons unknown, was opened there on May 13, 1840, with Thomas W. Pope, pm. The L&N RR extended its Lebanon Branch to this point in 1870 and est the Livingston Station, named for James Livingston, an early settler. In 1879 the po was renamed Livingston Station and became simply Livingston in 1882, by which name the town had been inc in 1880. 458, 1080.

Livingston County: *lihv*/ihŋ/stən. 312 sq mi. Pop 9,500. Seat: Smithland. This co was est in 1798 from part of Christian Co and named for Robert R. Livingston (1746–1813), member of the Continental Congress (1775–77 and 1779–81) and its secretary for foreign affairs (1781–83). He helped to draft the Declaration of Independence and, as Jefferson's minister to France (1801–4), helped negotiate the treaty that gave Louisiana to the US.

Livingston PO (Livingston). See *Iuka*

Livingston Station PO (Rockcastle). See *Livingston*

Lloyd (Greenup): loyd (Greenup, Wheelersburg). This village, with a Greenup branch po, extends for over 1 mi n of the mouth of Smith Branch of the Ohio R, 3 mi nnw of Greenup, between new US 23 and the r. At the mouth of Smith Branch was the town of Smith Branch, which like the stream was named for its first settler, Godfrey Smith, a Revolutionary War veteran, who arrived from Pennsylvania in 1810. On July 30, 1913, about a mi down the r, the Oliver po [*ahl*/əv/ər] was est and allegedly named for a relative of the first pm, Millard F. Logan. It was discontinued in 1923. In 1930 George E. Riggs reest the local po as Riggs and in 1952 it was renamed Lloyd by Mrs. Winnie M. Herald, then pm, for her youngest son, Irvin Lloyd Herald. 23, 1213, 1451.

Loafersburg (Green). See *Pierce*

Lock No. 4 PO (Butler). See *Woodbury*

Lockport (Henry): *lahk*/pawrt (Gratz). This hamlet with po lies where Sixmile Creek joins the Kentucky R, 10½ mi e of Newcastle. It was named in 1840 for Lock No. 2, which had just been located there by the state, and may also have been known as Wallace's Warehouse for a pioneer family. The Lockport po was est on July 3, 1840, with Alexander D. Williams, pm. 59, 1256.

Lockwood (Boyd): *lahk*/wo͞od (Burnaugh). This extinct po and station were on the old Chatteroi (now C&O) RR and US 23, 7 mi s of Catlettsburg. The first Lockwood po, in operation between 1860 and 1865, was named for Jacob Lockwood, son-in-law of pioneer David White who had deeded the land to him in 1809. Lockwood or Lockwood Station was est in 1881 on land then owned by John Lockwood (1834–99), Jacob's grandson, as a stop on the Chatteroi. Also in 1881 the po was reest as Staley by John, who had it renamed Lockwood in 1892. It closed in 1933. 509, 1091.

Locust Forest PO (Butler). See *Sugar Grove*

Locust Landing PO (Union). See *Uniontown*

Locust Port (Union). See *Uniontown*

Logan County: *loh*/ghən. 556 sq mi. Pop 24,059. Seat: Russellville. This co was est in 1792 from part of Lincoln Co and named for Gen. Benjamin Logan (1743–1802), pioneer, Indian fighter, delegate to the several Danville conventions to arrange Kentucky's separation from Virginia and, later, to draft Kentucky's first constitution, and twice an unsuccessful candidate for governor. The co, then comprising all of Kentucky s of the Green R, was one of the 7 organized in the new state's first legislative session. It included all of 23 and part of 6 cos subsequently created.

Logan Court House (Logan). See *Russellville*

Logans Crossroads (Pulaski). See *Nancy*

Logansport (Butler): *loh*/ghənz/pawrt (Cromwell). This hamlet with Morgantown branch po is in the Big Bend of the Green R, now on KY 403, ½ mi w of the r and 5½ mi nw of Morgantown. Early in this cent it was located about 1¼ mi se, and in the 19th cent was, as the name suggests, a port on the Green R. As such it was first called Carsons Landing for Thomas C. Carson, its owner. According to tradition, the winter of 1852 was exceptionally cold and the r froze over. The steamboat *Captain* (some say *General*) *Logan* was trapped for 2 months in ice some 18 inches thick. "When the spring thaws came, the boat was crushed by the impact of the ice and sank." The po, est on May 5, 1854, with Carson as pm, was named for the boat whose smokestack was visible for years. 578, 1019.

Log Lick (Clark): *lâhgh* lihk (Palmer). This hamlet with extinct po is on the ridge between Lulbegrud and Log Lick Creeks, 11½ mi se of Winchester. The creek for which it was undoubtedly named joins the Red R 6 mi above the latter's confluence with the Kentucky R. According to Daniel Boone's deposition of Sept 15, 1796, it was named for the lick at or near which William and Major Beezley in 1775 built a log trap or blind behind which they hid to shoot at game attracted to the nearby saline spring. They, or perhaps it was Boone, thus called it "The Log Lick." Some historians think it was Boone himself or Boone and John Finley who prepared the log blind. The Log Lick po was est on May 16, 1876, with John M. Elkin, pm, and closed in 1944. 883, 975.

Logville (Magoffin): *lahgh*/vihl (Salyersville North). This po on KY 364 and Rockhouse Creek, 8 mi n of Salyersville, was est in Morgan Co in 1905 and named for a local logging camp. It was moved to Magoffin Co during World War II. 840.

Lola (Livingston): *loh*/lə (Lola). This village with po is centered at the jct of KY 133 and 838, 12½ mi nne of Smithland. The po was est on Aug 23, 1881, and named for the daughter of the first pm, Robert P. Mitchell. 1382.

Lombard PO (Powell). See *Nada*

London (Laurel): *luhn*/dən (London, Lily). This 4th class city and seat of Laurel Co is on US 25 and KY 80, just e of I 75, is the w terminus of the Daniel Boone Parkway, and is 111 mi se of downtown Louisville. According to the most accepted account, the act creating the co in 1825 provided for a popular vote on the choice of the co seat. John and Jarvis Jackson's offer of this site was accepted along with their suggestion of the name London, probably for their English ancestry and their hope that the new town might grow to be like its name source. London was officially founded in 1826 and its po est on Feb 4, 1831, with Branham Hill, pm. It was inc in 1866. 259, 777, 1282.

Lone Oak (McCracken): *lohn* ohk (Paducah West). This village with extinct po is on US 45, just ssw of Paducah. On this site in 1873 a Dr. Pepper is said to have built a flour mill and the community that grew up around it was first called Pepper's Mill. It may also have been known as Pottsville, for D. M. Potts who opened a store in that vicinity. The po was est as Lone Oak on Mar 14, 1892, with Robert C. Potter, pm, and named for a huge oak tree that stood alone in a large cornfield. In 1898 the Post Office Department combined the words of the name but residents continued to spell it as 2 words. The po was closed in 1908. 466, 1014.

Long Falls Creek Po (McLean). See *Glenville*

Longlick (Scott): *lawŋ*/*lihk* (Stamping Ground). This settlement with extinct po at the jct of KY 32 and 1059, 9 mi nnw of Georgetown, was probably named for its location on Longlick Branch of Lytles Fork of Eagle Creek, on whose banks the buffalo herds would gather for long licks of the salt rock on their migrations to the Ohio R. The po was est as Long Lick on Jan 16, 1828, with Hiram Kelly, pm, and respelled Longlick in 1895. It was discontinued in 1902. 235.

Long Pond PO (Caldwell). See *Otter Pond*

Long Ridge (Owen): *lâhŋ rihdj* (Owenton). This hamlet with extinct po at the jct of US 127 and KY 36 is on a long ridge about 3 mi n of Owenton. The po was est on Jan 16, 1873, by Ed Porter Thompson and named Harrisburg Academy for the local coeducational preparatory school he headed, which had been named for the family on whose land it was located. In 1875 Thompson renamed the po Harrisburg. The name was changed to Long Ridge in 1909 to end the frequent misdirection of mail to Harrodsburg in Mercer Co. The po closed in 1966. 625, 1292.

Lookout Heights (Kenton). See *Fort Wright*

Loopee PO (Daviess). See *Stanley*

Loper (Greenup): *loh*/pər (Brushart). This virtually extinct rural settlement lies near the head of Schultz Creek, 12 mi w of Greenup. It was named for Jeff Loper, an early settler and once the owner of most of the land in the vicinity. It never had its own po. 1447.

Loretto (Marion): loh/*reht*/ə (Loretto). This 6th class city with po is centered at the jct of KY 49 and 52, 7 mi nw of Lebanon. It was named in the early 19th cent when an academy was founded here by the Sisters of Loretto at the Foot of the Cross, an order est at nearby St. Mary's in 1812. The order had been named for the town in the Italian Marches noted for its shrine to the Blessed Mother. The po of Loretto was est on Mar 14, 1833, with Thomas Livers, pm, and the town was inc in 1866 and reinc in 1966. 1399.

Lost Creek (Breathitt): *lâhst kreek* (Haddix). This hamlet with po lies at the jct of KY 15 and 476, 5 mi se of Jackson. It was named for the creek that flows into Troublesome Creek just across from the po. The creek was isolated in early settlement times and a number of hunters and travelers are said to have gotten lost when straying too far from its banks. According to one account, an accident befell a family on a particularly icy stretch and they lost all their possessions. The po was est on Oct 11, 1849, with Joseph E. Haddix, pm. 1310.

Lost River (Warren): *lâhst* rihv/ər (Bowling Green South) This is now a residential suburb centered at the jct of US 31W and KY 1484, just s of the Bowling Green city limits. It was named for a stream that came out of the ground nearby, flowed through a ravine for about 300 yards, and disappeared in a cave under a bluff over 100 ft high. The stream emerged further on to form Jennings Creek, a tributary of the Barren R. The community has never had its own po. 676, 1312.

Lot (Whitley): laht (Jellico East). This settlement with extinct po, ½ mi from the Tennessee line and 9½ mi sse of Williamsburg, is said to have first been called Boston for Boss Faulkner, a prominent early resident and possibly storekeeper. This form of the name may have been suggested by allusion to Boston, Massachusetts. The po, est as Lot on July 6, 1855, with James Faulkner, pm, was allegedly named for its fertile and level setting, reminiscent of the biblical Plains of Lot. The town was inc in 1880. The po closed in 1917. The Boston name survives in that of the nearby hill and the local school and church. 1380.

Louellen (Harlan): lū/*ehl*/ən (Louellen). This hamlet with po on Clover Fork of the Cumberland R, 12½ mi ene of Harlan, grew up around a former coal camp est in 1921 by the Cornett and Lewis Coal Co. and named by its president, Denver B. Cornett, for his daughter. The po dates from Dec 3, 1921, when Arthur B. Babbage became the first pm. At that time the L&N RR station there was called Lisbon but is now Closplint No. 2. 1015, 1044, 1173.

Louisa (Lawrence): lū/*eez*/ə, lū/*eez*/ee (Louisa). This 5th class city and seat of Lawrence Co is on US 23 at the forks of the Big Sandy R, 159 mi e of downtown Louisville. The town was est as the new co's seat on Dec 11, 1822, just below the site of Charles Vancouver's abortive settlement of 1789 at The Point or that area within the forks of the r. The first po was est on Nov 3, 1819, as the Forks of Big Sandy with Andrew Johnson, pm. Nothing more is known of it, but the po of Louisa itself was est on Sept 26, 1822, with Hiram Chadwick, pm. The name may have been imported by early settlers from Louisa Co, Virginia, or derived from that allegedly applied to the w fork of the r but later corrupted to Levisa. Or the place may have been named for the daughter (1805–77) of Neri Swetnam, a pioneer settler of nearby Blaine, or for the first white child born (ca. 1798) at the Forks, the daughter of Neri and Elizabeth Ward. It was probably not named for the daughter of Joseph R. Ward, the first co court clerk, as has also been claimed, for her obituary revealed that she was born in 1823. 194, 234.

Louisville (Jefferson): *lū*/ə/vəl (Louisville East, Louisville West, Jeffersonville, Jeffersontown). Kentucky's only 1st class city lies at the falls of the Ohio R. In 1773 Capt. Thomas Bullitt was commissioned by Virginia's colonial Gov. Lord Dunsmore to locate land warrants granted to Virginia's veterans of the French and Indian War. He surveyed 2000 acres on the site of early Louisville. In May 1780 the Virginia legislature authorized the est of the town to be named for the French King Louis XVI who had aided the American Revolutionary cause. Later that year it became the seat of Jefferson Co, one of the 3 created in the division of Virginia's Kentucky Co. The po was est on Jan 1, 1795, with Michael Lacassagne, pm, and the city was inc by the Kentucky legislature in 1828. For some years after the first settlement, and even after the name Louisville had been officially applied, the site was identified merely as the Falls of the Ohio. According to George Rogers Clark's Revolutionary War memoirs, the name was pronounced "*lū*/ihs/vihl" as early as 1789. This alternated with "*lū*/ee/vihl" as the accepted local pronunciation for much of the 19th cent. It was only with the 20th cent that the current local pronunciation came to be accepted. 357, 917, 1296.

Lovelaceville (Ballard): *luhv*/ləs/vəl (Lovelaceville). This village with po is on US 62, 13½ mi e of Wickliffe. The vicinity was settled in 1820 by Andrew Lovelace for whom the village, founded in the mid 1830s, was later named. The local po, est by A. J. Burnett on July 2, 1836, was named Sugar Creek for the local stream and renamed Lovelaceville on Feb 3, 1872. 169.

Loveland (Morgan). See *Redwine*

Lovely (Martin): *luhv*/lee (Kermit). This village with po is centered at the jct of KY 292 and 1714, on Tug Fork of the Big Sandy R, 6½ mi ese of Inez. In early settlement times, it is said to have been a rough place where area men would gather to drink and shoot their guns "and make the air right smoky." It thus came to be called Smoky Bottom, and still is by some, though most local persons now consider the name a disparagement. The po was est in 1931 with M. E. Williamson, pm, and named for local storekeeper S. L. Lovely who helped to get it started. It was laid off as a town in 1921 at which time it was also known as South Kermit, referring to its location 1 mi above this West Virginia town. 1360, 1361, 1362.

Lower Blue Licks PO (Nicholas). See *Blue Licks*

Lower Greasy PO (Johnson). See *Offutt*

Lower Kings Addition (Greenup). See *South Shore*

Lower Slickford (Wayne). See *Slickford*

Lowes (Graves): lohz (Lovelaceville). This village with po lies at the jct of KY 339, 440, and 849, 11 mi nw of Mayfield. It was originally called Lowes Crossroads, having been named for the influential family of pioneer settler Levi Lowe who arrived in 1837. The Lowes po was not est until Mar 27, 1872, by Arthur Smith, and the town of Lowes was inc in 1888. 14, 667, 1228.

Lowes Crossroads (Graves). See *Lowes*

Loyall (Harlan): *law*/əl (Harlan). This 5th class city with po is just below the forks of the Cumberland R and about a mi w of Harlan. It developed as a coal shipping point around an L&N RR switching yard and maintenance facility est in 1920 on land acquired from the local Creech family. The yard was named Loyall, some say for a company official, though no record of such a person has yet been found. The local po, est on Sept 2, 1922, as Shonn (a local name for a rail siding), was renamed Loyall in 1932. 1063, 1173.

Ludlow (Kenton): *luhd*/loh (Covington). This 4th class industrial and rr city is on a hill overlooking the Ohio R and Cincinnati and just w of the Covington city limits. The site was settled around 1790 by Cincinnati residents seeking more open spaces. By 1836 Israel Ludlow had acquired the site and laid out the town that bears his name. The Ludlow po was est on Aug 22, 1864, with John McCormick, pm, and in that year the city was chartered by the Kentucky legislature. The po closed in 1906. 105, 771.

Lula (Letcher). See *Kona*

Lunar PO (Nelson). See *Howardstown*

Lunsford PO (Knox). See *Kayjay*

Luretha PO (Pulaski). See *Ferguson*

Lusby PO (Owen). See *Lusbys Mill*

Lusbys Mill (Owen): *luhz*/beez *mihl* (Lawrenceville). This hamlet on KY 330 and Eagle Creek, 6 mi e of Owenton, may have occupied a site early settled by the family of Samuel Cobb, a Revolutionary War veteran from South Carolina. A mill is said to have been built there for a Stafford or William Jones. Shortly thereafter Jones is said to have sold it to William Cobb and it was called Cobb's Mill (ca. 1842), which name the community may also have borne. Sometime before 1852 John or William Lusby acquired the mill, and it and the village came to be known as Lusbys Mill. The po was est as Lusbys Mill on Aug 4, 1852, with W. C. Warring, pm, succeeded on Sept 16, 1852, by William Lusby. From 1894 till it closed in 1904, the po was called simply Lusby. The community was inc in 1869 as Lusbys Mill. 102, 1292.

Lutherheim (Lincoln). See *Ottenheim*

Luzerne (Muhlenberg): lū/*zɜn* (Greenville). This coal town with extinct po is on the Illinois Central RR, 1 mi w of the present Greenville city limits. William Graham Duncan, a Scottish-born coal operator, acquired this site in 1900, opened a mine here, and founded the town for his employees. Luzerne was chosen as the name for both the station and the po, which opened Jan 14, 1901, when the preferred name, Welling, was rejected by both the rr co. and the Post Office Department. According to a Duncan descendant, Luzerne had "no particular significance historically or personally." The community is also known as Skibo for another Duncan-owned mine in the area. (See also *Graham.*) 389.

Lynch (Harlan): lihnch (Benham). This 5th class city with po extends 2½ mi along KY 160, in the narrow Looney Creek valley, beginning at a point 23 mi ene of Harlan. It was founded in 1917 to house the workers of the newly developed coal operations of the US Coal & Coke Co., a subsidiary of US Steel, and was named for Thomas Lynch, the first president of the co. The po, est as Lynch Mines on Jan 19, 1918, with Frank A. Kearns, pm, became simply Lynch in 1922. The town was inc in 1963. 97, 335, 552, 1173.

Lynch Mines PO (Harlan). See *Lynch*

Lyndon (Jefferson): *lihn*/dən (Anchorage). This 5th class city and suburb is centered at the jct of LaGrange Rd (KY 146) and Lyndon Lane, 8½ mi e of downtown Louisville. It was inc in 1965 to avoid annexation by St. Matthews on the w. Sometime after 1865, the Louisville & Frankfort (now L&N) RR promised to est a station there if Alvin Wood, the local landowner, donated the land and built it for them. He did, and named it Lyndon though no one knows why. Some have suggested that the name refers to Linn's Station, a pioneer fort on nearby Beargrass Creek built by or for William Linn, one of George Rogers Clark's officers. A community grew up around the po est in the depot on Apr 1, 1871, the year the station was opened. In 1963 the po became a branch of the Louisville po. 717.

Lynn (Greenup): lihn (Load). This now all but extinct village lies at the mouth of Coal Branch of Tygarts Creek, 5 mi w of Greenup. Settled around 1800 by Virginia farmers, it was first named Liberty, which name the local church, about a mi below the old village site, still bears. In 1846 a shoe factory was opened and the place may have been renamed for the Massachusetts city which was then the country's leading shoe producer. The Tygarts Creek po, est on July 11, 1833, by Basil Waring, was renamed on Sept 7, 1857, to conform to it. Jesse Stuart once debunked the popular impression that this was a settlement of New Englanders who envisioned another shoe-manufacturing city on the scale of old Lynn, for he could find almost no early residents who had come from that part of the country. The po closed in 1959. 23, 762.

Lynn Camp (Whitley). See *Corbin*

Lynnford PO (Jefferson). See *St. Matthews*

Lynn Grove (Calloway): *lihn ghrohv* (Lynn Grove). This hamlet with po lies at the jct of KY 94 and 893, at the head of Mayfield Creek and 5½ mi w of Murray. On Jan 2,

1873, Lilburn C. Linn est a po in a large grove of trees and called it Linn Grove. After 18 months it was discontinued, but on June 8, 1886, another po was est in the vicinity called Leonville for Leon Blythe, the first storekeeper. On Apr 6, 1892, this po was renamed Lynn Grove. No reason is given for the change in spelling; perhaps a postal clerk's error was responsible. 1401, 1441.

Lynn (Station) (Pendleton). See *Boston*

Lyon County: *lah*/yən. 209 sq mi. Pop 6,200. Seat: Eddyville. Lyon Co was est in 1854 from part of Caldwell Co and named for Chittenden Lyon (1787–1842), son of pioneer settler Matthew Lyon, and local merchant and farmer who represented his district in the Kentucky legislature (1813–14 and 1822–25) and the US Congress (1827–35).

Lyons (LaRue): *lah*/ənz (New Haven). This onetime lumber town with rr station and extinct po is on KY 52, 9 mi ne of Hodgenville. The po was est as Lyons Station of the L&N RR on Apr 8, 1890, and probably named for William H. Lyons, the first pm, who may also have been the manager of the local operations of the Adler Lumber Co. of Louisville. In 1902 the po became simply Lyons. 559.

Lyons Station PO (Larue). See *Lyons*

Lytten (Elliott): *liht*/ən (Sandy Hook). This hamlet with po is now on KY 173, at the head of North Ruin Creek, 5 mi w of Sandy Hook. Until the po was est on June 17, 1898, at the head of Fulton's Fork of Devils Fork, a branch of the North Fork of the Licking R, the vicinity may have been called Devils Fork. The po was named for a local family. In 1959 it was moved to its present site. 1412

Mac (Taylor): maek (Saloma, Hibernia). This hamlet recently moved to its present location on KY 210, 8½ mi nw of Campbellsville, from the jct of KY 424 and 569, 1⅓ rd mi sw. Nothing remains at the original site, popularly identified as Old Mac, but the building that housed the Mac po. This was est on June 21, 1899, and is said to have been named for Mac Beans, then the boyfriend of the daughter of the first pm, William W. Kirtley. The po is no longer in operation. 1291.

McAfee (Mercer): *maek*/ə/fee (Harrodsburg). This hamlet with extinct po is centered at the jct of US 127 and KY 1160, 4½ mi n of Harrodsburg. It is a part of the 1400-acre McAfee Brothers preemption, which they surveyed in 1773. One brother, Robert McAfee, wrote in his journal of having reached "Eldorado" when he arrived in this vicinity, and the town of McAfee, est in 1851, was sometimes referred to as Eldorado. In fact, on June 8, 1849, the McAfee po, which had been est 4 months before with James M. Thompson, pm, adopted the Eldorado name on the suggestion of Peter Dunn, the area's wealthiest landowner. Since most of his neighbors preferred McAfee, however, that name was reinstated on Jan 9, 1850. 1264.

McAndrews (Pike): maek/*aen*/drūz (Belfry). This village with po extends for over 1 mi s along KY 199 and Pond Creek, from the mouth of Mullen Fork to above the mouth of Pinson Fork, and is 13 mi ene of Pikeville. The po, est on Jan 10, 1921, with Isaac L. Andrews, pm, is on the original site of the *Pinsonfork* po, now 1½ mi s. McAndrews was named for the owner of a store at the mouth of Pinson Fork. For years the Norfolk and Western RR station ½ mi n of the po was called Pinson, for an important Pike Co family. 1143.

McBride PO (Webster). See *Sebree*

McCall PO (Greenup). See *South Shore*

McCombs (Pike): mə/*kohmz* (Thomas). This hamlet with po is on KY 194 and Johns Creek, 11 mi n of Pikeville. The po was est on Aug 11, 1905, with Miles E. Hunt, pm, and named for Miles McCombs, a local resident. 1198.

McCools Creek Settlement (Carroll). See *Ghent*

McCormick PO (Powell). See *Natural Bridge*

McCracken County: mə/*kraek*/ən. 251 sq mi. Pop 62,700. Seat: Paducah. This co was est in 1824 from part of Hickman Co and named for Capt. Virgil McCracken, one of the 9 officers killed in the Battle of River Raisin, Jan 22, 1813, for whom Kentucky cos were named.

McCrarysville (Ohio). See *Rochester*

McCreary County: mə/*kreer*/ee, mə/*kreer*/ə. 427 sq mi. Pop 15,557. Seat: Whitley City. The last co est in Kentucky, in 1912, from parts of Whitley, Pulaski, and Wayne cos, was named for James B. McCreary (1838–1918), twice governor of Kentucky (1875–79 and 1911–15).

McDaniels (Breckinridge): maek/*daen*/əlz (McDaniels). This hamlet with po is on KY 259, 11 mi s of Hardinsburg. It is said that its founder, Sam Spencer, a pioneer and Indian fighter, named it for William McDaniels, a fellow member of Col. William Hardin's party at Fort Hardin (now Hardinsburg). McDaniels, who arrived at Fort Hardin in 1780, was killed by Indians before the turn of the cent. On Sept 4, 1860, William McDaniel (*sic*), no known kin to the pioneer, est the short-lived po of McDaniels Store. On July 7, 1874, another po was est by James F. Armes across the rd and called McDaniels. In 1976 the po was moved about a mi down the rd. 214, 935, 1398.

McDaniels Store PO (Breckinridge). See *McDaniels*

McDowell (Floyd): mək/*dow*/əl (McDowell). This village with po is on Hall Fork of the Left Fork of Beaver Creek and KY 680, just e of its jct with KY 122, 14 mi s of Prestonsburg. It may have been named by and for Walter B. McDowell, a North Carolina-born school teacher who settled there in the 1870s. He is said to have been instrumental in getting the po est on July 17, 1879, with Wilburn Hall, pm. 1370.

Maceo (Daviess): *mā*/see/oh (Maceo). This village with po and rr station stretches over 8 mi ne of Owensboro. The community was settled just after the Civil War by freed slaves on land given to them by their ex-masters. There the Louisville Henderson & St. Louis (now L&N) RR laid out a town and est a po in 1890 or 1891 named Powers Station for Col. J. D. Powers of Owensboro, a rr official. To avoid confusion with Powers Store, another Kentucky po, pm Edwin P. Taylor suggested that his po be renamed Maceo for Capt. Alonzo Maceo, a Cuban mulatto then in the news for having been killed in the early stages of the Cuban revolt against Spain. This change was effected on Feb 3, 1897. 930, 1348.

McHargue (Laurel): mə/*kahrgh* (Lily). This settlement, 1¼ mi from the Knox Co line and 8 mi sse of London, was named for William McHargue, progenitor of a large family, who arrived here from Pennsylvania in 1806. In 1812 he built a gristmill on Robinson Creek, a tributary of Laurel R. Another William McHargue est the po of McHargues Mills at this site on Jan 21, 1851, but it closed in 1853. 1282.

McHargue Mills PO (Laurel). See *McHargue*

McHenry (Ohio): maek/*hehn*/ree (Hartford, Paradise). This 6th class city is on US 62, 4 mi s of Hartford. At or close to this site, a village identified as Hamelton in the 1850 Ohio Co Census was inc on Feb 23, 1874. The po of Render Coal Mines, est here on Mar 29, 1872, and named for the local Render Mine which opened in 1871, was renamed McHenry in 1874 with Andrew Duncan, the superintendent of the local McHenry Mine, as pm. McHenry was named for Col. Henry D. McHenry (1826–90), an Ohio Co lawyer and US congressman from Kentucky's 4th District who, with

Duncan, est the McHenry Coal Co. in 1873 to mine the local coal. The town was reinc as McHenry in 1880. 598, 640, 826.

McKee (Jackson): mə/*kee* (McKee, Sandgap). This 5th class city and seat of Jackson Co lies at the jct of US 421 and KY 89, 104 mi se of downtown Louisville. It was founded as the co's seat in 1858 and probably named for George R. McKee, a co judge and state legislator from that area. The McKee po was est on Oct 25, 1858, with Harris Freeman, pm, and the town was inc in 1882. 1418.

McKinney (Lincoln): mə/*kihn*/ee (Hustonville). This village with po at the jct of KY 198 and the Southern Ry, 6½ mi sw of Stanford, is close by the site of the pioneer fort built by William Montgomery in 1779. It was destroyed by Indians sometime before 1789 when Archibald McKinney (1750–1823) arrived from Bourbon Co, rebuilt it, and renamed it McKinneys Fort. By this name the community, built up around it, was known until 1874 when the Cincinnati Southern (now Southern) Ry came through and the name was changed to McKinney Station. The po, est as McKinneys Station on Sept 12, 1877, with Thomas J. Christerson, pm, was renamed McKinney in 1880. 60.

McKinneysburg (Pendleton): mə/*kihn*/eez/bergh, mə/*kihn*/ihz/bergh (Kelat). This settlement and extinct po on the Licking R, 6 mi sse of Falmouth, were named for the many McKinneys in that vicinity. The po, est on Dec 3, 1890, with Jacob D. Doubman, pm, closed in 1929. 1230.

McKinneys Fort (Lincoln). See *McKinney*

McKinneys Station PO (Lincoln). See *McKinney*

Mackoy PO (Greenup). See *Graysbranch*

Mackville (Washington): *maek*/vəl (Mackville). This 6th class city with po extends e 1 mi along KY 152 from a point 7½ mi ene of Springfield. An act to est the town of Maxville (*sic*) on part of a 700-acre tract granted by the Virginia government to Capt. John M. McKittrick, a Revolutionary War veteran, was approved by the Kentucky legislature on Dec 28, 1818. It is not known why the name of Captain McKittrick, for whom the town is said to have been named, was corrupted to Maxville or why the po was est, on Jan 9, 1826, as Mackville. 16, 979.

McLean County: mə/*klān*. 256 sq mi. Pop 10,800. Seat: Calhoun. This co was est in 1854 from parts of Daviess, Ohio, and Muhlenberg cos and named for Judge Alney McLean (1779–1841), US congressman (1815–17 and 1819–21) and circuit judge (1821–41) for the district which included this future co.

McLeans Mill PO (Todd). See *Kirkmansville*

McPherson PO (Knott). See *Hindman*

McQuady (Breckinridge): mə/*kwā*/dee (Glen Dean). This crossroads hamlet with po at the jct of KY 105 and 261, 5 mi sw of Hardinsburg, grew up around a stagecoach stop and store called Jolly Station for the family of Nelson Jolly, the local landowner. On Aug 25, 1890, when the Fordsville Branch of the Louisville Hardinsburg & Western (later a branch of the Louisville Henderson & St. Louis) RR was completed to this site, a po was est and named for the family of its first pm, Annie McQuady. 558, 1398.

McRoberts (Letcher): mək/*rahb*/ərts (Jenkins West). This coal town with po, strung out along the upper reaches of Wrights Fork of Boone, a tributary of the North Fork of the Kentucky R, and 9½ mi ne of Whitesburg, was founded by the Consolidation Coal Co. in 1912 and named for Samuel McRoberts, a New York City banker and later (1918–28) a co. director. On Mar 30, 1912, the McRoberts po was est with Daniel P. Looney, pm. 1265.

McWhorter (Laurel): mək/*wɜt*/ər (Portersburg, London). This hamlet with recently discontinued po is on KY 578/638 and the South Fork of the Rockcastle R, 7 mi ne of

London. The po was est on Feb 8, 1884, with Elijah C. McWhorter, pm, and named for his family of farmers and timber and stock raisers, perhaps specifically for Cannon McWhorter, a local merchant. 1282.

Maddensville (Boone). See *Florence*

Maddoxtown (Fayette): *maed*/əx/town (Centerville). This predominantly black settlement extends about ½ mi along Huffman Mill Rd, just w of its jct with Russell Cave Rd, 4 mi nne of Lexington's New Circle Rd. It was founded by Samuel Maddox, a Maryland native and Scott Co farmer, on land he subdivided in 1871 and sold in lots to freed slaves to help them form their own village. Government maps today err in spelling it "Mattoxtown." 33.

Madge (Lawrence): maedj (Adams). This extinct po was somewhere on Dry Ridge, between KY 32 and Blaine Creek, about 6 mi wsw of Louisa. It was est on June 21, 1893, with Jesse K. Woods, pm, and named for Madge Carter Swetnam, the daughter of Millard and Jennie Clayton Carter of that vicinity. The po was discontinued in 1927. 1053.

Madison County: *maed*/ə/sən. 443 sq mi. Pop 53,315. Seat: Richmond. This co was est in 1785 from part of Lincoln Co and was one of the 9 cos formed while Kentucky was still a part of Virginia. It was named for James Madison who was to become the 4th president of the US.

Madisonville (Hopkins): *maed*/əs/ən/vihl (Madisonville East, Madisonville West). This 4th class industrial city and seat of Hopkins Co lies at the jct of US 41 and 41A and the Illinois Central Gulf and L&N RRs, 106 mi sw of downtown Louisville. In 1807 it was est as the seat of Hopkins Co on 40 acres donated by Daniel McGary and Solomon Silkwood and named for James Madison, then US secretary of state and later the 4th president. The Hopkins Court House po, est on Oct 1, 1809, with Joshua Barnes, pm, was renamed Madisonville in 1813. 159.

Maggard (Magoffin): *maegh*/ərd (Salyersville North). This hamlet with po is on KY 1081 and Raccoon Creek, 4½ mi n of Salyersville. The po, est on Jan 30, 1929, with Reuben Arnett, pm, is said to have been named for Hiram Maggard, local storekeeper. 1422.

Maggie (Trigg): *maegh*/ee (Cadiz). This extinct po was in what is now aptly called the Oakland Community [*ohk*/lənd], centered around the Oakland Church, less than ½ mi e of KY 139 and 5½ mi s of Cadiz. The po was est on June 4, 1894, and named for Maggie L. Porter, who became pm from 1900 until the po closed in 1907. Oldtimers still identify the vicinity as Maggie. 98, 1325.

Magness (Marshall): *maegh*/nəs (Oak Level). This extinct po on KY 299, 5½ mi s of Benton, was in operation from 1891 to 1907. It was probably named for its first pm, Zachariah Magness, or his family. 1337.

Magnolia (LaRue): maegh/*nohl*/yə (Magnolia). This village with po, centered at the jct of US 31E and KY 470, 8 mi s of Hodgenville, extends about a mi along both rds. The po was est on Apr 14, 1851, at a stage stop on the Louisville-Nashville Turnpike (now US 31E), 1 mi n, and is said to have been named by the first pm, David J. Harris, for his wife. After the Civil War, Aaron F. Smith moved the po to its present site, by then called Centerpoint, either for its location (1) on the dividing line of the headwaters of the Green and Nolin rs, (2) midway between Louisville and Nashville and at the highest point on the pike between those 2 cities, (3) between Hodgenville and Aetna Furnace (it is known to have early served as a shipping point for the iron works there), or (4) midway between the stage stop and the Tate house to the s; or because it served as the neighborhood social center. 621, 1436.

Magoffin County: mə/*ghahf*/ən. 310 sq mi. Pop 13,455. Seat: Salyersville. This co was est in 1860 from parts of Morgan, Johnson, and Floyd cos and named for Beriah Magoffin (1815–85), governor of Kentucky (1859–62), who is said to have resigned when his southern sympathies precluded his meeting Lincoln's call for troops.

Mahan (Whitley). See *Wofford*

Mains PO (Pendleton). See *Bachelors Rest*

Majestic (Pike): mə/*djehs*/tək (Majestic). This coal town with po is on KY 194 and Poplar Creek, 21½ mi e of Pikeville. It was named for the operator of the local mines, the Majestic Collieries, so named for the presumed magnitude of the deposit. The po was est on July 13, 1909, with Thornton M. Epperson, pm. 257, 1354.

Malone (Morgan): mə/*lohn* (Cannel City). This hamlet with po is in the Caney Creek Valley and on KY 191, 2½ mi s of West Liberty. The community is said to have been first called Mudville for the condition of its rds in winter. The po, est on Mar 20, 1896, with Lula M. Lykins, pm, was named for Malone Lykins, a resident and descendant of pioneer John Barker who settled in 1821 near the mouth of nearby Barker Branch of Caney. 112, 1027.

Maloneton (Greenup): mə/*loh[n]*/tən (Portsmouth). This rural settlement with po is on KY 7 and Tygarts Creek, 8 mi nnw of Greenup. It was probably named for its first pm, William Malone, when the po was est on June 20, 1884. It was then and afterwards also referred to as Fairview Community, probably a commendatory name. 1213, 1447.

Malt (LaRue): mâhlt (Hibernia). This extinct mill town and po were on the West Fork of Otter Creek, a branch of the Rolling Fork R, 8 mi se of Hodgenville. At the site of his mill and store, James M. Howell est the Otter po [*âht*/ər] on July 31, 1886, named for the creek that in turn had undoubtedly been named for the animals found by early settlers on its banks. In Dec 1897 the po was moved by Robert J. Skaggs some 3 mi w, where it continued to operate as Otter. In 1899 Howell requested another po at the original site, but since the Otter name was still in use, another was sought. According to local accounts, the name Malt was suggested by a store clerk who had spotted some cans of malt on a grocery shelf. 348, 1306.

Mammoth Cave (Edmonson): *maem*/əth *kāv* (Mammoth Cave). This po is at the Mammoth Cave Historic Entrance, 3 mi n of KY 70 at Sloans Crossing and 8½ mi e of Brownsville. The po was est on Dec 23, 1842, with Archibald Miller, pm. After an intermittent existence it closed in 1874, to be reest as Mammoth on May 20, 1881, and renamed Mammoth Cave some 3 months later. The now defunct city of Mammoth Cave was inc at that site on Mar 9, 1871.

Mammoth PO (Edmonson). See *Mammoth Cave*

Manchester (Clay): *maen*/chehs/tər (Manchester). This 4th class city and seat of Clay Co lies at the jct of US 421 and KY 11, 123 mi se of downtown Louisville. In May 1807 the newly organized Clay Co Court authorized the location of the co seat on a 10-acre tract ½ mi below the Lower Goose Creek Salt Works and stipulated that it be called Greenville for Gen. Green Clay (1757–1826), the Virginia-born legislator and later hero of the War of 1812, for whom the co was also named. Another Greenville in Kentucky led to the replacement of the name, in Dec 1807, by Manchester, but the derivation of this name seems to have long been in dispute. The popular notion that it was suggested by Lucy Burman Lees, the 2nd wife of Gen. Theophilus Toulmin Garrard, for her hometown in England, is unfounded. She was born in 1825, long after the name had come into use, and it is thought she came from Virginia. The more credible explanation is that it was named by its founders, members of the White, Garrard, and Gilbert families, following their development of the famed Goose Creek Salt Works, who envisioned the genesis of an industrial city on the order of Manchester, England. The po was est on Jan 1, 1813, as Clay County Court House with John M. Slaughter, pm. 809, 1301, 1329, 1418.

Mangum (Pulaski): *maeŋ*/əm (Mintonville). This po on KY 1676, 9 mi nw of Somerset, was est on Aug 31, 1908, by George Cleve Gifford, who named it for the seat of sw Oklahoma's Greer Co where he had formerly lived. 1410.

Manila (Johnson): mə/*nihl*/ə (Oil Springs). This hamlet with po is 1½ mi up Colvin Branch of Paint Creek and 5½ mi wnw of Paintsville. The po was est on July 1, 1898, with William McDowell, pm, and named for the Spanish American War battle of Manila Bay (May 1, 1898). 1353.

Manitou (Hopkins): *maen*/ə/tū (Madisonville West). This hamlet with po at the jct of US 41A and KY 630, 3 mi wnw of Madisonville is what remains of a well known 19 cent health resort. At what may have been called Tywhopity [tə/*wahp*/ih/tee], allegedly the aboriginal name for the local sulphur and salt spring, a community was founded and named Steubens Lick [*styū*/bənz lihk]. For his services to the American cause in the Revolutionary War, the Virginia legislature granted Friederich Wilhelm, Baron von Steuben (1730–94), a large acreage in this vicinity and the name was allegedly applied after his exploratory visit in 1787. A short-lived Steubens Lick po (1878–79) was reest on Nov 7, 1882, as Manitou, this name having been suggested by C. J. Pratt who had noted on a recent visit to Manitou (Springs), Colorado, the close similarity between the 2 springs. Manitou, an Algonquian word referring to the spirit or presence believed to pervade all living things, has a secondary meaning of "powerful," which was said to describe aptly the healing effects of the water. A folk etymology has also been offered for the name: The man sent by the L&N RR to investigate the possibility of extending its line through that place, when asked what he had seen, replied, "only a man or two." 159, 466, 1320.

Mann (Metcalfe). See *Curtis*

Manns Lick (Taylor). See *Mannsville*

Mannsville (Taylor): *maenz*/vihl (Mannsville). This village with po on Robinson Creek lies at the jct of KY 70 and 337, 7½ mi e of Campbellsville. It was first called Manns Lick for a local salt deposit on land owned by its pioneer settler, Moses Mann (1757–1849), a Revolutionary War veteran and Indian fighter. It became known as Mannsville before or at the time the po was est on Mar 4, 1852, with Lewis G. Pennington, pm. It may also have been called Buena Vista for the Mexican War battle. 1291.

Manse (Garrard): maens (Paint Lick). This hamlet with extinct po on KY 52, centered on the Old Paint Lick Church, 7½ mi e of Lancaster, may first have been called Old Paint Lick, for the Presbyterian church built around 1784. According to local tradition, it was renamed for the home of the preacher by residents who wished to distinguish their community from the village of Paint Lick, 2 mi ne. The Manse po was in operation from 1890 to 1906. 746.

Manuel (Perry): *maen*/yū/əl (Krypton). This extinct po on Grapevine Creek and KY 28, 8 mi nw of Hazard, was est on June 25, 1910, and is said to have been named by its first pm, Shade Davidson, for his son Manuel, a carpenter. 1272.

Maple Grove (Trigg): *māp*/əl *ghrohv* (Canton). This extinct po on Beechy Fork of Donaldson Creek and KY 1062, 6 mi ssw of Cadiz, was in operation from 1873 to 1913. Named for a grove of large maple trees, it served an area among whose earliest settlers were Drewry Bridges and his family who had arrived from Edgecomb Co, North Carolina, in 1804. Drewry's grandson, Cullen T. Bridges, was the only pm. 98.

Maple Mount PO (Daviess). See *St. Joseph*

Maplesville (Laurel): *māp*/əlz/vihl (London). This extinct po on KY 586, less than ¼ mi n of its jct with KY 472 and 2½ mi e of London, was named for the family of its first pm, William R. Maples. The po was est on May 14, 1890. 1282.

Marcum (Clay): *mahr*/kəm (Creekville). This po is now on KY 66 and Red Bird R, 11 mi ese of Manchester. It was est near the mouth of Big Creek, over 4 mi downstream, on Mar 11, 1908, with Henry B. Marcum, Jr., pm, and named for the family of Thomas Marcum, a Clay Co pioneer. 1340, 1418.

Mare Creek (Floyd). See *Stanville*

Maretburg (Rockcastle): *mehr*/ət/bergh (Maretburg). This hamlet with extinct po on US 150, 1½ mi w of Mount Vernon, was once a station on the L&N RR's Lebanon Branch called Mt. Guthrie for James Guthrie, the rr's 3rd president (see *Guthrie*). Around 1882 it was renamed by the rr for James Maret (1855–1936), then station agent and telegraph operator at the Mount Vernon Station, after he prevented the collision of 2 trains at this point. Maret, later a Mount Vernon businessman, was to found the co's first newspaper and telephone exchange but was best known as the promoter of the famed Boone Way which later became the Dixie Highway or US 25. The po was est as Maretburgh on Mar 27, 1885, with Benjamin F. Sutton, pm. 34.

Mariba (Menifee): *mε*/ə/bee, *mε*/ə/bə (Scranton). This hamlet with po on US 460, 3 mi se of Frenchburg, is said to have been named by William C. Taylor, merchant, lumberman, co judge, school superintendent, pm, and large landowner, for his wife, Mariba Osborne Taylor. The po was est as Hariba, probably a spelling error, on May 10, 1882, with Jonathan Osborne, pm. Taylor became pm in 1883, and Mariba herself succeeded him in 1886 and had the name changed to Mariba. The community may also have been nicknamed *Pokeberry*. 980, 1154.

Marion (Crittenden): *mε*/yən (Marion). This 4th class city and seat of Crittenden Co is on US 60 and 641, 132 mi sw of downtown Louisville. It was founded in 1842 on land donated by Dr. John S. Gilliam for the new co's seat and named for Revolutionary War Gen. Francis Marion. It was inc 2 years later. The po est as Oxford on Apr 29, 1843, on the grounds of the Oxford Academy, several mi se, was moved to and renamed Marion in 1846. 806.

Marion County: *maer*/yən. 347 sq mi. Pop 17,618. Seat: Lebanon. This co was est in 1834 from part of Washington Co and named for Gen. Francis Marion (1732?–95), the so-called "Swamp Fox" of the American Revolution.

Marksbury (Garrard): *mahrx*/behr/ee (Bryantsville). This extinct po on US 27, 4½ mi nw of Lancester, was named by and for William D. Marksbury, the local storekeeper, who est it on Apr 4, 1883. It closed in 1915. 1225.

Marlowe (Letcher): *mahr*/loh (Mayking). Now considered suburban Whitesburg, this former coal camp is on KY 931, ½ rd mi n of Whitesburg's nw city limits. It was est in the early 1920s and named for M. K. Marlowe, the cofounder of the local Elkhorn and Jellico Coal Co. 615, 1265.

Marrowbone (Cumberland): *maer*/bohn (Dubre, Waterview). This village is strung out for almost 2 mi along KY 90 and the stream for which it was named, 6½ mi wnw of Burkesville. The community was founded in 1809 and its po est on Jan 15, 1829, with Richard Wade, pm. Several accounts have been given for the naming of the highly fertile Marrowbone Creek. The most fanciful of these refers to one of the 11 children of pioneer settler Jane Allen, who became violently ill from eating the marrow of a bear shot by his older brothers. It is said he would eat no more of "that marrowbone meat." Or, the creek was named by early settlers who likened the rich farmland there to the marrow of a bone. Contemporary historians are fairly sure that the creek was named around the turn of the 19th cent by either the Allens or the children of Capt. John Pace, the earliest settlers, for the Marrowbone Creek in their native Henry Co, Virginia. 223, 642, 897, 1385.

Marrowbone (Pike). See *Regina*

Marshall (Mason). See *Lewisburg*

Marshall County: *mahr*/shəl. 304 sq mi. Pop 24,400. Seat: Benton. This co was est in 1842 from part of Calloway Co and named for John Marshall (1755–1835), the first chief justice of the US Supreme Court (1801–35).

Marshallville (Magoffin): *mahrsh*/əl/vihl (Ivyton). This po on KY 867, 5½ mi se of Salyersville, serves the families of upper Gun Creek, a tributary of the Licking R. The po, est in 1941, was named for local families. 1422.

Martha Mills (Fleming). See *Tilton*

Martin (Floyd): *mahr*/tən (Martin, Harold). This 4th class city with po lies at the forks of Beaver Creek, 5 mi ssw of its confluence with the Levisa Fork of the Big Sandy R, and 6 mi s of Prestonsburg. It was founded as a coal-mining community in the early 20th cent. The po, est on Mar 7, 1910, as Bucks Branch for this tributary of Beaver Creek, was renamed Smalley in 1913 for Smalley Crisp, the local landowner, when Martin Van Allen was appointed pm. Though in 1926 the po officially assumed Allen's given name, a 1915 map shows that this name had already come to identify the community at the mouth of Bucks Branch.

Martin County: *mahr*/tən. 230 sq mi. Pop 13,924. Seat: Inez. This co was est in 1870 from parts of Johnson, Floyd, Pike, and Lawrence cos and named for John P. Martin (1811–62), Kentucky legislator (1841–43 and 1857–61) and US congressman (1845–47).

Martin PO (Lewis). See *Queens*

Martinsburg (Elliott). See *Sandy Hook*

Martins Fork PO (Lewis). See *Queens*

Martinsville (Warren): *mahr*/tənz/vihl (Meador). This extinct community, with a po in operation from 1820 to 1850, lay 1 mi n of the Barren R 1½ mi s of the jct of KY 101 and 1402, and 10½ mi e of Bowling Green. It was laid off as a town in 1820 by its first settler, the pioneer physician Hudson Martin, who most likely named it for himself. 836.

Martwick (Muhlenberg): *mahrt*/wihk (Central City East). This coal town with branch po is on KY 1381, just n of the Illinois Central Gulf RR, US 62, and the Western Kentucky Parkway, and 10 mi ne of Greenville. It grew up around the Martwick Mine, opened in 1910 by Greenville coal operators Charles M. Martin and Judge William A. Wickliffe, for whom it was named. The po was est on Mar 15, 1912, with Arthur C. Howard, pm. 773, 1253.

Mary Alice (Harlan): *mɛ*/ee *ael*/əs (Harlan). This coal town with po is on KY 72 and Catron Creek, a branch of Martins Fork of the Cumberland R, 3½ mi s of Harlan. It was named by the owner of the Mary Alice Coal Co., Dr. H. K. Buttermore, for his 2 daughters, Mary Jane and Ruth Alice. The po was est in 1945. 1207.

Marydell (Laurel): *mɛ*/ee/dehl, *mɛ*/ee/dāl (Blackwater). This po is on KY 1803, 8½ mi e of London. The po was est on July 25, 1884, with Newton M. Gregory, pm, and named either for Mary, the daughter of a local resident, and her friend, Dell Nicholson, or, possibly, for a Marydell Spivey. 1141, 1282.

Mary Helen (Harlan): *mɛ*/ee *hehl*/ən (Harlan, Evarts). This coal town with po extends up Turtle Creek and its branches from a point about 1 mi from the confluence of Turtle and Martins Fork of the Cumberland R, and 3½ mi se of Harlan. It was founded and named around 1917 by the Mary Helen Coal Corp. The po was est on Nov 1, 1919, by Silas J. Dickenson as Coalgood, the transposition of the words aptly describing the quality of the coal being mined there. While the po still bears this name, the local L&N RR station has always been Merna, for reasons unknown. 1026, 1173.

Maryhill Estates (Jefferson): *mɛ*/ee/hihl ehs/*tāts* (Jeffersonville). This 6th class city lies between Cherrywood Village on the s and Brownsboro Rd on the n, 6 mi e of downtown Louisville. Inc in 1963, it had been developed as a subdivision in 1960 by John A. Walser on hilly land purchased from the Archdiocese of Louisville just after World War II and named for both the Blessed Virgin Mary and Walser's mother and daughter. It has never had its own po. 1168.

Maryville (Bullitt). See *Hillview*

Maryville PO (Ballard). See *La Center*

Mashfork (Magoffin): *maesh*/*fawrk* (Oil Springs, Salyersville North). This po on new US 460, 4 mi e of Salyersville, is at the e end of the Mashfork settlement, which extends for about a mi along the stream for which it is named, a branch of State Road Fork of the Licking R. The po was est on July 13, 1922, by Ogie Williams, who is said to have wanted to name it Marsh Fork for the soggy and marshy land in that area; since this name was already in use, she settled for the name of the creek. Several explanations of the latter have been offered. Years ago hogs would be turned loose to feed on a mash of beechnuts and acorns and thus the name may be a corruption of "mast." The name is less likely to refer to the craft of whiskey making. 1180, 1421.

Mason (Grant): *mās*/ən (Mason). This hamlet with po extends along US 25 and the Southern Ry for 1½ mi from KY 1933 n to a point 3½ mi s of Williamstown. Its po, est on July 26, 1855, as Gouge's [*ghowdj*/əz], was named for a local tavern run by James Gouge and his brother, who had arrived in the vicinity in 1798. In 1876 the Southern Ry built a station there and named it Gouge's or Turner's Station, for the station agent. The following year the po and station were renamed Mason, presumably for one of the rr's contractors. 530, 1342.

Mason County: *mā*/sən. 241 sq mi. Pop 17,534. Seat: Maysville. This co was est in 1788 from part of Bourbon Co. It was one of the 9 cos formed while Kentucky was still a part of Virginia and was named for George Mason (1725–92) who drafted Virginia's Declaration of Rights (1776), the basis of the first 10 amendments to the US Constitution. All or part of 19 other cos were later carved from its original territory.

Mason Creek PO (McLean). See *Beech Grove*

Masonville (Christian): *mā*/sən/vihl (Hopkinsville). This settlement is on the Illinois Central Gulf RR, on US 41A just s of its jct with KY 1027, and 4½ mi s of Hopkinsville. It was est in 1903 as a stop in the then Tennessee Central RR and named for the local landowning Mason family. Since the Mason farm was in the shape of a square, very unusual for this part of the country, local people came to refer to it simply as The Square. A po of this name was est there on May 7, 1891, with Clinton T. Mason, pm, but when the po closed in 1901, The Square ceased to exist as a name. 1403.

Masonville (Daviess): *mās*/ən/vihl (Sutherland). This hamlet extends n on US 231 for about 1½ mi from its jct with Lashbrook Rd, about 5 mi sse of Owensboro. Settled shortly after the War of 1812, it was laid out as a town by Judge Triplett and named for either George Mason (1725–92), the author of Virginia's Declaration of Rights (1776), who had owned 60,000 acres along Panther Creek and Green R, or his grandson, George R. Mason, who lived at the site of the later Green R steel mill. The Masonville po was est on Aug 21, 1856, with Henry F. Carpenter, pm, and closed in 1907. At some unknown location another Masonville po was begun by Samuel Haynes on July 16, 1842. Eight years later it was moved to and/or renamed Fillmore, and with this name was in operation until Dec 1855. 99, 1348.

Massac (McCracken): *maes/aek* (Paducah West). This crossroads settlement with extinct po lies at the jct of KY 786 and 1322, 5 mi sw of Paducah. The po was est as Massack on June 30, 1851, with Thomas B. Hines, pm, and named for the creek 2 mi e, which in turn had been named for the old Fort Massac just e of Metropolis, Illinois. The fort had been built in 1757 by the French to contain English settlement along the Ohio R. First called Ft. Ascension, it was later renamed Ft. Massiac for the French minister of Marine in the Seven Years War. The fort was destroyed by a band of Cherokees and rebuilt in 1794 by Americans who simplified the spelling to its present Ft. Massac. The po of Massac in Kentucky was discontinued in 1908. The name of community and creek was spelled as both Massac and Massack on maps for nearly a cent until, in the 1930s, the Board on Geographic Names confirmed local usage that favored the former spelling. 72, 204, 988.

Massack PO (McCracken). See *Massac*

Matanzas (Ohio): mə/*taen*/zəs, mae/*taen*/zəs (Equality). This extinct po on KY 85, 8 mi w of Hartford, was est on Mar 9, 1900, with Fritz J. Jenny, pm, and named for the Cuban seaport where US soldiers were stationed during the Spanish-American War. It was discontinued in 1912. 905.

Mater PO (Letcher). See *Kona*

Matlock (Warren): *maet*/lahk (Drake). This hamlet with extinct po lies at the jct of I 65 and KY 240, 7 mi s of Bowling Green. It may have been named for Rile Matlock, an early settler. The po was est on May 6, 1892, with Charles A. Matlock, pm, and closed in 1904. 1312.

Mattie (Lawrence): *maet*/ee (Adams). This extinct po on the Right Fork of Little Blaine Creek, 9 mi sw of Louisa, was est on Apr 29, 1898, and named for Mrs. Mattie Chaffin McKinster, the first pm. It was discontinued in 1940. 1095.

Mattingly (Breckinridge): *maet*/ihŋ/lee (Mattingly). This hamlet with extinct po lies at the jct of KY 629 and 992, 7 mi w of Hardinsburg. This site was called Balltown prior to the est on Nov 9, 1881, of the Mattingly po. The first pm, Richard T. Mattingly, was a descendant of Richard Mattingly, a Maryland native (born 1756) who had settled his family on Long Lick Creek, in what was to become Breckinridge Co, in 1791. The po was probably named for the family. 214, 290.

Maud (Washington): mâhd (Maud). This hamlet with po is on KY 55, just e of the Beech Fork of the Rolling Fork R and 9 mi nnw of Springfield. It was first called Rays Mill for a water-powered gristmill built by a Mr. Ray. After a Mr. Bascum had settled in the vicinity, the settlement came to be known as Racum, and was later called Glenville for its picturesque valley location. Another po with the latter name led to the adoption, on Aug 2, 1880, of the name Maud for the local po, honoring a famous trotting horse of that period. 1007.

Mavity (Boyd): *maev*/iht/ee (Boltsfork). This settlement with extinct po lies at the jct of

KY 3 and 1937, 6 mi sw of Catlettsburg. It is said to have been named for William Fletcher Mavity, a local farmer and preacher and the son of John Mavity, a native Virginian. The po was est on June 9, 1884, with Charles L. Williams, pm, and closed in 1912. 509.

Maxon (McCracken): *maex*/ən (Paducah West). This settlement at the jct of KY 305 and 786, 3½ mi w of Paducah, grew up around the Relief Mill, a gristmill on the banks of Massac Creek, est around 1870 by Morris I. Maxon (1831–1903), a Pennsylvania-born miller. According to local tradition, Maxon received his customers' mail for them at his mill, and soon mail was coming into the community addressed to Maxon's Mill. When the po was opened there on Nov 3, 1870, it was given this name and Maxon was appointed pm. The name was shortened to Maxonmill in 1895. When the Illinois Central RR's Paducah & Cairo line was built through in the 1920s, a station was erected ¾ mi sw that came to be known as Maxon Station. In 1925 the po was moved to a site between the mill and station, the jct of KY 305 and 725, and renamed West Paducah, which it remains to the present. The settlement by the mill site is now known simply as Maxon. 881, 1132.

Maxonmill (McCracken). See *Maxon*

Maxon's Mill PO (McCracken). See *Maxon*

Maxville (Washington). See *Mackville*

Mayfield (Graves): *mā*/feeld (Mayfield, Hickory, Farmington). This 3rd class industrial city and seat of Graves Co is on US 45 and KY 80, just off the Western Kentucky Parkway, and 177 mi sw of downtown Louisville. It is believed to have been settled by John Anderson and his wife, of South Carolina, in 1819. Anderson presumably est the Mayfield po on Aug 15, 1823, while the legislative act creating Graves Co in Dec of that year also est Mayfield as its seat. While everyone agrees the city was named for the nearby creek, no one is certain for whom the creek was named. One suggestion is that it was named for a George Mayfield, close friend and hunting companion of Davy Crockett, who accompanied the latter to Texas where both were killed at the Alamo. There is, however, no record of a George Mayfield having been in this section of Kentucky. The more acceptable but still unauthenticated tradition refers to the kidnapping and murder of a Mr. Mayfield, a wealthy Mississippian. While enjoying himself at the races at or near the present Hickman, he was abducted and taken to the future site of Mayfield, presumably to be held for ransom. While there, for some reason he saw fit to carve his name on a tree. Later, in an attempted escape, he was shot and his body fell into the creek and was never seen again. All that was ever found of him was his name carved on the tree. 54, 264, 1228.

Mayking (Letcher): *mā*/kehŋ (Mayking). This village with po is on US 119, where Bottom Fork and Pine Creek join the North Fork of the Kentucky R, 2½ mi ene of Whitesburg. The large bottom land in the immediate vicinity was first settled by Benjamine Webb, the son of James, a leader of the pioneer Adams colony. An early community there may have been called Bottom Fork. The origin of the Mayking name has long been debated. Some say that when the first pm, Isom Gibson, failed to win approval of any of the names he had submitted to the Post Office Department, he was forced to accept the name suggested to him, that of a recently deceased friend of a postal official. Gibson is said to have later received a letter from a Leominster, Massachusetts, resident stating that she had named the po for a girl friend. More likely it was named for the oldest daughter of an early settler named King, or for the wife of the man who had est in that vicinity one of eastern Kentucky's earliest locally financed coal operations. The po has been in operation since Jan 25, 1894. 74, 194, 1254, 1265, 1435.

Maynard (Allen): *mā*/nərd (Austin). This hamlet with extinct po on KY 98, 5 mi e of Scottsville, may once have been called Buncombe [*buhŋk*/əm]. It sprang up around a store opened by Hick Maynard, a Tennessean, during or just after the Civil War. The Maynard po was est in this vicinity on Mar 17, 1898, by Sim Maynard and allegedly named for Hick. The po was discontinued on Oct 31, 1907. 101, 1281.

Mays Lick (Mason): *māz* lihk (Mayslick). This village with po lies at the jct of old US 62 and KY 324, 9 mi ssw of Maysville. The vicinity was first settled in 1788 by 5 related families from Plainfield or Scotch Plains, New Jersey, who purchased 1400 acres from William May 1752–ca. 1825). They named it for him and a nearby salt spring. The po was est on July 1, 1800, with James Morris, pm. 77.

Maysville (Mason): *māz*/vihl (Maysville East and West). This 3rd class industrial city and seat of Mason Co lies at the confluence of Limestone Creek and the Ohio R, 102 mi ene of downtown Louisville. In 1785, 800 surveyed acres at this site were granted by the Virginia legislature to John May (1744–90), a delegate of the Kentucky District to that body, which had earlier sent him to Kentucky to adjudicate land disputes. The settlement that shortly developed there was called Limestone for the creek, which is said to have been so named by Capt. John Hedges in 1773. On Dec 11, 1787, a town called Maysville was formally created and named for May. Yet the local po was est on Oct 1, 1794, as Limestone with George Mitchell, pm, and not officially renamed Maysville until around 1799. The Limestone name actually persisted in use for many years; in 1824 the town was still being called by both names. In 1884 Maysville succeeded in attracting the co seat from *Washington*. 649, 803, 858, 1246.

Maytown (Floyd): *mā*/town, *lae*ŋ/lee (Martin). This village with po is on KY 80 and the Right Fork of Beaver Creek, 9 mi s of Prestonburg. The community has always been called Maytown for a prominent May family whose Beaver Creek ancestor, Reuben May, settled in the vicinity in the 1820s. Since that name had been preempted by a po in Morgan Co, the po est here on Nov 13, 1890, was named Langley, probably for John W. Langley (ca. 1862–1932), a state legislator from 1887 to 1891 who was to represent that district in the US Congress from 1907 to 1926. 128.

Maytown (Morgan): *mā*/town (Hazel Green). Little remains but the po of this 19th cent mill town at the head of Blackwater Creek and the jct of KY 946 and 1010, 12 mi wsw of West Liberty. The po was est on Feb 3, 1848, as Morgan, probably for the co. In June 1849 it became known as Blackwater for the creek and retained this name through its discontinuous existence, until in 1882 Elijah B. May, then pm and storekeeper, had it changed again to Maytown, for his family or specifically for his father Caleb. The creek is said to have been named for the dark appearance leaves made of its waters in the fall and winter. 503, 968.

Mazie (Lawrence): *mā*/zee (Mazie). This po is on KY 32 and the Right Fork of Blaine Creek, just above the mouth of Mill Creek, and 20 mi wsw of Louisa. Britt Maxie is said by some to have submitted his own name with his request for the local po, but postal officials apparently misread it as Mazie, and with this name the po was est on Apr 27, 1899, with Solvinon Sparks, pm. For some reason the error was never corrected. Others dispute this, claiming it was named for an elderly resident, the mother or grandmother of the local preacher. Maxie became pm in 1921. 1094, 1249, 1362.

Meade County: meed. 306 sq mi. Pop 22,856. Seat: Brandenburg. Meade Co was est in

1823 from parts of Breckinridge and Hardin cos and named for Capt. James Meade, one of the 9 officers killed in the Battle of River Raisin, Jan 22, 1813, for whom Kentucky cos were named.

Meador (Allen): *mehd*/ə (Meador). This crossroads settlement with extinct po on KY 101, 9 mi n of Scottsville, was probably named for its first pm, Asberry P. Meador, who est the po on Mar 9, 1891. 101, 1281.

Meadow Creek Community (Wayne). See *Betsey*

Means (Menifee): meenz (Frenchburg). This hamlet with po extends ½ mi along US 460, between the n and s routes of KY 713 and 7 mi w of Frenchburg. The po was est on Apr 10, 1901, and named for the local storekeeper and first pm, Wilbur W. Means.

Medcalf PO (LaRue). See *Athertonville*

Medina (Johnson). See *Oil Springs*

Melber (McCracken and Graves) *mehl*/bər (Melber). This village with po is centered at the jct of KY 339 and 1820, roughly half in each co, 7½ mi ssw of Paducah and 13 mi nnw of Mayfield. The community was first called Lewisburg (not Louisberg as given in an 1880s Graves Co atlas) for Lewis Helfer, the owner-operator of a water mill on Mayfield Creek, 1 mi n. When he est the local po on Apr 17, 1882, he found that another po had preempted his name, and offered instead that of the local Melber family. Oldtimers occasionally still refer to the village as Burg. 1074.

Melbourne (Campbell): *mehl*/bərn (Withamsville). This 6th class city with po is in the Ohio R bottom n of KY 8, over 6½ mi se of the Newport po. The town was founded and laid out in 1890 on land owned mostly by Hubbard Helm and said to have been named by him for the city in Australia whence he had come. The po was est on June 18, 1891, with Robert A. Carnes, pm, and the town was inc in 1912. 1062, 1075.

Mellensburg (Lawrence). See *Peach Orchard*

Melrose (Greenup). See *Worthington*

Melson Ridge (Adair). See *Cundiff*

Memphis Junction (Warren): *mehm*/fəs *djuhŋk*/shən (Bowling Green South). This is now a suburb just s of the Green River Parkway, ¼ mi w of US 31W, and less than 1 mi s of Bowling Green. This small community grew up around the point where the L&N RR's Memphis line switched off from the main line to Nashville. The Memphis Junction po was in operation from 1868 to 1909. 1252.

Menelos PO (Madison). See *Berea*

Menifee County: *mehn*/ə/fee. 203 sq mi. Pop 5,080. Seat: Frenchburg. This co was est in 1869 from parts of Bath, Morgan, Powell, Montgomery, and Wolfe cos and named for Richard Hickman Menefee (1809–41), who represented this district in the Kentucky legislature (1836–37) and in the US Congress (1837–39). An explanation for the spelling discrepancy cannot be given.

Mercer County: *mʒ*/sər. 250 sq mi. Pop. 18,844. Seat: Harrodsburg. Est in 1785 from part of Lincoln Co, Mercer was one of the 9 cos formed while Kentucky was still a part of Virginia. It was named for Gen. Hugh Mercer (1725–77), an officer in the Continental Army who was mortally wounded at the Battle of Princeton.

Mercer Station PO (Muhlenberg). See *Hillside*

Meredith (Grayson): *mʒ*/ə/dihth (Clarkson). This hamlet with extinct po lies at the jct of KY 259 and 226, 5½ mi sse of Leitchfield. The po was est on Mar 25, 1902, and named for the family of its first pm, Lewis T. Meredith. 243.

Meridian PO (Pendleton). See *Boston*

Merino PO (Breckinridge). See *Irvington*

Merna (Harlan). See *Mary Helen*

Merrill PO (Powell). See *Rosslyn*

Merrimac (Taylor): *mehr*/ee/maek, *mɛ*/ee/maek (Bradfordsville). This extinct po lies near the head of Robinson Creek, a Green R tributary, 11 mi ene of Campbellsville. To serve the community known as Robinson Creek Church since 1825, Ulysses C. Clarkson est a po on Sept 28, 1882, which he named Merrimac at the suggestion of Oliver Murrell, a 12-year-old schoolboy. The boy is said to have been impressed with the tale of the Civil War battle of the 2 ironclad warships, the Monitor and the Merrimac, that had fought to a draw at Hampton Roads, Virginia, on Mar 9, 1862, and felt that the Merrimac had been unduly slighted in memorials of the battle. 323.

Merry Oaks (Barren): *mehr*/ee *ohx* (Park City). This hamlet with extinct po lies at the jct of US 68 and KY 1186, 9 mi w of Glasgow. It is said to have been named for a large oak tree there, and, as horse racing was a popular early 19th cent local pastime, for the famed English track of the same name. The po, est on Jan 30, 1836, with Isaac Denton, pm, was closed in 1904. 733, 920.

Mershons (Laurel) *mɜsh*/ənz (Livingston). This extinct po on KY 490, 9 mi n of London, was probably named for William Titus Mershon (ca. 1756–1842), a native New Jersian and Revolutionary War veteran who settled at the jct of the Wilderness Rd and a rd leading to the Clay Co salt works sometime before 1813. This allegedly became Mershons Cross Roads. With this name, and presumably at this site, a po was est on Apr 1, 1837, with Cornelius Mershon, pm. This was renamed Bethel Cross Roads in 1860 and discontinued on Feb 19, 1861. On Sept 13, 1861, another Mershons Cross Roads po was est at the same site or nearby, and this was renamed Mershons in 1895. Since the present Mershons is not at a crossroads, it may be that the name was transferred from the other location. 63.

Mershons Cross Roads (Laurel). See *Mershons*

Meta (Pike): *mee*/də (Meta). This hamlet with recently closed po is centered at the jct of US 119 and KY 194, just ne of the mouth of Bent Branch of Johns Creek, and 6 mi nne of Pikeville. The po, est on June 15, 1896, with Samuel M. Ford, pm, is said to have been named for Meta Smith, a West Virginia girl who was visiting the Fords at the time a name was being sought for the new po. 1345.

Metcalfe County: *mehd*/kaef. 291 sq mi. Pop 9,444. Seat: Edmonton. This co was est in 1860 from parts of Adair, Barren, Cumberland, Green, and Monroe cos and named for Thomas Metcalfe (1780–1855), US congressman (1819–28) and senator (1848–49), and 10th governor of Kentucky (1828–32).

Metcalfe Furnace PO (Carter). See *Star, Coalton*

Metcalfes Landing PO (Bracken). See *Bradford*

Mexico (Crittenden): *mehx*/ee/koh (Fredonia). This hamlet is strung out along KY 70 and the Illinois Central Gulf RR, 6 mi s of Marion. According to local tradition, people moved into the area when fluorspar mining operations began before 1900. The Mexico po est by John A. Myers on Jan 13, 1896, may have been named in recognition of that country's role as a producer of the mineral. The po closed in 1957. 1324.

Middleburg (Casey): *mihd*/əl/bergh (Yosemite). This village with po lies on the Green R at the jct of KY 198 and 1552, 5 mi ene of Liberty. In 1784 Abraham Lincoln, grandfather of the future president and himself a Revolutionary War veteran, laid off an 800-acre patent in this vicinity which was later acquired by pioneer settler Christopher Riffe. Sometime after 1800, Riffe built near his home a water-powered mill which he sold to Jesse Coffey. The mill became the nucleus of a community first called

Coffey's Mill. On Feb 11, 1837, Coffey est a po he called Middleburg either for Middleburg, Virginia, or for its location midway between Liberty and Hustonville and Liberty and McKinney, or both. 212, 1397.

Middleburg (Nelson). See *Bloomfield*

Middle Creek PO (Floyd). See *West Prestonsburg*

Middle Elk Station (Pike). See *Argo*

Middlesboro (Bell): *mihd*/əlz/buhr/ə (Middlesboro North and South). This 3rd class city is 1 mi w of the Cumberland Gap and 8 mi s of Pineville. At or near the site of a pioneer Yellow Creek settlement made around 1810 by John Turner of Virginia, Alexander Alan Arthur, a Canadian resources developer, bought up thousands of acres of Yellow Creek bottom land, attracted investment capital from a number of English businessmen, and by 1889 began to build his city. The Middlesborough po had already been est on Sept 14, 1888, with George C. Whitlock, pm, the name having been selected from a list of names allegedly offered by the investors, or else suggested by a Mr. Watts, a hotel owner at the Gap who had come from the English city of Middlesbrough. Arthur's boom busted with the crash of 1893. In 1960 the Board on Geographic Names ruled in favor of what was by then the preferred spelling, Middlesboro, which the po had assumed in 1894 and the rr and a number of local businesses had used for years. Yet by the Act of Incorporation in 1890 it had been spelled "Middlesborough" and this is still the official form. 197, 894.

Middleton (Simpson): *mihd*/əl/tən (Auburn, Prices Mill). This hamlet lies at the jct of KY 100, 103, and 665, ½ mi e of the Logan Co line, and 7 mi w of Franklin. James W. Baird is said to have opened a store on the Logan Co side of the line around 1856. By 1869 the community had shifted to its present location. It was served by 2 pos: Millikens Store, est on Sept 17, 1878, by George H. Milliken, the storekeeper and first pm, which was discontinued in 1884, and Stowers, in operation in James Stowers's store from 1881 to 1910. Their precise locations are not known. Neither is the date of application of the Middleton name; we are told the names were not used interchangeably. The community may have been named for its original location about halfway between Russellville and Franklin, or for Thomas Middleton who early represented the co in the Kentucky legislature. 18, 1024.

Middletown (Bourbon). See *North Middletown*

Middletown (Jefferson): *mihd*/əl/town (Jeffersontown, Anchorage). This now unincorporated suburb is centered on US 60/460, 11 mi e of downtown Louisville, but bounded roughly by the Jefferson Freeway on the e, I64 on the s, Dorsey Lane on the w, and Anchorage and LaGrange Rd on the n. The town was laid out by William White, who built one of the first houses there in 1784, and was inc in May 1797. It is thought to have been named for its location midway between Shelbyville and Louisville. The po, est before 1809, is now a branch of the Louisville po. Middletown was disincorporated in 1962. 721.

Middleway (Woodford). See *Midway*

Middlewood (Grayson). See *Millwood*

Midland (Bath): *mihd*/lən(d) (Farmers). This village on US 60 and the C&O RR, 9 mi e of Owingsville. First called Midland City, it is said to have been named by the C&O crews for its location halfway between Lexington and Ashland. Across the tracks from the depot was a sawmill and the land across the rd from the mill was sold off in lots around 1890. It never had a po. 416, 1321.

Midland City (Bath). See *Midland*

Mid PO (Magoffin). See *Gunlock*

Midway (Calloway). See *Tobacco*

Midway (Crittenden): *mihd*/wā (Salem). This hamlet strung out along US 60 was named for its location halfway between Marion, 4½ mi ene, and Salem in adjacent Livingston Co. From 1881 to 1908 the vicinity was served by the Levias po, ¼ mi nw of US 60. 1324.

Midway (Edmonson). See *Lindseyville*

Midway (Woodford): *mihd*/wā (Midway). This 5th class city with po is on US 62, just s of its jct with US 421 and of I 64, and 5 mi nne of Versailles. The town was created by the Lexington and Ohio (now L&N) RR in 1835 on over 200 acres acquired from John Francisco and was first called Middleway for its location on the rr halfway between Lexington and Frankfort. A po, est as Stevenson's on Feb 8, 1832, by Thomas Stevenson at a site just n was moved to the tracks in Apr 1834 and renamed Midway in Mar 1837. The town was inc in 1846. 360, 591, 1269.

Mifflin PO (Menifee). See *Scranton*

Mike PO (Floyd). See *Hueysville*

Milburn (Carlisle): *mihl*/bərn (Milburn). This village with po is centered at the jct of KY 80 and 1371, 7 mi se of Bardwell. It was settled in 1822 by a Marylander, William Milburn (1772–1858), who with a neighbor, William Reddick, laid out the town and named it. The po was est Sept 29, 1837, with James B. Quigley, pm. 86.

Miles PO (Fulton). See *Jordan*

Milford (Bracken): *mihl*/fərd (Claysville). This hamlet with po lies on the North Fork of the Licking R and KY 19, just n of its jct with KY 539, 7½ mi sw of Brooksville. It was founded in 1831 by John Ogdon, the co-owner of a local store, and named for a water-powered grain mill and a ford across the r at that point. The po was est on June 10, 1850, with William M. Best, pm. 27, 1240.

Millard (Pike): *mihl*/ərd (Millard). This village with extinct po is centered where Russell Fork joins the Levisa Fork of the Big Sandy R, 6 mi se of Pikeville, and earlier was called simply The Forks. Until it closed in 1965, the po was located on Lower Pompey Branch of the Levisa, near its mouth, over 1 mi ne of the forks. It was est on Mar 11, 1892, and named for Millard Hamilton, the son of the first pm, Louise A. Hamilton. 1033, 1085.

Millersburg (Bourbon): *mihl*/ərz/bergh (Millersburg). This 5th class city with po lies where US 68 and the L&N RR cross Hinkston Creek, 7 mi ne of Paris. It was named for Maj. John Miller (1752–1815), who in 1798 founded the town on 100 acres of his farm. Miller was one of a party from Shermans Valley near Carlisle, Pennsylvania, that had preempted the land in 1778. The Millersburg po was est on Oct 1, 1804, by George Selden. 167, 673.

Millerstown (Grayson): *mihl*/ərz/town (Millerstown). This hamlet with extinct po is on the Nolin R, 12½ mi ese of Leitchfield. Its first settler is believed to have been a Jacob Miller and the po est sometime before 1828 may have been named for him, or for Nicholas Miller. The po closed in 1867. A 2nd Millerstown po was est at or near its original site on May 27, 1881, and first called Skaggs [skaeghz] by and for its first pm, Jefferson G. Skaggs. It was renamed Millerstown the following year when Eppy W. Ferguson became pm. 608, 1307.

Millersville (Adair). See *Crocus*

Millikens Store PO (Simpson). See *Middleton*

Million (Madison): *mihl*/yən (Valley View). This extinct po and station were on the long defunct Richmond Nicholasville Irvine and Beattyville (later L&N) RR and KY 169, 4½ mi wnw of Richmond. On Dec 23, 1881, Richard C. Fain est the Fain po, which was moved to and/or renamed Million in 1884, probably for the family of B. B. Million, large landowner and merchant there. 875.

Mill Pond (Clay): *mihl* pahnd (Barcreek). This extinct po was on KY 11 and Laurel Creek, about 1½ mi above its confluence with Goose Creek, and 5 mi n of Manchester. There is a lack of agreement on what kind of mill the name refers to and thus what kind of pond may have been created by it. According to some, it was named for a big flour mill built by Joe Hornsby in the 1880s and the pond adjacent to it designed to catch the water. Others say there was an old sawmill there and the pond was built to wash the mud from the logs before they were processed. The po est on May 14, 1821, in Oscar Hornsby's store closed in 1963. The mill is also gone. 1329, 1340.

Mills (Knox): mihlz (Scalf). This po at Nasby Mills's store on KY 718 at the mouth of Acorn Fork, 13½ mi e of Barbourville, was est on May 27, 1891, by Isaac Mills and named for his family. 1409.

Millseat (Boyd). See *Westwood*

Mills Pt. (Fulton). See *Hickman*

Mill Springs (Wayne): *mihl sprihŋz* (Mill Springs). This hamlet is centered on its po at the jct of old KY 90 and 1275, 500 ft s of Lake Cumberland and the mill just below the mouth of Meadow Creek for whose antecedent it was named. It is 6 mi nne of Monticello. The first of at least 3 mills here was a gristmill probably built by or for John, Charles, and James Metcalfe in 1816–17. Clark B. Firestone once described the springs: "Fourteen springs gush from the hillside in a stretch of perhaps a hundred yards, and their waters are impounded by a stone wall into a sort of canal shaded by tulip poplars. It is something like an underground river bursting into the sunlight wherever it can force an opening. A flume leads the collected waters to an overshot wheel on the downward side of the mill." On July 30, 1825, the Mill Springs po was est near the mill with John Metcalfe, Jr., pm. 73, 862, 1405, 1408.

Millstone (Letcher): *mihl*/stohn (Mayking). This coal town with po lies at the confluence of Millstone Creek and the North Fork of the Kentucky R, 4½ mi ne of Whitesburg. A po was est here on Dec 17, 1878, and named Craftsville for the family of Enoch Craft, a Confederate Army veteran. Nelson R. Craft renamed it Millstone on June 19, 1918, and the South East Coal Co. built a camp here that year. According to Post Office Department records, another Millstone po had been est at an unknown location on Oct 7, 1890, with Joseph Hall, pm. Inexplicably, the same year that Craftsville became Millstone, the other po, then with Sarah J. Franklin, pm, became Craftsville. Nothing more is known about it, nor is anything known about the mill for which the creek was named. 1265.

Milltown (Adair): *mihl*/town (Gradyville). This hamlet with po on KY 768 and Russell Creek, 4½ mi w of Columbia, was once a thriving village in the vicinity of a 19th cent grist- and sawmill built by the Townsend family. The community was first called Townsends Mill, but after it was acquired by N. S. Mercer it became simply *Milltown*. The po was est as Mill Town on Oct 28, 1853, with Chapman Dohoney, pm, and the name was later spelled as one word. 595, 1426.

Millville (Woodford): *mihl*/vihl (Frankfort East). This hamlet extends for over 1 mi on KY 1659 and Glenns Creek, a Kentucky R tributary, 6½ mi nw of Versailles. It was named for several 19th cent water-powered grist and flour mills in the vicinity. The po, est on July 25, 1854, with Samuel Miles, pm, was discontinued in 1907. 399, 1269.

Millwood (Grayson): *mihl*/wood (Caneyville). This village with po on US 62 and the Illinois Central Gulf RR, 4½ mi sw of Leitchfield, may first have been called Middlewood for its location between Hardin and Ohio cos, and renamed Millwood when a large sawmill was opened there. A po with the latter name was est on Apr 6, 1871, by Warren Kefauver. 347, 1307.

Milton (Trimble): *mihl*/tən (Madison East, Madison West). This 6th class city with po in the Ohio R bottom extends for over ½ mi up Tiber Creek and for 3 mi along US 421 toward Bedford, 7 mi s. The town, est by the Virginia legislature in 1789, was first situated between Canip Creek and Tiber Creek (earlier called Town Branch). Years later the town of Kingston was founded below Town Branch, and in 1872 inc into Milton. The Milton po was est by John or Robert Moffett sometime in the first decade of the 19th cent. No one knows why or how it acquired its name. There is no evidence for the suggestion that it was a corruption of Milltown or that the town was ever called this, or that it was a combination of Milltown and Kingston. 761, 913.

Mine 18 (McCreary). See *Blue Heron*

Minerva (Mason): mə/*nɜv*/ə (Germantown). This hamlet with po is centered at the jct of KY 435 and 1235, 8 mi wnw of Maysville. The po, est on July 10, 1812, with James M. Runyon, pm, is alleged to have been named for Minerva Green, the first white woman to reside there. 858.

Mingo (Johnson). See *Tutor Key*

Mining City (Butler): *mahn*/ihŋ *siht*/ee (South Hill). Virtually nothing remains of a thriving 19th cent Green R landing and coal shipping port at the mouth of Muddy Creek, just off KY 1117, 4½ mi w of Morgantown. It is believed to have been early called The Bark Yard and Suffolk. The Mining City po was est on Nov 27, 1876, with Elbridge P. Aspley, pm, and named for the deep coal mines in the vicinity. 571, 1341.

Minks PO (Lincoln). See *Moreland*

Minor Lane Heights (Jefferson): *meyen*/ər lān *heyets* (Brooks, Louisville East). This 5th class city and suburban community without po lies between the Outer Loop and South Park Rd, 9 mi s of downtown Louisville. It was inc in 1960, to get a favorable rate on sewer installations, it has been said. It was probably named for the rd that forms part of its eastern boundary, which in turn may have been named for the family of Jefferson Co pioneer Maj. Spencer Minor, a veteran of the War of 1812, who arrived in Kentucky with his father from Loudoun Co, Virginia, in 1797. 100, 597.

Minorsville (Scott): *meyen*/ərz/vihl (Stamping Ground). This hamlet with extinct po centered at the jct of KY 227 and 1874, 10 mi nw of Georgetown, may have been settled in the 1830s on part of a 2000-acre military grant received by Jeremiah Minor for Revolutionary War services and undoubtedly named for him. A po was est on Aug 29, 1870, with storekeeper S. T. Reynolds as pm and discontinued in 1902. 235.

Mintonville (Casey): *mihn(t)*/ən/vihl (Mintonville). This hamlet with po lies at the jct of KY 837 and 1676, 11 mi se of Liberty. The town, laid out in 1849, was named for pioneer settler "Uncle Bobbie" Minton, whose name was also applied to the po est by James Wesley on Oct 3, 1851. 220, 1397.

Miracle (Bell) *mahr*/ək/əl (Balkan). This po and station on the Kentucky & Virginia RR (a branch of the L&N) lie where KY 987 crosses the Cumberland R, 5½ mi e of Pineville. The po, est on May 16, 1912, with Willie A. Hoskins, pm, was named for a local family. 1416.

Mirror PO (Lincoln). See *Ottenheim*

Mistletoe (Owsley): *mihs*/əl/toh (Mistletoe). This po lies at the mouth of Rockhouse Branch of the Right Fork of Buffalo Creek, 11½ mi sse of Booneville. It was est on Nov 15, 1900, with Jeremiah Burns, pm, and named for the profusion of mistletoe and holly that grow in that vicinity. 1287.

Mitchellsburg (Boyle): *mihch*/əlz/bergh (Parksville). This village with L&N RR station and po is centered at the jct of KY 34 and 1856, 9 mi wsw of Danville. It was probably named for the family of the first pm, James P. Mitchell. The po has been in intermittent operation since Feb 19, 1853.

Mitchellsville (Boone). See *Bullittsville*

Mixville PO (Carlisle). See *Arlington*

Moberly (Madison): *mahb*/ər/lee (Moberly). This hamlet with extinct po extends for nearly a mi along KY 52 and the route of the extinct Richmond Nicholasville Irvine & Beattyville (later L&N) RR, 4½ mi e of Richmond. The po was est on Oct 31, 1891, by John S. Moberley and named for his pioneer family, the Moberleys, whose progenitor, Rev. Richard Moberley, is said to have arrived in that area from his native Virginia before 1800. The inconsistency in spelling has not been explained. 172, 1294.

Mobley Stand (Henry). See *Bethlehem*

Model Mills PO (Muhlenberg). See *Skilesville*

Modoc (Cumberland): *moh*/dahk (Frogue). This rural settlement with extinct po is on KY 449, 4½ mi se of Burkesville. On Mar 24, 1868, the Bear Creek po was est on the ridge overlooking the creek for which it was named. In 1869 the name was changed to Cherry Hill, and after an intermittent existence it closed in 1876. At or near this site, on June 6, 1892, local storekeeper John G. Jones est the Modoc po, which he probably named for his former home in Modoc Bend of the Cumberland R just over the Tennessee line. Around 1930 the store and po were moved about ½ mi nw, and the po closed in 1935. No one knows why the name was changed to Cherry Hill, not the name of any local feature. It has been suggested that since this is a strong Baptist area, the name may refer to a Cherry Hill of some significance to that faith. Cumberland Co's late historian J. W. Wells offers this folk etymology for the Modoc Bend name: When Jones complained to his wife that all he did lately was mow dock (troublesome weeds with long roots), his wife thought this would be a good name for the po; it was submitted to the authorities and accepted. 223, 1385.

Monkeys Eyebrow (Ballard): *muhŋk*/eez *ah*/brow (Bandana). This now extinct hamlet was on Sand Ridge, a 10-mi-long ridge of sandy loam, 2 mi from the Ohio R and 15½ mi nne of Wickliffe. It was settled before the turn of the cent by the brothers John and Dodge Ray, but never had its own po. No one is sure how the name came to be applied, but it has inspired several folk accounts. The most plausible refers to the crescent-shaped elevation called Beeler Hill behind Ray's store, the tall grass growing from which seemed to resemble in someone's imagination the eyebrows of a monkey. A variant account of a traveling salesman who saw the resemblance of the bush covered roadbank to a monkey's eyebrow, is not as acceptable to some former residents. Another account, reported by the late Allan Trout, refers to the traditional rivalry between Monkeys Eyebrow and Needmore, a hamlet 2.3 mi e. Between them lay a brush covered bluff directly under which was Ray's store. From the Needmore side, the store and Ray's home, directly across the road, seemed to resemble eyes and the brush above them looked like eyebrows. It is said that Luther Childress, from the vicinity of Ray's store, used to shop at Needmore instead and when asked why he didn't patronize his neighbor's place reported, "I aint buyin' no grub at no place that looks like a monkey's eyebrow." The least likely account was recorded by a WPA researcher. Robert Arivett, it was said, was always finding fault with the place and its other residents and seemed fond of reviling both with such gratuitous remarks as "this place is only fit for a bunch of monkeys" or "this place is populated with monkeys . . . and their eyebrows look exactly like the brows of monkeys and they belong to the monkey class.'' For some reason, according to this account, the epithet became the community's official name. 528, 690, 784, 1012.

Monroe (Hart): *muhn*/roh (Center). This hamlet with extinct po is at the jct of KY 88 and 677, 10 mi e of Munfordville. The now extinct town of (Old) Monroe, about a mi n, was named for Thomas Monroe who, with William I. Adair, est it in 1819 as a contender for the co seat. Sometime before 1826 Joshua Brents acquired the land and built a tavern for travelers between Lexington and Nashville. On Jan 30, 1826, he est the Monroe po, which in 1864 was moved to the Green R community of *Oceola*. Shortly after the Civil War, Thomas C. Young founded a community he called Young Town, which became New Monroe or simply Monroe when he est a po there on Sept 16, 1878. It closed in 1919. 863.

Monroe County: muhn/*roh*, *mahn*/roh, *muhn*/roh. 331 sq mi. Pop 12,277. Seat: Tompkinsville. This co was est in 1820 from parts of Barren and Cumberland cos and named for James Monroe, 5th president of the US (1817–25).

Montago (Perry). See *Vicco*

Monterey (Muhlenberg). See *Paradise*

Monterey (Owen): *mahn(t)*/ər/ā (Monterey, Gratz). This 6th class city with extinct po is centered at the jct of US 127 and Cedar Creek, less than a mi above Cedar's confluence with the Kentucky R, 7 mi s of Owenton. It was first called Williamsburg for the brothers James and Alexander Williams, Marylanders who founded a trading post there around 1805. The po was est by Turner Branham on Feb 1, 1817, and named Mouth of Cedar Creek for its original location. It became Cedar Creek probably in 1825 and may then have moved to its present site. It was renamed on Feb 23, 1847, to commemorate the Mexican War battle of Monterey, which had been fought the preceding Sept. It has been said that the community's then well deserved reputation as a violent place could not be equalled by the accounts brought back by veterans of that battle. The town was est by legislative act in 1847, and inc in 1874 and again in 1955. 600.

Montgomery (Trigg): mahnt/*ghahm*/ər/ee (Gracey). This hamlet with extinct po at the jct of US 68 and KY 276, 4 mi e of Cadiz, was named for Thomas Montgomery, pioneer settler and large landowner, who arrived in that vicinity in 1816. The po was est as Montgomery on Dec 13, 1853, by Harrison Ashford, the storekeeper, and the town itself was laid out in 1866 by Gen. John G. Gaines, who had by then acquired the site. The po closed in 1916. 98, 166, 1325.

Montgomery County: mahn(t)/*ghuhm*/ər/ee. 199 sq mi. Pop 20,072. Seat: Mt. Sterling. This co was est in 1797 from part of Clark Co and named for Gen. Richard Montgomery (1738–75), a Revolutionary War officer killed in the assault on Quebec.

Montgomery Court House PO (Montgomery). See *Mt. Sterling*

Monticello (Wayne): mahn/(t)ə/*sehl*/oh, mahn/(t)ə/*sehl*/ə (Monticello). This 4th class city and seat of Wayne Co is centered at the jct of KY 90 and 92, 102 mi sse of downtown Louisville. The town was founded as the seat of the new co in 1801 on 13 acres owned by William Beard. According to tradition, the pioneer Jones family wanted to name the new town Jonesboro, but the 15-year-old co court clerk, Micah Taul, asked by others to suggest another name, offered Monticello after Jefferson's Virginia home. The po was est as Monticello Court House on Jan 1, 1803, with Roger Oatts, pm. For some reason, the town was not inc by the Kentucky legislature until Jan 18, 1810. 65, 113.

Monticello Court House PO (Wayne). See *Monticello*

Moon (Morgan): mūn (Dingus). This po is on KY 172, near the upper end of Open Fork of Paint Creek, 11 mi ene of West Liberty. The name, one of those submitted to the postal authorities by James F. Wallin, the first pm, is said to have been inspired by the moonlit night in 1905 on which it was conceived. 112, 749.

Moorefield (Nicholas): *mawr*/feeld (Moorefield). This hamlet with po extends for almost a mi along KY 57 near its jct with KY 36, 5 mi se of Carlisle. The po was est on Jan 29, 1818, in Alexander Blair's store and named by Mrs. Benjamin Hall for Moorefield, Virginia (now West Virginia), whence she and her family had come in 1796. 196.

Moores Ferry (Bath): *mawrz fehr*/ee (Farmers). This hamlet with extinct po is now on KY 211, ½ mi s of the Licking R, and 7½ mi e of Owingsville. It is apparently the relocation of a thriving late 19th cent community that centered on a Licking R ferry owned by a Mr. Moore and a po in operation from 1888 to 1913. 186.

Moores Station (Owsley). See *Booneville*

Moorman (Muhlenberg): *mawr*/mən (Livermore). This village with po and rr station is at the jct of 2 L&N RR Evansville Division lines just w of US 431 and 10 mi n of Greenville. The po was est on Mar 4, 1890, as Godman, probably to honor John W. I. Godman (1798–1852), Muhlenberg's first elected co judge, who had lived in the vicinity. It was renamed in 1907 for the Moorman family, perhaps for James C. Moorman, a Breckinridge Co native, who had represented Muhlenberg Co in the Kentucky legislature in 1871–72. 189, 1253.

Moranburg (Mason): mə/*raenz*/bergh (Maysville West). This hamlet with extinct po lies at the jct of KY 10 and 1597, 2 mi wnw of Maysville. Its po, est on June 24, 1886, and named by and for its first pm, William L. Moran, closed in 1907. 1246.

Morehead (Rowan): *mawr*/hehd (Morehead). This 4th class city and seat of Rowan Co is on US 60 and KY 32, just s of I 64 and 116 mi e of downtown Louisville. The po was est as Triplett on Apr 1, 1817, with Jacob Powers, pm, and changed to Morehead Court House when Rowan Co was est in 1856 and Morehead became its seat. The town and seat, inc in 1869, were named for James T. Morehead, Kentucky's governor from 1834 to 1836. The name Triplett is retained in that of the local creek, a branch of the Licking R. 231, 605.

Morehead Court House PO (Rowan). See *Morehead*

Moreheads Horse Mill (Muhlenberg). See *Central City*

Moreland (Lincoln): *mawr*/lən(d) (Junction City). This hamlet with extinct po extending for nearly 1½ mi along US 127, 8 mi w of Stanford, was founded in 1877–78 when the Cincinnati Southern (now Southern) Ry was built through that section and named for Elliott Moreland who donated the land for the station. On Apr 27, 1886, James H. Minks moved his Minks po to the station and renamed it Moreland. The po closed in 1975. 365.

Morgan (Pendleton): *mawr*/ghən (Berry). This hamlet with extinct po lies on the South Fork of the Licking R, just above and opposite the mouth of Fork Lick Creek, 5½ mi sw of Falmouth. The site may first have been called Fork Lick, and the station est there with the arrival of the Covington and Lexington (now L&N) RR may first have been called Stowers Station for Richard Stowers, a resident and one of the directors of the rr. For reasons yet unknown, the name Morgan was applied to the local po, which was est on Jan 3, 1856 with Benjamin F. Hume, pm. 845, 847.

Morgan County: *mawr*/ghən. 382 sq mi. Pop 12,080. Seat: West Liberty. This co was est in 1822 from parts of Floyd and Bath cos and named for Gen. Daniel Morgan (1736–1802), Revolutionary War officer and US congressman (1797–99).

Morganfield (Union): *mawr*/ghən/feeld (Morganfield). This 4th class industrial city and seat of Union Co is on US 60/641, 116 mi wsw of downtown Louisville. In 1811 Presley O'Bannon, while representing Henderson Co in the Kentucky legislature, helped secure passage of the act creating Union Co. The commission appointed in this act to locate the co seat recommended the site of Jeremiah Riddle's home on land that had been acquired by O'Bannon from the heirs of Gen. Daniel Morgan (1736–1802), for whom it was named. It was part of the 1500-acre military grant awarded Morgan in 1783 for his Revolutionary War services. It was laid out in 1811 and said to have been first called Morgan's Field; within a short time the "s" was dropped and the words were written as one. The po was est on Mar 23, 1813, as Morganfield Court House with Ebenezer Boggs, pm. 151, 157.

Morganfield Court House PO (Union). See *Morganfield*

Morgan PO (Morgan). See *Maytown*

Morgantown (Butler): *mawr*ghən/town (Morgantown). This 5th class city and seat of Butler Co is on US 231 and KY 79, just e of the Green River Parkway, and 82 mi ssw of downtown Louisville. The town was founded and laid out in 1811 by Christopher Funkhouser on a 60-acre tract that may first have been called Funkhouser Hill. He is said to have named it Morgan Town (*sic*), though historians do not agree on its derivation. Some say it was named for Daniel Morgan Smith, the first white child born there on Dec 14, 1811. Others claim the name was applied before his birth. In 1811 the town was made the permanent seat of the newly est co. It was inc by the legislature on Jan 6, 1813, and the po was organized as Butler Court House or Morgantown on Apr 12, 1813, with David Morrison, pm. 28.

Morning View (Kenton): *mawr*/nihŋ *vyū* (Demossville). This village with po is on KY 177 and the Licking R, 17 mi s of downtown Covington. While the Covington & Lexington (now L&N) RR station there was est in 1855 as Mullins Station, presumably named for George H. Mullins, the po was created on Oct 5, 1855, as Morning View with Mullins as pm. Robert S. Tate recorded the traditional account of its naming: "One morning . . . some railroad officials were riding through on a hand car . . . when the sun was rising. They exclaimed on the wonderful 'morning view' and later when designating the place officially they would add 'where they have the wonderful morning view.' This . . . was condensed to Morning View and [the village] has carried the name ever since." 771.

Morrill (Jackson): *mâhr*/əl (Big Hill). This hamlet with po extends for ½ mi along US 421, just e of the Madison and Rockcastle Co lines, and 12 mi nw of McKee. The po, est on Jan 25, 1867, in Rockcastle Co, was probably named for a local family. In 1903 it was moved to a site in Jackson Co and was discontinued in 1905. It was reest in Madison Co in 1929, but in 1931 it returned to Jackson Co. 1251.

Morris Fork (Breathitt): *mâhr*/əs *fawrk* (Cowcreek). This hamlet with po lies on Morris Fork of Long Creek, ¾ mi s of KY 28 and 13 mi sw of Jackson. From a remote and disreputable section of the co in the early 20th cent, it became one of the more progressive rural communities in e Kentucky following the arrival in the mid-1920s of the Rev. and Mrs. Samuel VanderMeer and the est of a Presbyterian mission. The stream, community and po (est on May 25, 1931 with James Cornett, pm) were named for early area families. 236, 792.

Morse (Graves). See *Water Valley*

Mortons Gap (Hopkins): *mawr*/tənz *ghaep* (Nortonville). This 5th class city lies just n of a natural gap in a ridge through which US 41A now passes, 5 mi s of Madisonville. In stagecoach days the rd through the gap was sometimes called The Buttermilk Road for the free crocks of buttermilk that farmers would leave out for travelers. Thomas C. Morton, a Virginian, settled here around 1804, and his descendants were still in possession of the site when the town was est after the Civil War by the South Diamond Coal Mining Co., whose mine was 1 mi s. Henry H. Morton est the local po on Nov 3, 1871, and the town was inc in 1888. 159, 309, 741.

Mortonsville (Morgan). See *Ezel*

Mortonsville (Woodford): *mawr*/tənz/vihl (Salvisa). This hamlet with extinct po is on KY 1965, 4½ mi s of Versailles. Settled around 1790 by Virginians attracted by its proximity to Gen. Charles Scott's landing, 5 mi w on the Kentucky R, it soon came to be known as Rucker's Big Spring for John Rucker who, with John Morton, built the first houses there just above the spring. Morton's son Jeremiah laid off the town sometime before 1812 and named it for himself or his family. William Shryock had a po there by Jan 1828 and the town was inc in 1835. The po closed in 1921. 951, 1269.

Moscow (Hickman): *mahs*/koh (Cayce). Now a hamlet on Bayou de Chien, ¼ mi w of KY 239 and 4 mi ssw of Clinton, this was a busy 19th cent rail center. It was settled in the early 1820s and chartered as a town in 1830 on land owned by Samuel McFall, its first merchant. The po was est on Jan 13, 1829, with Howard Cassity, pm, and closed in 1955. No one knows how Moscow got its name. Some say it was a corruption of some Indian word or name. Despite the similarity in names it was not named for John Muscovalley, a Greek-born pioneer settler of the western part of the co. George R. Stewart suggests that the 15 Moscows in the US were named in the 19th cent fashion of naming places for foreign capitals. 162, 204, 614.

Moseleyville (Daviess): *mohz*/lee/vihl (Panther). This hamlet is strung out for ½ mi on KY 81, s of Old Panther Creek and 6 mi s of Owensboro. The po, in operation there from 1886 to 1909, was named for the local Moseley family, one of whose members, Presley T. Moseley, was the first pm. 1348.

Mossy Bottom (Pike): *mâhs*/ee *baht*/əm (Broad Bottom). This settlement with extinct po lies on the Levisa Fork of the Big Sandy R, across from US 23/460 and opposite the mouth of Cowpens Creek, 3 mi nw of Pikeville. It was aptly named for its location in the low-lying area between the C&O RR tracks and the r. The po, est on Mar 30, 1906, with Tobias Wagner, pm, was discontinued around 1940. The local C&O RR station of Wagner was named for Tobias, a pre-Civil War immigrant from Germany who later became a Pike Co judge. 1138, 1354, 1371.

Motier PO (Pendleton). See *Carntown*

Motley (Warren): *maht*/lee (Polkville). This hamlet with extinct po, just n of KY 1288 and 7 mi ese of Bowling Green, was inhabited by Motleys, descendants of Matthew Page Motley who built his home there in 1853. One of Matthew's sons, John K. Motley, est the po on May 15, 1890. It closed in 1905. 209.

Motte PO (Madison). See *Bobtown*

Mountain Ash (Whitley): *mown(t)*/ən *aesh* (Williamsburg). This is now a residential settlement with extinct po on Clear Fork of the Cumberland R, just e of I 75 and US 25W and 5 mi s of Williamsburg. Here some Welsh coal developers opened a mine in the early 1890s and named their camp and the town that grew from it for a town in Wales. The po was est on July 28, 1892, with Enoch Griffith, pm. 1380.

Mt. Carbon (Johnson). See *Whitehouse*

Mt. Carmel (Fleming): mownt *kahr*/məl (Flemingsburg). This village with extinct po extends for ½ mi along KY 57, 6 mi ne of Flemingsburg. It is said to have been named before 1820 by those who were reminded of the biblical Mt. Carmel and was est as a town by legislative act in 1825. The po, begun by John B. Clark on Nov 24, 1831, closed in 1932. 493, 1369.

Mt. Eden (Spencer and Shelby): mownt *ee*/dən (Mt. Eden). This village with po is on KY 44/53, midway (10 mi) between Taylorsville and Shelbyville. The beauty of the countryside and the fertility of its soil made it a most attractive place to early settlers, who are said to have compared it with their conception of the biblical Eden. In pioneer times its site may have resembled a mountain to those who viewed it from a distance. The po has moved several times across the co line since it was est on June 8, 1831, with Vincent Redman, pm, in Spencer Co, to which it returned for good in 1917. 902, 1239.

Mt. Guthrie (Rockcastle). See *Maretburg*

Mt. Hebron (Garrard). See *Bourne*

Mt. Holly (Jefferson). See *Fairdale*

Mt. Olive (Casey): mownt *ahl*/əv (Yosemite). This hamlet with extinct po on KY 837, 8½ mi ese of Liberty, was settled at least by the 1830s. It is not known when the name Mt. Olive was first applied to the community, though it was probably derived from the still-active Mt. Olive Christian Church. It is generally believed to predate the est, on Aug 19, 1881, of the local po as Humphrey [*uhm*/free], named for William T. Humphrey, the first pm. The po closed in 1948. 1397.

Mt. Olivet (Robertson): mownt *ahl*/ə/vət (Mt. Olivet). This 5th class city and seat of Robertson Co is centered at the jct of US 62 and KY 165, 88 mi ene of downtown Louisville. It was founded around 1820, inc in 1851, and designated the seat of the newly est co in 1867. The po was est on Apr 26, 1850, with Joshua Burlow, pm. The name is of biblical origin but no one knows why or just when it was applied. There is no evidence that it was first called Hell's Half Acre as is popularly believed. 1365.

Mt. Pleasant (Harlan). See *Harlan*

Mt. Pleasant (Trimble): mownt *plehz*/ənt (Bethlehem). This extinct crossroads hamlet and po were on KY 625, 4 mi wnw of Bedford. The po, in operation from 1892 to 1907, was aptly named for its location at one of the highest points between Louisville and Cincinnati. 913.

Mount Pleasant PO (Carter). See *Boone Furnace*

Mount St. Joseph (Daviess). See *St. Joseph*

Mt. Savage (Carter): mownt *saev*/ədj (Grayson). Nothing remains of this community with C&O RR station on KY 773 and Strait Creek, a tributary of Little Fork of the Little Sandy R, 4½ mi s of Grayson. It grew up around an iron furnace built in 1848 by Robinson M. Biggs and others and named for Edward Savage on whose land it was located. The po, est on Oct 25, 1848, closed in 1916. 36, 191.

Mt. Sterling (Montgomery): mownt *stɜl*/ihŋ (Mt. Sterling). This 4th class city and seat of Montgomery Co is on US 60 and 460, just s of I 64, and 92 mi e of downtown Louisville. The settlement that grew up on Enoch Smith's farm is said to have been first called Little Mountain Town for a large Indian mound at the jct of the present Maysville and Locust Sts. But Hugh Forbes, one of the proprietors, thought this name unsuitable for what he hoped would become an important town, and suggested instead that of the city in Scotland where he had been raised. Perhaps by way of compromise the place was christened Mt. Stirling but somewhere in the recording of the name it was corrupted to its present spelling and never corrected. In Dec 1792 it was chartered as Mt. Sterling by the fledging Kentucky legislature, and when the co was created in 1797 it became its seat. On Oct 1, 1801, the po was est as Montgomery Court House with Joseph Simpson, pm, but became Mt. Sterling in 1807. 184, 1237.

Mt. Tabor (Rowan). See *Wagners Store*

Mountvernon (Bullitt). See *Mt. Washington*

Mount Vernon (Rockcastle): *mownt v3n*/ən (Mount Vernon). This 5th class city and seat of Rockcastle Co is on US 25 and 150, 92 mi se of downtown Louisville. It is said that when the co was est in 1810, this place was called White Rock for the big white rock at the site of the present fertilizer factory. The name Mount Vernon was applied when the po was est on Sept 26, 1811, and referred to Washington's home in Virginia. However, according to John Lair, Col. Richard Henderson, of Transylvania fame, may have maintained a log home here during his trips between Boonesborough and North Carolina that he called Mount Vernon, for its situation seemed to resemble that of Washington's home. The future co seat which grew up around it retained this name and was so inc in 1818. 529, 1251.

Mount Victory (Pulaski): mownt *vihk*/tree (Dykes). This hamlet with extinct po is on KY 192, 11 mi ese of Somerset. It may have been named for a victory over renegade Indians by a small patrol headed by Lt. Nathan McClure in May 1788. Assigned to escort early settlers to Kentucky, this Revolutionary War veteran was fatally wounded in the skirmish which his men later won on a ridge between the Rockcastle R and Buck Creek. Or, it was named by Ella P. Darr, wife of Rev. Timothy T. Darr, a Methodist minister, who had arrived in the area in the 1890s. She and her colleagues considered it a religious victory that they were able to est a church and school there. Or, it was named for a successful revival once held there. Finally, this tale is told, though usually discredited, that 2 local teachers agreed to carry the mail free for one year if they could get a po. They succeeded and the po was named in honor of their achievement. The po was est on Mar 5, 1900, with John B. Edwards, pm. 336, 925, 1410.

Mt. Vitio PO (Bullitt). See *Brooks*

Mt. Washington (Bullitt): mownt *wahsh*/ihŋ/tən (Mt. Washington). This 5th class city with po is centered at the jct of US 31E/150 and KY 44, 7½ mi ene of Shepherdsville. By the early 19th cent, as Crossroads, this was a thriving community and important stage stop on the route between Louisville and Nashville. It was chartered in 1822 as Mountvernon presumably for Washington's Virginia home. Because the Mt. Vernon name had been preempted by the seat of Rockcastle Co, petitioners for the po in 1830 called it Mt. Washington instead. The town was inc in 1833, and reinc in 1955. 31, 1352.

Mt. Zion (Greenup). See *Frost*

Mousie (Knott): *mow*/see (Handshoe). This village with po is centered on KY 80 at the mouth of Ball Branch of Jones Fork of Right Beaver Creek, 6½ mi ne of Hindman. The po was est on July 31, 1916, some 2 mi up the fork with Ollie M. Gibson, pm, and named for Mousie (Mrs. Mart) Gibson (1896–1976), the daughter of Clay Martin, a large landowner of that area. The po was later moved to its present location but retained the name. According to Mrs. Gibson, a long time resident of Martin, her own name was suggested by her grandfather, W. J. Martin, since she had an older sister named Kitty. Mousie, however, is not an uncommon female given name in eastern Kentucky. 785.

Mouthcard (Pike): *mowth*/*kahrd* (Lick Creek). This hamlet with po at the jct of US 40 and KY 1499, 15 mi ese of Pikeville, was named for its location at the mouth of Card Creek, a tributary of the Levisa Fork of the Big Sandy R. Its po, est as Mouth of Card on Aug 4, 1853, with Isaac Epling, pm, had become simply Mouthcard before 1900. 1354.

Mouth of Beaver PO (Floyd). See *Allen*

Mouth of Card PO (Pike). See *Mouthcard*
Mouth of Cedar Creek PO (Owen). See *Monterey*
Mouth of Gasper (The) (Warren). See *Rockland*
Mouth of Hood (Lawrence). See *Blaine*
Mouth of Laurel PO (Lewis). See *Camp Dix*
Mouth of Raven PO (Harrison). See *Colemanville*
Mouth of Salt River (The) (Hardin). See *West Point*
Mouth of Smoot Creek (The) (Letcher). See *Hot Spot*
Muddy Branch PO (Johnson). See *Thealka*

Muddy Ford (Scott): *muhd*/ee *fawrd* (Delaplain). This settlement just off KY 922, 6½ mi nne of Georgetown, was named for its location near the mouth of Muddy Ford Creek, a branch of the West Fork of Eagle Creek. The creek, first settled by the Barnhills of Buchanan Co, Virginia, in 1792, is said to have been named for the large quantities of mud it deposited when it overflowed its banks, probably at some natural fording place. Hugh Shannon, the local storekeeper, maintained the po from its inception on Oct 21, 1890, till it closed less than 3 years later. 914, 1293.

Mud Lick (Monroe): *muhd lihk* (Freedom). This hamlet lies at the jct of KY 63 and 870, 5 mi nw of Tompkinsville. Its recently discontinued po was est on Feb 19, 1853, with Thomas Webb, pm. It is said to have been named for either a salt stream made muddy by animals coming to drink or the abundance of clay mud in the vicinity. 1395.

Mudville (Morgan). See *Malone*

Muhlenberg County: *myū*/lən/bergh. 478 sq mi. Pop. 32,000. Seat: Greenville. This co was est in 1798 from parts of Logan and Christian cos and named for Gen. Peter Muhlenberg (1746–1807), preacher turned Revolutionary War officer and, later, US congressman and senator.

Muldraugh (Meade): *muhl*/droh, *mahl*/droh (Ft. Knox). This 5th class city, (with po) now surrounded by Ft. Knox, extends n and s for over 1 mi between US 31W/60 and the Ft. Knox Military Reservation, 9½ mi ese of Brandenburg. It may have been named for William (or John) Muldraugh (or Muldrow), who is said to have settled briefly in the area before moving on. The po was est on June 22, 1874, with Thomas W. Summers, pm. The town was inc in 1952. A popular account of the name, patently absurd but amusing, has been offered for both the community and the important Muldraugh Hill to the s. The latter, a very steep hill (actually a ridge), was very difficult to climb and pioneer teamsters were often dependent on mulepower to get them up the hill. One enterprising man purchased a number of mules for rental use and set himself up at the foot of the hill at a place he called Mule-Draw Station. Soon the hill came to be known as Mule-Draw Hill. 616, 650.

Mullanixville (Grant). See *Corinth*
Mullins PO (Laurel). See *Bernstadt*
Mullins Station (Kenton). See *Morning View*

Mullins Station (Rockcastle): *muhl*/ənz *sta*/shən (Livingston). This settlement and L&N RR station with extinct po on Roundstone Creek, 5½ mi e of Mount Vernon, were named for the local Mullins family. The po, est on June 18, 1886, however, was always known as Withers for the family of the first pm, Mary A. Withers. 1243.

Mummie (Jackson): *muh*/mee (Sturgeon). This recently discontinued po lay where KY 30 crosses Blackwater Creek, a branch of Sturgeon Creek, 7 mi ese of McKee. The name is said to have been submitted to the Post Office Department by Bobby Farmer to commemorate the discovery there by early settlers of a mummified human body. Hiram V. Montgomery became the first pm on Nov 8, 1915. 1338, 1419.

Munfordsville Court House PO (Hart). See *Munfordville*

Munfordville (Hart): *muhn*/fərd/vihl (Munfordville). This 5th class city and seat of Hart Co is on US 31W, between the Green R and I 65, 63 mi s of downtown Louisville. It was named for Richard Jones Munford (1776–1843), pioneer settler and proprietor of what was first called Big Buffalo Crossing, who in 1816 gave 100 acres for the est of the town that became the seat of the new co in 1819. The po was organized as Munfordsville Court House on Apr 16, 1820, and the town was inc in 1858. The medial "s" was retained through the 19th cent but is no longer in official use, though many persons still follow the central Kentucky custom of sounding an "s" where one does not exist. 581, 617, 1331.

Munk (Gallatin): muhŋk (Verona). This extinct po and L&N RR station were on a dead-end rd just n of the Grant Co line and 11 mi e of Warsaw. This vicinity was home to a Webster family, who were called "The Munk Websters" to distinguish them from another Webster family in the area. The po was est on Apr 9, 1900, with Ina N. Webster, pm, as Munk. It closed in 1939. 1460.

Murphysville (Mason): *mɜ*/feez/vihl (Mayslick). This settlement with extinct po at the jct of US 62 and the North Fork of Licking R, 7 mi sw of Maysville, may have been named for William Murphy, an early settler. The po, in operation until 1906, was est on Nov 13, 1830, with Joseph Howe, pm. 858.

Murray (Calloway): *muhr*/ee (Murray). This 3rd class city and seat of Calloway Co on US 641, 168 mi sw of downtown Louisville, was est in 1842 on 80 acres then owned by Charles Curd and James Price, and named for Wadesboro attorney and US Congressman John L. Murray. This vicinity may first have been settled by James Willis, a dealer in tobacco and hides, in or before 1825. He is known to have est a po called Williston, at the jct of the present 4th and Sycamore Sts, on May 28, 1830. Shortly thereafter he sold out his holdings to Robert Pool, and the trading community that grew up around the Williston po came to be known as Pooltown, later Pleasant Hill. After the creation of Marshall Co from Calloway Co in 1842, a site in the vicinity was selected as more centrally located than Wadesboro for the seat of what remained of Calloway. Curd, then the Williston pm, renamed the po Murray on May 23, 1843, and the town was inc under this name in 1844. 787, 799, 1401.

Muses Mills (Fleming): *myūz*/əz *mihlz* (Plummers Landing). This hamlet with po is on KY 1013 and Fox Creek, 11 mi ese of Flemingsburg. The po was est on May 4, 1876, with George W. Manchester, pm, and named for the local grain and sawmill, which in turn was named for George Muse, Sr., a Revolutionary War veteran, who died there in 1827. 1369.

Myers (Nicholas): mahrz (Moorefield). This hamlet with extinct po on KY 32, 4 mi ne of Carlisle, was named for the Myers family that settled there around 1790 on George Myers' Revolutionary War grant. The po was est as Black Hawk, for reasons unknown, on Mar 25, 1854, with Henry V. Myers, pm. It was discontinued in 1856 and reest in 1872. In 1873 Myers Station was built by the Kentucky Central (now L&N) RR for its Paris–Maysville line and the po was renamed Myers in 1882 with Michael J. Myers, pm. From Dec 11, 1871, to Jan 15, 1873, a Myersville po was in operation somewhere in this vicinity. 47, 1374.

Myersville PO (Nicholas). See *Myers*

Myra (Pike): *mah*/ruh (Dorton). This po on US 23/119 and Shelby Creek, at the mouth of Beefhide Creek, 12½ mi s of Pikeville, was est on May 24, 1905, and named by its first pm and local storekeeper, Marquis D.L. Greer, for his daughter. 1198.

Myrtle PO (Johnson). See *Whitehouse*

Nada (Powell): *nā*/dee, *nā*/duh (Slade). This hamlet with extinct po extends over ½ mi along KY 77 e of its jct with KY 11/15 and the Mountain Parkway, 6½ mi ese of Stanton. It was est for its workers by the Dana Lumber Co., which built a mill there at the jct of its spur line with the old Lexington & Eastern Ry around 1911. The town's name was derived from that of the co. Its po was originally est .8 mi nw as Lombard, at the terminus of another spur line, built by J. T. Lombard. The spur closed in 1909, and the Lombard po and depot were moved to Nada in 1911. The po closed in 1968. 1109, 1334.

Nancy (Pulaski): *naen*/see (Delmer, Faubush). This village with po extends w for over 1 mi along KY 80, 5½ mi w of Somerset. It was first called Logans Crossroads for the family of William Harrison Logan (1811–84). The po was first est as Lincolnville for the late president on June 27, 1865, with Logan as pm. It was discontinued in 1875 and reest on Sept 4, 1884, as Nancy for Logan's wife, Nancy Lester Logan (1834–96), the daughter of Vincent Lester. 978, 1410.

Naomi (Pulaski): nā/*oh*/mee, nā/*oh*/mə, nee/*oh*/mee, nə/*yoh*/mə (Faubush). This hamlet with extinct po lies at the jct of KY 761 and 1664, 9½ mi sw of Somerset. The po, in operation from July 9, 1897, to 1962, was named for Naomi Trimble Tarter (1860–98), who is said to have run the po for her husband, storekeeper Samuel Tarter, the first pm of record. 1410.

Napfor (Perry): *naep*/fər (Krypton). This hamlet with po on the North Fork of the Kentucky R, opposite the mouth of Napier Branch and 7 mi nw of Hazard, was formerly a coal town with L&N RR station. It was est in 1917 by the Lincoln Coal Co. and named for the local Napier families and a Mr. Foreman, a co. official. The po has been in operation since Oct 29, 1921, when Homer H. Givin was appointed pm. 744.

Napier (Clay). See *Burning Springs*

Napier (Leslie): *nā*/pyər (Bledsoe). This hamlet with recently closed po lies on Greasy Creek, just below the mouth of John Miniard Branch, 12½ mi sse of Hyden. The po was est on June 6, 1902, with Felix G. Turner, pm, and named for a local family. 1248.

Napoleon (Gallatin): nə/*poh*/lyən (Patriot). Now but a hamlet on KY 16, 6 mi ese of Warsaw, this was once a prosperous 19th cent trade center. Settled in the first decade of the 19th cent, it was laid out and named about 1821 by Joseph Spencer Lillard, local merchant. Although some wanted to call the new town Madisonville for the president, others wished to show their gratitude for France's aid in our Revolution by naming it for her great leader. The po of Conner's, est by Samuel Conner before 1831, was renamed Napoleon on Jan 30, 1841, and the town was inc under this name the following month. The po closed in 1912. 87.

Narrows (Livingston). See *Grand Rivers*

Natlee (Owen): *naet*/lee (New Columbus). This settlement with extinct po lay where KY 607 crosses Eagle Creek, 10½ mi se of Owenton. Sometime before 1849 Nathaniel ("Nat") Lee, Sr., built a water-powered gristmill at this site. On June 2, 1849, his brother Grandison R. Lee, a physician, est the Lee's Mills po there, which in 1854 was moved 1½ mi ne and renamed New Columbus. The po at the mill was reest on Feb 16, 1898, as Natlee, 6 years after Nathaniel's death. It was discontinued in 1905. 275.

Natural Bridge (Powell): *naech*/ər/əl *brihdj* (Slade). This extinct po was at the mouth of Whittleton Branch of Middle Fork of the Red R, just e of KY 11 and 9 mi se of Stanton. In 1898 Floyd Day built the Mountain Central Ry from a jct here with the Lexington and Eastern (later L&N) Ry to Campton, and named the site Campton Junction. The po of McCormick was est here on May 29, 1902, to serve the rr's employees. It was renamed Natural Bridge in 1908 for the nearby scenic bridge. 208, 1334.

Nazareth (Nelson): *naez*/rəth (Bardstown). This po and rr station are almost a mi w of US 31E and 1½ mi n of Bardstown. The Motherhouse of the Sisters of Charity of Nazareth, founded in 1812 in St. Thomas, moved here in 1822. Nazareth Academy, later College, founded in 1814, also moved from St. Thomas and was chartered here in 1829. In 1860 the Sisters granted the right-of-way through their property to the Louisville & Bardstown (now L&N) RR. Since the Sisters later built the depot, the station was called Nazareth, as was the po est on Apr 14, 1863, with Mother Columba Carroll, pm. The po closed the following month but reopened in 1888. 123, 702, 739, 1104.

Neafus (Grayson): *nā*/fəs (Spring Lick). This rural settlement with po is less than ¼ mi e of the jct of Ohio, Butler, and Grayson cos and 17 mi wsw of Leitchfield. The po was est on Apr 2, 1900, with John M. Lykins, pm, and named for a local family. 1307.

Neatsville (Adair): *neets*/vəl (Knifley). This hamlet on KY 206, ½ mi s of the Green R and 10 mi ne of Columbia, is all that remains of a flourishing 19th cent Green R town named for the pioneer Neat family who had settled there before 1810. Sometime before World War I, a destructive flood forced its relocation from the n to the s bank of the r. A second relocation to its present site came with the impoundment for the Green River Reservoir in the 1960s. Though the po was est as Neatsville on Mar 13, 1844, with John S. Campbell, pm, the name was inexplicably spelled Neetsville from 1876 until the po closed in 1886. 669.

Nebo (Hopkins): *nee*/boh (Nebo). This 6th class city with po centered at the jct of US 41A and KY 502, 6½ mi wnw of Madisonville, was founded by Virginia-born pioneer Alfred Townes (born 1794) and named for the biblical Mt. Nebo, from which Moses viewed the promised land. In his store he est the Nebo po on Nov 18, 1840. The town was inc in 1861. 159, 535.

Ned (Breathitt): nehd (Haddix). This hamlet with po is on KY 15 and Lost Creek, 10½ mi sse of Jackson. The po was est on Feb 26, 1886, by Jeremiah Combs in his home at the mouth of Cockrell's Fork, about 600 yards n, and named for his son-in-law, Ned Turner. 1082.

Needmore (Ballard): *need*/mawr (Bandana). This crossroads hamlet is 2½ mi from the Ohio R and 16 mi nne of Wickliffe. The Ogden po, which was originally est at Ogden's Landing on the Ohio R, 3½ mi ne, on May 13, 1870, by Alfred N. Shelby, was moved here on Aug 10, 1888, to Thomas Brown Ogden's store. Sometime before 1900 the nickname Needmore was applied to Ogden's store because, according to tradition, its customers "always insisted they needed more than they could buy." Confusion over these 2 names led to a Board on Geographic Names decision in 1900 in favor of Ogden, but a 2nd decision made in 1967, based on the closing of the Ogden po in 1908 and common usage since World War I, made Needmore the official name. 38, 1002.

Needmore (Calloway). See *Tobacco*

Needmore (Lewis). See *Ribolt*

Needmore (Nelson): *need*/mawr (Bardstown). This extinct hamlet was on KY 605, just e of its jct with US 150, and 3 mi e of Bardstown. Local people would ask for so many things not stocked by the store that they began calling it Needmore. 1386.

Nehemiah PO (Magoffin). See *Wheelersburg*

Nelson County: *nehl*/sən. 424 sq mi. Pop 27,466. Seat: Bardstown. This co was est in 1784 by the Virginia legislature and named for the ex-Virginia governor and signer of the Declaration of Independence, Thomas Nelson (1738–89). It was taken from Jefferson Co, one of the 3 cos into which Kentucky Co, Virginia, was divided in 1780. From its original territory were created all of 11 and part of 9 other cos.

Nelson Junction PO (Bullitt). See *Bardstown Junction*

Neola PO (Wolfe). See *Helechawa*

Neon (Letcher): nee/*awn, nee/âhn* (Jenkins West). Having recently merged with adjacent *Fleming*, this is now part of a 5th class city extending over 2 mi along Wright Fork from a point ¼ mi above its junction with Potter Fork to form Boone Fork, and 6½ mi ne of Whitesburg. Neon was founded in 1913 as a trading center for the just est coal towns of Fleming, Hemphill, and McRoberts. It was first served by a po called Chip, ½ mi n of the forks of Boone Creek, which began Dec 11, 1902, with Ibby V. Holbrook, pm, and was discontinued in Apr 1915 when its papers were transferred to Fleming. The name Chip may have some connection with early timbering in the area; why it was not retained is uncertain but it may just be that the name lacked the degree of sophistication desired for an aspiring economic center. But the reason for the Neon name is the most problematic of all. It has been suggested that the name was first applied to the local rr stop, reflecting an old black conductor's command to passengers boarding the train on what at that time may have been but an old tree stump to "put your knee on and get up; knee on. . . ." According to tradition, this became known as the "knee-on" place. A more plausible explanation is that some early merchant bought a neon sign for his business, a rarity in those days. The town was inc in 1917 and the active Neon po was est on May 5, 1926, with Willie M. Quillen, pm. 1265.

Nepton (Fleming): *nehp*/tən (Elizaville). This hamlet with extinct po is at the jct of the present KY 367 and the L&N RR tracks, 5 mi w of Flemingsburg. When the rr was built through in the early 1870s, the station located here may first have been called Elizaville Station for the nearby community it served. The Nepton po est on Apr 13, 1881, was named by James Slicer, a local resident, for his recently deceased infant daughter Penelope, nicknamed "Neppie." It closed in 1958. 425.

Nerinx, Nerinckx (Marion): *neer*/ihŋx (Loretto). This religious community with po, the site of the convent of the Sisters of Loretto, lies 1 mi n of the jct of KY 49 and 152, and 9½ mi nw of Lebanon. The community was founded in the very early 19th cent as the home and headquarters of Fr. Stephen Theodore Badin, the first priest ordained in the US (1793), and named St. Stephens [sānt *steev*/ənz] by him for his patron saint. It may also have been called Priestland [*preest*/laend]. The Sisters of Loretto (see *Loretto*) moved to this site around 1820 from St. Mary, where the order had been organized by Fr. Charles Nerinckx in 1812. The community was later renamed for Fr. Nerinckx, a Belgian-born missionary. The Nerinx po was est on Sept 5, 1899, with Sr. Mary Rosina Green, pm. Though the name is spelled Nerinx on all current maps and documents, historians still accept Nerinckx as the proper spelling. 1399.

Neville (Carlisle). See *Arlington*

Nevisdale (Whitley): *nehv*/əs/dāl (Saxton). This hamlet with po is on KY 904, some 3 mi up Patterson Creek from the Cumberland R and 6½ mi ese of Williamsburg. According to Thomas Childers, when the Pine Mountain RR–West, a branch of the L&N, was built to this point early in this cent, a foreman named Gillreath was asked to name the new station. He suggested that "dale" be added to the name of his son, Nevel, and for some reason it became Nevisdale. The po of this name was est on Mar 19, 1917, with John Goins, pm. 1121.

New (Owen): Nyū (Monterey). This extinct po on Sandridge Creek, just off KY 607, 7 mi s of Owenton, was named by and for its first pm, William J. New, when it was est on Oct 23, 1895. 1292.

New Allen (Floyd). See *Allen*

New Allenville (Todd). See *Allensville*

Newby (Madison): *nyū*/bee (Valley View). This hamlet with extinct po is on KY 1984, 5 mi w of Richmond. The po was est on Mar 14, 1891, with James A. Stapp, pm, and named for a local family. 1294.

New Campbellsburg (Henry). See *Campbellsburg*

New Canton PO (Kenton). See *Visalia*

New Castle (Henry): *nyū* kaes/əl, *nyū kaes*/əl (New Castle). This 6th class city and seat of Henry Co is on US 421, 30 mi ene of downtown Louisville. The town was founded as the seat of the new co in 1798 and its po was est as New Castle or Henry Court House on Apr 1, 1805, with Dennis Abbott, pm. The derivation of its name is unknown but it may be assumed to refer either to the city in Pennsylvania, named for the English city in 1802, or to the earlier town in Delaware, which honored the Earl of Newcastle. The Kentucky town was inc in 1817.

New Columbus PO (Owen). See *Natlee*

New Concord (Calloway): nū *kahŋk*/awrd, nu *kahn*/kawrd (New Concord). This hamlet with po is on KY 121, 8½ mi se of Murray. Historians believe the place was first settled by immigrant Germans and Norwegians, humble God-loving folk who named it Humility, and a po with this name was est there on Mar 1, 1833, with James Barnett, pm. Two years later settlers from Concord, North Carolina, seeking a more appropriate name for a growing town, had it inc as Concord. There being another Concord in Lewis Co, the town and po were renamed New Concord in 1841. 137, 437, 585.

New Cuba (Graves). See *Cuba*

New Elk Horn (Taylor). See *Elk Horn*

Newfoundland (Elliott): n(y)ū/*fown*/lən(d) (Bruin). This hamlet extends along KY 7 for about a mi in each direction from its jct with KY 32, 2 mi nne of Sandy Hook. The po est here on July 15, 1869, by John A. Davis, was recently moved ½ mi down KY 7. According to tradition, the place was called by its earliest settlers "a new found land." For many years this section was also popularly known as Crackers Neck, referring to the instructions offered by a partisan in a local fight to his champion to "crack the neck" of his opponent. 1412.

New Haven (Nelson): *nyū* hāv/ən (New Haven). This 6th class city with po is centered at the jct of US 31E and KY 52, on the Rolling Fork R and 11 mi ssw of Bardstown. It is very close to the site of Pottinger's Landing [*paht*/əndj/erz *laend*/ihŋ], which served the pioneer station Col. Samuel Pottinger and other members of James Harrod's co. est on nearby Pottinger's Creek in 1781. Pottinger is said to have later renamed the landing New Haven for the city in Connecticut of which he was fond. The town was officially founded in 1820, the po was est by 1832, and the town was inc in 1839. 199.

New Liberty (Owen): nyū *lihb*/ər/tee (New Liberty). This village with po extends for over ½ mi along KY 227, 5½ mi nw of Owenton. It was settled before 1800, and may have early been called Adams Town for pioneer settler Reuben Adams. It was laid out as a town in 1815 and its po was est by Adams on Aug 17, 1816, as Twin Meeting House. This honored the local Baptist Church, organized and so named in 1801 for its location between the 2 branches of the Kentucky R known as (the) Big Twin and Little Twin Creeks. The po was renamed New Liberty for reasons unknown, and the town was inc under this name in 1827. 160, 1292.

Newman (Daviess): *nū*/mən (Read). This crossroads hamlet with recently discontinued po is on US 60, 9 mi wnw of Owensboro. At this site or close by it was Worthington Station, founded by J. Worthington on the old Louisville Henderson & St. Louis (now

L&N) RR. The Newman po was est on May 28, 1890, and may have been named for Alexander Newman, a local storekeeper who was one of the first settlers. 930, 1348.

Newman Stand (Estill). See *Winston*

New Monroe (Hart). See *Monroe*

New Peach Orchard (Lawrence). See *Peach Orchard*

Newport (Campbell): *nū*/pawrt (Newport). This 2nd class industrial city with po is across the Licking R from Covington, across the Ohio R from Cincinnati, and 83 mi ne of downtown Louisville. The town was laid out in 1792 by Hubbard Taylor on land owned by his father, James, and named for Capt. Christopher Newport who had commanded the ships bringing the first English colonists to Jamestown in 1607. It was chartered as a town by the Kentucky legislature on Dec 14, 1795. The co seat, est in 1793 at Wilmington on the Licking R, 22 mi s, was moved to Newport at the time of its creation. In 1827 it was moved again, to the more centrally located *Visalia,* now in Kenton Co, but in 1840 was returned to Newport. Later that year, when Kenton Co was separated from Campbell Co, the seat was moved to its present location in *Alexandria* 10 mi sse. The local po was est on Oct 6, 1800, as Newport Court House or Campbell Court House with Daniel Mayo, pm, but later became simply Newport. The town was inc in 1834. 93, 165.

Newport Court House PO (Campbell). See *Newport*

New Randolph (Metcalfe). See *Randolph, Wisdom*

New Roe (Allen): *nyū* roh (Hickory Flat). This hamlet with extinct po lies on Smyrna Creek, a branch of Sulphur Fork of Middle Fork of Drakes Creek, and 11 mi sw of Scottsville. According to A. H. Hill, a New Roe teacher in the late 19th cent, 3 Virginia families—the Harrells, the Chaneys, and that of Joseph Anthony—settled in the area in the first decade of that cent and named their community New Roe after the town of Roe in Virginia. Louise Horton, however, thinks that it may have been named for Roe's (or Row's) Mill on Drakes Creek in the present Simpson Co. The name was variously spelled New Roe and New Row on 19th cent maps. The po was est as New Roe on Feb 23, 1847, with Charles A. Spear, pm, and the town was so inc by the Kentucky legislature in 1858. 101, 483, 1281.

New Salem (Crittenden) nyū *sāl*/əm (Salem). This settlement extends along US 60 for about a mi in either direction from the site of the school and church for which it was named, 6 mi wsw of Marion. The name also implies proximity to *Salem,* the town 3 mi sw. 1336.

Newstead (Christian): *nū*/stehd (Caledonia). This hamlet with extinct po lies at the jct of KY 117 and 164, 6 mi sw of Hopkinsville. According to tradition, the name was suggested for the po est on Jan 15, 1847, in John C. Whitlock's store by his sister, who had come across a literary reference to Newstead Abbey in England. When the Indiana Alabama & Texas (later L&N) RR was built through to a point about ½ mi away the Newstead store, po, and name were moved to the site of the new depot, now defunct. The po closed in 1906. 1403.

New Store PO (Lincoln). See *Hustonville*

New Sweeden PO (Edmonson). See *Sweeden*

Newtown (Harrison). See *Kentontown*

Newtown (Scott). See *New Zion*

New White Plains (Hopkins). See *White Plains*

New Woodburn PO (Warren). See *Woodburn*

New Zion (Scott): nū *zah*/ən (Centerville). This black community is on KY 922 and North Elkhorn Creek, 3½ mi se of Georgetown. It is said to have been settled around

1878, perhaps by a Mr. Clay, and may have been named for the local Zion Church, with the "New" derived from its proximity to Newtown, 3.7 mi nne. It never had a po. 1293.

Niagara (Henderson): neye/*aegh*/rə (Delaware). This hamlet with extinct po lies at the jct of the Present KY 136 and 416, 7½ mi sse of Henderson. As the voting center for area residents, it was first called Tillotson's Precinct for James Tillotson (born 1800). After his death it was called Cross Plains, presumably for its site. It is not known when the name Niagara was first applied, but the po was called this when it was est on Sept 27, 1881, with John W. Porter, pm. It is said to have been named, in reminiscence of the famed falls in upstate New York, for a local falls on land then owned by the Porter family. The po closed in 1906. 12, 1221.

Nicholas County: *nihk*/əl/əs. 197 sq mi. Pop 7,172. Seat: Carlisle. This co was est in 1799 from parts of Bourbon and Mason cos and named for George Nicholas (1743–99), Revolutionary War officer and Kentucky's first attorney general, who is considered the "Father of the Kentucky Constitution" for his role in its drafting.

Nicholasville (Jessamine): *nihk*/ləs/vihl (Nicholasville, Little Hickman). This 4th class industrial city and seat of Jessamine Co is on US 27, 64 mi ese of downtown Louisville. It was laid out as the co's seat by Rev. John Metcalfe and named by him for George Nicholas (1743–99), Virginia-born lawyer and Revolutionary War veteran, who was Kentucky's first attorney general and was instrumental in framing its first constitution. The po was est on Jan 14, 1806, by Maj. Benjamin Netherland and the city was chartered by the legislature in 1812. 240, 620.

Nickells PO (Livingston). See *Grand Rivers*

Nihizertown (Fayette): *neye*/zər/town (Ford). This predominantly black settlement is bounded by Cleveland Pike, Todds Rd, and Sulphur Wells Pike, 5 mi e of Lexington's New Circle Rd. It was named for John Nihizer for it was on land he had subdivided to provide homes for freed slaves after the Civil War. 33.

Nina (Garrard): *neye*/nə (Kirksville). This hamlet with extinct po is 1 mi from Paint Lick Creek, which separates Garrard and Madison cos, and 6 mi ne of Lancaster. The first po, in operation from 1867 to 1870, was named Spoonville [*spūn*/vihl] for local storekeeper Robert E. Spoon[e]. When it was reest on Mar 10, 1886, it was named Nina for the daughter of the new school teacher, who is said to have also given her name to the local school. The po closed for good in 1913. 35, 1041.

Noble (Breathitt): *noh*/bəl (Noble). This recently discontinued po was most recently on Buckhorn Creek, a branch of Troublesome Creek, just above the mouth of Long Fork, 11½ mi se of Jackson. It was est on Troublesome Creek, ½ mi w of the Perry Co line, on Oct 28, 1889, with James Hudson, pm, and named for the pioneer Noble family.

Nobob (Barren): *noh*/bahb (Freedom). Little remains of a once thriving 19th cent village on the present KY 839, 10½ mi se of Glasgow. The name was first applied to the creek on which it is located, a branch of Skaggs Creek. The creek may have been named for one Robert (or Bob) Todd, a hunter for a party of Virginia military land grant surveyors that had made camp near the site of the future settlement. According to tradition, Todd failed to return to camp one night, and for days his companions searched for him only to return each night to report "No Bob!" The stream was often called Flathead Creek, allegedly for "a man who had his head flattened when he was thrown into the creek" by a powder mill explosion. The Nobob po, est on Apr 28, 1854, with Newberry M. Wilson, pm, is no longer in operation. (See also *Nolin.*) 83, 487.

No Creek (Ohio): *noh* kreek (Hartford). This narrow strip of land extending for about a mi along KY 136, some 3 mi nw of Hartford, was one of the oldest settled areas of the co. It was named for the stream that parallels it less than ½ mi to the n. This stream, a tributary of Rough R, is said to have been named by surveyors sometime before 1798 for its perceived dry bed, leading them to consider it "no creek at all." The first settler, John Bennett, a Revolutionary War veteran, arrived in the area in 1798. The No Creek po, est on Feb 9, 1848, with A. A. Rowan, pm, was discontinued in 1849 and reest on Jan 17, 1901. It closed for good in 1907. 216.

Nola PO (Magoffin). See *Fritz*

Nolin (Hardin): *noh*/*lihn* (Sonora). This station on the L&N RR lies at its jct with KY 1407, 8 mi s of Elizabethtown. A flourishing mill town here at one time was undoubtedly named for its location on the Nolin R, a tributary of the Green R. It is traditionally believed that the r was named for Col. Benjamin Lynn, one of James Harrod's associates, who, in 1779, while hunting with his companions, became separated from them. Men sent to search for him would come back each night to report "No Lynn." Later he was found camped on another stream, in Hart Co, which came to be called Lynn Camp Creek (*sic*). A Nolin po was in operation from 1836 to 1859 though its precise location is not known. The po at or near the rr station was est as Phillipsburg, for reasons unknown, on Nov 24, 1858. Its pm, Ben Hardin, had it renamed Nolin on Apr 22, 1859, about the time the station was opened. The po is extinct. (See also *Nobob.*) 1420.

Nonesuch (Woodford): *nuhn*/suhch (Salvisa). This hamlet with extinct po lies at the jct of KY 1965 and the Cummins Ferry Rd, 9 mi s of Versailles. The po was est on Apr 8, 1890, by Henry D. Wilson, who had opened the first store there in the 1870s. Some say the name was suggested by Samuel McCauley, a local magistrate, who once observed of the highly productive farmland of that area, "there is no other place like it." Or, it could have been named for the Virginia None-Such (*sic*). This, according to George R. Stewart, was a plantation or hundred so named because its owners thought that "no place was so strong or pleasant or delightful." C. R. Mason of Bristol, Virginia, believes the name spread from the plantation to which it was originally assigned to the surrounding area, but no one seems to know where this was located. In colonial times Virginians would often refer to their community by the name of its dominant plantation. Kentucky's Nonesuch po was discontinued in 1925. 205, 1107, 1269.

Nonnel (Muhlenberg): nahn/*ehl* (Drakesboro). This coal town with extinct po on the L&N RR, just e of US 431/KY 70 and 5½ mi ene of Greenville, was first known as Elk Valley. It was renamed for John Lennon (the letters of his name reversed), an L&N maintenance superintendent. From 1919 to 1931 the local po was called Tarma, for reasons unknown. The name continues to be spelled with 2 "l"s on topographic and state highway maps reflecting, perhaps, the stress on its 2nd syllable. 1253.

Nonsuch (Grant and Owen). See *Jonesville*

Norfleet (Pulaski) *nawr*/fleet (Faubush). This extinct po on KY 1664, 9½ mi wsw of Somerset, was est on Aug 1, 1906, with Rufus Tarter, pm, and named for Wyatt Norfleet, M.D. (1836–1906) whose family ran the local store and who gave the land for the local school. 1410.

Northfield PO (Pulaski). See *Jugornot*

North Fork PO (Mason). See *Lewisburg*

North Liberty (Jessamine). See *Keene*

North Middletown (Bourbon): nawrth *mihd*/əl/town (North Middletown). This fifth class city with po is centered at the jct of US 460 and KY 13 and 957, 8 mi se of Paris. It was first called Swinneytown for a Mr. Swinney who had early est a station at the site but was unsuccessful in securing a po. It was to have been called Middletown for its location halfway between Paris, Mt. Sterling, Winchester, and Millersburg, but the North was prefixed to it when it was inc in 1818 to distinguish it from the Middletown in Jefferson Co. John B. Stivers est the po. According to Jillson's *Pioneer Kentucky,* it was still being called Swinneytown by older residents in the 1920s. 109, 167.

North Pleasureville (Henry). See *Pleasureville*

North Tower PO (Jessamine). See *High Bridge*

North Town (Henry). See *Pleasureville*

Norton (Hopkins). See *Nortonville*

Norton Branch (Carter): *nawr*/tən *braench* (Rush). This hamlet with extinct po is on KY 1654, just below the mouth of Norton Branch of Williams Creek, a tributary of the Little Sandy R, and 5 mi e of Grayson. The stream, community, and po, in operation from 1910 to 1912, were named for the Norton Iron Works, whose area mines furnished coal for the Norton Furnace in Ashland. The co. was est in 1872 by Col. E. M. Norton and his brothers from Wheeling, West Virginia, and their furnace began operation the following year. 7.

Norton Village (Hopkins). See *Nortonville*

Nortonville (Hopkins): *nawr*/tən/vihl (Nortonville). This 5th class city with po lies at the jct of US 41A and 62, 8 mi s of Madisonville. In 1870 W. E. Norton, a recent settler attracted by the possibilities for the economic development of the area with the completion of the L&N and Illinois Central rrs then being built, bought 2000 acres at the place where they would join and laid off the town he called Norton. With this name the local po was est on Apr 10, 1871, and the town was inc on Jan 10, 1873. It was later called Norton Village and then, officially, Nortonville. 505, 1320.

Nottsville (Daviess). See *Knottsville*

Nuckles PO (Bell). See *Beverly*

Nuckols (McLean): *nuhk*/əlz (Utica). This hamlet with recently discontinued po lies at the jct of US 431 and KY 1080, 7½ mi e of Calhoun. This, or the point where 1080 crosses the L&N RR tracks less than ¼ mi w, was first called Tichenors Station for Manley Berry Tichenor, a nearby landowner. When the then Owensboro & Nashville RR arrived here in 1867, a station was built that came to be called Nuckols Station for Neverson "Nef" Nuckols, a local farmer and merchant who had settled in McLean Co in 1870. The po was est on July 2, 1895, with Hiram McMillion, pm. 932.

Nugent PO (Woodford). See *Nugents Crossroads*

Nugents Crossroads (Woodford): *nū*/djənts *kraws*/rohdz (Versailles). This crossroads settlement at the jct of US 62 and the old Frankfort Pike (KY 1681), 4 mi nne of Versailles, grew up around the famed Offutt-Cole Tavern, an early 19th cent stagecoach stop halfway between Frankfort and Lexington. The original log structure may have been built by John Lee or his father, Hancock Lee, sometime before 1800. In 1802 the building was leased as a tavern by Horatio J. Offutt. By then the hamlet of Leesburg had been est around the tavern, but it shortly came to be called Offutt's Cross Roads [*ahf*/əts]. In 1812 Richard Cole, Jr., bought the tavern and it became known as Coles Tavern and later the Black Horse Tavern. Cole had a po there around 1818 called Coles. In the 1870s, when the Nugent family built a store across the rd from the tavern, the community came to be known as Nugents Cross Roads. On Feb 8, 1884, James Nugent est the Nugent po in the store. This was moved in 1886 .3 mi e on the Frankfort Pike to property owned by the descendants of Judge Caleb Wallace. It was renamed Wallace Station for the station est on the Versailles & Midway (later Southern) Ry.

The po became simply Wallace in 1903, by which time a settlement had sprung up there. The po closed in 1913. 629, 816, 1269.

Oak Forest PO (Wayne). See *Steubenville*

Oak Grove (Christian): *ohk ghrohv* (Oak Grove). This loosely integrated community, centered on a prosperous 5th class city, extends for about 2 mi along US 41A to a point n of KY 911 and e to at least KY 115 at Hensleytown, some 12 mi s of Hopkinsville. The po of Oak Grove, whose original location in this area has not been precisely determined, was est in 1828 or earlier by Samuel Gordon, a pioneer settler. After an intermittent existence, the po was probably moved to the present site of Hensleytown, at the jct of KY 115 and 911, in 1887 and so named, though it was spelled Hinsleytown. Some 2 weeks later another Oak Grove po was est, probably at or near its present site. With the completion in 1903 of the Tennessee Central (now Illinois Central Gulf) RR, less than ½ mi e of the present US 41A, the po, retaining the Oak Grove name, was moved to the station which was then called Thompsonville. Recently the po returned to US 41A. The name Oak Grove was derived from a grove of oak trees. 1403.

Oak Grove (Trigg): *ohk ghrohv* (Cadiz). This rural settlement, focused on the Oak Grove Church at the head of Burge Creek, 4 mi s of Cadiz, was settled by the family of Starkie Thomas. Named for a local grove of oak trees, it has never had a po. 98.

Oak Hill (Pulaski): *ohk hihl* (Delmer). This rural settlement, 1 mi e of Lake Cumberland's Fishing Creek embayment and 1¼ mi w of Somerset, was allegedly named for an old Baptist church on a slight rise in the midst of a grove of oak trees. It has never had its own po. 978.

Oakland (Trigg). See *Maggie*

Oakland (Warren): *ohk*/lənd (Smiths Grove, Bristow). This 6th class city with po and rr station is ½ mi nw of an I 65 interchange and 8½ mi ene of Bowling Green. William Radford, the first storekeeper, is said to have named the L&N RR station there in 1859 for the many large oak trees in the vicinity. He est the local po as Oakland Station on Apr 13, 1860, and became its first pm. The name was shortened to Oakland in 1887. 872.

Oakland Station PO (Warren). See *Oakland*

Oak Level (Marshall): *ohk lehv*/əl (Oak Level). This hamlet with extinct po on KY 1949, 5 mi w of Benton, is believed to have been first settled before 1850 by Allen Nance who built a store there. The po, in operation from 1876 to 1907, was named for the thick oak forest on a fairly level stretch of land that has locally been referred to as The Flat Woods. 76, 1337.

Oaks (McCracken): ohx (Symsonia). This rural settlement with a station on the L&N RR's Paducah and Memphis Subdivision lies where the tracks cross KY 450, just w of the West Fork of Clarks R and 6 mi sse of Paducah. It was named for the many oak trees in the area. It has never had its own po.

Oakton (Hickman): *ohk*/tuhn (Oakton). This hamlet with po extends for about ½ mi along KY 123 from the Illinois Central Gulf tracks, 3½ mi w of Clinton. It grew up around the Mobile and Ohio RR station est around 1860 as Clinton Station to serve the co seat. When, by 1870, plans for the Illinois Central RR to come through Clinton itself precluded the further need for a station here to serve it, the community was renamed Oakville. The po was est as South Oak on Nov 23, 1874, with John B. Cave, pm, and became Oakton in 1882. It was named for a large oak tree. 162, 1118.

Oakville (Hickman). See *Oakton*

Oakville (Logan): *ohk*/vihl (Adairville, Dot). This po is on KY 739, 5½ mi s of Russellville. This site, once in a dense forest of red oak trees, suggested the name Red Oak to early settlers Henry Barker and Charles H. Johnson and by this name the community was known, though the po which served it from 1856 to 1863 was called Escipion. This po was reest by Johnson in early 1884. He renamed it Oakville on May 16 of that year when he learned that the name Red Oak was already in use. Yet that name continued to be borne by the Owensboro and Nashville RR station there until it closed in 1933. Now the name survives only in the Red Oak Church 2 mi nw. 206.

O'Bannon (Jefferson): oh/*baen*/ən (Anchorage). This hamlet with extinct po and L&N RR station is centered where Factory and Collins Lanes join LaGrange Rd (KY 146), 13 mi e of downtown Louisville. The po was est as Williamson on Feb 12, 1850, with John B. O'Bannon, pm, and named, as was the rr station, for the family of pioneer John Williamson, owner of several thousand acres in that area. In 1859 the name was changed to O'Bannon for John B. or his family. John B., son of Virginian Isham O'Bannon (1767–1845), was a farmer and businessman who built his home on LaGrange Rd around 1830. The po closed in 1964. 100, 720.

Oddville (Harrison): *ahd*/vihl (Shady Nook). This hamlet with extinct po is on US 62, 4½ mi nne of Cynthiana. The first settlers of the site were the family of Josiah Whitaker, a Methodist preacher, who arrived in 1799. In 1851, Hezekiah Whitaker, the local storekeeper, applied for the po and forwarded Rev. J. C. Crow's request that it be named Mt. Washington. When informed that there were already too many Washingtons in the country and that a unique name should be selected instead, Crow suggested Oddville. The po was in operation from June 5, 1851, to 1903. 808.

Offutt (Johnson): *ahf*/ət (Offutt). Little but the po remains of a once prosperous rail center on the Levisa Fork of the Big Sandy R, just above the mouth of Greasy Creek and 4 mi ne of Paintsville. It was first called Ward City [*wâhrd siht*/ee] for several local families. A po with this name from 1876 to 1897 was reest in 1908 as Lower Greasy [*loh*/ər *ghreez*/ee]. About this time the community was renamed for James Offutt, the president and general manager of the Rockcastle Lumber Co., and came to serve as the terminus of narrow gauge rrs from the co.'s mills on Greasy and the cannel coal mines on nearby Two Mile Creek. The po was renamed Offutt in 1914. 89, 128, 1353.

Offutt's Cross Roads (Woodford). See *Nugents Crossroads*

Ogden PO (Ballard). See *Needmore*

Ogden's Landing (Ballard). See *Needmore*

Ohio County: oh/*hah*/yoh, oh/*hah*/yə. 596 sq mi. Pop 21,900. Seat: Hartford. Ohio Co was est in 1798 from part of Hardin Co and named for the Ohio R which originally formed its northern boundary.

Oil Springs (Allen). See *Petroleum*

Oil Springs (Clark): *oy*/əl *sprihŋz* (Levee). Almost nothing remains of resort developed around several mineral springs on Lulbegrud Creek, 11 mi ese of Winchester. The medicinal waters of these springs and the rock oil that seeped from at least one of them were used by Indians and pioneers alike to treat wounds, rheumatism, and other ailments. The crude oil seepage gave the community its name. The community never had its own po. 404.

Oil Springs (Johnson): *awl sprihŋz* (Oil Springs). This hamlet with po extends nearly 1½ mi along KY 40 (old US 460) ca 7 mi w of Paintsville. It was named for its proximity to the first recorded natural oil spring in the co, said to have been discovered by the Indians who used it for medicinal purposes. The po was est on Jan 29, 1868, with Hamilton Litteral, pm. The community may also have been known for a while as

Medina [mə/*dah*/nə] for the Medina Seminary, a boarding school est there in the 1870s by John Riggs Long, an instructor at Ohio's Rio Grande College. 1411.

Oil Works PO (Greenup). See *Wurtland*

Oklahoma (Wolfe). See *Rogers*

Okolona (Jefferson): ohk/ə/*lohn*/ə (Louisville East, Brooks). This sprawling, unincorporated suburb without po is centered at the jct of Preston Highway and Outer Loop, 9¼ mi sse of downtown Louisville. The greater Okolona area was first served by a po called Cross Roads, in operation from 1850 to 1879 at the jct of the Preston Highway and Cooper Chapel Rd, 2.8 mi s of Okolona's present business center. The Okolona po itself was est on Aug 16, 1889, with George B. Kyser, pm, and discontinued in 1902. Patrons wanted to call it Lone Oak for the large tree that stood near the business center, but another po of this name in McCracken Co led to a reversal of the words and a slight change in the spelling. The community was named for the po. 155, 375, 692.

Olaton (Ohio): oh/*lā*/tən (Olaton). This hamlet with po is on Caney Creek, at the jct of KY 878 and the Illinois Central Gulf RR, 12 mi ene of Hartford. The first po to serve that vicinity was est as Sheaffers Mill on July 16, 1842, with Anthony Scheaffer (*sic*), pm. In 1851, several years after Benjamin R. Briggs, owner of a nearby water-powered gristmill, became pm, the po was moved to and/or renamed Briggs Mills. This po closed in 1866. On the hill several hundred yards w of Caney Creek, Joel Payton est another po on July 18, 1883. As the name he preferred, believed to have been Viola, was already in use, he submitted a combination of the name of his niece, Ola Wilson, daughter of John Wilson, and the last syllable of his own surname. 905, 1140.

Old Allen (Floyd). See *Allen*

Old Campbellsburg (Henry). See *Campbellsburg*

Old Christiansburg (Shelby). See *Christiansburg*

Old Cromwell (Ohio). See *Cromwell*

Old Cuba (Graves). See *Cuba*

Old Deposit (Jefferson). See *Fairdale*

Old Elk Horn (Taylor). See *Elk Horn*

Old Elkton (Todd). See *Elkton*

Old Feliciann (Graves). See *Feliciana*

Old Flat Lick (Knox). See *Flat Lick*

Oldhamburg PO (Oldham). See *Skylight*

Oldham County: *ohl*/dəm. 190 sq mi. Pop 27,712. Seat: La Grange. This co was est in 1823 from parts of Jefferson, Shelby, and Henry cos and named for Col. William Oldham, Revolutionary War veteran, who as the commander of a Kentucky militia regiment was killed by Indians in the so-called Battle of St. Clair's Defeat in 1791.

Old Harrison (Pulaski). See *Faubush*

Old Landing (Lee): ohld *laend*/ihŋ (Cobhill). Little but the po remains of community with L&N RR flagstop and landing on the Kentucky R, 6 mi nw of Beattyville. It is said that the community grew from an overnight lodginghouse for the loggers who would tie up their rafts in the bottom across the r. The local po, est on Mar 26, 1883, with Mrs. Delina McGuire, pm, was first called Whynot, allegedly pronounced "weye/*naht*," but renamed Old Landing in 1904 when Ambrose Durbin took it over. The story of the logger who suggested that "we tie up here" and got the answer "why not?" has been discounted, but no other explanation has been offered. The name Old Landing may predate the Whynot po, for according to postal records, an Old Landing po was in operation from 1871 to 1874 and another po called Old Landing Sinks was in existence for nearly 9 months from Apr 1878. It is not known where either of these po's was located. 1372.

Old Landing Sinks PO (Lee). See *Old Landing*

Old Monroe (Hart). See *Monroe*

Old Olga (Russell). See *Olga*

Old Olive Hill (Carter). See *Olive Hill*

Old Paint Lick (Garrard). See *Manse*

Old Pine Grove (Clark). See *Pine Grove*

Old Pryorsburg (Graves). See *Pryorsburg*

Old Randolph (Metcalfe). See *Randolph, Wisdom*

Old Rockport (Ohio). See *Rockport*

Old Sparta (Gallatin and Owen). See *Sparta*

Old Stephensburg (Hardin). See *Stephensburg*

Oldtown (Greenup): *ohld*/town (Oldtown). This hamlet with po on KY 1, near the Little Sandy R and 9½ mi ssw of Greenup, may have been named for the early evidence of an old Indian town at that site. Some have suggested that it was a way station for Indian hunting parties attracted to a local spring or even the scene of a battle among prehistoric Indians. It was settled by Virginia families before 1800, and the po was est on Mar 15, 1836, by Samuel Osenton. 23, 109, 636.

Old Volney (Logan). See *Olmstead*

Olga (Russell): *ahl*/ghə (Creelsboro). This hamlet with extinct po lies at the jct of KY 55 and 379, 4½ mi sw of Jamestown. On Apr 6, 1905, Joseph Barnes est the po in his store at the jct of the present KY 379 and 1058 and named it for Olga Kimper, the daughter of a friend. In the 1920s, M. E. Antle moved the po to its present site 2 mi n, where it continued as Olga until it closed in 1941. The original po site is locally known as Old Olga. 1100.

Olive Hill (Carter): *ahl*/əv *hihl, heel* (Olive Hill). This 4th class city stretches about 2 mi along US 60 and Tygarts Creek, 11 mi w of Grayson. A rural trade center was early est on land settled by the Henderson brothers in the first decade of the 19th cent. The origin of the name is not known. There is no evidence for the popular contention that Elias P. Davis, when he est the po on Apr 3, 1838, named the town for his friend Thomas Oliver. With the arrival of the Elizabethtown Lexington and Big Sandy (now C&O) RR in 1881, the town was moved from its hillside location to the tracks, leaving the hillside, as Old Olive Hill, an exclusively residential area. Inc in 1884, it became the seat of the short-lived Beckam Co, organized in 1904 from parts of Carter, Elliott, and Lewis Cos and named for the then Kentucky governor. 36, 638, 1326.

Oliver PO (Greenup). See *Lloyd*

Ollie (Edmonson): *ahl*/ee (Rhoda, Nolin Reservoir). This po on the Houchens Ferry Rd, 5½ mi ne of Brownsville, was est on Mar 30, 1898, by Joseph L. Sanders, the first pm, and named by his wife, Nealie, for her mother, Ollie Easter.

Olmstead (Logan): *ahm*/stəd (Olmstead). This hamlet with po and former L&N RR station lies where the tracks cross KY 775, 7 mi sw of Russellville. The site may first have been known as Hogan's Station for Martin Hogan who settled there shortly after 1800. Some 2 mi n, on the present US 79, Volney Walker's name was applied as early as 1816 to a stagecoach relay station and a school called Volney Institute. On Jan 8, 1850, George A. Williams est the Volney po at the Institute site, but after the L&N completed its Memphis Branch through this section in 1860, the po was moved to the tracks and renamed Volney Station. On July 15, 1862, it was renamed Olmstead by Jonathan Baker, pm, for the popular rr construction boss, perhaps, as has been suggested, to give the community a more independent identity. Volney was by that time known as Old Volney. 42, 206, 1344.

Olympia (Bath): oh/*lihm*/pyə (Olympia). This hamlet with po is centered on the jct of KY 36 and the C&O RR, 4 mi se of Owingsville. A town was laid off here sometime after 1876 and a po named Puck, for reasons unknown, was est on Nov 28, 1881, with Thomas J. Eubank, pm. By the following Mar, the po had been renamed Olympia for the Olympian Springs health resort, 2½ mi s, and the town was inc as Olympia that Apr. 15. 186.

Olympian Springs (Bath): oh/*lihm*/pyən *sprihŋz* (Olympia). Nothing remains of this 19th cent vacation and health resort on KY 36, 7 mi se of Owingsville. It has been said that William Ramsey, having discovered 8 different mineral springs here, which he collectively called Mud Lick Springs, built a boarding house and cabins. Around 1800 Col. Thomas Hart acquired the property, renamed it Olympian Springs apparently for Mt. Olympus, a 1200-ft elevation in a short distance to the se (which in turn undoubtedly referred to the mythical home of the Greek gods), and built a hotel. On Dec 13, 1811, the Olympian Springs po was est with William Bashaw, pm, and operated intermittently until 1882 when its papers were transferred to *Olympia,* 2½ mi n. Now the site is again called Mud Lick for nearby Mud Lick Creek. Most maps and atlases today spell the name Olympia Springs. 186, 332.

Omarsville PO (Leslie). See *Kaliopi*

Onedia PO (Clay). See *Oneida*

Oneida (Clay): oh/*need*/ə, oh/*need*/ee (Oneida). This village with po is on KY 11 where the Red Bird R, Goose Creek, and Bullskin Creek come together to form the South Fork of the Kentucky R, 9½ mi ne of Manchester. It is said by some, though disputed by others, that James Anderson Burns named the Oneida Baptist Institute, which he est here in 1898, and the community for the Indian tribe on the suggestion of a New York State resident. It is more likely that the community and the name preceded the school: The po was est as Onedia, an obvious error, on June 25, 1892, with William Lunsford, pm. The spelling was corrected to Oneida in 1906. No one today can account for the unusual pronunciation. 1259, 1340.

Ono (Russell): *oh*/noh (Jabez). This hamlet with extinct po is on KY 1611, 4½ mi e of Jamestown. The po was est on May 5, 1899, with William T. Wilson, pm, and undoubtedly named, though for reasons unknown, for the biblical town of Ono (mentioned in 1 Chron. 8:12). The obvious folk etymology offered for the several other Onos in the US has also been suggested for this one: A public meeting was held to choose the name of the new po. To every suggestion made there would be an "Oh, no!" from the group assembled. Finally, in desperation, they decided to name it Ono because that seemed to be the only thing people could agree on. The po closed in 1948. 1233.

Onton (Webster): *ahn*/tən (Beech Grove). This hamlet with recently discontinued po is centered at the jct of KY 147 and 370, 13 mi e of Dixon. The community was first called Orton for an early family, but another Orton in Kentucky compelled the adoption of the name Onton for the po est on Sept 28, 1882, with Franklin P. Tilford, pm. 1174.

Oolite (Meade): *ū*/leyet (New Amsterdam). This extinct po and co. town was on the Ohio R, 7 mi nw of Brandenburg. The town was founded in the first decade of the 20th cent with the est of a limestone quarry there and named for the oolitic nature of its rock. The po opened on June 9, 1910, with William H. Tompkins, pm, and closed in 1958. 641, 1260.

Orangeburg (Mason): *ahr*/əndj/bergh (Orangeburg). This hamlet with extinct po is on Stone Lick Branch of the North Fork of the Licking R and at the jct of KY 1234 and 1449, 5 mi se of Maysville. The site was part of Francis McDermid's 1400-acre tract that he conveyed to his daughter, Catherine (Mrs. Charles) Williams. Henry Parker and Charles's son John formally laid out the town in 1796, calling it Williamsburg for John Williams. A po of this name was est on Jan 1, 1814, with Elijah Thornberry, pm. A legislative act in 1836 authorized a name change to Orangeburg to honor a local tailor and leading citizen, Providence Orange Pickering. The po was also renamed in 1850, but closed in 1906. 51, 850.

Ordinary (Elliott): *awr*/dən/ehr/ee (Ault). This extinct po on KY 32, 5 mi nw of Sandy Hook, was est by George W. Carter on Aug 11, 1884. According to local tradition, while trying to think up a name for the new po, someone (perhaps Nelson Eagen) said that this was such an ordinary place it would be hard to find a name for it. So they called it Ordinary. It may, however, have been named for a local tavern, for Ordinary was the generic name for taverns in early pioneer times. The po closed in 1953. 658, 1412, 1415.

Oregon (Campbell). See *California*

Organette PO (Christian). See *Herndon*

Orion PO (Hickman). See *Spring Hill*

Orr (Anderson). See *Glensboro*

Orton (Webster). See *Onton*

Osceola (Green): oh/see/*oh*/lə (Center). Nothing remains of a once prosperous mill town at the point where KY 88 now crosses the Little Barren R, the site of Oceola Ford (*sic*), 9½ mi w of Greensburg. The town was founded in 1864, about the time the Hart Co po of *Monroe* was moved 1½ mi e, to the e side of the Little Barren, and renamed for the ford. No one knows why the ford was so named but it is assumed that someone wished to honor the famed Seminole chief (1804–38). The town was inc as Osceola in 1868 on 100 platted acres. 520, 774, 1043.

Otisville PO (Livingston). See *Grand Rivers*

Ottenheim (Lincoln): *aht*/ən/heyem (Crab Orchard). This settlement is centered at the jct of KY 643 and 1948, 7 mi sse of Stanford. According to co historians, Jacob Ottenheimer, a rr and steamboat passenger agent in New York City, bought a considerable amount of Lincoln Co land in 1873, on which he arranged for the settlement of some 90 families. The first settlers arrived in 1884 and built a Lutheran church in whose honor the settlement was first called Lutherheim. The Mirror po est by James Oaks on Mar 22, 1881, was renamed Lutherheim on Feb 19, 1885, by its then pm Xover Stokeler. Ostensibly to meet the objections of the local Catholic pop, the po and community were renamed Ottenheim in 1886. The po closed in 1907. 60, 470.

Otter PO (LaRue). See *Malt*

Otter Pond (Caldwell): *aht*/ər pahnd (Princeton East). This extinct hamlet, Illinois Central Gulf RR station, and po on KY 128, 5 mi se of Princeton, were named for a clear water lake ¼ mi s, once probably inhabited by otters. Now called Otter Pond, the lake was once some 20 acres in size and may early have been called Long Pond, perhaps suggestive of its shape then. The local po was est as Long Pond on Dec 23, 1847, with George S. Massey, pm, and discontinued in 1871. It was reest as Godwin (a spelling error, for it honored the local Goodwin family) on Apr 19, 1888, but became Otter Pond in June of that year. The po closed for good in 1941. 1196, 1278.

Oven Fork (Letcher): *uhv*/ən *fawrk* (Whitesburg). This hamlet of scattered homes extends some 2½ mi along US 119 on the upper reaches of the Poor Fork of the

Cumberland R, 3½ mi s of Whitesburg. The Bach family and others from Thuringia, Germany, settled here before 1800. Two accounts of the name have been offered: The earliest German settlers produced bricks for local chimneys from an open oven or, more likely, they baked their bread in such ovens. In the typical pattern of pioneer settlements, the name was probably first applied to the local stream, which is now Franks Creek, a branch of Poor Fork, and then transferred to the po est near its mouth on Feb 6, 1879. 1265.

Owen (Owen). See *Sweet Owen*

Owen County: *oh*/ən. 354 sq mi. Pop 8,713. Seat: Owenton. Owen Co was est in 1819 from parts of Scott, Franklin, and Gallatin cos and named for Col. Abraham Owen (1769–1811), Indian fighter and Kentucky legislator, who was killed at the Battle of Tippecanoe.

Owensboro (Daviess): *oh*/ənz/buhr/ə (Owensboro East, Owensboro West, Sutherland, Panther). This 2nd class city and seat of Daviess Co is on the Ohio R, 75 mi sw of downtown Louisville. The site was first called Yellow Banks as early as 1776 by r travelers, though the first recorded use of this name was in 1798. The name was applied to the whole bank for its yellowish appearance and specifically to the place where William Smeathers (Bill Smothers) (1762–1837), an Indian fighter and hunter, made the first permanent settlement in the area. Some historians have reported a frontier military post at the banks as early as 1795. The name Yellow Banks was given to the po est on July 1, 1806, but this was changed to Owensborough on Mar 9, 1816. In that year the town was surveyed and platted by Col. James W. Johnston and the name Rossboro (or Rossborough) was proposed to the Kentucky legislature. This was to have honored David Ross (died 1817), one of the wealthiest Virginia merchants and landowners of his day and a friend of Thomas Jefferson. But the proposal was rejected by the legislature in favor of a name to honor one of its own, Col. Abraham Owen (1769–1811) who had fallen at Tippecanoe (see *Owenton* and *Owen Co*). The town thus officially became Owensborough in 1817 and Owensboro, by virtue of a change in Post Office Department policy, in 1893. 99, 104, 648.

Owensborough Junction PO (Muhlenberg). See *Central City*

Owenton (Owen): *oh*/ən/tən (Owenton). This 5th class city and seat of Owen Co is on US 127 and KY 22, 48 mi ene of downtown Louisville. A tract of 50 acres on this site was surveyed in 1822 prior to its acquisition for the co's second seat (see *Hesler*). Both town and co were named for Virginia-born Col. Abraham Owen (1769–1811), a Kentucky legislator and Indian fighter who had fallen at the battle of Tippecanoe (see *Owensboro*). The po was est on Apr 6, 1822. 324, 1292.

Owingsville (Bath): *oh*/ihnz/vəl (Owingsville). This 4th class city and seat of Bath Co is on a plateau 1 mi n of I 64 and 102 mi e of downtown Louisville. According to tradition, the new co's seat was to be located in Catletts Flat, 1 mi s, but this was rejected in favor of the present site, where several important families had already est their homes. Among these were Richard Menifee and Thomas Deye Owings, each of whom donated land for the new seat and town laid out in 1811. To determine for which the town would be named, these 2 well-est gentlemen agreed to a race to build the finest home in the shortest time. Owings won. Owings, a Marylander, had come to Bath Co around 1800, distinguished himself as an ironmonger, and was to represent his co in the War of 1812 and later in the state legislature. The po was organized on July 1, 1814, as Bath Court House or Owingsville with Edward Stockton, pm, and the town was inc in 1829. 15, 662, 1321.

Owsley County: *owz*/lee. 198 sq mi. Pop 5,704. Seat: Booneville. This co was est in

1843 from parts of Clay, Estill, and Breathitt cos and named for William Owsley (1782–1862), judge of Kentucky Court of Appeals and 16th governor of the state (1844–48).

Owsley Court House PO (Owsley). See *Booneville*

Oxford PO (Crittenden). See *Marion*

Packard (Whitley): *paek*/ərd (Saxton). This abandoned coal town with extinct po was 7 mi se of Williamsburg, 0.6 mi up a hollow w of Polly Camp, which is on Patterson Creek, 1.7 mi s of KY 904. The town, its po, est on Nov 27, 1908, and the station on the Long Branch Spur of the Pine Mt. RR-West (L&N) all served the Packard Coal Co., which is said to have been named for Amelia Packard, a Brooklyn, New York-born Whitley Co school teacher. 1380.

Pactolus (Carter): paek/*toh*/ləs (Grayson). This hamlet between the Little Sandy R and KY 1, just below the jct of that rd and KY 7, and 1½ mi n of Grayson, was the location of a charcoal-fueled iron furnace built in 1824 by Joseph McMurtry and David L. Ward. The furnace was undoubtedly named for the Pactolus Torrent, which flowed through Sardis, the seat of the ancient kingdom of Lydia in Asia Minor and which, according to tradition, covered a bed of pure gold. Though it must be assumed that such a name, suggesting the potential of great wealth, was inspired by the great faith of the furnace builders in the success of their efforts, the furnace was abandoned in 1834. The Pactolus po, est on Apr 7, 1882, with William Osenton, pm, was discontinued in 1956. The name has long inspired folk etymological explanations. Some people would mention a Mr. Toll who owned a good pack mule or ass which he called "Pac"; hence "Pac, Toll's Ass." According to another account, farmers would pack their grain to Richard Deering's mill in the vicinity and tell the miller "here's my pack, toll it for us" which was then easily corrupted to Pack-tol-us. 36, 188, 1010, 1057, 1322, 1366.

Paducah (McCracken): pə/*dū*/kə (Paducah East, Paducah West). This 2nd class city and seat of McCracken Co lies just below the confluence of the Tennessee and Ohio rs, 164 mi wsw of downtown Louisville. James and William Pore are said to have built the first house on the site in 1821, and they were soon joined by others to form a community called Pekin, for reasons unknown. On May 26, 1827, the town was laid out by William Clark, who had earlier distinguished himself with Merriwether Lewis on an expedition to the northwest, and named Paducah. The po of that name was est on Feb 25, 1828, with Francis A. Harrison, pm. In 1832 the co's seat was moved to this site from Wilmington near Massac Creek where it had been first located. Paducah is said to have been named for the legendery "Chief Paduke" of a subtribe of Chickasaw Indians known as "the Paducahs." According to noted author Irvin S. Cobb, the name of the chief and the subtribe "were derived from a compound word in the Chickasaw tongue meaning 'wild grapes hanging' or, more properly, 'place where the grapes hang down.' This place is spelled by the whites . . . Pakutukah or Pak'tuka." Cobb believed that the site of the later city was named for the wild grape vines there or that the "chief" was called some form of that word meaning "wild grape." The chief is said to have died in 1819 and been buried at the site of the later town. Authorities on the Chickasaw Indians, however, say there was never such a subtribe or chief by that name or anything like it, nor such a word in their language. It is now believed that Clark adopted the name by which the Comanche Indians, with whom he was acquainted, referred to themselves—"Padoucas." 153, 443.

Page (Bell). See *Calvin*

Pageville (Barren): *pādj*/vihl (Lucas). This extinct po was where the old Glasgow–

Scottsville Rd crossed Peter Creek just above its confluence with Barren R, 9½ mi sw of Glasgow. This site is now in the Barren River Reservoir. The po, est on Apr 16, 1851, with John E. Holman, pm, was named for the family of the local storekeeper. The community may also have been called Chaplinton or Chaplaintown for pioneer Abraham Chaplin who is said to have tried unsuccessfully to found a town there on land he had acquired in early settlement times (see *Chaplin*). A po called Chaplaintown was in operation in the vicinity from Apr 7 to May 20, 1851, with John F. F. Jewell, pm. Jewell also served as Pageville pm from May 1853 to Dec 1864. The Pageville po was discontinued in 1916. 791, 1368.

Paint Creek PO (Johnson). See *Paintsville*

Paint Lick (Garrard): *pānt lihk* (Paint Lick). This village with po is on KY 52 and Paint Lick Creek, 8½ mi e of Lancaster. It was named for the creek along whose banks Indians are said to have painted rocks and trees to mark a good spot to hunt animals that came to lick the salt. Col. William Miller (1717–1811), a Virginia-born Revolutionary War veteran who had acquired some 2000 acres on the creek, built a log fort at the lick in 1776 and initiated settlement. The Paint Lick po was est sometime in the second decade of the 19th cent. A fanciful, certainly unsubstantiated account of the name was once offered by Clay Sutton of Lancaster in the *Lexington Herald:* A hunter once ambushed a squaw on the upper reaches of the creek. He was soon captured by the Indians and hung by his heels from a tree with his throat cut. His blood was splashed on the white trunks of nearby sycamore trees and his body was left hanging as a warning to other white men. 302, 766.

Paintsville (Johnson): *pānts*/vəl (Paintsville). This 4th class city and seat of Johnson Co extends for over 1 mi along the broad bottoms of Paint Creek from its jct with the Levisa Fork of the Big Sandy R, 151 mi ese of downtown Louisville. In 1826 Rev. Henry Dickson or Dixon, a North Carolina-born preacher and farmer, laid out the town on the site of Paint Lick Station, a trading post of uncertain origin, which he and others purchased by auction in 1812 from part of the 19,050-acre George Lewis Tract. It was not until 1834, however, that the town was officially est by the Kentucky legislature. The po may have been called Paint Creek by 1831 when James Hayden became pm, but was Paintsville by 1843. In the same year the town became the seat of newly est Johnson Co. The name Paintsville, which may have been derived by Dixon from the station or the creek as early as 1826, refers to the red and black painted figures of animals and birds found by early hunters on the denuded trunks of many large trees along the creek. Painted trees found in the vicinity of briny springs which attracted game animals led to the licks being designated by the hunters as "painted licks" and the stream as Paint Lick Creek, by which name it appears on early maps. 194, 222.

Palsgrove Store PO (Franklin). See *Polsgrove*

Panola (Madison): pə/*noh*/lə (P nola). This hamlet with extinct po on KY 499, 10 mi ese of Richmond, was esser ally a station on the Richmond Nicholasville Irvine & Beattyville (later L&N) RR and was probably founded and named when the rr was built through in 1890. According to tradition, it was first called Hispanola, for reasons unknown, but was shortened at the suggestion of postal officials when the po was est on Nov 27, 1891. Since cotton was grown in Madison Co in the 19th cent, it's conceivable that the name derived from the Choctaw word for cotton. 962, 1294, 1373.

Panther (Daviess): *paen*/thər (Panther). This hamlet with extinct po lies at the jct of KY 554 and 1514, 8 mi ssw of Owensboro. The Panther po was est on May 12, 1881, in John P. Burns's store and named for Panther Creek, a stream 4 mi n. The name was applied to the creek in the 1780s by surveyors for George Mason of Virginia after a large animal was spotted on this tributary of the Green R. An earlier Panther Creek po est on the creek in 1830 was renamed Howardsville 9 years later and discontinued in 1843. 885.

Panther Creek PO (Daviess). See *Panther*

Paoli (Paeola) (Washington). See *Willisburg*

Paoli PO (Clinton). See *Albany*

Paradise (Muhlenberg): *paer*/ə/deye(s) (Paradise). This once thriving, now extinct Green R town was 10½ mi ene of Greenville. By the very early 19th cent, this site was called Stum's Landing for the local ferry, landing, and store owned by Leonard Stum and his sons. No one knows how, why, or when the name was changed to Paradise but the story has been told since earliest times that a family traveling upstream with a sick child decided to spend the night at the landing; when they awoke the next day the baby had completely recovered and the grateful parents said, "This truly must be Paradise." The place may have been called Monterey [*mahn(t)*/ə/rā] for a while after the Mexican War but the po was est as Paradise on Mar 1, 1852, with Robert Duncan, pm, and the town was inc under this name in 1856. The po closed in 1967. 287, 320, 361.

Paris (Bourbon): *paer*/əs (Paris East, Paris West). This 3rd class city and seat of Bourbon Co is centered at the jct of US 27, 68, and 460, 75 mi e of downtown Louisville. Joseph Houston est a station in the vicinity in 1776. This site was later preempted by John Reed and others. In 1786 Lawrence Protzman bought part of Reed's land, divided 250 acres of it into town lots, and offered it as the seat for the new Bourbon Co created that year. At his request, the Virginia legislature in 1789 chartered the town as Hopewell for his hometown in New Jersey, but renamed it Paris in 1790 to conform to the co's name, given to honor the French royal family for its aid in the American Revolution. The po was est as Bourbontown (or Bourbonton) on Jan 1, 1795, with Thomas Eades, pm. It is believed that the name Paris was in official use by 1815 when James Paton became pm. There is no evidence that the Bourbonto(w)n name was ever applied to the town itself. The mundane derivation of Hopewell notwithstanding, more romantic local traditions have suggested that pioneer teamsters on the old Limestone–Lexington pike hoped to reach the security of Houston's blockhouse by nightfall, or else that "hope was . . . dawning in the . . . hearts of settlers after years of horrible Indian atrocities." 109, 167, 254, 538, 1414.

Park (Barren): pahrk (Park). This hamlet with extinct po lies at the jct of KY 740 and 1243, 10½ mi ne of Glasgow. On Jan 20, 1853, the po of *Three Springs,* est in 1841 in Hart Co, was moved 3 mi se to this site by John C. Green, a physician, and renamed Park. This name was derived from that of his home, Green's Park. 791.

Park City (Barren): *pahrk sih*/tee (Park City). This 6th class city with po is on US 31W, just w of its jct with I 65, and 7½ mi nw of Glasgow. In the 1820s a stagecoach relay station was located at this site where the Glasgow and the Bardstown rds joined the Louisville and Nashville Pike. A po est here on Oct 24, 1827, with William Bell, pm, was thus called Three Forks. About this time Bell acquired a 1500-acre plantation in the vicinity and built Bell's Tavern, a famous meeting place until it burned in 1860. Part of Bell's plantation was later divided into lots and sold to the founders of Glasgow Junction inc in 1871. A spur from this point on the L&N RR's main line, completed in 1859, was extended 11 mi to Glasgow and the po became known as Glasgow Junction on Dec 15, 1863. On Apr 1, 1938, the po officially became Park City, as had the rr station and town, to avoid confusion with Glasgow and because it was the closest rr and highway stop to Mammoth Cave National Park. 549, 576, 730.

Parkers Lake (McCreary): *pahrk*/ərz *lāk* (Wiborg). This hamlet with po at the jct of US 27 and KY 90, 7½ mi n of Whitley City, was named for Joe Caldwell Parker, a land speculator who sought to capitalize on the extension of the Cincinnati Southern (now Southern) RR through that section. The lake was made by the rr to supply its locomotives with water. The local station was called Cumberland Falls Station for it "was the point of debarkation" for the falls, some 8 mi e, and the po was est as Parkers Lake on Feb 21, 1889, with Parker as pm. 174, 1384.

Parkersville (Lyon). See *Lamasco*

Park Hills (Kenton): *pahrk hihlz* (Covington). This 4th class city and residential suburb without po, adjacent to Covington's western boundary, is centered on US 25/42/127. Around 1845 part of the site was subdivided and laid off as a town by Messrs. Coran, Spencer, and Corry; lots were sold and some buildings erected. But it was not until 1926 that the present Park Hills was formally est by D. Collins Lee and Robert Simmons. The "Park" refers to the 550-acre Devou Park, which it overlooks on the n, most of which William P. Devou's children donated to the city of Covington in 1910. 771.

Parksville (Boyle): *pahrx*/vihl (Parksville). This hamlet with po at the head of Chaplin R is centered at the jct of KY 34 and 300, 6 mi wsw of Danville. The po, est on Feb 12, 1859, was probably named for James Parks, who was to donate the land for the L&N RR station built there in 1865. 908.

Parmleysville (Wayne): *pahrm*/leez/vihl (Parmleysville). Little remains of this hamlet on KY 1756 and the Little South Fork R, a tributary of the Big South Fork of the Cumberland R, 11 mi sse of Monticello. It is said to have been settled around 1780 and was named for John Parmley, a Revolutionary War veteran, or his son, Robert, a prosperous local businessman. The po was est on Feb 15, 1861, with James H. Burnett, pm, but at some undetermined date it was moved several hundred yards upstream where it remained until it closed in 1958. 1247.

Parrot (Jackson): *paer*/ət (Parrot). This hamlet with po at the jct of KY 2002 and 2003, 8 mi ssw of McKee, may have been named for Dan Parrot, a resident, or at least for the local Parrot family. Locally it is still known as Letter Box, the name of its recently closed elementary school. Long before the po was est on Sept 7, 1898, with John Lear, pm, the postal needs of the community were served by a letter box tacked to a tree by the side of the rd. 1338, 1418.

Patesville (Hancock): *pāts*/vihl (Cloverport). This crossroads settlement, a thriving trade center in the late 19th cent, is on KY 144, 7½ mi s of Hawesville. It was named for its founder, William Minor Pate (1775–1853), who by 1803 had est an inn he called Pate's Station here. Postal service initiated by Pate on Oct 19, 1812, ended in late 1966. 674, 675.

Patsey (Estill): *paet*/see (Cobhill). This po, over 1 mi w of the Lee Co line and 9 mi e of Irvine, was est on July 31, 1882, when the ne section of Estill was in Powell Co. It was named for its first pm, Patsey Wells, through whose efforts, it is said, the po was secured for this isolated ridgetop area.

Patterson's Ferry (Marshall). See *Altona*

Pattonsville (Lee). See *Primrose*

Pauley (Pike): *pahl*/ee (Pikeville). This residential community on the Levisa Fork of the Big Sandy R, formerly a northside suburb of Pikeville, was recently inc into the city's limits. The now extinct po was est on July 8, 1922, with Astace K. Steele, pm, and named for the Pauley family. 1456.

Paw Paw (Pike): *pah*/pâh (Hurley). This hamlet with po is centered at the mouth of

Rockhouse Fork of Paw Paw Creek, 20½ mi e of Pikeville. The po, est on Oct 4, 1878, with Daniel B. Coleman, pm, and the creek, which joins Knox Creek 3 mi e in Virginia, were named for the growth of paw paw trees in the area. 1371.

Paynes Depot (Scott): *pānz dee*/poh (Georgetown). This rail center is where the L&N RR crosses US 62, 4½ mi sw of Georgetown. From 1792 to 1834 when the Lexington & Ohio RR est a station there on its Lexington–Frankfort route, this site was a supply point for freight hauled by wagon. The station was named for the Payne family of local landowners whose progenitor, Gen. John Payne, had succeeded John Floyd as Virginia's surveyor of Kentucky lands and was Scott Co's first justice. The po of Payne's Depot was est on Jan 31, 1852, with General Payne's son Asa as the first pm. It closed in 1925. 13, 914.

Payne's PO (Knox). See *Fount*

Paynesville (Union). See *Waverly*

Payneville (Meade): *pān*/vihl (Irvington). This village with po extends for over ½ mi on KY 144, around its jct with KY 376, 7 mi w of Brandenburg. The community was first called Caseyville, but a po of this name in Union Co led to the Meade Co po being est on July 26, 1868, as Payneville to honor a local family. 1260.

Peach Grove (Pendleton): *peech* ghrohv (Butler). This hamlet with extinct po at the jct of KY 10 and 154, 10½ mi nne of Falmouth, was named for its location in what was once an important peach-growing area. Its po was in operation from 1875 to 1907. 1230.

Peach Orchard (Lawrence): *peech* awr/chərd (Milo). This name was given to 2 extinct coal towns on Nats Creek, a tributary of the Levisa Fork of the Big Sandy R, 11–12 mi s of Louisa. The first of these, also known as Mellensburg, was est around 1850 by William B. Mellen, who had been hired by the Peach Orchard Coal Co. to develop and manage the mining operations on its 2000-acre tract purchased 3 years before from Archibald Borders. On Apr 11, 1851, the local po was est as Peach Orchard and the community soon adopted this name. This po closed in 1871. When a new mine was opened in 1881 on the Left Fork of Nats Creek, 3 mi e of the r, a 2nd town, called New Peach Orchard, was built in that vicinity. George S. Richardson assumed control of the co., which by then had become the Great Western Mining and Manufacturing Co., and on Dec 14, 1881, he reest the Peach Orchard po, which remained in operation until 1919. 19, 867.

Peacock PO (Laurel). See *Pittsburg*

Peaks Mill (Franklin): *peex mihl* (Switzer). This hamlet with extinct po is strung out along the Peaks Mill Rd on Elkhorn Creek, 5 mi n of Frankfort. In 1817 Thomas H. Gouldman built a water-powered grist- and sawmill at the site. In 1838 his widow sold it to John J. Peak (1789–1855), a Virginian, whose widow in turn sold it in 1871 to John W. Gaines. In 1856 a Pecks Mill (*sic*) po was est by Asa B. Tarrant. It became known as Tiger for a very brief period before it closed in Dec 1859. The town of Peaks Mill was inc by the Kentucky legislature in 1873 and another po, this time with the correct spelling, was est on May 4, 1877, by Samuel G. Gaines. It closed in 1907. 372.

Pearl (Whitley and Bell) pɜl (Frakes). This settlement with extinct po is centered at the jct of KY 190 and 1595, 13 mi se of Williamsburg and 15½ mi sw of Pineville. The po was est in Bell Co on June 17, 1907, and named for the daughter of the first pm, James L. Fletcher. The po, which moved to the Whitley Co side in 1924, was discontinued in 1968. 1161.

Pebble (Bath): *pehb*/əl (Sherburne). This settlement with extinct po lies where KY 1602 crosses Lick Branch, 8 mi n of Owingsville. Until 1905 the community was called Lick

Branch for the rocky stream that joins the Licking R some 2 mi n, and was also known at times as Fairview for the church on a nearby hill. In 1905 John G. McClure, the storekeeper, applied for a po. As his name was already in use an alternative suggestion, Pebble, for the texture of the stream bed, was adopted instead. The po closed in 1922. 755.

Pecks Mill PO (Franklin). See *Peaks Mill*

Peedee (Christian): *pee*/dee (Caledonia). This crossroads hamlet with extinct po lies at the jct of KY 164 and 287, 9½ mi sw of Hopkinsville. The po, est as Pee Dee on May 22, 1876, with Joseph B. Pollard, pm, was named for Pumphrey David (locally called "P.D.") Smith, a highly respected local landowner, who had settled in the area sometime before the Civil War. While Smithland, Smithfield, and other forms of his name were rejected in turn by the Post Office Department as already in use, there seemed to be no objection to the spelling out of his initials as 2 words. Sometime over the years, however, the 2 words were combined into one. The po closed in 1909. 95, 1403.

Peeled Oak (Bath): *peeld ohk* (Preston). Little remains of a once thriving village on the present KY 1331, 5½ mi ssw of Owingsville. According to tradition, early settlers happened upon a large chestnut oak tree at the edge of a nearby stream, the bark of whose trunk and every limb had been thoroughly peeled. It was assumed that this had been done by Indians or perhaps by a pioneer to mark a boundary line. The local po was est Apr 26, 1822, and operated with many intermissions until 1874. 186, 618.

Peg Station (Pike). See *Pinsonfork*

Pekin (McCracken). See *Paducah*

Pellville (Hancock): *pehl*/vihl (Pellville). This hamlet with po is on KY 144, 10 mi ssw of Hawesville. It is said to have been called Bucksnort for years until the po of Blackford—probably located on or near the creek of that name—was moved and renamed Pellville on May 23, 1868. The name Bucksnort traditionally refers to the tale of the pioneer who thought he heard a deer snorting in the brush by the side of the rd, while Pellville was named for Samuel B. Pell (1796–1864), a state legislator and long-term Hancock Co sheriff who often visited the place. 164, 262, 1332.

Pellyton (Adair): *pehl*/ə/tən (Dunnville). This hamlet with extinct po is on KY 206, 13 mi ne of Columbia. The po was est on Sept 1, 1887, with James W. Perryman, pm, and like the community was named for the Pelly or Pelley family of early settlers. 1426.

Pembroke (Christian): *pihm*/brohk, *pihm*/br o͞o k (Pembroke). This 6th class city with po is on US 41, 7 mi se of Hopkinsville. The po was est on Sept 9, 1836, and named by Dr. Lunsford Lindsay, local merchant, for the Earl of Pembroke, a much-admired character in Jane Porter's historical novel *Thaddeus of Warsaw* (1803). The town was inc on Mar 6, 1869. 145, 1403.

Penchem (Todd). See *Pinchem*

Pendleton County: *pehn*/dəl/tən. 281 sq mi. Pop 10,900. Seat: Falmouth. This co was est in 1798 from parts of Bracken and Campbell cos and named for Edmund Pendleton (1721–1803), a member of the Virginia House of Burgesses (1752–74) and the First Continental Congress, governor of Virginia (1774–76), and chief justice of the Virginia Court of Appeals (1779–1803).

Pendleton Court House PO (Pendleton). See *Falmouth*

Penny (Pike): *pihn*/ee (Dorton). This hamlet with extinct po is on Shelby Creek, ½ mi w of the mouth of Caney Creek, and 7½ mi s of Pikeville. It is said to have been named for Orville Roberts's daughter Penny, who was killed there by some unknown animal or person. The Penny po was est on Apr 13, 1909, with Laura Branham, pm. 1456.

Penrod (Muhlenberg): *pihn*/rahd, *pehn*/rahd (Dunmore). This hamlet with L&N RR station and po extends for about 1½ mi along KY 949 just e of US 431 and 11 mi se of Greenville. The local po was est as Albrittain [*awl*/briht/ən] on May 6, 1882, with Albrittain (or Albritton) J. Drake as pm. Drake was probably a descendant of Albritton Drake, a Revolutionary War veteran who settled in the area in 1806 and died there in 1834. In 1884 the community was inc as Home Valley, for reasons unknown, and officially renamed Penrod in 1886 to conform to the name the po had assumed on May 19, 1885. In 1881 Henry C. Penrod had become pm and he is said to have renamed the po for his ancestor, Tobias Penrod, a Pennsylvanian who had settled in the area around 1797. 189.

Peoples (Jackson): *peep*/əlz (Parrot). This po is at the jct of KY 30 and 2002, 10 mi ssw of McKee. Est on the Laurel Co side of the nearby Rockcastle R on Apr 13, 1881, with W. A. Spence, pm, it was allegedly named for William Peoples, a Harlan Co man who had married a Miss Ball then living near the site of the po. The po was moved to its present site in 1888. 1419.

Pepper's Mill (McCracken). See *Lone Oak*

Perry County: *pehr*/ee. 341 sq mi. Pop 33,341. Seat: Hazard. Perry Co was est in 1820 from parts of Clay and Floyd cos and named for Commodore Oliver Hazard Perry (1785–1819), the hero of the Battle of Lake Erie (1813), for whom Hazard was also named.

Perry Court House PO (Perry). See *Hazard*

Perry Park (Owen): *pehr*/ee *pahrk* (New Liberty, Worthville). This resort and retirement community with po is on KY 355 and the Kentucky R, between the mouths of Mill and Big Twin creeks, 8 mi w of Owenton. According to tradition, this site was first called Lick Skillet "by a party of pioneer surveyors. . . . Hunters for the party were so busy with guard duty [against an especially ferocious band of Indians] that little game was killed; so short on rations were they that they said, 'We would eat everything in sight, then lick the skillet.' " Years later a settlement was est there called Cleveland, probably for Grover Cleveland, and then Balls Landing for James Ball who operated the local steamboat landing and founded the Balls Landing po on Apr 6, 1887. In 1933 this po was renamed Perry Park for John M. Perry, Sr., whose forebears had owned a considerable amount of land s of Mill Creek. After some years as a New York-based owner of a chain of newspapers, Perry returned home, acquired some 2600 acres of Kentucky R bottom land, and est the Perry Park community. 515, 1159, 1292.

Perryville (Boyle): *pehr*/ə/vəl, *pehr*/ə/vihl (Perryville). This 5th class city with po is on Chaplin R and US 68 and 150, 7½ mi w of Danville. The site was first settled in 1781–82 by a party led by James Harberson and was called Harberson's Fort and later Harberson's Crossing (for its location at the jct of rds between what became the towns of Harrodsburg, Danville, Lebanon, and Louisville). The town was laid out in 1815 by Edward Bullock and William Hall and named in honor of Oliver Hazard Perry's Lake Erie victory in 1813. Bullock est the Perryville po on Feb 12, 1816, and the legislature chartered the town in 1817. 92.

Peru PO (Oldham). See *Glenarm*

Petersburg (Boone): *pee*/tərz/bergh (Lawrenceburg, Indiana). This recently disincorporated city with po is on KY 20 and the Ohio R, 8 mi wnw of Burlington. It was laid out and named by John J. Flournoy, proprietor of the land, in 1817–18 on the site of Tanner's Station (allegedly also known as Caledonia), est around 1790 by John Tanner, A Baptist minister (ca. 1732–1812). Flournoy also became the first Petersburg pm in Jan 1819. The origin of the name is not known. 315, 891.

Petersville (Lewis): *pee*/tərz/vihl (Stricklett). This hamlet with extinct po lies at the mouth of Dunaway Branch of Kinniconick Creek and the jct of KY 344 and 559, 12½ mi sw of Vanceburg. It was named for its founder, Peter D. Lykins, who had been forced by his Unionist sympathies to flee his Morgan Co home during the Civil War. The po was est on Apr 17, 1878, with James M. Lawlyes, pm, and closed in 1955. 1103.

Petrie Station (Hancock): *pee*/tree *stā*/shən (Tell City). This L&N RR freight siding and extinct po where the tracks cross KY 271, ¼ mi ne of US 60 and 2½ mi wnw of Hawesville, was est as a station on the old Louisville St. Louis & Texas Ry, and probably named for Fred Petrie or his family. Fred operated the Petri Station (*sic*) po here from 1889 to 1904. Area residents still call this place Petrie Station, not just Petri, and insist that this is the correct spelling. 1332.

Petri Station PO (Hancock). See *Petrie Station*

Petroleum (Allen): pə/*troh*/lee/əm (Petroleum). This hamlet with extinct po lies on Little Trammel Fork of Trammel Fork of Drakes Creek, just off US 31E and less than 4 mi sw of Scottsville. This was long an oil-producing area, and there was once a settlement called Oil Springs nearby. The local po was est on Dec 13, 1886, with Joseph U. Tiffany, pm. According to tradition, the founders preferred the name Oil City, but it was already in use and Petroleum was offered as 2nd choice. 101, 247, 1281.

Petros (Warren): *peet*/rohs, *pee*/trâhs (Rockfield). This hamlet on US 68/KY 80 was once a flag stop on the Memphis Branch of the L&N RR where rd and tracks almost come together, 7½ mi sw of Bowling Green. Thomas McDavitt gave the land for the rr's right-of-way. It is said to have been named for the old roadbed, over which rock was hauled, that was considered as hard as rock itself. Petros never had its own po. 1158.

Pewee Valley (Oldham): *pee*/wee *vael*/ee (Crestwood). This 5th class city with po lies just short of the Jefferson Co line and 7½ mi sw of LaGrange. Which Smith is to be credited with founding the town in 1852 and giving his name to Smiths Station on the Louisville & Frankfort (now L&N) RR, by which the place was first known, has long been a matter of debate. It may have been Thomas Smith, a Virginia-born veteran of the War of 1812, who was a local storekeeper and station agent, or it may have been Henry S. Smith (1802–83), the son of a pioneer settler, who is said to have laid out the town in 1856 on land he had earlier acquired from his father. The po was est as Pewee Valley on Feb 8, 1856, with Henry's son Charles Franklin Smith as pm. The story goes that when the town fathers were considering a name for this po, the distinctive call of a wood pewee (or phoebe), a bird common to the area, was heard and everyone agreed that this would make a dandy name. Yet no one has since been able to explain the "Valley" part of the name since the town lies on a ridge. In a more romantic vein, it may be recounted that, at the height of a rather spirited debate over the name, "a flock of pewee birds alighted just outside the windows and began to chatter noisily. The resemblance of the din to that of the meeting itself struck several of those present. Good humor was restored and the name was adopted." The town was inc in 1870. 198, 449, 687, 737.

Peytona (Shelby): pā/*tohn*/ə (Waddy). This settlement with extinct po is at the jct of Old US 60 and KY 395, 8 mi e of Shelbyville. The po, in operation from 1874 to 1902, was named for John Peyton, the owner of the site. The terminal "a" is said to have been added at the suggestion of a neighbor, Squire James Gill, to make a better-sounding name. 902.

Peytonsburg (Cumberland): *pā*/tənz/bergh (Blacks Ferry). This hamlet with recently closed po is on KY 61, 10 mi s of Burkesville. The po, originally located on Sulphur Creek, was est by and named for Peyton Parrish, the local storekeeper, on Apr 28, 1871. He was the son of John Parrish, Sr., a pioneer settler from Henry Co, Virginia, who settled in 1810 on Howards Bottom, ne of Burkesville. About the time Dale Hollow Lake was formed, the po was moved up to Pea Ridge to the site now identified as Peytonsburg. 223, 1385.

Peytontown (Madison): *pā*/tən/town (Richmond South). This almost exclusively black settlement with extinct po, 1 mi w of I 75 and 4 mi ssw of Richmond, may have predated the Civil War. It was named for the Peytons, a once prominent family in the co. The po, est on June 22, 1899, with Wiley E. Harris, pm, was closed in 1910. 1294, 1373.

Pherba (Cumberland): *fɜ*/bee/yə (Burkesville). This extinct po was near the mouth of Vaughn Creek, a branch of Bear Creek, about 4 mi ese of Burkesville. It served the community now called Bear Creek [*bɛ* kreek], along KY 90 and the stream for which it was named. The po, in operation from 1918 to 1922, was est by its only pm, Charlie C. Smith, and named for his paternal grandmother, Pherba or Ferba Rush Smith. 1385.

Phil (Casey): fihl (Phil). This hamlet, once an important rural trade center, lies at the jct of the present KY 501 and 910, 6 mi s of Liberty. The po, est by F. P. Combest in 1882 and named for US Congressman Phil Thompson of Harrodsburg, was discontinued in Dec 1968. 1397.

Phillipsburg PO (Hardin). See *Nolin*.

Philpot (Daviess): *fihl*/paht (Philpot). This suburban community with po is now centered at the jct of KY 54 and 142, 5 mi e of Owensboro. Its first po was est on June 3, 1872, as Philpott (*sic*) by Augustus J. Philpot (or Philpott) and named for his very early Daviess Co family. It lasted but a year, to be reest in 1875 as Philpots Station at the jct of the Illinois Central RR and the Old Leitchfield Rd, ½ mi e of its present site. In 1882 the po became just Philpot and sometime later was moved to its present location. 885, 1348.

Philpots Station PO (Daviess). See *Philpot*

Phyllis (Pike): *fihl*/əs (Lick Creek). This hamlet extends over 1 mi along KY 194 and Grapevine Creek, with its po at the mouth of Dicks Fork, 9 mi sse of Pikeville. The community, settled in the 19th cent, was first called Grapevine for the tributary of the Levisa Fork of the Big Sandy R, which according to tradition was named for a large grapevine that some early settlers had split to make fence rails. On Mar 29, 1917, a po was est on the creek at a site just above the present po and named Rowton [*roh*/tən] for its first pm, Grover C. Rowe. It closed in the mid 1930s. In 1947 Ervel Reynolds reest the local po ¾ mi from the mouth of Grapevine but his choice of Orlendo for his grandfather, Orlendo Reynolds, a pioneer settler, was rejected and the po was named Phyllis for the daughter of a Post Office Department official. When the Fishtrap Reservoir was created in 1968, Phyllis was moved 2 mi up the creek. 934, 1137, 1364.

Pierce (Green): peers (Exie). This hamlet with extinct po is on KY 218 at its jcts with KY 729 and 1464, 7 mi sw of Greensburg. It was founded in the early 19th cent by a family of Brewers who had a legal distillery there and named their community Brewersburg. The po, est on July 16, 1886, was named Pierce for local storekeepers William Franklin and John Pierce. John was the first pm. The community was often referred to as Loafersburg for some of the residents could be observed whiling away the hours in front of a local store. 1339, 1446.

Pig (Edmonson): pihgh (Rhoda). This crossroads settlement with extinct po lies at the jct of KY 259 and 422, 6 mi se of Brownsville. According to tradition, some local residents assembled to name the new po, est on Sept 23, 1880, could not agree on what to call it, for each wanted it named for himself. Finally when the deliberations seemed about to break down, one man said in disgust, ''I see a small hog outside on the road and that prompts me to suggest that we name the post office Pig.'' The Post Office Department apparently accepted the suggestion, and the community was then named for the po. The latter closed in 1904. 747.

Pigeonroost (Clay): *pihdj*/ən/rūst (Hima). This coal town with extinct po is on KY 80 and Horse Creek, about 2 mi below the mouth of Pigeon Roost Branch, and 3½ mi sw of Manchester. The po was est as Pigeon Roost on May 11, 1888, with Jefferson D. Rowland, pm, and probably named for the branch on which early settlers had observed such large numbers of pigeons roosting in the timber that they seemed to ''break the branches out.'' In 1894 the Post Office Department ordered the 2 words of the name combined, which spelling was retained until the po recently closed. 906, 1259.

Pigeon Roost PO (Ohio). See *Rosine*

Pike County: peyek, pahk. 785 sq mi. Pop 80,777. Seat: Pikeville. Pike Co was established in 1821 from part of Floyd Co and named for Gen. Zebulon M. Pike (1779–1813), the frontier explorer who was killed in the assault on York, Canada, in the War of 1812.

Pike PO (Pike). See *Pikeville*

Piketon PO (Pike). See *Pikeville*

Pike View (Hart): *peyek* vyū (Hammonsville). This hamlet with recently discontinued po lies at the jct of KY 936 and the old route of US 31E, 10 mi ne of Munfordville. The po, in operation from 1891 to 1908, was named for its location on the pike to Nashville from which early travelers could enjoy a picturesque view of the countryside. It is said that when the po was reest there in 1910, another name was requested by the postal authorities to avoid confusion with Pikeville in Pike Co. Dowagiac [*dow*/djaek] was suggested by someone who had spotted that name on an old wheat drill in the vicinity. The po retained this name until Pike View was recently readopted. It is believed that the name Dowagiac was ultimately derived from the town in Michigan which, according to George R. Stewart, bears a Potawatami name probably referring to ''a place where fish can be netted.'' 204, 863.

Pikeville (Pike): *pahk*/vəl (Pikeville). This 4th class city and seat of Pike Co is on US 23/460 and 119, 172 mi ese of downtown Louisville. Public disapproval of the first site of the new co's seat at the present site of Garden Village led to the decision of a commission on Dec 24, 1823, to locate the seat here on land donated for this purpose by Elijah Adkins. The town was probably called Pikeville from its inception though its po was est as Pike on Aug 5, 1825, with William Smith, pm. The po name was changed to Piketon in 1829 and the town was inc under this name in 1848. The town officially became Pikeville in 1850 though the po did not assume this name until 1881. The town and co were named for Zebulon M. Pike (1779–1813), US Army officer-explorer and the discoverer of Pike's Peak. 194, 406, 1354.

Pilgrim (Martin): *pihl*/ghrəm (Kermit). This hamlet with po is on KY 1714, 3½ mi up Wolf Creek from its confluence with the Tug Fork of the Big Sandy R, and 7 mi se of Inez. The po was est on June 30, 1891, with Moses Parsley, pm, and may have been named for the Pilgrim Home United Baptist Church there. 1392.

Pilot Oak (Graves): *pahl*/ət *ohk* (Cuba). This hamlet with extinct po at the jct of KY 94 and 129, 12 mi ssw of Mayfield, was named for a tree to which travelers could refer for the direction to Paducah, due n. The po was in operation from 1876 to 1906. 466.

Pilot View (Clark): *pah*/lət vyū (Hedges). This hamlet with extinct po 5½ mi e of Winchester, at the jct of KY 15 and the Schollsville Rd, originated and was named when these 2 rds were built to this site in 1868. According to tradition, the impressive view of Pilot Knob, Daniel Boone's famed reference point 15 mi se in Powell Co, inspired either Franklin H. Ramsey, local storekeeper, or Maj. John N. Conkwright to suggest its name. The Pilot View po operated from 1893 to 1904. 975, 1349.

Pinchem (Clark): *pihn*/chəm (Winchester). This hamlet extending for about a mi down Four Mile Creek, a branch of the Kentucky R, and KY 974, 4 mi s of Winchseter, has long been called Pinchem. Three accounts of the name's origin have been suggested. Clark Co historian Kathryn Owen, a descendant of the community's pioneer settlers, prefers that of the early storekeeper who was so tight that customers would come away feeling they had been pinched in the trade. After a while they called his the Pinchem Store and eventually the community was called just Pinchem. Or, the name may have been derived from Pinchem Slyly; the story is told that when the co was dry, anyone wanting a quart would come to the store and pinch the local bootlegger in a subtle fashion. Or, the area farms were so poor that everyone suffered from lack of nourishment; even the cattle had a pinched appearance, and were so skinny that one could pinch a calf and there would not be anything between his sides. Miss Owen discredits this last account, for though the place is rocky it has always been fairly good grazing country. When he came to est the local po, on Mar 13, 1888, pm-designate William Perry Owen, finding that *Pinchem* was already the name of a po in Todd Co, suggested the name Tulip, that of a town in Missouri that had impressed him on a recent visit. Some 5 years before the descendants of Jonathan Hunt had est the Hunt po in their store 1 mi down the creek. The Tulip po closed in 1908, the Hunt po a year later. 1349.

Pinchem (Taylor). See *Saloma*

Pinchem (Todd): *pihnch*/əm (Guthrie). This crossroads hamlet, at the jct of KY 181 and 848, 7 mi ssw of Elkton, is the center of a community of Old Order Amish. It is not known how old the community is or when this unusual name was first applied to it. At some time in the past, Green Simms (Sims) owned a "blind tiger" here. To announce their intentions and avoid being mistaken for lawmen in that age of dryness, customers would follow a prearranged procedure and pinch the proprietor in a sly fashion. Over the years the place came to be known as Pinchem Slyly, which was later simplified to Pinchem and even corrupted to Penchem. On July 1, 1882, the po of Pinchem was est with William L. Adams, pm. It lasted only 12 years. 1235.

Pinchem Slyly (Todd). See *Pinchem*

Pine Grove (Clark): *pahn ghrohv* (Clintonville). One of the 2 Pine Groves extant in Clark Co, also called Pine Grove Station, is the remains of a village and station where the C&O RR crosses the Combs Ferry and Old Todds rds, 6 mi w of Winchester. This was named for an older village of Pine Grove, shown on contemporary maps as Old Pine Grove, at the jct of US 60 and KY 1678, 4 mi wnw of Winchester. The latter in turn was named for a grove of pine trees on US 60. At one of the 2 sites, probably the one on the rr, was the Pine Grove po, which in Jan 1850 had been moved from *Chilesburg* in Fayette Co, less than 2½ mi w of Pine Grove Station. This po closed in 1964. 975, 1349.

Pine Grove (also called **Watauga**) (Clinton): pahn *ghrohv* (Cumberland City). This rural settlement, extending for some 3 mi along KY 588, and 10 mi nne of Albany, was served by the extinct Watauga [wah/*tâh*/ghə] po. Before the po was est on Feb 23, 1901, with George F. Brown, pm, the community was called Piney Woods for the tall pine trees in the vicinity. The name Watauga was requested for the po because many of the area's first residents had come from the old Watauga settlement in Tennessee. With the closing of the po in 1954 the community has been locally called Pine Grove for the neighborhood school (also closed) and Methodist church. It is doubtful whether the Watauga name is used anymore. 1263.

Pine Hill (Rockcastle): *pahn hihl* (Mt. Vernon). This settlement with extinct po is on US 25 and the L&N RR, 3½ mi ese of Mount Vernon. The po was est on Apr 16, 1867, with Rees B. Ward, pm, and named for the local pine trees. It is now a rural branch of the Mount Vernon po. 1251.

Pine Knob (Grayson): *pahn*/*nahb* (Spring Lick). This hamlet, dating back to pre-Civil War times, is in the valley of Pine Knob Creek, 11 mi w of Leitchfield. It was named for the 760-ft knob to the w, and may also have been called Hoodoo, by which name it is identified on a 1925 topographic map; nearby is Big Mouth Cave, haunted by victims of the notorious Dock Brown gang. It has had no po. 609, 1307.

Pine Knot (McCreary): *pahn* naht (Whitley City). This village with po is on old US 27 and KY 92, 3½ mi s of Whitley City. Katie Branham's inn was a favorite of antebellum travelers on the old toll rd between Lexington and Jacksboro, Tennessee. According to tradition, Katie charged a customer for corn for his horse, but put only pine knots in the feed bucket and later retrieved them so he would not know the difference. After he discovered Katie's deception and spread the word of what had happened, the inn came to be called Katie's Pine Knot and, after her death, the Pine Knot Inn. When the po was est there on June 19, 1874, with James H. Wilson, pm, it too was called Pine Knot. It closed in 1878 and reopened in July 1879 at this site or nearby as Commercial Summit. In 1887 it again became known as Pine Knot. The community that grew up around the inn and po was inc in 1913, but is no longer. 1367.

Pine Mt. Station (Harlan). See *Totz*

Pine Ridge (Wolfe): *pahn rihdj* (Pomeroyton). This hamlet with po is centered at the jct of KY 15 and 715, 3½ mi wnw of Campton. It was named for its location on a ridge dominated by scrub pine and near the Rock Bridge section of the co said to contain "one of the largest strands of eastern white pine in Kentucky." The po was est on Mar 6, 1907, with Henry C. Lacey, pm. 67, 708, 1236.

Pineville (Bell): *pahn*/vəl, *pahn*/vihl (Pineville). This 4th class city and seat of Bell Co is on the Cumberland R and US 25E and 119, 141 mi se of downtown Louisville. The site was settled early (ca. 1781) since it was at the point where the Wilderness Rd crossed the Cumberland R. Thus the community was first called Cumberland Ford and the po of this name was est on Mar 31, 1818, with Moses Dorton, pm. Though the settlement may have been aptly called Pineville as early as 1825, it was not until 1867 that the town was actually laid off. In 1869 J. J. Gibson donated land for the seat of Josh Bell Co, which had been created 2 years before. The po name was changed to Pineville in 1870, and the town was inc as Pineville in 1889. 20, 217, 462.

Piney Woods (Clinton). See *Pine Grove*

Pin Hook (Bourbon). See *Plum*

Pin Hook (Clay). See *Fall Rock*

Pin Hook (Fleming). See *Tilton*

Pin Hook (Grant). See *Crittenden*

Pin Hook (Morgan). See *Caney*

Pink PO (Jessamine). See *Little Hickman*

Pinson (Pike). See *McAndrews*

Pinsonfork (Pike): *pihn*/sən/*fawrk* (Belfry). This village with po extends for almost 1 mi along KY 199 and Pond Creek, 13 mi ene of Pikeville. The po was est as Pinsonfork on June 6, 1890, conforming to the Post Office Department's preference for one-word names, and was undoubtedly named for its first location at the mouth of Pinson Fork of Pond, the site of the present village of *McAndrews*. It was later moved 1½ mi up Pond Creek. The fork was named for the Pinson family, probably the descendants of Pike Co pioneer Allen Pinson, a Virginian who settled on Johns Creek around 1800. The local Norfolk and Western RR station has been called Peg Station, allegedly for an old man with a wooden leg. 173, 1143, 1146.

Pippapass (Knott). See *Pippa Passes*

Pippa Passes (Knott): *pihp*/ə *paes*/əz (Hindman, Kite). This village with po, home of Alice Lloyd College, extends ne along the upper reaches of Caney Creek for about a mi from a point 4½ mi e of Hindman. When Alice Geddes Lloyd of Boston est Caney Creek Junior College here in 1923, among the groups from whom she solicited funds were the Robert Browning Societies of New England. They agreed also to build the local po and are said to have suggested its name for the poet's heroine, the devout and simple mill girl Pippa, who, as she passes through her town on New Year's Day, innocently touches the lives of those who hear her songs of joy and fulfillment. The Post Office Department's preference for one-word names led to the po's est, on Dec 31, 1917, as Pippapass, a meaningless name retained until July 1, 1955, when pressure brought about a return to the intended spelling. Local people still call their community Caney or Caney Creek as they always have. 177, 403.

Piqua (Robertson): *peek*/wā (Piqua). This hamlet with extinct po lies just s of KY 165, 4 mi s of Mt. Olivet. The community was founded by Isaac Chamberlain, a school teacher who had come from Piqua, Ohio, the birthplace of Tecumseh and the site of a principal village of the Piqua subtribe of the Shawnee nation. The po was in operation from 1889 to 1937. 1365.

Pisgah (Pulaski): *pihz*/ghə (Delmer). This residential settlement with extinct po just w of US 27, 2 mi s of Somerset, was est around a Presbyterian church organized in 1828 by Rev. William Dickson on land donated by Richard Goggin. The church was named Pisgah in 1830 for the mountain from which Moses viewed the promised land as early settlers stood on the local hill and looked over the land below. The po organized on June 30, 1864, to serve this vicinity was called Stigalls Ferry [*stihgh*/ahlz] until, in 1867, Samuel R. Owens renamed it Garden Cottage for the house built for Rev. James E. Barnes, the church's pastor. The po was discontinued in 1884. 215.

Piso (Pike): *peye*/soh (Varney). This po lies at the mouth of Big Lick Branch of Brushy Fork of Johns Creek, 10 mi nne of Pikeville. After several proposed names were rejected by the Post Office Department, Bud Williamson submitted Piso, the name of a patent medicine, an ad for which he had seen in an almanac. The po was est on Apr 27, 1904, with Williamson as pm. 1013.

Pittsburg (Laurel): *pihts*/bergh (London). This village with po, extending for over 1 mi along US 25 and the L&N RR from a point ½ mi n of London, may have been named for the pioneer Pitman (*sic*) family. The brothers Lot and Holland Pitman, sons of Richard Pitman, and the neighboring McNeills were the first settlers of the vicinity; the first house is said to have been built by Holland before 1817. Soon after the Kentucky Central (now L&N) RR arrived around 1881, the coal lands owned by the Pitmans and McNeills were developed and the community grew up around the mines; the rr station came to be known as "The Pittsburgh of the South." The town was inc in 1884. The po, est as Peacock on June 13, 1882, with Michael Hope, pm, was renamed Pittsburgh on Mar 16, 1883, and then respelled Pittsburg in the 1890s. 570, 777, 1282.

Pitts Point (Bullitt): *pihts point* (Pitts Point). All that remains of a prosperous 19th cent village and steamboat port at the mouth of the Rolling Fork of Salt R, 7 mi sw of Shepherdsville, is "scattered foundation stones" in the Ft. Knox Military Reservation. The town was laid off by the brothers James G. and John S. Pitt on 600 acres they purchased in 1831 from the Fromans and was first called Pittstown. However, the po est on Mar 11, 1850, with John Greenwell, pm, was called Pitts Point, by which name the town was also inc in 1861. The po closed in 1907. The similarity of the name of this town to Pittsburgh, Pennsylvania, also located at the convergence of 2 large streams, has suggested a variant source of the name but it seems much less likely. 31, 296, 353.

Pittstown (Bullitt). See *Pitts Point*

Place PO (Knox). See *Siler*

Plank (Clay): plaeŋk (Ogle). This po some 2½ mi up Martins Creek, a branch of Goose Creek, 8 mi se of Manchester, was est on Dec 7, 1906, with George W. Walker, pm. "In this area," writes Marian Martin, "there was very fine virgin timber and sawing lumber was big business. Each sawmill owner liked to boast of the largest boards or planks they had sawed. When the po was named they called it Plank because they had possessed the largest plank that had been sawed in the whole area." 940.

Pleasant Bend (Wayne). See *Cooper*

Pleasant Green PO (Daviess). See *Whitesville*

Pleasant Grove (Wayne). See *Steubenville*

Pleasant Hill (Calloway). See *Murray*

Pleasant Hill (also called **Shakertown**) (Mercer): *plehz*/ənt *hihl*, *shā*/kər/town (Wilmore). This is a restored religious community at the jct of old US 68 and KY 29 and 33, ¼ mi n of new US 68, and 6 mi ne of Harrodsburg. From a colony est in 1805 on a 140-acre farm on nearby Shawnee Run, the Shakers soon moved to the Pleasant Hill site, laid out their village, and eventually expanded their farm holdings to some 4500 acres. Shaker Landing, a Kentucky R steamboat landing, was 1 mi e. A short-lived Pleasant Hill po was est on Mar 12, 1818, with Francis Varis, pm, reest as Shawnee Run on Jan 22, 1834, and renamed Pleasant Hill in 1851. The po closed in 1904 and the colony was formally disbanded in 1910. From then until the restoration of the Shaker colony began in 1961, Pleasant Hill was a small village of privately owned homes and businesses. The several names associated with this religious group and its colony have long confused the uninitiated. Referring to themselves as the United Society of Believers in Christ's Second Appearing and to their settlement as the Pleasant Hill Colony, they were almost universally known to others as Shakers. At first they resented this label but soon came to accept it and even to refer to their colony as Shakertown, a name still popularly applied to the community as evidenced by the name it bears on the topographic maps. State highway maps, however, continue to identify the place as Pleasant Hill. 300, 457.

Pleasant Point PO (Lincoln). See *Kings Mountain*

Pleasant Ridge (Daviess): *plehz*/ənt *rihdj* (Pleasant Ridge). This hamlet is now on US 231 and the Ohio-Daviess Co line, 11 mi sse of Owensboro. Before 1950 it was centered on a po on KY 764, est on Aug 3, 1859, by storekeeper Elijah Hatfield and named for the attractive view from the ridge on which it was situated. The po closed in 1913. 930, 1348.

Pleasant Ridge PO (Bracken). See *Berlin*

Pleasant Run (Morgan). See *Yocum*

Pleasant Valley (Carter): *plehz*/ənt *vael*/ee (Grahn). This hamlet lies at the jct of US 60 and KY 182, just s of I 64 and 8½ mi w of Grayson. This was originally called Counts Cross Roads for Philip Counts, a Virginian, who had arrived by 1850 and, with his 5 sons, ran the local store. The Counts Cross Roads po was est on Sept 24, 1873, with Van Buren B. King, pm, but the community was inc on May 9, 1890, as Pleasant Valley, a commendatory name. 36, 1322, 1326.

Pleasant View (Whitley): *plehz*/ənt *vyū* (Williamsburg, Saxton). This settlement with station on the present Knoxville and Atlanta Division of the L&N RR is centered on the jct of US 25W and KY 628, just e of I 75, and is suburban to Williamsburg, 3½ mi nnw. It was aptly named for its view of the nearby hills. Its po, est on Nov 13, 1870, with Robert Bird, pm, is now a rural branch of the Williamsburg po. 1380.

Pleasant View PO (Todd). See *Kirkmansville*

Pleasure Ridge Park (Jefferson) *plehʒ*/ər rihdj *pahrk* (Louisville West). This unincorporated suburb of Louisville with extinct po is centered at the jct of US 31W/60 and Greenwood Rd, 9 mi ssw of downtown Louisville. It was named for a 19th cent dance hall in a large park on the ridge just e of the highway and the Elizabethtown & Paducah (now L&N) RR tracks, which had been completed to this point by 1874. The local po, est as Lacona in 1850, was renamed Pleasure Ridge Park in 1876. This po was discontinued in 1903, reest in 1948, and closed for good in 1964. 723.

Pleasureville (Henry and Shelby) *plehʒ*/ər/vihl (North Pleasureville). This 6th class city with po is on US 421 and KY 241, 5½ mi se of New Castle and 10 mi nne of Shelbyville. In 1784 some 30 families of a Dutch Huguenot colony in Mercer Co acquired 10,000 acres in the area from Squire Boone and built a fort about 1½ mi e of what was to become North Pleasureville. Their land, owned and cultivated in common and managed by Abraham Banta, has been identified historically as The Dutch Tract or Low Dutch Settlement. North Pleasureville was first called Bantatown [*bahn*/tə/town, *bahn*/tee/town], but its po was est as Pleasureville perhaps as early as 1828 and it was inc under this name in 1842. The name is traditionally believed to have been derived from a visitor's remark about his pleasure in being there among such pleasant people. In 1858, what later became a part of the L&N RR was built through to a point 1 mi s, and another town developed around the depot. In 1874 the Pleasureville po was moved here, retaining this name; in 1879, another po, called North Pleasureville, was est at the original site. The 2 towns finally merged in 1962. Many of the older residents, however, still refer to the 2 component communities as simply North Town and South Town. 786, 950, 1256.

Pluckemine (Jessamine). See *Little Hickman*

Pluckum (Casey). See *Linnie*

Plum (Bourbon): pluhm (North Middletown). This crossroads hamlet lies at the confluence of Plum Lick and Boone Creeks, 11 mi e of Paris. Historians suggest it was first called Pinhook or Pin Hook but cannot tell us when or why. It was called The Levy when in 1873 Andrew B. Thomason moved his po here from Flat Rock (now Little Rock), 1½ mi nw. Historians are equally mystified by the name The Levy but its pronunciation as "*lehv*/ee" and the definite article suggest a corruption of that geographic term; perhaps there was a levee somewhere in the vicinity. On Apr 20, 1874, Thomason renamed his po Plum Lick, probably for the stream, and in May 1894 it became simply Plum. This name is said to have derived from a grove of wild plum trees. Local tradition has it that a band of Indians en route to or from their homes in Ohio ate plums from a supply in their knapsacks and threw the stones on the ground, where they germinated. The name The Levy is once more locally applied. The po was discontinued in 1905. 304, 538, 1414.

Plum Grove (Greenup): *pluhm ghrohv* (Greenup). This rural settlement lies on Shackle Run, a tributary of the Little Sandy R, just s of W Hollow, w of KY 1, and 1½ mi s of Greenup. The community was named for the many wild plum trees there. It has never had a po. 946, 1447.

Plum Lick PO (Bourbon). See *Plum*

Plummers Landing (Fleming): *pluhm*/ərz *laend*/ihŋ (Plummers Landing). This hamlet with po near the confluence of Stocktons and Fox creeks, 11 mi se of Flemingsburg, was named for the landing maintained for stock drovers by George Plummer in the early 19th cent. The first po to serve this area was est on Feb 8, 1849, at Plummer's Mill by George's son Benjamin. The mill, built by a Captain Seavers, Benjamin's father-in-law, whom he succeeded in its operation, was 2 creek mi below the Landing. On Jan 3, 1862, Samuel Maguire moved the Plummers Mill po a mi up Stockton's Creek from the Landing and called it Belle Grove, a commendatory name, and renamed it Belle Grove Springs for the sulphur springs there. For some reason the po was again moved in Sept 1862, to the Landing, where it was renamed Plummers Landing. A po est as Crane Creek in 1865 moved 2 mi up Fox Creek to Plummers Mill in 1867, where it went by that name until it closed in 1877. The hamlet of Plummers Mill is now called Butler for another local family, and sometimes Watson's Store for the local store. 380, 1369.

Plummers Mill PO (Fleming). See *Plummers Landing*

Plum Springs (Warren): *pluhm sprihŋz* (Bowling Green North). This 6th class city and suburban residential community without po is on the Plum Springs Rd (KY 957), just n and w of US 31W and 1½ mi ene of Bowling Green. It was inc on Jan 27, 1966, and probably named for its location.

Poages Settlement (Boyd). See *Ashland*

Point Curve PO (Graves). See *Wingo*

Point Isabel PO (Pulaski). See *Burnside*

Pokeberry (Menifee). See *Mariba*

Polin (Washington): *poh*/lən (Brush Grove). This hamlet with extinct po lies where KY 433 crosses Lick Creek, just above its confluence with Long Lick Creek, and 8 mi n of Springfield. It is said to have grown up around the site of Walton's Lick, a late 18th cent salt lick named for and probably owned by Gen. Matthew Walton (1759–1819), a Virginia-born surveyor and extensive landowner (see also *Springfield*). The local po, in operation from Sept 23, 1879, to June 6, 1881, was called Walton's Lick [*wâhl*/tənz *lihk*]. It was reest by Enos Polin as Polin on Mar 1, 1888. Enos was the son of an Irish-born pioneer, John Polin (1816–97) who lived on Little Beech Fork. This po closed in 1908. 1314.

Polkville (Warren): *pohk*/vəl (Polkville). This crossroads hamlet with extinct po lies at the jct of KY 1182 and 1297, 7 mi e of Bowling Green. The po was est on July 29, 1846, with Nathan Howard, pm, and probably named for James K. Polk, then president of the US. It closed in 1903.

Pollards Mill (Boyd). See *Ashland, Westwood*

Polsgrove (Franklin): *pâhlz*/ghrohv (Polsgrove). This extinct po and hamlet were on the Kentucky R just above the mouth of Flat Creek and on KY 12, 9 mi n of Frankfort. The local po was est on July 7, 1870, as Palsgrove Store with William H. Palsgrove (*sic*), pm and probably the store's owner. The po was discontinued in 1875 and reest on Apr

19, 1880, as Polsgrove. The community was for years called Polsgrove Landing and this name identified it in an 1882 atlas. Polsgrove is generally considered the correct spelling of the name of this early Franklin Co family whose progenitor, George Polsgrove, settled on Flat Creek in 1821. The po closed for good in 1962. 864, 1290.

Polsgrove Landing (Franklin). See *Polsgrove*

Pomp (Morgan): pahmp (West Liberty). This hamlet with extinct po lies at the jct of KY 7 and 1161, at the mouth of Lick Fork of Elk Fork of the Licking R, 2 mi nnw of West Liberty. The po was est on Dec 23, 1891, with John Milton Perry, pm, and named for Walter D. (''Pomp'') Kendall, a resident. It closed in 1956. 112.

Pond Fork PO (Jackson). See *Welchburg*

Pontotoc (Fulton). See *Fulton*

Poole (Webster): pūl (Poole). This village with po lies at the jct of US 41A and KY 56 and 145, 8 mi n of Dixon. The brothers John H. and James Poole, first cousins to Sam Houston of Texas fame, arrived here from Nelson Co, Kentucky, in 1826 to settle on a 2400-acre military grant. John (1776–1862), a millwright, built a horse-powered gristmill and brick factory. The town was first called Poole's Mill, as was the po est on Jan 29, 1855, with John's son William W. as pm. The town was later called Pooleville; it and the po were renamed Poole in 1894. 12, 1174.

Poole's Mill (Webster). See *Poole*

Pooleville (Webster). See *Poole*

Pooltown (Calloway). See *Murray*

Poor Fork (Harlan). See *Cumberland*

Poortown (Washington). See *Litsey*

Poplar Creek (Whitley). See *Siler*

Poplar Grove (Owen): *pahp*/lər *ghrohv* (Glencoe). This settlement with extinct po centers just s of the Poplar Grove Baptist Church at the jct of US 127 and KY 1316, 8 mi n of Owenton. The church, org in 1827, and the po, in operation from 1838 to 1903, were named for a local grove of yellow poplars. 1292.

Poplar Plains (Fleming): *pahp*/lər plānz (Hillsboro). This hamlet with extinct po at the jct of KY 111 and 156, 4½ mi se of Flemingsburg, is believed to have been settled before 1792 by William Pearce, Sr., and his family. An attempt by the Pearces to name the community Pearceville was rejected by the other early residents who favored The Poplar Plains, later shortened to Poplar Plains, for its situation in a grove of yellow poplars on a level stretch of land. The local po of this name was est on or before Oct 31, 1826, with William Pearce (probably a son) as pm. The po closed in 1926. 1369.

Poplarville (Pulaski): *pahp*/lər/vihl (Dykes). This po on KY 1097, 10 mi se of Somerset, was est on Mar 11, 1903, with Lawrence Sears, pm, and named for the many poplar trees in the vicinity. 1410.

Porter (Knott). See *Betty*

Porters Landing PO (Ohio). See *Cromwell*

Port Oliver (Allen): pawrt *ahl*/ə/vər (Meador). This extinct community on the Barren R is believed to have been midway between the mouth of Big Difficult Creek and the gauging station of the Barren R Reservoir, 9 mi n of Scottsville. It was probably named for George Washington Oliver, who settled in that vicinity in the 1790s and began the exploitation of a natural salt deposit on the r. Taking advantage of the buffalo trace that had recently been surveyed and developed for travel between Lexington and Nashville, the so-called Stovall Rd, Oliver also opened a trading post and r shipping port. This settlement apparently grew sufficiently by 1815 to justify its being laid out as a town. On May 17, 1824, a po called Port Oliver was est with Fielding Fant, pm. In

1825 it was removed to Rocky Hill some 6 mi ne, in Barren Co, with Franklin Settle, pm. In 1833 a Barren Co po called Lewis was est by John Lewis at some undetermined site (perhaps the present Finney), though near enough to Port Oliver to be considered by at least one source to have served that community until it closed in 1846. On the current topographic map the site is marked as Port Oliver Ford. 101, 810.

Portsmouth PO (Breathitt). See *Wilstacy*

Port William (Carroll). See *Carrollton*

Possum Trot (Marshall): *pahs*/əm traht (Little Cypress). This concentration of businesses at the jct of US 62, KY 1610, and the old Paducah–Calvert City Rd, 10 mi nnw of Benton, can be traced back only to the construction of US 62 between Paducah and the Kentucky Dam. According to local tradition, Sol King and Buck Bolen were possum hunting in the area around the turn of the cent, and one said to the other, "If we dont catch one soon, these possums are going to trot across the road and be gone." A recent effort to change the name to Fairview was unsuccessful when, after an informal poll, it was decided to retain the more colorful name. The community has never had a po. 1337.

Potters Fork (Letcher): *paht*/ərz *fawrk* (Jenkins West). This settlement with extinct po is strung out along US 119 on Potters Fork, of Boone Fork of the North Fork of the Kentucky R, below the mouth of Grays Branch, 8½ mi ne of Whitesburg. The po was est on Dec 23, 1891, and named for the creek which had been named for the Potter family, among that area's earliest and most distinguished residents. The po was discontinued in 1913. 1265.

Pottertown (Calloway): *paht*/ər/town (New Concord). This rural settlement with extinct po on KY 280, 5½ mi e of Murray, was named for the pottery works that developed there after the discovery of local clay deposits before the Civil War. It is not known when or by whom the vicinity was first settled or who actually developed the pottery industry there. Some say it was John Shell; others credit Willis Bonner. The Pottertown po operated only from 1888 to 1905. 436, 586.

Pottertown (Lyon). See *Carmack*

Pottsville (McCracken). See *Lone Oak*

Poverty (McLean): *pahv*/ər/tee (Calhoun). This settlement with extinct po lies at the jct of KY 140 and 256, 3½ mi wnw of Calhoun. The name is said to have been applied to the short-lived po (1902–6) by a local physician, William Short. According to tradition, this was his way of ridiculing his snobbish neighbors who, having formed themselves into a group known as "the Social Circle," held that property, breeding, and cultural attributes clearly placed them a cut above everyone else in the community, including the doctor. Much to their chagrin, the name has officially identified the place ever since, though recently some residents have expressed a preference for Eureka, the name of the community's old church and school. 311, 932.

Powderly (Muhlenberg): *pow*/dər/lee (Greenville). This 6th class city with po is contiguous on the s with Greenville. The town sprang up around the Cooperative Coal Co. mine opened in 1887 by Terence V. Powderly, an early labor organizer. The po was est on Jan 14, 1888, with William H. Smith, pm, and the town was inc in 1963. 189, 547.

Powder Mills (Hart): *pow*/dər *mihlz* (Hudgins). This extinct community on Lynn Camp Creek, 11 mi ne of Munfordville, was the site of Kentucky's first commercial powder mills. Built in 1811 by John Courts, these are said to have supplied Jackson's troops at the Battle of New Orleans and Union soldiers in the Civil War. The town's first po, Fountain Powder Mills, was in operation from 1826 to 1846. The now extinct Powder Mills po was est on May 24, 1876, with Milton P. Ligett, pm. 44, 661, 863.

Powell County: *pow*/əl. 180 sq mi. Pop 11,073. Seat: Stanton. This co was est in 1852 from parts of Montgomery, Clark, and Estill cos and named for Lazarus W. Powell (1812–67), governor of Kentucky (1851–55) and US senator from Kentucky (1859–65).

Powell Valley (Powell): *paelz vael*/ee (Clay City). This hamlet lies at the jct of KY 15 and 82, just off the Mountain Parkway, 4 mi w of Stanton. The community was named for the progenitor of the local Powell family. It has never had a po. 1334.

Power PO (Magoffin). See *Lakeville*

Powersburg (Wayne): *pahrz*/bergh, *paer*/əz/bergh (Powersburg). This hamlet with extinct po is now centered at Hurts's store on KY 200, 9 mi sw of Monticello. The po was est on Aug 4, 1876, with Daniel D. Powers, pm, and named for the influential Wayne Co Powers family, whose progenitor was Virginia-born Revolutionary War veteran and pioneer settler Jesse Powers. The po was discontinued in 1972. 113, 1309.

Powers Station (Daviess). See *Maceo*

Powersville (Bracken): *pow*/ərz/vihl (Brooksville). This hamlet with extinct po at the jct of KY 10 and 19, 2 mi sw of Brooksville, was est at some unknown date on the site of a travelers' inn between Augusta and Cynthiana. It was named for a local family. The local po, est on Nov 13, 1841, with James W. Morford, pm, closed in 1904. 27.

Praise PO (Pike). See *Elkhorn City*

Praters Fort (Magoffin). See *Salyersville*

Preachersville (Lincoln): *preech*/ərz/vihl (Lancaster). This hamlet with extinct po extends for over 1 mi along KY 39 from a point 6 mi e of Stanford. The po, est on May 18, 1854, was named for the several preachers who lived there at that time. It closed in 1911. 746.

Premium PO (Letcher). See *Hot Spot*

Preston (Bath): *prehs*/tən (Preston). This hamlet with C&O RR station and po is 3½ mi s of Owingsville. It was founded in 1881 as Preston Station and named for William Preston who donated the right-of-way to the then Elizabethtown Lexington & Big Sandy Ry on condition that a station named for him be maintained there. The local po was est on Aug 21, 1882, as Crooks for a prominent area family and renamed Preston in 1913. 186.

Prestonsburg (Floyd): *prehs*/tənz/bergh (Prestonsburg, Lancer). This 4th class city and seat of Floyd Co extends for some 6½ mi along the Levisa Fork of the Big Sandy R and is centered at the jct of the eastern terminus of the Mountain Parkway (KY 144) and US 23/460, at the mouth of Middle Creek, 156 mi ese of downtown Louisville. It was founded and laid out in 1797 as Preston's Station on part of John Preston's 100,000-acre grant, which had first been settled in 1791 by John Spurlock of Montgomery Co, Virginia. When Floyd Co was est in 1799 it became its seat and was inc as a town in 1818. The po was created as Floyd Court House on Apr 1, 1816, with John Havens, pm, and was renamed Prestonsburg or Prestonsburg Court House in the late 1820s. 194, 699.

Prestonsburg Court House PO (Floyd). See *Prestonsburg*

Preston's Station (Floyd). See *Prestonsburg*

Preston Station (Bath). See *Preston*

Prestonville (Carroll): *prehs*/tən/vihl (Carrollton). This recently disincorporated suburban town on the Ohio R, across the mouth of the Kentucky R from Carrollton, was named for Col. William Preston of Virginia. A surveyor for Fincastle Co, Virginia, he had made his camp here in 1773–74 and later received a grant of several thousand acres, including the site of the future town, for his services in the Revolutionary War.

In 1797 the town was chartered by the Kentucky legislature, and on Nov 26, 1844, a po was est by G. W. Lee. It closed in 1849. Another po, called Wideawake, was est somewhere in the vicinity on Aug 12, 1880, with Joseph S. Colyer, pm; in 1893 it was moved to and/or renamed Prestonville. It has since closed. 44, 219, 646, 670, 1330.

Price (Floyd): prahs (McDowell). This coal town with po is on KY 122 and [the] Left [Fork of] Beaver Creek, 17½ mi s of Prestonsburg. The community and its po, est on Aug 1, 1923, with Columbus Jackson, pm, were first called Gearheart for Robert Gearheart, a local resident. In 1948 they were renamed for Emory R. Price, then general manager of Inland Steel Co.'s operations on Left Beaver and a highly respected community leader. 807, 981, 1197.

Priceburg (Grant). See *Keefer*

Prices Mill (Simpson): *prahs*/əz *mihl* (Prices Mill). This hamlet with extinct po is on the Red R, at the jct of KY 591 and 1885, 7 mi wsw of Franklin. It was named for a water-powered flour mill built by J. C. Price in 1844. The po was est on Apr 30, 1879, with Marion L. Fugate, pm, and closed in 1909. 18, 1024.

Pricetown (Casey): *prahs*/town (Liberty). This hamlet with extinct po is on US 127, just over 1 mi ssw of Liberty. This vicinity may first have been settled by Hansfords and was early known as Walnut Hill for a large stand of walnut trees. The po was est on Feb 4, 1925, as Pricetown for Ed Price, who then owned half the land on Walnut Hill Ridge, e of the present highway. His was the name chosen by the Post Office Department from a list submitted by John W. Weddle, Sr., storekeeper, and brother of Rupert C., the first pm. The po closed in 1959. 212, 1397.

Pricetown (Fayette): *preyes*/town (Ford). This predominantly black settlement on Todds Rd, 5 mi e of Lexington's New Circle Rd, was named for Dr. Sanford Price who subdivided land his father, Willis, had inherited from his pioneer family, and est this settlement for freed slaves. 33.

Priceville (Hart): *preyes*/vihl (Munfordville, Upton). This hamlet with extinct po is at the jct of KY 728 and 1140, 7 mi nw of Munfordville. It was founded in 1848 on land owned by James Corder and named for pioneer settler Meridith (or Marida) Price. The po was est as Vanfleet on Apr 4, 1882, and named for Ideral Vanfleet, the first pm. His successor, Thomas H. Bowles, renamed it for the community in 1886. 5, 340.

Pride (Union): preyed (Sturgis). This hamlet and former rail shipping point is at the jct of KY 141 and 758, 8 mi s of Morganfield. In 1906 it was laid off as a town around the station est the year before by the Morganfield and Atlanta RR on land purchased from Mr. and Mrs. D. T. Pride. It has never had its own po. 151.

Priestland (Marion). See *Nerinx*

Primrose (Lee): *prihm*/rohz (Tallega). This hamlet with po is on KY 2017, 5 mi ene of Beattyville. It is said to have been first settled by a Mr. Grey, a Lexington silversmith, in the 1830s, and may first have been called Greys Bend. He sold off his land to other settlers, one of whom, Patton Coomer, became the leading citizen, and the community came to be known as Pattonsville. Joseph Hieronymus est the po on July 21, 1893, and named it for the yellow flowers that bloomed in profusion in that area. 132, 1372.

Princess (Boyd): *prihn*/səs (Ashland). This hamlet with extinct po on Williams Creek, at the jct of US 60 and KY 5, 6 mi sw of Ashland, grew up around the short-lived Princess Coal Mine and Iron Furnace for which it was named. These were est in the mid 1870s by a co. headed by Thomas W. Means. A Princess po served the area from 1887 to 1924. 188, 1415.

Princeton (Caldwell): *prihns*/tən (Princeton East, Princeton West). This 4th class city and seat of Caldwell Co is on US 62 and the Western Kentucky Parkway, 130 mi sw of downtown Louisville. First called Eddy Grove for its location by a big swirling spring that was the head of Eddy Creek, it was renamed in 1817 for, and probably at the request of the heirs of, William Prince, a Virginia-born pioneer settler (1752–1810) who acquired some 1700 acres there for Revolutionary War service. According to some accounts, his heirs donated 40 of these acres for the relocation of the co's seat from Eddyville. In July 1817 the co court ordered that the town, laid off on land owned by Prince and Thomas Frazier, be called Princetown, which shortly thereafter became Princeton. The po for this vicinity was est as Eddy Grove on Oct 1, 1805, with Elisha Prince, pm, but by Dec 19, 1817, it too had become Princeton. 1278.

Princetown (Caldwell). See *Princeton*

Printer (Floyd): *prihn*/tər (Harold). This hamlet with po is on KY 122, at the mouth of Spurlock Creek, a branch of [the] Left [Fork of] Beaver Creek, and 9 mi s of Prestonsburg. The po was est on May 26, 1909, with Henry H. Justice, pm, and named for John Printer, a local resident. When the Long Fork (now C&O) RR was built up Left Beaver around 1918, the station of Salisbury was est, for this had been the site of an early settlement of Salisburys. 194, 976, 1280, 1370.

Proctor (Lee): *prahk*/tər (Beattyville). This is now a residential suburb with po just below the forks of the Kentucky R and is across the r from Beattyville. The area may have been settled in the very early 19th cent by pioneer and Indian fighter Archibald D. McGuire and named for Rev. Joseph Proctor (1754–1844), a North Carolina-born Indian fighter turned Methodist minister and one of the first permanent settlers of Estill Co. The Proctor po was est on Apr 4, 1843, with Nathan Jacobs, pm, and discontinued in 1918. 132, 1372.

Prospect (Jefferson): *prahs*/pehkt (Anchorage). Though this 5th class city extends along a 2½ mi stretch of US 42 from the Oldham Co line, it is centered at its po at the jct of US 42 and Rose Island Rd, 11 mi ne of downtown Louisville. This point was once the terminus of the now defunct Louisville Harrod Creek & Westport (later L&N) RR. The station is said to have been named in the late 1870s when the rr was almost completed to what was, till then, aptly known as Sand Hill. Either someone admired the view from the hilltop, or the prospect of completing the line was then in question. (It never did reach Westport.) The local po of Wilhoyte, est on Feb 15, 1886, with A. C. Wilhoyte, pm, was renamed Prospect the following month. 724, 772, 916.

Prosperity (Edmonson): prahs/*pehr*/ə/tee (Bee Spring). This rural settlement is on the New Salem Church Rd, 9 mi n of Brownsville. According to Lancie Meredith, sometime in the early 20th cent the local storekeeper observed that "this place is really beginning to prosper" and suggested this commendatory name. It failed to live up to its name, never even acquiring a po. 942.

Providence (Webster): *prahv*/ə/dəns (Providence, Nebo). This 4th class city with po is on the Hopkins Co line, 6½ mi ssw of Dixon. It was founded by Richard Savage who arrived there with his wife in 1820. The settlement that grew up around his store was first called Savageville but was renamed Providence when the po was est on Oct 16, 1828. The name is traditionally believed to have been suggested by an old trader who, on his way from Henderson to Madisonville, had avoided serious calamity thanks to the good samaritan efforts of local farmers. He was ever to bear witness that his succor had been an act of Providence. The city of this name in Rhode Island may also have influenced the naming of the Kentucky community, which was chartered in 1840. 501.

Provo (Butler): *proh*/voh (South Hill). This settlement is centered on its po on KY 1117, 7½ mi w of Morgantown. The po was est on May 7, 1901, with William A. Pendley, pm, and named by Lena Stall and Hardin Rone for the city in Utah. The latter, according to George R. Stewart, had been named for Etienne Provost, "a French-Canadian trapper who explored the region in the 1820s." 204, 1087.

Pryorsburg (Graves): *prah*/yərz/bergh (Mayfield). This village with extinct po is on US 45 and the Illinois Central Gulf RR, just e of the Purchase Parkway and 3 mi sw of Mayfield. The po was est as Depot on Apr 3, 1855, with Melbourn Saxon, pm, probably in anticipation of the arrival of the New Orleans & Ohio RR 2 years later. By that time the community may already have borne the name of its most influential landowner, Jonathan Pryor, a Virginian who settled there by 1840. In its early years the community may also have been known as Boggy or Bogey, for wheeled vehicles would often bog down in the poorly drained roadbed. The po, renamed Pryorsburg on May 14, 1860, operated intermittently until it closed in 1960. Old Pryorsburg on the rr has since been largely bypassed by the new settlement on the highway. 731, 1228.

Pryse (Estill): prahs (Cobhill). This hamlet with po and defunct L&N RR station lies in the Kentucky R bottoms, 5 mi ese of Irvine. David Pryse, a Welsh immigrant, is known to have purchased several hundred acres between the L&N tracks and the r and built one of the co's first brick houses. On Mar 9, 1904, he est and named the Pryse po. A thriving co. town grew up around a Texas Oil Co. refinery there by 1926 and was called Texola or Texola Station. When the co. pulled out in 1945 the community returned to its previous rural status and is once again known only as Pryse. 865.

Puck PO (Bath). See *Olympia*

Pughville (Harrison). See *Sunrise*

Pulaski (Pulaski): pyū/*laes*/kee, pyə/*laes*/kee (Science Hill). This hamlet with po on KY 1247, 6 mi n of Somerset, probably occupies the site of an old stagecoach stop called Higgins Station, named for Aaron Higgins, local teacher and farmer. The po was est on Apr 18, 1828, as Adam's Mill for the mill built there and operated by Alexander Adams (1799–1849) who was also the first pm. The po was renamed Pulaski Station in 1879 for the station on the Cincinnati Southern (now Southern) RR, and became simply Pulaski in 1880. 1410.

Pulaski County: pəl/*aes*/kee. 660 sq mi. Pop 45,697. Seat: Somerset. This co was est in 1798 from parts of Lincoln and Green cos and named for Count Casimir Pulaski (1748–79), the Polish patriot who gave his life in the American Revolutionary cause at the Battle of Savannah.

Pulaski Station PO (Pulaski). See *Pulaski*

Pulltite (Hopkins). See *Beulah*

Puncheon (Knott): *puhnch*/ən (Kite). This po, ¾ mi up Puncheon Branch of the Right Fork of Beaver Creek, 10 mi ese of Hindman, was est on Apr 4, 1900, with John Franklin, pm. It is said to have been named for the puncheon flooring of the building in which it was located. However, if the stream bore this name before 1900, it may well have been named for a local industry, the splitting of poplar logs for the floors of early cabins. 1391.

Punkin Center (Harlan). See *Dizney*

Quality (Butler): *kwahl*/ə/tee (Quality). This hamlet with po is on KY 106, 13 mi sw of Morgantown. The po, est as Quality Valley on May 13, 1853, with Moses G. Watkins, pm, was allegedly named for the "high tone of the people and the land." It became simply Quality in 1894. 1214.

Quality Valley PO (Butler). See *Quality*

Queens (Lewis): kweenz (Concord). This settlement with extinct po is on KY 984, at the mouth of Martin[s] Fork of Quicks Run, an Ohio R tributary, and 6½ mi wnw of

Vanceburg. The po was est as Martin on Mar 25, 1891, with George Queen, pm, and named for pioneer and Indian fighter James Martin who had acquired a large tract of land in this area before 1800. A Martins Fork po was also in operation in this vicinity between 1851 and 1860. Forrest Queen, storekeeper and later pm of the Martin po, renamed it for his family on Mar 16, 1926, probably to avoid confusion with the new city of Martin in Floyd Co. The po closed in 1951. 179, 1103.

Quicksand (Breathitt): *kwihk*/saend (Quicksand). This hamlet with po lies on the North Fork of the Kentucky R just opposite the mouth of Quicksand Creek for which it was named, and less than 1½ mi se of Jackson. The po was est as Quick Sand Mills on Mar 18, 1878, with Fletcher McGuire, pm, and renamed Quicksand in 1888. The several-forked Quicksand Creek, which drains much of eastern Breathitt Co, was, according to tradition, named for the "treacherous shifting sands," which caused considerable difficulty for 19th cent travelers and residents alike. 700, 974, 1222.

Quick Sand Mills PO (Breathitt). See *Quicksand*

Quinn PO (Caldwell). See *Fryer*

Quinton (Pulaski): *kwihn*/tən (Frazer, Burnside). This hamlet with extinct po is on KY 790, 7 mi s of Somerset. Though there is a difference in spelling, co historians insist that the po, est on Feb 24, 1908, with John A. Simpson, pm, was named for then President Roosevelt's son Quenton. 1410.

Quirey (Union). See *Sullivan*

Rabbit Hash (Boone): *raeb*/ət haesh (Rising Sun). This hamlet where KY 536 joins the Lower [Ohio] R Rd, 8½ mi sw of Burlington, was a busy 19th cent steamboat landing across the Ohio from Rising Sun, Indiana. Its colorful name is derived from the monotony of its early enforced diet of rabbit. The story is told that in 1816 2 travelers proceeding in opposite directions met at Rising Sun. One asked the other if he could get anything to eat at Meek's Ferry Landing on the Kentucky shore. The other said "Yes, plenty of rabbit hash." The river was receding from flood stage and rabbits by the thousands had been driven to the hillsides where they were killed for food. On Jan 3, 1879, the local po was est as Carlton, for a local family. In 2 months it was changed to Rabbit Hash to avoid confusion with nearby Carrollton. It closed in 1912. 239.

Rabbit Town (Clark): *raeb*/ət town (Hedges). This rural settlement on the present KY 974, 10 mi se of Winchester, was allegedly named by an itinerant school teacher for the many wild rabbits on which he had to rely for sustenance while teaching there. It has never had a po. 975.

Raccoon (Pike): rae/*kūn* (Millard). This hamlet with po is on KY 1441 and Raccoon Creek, 3 mi e of Pikeville. The creek, community, and po est on Jan 16, 1919, with Carolyn Coleman, pm, were named for the large number of raccoons observed and trapped there. 1354.

Raceland (Greenup): *rās*/lən(d) (Ironton). This 5th class city and suburb of Ashland is on US 23, 4½ mi ese of Greenup. This site and adjacent land were part of a 5000-acre Revolutionary War grant to Abraham Buford, which his son and heir Charles divided and sold in farm tracts. One of these was acquired by the widow of Benjamin Mead and later laid out and sold in town lots by her grandson Benjamin Chinn who named the new community Chinnville. A po of this name was est on Mar 7, 1910, with Mollie Schrope, pm. In 1924 J. C. Keene and others of Lexington racing fame opened a racetrack about a mi below town to which a rail spur line was laid, and a station there was called Raceland Junction. On Aug 1, 1925, Raceland replaced Chinnville as the name of the local po. For a brief period after the track was abandoned 3 years later, the po resumed the Chinnville name, but on Apr 1, 1930, it again assumed the Raceland name, which it retained until it was discontinued in 1958. 22, 682, 1447, 1451.

Raceland Junction (Greenup). See *Raceland*

Racum (Washington). See *Maud*

Radcliff (Hardin): *raed*/klihf (Vine Grove). This 4th class city with po is contiguous on the w with the Fort Knox Military Reservation and 6 mi nnw of Elizabethtown. It is said to have been est around 1919 by H. E. McCollum who named it for his friend, a Major Radcliffe (*sic*), then the Commander of the Quartermaster Corps at Camp (later Fort) Knox, and a very popular officer. The place name was originally spelled with a terminal "e," but for some reason this has since been dropped. The town was inc in 1956 and the po was est on Sept 14, 1962, with Jerry W. Davis, pm. 409, 1420.

Radford PO (Calloway). See *Kirksey*

Ragland (McCracken): *raegh*/lən(d) (Bandana). This extinct po lay at the jct of KY 358 and the Crawford Lake Rd, 13½ mi wnw of Paducah. It was est on May 18, 1888, and named for its first pm, William N. Ragland, or his family. It closed in 1908.

Rail PO (Floyd). See *Weeksbury*

Rains (Whitley): rānz (Frakes). This extinct po lay on Goldens Creek, a branch of Poplar Creek, tributary of the Cumberland R, 11½ mi e of Williamsburg. It was est in Knox Co as Rain on Feb 16, 1906, with William F. Davis, pm, and shifted to Whitley Co shortly before World War I. Though still shown on records and maps as Rain, it is locally spelled with a terminal "s," for it was named for the Rains family. 1267.

Ralph (Ohio): raelf (Dundee). This extinct po on KY 1414 and the South Fork of Panther Creek, 11½ mi n of Hartford, was est on Apr 5, 1899, on land owned by H. W. Ralph and named for him. It was discontinued in 1910. The Ralphs are descendants of John L. Ralph, Sr., who had brought his family to this site in 1827. 170, 905.

Ramsey Island (Wayne). See *Stop*

Randolph (Metcalfe): *raen*/dahlf (Summer Shade). This hamlet with extinct po lies at the jct of KY 640 and 861, 4½ mi w of Edmonton. On Aug 12, 1873, the Randolph po that had been est in 1846 at the present site of *Wisdom,* 2½ mi n, was moved here with Samuel J. Oldham, pm. The name Randolph was retained though the place has often been referred to as New Randolph to distinguish it from Old Randolph or Wisdom. It is said that the original po was named for "the Virginia statesman" though it has never been clear which member of that illustrious family was intended. 142, 1193.

Randville (Lewis). See *Kinniconick*

Ransom (Pike): *raen*/səm (Matewan). This hamlet with po lies 4½ mi up Blackburn Creek from its confluence with the Tug Fork of the Big Sandy R, 17 mi ene of Pikeville. The po was est on May 16, 1898, with William J. Hatfield, pm, and named for Ransom Hatfield, a local resident. 1198.

Ravenna (Estill): rə/*vehn*/ə (Irvine). This 5th class city with extinct po is 1 mi se of Irvine across the narrow Chamberlin Branch, a tributary of the Kentucky R. The L&N RR's Eastern Kentucky Division completed its headquarters here on land purchased from the Cockrell and Park families in 1915. In that year the Ravenna Realty Co. was organized by John D. Sawyer to dispose of the co.'s land by sales of lots to its employees. A town was founded and named for the realty firm, which presumably had been named by its secretary, Kate H. Sawyer, for a city in Ohio. The latter is said to have been named around 1808 by its proprietor for the Italian city he had visited and admired. The Ravenna po was est on May 12, 1916, with Mrs. Hallie T. Vaughn, pm. On Jan 18, 1921, the town was inc. The po was discontinued in 1972. Irvine and Ravenna seem to be so physically and economically related that "they are sometimes called 'The Twin Cities' and this is the name used by several businesses'' in both cities. 226, 865.

Rays Mill (Washington). See *Maud*

Raywick (Marion): *rā*/wihk (Raywick). This village with po is on Prather Creek, a branch of the Rolling Fork R, and at the jct of KY 84 and 527, 9½ mi w of Lebanon. The site was first settled by James and John Ray and Henry Prather in 1778 and named for the pioneer Ray and Wickliffe families whose association was solemnized with the marriage in 1811 of Loyd Ray and Nancy Wickliffe. The po was est on Jan 28, 1833, with John S. Ray, pm, and the community was inc in 1838. 927.

Razorblade (Knott). See *Democrat*

Rectorville (Mason): *rehk*/tər/vihl (Orangeburg). This growing village with extinct po extends for about a mi along KY 10, 6 mi se of Maysville. The po, in operation from 1873 to 1915, was named either for Rector Marshall, who may have been a descendant of Col. Thomas Marshall (father of Supreme Court Justice John Marshall) or for the cousins Albert Rector Glascock and William Rector Glascock, descendants of the Rector family that settled in Orange Co, Virginia, before 1714. 858, 1246.

Redbird (Whitley): *rehd*/bird (Wofford). This settlement with extinct po lies on the Cumberland R, at the jct of KY 204 and 478, less than 3 mi wnw of Williamsburg. Like the Red Bird R in Bell and Clay cos, it was probably named for the Cherokee subchief Red Bird who had settled on that stream to hunt and trap, and who was later murdered by white hunters. He and his companion, Crippled Willie, are said to have frequently traveled through the present Whitley Co on their way to market their furs. His name had been applied to the community before the est of the Redbird po on Jan 5, 1898, with Simon C. Steely, pm. 1267, 1380.

Red Bird PO (Bell). See *Beverly*

Redbush (Johnson): *rehd*/b$\overline{oo}$sh (Redbush). This hamlet with po lies on Upper Laurel Creek, at the jct of KY 172 and 469, 10½ mi nw of Paintsville. The po was est on May 2, 1890, with William A. Williams, pm, and named for the profusion there of small pin oak trees whose leaves turn red in the fall. 1353.

Red Hot (Greenup). See *Warnock*

Redhouse (Madison): *rehd*/hows (Richmond North). Little remains of a once thriving trade center with po and L&N RR station at the jct of KY 388 and Otter Creek, 4 mi n of Richmond. It may have been named for the Red House Tavern, which catered to Kentucky R loggers in the 19th cent. Or, it may have been named for someone's ancestral home in England. Historians now doubt the tradition that it was named for a big red house on the projected route of the then Kentucky Central RR being built through that area in the 1880s, since references to the Red House (*sic*) community there precede the coming of the rr by at least a decade. Most likely the name was derived from some old large red brick building that housed a pioneer family in the mid 19th cent. The late French Tipton claimed the community was est in the 1840s and that John Manley had built a horse mill there in 1859. A po called Sturgel, est on Aug 31, 1883, with Jonathan F. Sturgel, pm, was moved to and/or renamed Red House 2 months later and officially respelled Redhouse in 1894. It has since closed. 415, 982, 1294.

Red Oak (Logan). See *Oakville*

Red River Iron Works PO (Powell). See *Clay City*

Red River PO (Wolfe). See *Lee City*

Redwine (Morgan): *rehd*/weyen (Sandy Hook). This hamlet with extinct po is on KY 711, at the head of the North Fork of the Licking R, 6 mi n of West Liberty. The po was est somewhere in that vicinity on Jan 15, 1883, and named for the family of the first pm, William B. Redwine. In 1908 the Morehead & North Fork RR was extended to this vicinity and the local station was also called Redwine. In 1914 the po was discontinued. In 1909 a po had been est nearby called Loveland with Mary Collins, pm. Its relative inaccessibility led to its relocation at the site of the station and it was given the Redwine name. The Redwine po closed for good in 1976. 112.

Reed (Henderson): reed (Reed). This hamlet and po are on US 60 and the L&N RR, 10½ mi e of Henderson. The po was est on Oct 3, 1891, with George Kerrick, pm, and named for Dr. W. H. Reed, then owner of much of the land in that vicinity. 1216.

Reedyville (Butler): *ree*/dee/vihl (Reedyville). This hamlet with extinct po on KY 185, 13½ mi e of Morgantown, was named for its location on a branch of Big Reedy Creek, a tributary of the Green R. The po was est on Mar 14, 1860, with Wiley Prewitt, pm. The community was shown on a 1923 topographic map as 1 mi n of its present site. 1214.

Reese's Settlement (Campbell). See *Cold Spring*

Reform (Fayette). See *Fort Spring*

Regina (Pike): rə/*djeyen*/uh (Hellier). This hamlet with po is centered at the jct of US 460 and KY 195 and the confluence of Marrowbone Creek and the Levisa Fork of the Big Sandy R, 9 mi se of Pikeville. The local C&O RR station is called Marrowbone [*mahr*/bohn, *mahr*/ə/bohn, *maer*/ə/bohn] for the creek, which some say was named for a human bone once found washed up on its bank. The po was est on Mar 13, 1895, with John E. Ratliff, pm, and allegedly named at the suggestion of a traveling salesman for his hometown in Canada. This is supposed to account for its peculiarly British pronunciation, for in the US as a girl's name it is pronounced "rə/*djee*/nuh." 934, 1354.

Reidland (McCracken): *reed*/lənd (Paducah East). This village without po is centered at the jct of US 68 and KY 284, just e of Clarks R and 3 mi se of Paducah. It was named for John Barton Reid who brought his family here from Charlotte, North Carolina, in 1855 and purchased 640 acres of the site. The po that served this community from 1884 to 1905 was at Epperson, a short distance n. 1014.

Reidsville PO (Rockcastle). See *Disputanta*

Relief (Morgan): rə/*leef* (Redbush). This hamlet centered on its now extinct po on KY 172, just above the mouth of Brown's Branch of the Open Fork of Paint Creek and 13½ mi e of West Liberty. It was est on June 29, 1859, with Wallace W. Brown, pm, and allegedly named by patrons who thought it would be a relief "not to have to go so far for their mail." Or else early travelers between Paintsville and West Liberty felt it was a relief to reach this point, roughly halfway in their arduous trip. The po closed on June 27, 1980, when its site and that of much of the community were appropriated for the Paintsville Reservoir. 112, 1066.

Render Coal Mines PO (Ohio). See *McHenry*

Renfro Valley (Rockcastle): *rehn*/froh *vael*/ee (Wildie). This hamlet with po is on US 25, just e of I 75 and 2 mi n of Mount Vernon. The valley formed by Renfro Creek, a tributary of Roundstone Creek, was probably named for James Renfro, the owner of considerable land in this area; his nephew John is said to have been the first settler in 1789. The Renfro Valley po was est in 1939. 1317.

Renfrow (Ohio): *rehn*/froh (Rosine). This extinct po, 11 mi e of Hartford, was est on May 13, 1886, and named by and for its first pm, John T. Renfrow. 905.

Revelo (McCreary): *rehv*/ə/loh, *rehv*/loh (Whitley City). This village with rr station and po are on KY 92, 2½ mi s of Whitley City. The po was est on June 29, 1928, with William B. White, pm, and named for a Mr. Oliver, the engineer in charge of the construction of the Cincinnati & Southern (now Southern) Ry line through this section. It is not known why or when the spelling of his name was reversed or why the "i" was corrupted to "e." For some time it was spelled Revilo. According to George R. Stewart, there is a Revilo in South Dakota that was probably named for J. S. Oliver, a local rr man. 204, 1162, 1308.

Revilo (McCreary). See *Revelo*

Reynolds Station (also called *Deanefield*) (Ohio): *rehn*/əldz *stā*/shən, *deen*/feeld (Whitesville). This village, also called Deanefield, is now centered around the Reynolds Station po on KY 54, 14½ mi nne of Hartford, and the station of Deanefield on the Illinois Central Gulf RR, just n of the po. The po was originally est on Apr 22, 1890, at a newly located depot 2¼ mi e. Both po and depot were named for J. S. Reynolds from whom the site was acquired. The adjacent coal town of Deanefield, inc in 1890, was allegedly named for Guy Deane of Owensboro and a Mr. Field who owned the local mine. A po est as Aetnaville on July 21, 1887, was renamed Deanefield in 1910 and closed in 1922. 905.

Rhoadsville (McLean). See *Calhoun*

Rhoda (Edmonson): *roh*/də (Rhoda). This hamlet with extinct po centered at the jct of KY 101 and 259, 2½ mi se of Brownsville, was named for the wife of the first pm, William W. Buford, when he est the po on Dec 5, 1891. The po closed in 1904. 1150.

Rhodelia (Meade): roh/*deel*/yə (Alton). A hamlet with po on KY 144, 13 mi w of Brandenburg. The site was first called Vessells Woods (*sic*) for its owners, Thomas and Sarah Vessels, and was settled around 1876 by their grandson, Samuel Joseph Manning. In 1878 Stephen K. Vessels and his brother opened a general store, and on Sept 4, 1879, Vessels est the po, which he named at the suggestion of (future governor) J. Proctor Knott for Elias Rhodes (1781–1868), a leading citizen of neighboring Breckinridge Co. 935.

Ribolt (Lewis): *reye*/bohlt (Tollesboro). This hamlet with extinct po just off KY 10, 10 mi w of Vanceburg, was originally called Needmore, but was renamed when the po was est on July 14, 1898, for local storekeeper Ribolt Harrison. The po closed in 1936. 1200.

Ricedale PO (Muhlenberg). See *Drakesboro*

Rice's PO (Laurel). See *Hazel Patch*

Rice Station (Estill): *rahs stā*/shən (Panola). This hamlet with extinct po, now on KY 52, 3 mi w of Irvine, was earlier centered on a now defunct rr station on the old Richmond Nicholasville Irvine & Beattyville (later L&N) RR, just n. The station was named for Charlie Rice who gave the land for the tracks and depot. The rr was completed to this site in 1890, and on Dec 16, 1891, the Rice Station po was est with John M. Kerby, pm. The po recently closed. 865.

Ricetown (Indian Creek) .(Owsley): *rahs*/town *ihn*/dyən *kreek* (Cowcreek). This po at the mouth of Stringtown Branch of Indian Creek, 5½ mi se of Booneville, was est as Floyd on Sept 13, 1901. It was named by Joseph Baker, its first pm, for his son. In 1905 Harvey Rice, the local storekeeper, renamed the office Ricetown for himself and had his wife Mary appointed pm. The community served by this po is now locally called Indian Creek for the stream, which flows into the South Fork of the Kentucky R some 5 mi nw. 1287.

Riceville (Johnson): *rahs*/vihl (Ivyton). This hamlet with po at the forks of Jennys Creek, 7 mi sw of Paintsville, is strung out for 1½ mi along KY 1867 and the C&O RR tracks from KY 825. The po was est on Oct 17, 1891, with George D. Rice, pm, and may have been named for Sherman Rice, prominent area farmer and merchant. Shortly thereafter the Dawkins Log and Mill Co. extended its Big Sandy & Kentucky River (now C&O) RR up Jennys Creek and opened a mill here. The community developed around the mill and the rail shipping operation. 89, 854, 1353.

Richardson (Lawrence): *rihch*/əs/ən, *rihch*/ərd/sən (Richardson). This po and C&O RR station are on the e bank of Levisa Fork of the Big Sandy R, just below the mouth of Nats Creek and 11½ mi s of Louisa. They were named for George S. Richardson, the Massachusetts-born manager of the Peach Orchard Coal Co. and a prime mover in the organization of the Chatteroi Railway Co. (forerunner of the C&O). The rr reached this point by May 1, 1883, and the Richardson po was est on May 25, 1883, with Patrick H. Vaughn, pm. 867.

Richardsville (Warren): *rihch*/ərdz/vihl (Bowling Green North). This hamlet with po extends about ½ mi along KY 263 from a point 5½ mi n of Bowling Green. The po was est on July 10, 1872, by Granville E. Speck, the first pm, who named it for Thomas Richards (1812–96), an English-born wagonmaker who settled in the area in the late 1840s. 1158.

Richmond (Madison): *rihch*/mənd (Richmond North, Richmond South). This 3rd class city and seat of Madison Co is on US 25/421, just e of I 75 and 78 mi ese of downtown Louisville. It is believed to have been settled in 1785 by Col. John Miller, a Virginia-born Revolutionary War veteran, who donated 50 acres for the transfer of the co's seat from Milford, 4½ mi sw, to a location more accessible to the co's other pop centers. The town was created by legislative act on July 4, 1798, and named by Miller for his birthplace in Virginia. The po was est on July 1, 1802(?), with William Miller, pm, and the town was inc in 1809. 57, 454.

Richmond Junction (Lincoln). See *Rowland*

Ridgeway (Harlan): *rihdj*/wā (Louellen, Nolansburg). This coal town with extinct po and station on the L&N RR's Clover Fork Branch is on Clover Fork of the Cumberland R, 10½ mi ene of Harlan, and was named for the Ridgeway Coal Co., which opened a mine there around 1921. The po was est on Oct 6, 1925, with James A. Evans, pm. 1173.

Riggs PO (Greenup). See *Lloyd*

Riggs PO (Metcalfe). See *Willow Shade*

Rightangle (Clark): *reyet*/aeŋ/əl (Hedges). This rural settlement with extinct po is on KY 974, 10 mi se of Winchester. Its name is said to have derived from that of a local Masonic lodge. The Rightangle po was est on July 9, 1883, by Henry H. Forman, and closed in May 1931. 1349.

Rileys Station PO (Marion). See *Gravel Switch*

Rineyville (Hardin): *reye*/nee/vihl (Cecilia, Vine Grove). This village with po is centered at the jct of KY 220 and the Illinois Central Gulf RR, 4½ mi wnw of Elizabethtown. The area was probably settled by John Wesley Pawley and his family, and the village itself grew up around Riney Station of the Illinois Central, built through there in 1874. Like the station, the po est on June 23, 1874, with Mancil G. Riney, pm, was named for the Riney family, who donated the land to the rr. The family's progenitor, Zachariah Riney, a Virginia-born Nelson Co pioneer, is said to have been Abraham Lincoln's first school teacher. 136, 824, 1420.

Ringgold (Pulaski): *rihŋ*/ohld (Delmer). This crossroads settlement with extinct po a mi n of the Cumberland Parkway and 1½ mi nw of Somerset was once an inc town (1848) named for Maj. Samuel Ringgold, the first American officer killed in the Mexican War, at the Battle of Palo Alto on May 8, 1846. It was not until Apr 10, 1914, that the Ringgold po was est with George R. McKiney, pm. 204, 870.

Ripyville (Anderson): *rihp*/ee/vihl (McBrayer). This extinct industrial hamlet and po were just n of the jct of old US 127 and the US 127 bypass, 2½ mi s of Lawrenceburg. The vicinity may have been settled in the 1830s but was unnamed until John Ripy from Co Tyrone, Ireland, opened a store there in 1855. On Feb 17, 1858, the area around his store was inc as Ripyville, and a po of this name was est on May 31, 1867, with Dickson G. McMichael, pm. It closed in 1905. 602, 1387.

Rislerville (Carroll). See *Sanders*

Risner (Floyd): *rahz*/nər (Martin). This po lies some 2½ mi up KY 1215 and Caney Creek from the latter's confluence with the Left Fork of Middle Creek, and 6½ mi ssw of Prestonsburg. It was est on May 12, 1923, with Harris Bradley, pm, and named for one or more local families.

Ritchie (Knott): *rihch*/ee (Carrie). This hamlet with recently discontinued po is on Clear Creek of Troublesome Creek and KY 721, 5 mi wsw of Hindman. The po was est on Jan 12, 1900, with Abbie Ritchie, pm, and named for the large number of local Ritchies, the descendants of pioneer Crockett Ritchie. 1288.

Rivals (Spencer): *rah*/vəlz (Taylorsville). This extinct po was on KY 1169 and Brashears Creek, 4½ mi nne of Taylorsville. A water-powered gristmill was built around 1790 at this site by the brothers Elijah and James Van Dyke, and a Vandykes Mill (*sic*) po was in operation there from 1848 to 1872. On June 23, 1900, the Rivals po was est with George W. Sloan, pm. Charles L. Stout, then the mill's owner, is said to have submitted 3 names to the Post Office Department. One of these is not recalled. Stout's preference was Boneset [*bohn*/seht], for an herb that, brewed with whiskey, makes a good tonic that was used locally as a medicine. In his search for a third name, he spied on a shelf in the local store a box of shotgun shells with the name Rivals on the label. Rivals was accepted. Less likely is the explanation that the name was derived from the rivalry of the pioneer Van Dyke brothers, which led to James's starting another mill further down the creek. The Rivals po closed in 1915. 1036, 1239.

River (Johnson): *rihv*/ər (Offutt). This hamlet with po was named for its location on the Big Sandy R's Levisa Fork, at the mouth of Wiley Creek, 4½ mi ne of Paintsville. The po was est on Sept 6, 1890, with Elbert J. Harris, pm. 1353.

Riverside (Warren): *rihv*/ər/seyed (Riverside). This hamlet and po, as far as anyone knows, have always been over 1 mi s of the Green R, on the present KY 263, 10½ mi nnw of Bowling Green. No one knows why it was thus called Riverside; it never had another name. The po was est on July 26, 1888, by John A. Simmons. 1128.

Riverview (Greenup). See *Russell*

River View PO (Jefferson). See *Kosmosdale*

Roaring Spring (Trigg): *rawr*/ihŋ *sprihŋ* (Roaring Spring). This hamlet with extinct po is on KY 164, 11 mi se of Cadiz. It was named for the large spring that, at certain times of the year, makes a roaring sound when it emerges from a limestone cave. This area may have had a po called Burnett Spring, for a local family, as early as 1816, though nothing is known of it. By 1849 the po of Roaring Spring was in operation in Charles A. Bacon's store, from which developed a thriving trade center that was inc in 1861. The po closed in 1909. 166, 431, 1325.

Robards (Henderson): *rahb*/ərdz (Robards). This settlement with po lies at the jct of the L&N RR and KY 416, 9 mi s of Henderson. It was named for J. D. Robards who built the first house and store there in 1867. A successful businessman and landowner, he helped get the L&N station and the po est there in 1868 and served as the first pm of Robard's Station. This was an obvious spelling error that was perpetuated in the official name change to Robard in 1883. A Board on Geographic Names decision in

1924 finally properly designated the name as Robards. Robards has often been called "The Sanctified Town," referring to Lucy Furman's tales of a religious sect there in the late 19th cent. 12.

Robard's Station PO (Henderson). See *Robards*

Robertson County: *rahb*/ə(rt)/sən. 100 sq mi. Pop 2,282. Seat: Mt. Olivet. This co was est in 1867 from parts of Bracken, Harrison, Mason, and Nicholas cos and named for George Robertson (1790–1874), Kentucky congressman (1817–21) and later chief justice of Kentucky's Court of Appeals.

Robertson's Station PO (Harrison). See *Robinson*

Robertsonville (Hardin). See *Colesburg*

Robertsville (Hardin). See *Colesburg*

Robinson (Harrison): *rahb*/ihn/sən (Cynthiana). This hamlet with po is on the L&N RR, 7 mi nnw of Cynthiana. According to local tradition, the Covington and Lexington (later Kentucky Central and now L&N) RR intended to name its new station here for James Robertson, but when his name was found to be a bit too long for the depot sign it was shortened to Robinson. Yet a Robertson's Station po, est on June 2, 1855, by George W. Robertson, was to retain this name until 1882 when it dropped the "Station"; then it too became Robinson in 1892. Robinson's 2nd pm, incidentally, was John R. Robinson. A Benjamin Robinson is known to have operated another Robinson po somewhere in the co from May 22, 1832 to July 15, 1833. 158.

Robinson Creek (Pike): *rahb*/əs/ən kreek (Pikeville). This village with po extends for some distance along US 23/119 and the creek for which it was named, 5 mi s of Pikeville. The creek was named for the family of Joseph Robinson, its pioneer settler. The first Robinson Creek po was est on May 27, 1848, with David May, pm. It was discontinued in Sept 1888 and its papers transferred to the nearby Little Creek po, which operated from 1867 until it was moved to and renamed Robinson Creek in Nov 1888. 1444.

Robinson Creek Church (Taylor). See *Merrimac*

Rochester (Butler): *rah*/chehs/tər (Rochester). This recently disinc Green R town with po is on KY 70, just above the mouth of Mud R and 10 mi w of Morgantown. Though the town per se was founded in the 1830s, it was really an outgrowth of a large pioneer settlement that extended into 3 cos in the vicinity of the confluence of the Mud and Green rs. Early travelers are said to have called this settlement simply The Mouth for its location at the mouth of Mud R. Two other 19th cent towns developing from this pioneer settlement were *Skilesville* in Muhlenburg Co and the now extinct McCrarysville in Ohio Co. Rochester was inc in 1839 and allegedly named by the descendants of John Rochester for his distinguished English family. John's brother Nathaniel is considered the founder and eponym of Rochester, New York. The Rochester, Ky. po was est on Sept 8, 1843, with William McDowell, pm. 28, 218, 575.

Rockcastle (Trigg): *rahk*/aes/əl, *rahk*/*aes*/əl (Lamasco). Now a retirement community on Lake Barkley, this was a 19th cent shipping port on the Cumberland R, 8 mi wnw of Cadiz. It was settled by the mid 1830s, when the first store opened, and named for Castle Rock in the limestone bluffs facing the r. The po was est as Rock Castle on Oct 12, 1852, with Washington L. Fuqua, pm, and the town was inc as Rockcastle in 1868, which spelling was applied to the po in 1895. It is not known why the words were transposed. The po closed in 1915. 98, 1325.

Rockcastle County: *rahk*/aes/əl. 318 sq mi. Pop 13,929. Seat: Mt. Vernon. This co was est in 1810 from parts of Knox, Lincoln, Madison, and Pulaski cos and named for the Rockcastle R, a tributary of the Cumberland R, which flows along its se border with Laurel Co. The r was first named Lawless R by Dr. Walker in 1750 for a member of his exploring party. It was renamed in 1767 by long hunter Isaac Lindsey, for a huge rock with an overhang that could provide shelter for a large number of persons; the pioneers often called these natural formations "rock castles" while their smaller counterparts were merely "rock houses." Historians have never agreed on the precise location of this rock. 529.

Rockfield (Warren): *rahk*/feeld (Rockfield). This hamlet with po stretches along KY 242 from US 68/KY 80 s past the L&N RR tracks, 5½ mi sw of Bowling Green. The community grew up around the L&N station and po est in 1866 and named for the rock-strewn fields in the vicinity. 1158.

Rock Haven (Meade): *rahk hāv*/ən (Rock Haven). This extinct 19th cent riverport and industrial town was at the foot of a high bluff overlooking the Ohio R, 6 mi ese of Brandenburg. Here in the early 1790s several Englishmen planned to build a large city called Ohiopiomingo, for the r and the chief of the Mingo Indians. (Though nothing came of this plan, the name appears on Russell's 1794 map of Kentucky.) It is assumed that Rock Haven was named for its location. The local po was in intermittent operation from 1848 to 1956. 856, 1260.

Rockholds (Whitley): *rahk*/hohldz (Rockholds). This village with po and L&N RR station, centered on the jct of KY 26 and 511, 5 mi n of Williamsburg, was probably named for its first storekeeper and pm, Thomas Rockhold, and was first called Rockhold's Store. The po was est as Rockhold's on July 18, 1838. 1267, 1380.

Rockhold's Store (Whitley). See *Rockholds*

Rockland (Warren): *rahk*/lənd (Hadley). This extinct po at the jct of KY 626 and 1435, 8 mi nw of Bowling Green, was est on Jan 29, 1875, with Commodore P. Burchfield, pm, and named for a large bluff ½ mi se, where the Gasper R flows into the Barren R. The bluff has since become known as Sally's Rock, honoring Sally Beck who, between 1900 and 1915, would stand on the rock and call to the pilots of passing r boats. The settlement about that po for years was known simply as The Mouth of Gasper and is now essentially a part of the nearby community of Hadley. 1343.

Rockport (Ohio): *rahk*/pawrt (Paradise). A 6th class city with po is now located mostly on the bluff overlooking the Green R between US 62 and the Illinois Central Gulf RR, just n of the Western Kentucky Parkway and 8½ mi ssw of Hartford. The first settler may have been Lewis Kincheloe (see *South Carrollton*), below whose cabin on the bluff the small settlement of Benton's Ferry was founded. With the est of the local po on May 7, 1863, the community became known as Rock Port and then Rockport. It was probably named for the steamboat landing and the large rocks on the r bank which looked to early settlers as if they had been "torn loose from the hill above . . . by a mighty giant and rolled there." What little remains of the section of town on the r is now known as Old Rockport. 778, 905, 1400.

Rockville (Lawrence). See *Buchanan*

Rockville (Rowan): *rahk*/vihl (Morehead). This extinct C&O RR station and hamlet were on US 60 in the vicinity of Cincinnati Hollow of Triplett Creek, about 2½ mi wsw of Morehead. They were named for the abundance of local freestone quarried in the area early in this cent. 688, 851.

Rockybranch (Wayne): *rahk*/ee/*braench* (Bell Farm). This po is now on Rocky Branch of Canadas Creek and KY 1756, 8½ mi se of Monticello. It was probably named for the wet weather branch, which in turn was named for the profusion of rocks lying about both in the stream and on the adjacent hillsides. The po was est on Oct 3, 1908, by C.

E. Bell in his home about 100 yards s of its present site, to which it was moved in the 1930s. 1258, 1406.

Rocky Hill (Barren): *rahk*/ee *hihl* (Lucas). This hamlet with extinct po lies at the jct of KY 252 and 255, 7 mi sw of Glasgow. The vicinity was first settled around 1800 by the family of William Settle, makers of the famed Settles Long Rifles. Though the area is rocky, the po moved from *Port Oliver* on Jan 17, 1825, to Franklin Settle's store, is said to have been renamed for a place in Fauquier Co, Virginia, whence the first settlers had come. After a noncontinuous existence, the po was renamed Game in 1911, a name of unknown derivation, which was applied because by then the Rocky Hill name had been assumed by another po in Edmonson Co. The Game po was discontinued in 1926 and the community is now called Rocky Hill. 920, 1368.

Rocky Hill (Edmonson): *rahk*/ee *hihl* (Smiths Grove). This village with po extends ½ mi along KY 259, 10 mi se of Brownsville. When the L&N RR was completed through here in 1859, the Dripping Spring po, est on July 17, 1828, was moved from its site several mi nw, set up at the new depot, and renamed Rocky Hill Station with William Newman, pm. It is not known when the Rocky Hill name was first applied or even exactly why. Some say the rocky terrain impeded early efforts to farm it. Others refer to the limestone outcropping and deep sinkholes in the area. The "Station" was dropped from the po name in 1923. 942, 1150.

Rocky Hill Station PO (Edmonson). See *Rocky Hill*

Rodbourn PO (Rowan). See *Rodburn*

Rodburn (Rowan): *rahd*/bern (Morehead). Several homes and businesses now occupy the site of an old sawmill town centered at the jct of US 60 and KY 32 at the ne fringe of Morehead. The mill and town were est in 1873–74 by the New York State-based Hixson-Rodburn Lumber Co. to process timber shipped from the vicinity of Cranston. The po est there as Rodbourn on July 3, 1888, with Amos Hixson, pm, closed in 1922. 688, 952, 1454.

Rodonnel (Clay). See *Blue Hole*

Roelosson's Settlement (Henderson). See *Smith Mills*

Roe's (Row's) Mill (Simpson). See *New Roe*

Roff PO (Breckinridge). See *Stephensport*

Rogers (Wolfe): *rahdj*/ərz (Zachariah). This hamlet with po is on KY 715, 4 mi w of Campton. The po was est on Aug 16, 1900, with Samuel P. Napier, pm, and named for Elihu Rogers, the local blacksmith. The community was settled by the Spencers on land acquired from a logging firm and first called Oklahoma, it is alleged, after some local men had returned, with fond recollections, from that western territory. 1038, 1236.

Rogersville (Hardin): *rahdj*/ərz/vihl (Vine Grove). This residential community extends s along US 31W and KY 447 from the city of Radcliff, of which it is generally considered a functional part, to a point less than 4 mi nnw of Elizabethtown. It was named for a local family and never had its own po. 1420.

Rogersville (Madison). See *Terrill*

Rome PO (Knox). See *Flat Lick*

Romine (Taylor): *rohm*/eyen (Cane Valley). This extinct po was on old KY 55 at the foot of Green R Hill, just e of Tebbs Bend of the Green R, and 6½ mi s of Campbellsville. The po was est on May 15, 1901, and named for the family of its first pm, Melvin Romine. 1291.

Rose Hill (Mercer): *rohz* hihl (Perryville). This hamlet with extinct po is on KY 152, 3 mi w of Harrodsburg. Its po was est on Aug 29, 1870, with William Jackson, pm, and closed in 1972. It was named for its hilly location and its abundance of wild roses. 53.

Rosine (Ohio): *roh/zeen* (Rosine). This village with po is on US 62 and the Illinois Central Gulf RR, 8 mi e of Hartford. It was founded in 1872, with the coming of the then Elizabethtown and Paducah RR, by Henry D. McHenry (see *McHenry*) and named for his wife, Jenny Taylor McHenry. In 1867 Mrs. McHenry, a writer and daughter of Rev. James Taylor of Hardinsburg, had used "Rosine" as a pen name to publish a book of poems entitled *Forget Me Not*. The po was est on Jan 16, 1872, as Pigeon Roost for the local creek, a branch of Muddy Creek. The creek is said to have been named in pioneer days for the hundreds of pigeons which had mysteriously come to roost in the large cedar trees on its banks; the pigeons were so numerous that they actually broke the limbs of the trees by their weight. The po was renamed Rosine in 1873. 75, 246, 704.

Rosslyn (Powell): *rahz*/lihn (Stanton). This hamlet with po is on KY 11/15, just s of the Mountain Parkway and just below the mouth of Cat Creek, a branch of Red R, 1 mi e of Stanton. In the very early 19th cent there was a water mill at the mouth of Cat Creek called Kirkpatricks Mill [ker/*paet*/rəx mihl]. Later when Hugh Maxwell acquired the mill it became Maxwell's Mill. It became Harrow's Mill [*haer*/əz mihl] when it came into the possession of D. P. Harrow in 1866. A po called Harrahs Mills (*sic*) was in operation there from 1872 to Jan 1874. By 1883 the mill had changed hands again and become the Mansfield Mill. In 1905, when George P. Burkes bought the mill, it became Burkes Mill. On Jan 2, 1880, Nick D. Merrill, local storekeeper and Powell Co court clerk, secured another po at the site of the mill, which he called Merrill. Reuben C. Mansfield, who ran the mill, became pm. In 1886 he renamed the po Cat Creek for the stream, which in early land grants was called Catamount Creek and later Cat and Owl Creek. Finally, in 1898, the Lexington & Eastern RR renamed the po and its station there Rosslyn, allegedly for the many wild roses growing locally. By 1900 the community had also come to be identified by this name. 1334.

Ross's Mill (Gallatin and Owen). See *Sparta*

Rough and Ready (Anderson). See *Alton*

Roundhill (Edmonson): *rownd* hihl (Reedyville). This hamlet with po is on KY 70, about ¼ mi e of KY 185 and 8½ mi wnw of Brownsville. The po, est in Butler Co on Oct 14, 1893, with John Willis, Jr., pm, and named for the shape of a local hill, was moved in 1937 to its present site.

Round Hill (Madison): *rownd hihl* (Kirksville). This crossroads settlement on KY 595, 6 mi sw of Richmond, was named for a mound alleged to have been built by an early tribe of Indians. It never had its own po. 1294.

Roundstone (Rockcastle): *rownd* stohn (Wildie). This hamlet with extinct po at the jct of US 25 and KY 1617 and 1786, 5½ mi n of Mount Vernon, is also located on Roundstone Creek, a branch of Rockcastle R, which was named for the round stones early found in its bed. The po, est as Round Stone on Mar 18, 1856, with James Sayers, pm, was discontinued in 1896. 1251.

Rousseau (Breathitt): *rū*/soh (Guage). This hamlet is centered at its po on KY 30 and Quicksand Creek, just below the mouth of Hunting Creek and 7 mi ene of Jackson. The po was est on Feb 28, 1882, with Jeremiah McQuinn, pm, and named for the operator of a local windmill. 1129.

Rowan County: *row*/ən. 282 sq mi. Pop 19,026. Seat: Morehead. Rowan Co was est in 1856 from parts of Fleming and Morgan cos and named for John Rowan (1773–1843), justice of the Kentucky Court of Appeals and later US senator from Kentucky (1824–30).

Rowdy (Perry): *row*/dee, *rah*/dee (Noble). This hamlet with po extends for over ½ mi along KY 476 n from its jct with KY 267 at the mouth of Rowdy Branch of Troublesome, for which it was named, and 8½ mi n of Hazard. For many years the community was also known as Stacy, for several local families, and the po there was est as Stacy on June 30, 1890, with Ira Allen, pm. Recently the po adopted the Rowdy name which is said to have long reflected the wild character of its residents. Curiously, postal records mention that Allen was also pm of a Rowdy po, in operation in that vicinity from July 18 to Oct 2, 1890, at the same time he was in charge of the Stacy po. 1272.

Rowena (Russell): roh/*ee*/nə, roh/*ee*/nee (Jamestown). This hamlet with extinct po is now on US 127, 7 mi s of Jamestown. It was est as a town by the Kentucky legislature on land owned by John Leveridge on the s bank of the Cumberland R on Feb 10, 1845, and named for the daughter of William D. Lair, or a member of the pioneer Leveridge (Leverage) family, or Rowena Leffler, who is said to have been the first child born there, of parents en route to the w. Rowena was across the r from a community est on Mar 1, 1847, as Lairsville, named for William D. Lair, its founder, which was later destroyed by a flood. The local po was est as Rowena on May 14, 1847, with Robert Tarpley, pm. After several changes in location, including a move to the Lairsville site and thence onto the ridge overlooking Lake Cumberland, it was discontinued in 1967. The community may also for a time have been called Wild Goose for its location near the Wild Goose Shoals of the Cumberland R. 3, 58, 758, 1156, 1233.

Rowland (Lincoln): *roh*/lən(d) (Stanford). This residential suburb with extinct po on US 150, just e of Stanford, occupies the site of the old Richmond Junction est by the L&N RR around 1868 as a jct for its Knoxville (now Lebanon) Branch and the then just completed Richmond Branch lines. It was named for the city of Richmond where the Richmond Branch connected with the Kentucky Central RR. A Richmond Junction po, in operation from 1879 to 1883, was reest as Rowland on June 4, 1886 and named for D. W. C. Rowland, then general superintendent of the L&N. It closed in 1912. 637.

Rowletts (Hart): *row*/ləts (Horse Cave). This village with po is just s of the jct of US 31W and KY 335 and 1 mi s of Munfordville. A station on the L&N RR's main line between Louisville and Nashville was called Rowlett's Depot for the first station agent, John W. Rowlett. Under this name Rowlett est the first po on Feb 9, 1860. A prosperous trade and shipping center soon developed, which was inc in 1874 as Rowletts Station. In 1880 the Depot was dropped from the po name and in 1882 the town was reinc as Rowletts. 863.

Rowlett's Depot PO (Hart). See *Rowletts*

Rowton PO (Pike). See *Phyllis*

Royalton (Magoffin): *raw*/əl/tən, *roi*/əl/tən (Salyersville South). This village with po is on KY 7 at the mouth of Gun Creek, a tributary of the Licking R, 4½ mi sse of Salyersville. It developed as a co. town around a large sawmill built before World War I by the Dawkins Log and Mill Co., a Canadian firm financed by the Royal Bank of Canada, for which the town was named. The Royalton po was est on Sept 20, 1920, with Mary K. Stephens, pm. Despite the prosaic account of the name, some local credence has been given to the tale of the Kentucky governor who, on viewing the town that had just grown up around the mill, was heard to remark "Well boys, you have a royal little town here." 149, 965, 1422.

Royrader (Jackson): *roi*/*rād*/er (Tyner). This settlement with extinct po is on KY 578 and Lewis Branch of Terrell Creek, 11½ mi sse of McKee. The po, est on Aug 30, 1927, with Etta McGee, pm, was named for the late Roy Rader, an executive of Bond-Foley Lumber Co., a major industry in the co at that time. No reason has been given for the odd spelling of this name. 1419.

Royville (Russell): *rojz*/vihl (Russell Springs). This residential suburb without po on KY 80, 5 mi nnw of Jamestown, was chartered in 1951 to avoid inc by the city of Russell Springs, adjoining it on the se. It was named for John Roy, then local storekeeper. It is no longer inc. 1037.

Rucker's Big Spring (Woodford). See *Mortonsville*

Ruckerville (Clark): *ruhk*/ər/vihl (Hedges). This rural settlement with extinct po on KY 89, 5 mi se of Winchester, was named for Reuben Rucker (1805–65), a pioneer settler from Culpeper Co, Virginia, who on his arrival in Clark Co in 1823 purchased 12 acres on the site from Alexander Pitcher. Here the Ruckerville po was est on Jan 24, 1850, with William Ritchie, pm. It was closed in 1906. 1349.

Ruddells Mills (Bourbon): *ruhd*/əlz *mihlz* (Millersburg). This hamlet with extinct po lies where Stoner and Hinkston Creeks join to form the South Fork of the Licking R, 5 mi n of Paris. It was named for the Ruddell family whose progenitor Isaac, a Virginian, built a cabin near the site in 1776. In 1779, the threat of Indian raids forced him to move his family 3 mi down r to an abandoned fort that was later captured by Col. Henry Byrd and his mixed band of British and Indians. After 4 years of captivity, the Ruddells returned to the Hinkston area and developed a large orchard. Isaac's son Abram operated a mill on Hinkston for which the community was named. The family is said to have spelled its name Ruddell but over time the spelling changed to Ruddel and Ruddle to conform to the local pronunciation. Contemporary historians prefer the original spelling and are not pleased to see the name misspelled on most maps and legal documents. The local po, est as Ruddles Mills on July 5, 1820 with John McKee, pm, has since closed. 167, 1414.

Rumsey (McLean): *ruhm*/zee (Calhoun). This village with po on KY 81 and across the Green R from Calhoun, was recently disincorporated. This was a small settlement in 1834 when work was begun on Lock and Dam No. 2. On Nov 12 of that year John M. Johnson est the po, which according to tradition was named for James Rumsey (1743–92), the pioneer of steam navigation, at the request of his nephew, Edward Rumsey, a Greenville attorney who was later to represent the area in the US Congress. Some historians aver that Edward (1800–1868) declined a suggestion that the place be named for him but accepted a compromise that attributed the name to his uncle. The town boomed with the completion of the Lock and Dam in 1837 and was inc in 1839. 189, 567.

Rush (Boyd): ruhsh (Rush). This hamlet extending for over 2 mi on KY 854 and along Rush Creek and its main stream, Williams Creek, centers at the Rush po just below the confluence, 10 mi wsw of Catlettsburg. Earlier known as Geigerville, for its pioneer family, this community rapidly grew up around a coal seam called Rush No. 5, developed by the Ashland Coal and Iron Ry Co. in 1870. The po was est on July 25, 1890, with Henry Artist, pm. The derivation of the name is not known; no Rush family lived in the area then. There is a local tradition that the coal boom brought a rush of people into the community to share in its anticipated prosperity. 7, 1311.

Russell (Greenup): *ruhs*/əl (Ironton). This 4th class city directly across the Ohio R from Ironton, Ohio, is 6½ mi ese of Greenup. It was founded in 1869 by John Russell (1821–96) and his colleagues of the Means and Russell Iron Co. on the site of the old

Amanda Furnace Tract. In response to the interest of Ohioans for Kentucky land and in anticipation of an extension of the C&O RR w of Huntington to Cincinnati, Russell laid off the Amanda lands, which his co. had earlier acquired from the Poages (see *Amanda Furnace*), into plots which the purchasers in turn developed into town lots. For some years this area had been known as Riverview, but in Nov 1872 property owners gathering to select another name accepted Dr. Frederick A. Long's suggestion of Russell for its founder, and with this name Long's po was est on Jan 3, 1873. The town was inc on Feb 23, 1874. 453.

Russell County: *ruhs*/əl. 250 sq mi. Pop 13,488. Seat: Jamestown. This co was est in 1825 from parts of Adair, Wayne, and Cumberland cos and named for Col. William Russell (1758–1825), veteran of the Revolutionary War, the Indian campaigns of the 1790s, and the Battle of Tippecanoe (1811), who succeeded William Henry Harrison as commander of American forces on the frontier. He later served in the Kentucky legislature.

Russell Springs (Russell): *ruhs*/əl *sprihŋz* (Russell Springs). This 5th class city with po on US 127 and the Cumberland Parkway, 2½ mi n of Jamestown, had a long history as a health resort. Known as Big Boiling Springs by 1850, the resort is said to have been founded by pioneer settler Sam Patterson around a chalybeate spring. The po, est as Russell Springs on May 17, 1855, with Timoleon Bradshaw, pm, was discontinued in 1865 and reest in 1888 as Kimble, honoring George Kimble, the town's leading businessman. In 1901 it was renamed Russell Springs to conform to the name the town had officially adopted shortly before. 419.

Russellville (Logan): *ruhs*/əl/vihl, *ruhs*/əl/vəl (Russellville). This 4th class industrial city and seat of Logan Co is on US 68, 79, and 431, 105 mi wsw of downtown Louisville. The date of its first settlement has been disputed. According to Logan Co's noted historian, Alex C. Finley (in 1879), the first house on the site was built by Gasper Butcher around 1780. W. R. Jillson has questioned this, finding no recorded evidence of a house there until Cook's Cabin or Station was built in 1790. It has been said that the name Big Boiling Spring was early applied to the place, for a spring that boiled up out of the ground, along with Gasper Butcher's Spring or Station (so he undoubtedly had something to do with its early history), and later Cook's Station until 1792 when, with the formation of the co, it became known as Logan Court House. Actually the first courthouse and community were 1 mi e of the present courthouse site. The town that was laid off in 1795 and named for Gen. William Russell centered in 1798 on the 2nd courthouse located on Russell's 2000-acre Revolutionary War military grant. Russell, (1735–93), the son of English immigrants, was a veteran of both French and Indian and Revolutionary War campaigns. The Russellville po was est on Apr 1, 1801, with Armestead Morehead, pm, but the town was not inc by legislative act until Jan 13, 1810. 42, 109, 206, 1344.

Ruth (Pulaski): rūth (Somerset). This hamlet with po is on KY 192 and Pitman Creek, 3 mi e of Somerset. The first po in this vicinity was est on July 19, 1888, with Matthew Warren, pm, and called Juno for reasons unknown. It was closed in 1896. In 1908 Rufe Ashurst, a local storekeeper, reest the po and named it for his daughter Ruth, and Warren again became pm. 1016.

Ryans Mill PO (Washington). See *Litsey*

Sacramento (McLean): saek/rə/*mehn*/toh (Sacramento). This 6th class city with po lies at the jct of KY 81/85 and 254, 8 mi s of Calhoun. On May 20, 1852, the Social Hill po was est at a settlement called Crossroads. Two years later George L. Helm laid off a town, which according to tradition was named at the suggestion of John Vickers for the town or r valley by Sutter's Fort in the California gold fields, from which he had recently returned. The McLean Co town was inc as Sacramento on Mar 1, 1860, and the po was renamed this on Oct 8, 1861. 798.

Sacred Wind (Lawrence): *sāk*/rəd *wihnd* (Mazie). This extinct po lay at the head of the Left Fork of Cains Creek, 17 m wsw of Louisa. It was est on July 24, 1903, and, according to tradition, named by its first pm, James N. Sturgill, for his father, a Baptist preacher, "it is said not for his preaching but for flatulence from which he suffered from time to time and his admirable artistry in relieving himself." The po was discontinued in 1947. 1175.

Sadieville (Scott): *sā*/dee/vihl (Sadieville). This 6th class city with po is on Eagle Creek where KY 32 crosses the Southern Ry tracks, 11 mi n of Georgetown. Founded on the Cincinnati Southern RR, completed through this site in 1876, it was named for Sadie Pack, a highly respected citizen. The po was est on Jan 14, 1878, by James W. Jones, who opened the first store there about that time. The town was inc in 1880. 13, 1293.

Sadler (Grayson): *saed*/lər (Bee Spring). This hamlet with po on KY 1133, 8 mi s of Leitchfield, was named for its first pm and storekeeper, E. Garner Sadler. Though the po was est on Feb 10, 1892, the community may have been settled earlier in the cent by the Ephriam House family from White River, Indiana. 589.

St. Anthony (Breckinridge). See *Axtel*

St. Catharine (Washington): sānt *kaeth*/rihn (St. Catharine). This settlement with po lies between US 150 and Cartwright Creek, 1½ mi nw of Springfield. It grew up around the St. Catharine Academy and Motherhouse of the Dominican Sisters in the US. Cofounded in 1822 by Mother Angela Sansbury and Rev. Samuel T. Wilson to provide a Catholic education for local women, the Academy was called St. Magdalen until 1851 when it was renamed for St. Catharine of Siena. The po was est on Feb. 27, 1900, as St. Catherines (*sic*) with Josie Holleran, pm, and the spelling error was corrected in 1903. 1314.

Saint Charles (Hopkins): sānt *chahrlz* (St. Charles). This 6th class city with po lies at the jct of US 62 and KY 454, just s of the Western Kentucky Parkway and 8 mi ssw of Madisonville. It was founded as a coal camp in or before 1872 on land deeded to the St. Bernard Mining Co. by J. I. D. Woodruff and called Woodruff when the local po was est with that name on Jan 15, 1873. The po and community were renamed St. Charles, for reasons unknown, when the town was inc in 1874. 159, 331.

St. Francis (Marion): sānt *fraen*/səs (Loretto, Raywick). This village with po centered at the jct of KY 52 and 527, 9 mi wnw of Lebanon, grew up around an unnamed settlement there before the co was created in 1834. The po, est on Sept 14, 1858, was named Chicago, allegedly in hopes that the place would someday rival the city in Illinois. This name was applied to the station on the Lebanon Branch of the L&N RR built through in 1865–66, and under this name the town was inc in 1870. On Jan 1, 1938, the Post Office Department, having approved the local request for a change of name on the ground that mail had frequently been missent to Illinois, renamed the po St. Francis. By this name, that of the local St. Francis of Assisi Church, the community has been officially known ever since, though oldtimers may still also refer to it as Chicago. 534, 904, 1219, 1399.

St. Helens (Jefferson). See *Shively*

St. John (Hardin): *sānt djahn* (Cecilia). This station on the Illinois Central Gulf RR and extinct po on KY 1357, 4 mi w of Elizabethtown, were est in 1874 to serve the Bethlehem Academy, 1½ mi w. They were named for the St. John the Baptist Catholic

Church, 1 mi nnw, which had been built by Fr. Charles Nerinckx in 1812 and is still active. 757, 1420.

St. Johns (McCracken): *sānt djahnz* (Melber). This hamlet is centered on and named for St. John's Catholic Church and School at the jct of US 45 and Contest Rd, 5½ mi s of Paducah. The church was est around 1832 to serve a community of German settlers. The hamlet never had its own po. 1014.

St. Joseph (Daviess): sānt *djoh*/səf (Curdsville). This hamlet with po at the jct of KY 56 and 500, 10 mi wsw of Owensboro, was named for the St. Joseph Academy est there in 1861 by Fr. Ivo Schacht of the local St. Alphonsus Church. Four years after the building was destroyed by fire in 1870, several Ursuline Sisters from Louisville reest the school as Mount St. Joseph Academy or, officially, the St. Joseph Female Ursuline Academy. A St. Joseph po was est there on May 4, 1886, with Emma J. Pike, pm. In 1912 Mount St. Joseph "became an . . . autonomous community of Ursuline Sisters." In Dec 1934 a separate po was opened on the Academy grounds and named Maple Mount [māp/əl *mownt*] for the maple grove planted there by Fr. Paul Joseph Volk in 1875. The Maple Mount po still serves the religious community. 1029.

Saint Mary (Marion): sānt *mɛ*/ee (Lebanon West). This hamlet with po is centered at the jct of KY 84 and 327, 4 mi w of Lebanon. It is said to have been part of the pioneer Hardins Creek Settlement, settled by the Hardin family shortly after 1785. Catholics from St. Charles Co, Maryland, arrived in the 1790s and est an early church they named St. Charles, by which name their parish and the local schools are still called. This was the home of the famed St. Mary's College founded in 1821 by Rev. William Byrne, and the town was named for the college when its po was est as Saint Mary's on June 7, 1858, with Green Forest, pm. It was renamed Saint Mary in 1893 but the station on the Lebanon Branch of the L&N RR has always been Saint Marys. It was inc as a town in 1865. 1399.

St. Matthews (Jefferson): sānt *maeth*/yūz (Jeffersonville, Louisville East). This 4th class city and residential suburb is centered at the jct of Shelbyville Rd. (US 60/460), Westport Rd. (KY 1447), and Chenoweth Lane, 5½ mi e of downtown Louisville. This vicinity was first called Gilman's Point for Daniel Gilman who operated an early store and stagecoach tavern there. The first po was Lynnford, est on Sept 25, 1849, probably referring to the pioneer Linn Station on the nearby Middle Fork of Beargrass Creek. This was renamed St. Matthews on Oct 1, 1851, for a local Episcopal church, organized in 1839. The po closed in 1931. The city was inc in 1950. 725, 838.

St. Paul (Lewis): sānt *pawl* (Friendship). This hamlet with po is on KY 10, at the edge of the Ohio R bottom, 13 mi ne of Vanceburg. In 1888 the C&O RR named its local flag stop for the St. Paul Methodist Church built in 1874 just across the tracks from the depot site. When Charles T. Booton est the po there on Dec 24, 1898, he too adopted the St. Paul name. 1065, 1103, 1122.

St. Regis Park (Jefferson): sānt *ree*/djəs pahrk (Jeffersontown). This 4th class city and residential suburb without po is e of Browns Lane and between I 64 and Taylorsville Rd (KY 155), less than 8 mi ese of downtown Louisville. Inc as a 6th class city in 1953, it had been est as the subdivision of St. Regis Park the year before, and probably named for the local St. Regis Catholic Church. 433, 550, 1296.

St. Stephens (Marion). *Nerinx*

Saldee (Copland) (Breathitt): *sael*/dee, *kohp*/lən(d) (Canoe, Haddix). This po is now on KY 1110 and the North Fork of the Kentucky R, 6 mi s of Jackson. It was est on July 9, 1919, with George Arrowood, pm, at the site of the L&N RR's Copland Station across the r and ¾ mi below its present site. It is said to have been named for the girl friend of a local resident, or else was the combination of the names of the 2 leading local families, the Salyers and the Deatons. In the late 1960s the po was moved to its present location but still serves the community of Copland, named for the station est in 1912, which had been named for the local Levi Cope family. 1049, 1222.

Salem (Livingston): *sā*/ləm (Salem). This 6th class city with po extends almost 2 mi along US 60 to a point 11 mi ne of Smithland. The origin of its name has never been confirmed but it is generally considered to have derived from the town in North Carolina that became Winston-Salem, whence the earliest settlers are said to have come. Kentucky's Salem was founded and named sometime shortly after 1800, and the Livingston Co seat was moved there from Centerville in 1809. It is not clear from Post Office records whether the po was est on Jan 1, 1807, with Jeremiah Walker, pm, or 2 years later; it depends on whether the po was created anew or transferred from Centerville, 8 mi e (see *Crayne*). With the creation of Crittenden Co from Livingston Co in 1842, the seat was moved to *Smithland,* its present site, to be more centrally located. The town was reinc in 1950. 138, 1189.

Salem (Morgan). See *Buskirk*

Salem (Russell): *sā*/ləm (Eli). This hamlet with extinct po, centered at the jct of KY 76 and 910, just s of the Cumberland Parkway, and 6½ mi ne of Jamestown, was probably named for a local church organized in 1869. The po, in operation from June 27, 1927, to Nov 15, 1928, was called Dallo [*dael*/oh] for Dallo Wilson, a local storekeeper. 1178.

Salem(town) (Nelson). See *Bardstown*

Salisbury Station (Floyd). See *Printer*

Salmons (Simpson): *saem*/ənz (Woodburn). This hamlet with extinct po lies at the jct of KY 1434 and the L&N RR's main line, 2½ mi n of Franklin. The po was est on Nov 14, 1893, with John W. Stallard, the first storekeeper, as pm, and named for a prominent Franklin family. The po was discontinued in 1955. 18.

Saloma (Taylor): sə/*lohm*/ə (Saloma). This hamlet with extinct po, at the jct of KY 527 and 744, 4 mi nw of Campbellsville, was est by legislative act in 1838 and inc in 1866. John Durham became the first pm on May 9, 1855. For some time during the 19th cent, the community was also known as Pinchem [*pihn*/chəm], for which several explanations have been given. The most generally accepted refers to the practice of customers at the local store of pinching the storekeeper when a bottle or jug of illicit whiskey was desired. According to another tradition, the storekeeper "was hard of hearing and would pinch a customer if he wanted him to repeat an order." The origin of the name Saloma is unknown, but an association with that of the Old Siloam Meeting House in Green Co, built around 1800, has been conjectured. 833, 1291.

Salt Creek PO (Perry). See *Cornettsville*

Saltillo (Oldham). See *Goshen*

Salt Lick (Bath): *sâhlt lihk* (Salt Lick). This 6th class city with po is centered at the jct of US 60 and KY 211, 7 mi e of Owingsville and only yards from the Licking R. Before it was laid out as a town in 1884 and named for the many salt springs in the area to which deer had long come to lick, it was a crossroads settlement with a po called Vail, est on Jan 17, 1882, with James M. Colliver, pm. The po was renamed Salt Lick on Aug 9, 1888, several months after the town was inc under that name. 15, 186.

Salt Lick Valley PO (Lewis). See *Charters*

Salt River PO (Anderson). See *Glensboro*

Saltsburg (Bullitt). See *Bullitts Lick*

Saltwell (Nicholas): *sawlt*/wehl (Piqua). This extinct hamlet and po were on Beaver

Creek, 6 mi nw of Carlisle. The po, est as Salt Well on June 28, 1878, with John A. Taylor, pm, was named for one or more early local salt wells. Discontinued in 1879, it was reest as Saltwell in 1886 but closed again in 1906. 47.

Salvisa (Mercer): sael/*veye*/sə (Salvisa). This village with po is just e of US 127, and 9 mi n of Harrodsburg. Laid out in 1816 by Robert B. McAfee and inc in 1828, it was most likely named for the 2 nearby streams, the Salt R and the Kentucky R, the latter said to have once been called the Levisa. Another account is that the name was coined from sal (salt) and visa (Latin for ''I see''). An obvious fabrication is the local legend that the name combined those of 2 elderly maiden sisters, Sally and Visa Britton, who allegedly lived there. The po was est on Mar 25, 1828, with Richard Holman, pm. 53, 1264.

Salyersville (Magoffin): *sah*/yərz/vəl, *sahl*/yərz/vəl, *sael*/yərz/vəl (Salyersville North, Salyersville South). This 4th class city and seat of Magoffin Co is on US 460 and KY 7, just n of the Mountain Parkway and 139 mi ese of downtown Louisville. The first permanent settlement in this vicinity was made around 1800 on the hill just below the later townsite by the Praters, Ebenezer Hannah, and others, and was called Prater's Fort or Licking Station as it overlooked the Licking R. In 1839 the po est as Burning Spring on Mar 3, 1829, was moved to this site and renamed Licking Station with Benjamin F. Gardner, pm. It was removed to the site of the present Salyersville in 1849 and renamed Adamsville for William (''Uncle Billy'') Adams, the son of pioneer Stephen Adams who had come to Kentucky from North Carolina around 1809. The po was renamed Salyersville in 1861. Here on land donated by Billy Adams, an extensive landowner and businessman, the new co's seat had been est in 1860 and named for Samuel Salyer (1913–90), the local representative who had introduced the bill in the state legislature to create the co. 149, 194.

Sams PO (Estill). See *Hargett*

Samuels (Nelson): *saem*/yū/əlz (Samuels). This hamlet with recently discontinued po lies at the jct of KY 245 and 609, 5 mi nw of Bardstown. The po of *Deatsville,* est on Oct 30, 1850, with Leander P. Bradshaw, pm, was moved to this site in 1860 when the Louisville & Bardstown (now L&N) RR was built through, and renamed Samuels Depot for the principal family in that area. The family's progenitor was Virginia-born William Samuels (ca. 1771–1836), who built a spring-powered gristmill on part of a 4000-acre grant in the vicinity and later opened the first commercial distillery in that section of the co. In 1894 the po became merely Samuels. 1386.

Samuels Depot PO (Nelson). See *Samuels*

Sanders (Carroll): *saen*/dərz (Sanders). This 6th class city with po on KY 36 and 47, 10 mi ese of Carrollton, was founded on the site of an old salt lick on the buffalo trace that extended from the mouth of the Licking R to Drennon Springs. A settlement grew up around a gristmill built and operated by Virginian Nathaniel Sanders and his son, George Washington Sanders, among the earliest settlers on Eagle Creek, and was early called Rislerville for John or William Risler, the local storekeeper, of whom nothing more is known. For a brief period from about 1816, it was served by a po called Sanders Mill, with Nathaniel as pm. From 1865 the Bramlette po, which may have been 2 or 3 mi away in Gallatin Co, provided mail service. When the Louisville Cincinnati & Lexington (Shortline) RR came through in 1867, residents named the station Dixie, but shortly thereafter the place was renamed Liberty Station for its new role as the shipping point for farmers and stockmen around New Liberty, 4½ mi s in Owen Co. About this time the po was moved to its present site and renamed Liberty Station. Until 1872 this site was a part of the narrow strip along Eagle Creek that was transferred from Gallatin to Carroll Co. According to Anna V. Parker, a co historian, the name Sanders was applied in 1874 at the suggestion of State Sen. Larkin Sanders to honor his father, George Washington Sanders. It was not until May 12, 1884, that the po officially became Sanders with John Q. Adams, pm. 87, 342, 412, 537, 646, 695, 1330.

Sanders Mill PO (Carroll). See *Sanders*

Sanders PO (Grant). See *Crittenden*

Sandersville (Fayette): *saen*/dərs/vihl (Lexington West). This extinct village was on the Sandersville Rd just w of the Southern Ry tracks, and ¾ mi n of Lexington's New Circle Rd. It was est in 1815 by Col. Lewis Sanders, merchant and industrialist, to accommodate the workers at his cotton factory there. In 1819, following the failure of the factory, it, the village, and Sanders' home, Sanders Garden, were sold by court order. Though the Sandersville name is perpetuated on most current maps and still identifies the rd, there is no longer a community there and locally the site is now known simply as Hillenmeyer's Nursery. 175, 392, 1335.

Sandford PO (Fleming). See *Goddard.*

Sandgap (Jackson): *saend*/*ghaep* (Sandgap). This village with po is centered at the jct of US 421 and KY 2004, 5½ mi nw of McKee. The community dates from pre-Civil War times. The local po was est on June 10, 1886, and named Collinsworth, probably for a local family, but was renamed Sandgap in 1902 for a slight but very sandy depression in the ridge that forms the dividing line between the Cumberland and Kentucky R watersheds. 1192, 1418.

Sand Hill (Greenup). See *South Shore*

Sandy Hook (Elliott): *saend*/ee *hōōk* (Sandy Hook, Isonville). This 5th class city and seat of Elliott Co is on KY 7, 132 mi e of downtown Louisville. It was settled in the 1820s at what was then the head of navigation of the Little Sandy R and named, by the time it was chartered by legislative act in 1850, for the "fishhook curve" of the r at that point. On Apr 5, 1869, this site was chosen for the seat of the new co over nearby Newfoundland on the basis of a generous offer of land by its proprietor, James K. Hunter. It was reinc as Martinsburg in 1872 to honor John P. Martin (1811–62), US congressman and later state senator from Floyd Co. However, since the po was est as Sandy Hook on Jan 12, 1874, there being another Martinsburg in Kentucky at that time, the town soon reassumed the Sandy Hook name. Some residents have long suggested that the Martinsburg name was also derived from the abundance of purple martins that once had threatened to take over the little village until some of the men caught them by the sackful and disposed of them. 410, 696, 794, 1412.

Sassafras (Knott): *saes*/ə/fraes, *saes*/ə/frəs (Vicco). This coal town with po is on Carr Fork of the North Fork of the Kentucky R, 7½ mi ssw of Hindman. On Mar 27, 1879, Manton Cornett is said to have est the po under a large sassafras tree at the mouth of Sassafras Creek, a branch of Carr Fork. Around the turn of the cent it was moved 2 mi down the fork to its present site at the mouth of Yellow Creek, and the community bearing its name grew up around it. 1130, 1288.

Sassafras Ridge (Fulton): *saes*/ə/fraes *rihdj* (Bondurant). This hamlet, centered at the jct of KY 94 and 653, 7 mi w of Hickman, has always been known locally as Sassafras Ridge for the trees that once grew there. Yet for some 35 years, until 1971, it was identified as Western on state highway maps for the local school est in 1935. The community is not known to have ever had its own po. 668.

Sasser (Laurel): *saes*/ər (Blackwater). This po, 1¼ mi s of KY 80 and 10 mi ese of

London, was est on Apr 14, 1902, with Malinda Gilbert, pm, and named for a local family. 1282.

Savage (Clinton): *saev*/ədj (Savage). This extinct po was on the present KY 696 and Duvall Creek (Stockton Valley), 4 mi e of Albany. It was est on Aug 14, 1882, by storekeeper George W. Savage, and named for one or more local families living at the head of the valley. It closed in 1951. 1263.

Savageville (Webster). See *Providence*

Savoyard (Metcalf): sə/*voy*/ərd, sə/*void* (Sulphur Well). This hamlet with extinct po at the jct of KY 314 and 1243, 10 mi nw of Edmonton, was first called Cross Plains, probably for its location at the northern edge of the Barrens (see *Barren Co*). For much of the 19th cent it was known as Chicken Bristle [*chihk*/ən *brihs*/əl], allegedly for the practice of leaving the pin feathers or bristles on chickens hurriedly killed and carelessly prepared for customers by an early 19th cent stagecoach inn. The Cross Plains po, in operation from 1869 to 1882, was reest as Savoyard on May 3, 1886, and named for a native son, Eugene W. Newman (1845–1923), a Washington correspondent for several American newspapers and respected political writer who wrote under the pseudonym of Savoyard. 142, 192.

Sawyer (McCreary): *saw*/yər (Sawyer). This po on KY 896, 13½ mi nne of Whitley City, was est on Dec 14, 1891, and named for its first pm, Thomas W. Sawyer, or his family.

Saxton (Whitley): *saex*/tən (Saxton). This hamlet with L&N RR switching station and extinct po is on KY 1804 and the Clear Fork of the Cumberland R, just e of I 75 and US 25W, and 7 mi s of Williamsburg. The name was applied to the station est in 1883. Co historians assume that, given the absence of Saxton families in the area, the name was imported by the rr co. or, possibly, was a misrendering of the common local family name Sexton. The po opened on June 6, 1889, with Henry L. Manning, pm. 1267, 1380.

Sayers Depot PO (Nelson). See *Deatsville*

Scalf (Knox): skaef (Scalf). This hamlet with po is on KY 223 and the Middle Fork of Stinking Creek, 2½ mi above its mouth, and 10 mi ene of Barbourville. Its po was est on July 13, 1883, as Scalfton with Peter Scalf, pm. It was discontinued in 1884 and reest as Scalf at or near the same site on Dec 23, 1897, with James M. Scalf, pm. 1409.

Scalfton PO (Knox). See *Scalf*

Schley (Logan): shleye, sleye (Dot). This settlement on the Red R, 10 mi s of Russellville, at the jct of KY 96 and 591, developed around a water-powered gristmill built by John Bailey, a Revolutionary War veteran, later acquired by the Orndorff family from Maryland. A po est there on June 21, 1898, by Felix G. Anderson, was named for Rear Adm. Winfield Scott Schley (1839–1911), who would come to fame in the Spanish-American War battle of Santiago fought about 2 weeks later. The po closed in 1904. 206, 1344.

Schochoh (Logan): *shahk*/oh (Adairville). This hamlet with extinct po lies at the jct of KY 663 and 664, 8 mi sse of Russellville. The po was est as Schochoh (though it was actually recorded as Shochoh) on July 1, 1875, with Marcellus E. Orndorff, pm, at the suggestion of Thomas O. Townsend for the biblical towns variously identified as Schocho, Soco, Shoco, Socho, and Sochoh. The po closed in 1904. 206, 1344, 1427.

Science Hill (Pulaski): *sah*/əns *hihl* (Science Hill). This 6th class city with po is on KY 635 and 1247, 4 mi n of Somerset. The name is said to have been applied to this vicinity by William J. Bobbitt, a scientist who had spent some time there collecting and analyzing rocks. William B. Gragg gave the name to the local po, which he est on June 19, 1874. The town was inc in 1882. 1410.

Scott County: skaht. 286 sq mi. Pop. 20,200. Seat: Georgetown. Scott Co was est in 1792 from part of Woodford Co, and was named for Gen. Charles Scott (1739–1813), Revolutionary War officer and Kentucky's 4th governor (1808–1812).

Scottsburg (Caldwell): *skahts*/bergh (Princeton East). This hamlet with extinct po on KY 91, 2½ mi se of Princeton, lies close to an Illinois Central RR station. Near here was an important stagecoach stop between Hopkinsville and Paducah that may have borne the Scottsburg name. The name was definitely applied to the station that was located there on land acquired in 1871 from Marquess LaFayette and Aaron, the sons of pioneer Stallard Scott (1790–1858), for whom it was probably named. On July 22, 1872, the local po was est by Joseph H. Miller. This was discontinued in 1917. 1196, 1278.

Scott's Station (Jessamine). See *Wilmore*

Scottsville (Allen): *skahts*/vihl (Scottsville). This 4th class city and seat of Allen Co is on US 31E and 231, 100 mi ssw of downtown Louisville. Settled in 1797, it was the site of an early stagecoach stop and relay station. Its central location on Bays Fork in newly organized Allen Co inspired its choice as the seat. The town was laid off in 1816 and named for Kentucky's 4th governor, Gen. Charles Scott (1739–1813), and its po was est in that year as Allen Court House or Scottsville with Daniel M. Jones, pm. Though it appeared on Munsell's 1818 Kentucky map as Scottsville, the earliest references to the place in the records of the Kentucky legislature omit the medial "s" as do some later maps. 101, 596.

Scranton (Menifee): *skraen*/tən (Scranton). This settlement with po, on Slab Camp Branch of Beaver Creek, just n of KY 1274 and 5 mi ene of Frenchburg, is all that remains of a thriving late 19th cent lumber town founded by lumbermen brought in from Scranton, Pennsylvania, to run the local sawmill. It was first called Slab Camp. The local po, whose precise location is unknown, was est as Mifflin on Apr 27, 1899, with George A. Williams, pm. On Oct 13 of that year it moved to and/or was renamed Scranton. 656, 1283.

Scuffletown (Henderson): *skuhf*/əl/town (Newburg). Nothing remains of this early Ohio R settlement that grew up around Jonathan Stott's tavern above the mouth of Green R. The tavern was an early 19th cent rendezvous for the rougher class of rivermen whose regular Saturday night free-for-alls gave the community the only name it is said to have ever had. The Scuffletown po was in operation from 1868 to 1914. 12, 1216.

Seagrave (Harlan). See *Highsplint*

Seaville (Washington): *see*/vəl (Ashbrook). This extinct po on KY 390, 16 mi ne of Springfield, was est on Mar 16, 1874, and probably named for its first pm, Leonard H. Sea, or his family. It was discontinued in 1914.

Sebastians Branch (Breathitt): sə/*baes*/chənz *braench* (Canoe). This hamlet with po is on KY 315 and the Middle Fork of the Kentucky R, just below the mouth of Sebastian Branch (*sic*), 9 mi sw of Jackson. The po was est in 1947 with Walter Sebastian, pm, and named for the stream, which had probably been named for John Sebastian of an important local family. 1147.

Sebree (Webster): *see*/bree (Sebree). This 5th class city with po is centered at the jct of US 41 and KY 56, 9½ mi ne of Dixon. It was founded in 1868 by William Scott and Col. E. G. Sebree and laid off for settlement when the L&N RR was built through in Oct of that year. It was to be called Springdale for the local mineral springs, but a po of this name already existed in Mason Co. The Webster Co po was first est as McBride on Aug 25, 1869, with James H. Priest, pm, but was renamed Sebree the following year for the Colonel, a Trenton native who was the first president of the St. Bernard Mining Co. of Earlington and influential in bringing the rr into that section of the state. The town was inc in 1871. 62, 1174.

Seco (Letcher): *see*/koh (Jenkins West). This coal town with po is on US 119 and Boone Fork, 1½ mi from its confluence with the North Fork of the Kentucky R, and 5½ mi ne of Whitesburg. It was founded in 1915 by A. D. Smith and Harry Laviers of the South East Coal Co. for which it was named. The po was est on Oct 2, 1915, with Dr. Benjamin Franklin Wright, the co.'s physician and later a political power in Letcher Co, as pm. 74, 671, 1265.

Sedalia (Graves): səd/*ăl*/yə (Farmington). This village with po centered at the jct of KY 97, 339, and 381, 5½ mi s of Mayfield, may have grown up around its po, est on Mar 5, 1879. It was recently disincorporated. The suggestion that it was named for Sedalia, Missouri, has never been substantiated, but co historians cannot account for the name in any other way. A local folk etymology, hardly taken seriously by anyone, is that the young men of the area were much taken by a local beauty named Dalia and asked where they were going of a night, they would say "to see Dalia." According to Ramsay, the Missouri city was named in 1857 by its founder, Gen. George R. Smith for his daughter Sarah, nicknamed "Sed." He preferred the Latin ending to the undistinguished "ville" that he is said to have first considered. 181, 1228.

Select (Ohio): *see*/lehk(t) (Flener). This settlement with extinct po was on KY 505, 10 mi se of Hartford. The po was est on Feb 10, 1885 with Lafayette Jones, pm. According to one tradition, when several names had been successively rejected by the Post Office Department, the petitioners suggested that the authorities furnish a list of acceptable names; this they did with instructions to "select one of them." The local people apparently stopped at the first word. Or, more likely, several names were submitted to the department with the request that the authorities make the selection. 1245, 1400.

Seminary (Clinton): *sehm*/ən/ehr/ee (Wolf Creek Dam). This settlement with extinct po is on KY 90, 6 mi nw of Albany. Shortly before 1900 the Methodist Church purchased land in the vicinity to est a college. For some reason the school was located in Columbia in Adair Co instead and became Lindsey-Wilson College. But the community was named Seminary anyway. The Seminary po was est on Jan 25, 1936, with Paul M. Pennycuff, pm, and closed in 1966. 1263.

Sergent (Letcher): *s3*/djənt (Mayking). This coal town with po is on the North Fork of the Kentucky R at the mouth of Webb Branch, some 3 mi ne of Whitesburg. Founded in 1886 and, with its po est on May 29, 1890, named for a prominent local family, it was a coal co. town from 1917 to 1930. 74, 1218, 1265.

Seventy Six (Clinton): *sehv*/ən/tee *sihx* (Wolf Creek Dam). This hamlet with extinct po is centered at the jct of KY 734 and 1286, 6 mi n of Albany. The po was originally located about a mi sw of what has long been called Seventy Six Falls. Actually, historians tell us, the falls of the Indian R that dropped "over a rocky shelf and into a deep gorge below" were more like 84 ft in height, though they could have measured 76 ft at the time the name was first applied. The vicinity was settled around 1806 by John Semple, who built water-powered grist and cotton mills and a store and laid out a town around the falls in 1817. On Apr 27, 1830, Joseph M. Goodson est a po there he called Goodson, which Charles D. Semple renamed Seventy Six in 1834. In 1890 Iverson L. Warinner moved the po to a large store he built about a mi up on the present KY 734.

The po closed in 1952. At least 2 other explanations have been offered for the unusual name by those who claim that the po was named prior to the falls. According to the late J. W. Wells, the po was "named for the station number in the original survey where they had built a shop and lodging quarters." Others insist that the name refers to the year of the Declaration of Independence. 124, 181, 223, 469, 1263.

Sewellton (Russell): *sū*/əl/tən (Jamestown). This settlement with extinct po is on US 127, 3 mi ssw of Jamestown. The po, est on May 14, 1894, and named for its first pm, P. Montfort Sewell, closed in 1958. 1233.

Sextons Creek (Clay): *sehx*/tənz *kreek* (Maulden). This po lies at the jct of KY 577 and 1350 and on Little Sexton Creek, about 2 mi above its confluence with Sexton Creek, a branch of the South Fork of the Kentucky R, 10½ mi n of Manchester. It was est on May 24, 1828 (or earlier), as Section Creek with Henry Clark, pm. Postal officials corrected this obvious misnomer in 1843 as Sexton Creek for the creek, which is said to have been named for a local family by 1815. 1418.

Shackelford PO (Casey). See *Gilpin*

Shady Grove (Crittenden): *shā*/dee *ghrohv* (Shady Grove). This hamlet lies on KY 139, nearly on the Caldwell Co line, and 10 mi e of Marion. The po was est on Sept 29, 1852, by Miles Malin and named for a grove of shade trees in the vicinity. It closed in 1950. 1324.

Shake Rag (Todd). See *Claymour*

Shakertown (Logan). See *South Union*

Shakertown (Mercer). See *Pleasant Hill*

Shanty (Henderson). See *Spottsville*

Sharer (Butler): *shε*/ə (Sugar Grove). This recently closed po on KY 1083, 11½ mi s of Morgantown, was est on Feb 15, 1900, and named for its first pm, Moses J. Sharer, or his family.

Sharkey (Fleming and Rowan): *shahrk*/ee (Farmers). This scattered community is centered at the jct of KY 158 and 801, 15½ mi sw of Flemingsburg and 7 mi wnw of Morehead. The Sharkey po, est in Fleming Co July 10, 1913, with Lewis H. Ratliff, pm, was discontinued in 1927 and reest in Rowan Co the following year with Samuel N. Sorrell, pm. It returned to Fleming Co in 1939, where it closed in 1958. According to local tradition, it was named for a resident, a professional boxer who fought under the name St. Ratliff Sharkey. Yet no one now recalls a family of Sharkeys ever having lived in that vicinity. A less likely theory is that the po was named for a champion rooster. 1369.

Sharon Grove (Todd): *shε*/ən ghrohv, *shaer*/ən ghrohv (Sharon Grove). This crossroads village with po, 7 mi nne of Elkton, was named for its location near a big grove of oak trees and the biblical name Sharon. The po was est as Sharon Grove on July 2, 1869 with Benjamin F. Smith, pm, but was changed to Sharongrove by orders of the Post Office Department on Feb 4, 1896. The community was inc on Apr 7, 1882. Oldtimers still refer to the vicinity by its nickname Frog Level, reflecting its low and swampy terrain that produced a surfeit of frogs. 1304.

Sharpsburg (Bath): *shahrps*/bergh (Sharpsburg). This 6th class city with po is on KY 11, 9 mi wnw of Owingsville. Moses Sharp (1747–1820), a Revolutionary War veteran from Virginia who had settled in the area in 1780, laid out the town in 1814 on his land. He is said to have named it Bloomfield for the "luxuriant growth of vegetation and the profusion of wild flowers which grew in the open spaces of what was then a vast forest." However, the po est there on Jan 16, 1821, by Josiah Reed was named for Sharp. The town was formally est by the Kentucky legislature in 1825. 15, 857.

Sharpsville (Washington): *shahrps*/vəl (Cardwell). This extinct po on KY 53, just s of the Chaplin R, 13½ mi ne of Springfield, was est on Mar 18, 1858, and probably named for its first pm, William Sharp, who had arrived shortly before from western Kentucky. It closed in 1907. 1314.

Shawhan (Bourbon): *shâh*/hahn, *shoh*/hahn (Shawhan). This hamlet with extinct po on KY 1893, 5½ mi n of Paris, was named for Daniel Shawhan (1738–91), pioneer settler and large landowner, as a condition made to the Kentucky Central (now L&N) RR by his descendants who donated the local depot and right-of-way. The first po to serve this vicinity was Townsend, est on Dec 2, 1854 by George F. Lilley at an unknown location, possibly on Townsend Creek, 2 mi w. It is said to have been named for an early preemptioner. In Oct 1855 Lilley renamed the po Lilleys Station, probably moving it to the tracks, and 2 years later it became Shawhan. 538.

Shawnee Run PO (Mercer). See *Pleasant Hill*

Sheaffers Mill PO (Ohio). See *Olaton*

Shelbiana (Pike): shehl/bee/*aen*/uh (Millard). This hamlet with rr station and po lies just e of the confluence of Shelby Creek, for which it was named, and the Levisa Fork of the Big Sandy R, 3 mi s of Pikeville. The local po was est on Nov 14, 1905, with William F. Morell, pm, soon after the C&O RR reached this point. The local station has long been called simply Shelby, and like the creek was named for Kentucky's first governor, Isaac Shelby (1750–1826). 1198, 1444.

Shelby (Pike). See *Shelbiana*

Shelby City (Boyle). See *Junction City*

Shelby County: *shehl*/bee. 385 sq mi. Pop 23,775. Seat: Shelbyville. This co was est in 1792 from part of Jefferson Co. It was one of the 7 co organized in the new state's first legislative session and was named for Gen. Isaac Shelby (1750–1826), veteran of the Revolutionary War and Indian campaigns, and Kentucky's first and 5th governor (1792–96 and 1812–16).

Shelby Gap (Pike): *shehl*/bee ghaep (Jenkins East). This hamlet with po at the jct of US 23/119 and KY 197, just s of the head of Shelby Creek, 17 mi s of Pikeville, was named for the creek (see *Shelbiana*). The po was est on the Letcher Co line as Jewell on Aug 15, 1882, and was moved 1½ mi down Elkhorn Creek and renamed Shelby Gap in 1914. 1456.

Shelbyville (Shelby): *shehl*/bee/vihl (Shelbyville). This 4th class industrial city and seat of Shelby Co is on US 60, just n of I 64, and 27 mi e of downtown Louisville. It was est as a town in 1792 on land donated by William Shannon, ending a long dispute with nearby Squire Boone's Station for the new co's seat. Like the co, it honors Kentucky's first governor, Isaac Shelby (1750–1826). The po was est on Apr 1, 1801, with James Wardlow, pm, and the town was inc in 1846. 228.

Shepherdsville (Bullitt): *shehp*/ərdz/vihl (Shepherdsville). This 4th class industrial city and seat of Bullitt Co is on Salt R just w of I 65 and 17 mi s of downtown Louisville. Attracted by its proximity to the salt works at nearby Bullitt's Lick, Adam Shepherd built a mill and store on this part of a 900-acre tract he had acquired and laid out the town which bears his name. It was chartered in 1793 and became the seat of the newly est co in 1796. On Jan 1, 1806, Thomas T. Grayson became the first pm. 31.

Shepola (Pulaski): shəp/*oh*/lə (Delmer). This extinct po was about ¼ mi s of KY 80 and 4½ mi w of Somerset. Local storekeeper Edd "Shep" Sheppard's nickname was submitted to the Post Office Department along with those of Ola Burton and other local residents. Postal authorities are said to have combined Shep and Ola to form the name and appointed Shep's wife, Grace as the first pm on Feb 10, 1926. 1410.

Sherburne (Fleming): *shз*/bən, *shз*/bern (Sherburne). Little remains of this town on KY 11 and the Licking R, opposite the mouth of Flat Creek and 9½ mi ssw of Flemingsburg. By 1807 a water-powered gristmill had been built at this site by Robert Andrews, a native of Sherburne, New York, to be joined later by a sawmill and other enterprises. His son John, who succeeded his father in the operation of the family's businesses, est the po of Sherburne Mills on Apr 1, 1815, and founded the town probably to accommodate his workers. The town was inc in 1847. In 1879 the po name was clipped to Sherburne, which it retained until it closed in 1958. 379, 1369.

Sherburne Mills (Fleming). See *Sherburne*

Sheridan (Crittenden): *shehr*/ə/dən (Salem). This hamlet with recently discontinued po strung out along KY 297, about 5 mi w of Marion, may early have been called Dog Trot for the style of the log dwellings along the rd. It was officially named before or when the po was est on Mar 13, 1888, by storekeeper and leading resident Richard Bebout for his favorite Civil War general, Philip Sheridan. 466.

Shields (Harlan). See *Lejunior*

Shiloh (Anderson). See *Sinai*

Shiloh (Webster). See *Lisman*

Shipley (Clinton): *shihp*/lee (Albany). This extinct po lay at the jct of KY 553 and the Lettered Oak Rd, 4 mi wsw of Albany. The po was est on Oct 31, 1892, with Samuel W. Bristow, pm, and named for several local families. It closed in 1934. 1263.

Shively (Jefferson): *sheyev*/lee (Louisville West). This 4th class city with extinct po is centered at the jct of US 31W/60, 7th Street Rd, and Crums Lane, 5 mi ssw of downtown Louisville. Here Jacob and Christian William Shively settled around 1780, and the area of large estates that developed around Christian's mill and tavern was first called Shively Precinct. In 1897 St. Helen's Catholic Church was est at the jct, and almost at once became the focal point of the community and the name by which it was to be identified for the next 40 years. Since the name St. Helens was already in use in Lee Co, the po est on Oct 30, 1897, was called Shively instead. In 1938 residents petitioning for inc to prevent annexation by Louisville, though still preferring St. Helens, again settled for Shively, by which the community, now without po, is officially known. 628, 727.

Shonn PO (Harlan). See *Loyall*

Shopville (Pulaski): *shahp*/vəl (Shopville). This hamlet with po is on KY 80 and Flat Lick Creek, 6½ mi ne of Somerset. The po was est on Apr 8, 1865, with William Hargis, pm, and named for the local blacksmith shop, then a very popular meeting place for area residents. 1410.

Short Creek (Grayson): *shawrt* kreek (McDaniels). This hamlet with extinct po is centered at the jct of KY 54 and 79, 9½ mi wnw of Leitchfield. The vicinity was settled in the early 19th cent and the Short Creek po, est on Nov 12, 1849, with Henry Haynes, pm, was named for its location near the head of Short Creek, a wet water branch of Spring Fork of Rough R. It is not known why the creek was so named since it is 12 mi in length, not particularly short. 610, 1307.

Shoulder Blade PO (Breathitt). See *Juan*

Shrewsbury (Grayson): *shrūz*/behr/ee (Caneyville, Ready). This hamlet with extinct po is on KY 187, 8 mi ssw of Leitchfield. As a thriving village it was first called Territory, but was renamed for Co Judge James W. Shrewsbury when the po was est on June 30, 1881. It was inc from 1895 to 1901. 611, 1307.

Shytown (Shelby). See *Claysville*

Sibert (Clay): *sah*/bert (Hima). This coal town and terminus of the Horse Creek Branch of the L&N RR's Cumberland Valley Division are 2 mi up KY 80 and Horse Creek from Horse Creek Jct just s of Manchester. The recently discontinued po was est on Aug 20, 1920, and named, like the station, for a local family. 1259, 1329.

Sidell (Clay): *seye/dehl* (Manchester). This recently discontinued po was on Rader Creek, a branch of Little Goose Creek, 4½ mi nw of Manchester. Robert P. Rawlings est the po on Nov 13, 1890, in his store down the creek from its final location and named it for a local family. 1259, 1329, 1418.

Sideview (Montgomery): *sahd*/vyū (Sideview). This hamlet with extinct po lies at the jct of US 460 and KY 645, 5 mi nw of Mt. Sterling. The po was est as Side View on Oct 22, 1858, with Jetson McDonald, pm, and closed in 1914. This probably descriptive name is now spelled as one word. 1237.

Sidney (Pike): *sihd*/nee (Belfry). This hamlet with po is centered at the jct of US 119 and KY 468, at the mouth of Road Fork of Big Creek, 11½ mi ne of Pikeville. The po, est on June 30, 1892, is said to have been named for the grandson of Thomas B. Pinson, the first pm. 1456.

Siler (Knox): *sahl*/ər (Corbin). This hamlet with extinct po is centered at the jct of old US 25E and KY 830, just s of the new route of US 25E, and 8½ mi nw of Barbourville. It was est as Silers Station on the L&N RR and honored a prominent Knox Co family. As another Siler po was already in operation in Whitley Co, the po est here on May 13, 1899, was named Place [plās] (derivation unknown), though the community and station continued to be called Siler and Silers. In 1970 the Board on Geographic Names approved the official use of Siler since the Place po had been discontinued in 1963. 1004, 1409.

Siler (Whitley): *sahl*/ər (Frakes). This hamlet with po is centered at the jct of KY 92 and 904, 11 mi ese of Williamsburg. Until the po was est on Oct 5, 1905, with Owen Peace, pm, local people referred to their home as Poplar Creek, for the local stream. Siler was named for J. W. Siler, local magistrate and preacher, probably a descendant of Jacob Siler who had come from the Yadkin Valley of North Carolina before 1795 and settled originally on nearby Mud Creek. 128, 1380.

Silers Station (Knox). See *Siler*

Silerville (McCreary). See *Strunk*

Siloam (Greenup): *sah*/lohm (Portsmouth). This community with extinct po and C&O RR station is in the Ohio R bottom, just n of US 23 and 11 mi nnw of Greenup. It was probably settled around 1800 by Mackoys from Campbell Co, Virginia. The local po was est as Little on June 24, 1889, by an Ohio riverboat captain, William Wallace Little (1825–97), who became its first pm. On Apr 22, 1910, it was renamed Siloam by its then pm-storekeeper Henry Green Richards for the local church which has always borne this biblical name. The po was discontinued in 1958. 23, 1451.

Silver Grove (Campbell): *sihl*/vər *ghrohv* (Newport). This 5th class city with po is in the Ohio R bottom just above the mouth of Four Mile Creek and 3 mi n of Alexandria. A summer resort at the mouth of Four Mile, named for a large grove of silver poplar trees, in turn gave its name to the town created by the C&O RR in 1912 to house the employees of its relocated yard and shops. The Silver Grove po was est on July 17, 1913, with Frank E. Neltner, pm. The town has been inc since 1950. The local C&O station is called Stevens. 985.

Silver Lake (Kenton). See *Erlanger*

Simmons (Ohio): *sihm*/ənz (Paradise). This former coal town with extinct po is on US 62 and the Illinois Central Gulf RR, 6 mi s of Hartford. It was owned by the Broadway Coal Mining Co. and named for its president, William Simmons of Memphis, Tennessee. The po was est on May 14, 1908, with Charles M. Mallam, pm, and discontinued in 1930 about the time the mines were closed. 640, 905, 1400.

Simpson County: *sihm(p)*/sən. 236 sq mi. Pop 14,627. Seat: Franklin. This co was est in 1819 from parts of Allen, Logan, and Warren cos and named for Capt. John Simpson, Speaker of the Kentucky House (1811) who was elected to the US Congress in 1812 but did not serve. He was one of the 9 officers killed in the Battle of River Raisin, Jan 22, 1813, for whom Kentucky cos were named.

Simpsonville (Shelby): *sihm*/sən/vihl (Simpsonville). This 6th class industrial and commercial city with po is on US 60, just n of I 64 and 6 mi w of Shelbyville. The town was founded in 1816 on the site of a stagecoach relay station and tavern and named for Capt. John Simpson, a Virginia-born Shelbyville lawyer and 4-term state legislator who was elected to the US Congress in 1812 only to be killed at the Battle of River Raisin in Jan 1813. The po was est in 1821 and the town was inc in 1832. 228.

Sinai (Anderson): *sah*/nee/eye (Ashbrook). This extinct po was on Beaver Creek and KY 53, nearly 8 mi sw of Lawrenceburg. It was est on Oct 24, 1876, by James M. Wash, and until it closed in 1973 it served a community dually known as Sinai and Shiloh. Both are scriptural names but it is not known why or by whom they were applied. The name Shiloh may have been derived from the Shiloh Christian Church organized around 1870, though some think it commemorated the Civil War battle of Shiloh. 958, 1387.

Skaggs PO (Grayson). See *Millerstown*

Skeggs Creek PO (Barren). See *Temple Hill*

Skibo (Muhlenberg). See *Luzerne*

Skilesville (Muhlenberg): *skahlz*/vəl (Rochester). This once thriving village is on KY 70 and the Green R, just below the mouth of Mud R and 14 mi e of Greenville. Early considered a part of the Butler Co community of *Rochester* ½ mi above, it was founded and named by 1837 and its po est on June 18, 1840, with Jacob Luce, pm. It was named for James Rumsey Skiles, a Warren Co resident, who introduced the first steamboat on the Green R and was influential in promoting navigation thereon. The po was discontinued on several occasions, during one of which, from 1855 to 1865, a po called Model Mills served the area. Little is known of the latter except that the name referred to the local grist and textile mills. Skilesville was inc in 1876. Its po was closed for good in 1907. 189, 1253.

Skillet (Ballard). See *Bandana*

Skillman (Hancock): *skihl*/mən (Cannelton). This extinct po and defunct L&N RR station were at the edge of the Ohio R bottom, some 3 mi e of Hawesville. The station that the then Louisville St. Louis & Texas Ry built in 1888 was named for A. B. Skillman who donated the land, and this name was also applied to the po est on July 26, 1889, with John C. Jarboe, pm. The name now identifies only the r bottom. 953, 1332.

Skullbuster (Scott): *skuhl*/buhst/ər (Stamping Ground). This rural settlement lies at the jct of the Skinnersburg, Stonewall, and Glass rds, on Lytle's Fork of Eagle Creek, 7½ mi nnw of Georgetown. Its name is derived from the original name of the Corinth Christian Church, sometime between 1837 and 1842. According to legend, a very tall man, on entering the original log structure, "struck his head against the cap of the door" after a friend, John Cartenhour, had warned him to "look out or he would bust his skull." This community has never had its own po. This is not a nickname; no other name is known to have been applied to the community. 13, 1293.

Skylight (Oldham): *skah*/leyet (Owen). This hamlet with extinct po on US 42, 7 mi wnw of LaGrange, is believed to have been first called Tippecanoe by early residents who had served with Gen. William Henry Harrison in his Indian campaigns. On Feb 7, 1854, the po was est as Oldhamburg [*ohld*/əm/bergh], probably for the co, with William Ladd, Jr., pm. This was discontinued in 1870, but when another po was opened to serve the community in 1888, it was given the name Skylight. No one seems to know why this name was selected, but a story is told of how "a group of residents were meeting on a very stormy day when a lady, looking out the window, observed 'how light the sky seems to be getting.'" The Skylight po closed in 1925. 1090.

Slab Camp (Menifee). See *Scranton*

Slabtown (Graves). See *Symsonia*

Slap Out (Fulton). See *Crutchfield*

Slaughters (Webster): *slâht*/ərz (Slaughters, Hanson). This 6th class city with po lies just w of US 41 and 9½ mi e of Dixon. According to local tradition, it was named for Gustavus G. Slaughter, local storekeeper, who in 1855 won the right to name the new town and po in a card game with his rival, blacksmith Frederick W. Stiman. The po was est as Slaughtersville on Jan 29, 1856, with Henry A. Prater, pm. Slaughter himself served as pm from 1860 to 1865 and was succeeded by Stiman. Though the po was renamed Slaughters in 1915, the town remained Slaughtersville from its inc in 1861 until 1967 when the Board on Geographic Names reversed an earlier decision and conformed to common usage and the present name of the po. 512, 1174.

Slaughtersville (Webster). See *Slaughters*

Slemp (Perry): slihmp (Tilford). This coal town with po is on KY 699, at the mouth of Owens Branch of Leatherwood Creek, 11 mi sse of Hazard. The po was est on June 26, 1905, with Henry Singleton, pm, and named for C. Bascom Slemp of Big Stone Gap, Virginia, an early coal buyer in that area. 554, 1272.

Slickaway (Fayette). See *Fort Spring*

Slickford (Wayne): *slihk*/fawrd (Powersburg). This hamlet with extinct po is now centered at Ina Stearns's store at the jct of Dry Hollow and Otter Creek, 9½ mi ssw of Monticello. It was named for the large flat rocks in the creek bed just below the store, which were so slick that horses and pedestrians alike would slip on them as they forded the creek. The po, est on June 23, 1892, with Carter T. Denney, pm, may first have been located at what is now called Lower Slickford, ½ mi below the mouth of Dry Hollow. It closed in 1956. 1383, 1389.

Slick Rock (Barren): *slihk rahk* (Hiseville). This settlement with extinct po on Beaver Creek, 5 mi e of Glasgow, was named for the condition of the rocks there. The po was est on Mar 26, 1867, with Robert W. Biggerstaff, pm. 791.

Slipaway (Fayette). See *Fort Springs*

Sloans Valley (Pulaski): *slohnz vael*/ee (Burnside). This rural settlement with po is on US 27, 9 mi sse of Somerset. It was named for Benjamin Sloan, a Virginian, who, attracted by the local saltpetre deposits, sugar trees, and wild game, settled there around 1789. The po was not est until Feb 5, 1879, with George P. Lester, pm. 978, 1410.

Slowgo PO (Monroe). See *Akersville*

Smalley PO (Floyd). See *Martin*

Smilax (Leslie): *smahl*/aex (Hyden East). This hamlet with po lies at the mouth of Polls Creek, a branch of Cutshin Creek, 5 mi ese of Hyden. The po was est on Apr 18, 1902, with John J. Baker, pm, and probably named for a locally found plant or vine of the smilax family. 29.

Smile (Rowan): smahl (Cranston). This recently discontinued po on KY 785 and Big Brushy Creek, a branch of the North Fork of Triplett Creek, 5 mi nnw of Morehead, was est on Sept 12, 1913, with Lydia J. Caudill, pm. According to tradition, local residents smiled when they heard that their application for a po had been approved.

Smith (Harlan): smihth (Rose Hill). This hamlet with po and a station on the Martins Fork Branch of the L&N RR's Cumberland Valley Division is on KY 987, just e of Martins Fork of the Cumberland R and 7½ mi sse of Harlan. The po, est on June 2, 1897, with Noble L. Smith, pm, was named for a local family. 1173.

Smith Branch (Greenup). See *Lloyd*

Smithburg (Whitley). See *Jellico*

Smithfield (Henry): *smihth*/feeld (Smithfield). This 6th class city with po is centered at the jct of KY 322 and 1861, 5 mi sw of New Castle. The community and its po, est on Mar 10, 1851, with Fleet H. Goodridge, pm, were named for Thomas Smith (1790–1850), a New Castle merchant and president of the Louisville & Frankfort (later L&N) RR, who was responsible for getting the tracks laid through this section of Henry Co. Inc in 1870, Smithfield is now little more than a hamlet. 59, 948.

Smithland (Livingston): *smihth*/lən(d) (Smithland). This 6th class city and seat of Livingston Co lies at the confluence of the Cumberland and Ohio rs, 153 mi wsw of downtown Louisville. An earlier settlement called Smithland, 3 mi below, was laid off by Zachariah Cox around 1780 but was extinct in less than 20 years. By this time Thomas Bullard had built a one-room log cabin at the present Smithland site, and a po of this name was est on Oct 1, 1802, with Isaac Bullard, pm. On Nov 4, 1805, the town was inc. It was named for James Smith, a Pennsylvanian, who in 1766–67 was one of the first to explore the lower reaches of the Cumberland and Tennessee rs. With the creation of Crittenden Co from Livingston Co in 1842, the seat was moved from Salem to benefit from Smithland's strategic location and greater promise of growth and prosperity. 138, 286, 1443.

Smith Mills (Henderson): *smihth mihlz* (Smith Mills). This village with po centered at the jct of KY 136 and 359, 5½ mi w of Henderson, is now locally called The Point. It was first called Roelosson's Settlement for its late 18th cent founder, William Roelosson, a Hessian soldier who deserted the British cause in the American Revolution to join the Continental Army. It was renamed for Col. Robert Smith's horse-powered gristmill and steam-operated sawmill there sometime before 1830. Smith, a veteran of the Battle of New Orleans, served as a local magistrate and sheriff. The po was est as Smith's Mills on Dec 23, 1830, with Smith's son Hosea as pm. After an intermittent existence, the po was renamed Smith Mills in 1893. 12, 1216.

Smith Ridge (Taylor). See *Atchison*

Smithsboro (Knott): *smihths*/buhr/ə (Blackey). The site of this extinct community on KY 15, at the mouth of Smith Branch of Carr Fork of the North Fork of the Kentucky R, and 6½ mi s of Hindman, is now under Carr Fork Lake. Its recently discontinued po, est on Oct 15, 1902, with George Francis, pm, was named for the brothers Jeremiah and Thomas Smith, local landowning sons of William and Millie (Combs) Smith, early Perry Co residents. 1262.

Smiths Creek (Carter): *smihth* kreek (Wesleyville). This hamlet with po lies at the head of Smith Creek, 6 mi from its confluence with Buffalo Creek, a branch of Tygarts Creek, and 15 mi nw of Grayson. On July 7, 1887, Dr. Hugh H. Williams est the po, which he named for the creek, which in turn was named for an early local family. No explanation has been given for the terminal "s" in the po name and most people today refer to the place without it. 1366.

Smiths Grove (Warren): *smihths ghrohv* (Smiths Grove). This 6th class city with po is on KY 101 and the L&N RR, just n of I 65 and 10½ mi ene of Bowling Green. The po was est on Sept 24, 1829, with Benjamin Ford, pm, and named for a grove at the foot of the small knob w of the present town and for the original landowner. This po was discontinued in 1834. A po est there as Cool Spring in 1836 was renamed Smiths Grove in 1844. The town was inc in 1871. 836, 1191.

Smiths Station (Garrard). See *Bryantsville*

Smiths Station (Oldham). See *Pewee Valley*

Smithtown (Garrard). See *Bryantsville*

Smith Town (McCreary): *smihth town* (Barthell). This hamlet with extinct po is centered at the jct of KY 92 and 791, 2 mi sw of Whitley City. It was named for the local Smith family, perhaps for Crit Smith, large landowner and storekeeper there when the po was est on May 20, 1922. This po closed in 1977. 1384.

Smithville PO (Harlan). See *Bailey Creek*

Smoky Bottom (Martin). See *Lovely*

Smoot Creek PO (Letcher). See *Hot Spot*

Snow (Clinton): snoh (Wolf Creek Dam, Albany). This extinct po was at the jct of US 127 and KY 734, 3½ mi n of Albany. The po, est on Apr 12, 1900, with James W. Stratton, pm, was named for one or more local families. It was discontinued in 1940. 1263.

Social Hill PO (McLean). See *Sacramento*

Soft Shell (Knott): *sâhft shehl* (Handshoe). This po on KY 1087 and Balls Fork of Troublesome Creek, 4 mi nne of Hindman, was est on May 4, 1926, with Sarah Slone, pm, and given the name popularly applied to the Regular Baptists to distinguish them from the Hard Shell or Primitive Baptists. 1391.

Soldier (Carter): *sohl*/djər (Soldier). This village with po on KY 174, 18½ mi wsw of Grayson, is rooted in the arrival of the Elizabethtown Lexington & Big Sandy (now C&O) RR in 1880. The local station is said to have been est as Triplett, but as this name was already in use by a po in Rowan Co, John W. Richards chose the name Soldier for his po and became the first pm on May 17, 1880. The true derivation of this name may never be known but a local legend derives it from that of a rr worker's dog that had been killed there a short time before. 734, 1119.

Somerset (Pulaski): *suhm*/er/seht (Somerset, Delmer). This 3rd class city and seat of Pulaski Co is on US 27, KY 80, and the e end of the Cumberland Parkway, 94 mi se of downtown Louisville. The town was created as the co's seat in 1801 on 40 acres donated by William Dodson and, according to local tradition, named for the home co of a group of settlers from New Jersey as a consolation for not getting the seat located on their land just n of the present city. The po was est on Jan 1, 1803, with Archibald M. Sublette, pm. 767, 955.

Somersville (Green). See *Summersville*

Sonora (Hardin): sən/*aw*/rə (Sonora). This 6th class city with po is centered at the jcts of the L&N RR and I 65 with KY 84, and 10 mi s of Elizabethtown. The L&N's main line station and the local po, est on Dec 21, 1859, with William Stuart, pm, are said to have been named for the home state of either a rr contractor of Mexican extraction or a Mexican cook who had been hired to feed the rr construction gangs. At or near this site was the rr construction camp of Buck Snort or Bucksnort with its own po from Aug 5, 1858, till the end of the following year. Two explanations of this name have been offered. One account refers to a herd of tame deer and a construction train engineer who would blow his locomotive's whistle just to hear the "bucks snort." In the other, the early locomotives were likened to snorting bucks, and when the first train arrived at the station site, someone is said to have shouted, "Did you hear that buck snort?" The town of Sonora was inc in 1865. 136.

Sorgho (Daviess): *sahr*/ghoh, *sawr*/ghoh (Owensboro West, Reed). This hamlet with extinct po is centered at the jct of KY 54 and 56, 5 mi w of Owensboro. Around 1868 a factory was opened by Drs. Stirman and Stewart to produce sugar from locally grown sorghum. The village that soon grew up around it and its po, est on July 15, 1869, with Martin Mattingly, pm, were called Sorghotown. In 1883 the po name was shortened to Sorgho. The po was discontinued in 1918. 99, 104.

Sorghotown (Daviess). See *Sorgho*

Sourwood (Clay and Jackson): *sah*/ər/wo͞od, *saer*/wo͞od (Maulden). This settlement extends along Buncomb Creek from Little Sexton Creek in Clay Co past the Jackson Co line, 12 mi n of Manchester and 11½ mi se of McKee. The local po, which was to occupy several locations on both sides of the co line, was est as Ethel on Aug 22, 1890, by William St. John and allegedly named for his oldest daughter. After it was discontinued in 1933, local pressure was exerted for the est of another po. Willie Bond, the local storekeeper, submitted the name Sourwood for the famed fiddle and dance tune, and the po was opened in his store on Buncomb in 1941. It closed in 1957. 499, 1419.

South (Grayson): sowth (Bee Springs). This hamlet with po on KY 187, 10 mi ssw of Leitchfield, was settled in the late 1870s by the Mays, South, and Deweese families and first called Bethel. When the po was est on Oct 24, 1889, it was named for Dr. John W. South, a local physician, or his family, and the community was renamed for the po. 601, 612.

South America (Bell). See *Frakes*

South Carrollton (Muhlenberg): sowth *kaer*/əl/tən (Central City West). This village recently disincorporated, with po, is on US 431 and the Green R, 7 mi n of Greenville. It was founded around 1838 by John Fentress on what was then called Randolph Old Farm. He named it Carrollton for his first grandson, Carroll McCown, the son of Louis McCown, and the South was added to distinguish it from the seat of Carroll Co, which had adopted that name in the same year. In 1848 Fentress had the po of Lewisburg moved from 2 mi up r and renamed for his town, which was inc in the following year. Lewisburg or Kincheloes Bluff, named for pioneer Lewis Kincheloe, was an early Green R landing. A Lewisburgh po was est there on Jan 1, 1805, with James Weir, pm, and a town was laid off around it in 1816–17. 189, 1212, 1253.

South Danville PO (Boyle). See *Junction City*

South Erlanger (Kenton). See *Elsmere*

South Fredonia (Caldwell). See *Fredonia*

Southgate (Campbell): *sowth*/ghāt (Newport). This 4th class city centers on the present US 27, just over 1 mi sse of the Newport po and 7½ mi nnw of the court house at Alexandria. It was est as a city in 1907 and named, it is said, by then Circuit Judge Albert S. Berry, for pioneer landowner Richard Southgate (1773–1857), a New York City-born lawyer who settled in Newport around 1795. It has also been suggested that Judge Berry sought as well to perpetuate the strategic significance of the place as "the southern entrance to Newport" for its location on a principal route between Newport and the bluegrass section of Kentucky. The name may have been doubly appropriate since the family's name was allegedly derived from their ancestors' role as keepers of the s gate of London. The community never had its own po. 127, 969.

South Hill (also called **Bethel**) (Butler): *sowth hihl, behth*/əl (South Hill). This hamlet with extinct po on KY 70, 7 mi sw of Morgantown, was once a prosperous farm trade center called Bethel, presumably for its extant pioneer church. In 1890 John W. Holman purchased 8 acres ¼ mi w of the church and opened a store in which he applied for a po. Since there already was a Bethel po in Bath Co, he asked that his be called South Hill, for its location on the s side of the local hill, and he became the first pm on Nov 13, 1890. Both names now locally identify the community though the po has been closed for several years. 657, 1341.

South Hills (Kenton). See *Fort Wright*

South Kermit (Martin). See *Lovely*

Southland (Grayson). See *Big Clifty*

South Oak PO (Hickman). See *Oakton*

South Park (Jefferson). See *Fairdale*

South Pleasureville (Henry). See *Pleasureville*

South Portsmouth (Greenup): sowth *pawrts*/məth (Portsmouth, Friendship). This village with po, extending for over 1 mi along KY 10, 13 mi nw of Greenup, is directly s of and across the Ohio R from the city of Portsmouth, Ohio. It was first called Springville for the many springs that issued forth from the foot of the nearby hills. One of these, Cooks Springs, gave its name to the first po, est by Thomas B. King on July 25, 1838. This was renamed Springville in 1839 and under this name the town was inc on Mar 3, 1876. The po was discontinued in 1879, and another in the vicinity, est in 1886 as Lawson by Joshua R. Lawson, was renamed Springville the following year. The name South Portsmouth is said to have been applied by the C&O RR after 1900 and the po's name was changed accordingly in 1905. A town called Beattyville, founded in 1849 by Reuben Thomson just below the Springville limits, is now part of South Portsmouth. 22, 23.

South Shore (Greenup): *sowth shawr* (Portsmouth). This extended 6th class city is across the Ohio R from Portsmouth, Ohio, 11 mi nnw of Greenup. The section of this community w of the mouth of Tygarts Creek was a part of Josiah Morton's Revolutionary War grant, which before 1890 was only sparsely settled by Fullertons, Warnocks, and Mortons from the Tygarts Valley. With the coming of the C&O RR and George D. Winn's ferry to Portsmouth in the 1890s, the area began to develop. Winn, petitioning for a po in 1893, is said to have submitted 3 names to the postal authorities—his, Philip Thompson's, and that of brothers Harvey and Harrison Fullerton. Fullerton [*fo͞ol*/ ər/ tən] was chosen, and on July 21 Winn became its first pm. Fullerton was inc briefly in 1919. Meanwhile, between Fullerton and Tygarts Creek, the Taylor Brickyard, started in 1895 by Clyde King, had become the major employer of the area's pop. The Taylor name was applied to the rr station located at the brickyard site. The McCall po, est on May 6, 1907, by Edward A. McCall, became Taylor po on Jan 16, 1930, and was renamed South Shore on Feb 1, 1940. By this time, an area e of the mouth of Tygarts, an old Indian battlefield and burial ground that had been the property of Thomas King, had come to be known as the Upper and Lower Kings Additions and Sand Hill. In Dec 1957 the eastern section of Fullerton and all the land almost to Tygarts Creek was inc as the city of South Shore. According to local historian J. Paul Davis, the South Shore site was developed by James E. Hannah, a local realtor, around 1928, and was named by his wife Hazel for its location on the s shore of the r. On Oct 4, 1957, the Fullerton and South Shore pos were consolidated and in 1958 they became the single po of South Shore. The community, to all intents, now includes its present inc, the Kings Additions, and even Sand Hill to the e. 22, 23, 659, 1447, 1451.

South Town (Henry). See *Pleasureville*

South Union (Logan): sowth *yū*/nyən (South Union). This hamlet with po at the jct of

KY 73 and the L&N RR, just s of US 68, and 11½ mi e of Russellville, has served 2 religious communities. The Shakers, officially the United Society of Believers in Christ's Second Appearing, arrived in this vicinity in 1807 and est their colony first as the Gasper Society, probably for the nearby r, and then as the South Union Society, for the Union Colony in Ohio. The South Union po opened on Apr 1, 1826, with David Smith, pm. The colony disbanded in 1922. A po called Shakertown was in operation for a 5 month period in 1889 and on dissolution its papers were sent to South Union. The Benedictine Order bought the Shaker colony's buildings and opened its St. Maur's Priory (now St. Mark's) here in 1949. 1148.

South Williamson (Pike): sowth *wihl*/yəm/sən (Williamson). This village without po is across the Tug Fork of the Big Sandy R from the city of Williamson, West Virginia, to which its name refers, 1 mi below the mouth of Pond Creek and 17 mi ne of Pikeville.

Spa (Logan): spâh (Sharon Grove). This rural settlement with extinct po is on KY 106, 8 mi nw of Russellville. The po was est on Oct 3, 1890, by Simeon W. Danks and named for the local sulphur springs, which as far as is known were never commercialized. The po closed in 1909. 343, 1344.

Sparksville (Adair): *spahrx*/vəl (Gradyville). This hamlet is centered at the jct of KY 61 and 768, 7 mi sw of Columbia. Its now extinct po was named for Charles W. Sparks who is said to have est it on Aug 11, 1884. 797.

Sparrow (Anderson): *spaer*/əz (Chaplin). This settlement with extinct po is on US 62, 14½ mi wsw of Lawrenceburg. It is not known when the community was settled but it was first called Wardsville for a local family and many persons still refer to it by this name. The po was est as Sparrow on Jan 15, 1883, with James B. Barnett, pm, to honor the many Sparrow families in the vicinity. So identified are these families with this area that the place has also been known as The Sparrows Nest. Though spelled without a terminal ''s'' the name is often pronounced as if it had one. 1387.

Sparta (Gallatin and Owen): *spahrt*/ə (Sanders). This 6th class city with po is centered at the jct of KY 35 and Eagle Creek, 6½ mi s of Warsaw and 9 mi nne of Owenton. Jacob Carlock and party from Virginia's Holston Valley settled around 1800 on the Owen Co side of the creek. This settlement was first called Ross's Mill and then Brock's Station, for David Ross, the local gristmill operator who arrived before 1805, and Granville Brock, who built a log house there around 1818 and later took over the operation of Ross's mill. Another local gristmill called Sparta Mill was probably the source of the name Sparta by which the community was inc on Jan 3, 1852, and the po was est on Feb 19, 1853. This community is now known as Old Sparta. With the location of the Louisville Cincinnati & Lexington or ''Short Line'' (now L&N) RR on the Gallatin Co side of Eagle Creek in 1869, the main section of the community shifted to Gallatin Co. Another po was est there on Jan 13, 1870, and called Sparta Station. The old Sparta po closed in May 1870, and Sparta Station was renamed Sparta in 1881. 87, 102, 795.

Sparta Station PO (Gallatin and Owen). See *Sparta*

Spencer County: *spehn*/sər. 192 sq mi. Pop 5,955. Seat: Taylorsville. This co was est in 1824 from parts of Nelson, Shelby, and Bullitt cos and named for Capt. Spear Spencer, a veteran of most of the post-Revolutionary War Indian campaigns who was killed in the Battle of Tippecanoe (1811).

Spoon Grove (Calloway): *spūn ghrohv* (Hico). Almost nothing remains of this short-lived village e of KY 94, 7 mi ne of Murray. The village was named for Alden Spooner, an itinerant carpenter, who under contract had built the local store in 1872 and several homes. The po was est as Spoon on June 1, 1883, and closed in Aug 1889. 440, 587.

Spoon PO (Calloway). See *Spoon Grove*

Spoonville PO (Garrard). See *Nina*

Spottsville (Henderson): *spahts*/vihl (Spottsville). This village with po is on the Green R, just s of US 60, and 7 mi e of Henderson. A settlement here prior to 1830 was called Knights for either John or Isaac Knight, the earliest landowners. In 1822 Maj. Samuel Spotts acquired 1400 acres of local land to which, in 1829, he sent his nephews, John and George Spotts of Wilmington, Delaware, to build grist- and sawmills. By the time these were in operation in 1830, the community had been renamed by John for his family, allegedly to locate his mills more effectively. Within a short time the vicinity may also have been nicknamed Shanty for a number of quarrymen's shacks between the rock-bearing hills and the r. After Green R's Lock No. 1 was built, it was even briefly called The Locks. The Spottsville po was est on May 4, 1858, with Robert S. Eastin, pm. The town was laid off in 1860 and inc in 1871. In the late 19th cent, residents began building on the hillsides and the town was more or less relocated there from the flats under the bluff. 936.

Spout Springs (Estill): *spowt sprihŋz* (Clay City). This rural settlement with extinct po is on KY 82, 8 air miles n of Irvine. It was named for several local springs, the largest of which comes out of a cliff as a "large stream of very cold, never failing limestone water" long considered the best tasting water around. Travelers used to stop there to water their horses, and people still come to get a drink or haul away the water in barrels. The Spout Spring po was est in the vicinity on Aug 5, 1892, with John M. Elkin, pm, but 3 years later the 2 words were combined and the po was known as Spoutspring until it closed in 1937. 865.

Springfield (Washington): *sprihŋ*/feeld (Springfield). This 4th class city and seat of Washington Co is on US 150 and KY 55, 45 mi se of downtown Louisville. The site of the court house of the first co est after Kentucky became a state in 1792 was originally called Washington Court House. In Dec 1793 the town itself was founded on a 50-acre site donated by Gen. Matthew Walton, a Virginia-born surveyor and one of pioneer Kentucky's largest landowners, and named for the many area springs. The po was est as Springfield Court House on Apr 9, 1796, with Isaac Lansdale, pm. 523, 1314.

Springfield Court House PO (Washington). See *Springfield*

Spring Grove (Union): *sprihŋ ghrohv* (Grove Center). This hamlet with extinct po on KY 56, 5 mi w of Morganfield, was named for a spring in a nearby grove which supplied water for the family of Solomon Blue, who may have settled there as early as 1803. The community grew up around a local coal mine opened in 1861 by James Stanfield, an Englishman. John W. Hall est the po in his store on Nov 16, 1876. The po closed in 1906. 157.

Spring Hill (Hickman): *sprihŋ hihl* (Clinton). This crossroads hamlet with extinct po at the jct of KY 288 and 1362, 4 mi n of Clinton, was named for its site on a hill from which flowed a good spring. The po est on Apr 26, 1866, as Spring Hill with John T. Porter, pm, became Orion in 1878 and closed a year later. In 1887 Henry J. Lamkin had his po of Trevor, est in 1881, renamed Spring Hill. This closed in 1905. 919.

Spring Hill Depot PO (Henry). See *Turners Station*

Spring Lick (Grayson): *sprihŋ link* (Spring Lick). Little but the po remains of this once thriving rail center on the Illinois Central RR, 4½ mi w of Caneyville and 13½ mi wsw of Leitchfield. This site was settled before 1850 and named for a nearby deer lick and an ever-flowing spring from which residents secured fresh water. The Spring Lick po was est on Apr 28, 1871, by Alphonso G. Rowe soon after the rr was built through. The town was inc in 1881. 269, 613.

Spring Station (Woodford): *sprihŋ stā*/shən (Midway). Little remains of a once busy freight station and extinct po on the old Lexington & Ohio (now L&N) RR, where the tracks cross KY 1685, 5½ mi n of Versailles. Settled early by families of Blackburns, Alexanders, and others, a village may already have been in existence when the rr came through in 1833. The po was est on May 6, 1856, as Spring Station with George Turner, pm, and the community may then have been called Big Spring Station. Station, po, and community were named for a large spring that bubbled up in several places a short distance from the depot. The po closed in 1973. 371, 938, 1176, 1269.

Springville (Greenup). See *South Portsmouth*

Sprout (also called **Buzzard Roost**) (Nicholas): sprowt, *buhz*/ərd rūst (Moorefield). Almost nothing remains of this crossroads hamlet with a po on Cassidy Creek and KY 57, 7 mi e of Carlisle. Although the name is still officially Sprout, locally people have always identified it as Buzzard Roost or simply (The) Roost. The po was est as Buzzard Roost on Mar 12, 1852, with Andrew W. Shrout, pm, and discontinued in 1861. According to tradition, a drummer passing through one day observed some of the local men sitting in a line on a whitwashed fence, all dressed up in their dark suits and hats, passing a jug. When he arrived at the next town he described what he had seen, and said he never did learn what the place was called but there were these fellers looking like a bunch of buzzards a-roosting on a fence. On July 7, 1882, the po was reest as Sprout with Millard F. Fuller as pm. Shrout was the name that Andrew's brother James had placed on his petition for a new po but this had been misread as Sprout and the postal officials refused to change it. This po was discontinued in 1907. The name Shrout was never used for the community. 167, 1374.

Spurlington (Taylor): *spɜl*/ihŋ/tən (Spurlington). This hamlet, with extinct po, a once prosperous rural trade center and L&N RR station lie where the present KY 634 crosses the tracks, 4½ mi ne of Campbellsville. The now extinct po est on Jan 2, 1880, was named for the pioneer forebears of its first pm, John Spurling, Sr. 308, 1291.

Squib (Pulaski): skwihb (Billows). This recently closed po, .2 mi s of KY 80 and 14 mi ene of Somerset, was est on Feb 24, 1923, with Louis H. Cress, pm. While local citizens were considering what to do after several names had been rejected by the Post Office Department, Henry Whitaker, a young fellow whose nickname was "Squib," arrived on the scene and inspired someone to suggest his name. It was submitted and accepted. 1410.

Squiresville (Owen): *skwah*/yərz/vihl (New Liberty). This extinct po on KY 1982, 5½ mi w of Owenton, was named for the several squires or magistrates said to have lived there at one time. In Kentucky one who has served in this capacity can use the title for the rest of his life. The po was in operation from 1871 to 1903. 625.

Stacy (Perry). See *Rowdy*

Stacy Branch (Perry). See *Allock*

Stacy Fork (Morgan): *stā*/see*fawrk* (Cannel City). This hamlet with po lies at the jct of KY 191 and 844, on Caney Creek opposite and just below the mouth of Stacy Fork, and 5 mi s of West Liberty. The first po to serve this area was Castle, est about a mi n of Stacy Fork on Mar 21, 1896, and named for and by Goldman D. Castle, the first pm. The po closed in 1907 but was reest in 1913 at the mouth of the creek for which it was named. Stacy Fork's first pm, Hezekiah Gullett, was also the agent at the Ohio & Kentucky RR's station at that point. The stream had been named for the many residents descended from pioneer Hugh Stacy. 112.

Staffordsville (Johnson): *staef*/ərdz/vihl (Paintsville). This village with po is on Paint Creek and US 460, and just nw of the Paintsville city limits. The po was est on July 14, 1882, as Frew with Millard F. Rule, pm. After Jessie Stafford became pm in 1893, its name was changed to honor the Stafford family which included John Frew Stafford. 1353.

Staley PO (Boyd). See *Lockwood*

Stambaugh (Johnson): *staem*/boh (Sitka). This hamlet with po is on KY 1559 at the mouth of Wells Branch of Toms Creek, 4½ mi n of Paintsville. The po was est on Feb 28, 1905, with Bessie L. Stambaugh, pm, and named for the descendants of Samuel and Philip Stambaugh, pioneer settlers of the vicinity. 90.

Stamping Ground (Scott): *staemp*/ihŋ ghrownd (Stamping Ground). This 6th class city with po is on KY 227 and Locust Fork of North Elkhorn Creek, 6½ mi nw of Georgetown. It has generally been assumed that large herds of buffalo, gathering at a salt spring here, trampled or stamped a considerable acreage of undergrowth and soil as they waited under the shade of the trees to taste the water. But Neal Hammon has offered another explanation: "As the animals shed the hair of their hindquarters, these portions became very sensitive to insect bites; for this reason they had recourse to rolling in mud or clay which forms a protective cover for several days. These stamping grounds or wallows would normally be found near water and on the established game trails. Here all the grass and underbrush would be trampled down, leaving a bare spot composing several acres." Three such "stamping grounds" were recorded in pioneer days but only this survives in the name of a community. A po called Stamping Grounds (*sic*) was est at or near the spring on Oct 1, 1816, with Alexander Bradford, pm, but was discontinued after only a few years. The town was laid out in 1817 and another po, est perhaps in 1823 as Herndonsville, was renamed Stamping Ground in 1834, the year the town was inc. 13, 235, 468, 763.

Standing Rock (Lee): *staend*/ihŋ *rahk* (Zachariah). This scattered settlement on KY 1036, 9 mi n of Beattyville, probably dates back only to the oil boom of the early 1920s. It is named for the "large sandstone slab of several hundred tons which stands on end like a huge grave marker . . . on top of a mountain." where Lee, Wolfe, and Powell cos come together. The rock, which is at "the corner of a number of old surveys" was also "an ancient landmark mentioned in pioneer history as having some sort of superstitious awe for Indians." It never had its own po. 750, 1210, 1372.

Stanford (Lincoln): *staen*/fərd (Stanford). This 5th class industrial city and seat of Lincoln Co is on US 27 and 150, 72 mi se of downtown Louisville. Less than 1 mi w of the courthouse is the site of the pioneer station of St. Asaph's [*sānt ās*/əfs], built by Col. Benjamin Logan in 1776. It was later generally referred to as Logan's Fort. According to generally accepted accounts, a Welshman in Logan's party suggested the name of a 6th cent Welsh saint on whose feast day, May 1, 1775, they arrived at this site. The saint himself had assumed the name of a Biblical psalmist and the leader of King David's choirs. An act of the Court of Quarter Sessions held for Lincoln Co on May 16, 1786, authorized the removal of the court to the town of Standford on lands conveyed to the court by Logan. The name is said to have been derived from that of the borough of Stamford in Lincolnshire, England. This was spelled Stanford in the Domesday Book and was famed as the site of several meetings of English nobles in opposition to royal authority during the Middle Ages. There is no basis at all to the popular notion that the name was corrupted from Standing Fort, alleged to have commemorated Logan's successful resistance to repeated Indian attacks. The Stanford po was est on Apr 1, 1798, with Joseph Welsh, pm. 677, 698.

Stanley (Daviess): *staen*/lee (Owensboro West). This village with po is centered at the jct of US 60 and the L&N RR, 6½ mi wnw of Owensboro. A po est as Loopee in 1883 with Robert M. Hagan, pm, was moved to the site of and/or renamed Stanley on May 18, 1889, for Nat Stanley, an early settler. No one today knows anything about Loopee. 930.

Stanton (Powell): *staen(t)*/ən (Stanton). This 4th class city and seat of Powell Co is just off the Mountain Parkway at KY 213 and 100 mi ese of downtown Louisville. On the old Virginia land grants this settlement was aptly recorded as Beaver Ponds and the po was est as such on July 7, 1849, with James M. Daniel, pm. When the community became the new co's seat in 1852, both it and the po were renamed for Richard H. Stanton, congressman (1849–1855) and later US senator. 954, 1334.

Stanville (Floyd): *staen*/vəl, *mε* kreek (Harold). This village with po is on US 23/460 and the Levisa Fork of the Big Sandy R, just above the mouth of Mare Creek, and 8½ mi se of Prestonsburg. On the site of a home built by pioneer Solomon Stratton from Montgomery Co, Virginia, this community was first called Mare Creek for the stream, and the po of this name was est on Aug 8, 1949, with Mrs. Mildred A. Hall, pm. It has been said that the stream was originally Marrow Creek, a name alleged to have been applied by the early Strattons for the large quantities of cracked bison marrowbones they had seen lying about its banks. From this was derived the tradition of the wandering Shawnees who had camped at the mouth with only buffalo bones to satisfy their hunger. They cracked them and consumed the marrow. Some years later, according to another account, James S. Layne, another pioneer settler of the area, located a strayed mare on the banks of the creek and, perhaps, Marrow was thus easily corrupted to Mare. When in 1960 residents objected to the rusticity of the name Mare Creek for their po, they succeeded in getting it changed to Stanville, honoring a local resident and former Floyd Co sheriff and judge, Robert E. Stanley. 194, 1370.

Star (Carter): stahr (Rush). This hamlet is on Star Creek, a branch of Williams Creek, and US 60, 6 mi e of Grayson. This was once the site of *Star Furnace*, a stone coal blast furnace built in 1848 by A. McCullough and the Lampton Bros. from Ohio and presumably named for their hopes that it would be the best or "star" of all the furnaces in the region. A po was est somewhere in the vicinity on Jan 24, 1848, and named Metcalfe Furnace with Samuel P. Williams, pm. It was renamed Star Furnace in 1850 but in 1865 it was moved some 2 mi ne to Coalton in Boyd Co, while another Star Furnace po opened in 1866 and closed 2 years later. Contemporary historians are unaware of any Metcalfe Furnace as such in the area, or of Star Furnace ever being called that. The creek, which may first have been called Rachel Creek, was also named for the furnace. 36, 1177, 1326.

Star Furnace PO (Carter). See *Coalton, Star*

Stark (Elliott): stahrk (Ault). This hamlet with po extends for over 2 mi along KY 649 on a ridge between Big and Little Caney Creeks, 5½ mi nw of Sandy Hook. Though the po was only est on June 30, 1890, with James M. Porter, pm, the community it serves is one of the oldest in the co and is said to have been named by its earliest residents for the Revolutionary War hero, Gen. John Stark, with whom their fathers had served. The community may also have been called Egypt in its early years, for area residents would come to the local store for their grain. 1202, 1412.

State Line PO (Fulton). See *Jordan*

Station Camp (Estill): *stā*/shən *kaemp* (Irvine). This hamlet with extinct po on the present KY 594, 2½ mi s of Irvine, was named for Station Camp Creek, which joins the Kentucky R opposite Irvine. The creek may have been named by Daniel Boone, who stayed here at the site of a Shawnee Indian Camping ground and trading post called Ah-wah-nee ("deep grassy place") en route to the Bluegrass in 1769. The po was est on Mar 27, 1828, by James Scrivner, and was discontinued in 1843. It was reest in 1878 by John Wilson, and closed for good in 1969. 116, 865.

Station Landing PO (Lewis). See *Carrs*

Staub PO (Perry). See *Harveyton*

Stearns (McCreary): stɜnz (Whitley City). This coal town with po 1 mi w of new US 27 and 1 mi s of Whitley City, was, until recently, the wholly owned co. town and headquarters of the Stearns Coal and Lumber Co.; after 1960 the firm's local holdings were sold to residents and utility cos. The site is said to have been settled in 1840 by Riley and Bailey Sellers and was first called Hemlock, probably for the local trees. In 1902 it assumed the name of Justus S. Stearns of Ludington, Michigan, who founded both the town and the co. that year. The Stearns po was est on Dec 29, 1902. The Hemlock name has long been preserved in the co.-controlled Kentucky and Tennessee Ry freight facilities and repair depot in town. 174, 208, 752, 1162, 1163.

Stedmantown (Franklin): *stehd*/mən/town (Frankfort East). This extinct mill town was on Elkhorn Creek, at the edge of the Indian Hills section of Frankfort. In 1834 the brothers Ebenezer and Samuel Stedman from Georgetown bought Amos Kendall's mill (which the future US postmaster general had built in 1823) and reest it as a paper mill. Within a few years they had located a village there for their employees and called it Stedmanville, under which name a po was in operation from 1855 to 1857. Mill and village flourished until after the Civil War. Later in the 19th cent, the community, by then known as Stedmantown, was centered on Samuel Martin's gristmill. 52, 369.

Steff (Grayson): stehf (Spring Lick). This hamlet with po on US 62, just n of the Illinois Central Gulf RR, and 16½ mi wsw of Leitchfield, was first called Goffs Crossing [*ghahfs kraws*/ihŋ] for a family that settled there about the time the rr was built through in 1870. The po of Goff was est on Aug 8, 1879, with Gideon T. Bunch, pm, but was discontinued in Apr of the following year. On Mar 13, 1918, Romey Payton est the Steff po at this site, and by this name, that of another local family, it is still known. Though a Board on Geographic Names decision in 1967 approved Steff over Goff(s) (Crossing) as the community's name, local people still use both names interchangeably. 1307.

Stella (Calloway): *stehl*/ə (Kirksey). This hamlet with extinct po at the jct of KY 121 and 299, 4 mi wnw of Murray, may be traced back at least to the 1840s when it was first called Goshen [*ghoh*/shən] for the local Methodist church. The po est on Feb 2, 1895, with Robert E. Dodd, pm, was named Stella for either the youngest daughter of a Mr. Scarborough who donated the land for it or the daughter of a Mr. Waterfield, a local storekeeper. While Stella is the official and generally recognized name for the community, many oldtimers still refer to it as Goshen as the church still bears this name. The po closed in 1904. 1401, 1441.

Stella (Magoffin): stehl/ə (Seitz). This po lies at the mouth of Cherry Orchard Branch of Cow Creek, 4½ mi w of Salyersville. It was est on Nov 3, 1910, by Jim Adams who named it for his daughter Stella. 1056, 1422.

Stephensburg (Hardin): *stee*/vənz/bergh (Summit). This village, 8 mi se of Elizabethtown, is made up of Old Stephensburg, with po, on US 62, and Stephensburg, with defunct Illinois Central Gulf RR station, ½ mi n. The po, est as Stevensburg on Dec. 23, 1829, was probably named by and for its first pm, Stephen Southern. This spelling was later corrected to Stephensburgh, and, in 1893, to Stephensburg. 1420.

Stephensport (Breckinridge): *stee*/fənz/pawrt (Rome). This village with po, once a prosperous Ohio R port, is at the mouth of Sinking Creek, 9 mi nnw of Hardinsburg. Probably settled before 1800, the town was founded on part of the 94,000-acre Revolutionary War grant to Richard Stephens that was later owned by his son, Daniel J., and was laid out in 1803. It was inc in 1825, in which year its po was est. Historians disagree on whether the place was named for Richard or Daniel J. Postmaster Lewis Roff's brief attempt to change the name of the po to Roff in Sept 1882 met with local opposition and the original name was reinstated the following month. 290, 384.

Steubens Lick (Hopkins). See *Manitou*

Steubenville (Wayne): *stū*/bən/vihl, *styū*/bən/vihl, *styū*/bən/vəl (Mill Springs). This hamlet is centered at its po on old KY 90, ¼ mi sw of its jct with KY 1808, and 7 mi ne of Monticello. The community is said to have been settled before 1800 by Revolutionary War veterans and named for Baron Friederich von Steuben (1730–94), the Prussian trainer of General Washington's troops. The first po to serve the vicinity was est as Oak Forest on July 16, 1842, with Stephen Scott, pm, probably just over 1 mi ne of its present location. The po was probably moved when its name was changed to Steubenville in 1851 as Charles H. Buster became pm. It closed in 1854 and was reest in 1871 with Joseph A. Bohon, pm. The community may also have been called Pleasant Grove, the name of the local church until 1894 when it became the Steubensville Baptist Church. 1405, 1413.

Stevens (Campbell). See *Silver Grove*

Stevensburg PO (Hardin). See *Stephensburg*

Stevenson's PO (Woodford). See *Midway*

Stick PO (Knott). See *Democrat*

Stigalls Ferry PO (Pulaski). See *Pisgah*

Stigalls Station PO (Rockcastle). See *Brodhead*

Stine's Station (Jefferson). See *Buechel*

Stipps Crossroads (Bourbon). See *Clintonville*

Stithton (Hardin): *stihth*/tən (Fort Knox). The site of this 19th cent trade center and Illinois Central RR shipping point is now wholly within the built up section of *Fort Knox,* centered at the principal Ft. Knox traffic circle, some 12 mi nnw of Elizabethtown. In the vicinity of a stagecoach stop on the old Louisville & Nashville Turnpike (now US 31W), the Illinois Central built a station in 1874. On August 19 of that year, a po was est and named Stithton for either Thomas Stith, a local resident who had served in the Mexican War, or the family of Milton Stith who had settled there soon after his purchase of 1000 acres in that vicinity in 1859. In 1918 Camp Knox (later Fort Knox) was est and immediately acquired and razed the Stithton site. Many of the residents moved a short distance away and created a New Stithton only to be forced to move a 2nd time when the military installation extended its boundaries in 1942. The Stithton po was officially renamed Camp Knox on May 15, 1925. 136, 1420.

Stithton PO (Hardin). See *Fort Knox*

Stockholm (Edmonson). See *Sweeden*

Stone (Pike): stohn (Belfry). This coal town with po is about a mi s of the jct of US 119 and KY 199 at Huddy and 13½ mi ne of Pikeville. It may have been named for E. L. Stone, the president of the Borderland Mines with headquarters in Borderland, West Virginia (ca. 1904). The po was est on Oct 17, 1912, with Phare Osburn, pm. 185.

Stone City (Lewis). See *Garrison*

Stonetown (Fayette). See *Bracktown*

Stop (Wayne): stahp (Parnell). Little remains of this hamlet on KY 1546, 6 mi w of Monticello. No one really knows how the po est on Dec 17, 1910, with John F.

Upchurch, pm, got its name. Some say this was the end of the local mail route, or that the rd stopped there. According to one published account, some visitors, asked by Mr. Upchurch for help in naming the po, could not decide and were about to leave when he called to them to "Stop! Let's talk about it some more." The po closed in 1933. Some recent maps err in referring to this community as Ramsey Island; this name is locally applied to a farming area within a 6-mi loop made by KY 1546, an area once owned by related families of Ramseys whose descendants still live there. As expected, the name Stop has inspired a number of anecdotes like the one about the man passing through who asked the name of the local po. "Stop," he was told. "I can't stop," he said, "I'm in a hurry to make Cabell [a nearby hamlet] by sundown." 427, 1355, 1356.

Stopover (Pike): *stahp*/oh/vər (Majestic). This coal town with po is on Turkey Creek, a branch of Knox Creek, at the jct of KY 194 and 2062, 22 mi e of Pikeville. The po was est in 1949 by S. H. Blankenship and named for the fact that travelers would often stop over here to seek directions to the area's mines. 1456.

Stouts Landing (Lewis). See *Carrs*

Stowers PO (Simpson). See *Middleton*

Stowers Station (Pendleton). See *Morgan*

Straight Creek (Bell): *strāt* kreek (Pineville). This coal town with po and L&N RR station extends e for over 1½ mi along KY 221 from its jct with KY 66, at the forks of the creek for which it was named, and less than 1 mi ene of Pineville. The po has been in operation since Mar 8, 1900. The creek, a tributary of the Cumberland R, is aptly named. 1416.

Strawberry (Pulaski): *straw*/bə/ree (Somerset). This extinct po was in Waddle Hollow on KY 769, 3½ mi se of Somerset. It was est on Apr 24, 1900, with William E. Kelly, pm, and named for the many local strawberry patches. 1410.

Stringtown (Anderson): *strihŋ*/town (Lawrenceburg). This hamlet is strung out for about 1½ mi s along US 127, from its jct with the Southern Ry tracks, ½ mi s of Lawrenceburg. It may have been settled before 1800 and has borne this name alone for as long as anyone can remember. It has never had its own po. 1387.

Stringtown (Boone): *strihŋ*/town (Burlington). This aptly named residential community is strung out along KY 8, on the Ohio R, 5 mi ne of Burlington. Though modern historians assume the name was derived from John Uri Lloyd's novel *Stringtown on the Pike* about nearby *Florence,* a community called Stringtown had a regular news column in the Covington *Daily Commonwealth* in 1881, 19 years before the novel was published. Stringtown has never had a po.

Stringtown (Knott). See *Larkslane*

Stringtown (Magoffin): *strihŋ*/town (Salyersville North). This residential community is strung out along KY 40 in a roughly ne direction from near the Salyersville city limits to the mouth of Twentytwo Miles Branch of State Road Fork of the Licking R. It has never had a po. 1422.

Stringtown (Mercer): *strihŋ*/town (Harrodsburg). This suburban community is strung along US 68 for about ½ mi from a point less than ½ mi ne of Harrodsburg. The Counter po, in operation from Jan 5 to May 14, 1904, was allegedly so named because the po was merely a counter in John D. Royalty's store. It was much later that the Stringtown name came to officially identify this community. 1264.

Stringtown on the Pike (Jefferson). See *Fern Creek*

Stroud City (Muhlenberg). See *Central City*

Stroud PO (Muhlenberg). See *Central City*

Strunk (McCreary): struhŋk (Whitley City, Winfield). This hamlet with po lies at the jct of old US 27 and KY 1470, 6½ mi sse of Whitley City. The po was est as Strunks Lane on Feb 18, 1892, with James H. Pemberton, pm, and probably named for George W. Strunk who owned the local store and mine. In 1894 the po became merely *Strunk.* The Southern Ry station in that immediate vicinity was called Silerville, probably for Bill Siler, and this had its own po between 1907 and 1915 when its papers were transferred to Strunk. The names Strunk and Silerville may have been used interchangeably to identify the same community. 1257, 1384.

Strunks Lane PO (McCreary). See *Strunk*

Strutsville (Grant). See *Keefer*

Stum's Landing (Muhlenberg). See *Paradise*

Sturgel PO (Madison). See *Redhouse*

Sturgis (Union): *stɜ*/djəs (Sturgis, Dekoven). This 4th class industrial city with po is on US 60/641, 9 mi ssw of Morganfield. The town was est in 1886 by the Cumberland Iron and Land Co. as the center of its developing coal-mining operations. It is said by some to have been named for Samuel P. Sturgis from whom the town site had been acquired. Others suggest that it was named by Col. Jordan Giles, the co's resident manager, for Samuel's sister, Alida Livingston Sturgis, the wife of Dr. P. G. Kelsey, president and general manager of the Ohio Valley RR Co., for "she had been kind to him at the time of his wife's death in Louisville and because, for many years, she and Dr. Kelsey had made him a welcome guest in their home." The po was est on Feb 17, 1888, with Stephen C. Hammack, pm, and the town was inc in 1890. In recent years Sturgis extended its s boundary to include the old settlement of Buffalo City, earlier called Buffalo Lick and Crossroads, which dated back to around 1860. It has also expanded on the w to include part of the late 19th cent mill town and Tradewater port of Commercial Point, now a residential area e of *Grangertown.* 238, 1229.

Sublett (Magoffin): *suhb*/lət (Salyersville South). This hamlet with po is a mi up KY 1635 and Oakley Creek, a branch of the Licking R, 5 mi s of Salyersville. The po was est on May 20, 1899, with Jasper Owens, pm, and was probably named for the family of David D. Sublett, a Bath Co native who arrived in Salyersville sometime after 1861 and became a prominent Salyersville attorney and state representative. 149.

Subletts Store PO (Taylor). See *Coburg*

Sublimity City (Laurel): sə/*blihm*/ət/ee *sih*/tee (Lily). This residential community on KY 1006, 1½ mi s of London, was est in 1937 as a New Deal experiment called Sublimity Forest Community. This was a planned community on 578 acres purchased by the federal government and divided into 66 subsistence homesites for selected farm families who could be taught modern farming practices "under controlled conditions." The name was derived from that given to the springs on the Rockcastle R by Dr. Christopher Columbus Graham, at which he est a grist- and sawmill as well as a 19th cent watering place. It may be assumed that the springs were so named by Graham because he thought the scenery there sublime. 395, 1282.

Sublimity Forest Community (Laurel). See *Sublimity City*

Sudith (Menifee): *sū*/dəth (Olympia). This po is on KY 36, 3½ mi n of Frenchburg. The po was est as Carrington on May 21, 1890, with Hiram B. Armitage, pm, and named for a nearby rock, which had been named for John Carrington, its pre-Civil War owner, who had operated a successful tannery there. In 1904 pm Charles F. Craig renamed the po Sudith for a prominent area family, one of whose members was then a state legislator. For many years the po lay about a mi n, where KY 36 crosses Salt Lick Creek. 980.

Suffolk (Butler). See *Mining City*

Sugar Creek PO (Ballard). See *Lovelaceville*

Sugar Grove (Butler): *shoogh*/ər *ghrohv* (Sugar Grove). This hamlet with extinct po is on KY 1083, 9 mi s of Morgantown. The po was est on Jan 26, 1832, as Locust Forest, presumably for the locust trees in the vicinity, and was renamed Sugar Grove in 1851 for the large sugar camp in the local grove of sugar maples. 764.

Sullivan (Union): *suhl*/ə/vən (Blackford, Sturgis). This village with po is centered at the jct of US 60/641 and KY 109 and 141, 12 mi s of Morganfield. In 1882 John F. Quirey and a Mr. McGraw deeded the right-of-way to the Ohio Valley (now Illinois Central Gulf) RR, which reached the site in 1887, and called the local station Quirey. On Aug 6, 1887, Quirey est the po there, which he named for A. M. ''Mike'' Sullivan, who had begun to develop a recently acquired timber acreage in the area, and his brother Frank, the owner of the local store. 238.

Sulphur (Henry): *suhl*/fər (Smithfield). This village with po is centered at the jct of KY 157 and 1606, on the Little Kentucky R, 6½ mi nw of New Castle. First called Abbottsford for Marion and Wash Abbott, early settlers, and renamed for the local sulphur springs, the village grew up around the depot built for the Louisville Cincinnati & Lexington (or Short Line, later L&N) RR on land donated by Thomas H. Hancock in 1867. The po was est as Sulphur Fork, for White Sulphur Fork, a nearby branch of the Little Kentucky, on Aug 24, 1869, with Hancock as the first pm. It became Sulphur Station in 1880 and Sulphur in 1882. 59, 1256.

Sulphur Fork PO (Henry). See *Sulphur*

Sulphur Lick (Monroe): *suhl*/fər *lihk* (Sulphur Lick). This hamlet with extinct po on KY 839 and 678, 7 mi n of Tomkinsville, is on a site settled around 1800 by Thomas White and George Keys. In presettlement times, buffalo and deer would come to lick the salt and sulphur from the rocks along the bed of Sulphur (now Skaggs) Creek, a branch of the Barren R. The healing properties of a nearby sulphur spring later attracted human visitors. A Sulphur Lick po was in operation from 1850 to 1952. 765.

Sulphur Springs (Ohio): *suhl*/fər *sprihŋz* (Dundee). This was the site of a turn of the century health resort est around both fresh water and white sulphur springs in the vicinity of the present KY 69, 8 mi ne of Hartford. The po of Hines Mills, est in 1846 at what is now *Dundee*, 1½ mi n, was moved here and renamed on Mar 26, 1872, with Jeremiah B. Cannon, pm. It was discontinued in 1907. 1400.

Sulphur Station PO (Henry). See *Sulphur*

Sulphur Well (Jessamine): *suhl*/fər *wehl* (Little Hickman). This 19th cent village, now a hamlet on KY 39, 2 mi sse of Nicholasville, was settled by Rev. John Walters, a Baptist preacher, and later named for a large well of black sulphur water whose medicinal benefits attracted many persons. The well was accidentally discovered while digging for a supply of drinking water sometime before Apr 7, 1852, when William W. Newland est the Sulphur Well po. This po was discontinued in 1869 and reest on June 15, 1881, as Ambrose, for pm Ambrose Cobb, as the Sulphur Well name had recently been applied to a new po in Metcalfe Co. Ambrose closed in 1904. 240, 1270.

Sulphur Well (Metcalfe): *suhl*/fər *wehl* (Sulphur Well). This hamlet with extinct po lies where KY 70 crosses the South Fork of the Little Barren R, 7½ mi n of Edmonton. Shortly before the Civil War, while drilling for salt, Ezekiel Neal discovered instead an artesian well of sulphur water with a high mineral content. Its evident medicinal value soon led to the est of a watering place. The village grew up around the hotels, and a po was started on July 30, 1879, with Thomas M. Quesenberry, pm. 232.

Summer Shade (Metcalfe): *suhm*/ər shād (Summer Shade). This village with po extends for over 1 mi along KY 90, 7 mi sw of Edmonton. On June 21, 1862, storekeeper Ezekiel Witty est the po as Glovers Creek for the nearby stream, which had been named for a local family. In 1876 the community was inc as Summer Shade for the local shade trees, and 2 years later that name was also applied to the po. 232.

Summersville (Green): *suhm*/ərz/vihl (Summersville). This village is centered at the jct of KY 61 and 323, 4 mi nnw of Greensburg. It was laid out on 75 acres of John Emerson's land and est as Somersville (probably in error) in 1817. On or before Sept 12, 1828, William Mudd started the local po as Summersville and with this spelling the community was inc in 1839. In 1865 the po was moved to nearby *Allendale*. On Mar 9, 1866, Samuel Bennett est a 2nd Summersville po at or near the original site. It was named for a local family of Summerses. 2, 912, 1339.

Summit (Boyd): *suhm*/ət (Ashland). This suburb of Ashland, centered on KY 716, between US 60 and KY 5, and 4½ mi w of Catlettsburg, was named for its location on an elevation traversed by the C&O RR tracks. 1311.

Sunfish (Edmonson): *suhn/fihsh* (Bee Spring, Ready). This hamlet with po lies at the jct of KY 187 and 238, 8½ mi nw of Brownsville. The po was est on June 27, 1856, by William H. Bush and named for nearby Sunfish Creek, which was probably named for the sunfish that inhabited it. Yet, wrote Lancie Meredith, "it has been said that the fish in this creek on occasion come very near the top of the water, thus giving the appearance of 'sunning' themselves. From this the name Sunfish evolved." 942, 1150.

Sunnybrook (Wayne): *suhn*/ee/brook (Powersburg). This hamlet with a recently closed po is centered at the mouth of Bertram Hollow on Carpenter Fork of Otter Creek, on KY 200, 12½ mi ssw of Monticello. The po was est in Carter D. Dalton's store on July 21, 1887, with Dalton as pm, and named for the perceived sunshine on the water of the 2 streams that come together at this point. 1231.

Sunrise (Harrison): *suhn*/reyez (Claysville). This hamlet with extinct po is on KY 1284, 10 mi n of Cynthiana. According to tradition its first name, Pughville, for a local family, was not considered an acceptable name for the po. But when the residents could not decide on one, a postal official on the scene proceeded to name it himself for "the prettiest sunrise I ever saw." James P. Hill became the first pm of Sunrise on May 22, 1889. 158.

Sunshine (Greenup): *suhn*/sheyen (Portsmouth). This hamlet is on Tygarts Creek and KY 7, at the mouth of Lower White Oak Creek, and 10½ mi nw of Greenup. Some say the settlement was named by the Indians for its location on their inland route from the Ohio Valley but others have suggested that it was named for a school built in 1868. It has never had its own po. 1333, 1447.

Sunshine PO (Ruseell). See *Whittle*

Superior PO (Lawrence). See *Torchlight*

Surran (Bell). See *Tinsley*

Sutherland (Daviess): *suth*/er/lənd (Sutherland). This hamlet with extinct po lies at the jct of KY 298 and the L&N RR, 4 mi s of Owensboro. The po, est on Oct 28, 1891, with Alva C. Leach, pm, was named for Arch Sutherland, large landowner and pioneer settler. 930.

Swamp Branch (Johnson): *swahmp braench* (Ivyton). This po on KY 825, at the mouth of Swamp Branch of Jennys Creek, 6 mi sw of Paintsville, was est on Dec 22, 1923, with Crate Rice, pm, and named for the aptly named stream. 1411.

Swampton (Magoffin): *swahmp*/tən (Salyersville South, Ivyton). This hamlet extends s along KY 7 for nearly 2 mi from the extinct po site, 6 mi sse of Salyersville. William Allen, the first pm, had a store at the mouth of Big Half Mountain Creek when the po was est there on Dec 20, 1887. Later the po was moved a short distance down the rd to the site it occupied until it closed in 1978. The name was most likely derived from the swampy condition of the Licking R bottoms there. 1421, 1422.

Swan Creek PO (Warren). See *Greencastle*

Sweeden (Edmonson): *swee*/dən (Bee Spring, Brownsville). This village with po extends for about ½ mi along KY 259, 4 mi n of Brownsville. It was founded and named by Larkin J. Proctor, a Glasgow attorney and land developer, as part of a scheme to promote the co's economic development. In 1883 he arranged for several families of Swedish immigrants then living in the Chicago area to move to this site. The po of New Sweden, est here on Dec 28, 1892, with Bradley Musick, pm, was changed to Sweeden in 1894. No one has ever been able to explain this curious spelling. Some 8 mi e, on KY 1352, are the remains of another Swedish settlement est by Proctor and called Stockholm [*stahk*/hohm], whose po of this name operated from July 3, 1882, to Nov 15, 1913. 812, 830.

Sweet Owen (Owen): *sweet oh*/ən (Owenton). This hamlet with extinct po is now at the jct of KY 22 and 845, 4 mi e of Owenton. It is believed that until the Breckinridge congressional campaign of 1851 the community, if it had a name at all, was called simply Owen for the co. As the story goes, Democrat John C. Breckinridge had all but lost his election bid to Leslie Combs, his Whig opponent, but refused to concede defeat. "Wait," he said, "for you've not yet heard from Sweet Owen." When all the returns were in, he found that Owen Co, staunchly Democratic, had given him sufficient votes to win. The co has been known as "Sweet Owen" ever since, but for some reason the name was officially applied to this community before or when it received its po on June 19, 1873. The community was originally located about a mi nw. The po closed in 1902. 102, 892, 1292.

Swinneytown (Bourbon). See *North Middletown*

Swiss Colony (Laurel). See *Bernstadt*

Switzer (Franklin): *sweyets*/ər (Switzer). This hamlet with extinct po is centered at the jct of KY 1262 and 1689, just w of North Elkhorn Creek, and 4 mi ne of Frankfort. The po was est on Mar 29, 1882, with John H. Switzer, pm, and named for his family whose local progenitor (ca. 1838) may have been James Switzer. When the Frankfort & Cincinnati Ry was built through this area, Kissinger Station was located here. The po closed in 1957. 864, 1290.

Symsonia (Graves): sihm/*sohn*/yə (Symsonia). This prosperous village with po is centered at the jct of KY 131 and 1348, 12½ mi nne of Mayfield. The community is said to have begun in the 1820s as Slabtown, still occasionally heard as a nickname, which may have referred to the planks early settlers laid down on the very muddy rds in that vicinity. No one knows the origin of Symsonia, with which name the po was est by James K. Wilson on Dec 23, 1847, but one logical hypothesis is that it was partially derived from the local Simmons family. 277, 1337.

Tailholt (Boone). See *Hebron*

Tail Holt (Livingston). See *Burna*

Tailton PO (Scott). See *White Sulphur*

Talbert (Breathitt): *tahl*/bərt (Canoe). This po is on KY 1933, at the mouth of Pipemud Branch of Turners Creek, ½ mi from where Turners joins the Middle Fork of the Kentucky R, and 9½ mi ssw of Jackson. The po was est on Feb 12, 1914, and probably named for its first pm, Talbert Turner. The community it serves is locally called Turners Creek. 1310.

Tampico PO (Taylor). See *Coburg*

Tanbark (Cumberland): *taen*/bahrk (Blacks Ferry). This extinct po on KY 485, 4 mi s of Burkesville, was est on Nov 27, 1920, with Thomas B. Guthrie, pm, and named for the local business of gathering oak bark to supply are a tanneries. The community it served is now generally referred to as Guthries Chapel for the local Methodist church. The Guthries, a pioneer landowning family, also gave their name to the ridge on which the community is located. The po closed in 1962. 223, 1385.

Tanksley (Clay): *taeŋk*/slee (Barcreek). This po on KY 11, in the Goose Creek bottom, 5 mi ne of Manchester, was est on July 31, 1882, and said to have been named for John, the father of James Tanksley, the first pm. Some co historians say the family spelled its name Tankersley and that the middle syllable was dropped in forming the po's name. 1455.

Tanner's Station (Boone). See *Petersburg*

Tannery (Lewis): *taen*/ər/ee (Garrison). This hamlet with extinct po near the mouth of Wolf Creek, a branch of the Trace Creek branch of Kinniconick Creek, 6 mi se of Vanceburg, was named for a pre-Civil War tanyard operated there by A. W. Fryer and the Greenslate family. A po was in operation from 1889 to 1957. 770.

Tarkiln (Lawrence): *tahr*/kihl (Sitka). This extinct po on Tarkiln Branch of Hood Creek, 14 mi sw of Louisa, operated between 1924 and 1931, with Judge Clayton Greene as its only pm. It was named for the creek, whose name referred to a traditional method of drying fruits and making tar for home use in a stone oven with a mud topped flue through the middle of it. 1362.

Tarma PO (Muhlenberg). See *Nonnel*

Tate's Store PO (Pulaski). See *Tateville*

Tateville (Pulaski): *tāt*/vəl (Burnside). This village with po is on US 27 and the Southern Ry, 6 mi s of Somerset. It was named for Maj. Samuel Bracken Tate (1775–1861), a large landowner who settled there around 1803. The po was est as Tate's Store on June 19, 1874, with T. G. Smith, pm, and changed 3 weeks later to Tatesville. The medial "s" was later dropped. 215.

Tattletown (Mercer). See *Kirkwood*

Tatumsville (Marshall): *tā*/təmz/vihl (Briensburg). This crossroads hamlet with extinct po on KY 1422, 4½ mi nne of Benton, was named for a local family. The po was est on June 30, 1897, with William W. Gregory, pm, and closed in 1907. 1337.

Taylor County: *tā*/lər. 270 sq mi. Pop 20,916. Seat: Campbellsville. This co was est in 1848 from part of Green Co and named for Zachary Taylor (1784–1850), Mexican War hero and 12th president of the US (1849–50).

Taylor Mill (Kenton): *tā*/lər *mihl* (Covington, Newport, Independence, Alexandria). This 4th class city and residential suburb without po is 3 mi s of downtown Covington and 2½ mi nne of the courthouse at Independence. Inc in 1956, it merged with neighboring Winston Park in 1972. It was named for a mill built by James Taylor on part of the 5000-acre patent issued to Raleigh Colston in 1790 by Virginia's Governor Randolph. 118.

Taylor Mines (Ohio): *tā*/lər mahnz, *tā*/lawr mahnz (Hartford). Only a church and several homes remain at the site of this extinct co. town, 4 mi s of Hartford. The town was founded in the vicinity of the coal mines est in the early 1870s on land owned by Harrison B. Taylor for whom it was named. A po was in operation from 1890 to 1910. 598.

Taylor PO (Greenup). See *South Shore*

Taylors Landing (Owsley). See *Beattyville*

Taylorsport (Boone): *tāl*/ərz/pawrt (Burlington). This small settlement, with extinct po, once an Ohio R port just above the mouth of Elijahs Creek, is on KY 8, 5 mi nne of Burlington. Until 1849 it was called Taylorsville for Gen. James Taylor who helped develop it as a town. By an act of the Kentucky legislature in that year it became Taylorsport and a po of this name, since closed, was est on May 15, 1909, with L. H. Sprague, pm. 1284.

Taylor Station PO (Jefferson). See *Eastwood*

Taylorsville (Boone). See *Taylorsport*

Taylorsville (Spencer): *tāl*/ərz/vihl (Taylorsville). This 6th class city and seat of Spencer Co is centered at the jct of KY 44 and 55, 25 mi se of downtown Louisville. By 1790 homes were being built here and in 1799 a town was laid and and named for Richard Taylor, the owner of a gristmill and a large tract of land at the confluence of Brashears Creek and Salt R. However, since the plat was not recorded until 1814, this is considered the year of founding. The po was est on Oct 1, 1817, with Mastin B. Shelburn, pm, and the town was inc in 1829. According to co historian Mary Frances Brown, the name Belgrade [*behl*/ghrād] was also suggested. "The way the creek meanders around the town it leaves a tract of land that is somewhat bell-shaped and that was considered at one time." But Taylorsville was the locally preferred name. 228, 651, 1239.

Tearcoat (Clinton): *tɛ*/koht (Wolf Creek Dam). This extinct po at the mouth of Tearcoat Creek, which joins the Cumberland R at the lower end of Wells Bottom, and 11½ mi nnw of Albany, was in operation between 1910 and 1920. The creek was, until recently, an almost innaccessible and inhospitable location that inspired legends of persons, for example the daughter of pioneer Daniel Clift, stumbling through the dense thicket along the creek and tearing their coats on the brambles as they attempted to elude pursuing bears. 223, 1263.

Teatersville (Garrard): *tee*/tərz/vihl (Buckeye). This hamlet with extinct po on KY 39, 5½ mi ne of Lancaster, was named for a very old and influential co family. The Teatersville po, est on June 1, 1893, with William Simpson, pm, was closed in 1912. 1225.

Teddy (Casey): *tehd*/ee (Phil). This hamlet with extinct po lies on Dry Fork of the South Fork of Green R and KY 910, 9 mi s of Liberty. It was named for Theodore Combest, son of Bill Roe Combest who est the local po on Mar 26, 1900. In Dec 1908 the po was moved from the Combest home to the Rodgers brothers' store and mill site, 1½ mi down Price Creek, and Thomas Rodgers assumed charge until it closed in 1932. 212, 1397.

Teges (Clay): *tee*/djəs (Oneida). This hamlet with po is on KY 11 and the South Fork of the Kentucky R, just below the mouth of Upper Teges Creek, and 10½ mi nne of Manchester. The Upper and Lower Teges Creeks and later the po, est on Dec 16, 1881, with Levi Abner, pm, were named for a pioneer resident, Adonirum Allen (1734–1838), a New Hampshire-born Revolutionary War veteran who was so particular that his ways seemed tedious to others, thus earning him the nickname "Tedious" or "Tejus" Allen. The creeks were actually identified as Tedious on some older maps. 150, 1259.

Tejay (Bell): *tee*/djā, tee/*djā* (Balkan). This L&N RR station and coal camp at the mouth of Toms Creek on the Cumberland R, 7 mi e of Pineville, was est by T[homas] J[efferson] Asher (1848–1935), an extensive landowner and one of the pioneer developers of the logging and coal industries in se Kentucky. Its name was simply a spelling out of his initials. Tejay never had its own po. 147, 1416.

Temperance PO (Simpson). See *Gold City*

Temple Hill (Barren): *tehm*/pəl *hihl* (Temple Hill). This village with extinct po extends for almost a mi along KY 63, 6½ mi sse of Glasgow. It was named for its location on a hill owned by the Temple family and early called Temple's Hill. The po, est as Skeggs Creek on Feb 26, 1839, with Benjamin M. Payne, pm, and named for the nearby stream—usually spelled Skaggs Creek—was moved to and/or renamed Temple Hill in 1858. The stream was probably named for Henry and/or Richard Skaggs, Long Hunters, who are known to have visited this section before the Revolution. 920.

Terrill (Madison): *tehr*/əl (Richmond South). This hamlet at the jct of US 25 and 421, 3½ mi s of Richmond, was an early stopping place for travelers on the Wilderness Rd and was first called Arcadia and then Rogersville for Adam Rogers who built his home there in 1811. A Rogersville po was in operation intermittently from 1849 to 1872. On Apr 6, 1883, the Terrill po was est there with George C. Francis, pm, and named for William Terrill, a local storekeeper and blacksmith. The po was discontinued in 1927. 4,.875, 962, 1294.

Territory (Grayson). See *Shrewsbury*

Terryville (Lawrence): *tehr*/ee/vihl (Redbush). This hamlet with extinct po is on KY 1715, near the head of Blaine Creek, and 21½ mi wsw of Louisa. The po was est on Mar 12, 1909, with storekeeper Samuel B. Terry as pm, and is said to have been named for pioneer settlers Miles and Nancy Skaggs Terry. The po closed in 1955. 1095.

Texas (Madison). See *College Hill*

Texola (Station) (Estill). See *Pryse*

Thealka (Johnson): thee/*ael*/kə, thee/*ael*/kee (Paintsville). This hamlet and one-time coal town with a po extends for about a mi up KY 581 and the aptly named Muddy Branch from its confluence with Levisa Fork of the Big Sandy R, ½ mi ne of Paintsville. The community was est by the North East Coal Co., and its po, first called Muddy Branch, was est on June 20, 1906, with Mary Matney, pm. She renamed it in 1911 for Alka Mayo, daughter of Greenville Meek—a Paintsville timberman and the owner of a fleet of steamboats—and wife of coal land magnate John C.C. Mayo. The name was also undoubtedly influenced by that given to one of Meek's boats built and named in 1899. He is said to have named the boat, the last of the Big Sandy sidewheelers, "The Alka" for his daughter, but a sign painter ran the letters together and it came out "Thealka." 194, 1353, 1411.

The Bark Yard (Butler). See *Mining City*

The Chapel (Morgan). See *Grassy Creek*

The Crossing (Scott). See *Great Crossing*

The Cross Roads (Rowan). See *Farmers*

The Cross Roads (Union). See *Waverly*

The Forks (Franklin). See *Forks of Elkhorn*

The Forks (Pike). See *Millard*

The Hall (Caldwell). See *Fryer*

The Joe Field(s) (Whitley). See *Woodbine*

The Levy (Bourbon). See *Plum*

Thelma (Johnson): *thehl*/mə (Paintsville). This hamlet with po is on KY 1107 and the Levisa Fork of the Big Sandy R, 1¼ mi e of Paintsville. When the C&O RR extended its Big Sandy line to this point in 1903, it opened a station called Buskirk [*buhs*/kɜk], named for an area family. The po est on June 5, 1905, as Thelma is said to have honored the daughter of either Bill Ward, a Paintsville coal operator, Warren Meek, the editor and publisher of the Paintsville *Herald*, or a Mr. Stratton, a local resident. Miss Ward was the wife of T. J. Spencer, a local storekeeper. The name *Buskirk* is no longer used. 310, 1045, 1353.

The Locks (Henderson). See *Spottsville*

The Mouth (Butler). See *Rochester*

The Point (Henderson). See *Smith Mills*

The Point (Shelby). See *Todds Point*

The Roost (Nicholas). See *Sprout*

The Square PO (Christian). See *Masonville*

The Sparrows Nest (Anderson). See *Sparrow*

The Stock Sale (Letcher). See *Isom*

Thomas (Floyd): *tahm*/əs (Thomas). This extinct po on KY 194 and Johns Creek, 7½ mi e of Prestonsburg, was est on Nov 21, 1889, and named by and for its first pm, Thomas James. It closed in 1965. 1370.

Thompsonville (Christian). See *Oak Grove*

Thousandsticks (Leslie): *thow*/zən(d)/stihx (Hyden West). This po is now at the jct of KY 118 and the Daniel Boone Parkway, 100 yards from its earlier site at the mouth of Thousandsticks Creek, a branch of Bull Creek, 2½ mi nw of Hyden. The po was est as Gad on Mar 1, 1905, at the mouth of Osborne Fork of Bull, ½ mi w of the present site, and named for one of the 12 tribes of Israel or for the prophet who counseled King David. It was moved in 1924 to the mouth of the creek, whose name it then assumed. Two accounts have been offered for the name, which has identified stream, mountain, post office, school, church, and even a newspaper published in Hyden. According to Harry Caudill, "the mountaineer from the earliest times applied the term [sticks] to the trunks of his great trees. Settlers on [this] stream . . . found hundreds of ancient trees which had died of old age. There were so many of them that it was called the 'Thousand Sticks Creek.'" Others recall the tale of the early travelers who came upon the remains of a forest fire—the "straight, charred stumps of trees" which resembled nothing less than a thousand sticks. 37, 106, 1248.

Threeforks (Martin): *three* fawrx (Kermit). This settlement with po lies 1 mi up Petercave Fork of Pigeonroost Fork of Wolf Creek, 8 mi sse of Inez. The po was est in 1938 and named for the 3 forks of Petercave. 1360.

Three Forks (Warren): *three fawrx* (Meador). This hamlet with extinct po at the jct of KY 101 and 1402, 11 mi e of Bowling Green, was probably named for its location at the forks of a rd rather than a stream. It was inc as a town in 1880 and had its own po from 1879 to 1903.

Three Forks PO (Barren). See *Park City*

Three Point (Harlan): *three point* (Harlan). This coal town with extinct po lies near the head of Lick Branch of Martins Fork of the Cumberland R, 6 mi sse of Harlan. It may have been named either for 3 nearby mountain peaks or for the 3 virtues—dependability, service, and quality—claimed for the local mine by its owner, the Three Point Coal Corp. The community, or at least the station at the end of the Lick Branch Spur of the L&N RR's Cumberland Valley Division, may have been called Coalville as early as 1921. The Three Point po was est on Aug 29, 1927, with Louis J. Hampton, pm. 335, 1173.

Three Prong (Greenup): *three* prâhŋ (Tygarts Valley). This now extinct rural settlement and po was on Three Prong Branch of Tygarts Creek, 14 mi wsw of Greenup. The branch was named for the 3 prongs of a nearby ridge. The po was to have been called

Buffalo, but was actually est on Sept 29, 1857, in nearby Carter Co as Three Prong with William A. Womack, pm. It shifted to Greenup Co sometime before 1861 when J. R. Warnock became pm, and was discontinued in 1867. 1369, 1447.

Three Springs (Hart): *three sprihŋz* (Center). This hamlet with extinct po lies at the jct of KY 218, 677, and 740, 10 mi se of Munfordville. This is likely an old settlement since the local church was organized in the early 1820s. The church and later the community and po were named for the 3 springs that emerge from and reenter the ground within a short distance and feed a large underground drainage network in the area. The Three Springs po, est on Feb 11, 1841, with Allen W. Durham, pm, was later transferred to *Park* in Barren Co, and was reest as Three Springs at its original location in 1853. The po was closed in 1919. 863, 1331.

Threlkel (Butler): *threhl*/kəl (Reedyville). Virtually nothing remains of a once thriving community on the Green R, 10 mi e of Morgantown. It and the now extinct po est on Jan 24, 1895, were named for the family of Christopher C. Threlkel, the first pm. 1341.

Thruston (Daviess): *thrū*/stən, *thɜ*/stən (Owensboro East). This hamlet with extinct po at the jct of KY 144 and 405, 4 mi ne of Owensboro, was a thriving trade center in the late 19th cent. The po, in operation from 1886 to 1906, was named for Col. Algernon S. Thruston, a pioneer resident who fought with Sam Houston in Texas's war for independence and was later a member of his cabinet. 1348.

Tichenors Station (McLean). See *Nuckols*

Ticktown (Montgomery). See *Jeffersonville*

Tidalwave (Whitley): *tah*/dəl wāv, *tah*/dəl *wāv* (Wofford). This rural settlement with extinct po is centered at the Tidal Wave Church on Carr Creek, 6½ mi n of Williamsburg. The po was est in this vicinity as Tidal Wave on Apr 12, 1878, with T. Foley, pm. It was respelled as one word in 1895. It is assumed by co historians that the name recalls an early flood, for such were often locally considered "tides" or "tidal waves." 1267, 1380.

Tiger PO (Franklin). See *Peaks Mill*

Tilford (Butler): *tihl*/fərd (Welchs Creek). This extinct po on KY 79, 12 mi ne of Morgantown, was named for N. C. L. Tilford who est it on Nov 11, 1896. George M. Willis was the first pm of record. 1215.

Tiline (Livingston): tah/*leen* (Dycusburg). This hamlet with po is on KY 70, a mi s of the Cumberland R, 8 mi ene of Smithland. The site was first called Cumberland Valley and for some years was owned by an Englishman, Joe D. Tweedle. It was served by the Hillsville po 2 mi e, which was est on June 11, 1890, and named for its local storekeeper and first pm, James I. Hill. Sometime during the 1890s the po was moved to the hamlet of Cumberland Valley, and closed in July 1901. When it reopened the following Oct with William A. Hilliard as pm, it was renamed Tiline for the oldest daughter of Willie A. Doom, in whose store the new po was located. 117, 138.

Tillotson's Precinct (Henderson). See *Niagara*

Tilton (Fleming): *tihl*/tən (Sherburne). This hamlet with extinct po on KY 11, 4½ mi s of Flemingsburg, was first called Pin Hook [*pihn*/hook], a term describing the sharp trading practices of pioneer storekeepers. The first po to serve this area was est on Mar 2, 1836, as Martha Mills [*mahr*/thuh *mihlz*] on Fleming Creek, about 1½ mi n. It was moved to Pin Hook in 1851 and given this name, and then renamed Tilton in 1855. Martha Mills was named for the wife of Jimmy Andrews, operator of the only mill there, a gristmill; it was thus for a time called Andrews' Mill. The po of Tilton and the town chartered under this name in 1854 were named for Richard Tilton, a prosperous landowner and local farmer. The po closed in 1905. 1369.

Timberlake (Kenton). See *Erlanger*

Tinsley (Bell): *tihnz*/lee (Artemus). This hamlet with po is on KY 92 and Greasy Creek, 1 mi above its confluence with the Cumberland R and 3 mi wnw of Pineville. The po was est on Apr 9, 1900, with Charles C. Smith, pm, and named for a local family involved in early coal mine operations in that vicinity. The local station on a spur from Yingling on the main line of the L&N RR's Cumberland Valley Division is Surran, named for W. L. Surran, a local trainmaster. 742, 1416.

Tippecanoe (Oldham). See *Skylight*

Tiptop (Magoffin): *tihp*/tahp (Tiptop). This coal town with extinct po is on KY 1635, 8 mi s of Salyersville. The po was est on Nov 22, 1926, with Frank Hurt, pm, and named for the local Tip Top Mine, which opened in 1924 at the very summit of a ridge. 1422.

Tobacco (Calloway): tə/*baek*/ə, tə/*baek*/ər (Murray). This extinct community was some 600 yards e of the present hamlet of Midway at the jct of US 641 and KY 1828, 2½ mi s of Murray. Around 1830 James Willis, attracted by the tobacco-growing potential of the area, built a tobacco factory here and on Mar 26, 1831, est the Willisville po, which closed in 3 months. A few years later a New Orleans–based firm bought the factory and the community of Tobacco was born. It was not until July 1, 1902, that the Tobacco po was est, with Christopher H. Redden, pm. The po was discontinued on Feb 28, 1927. The community may once also have been known as Needmore for the "scarcity of goods" at the local store. Midway was named for its location halfway between Murray and Hazel. 1401, 1441.

Todd County: tahd. 377 sq mi. Pop 11,640. Seat: Elkton. Todd Co was est in 1819 from parts of Logan and Christian cos and named for Col. John Todd (1750–82), who served with Gen. George Rogers Clark in his Illinois campaigns and was killed in the Battle of Blue Licks.

Todds Point (Shelby): *tahdz poynt* (Ballardsville). This settlement on KY 362, 7 mi nw of Shelbyville, was named for the pioneer Todd family. Its po was est on Apr 18, 1867, with Thomas A. Fountain, pm, and closed in 1913. It is now locally called just The Point. 1378.

Toler (Pike): *toh*/lər (Williamsson). This village with po and a Norfolk & Western RR station is centered at the mouth of Blackberry Fork of Pond Creek, 3 mi from Pond's confluence with the Tug Fork R, and 15½ mi ne of Pikeville. The po, est on June 4, 1907, was probably named for the family of its first pm, James M. P. Toler.

Tolesboro PO (Lewis). See *Tollesboro*

Tollesboro (Lewis): *tohlz*/buhr/oh (Tollesboro). This 6th class city with po is centered at the jct of KY 10 and 57, 13½ mi w of Vanceburg. The early history of the community is not known except that it was served by a po called White House, at some unknown site, from 1839 to 1845. The po was either renamed or moved to what became known as Tolesboro (*sic*) on Oct 23, 1845, with Herman Ebersole, pm. By the 1850s the name was spelled Tolesborough, but it was not until 1916 that the current spelling was formally adopted by the Post Office Department. It was named for the Tolle family, known to have lived in that area since 1809. The town was inc as Tollsboro in 1860, as Tollesboro in 1871, and again as Tollesboro in 1977. 1103, 1200.

Tolu (Crittenden): *tū*/lū (Cave in Rock). This hamlet with po lies on Caney Fork, just above its confluence with Hurricane Creek and ½ mi above the Ohio R, 10 mi nw of

Marion. From 1849 to 1852 a po called Cookseyville served an Ohio R landing at the mouth of Hurricane. It was reest as Hurricane [*h*ɜ/ək/ən] in 1867, and in 1890 was moved ½ mi up the creek to a store and sawmill site owned by J. M. Guess, and renamed Tolu. This name had by then been ''applied'' to Guess's store, which served in an otherwise dry area a whiskey-based tonic made with the extract of tolu prepared from the bark of the Colombian tolu tree. 362, 1336.

Tomahawk (Martin): *tahm*/ə/hawk (Inez). This hamlet with po is on KY 40 and Rockhouse Fork of Rockcastle Creek, 3 mi w of Inez. The po was est as Wells on Aug 20, 1886, and named for its first pm, Richard M. Wells. It was discontinued in 1894 and reest on Nov 4, 1898, as Tomahawk for the *Tomahawk News,* a newspaper then being published in Inez, which apparently had an appeal for the local residents. 1353.

Tompkinsville (Monroe): *tahm*/kihnz/vihl (Tompkinsville). This 5th class industrial city and seat of Monroe Co is 100 mi s of downtown Louisville centered on the jct of KY 100 and 163. In 1809 J. C. Watson, a Virginian, built a log store on the site and a village called Watsons Store soon grew up around it. The town was formally laid out in 1816/17 by Abijah Marrs and included part of his father Samuel's 50-acre farm. By popular vote in 1819 the new town, by then called Tompkinsville for US Vice Pres. Daniel D. Tompkins (1774–1825), was selected as the seat of the new co, which had been named for then Pres. James Monroe. The po of Tompkinsville was est on Jan 17, 1819, with Joseph G. Hardin, pm. 779, 1395.

Toner PO (Perry). See *Leatherwood*

Tongs PO (Greenup). See *Limeville*

Tonieville (LaRue): *tohn*/ee/vihl (Tonieville). This extinct po and station on an Illinois Central Gulf RR spur line, were merely yards from Middle Creek, ¾ mi sw of KY 61, and 3½ mi nw of Hodgenville. The po was est on June 6, 1888, with Robert A. Hubbard, pm, and like the station set up at that time was named for 2 local landowners, Anthony Vernon Goodin and Anthony Kennedy, who were both apparently nicknamed ''Tone.'' 1268, 1319.

Torchlight (Lawrence): *tawrch*/leyet (Louisa). Nothing remains of this late 19th cent coal town on the Levisa Fork of the Big Sandy R, 4 mi s of Louisa. On the site of John Hammond's settlement with store, sawmill,and stave factory, Col. Jay H. Northup est the Torchlight Mine and the community to serve it and house its workers. He is also said to have suggested its name, recalling the customary torchlight parades held on election nights in many eastern Kentucky towns. He referred to the particular event a few weeks earlier when one man dropped or threw his pine torch onto the porch of a Greenup hotel and burned it to the ground. Historians seem to favor this account of the name to other local traditions that refer to residents lighting their way at night with pine torches and to an ever-burning torch that allegedly stood at the mine entrance. On Sept 16, 1902, Torchlight acquired its po with Harry D. Lambert, pm. In 1920–21 the po was known briefly as Superior for the Superior Brick, Tile, and Coal Co., which then had some interest in the place, but the Torchlight name was soon restored. The po closed in 1943. 1194, 1353.

Torrent (Wolfe): *tawr*/ənt (Zachariah). Almost nothing remains of this once prosperous resort community on KY 11 in the narrow valley of the Middle Fork of Red R, 6 mi wsw of Campton. Around 1890 W. A. Byrd built a hotel at the site and on Dec 1 of that year est the Torrent po, aptly named for the huge volume of water that still falls year round from the highest cliff in the area. The rr station and po closed in the 1930s. 67, 1236.

Totz (Harlan): tahts (Louellen). This coal town with po and station on the Poor Fork

Branch of the L&N RR's Cumberland Valley Division is on US 119 and the Poor Fork of the Cumberland R, 12 mi ne of Harlan. It was named for Harry Totz of West Virginia who had acquired the local mine by 1921. The Totz po was est on Apr 18 of that year with Edgar L. Bradley, pm. The station, early called Colton, is now known as Pine Mt. Station for its location at the foot of the Pine Mt. Ridge. 1173.

Touristville (Wayne): *tūr*/ihst/vihl (Mill Springs). This recently closed po was on old KY 90, 7½ mi ne of Monticello. It was est on July 20, 1929, by John R. Wright at a site ¼ mi ne. Three names were submitted to the Post Office Department by his son, Alfred: Wrightsville, Green Valley (his choice), and Touristville, and the 3rd was selected. In retrospect, that name was most aptly applied, for, as was Wright's intention, the po capitalized on the developing tourist trade in nearby *Mill Springs*, 1½ mi nw. In 1934 the po was moved to an old red brick building at the jct of KY 90, 1275, and 1619, believed to have been one of the sites of the Weaverton po, est by and probably named for Stephen A. Weaver and in operation from 1859 to 1887. In 1956 Mrs. Grace Poore moved the Touristville po to its last location. For a number of years, the jct itself was locally known as Crossroads. 1005, 1165, 1424.

Tousey (Grayson): *tow*/see (Falls of Rough). This rural settlement with extinct po at the head of Spring Fork of Rough R, on KY 878, and 13 mi w of Leitchfield, once supported a store and a water-powered mill owned by a Mr. Tousey for whom it was named. The po was est by James D. Wilson on Nov 18, 1880. 1307.

Towers (Kenton). See *White Tower*

Townsend PO (Bourbon). See *Shawhan*

Townsends Mill (Adair). See *Milltown*

Tracy (Barren): *trā*/see (Tracy). This hamlet with extinct po at the jct of KY 87 and 921, 12 mi s of Glasgow, was named for Isaac and Erasmus, 2 sons of Timothy Tracy, pioneer settlers. Timothy settled on a patent on nearby Peters Creek shortly after 1800, while sometime before 1821 Isaac built a home some 200 yards n of the jct. The po was est on Jan 22, 1861, with James M. McAdams, pm. 713.

Tradewater Station (Hopkins). See *Dawson Springs*

Tram (Floyd): traem (Harold). Many of the residents of this village with po on the Levisa Fork of the Big Sandy R, 8 mi sw of Prestonsburg, are the descendants of the natural son of James Shannon Layne, an early landowner, and one of his slaves. The po was est on Mar 5, 1902, with Frank M. Layne, pm, and named for a local tram rd on which logs were moved to the r at that time. 1370.

Trammel (Allen): *traem*/əl (Allen Springs). This crossroads settlement with extinct po lies between the Trammel and Middle Forks of Drake Creek, 8½ mi w of Scottsville. The po, est as Trammel on July 22, 1881, with John B. Russell, pm, was probably named for the stream, which in turn may have been named for Nicholas and Philip Tramel (*sic*), who, according to Collins's *History*, hunted in that section in 1779. One of them is supposed to have been killed by Indians near the mouth of Trammel Fork. 101, 760.

Transylvania (Jefferson). See *Harrods Creek*

Trapp (Clark): traep (Hedges). This hamlet with extinct po lies at the jct of KY 89 and 974, 9 mi se of Winchester. The animal traps hanging from the walls of Berryman's store are said to have inspired the naming of this po on Mar 5, 1904, as Trap to which the 2nd "p" was later added for reasons unknown. The po was discontinued in 1908. 1349.

Travellers Rest (Owsley): *traev*/lərz *rehst* (Sturgeon). This hamlet with extinct po lies at the jct of KY 30 and 847, on Little Sturgeon Creek, 5½ mi wsw of Booneville. The po, est on July 23, 1817, with Benjamin Bondurant, pm, may have been named for a local tavern, then referred to as "travelers' resting places" or simply "travelers' rests," and/or perhaps was suggestive of Isaac Shelby's home, Travelers Rest, s of Danville. The po was converted to a rural station of Booneville in 1964. Some local residents now refer to their home as simply "on Sturgeon." 1287.

Travellers Rest (Pendleton). See *Havilandsville*

Trenton (Todd): *trehn(t)*/ən (Trenton). This 6th class city with po is centered at the jct of US 41 and KY 104, 7 mi sw of Elkton. The site is believed to have been settled in 1796 by a Virginian, Brewer Reeves, and his family. By 1819 the settlement had come to be called Lewisburg for Lewis Leavell who had by then acquired most of the land in the area. Leavell laid out the town in that year. When he learned that another Lewisburg po was in operation in Muhlenberg Co, he suggested the name Trenton, for reasons unknown, and a po of this name was est on Feb 4, 1819, with himself as pm. The town was inc by the Kentucky legislature in 1840 and reinc in 1868 after the coming of the L&N RR brought an addition to the town. 225.

Trevor PO (Hickman). See *Spring Hill*

Trickum (also called *Breckinridge*) (Harrison): *trihk*/əm, *brehk*/ən/rihdj (Breckinridge). This crossroads hamlet with extinct po lies at the jct of KY 36 and 1842, 5 mi nw of Cynthiana. At or near this site was one of the many stops on a well-traveled route between Lexington and Covington which became notorious for its deceptive trading practices, impelling travelers and local people alike to refer to the place as "where they trick 'um" or simply "Trickum." In fact the name Trickum was applied to the local po in operation from 1879 to 1883. This po was reest in 1890 as Breckinridge by Robert L. Clifford, a storekeeper, but closed in 1909. Though the community is identified on maps solely as Breckinridge, most co residents still refer to it as Trickum (generally spelled Tricum). 158, 167, 1227.

Trigg County: trihgh. 421 sq mi. Pop 10,000. Seat: Cadiz. Trigg Co was est in 1820 from parts of Caldwell and Christian cos and named for Col. Stephen Trigg, an early Kentucky pioneer who represented his new home in the Virginia legislature and was killed at the Battle of Blue Licks, Aug 19, 1782.

Trigg Furnace (Trigg): *trihgh f3n*/əs (Lamasco). Nothing remains of a village on KY 274 and Dyers Creek, 5½ mi w of Cadiz, at the site of the iron furnace for which it was named. This hot blast furnace was built by Tennesseean Daniel Hillman in 1871 and operated for only 7 years. The Trigg Furnace po was in operation intermittently from 1871 to 1915. 166.

Trimble (Pulaski): *trihm*/bəl (Delmer). This hamlet with po is on KY 235, 7 mi sw of Somerset. The po was est on Feb 6, 1882, with John C. Ford, pm, and named for a local family. 1410.

Trimble County: *trihm*/bəl. 148 sq mi. Pop 5,900. Seat: Bedford. This co was est in 1836 from parts of Gallatin, Henry, and Oldham Cos and named for Robert Trimble (1777–1828), justice of the Kentucky Court of Appeals (1807–9), US district judge (1817–26), and associate justice of the US Supreme Court (1826–28).

Triplett (Carter). See *Soldier*

Triplett PO (Rowan). See *Morehead*

Trixie (Clay): *trihx*/ee (Oneida). This extinct po lay on the South Fork of the Kentucky R, 13 mi nne of Manchester. The po was est on Jan 6, 1931, and named by the first pm, Jobe Baker, for his dog. It closed in 1966. 1259.

Trosper (Knox): *trahs*/pər (Artemus). This hamlet with po on KY 225 and Brush Creek, a branch of the Cumberland R, 5½ mi se of Barbourville, is said to have been named for Jim Trosper, local landowner. There was probably a community there before the po was est on May 20, 1900, with John R. Trosper, pm. The local rr station, now extinct, was called Bennettsville for Dr. Samuel Bennett, another area landowner who also operated several local coal mines. 1068, 1409.

Trunnelton PO (Bullitt). See *Bardstown Junction*

Tuffy (Fleming). See *Goddard*

Tulip (Clark). See *Pinchem*

Tunnel Mill PO (Perry). See *Dwarf*

Turk (Adair). See *Bliss*

Turkey (Breathitt): *t3k*/ee (Cowcreek). This po on KY 30, 1 mi up Terry Fork of Turkey Creek, and 8½ mi sw of Jackson, serves the Turkey Creek community. It was est on Mar 8, 1894, with Jacob Terry, pm, and named for the creek that was so thickly populated by wild turkeys. Though the community is officially Turkey Creek, local people have always referred to it simply as Turkey. 1310.

Turkey Creek (Breathitt). See *Turkey*

Turkeyfoot (Scott): *t3k*/ee/fo͞ot (Delaplain). Little remains of this 19th cent industrial town on KY 620, 8 mi nne of Georgetown. The area was settled around 1790 and named, possibly by Col. Robert Patterson, for the resemblance to a turkey's foot of the jct of the 3 forks of Eagle Creek. The town of Turkeyfoot was founded around 1817 and the local po was est on Jan 31, 1831, with Bushrod W. Wash, pm. After an intermittent existence, it closed in 1886. 274.

Turmans Ferry PO (Lawrence). See *Buchanan*

Turners Creek (Breathitt). See *Talbert*

Turner's Station (Grant). See *Mason*

Turners Station (Henry): *t3n*/ərz *stā*/shən (Campbellsburg). This recently disincorporated city with po and RR station is centered at the jct of KY 574 and the L&N tracks 8 mi n of New Castle. When the Louisville Cincinnati & Lexington (or Short Line, now L&N) RR was being built through this area in 1867–68, Joseph T. Ransdell donated land there for a right-of-way and depot and on Sept 20, 1869, est a po he called Spring Hill Depot for its location near the foot of the hill above Barker's Spring. A town grew up around the depot and po and in 1876 was inc as Turners Station for the large number of local Turners, the descendants of Virginia-born pioneer Joseph B. Turner. The po was renamed Turners Station in 1879. 59, 64.

Turnersville (Lincoln): *t3n*/ərz/vihl (Halls Gap). This crossroads hamlet with extinct po at the jct of KY 78 and 198, 4 mi sw of Stanford, was named for the family that ran the local store and lived on a nearby farm. The po was est on Feb 6, 1895, with Ellerson O. Livingston, pm, and closed in 1909. Another Turnersville po, at an unknown location in the county, had been in operation from Nov 1851 to Dec 1853. 1448.

Turnertown (Butler). See *Berrys Lick*

Tutor Key (Johnson): *tū*/dər *kee* (Paintsville). This hamlet with po is on Toms Creek, centered at the jct of KY 581 and 993, and less than 2½ mi ne of Paintsville. It is said to have been first called Mingo at the suggestion of Rev. E. J. Harris, who may have been from Mingo Co, West Virginia, and the local po was est with this name on July 3, 1897, with Amanda Preston, pm. In the late 1930s, to avoid the missending of mail to Wingo in Graves Co, the name was changed to Tutor Key. The new name is supposed to have been suggested by Lon Daniels after he had observed a box of shoe polish with this name on a local store shelf. 1134, 1353, 1388.

Twenty Six (Morgan): *twehn(t)*/ee sihx (West Liberty). This extinct po was on KY 772, just w of the Licking R and 5 mi wnw of West Liberty. The first pm, Mrs. Martha

Rowland, is said to have submitted a list of 25 names to the Post Office Department and then added a 26th, simply the year in which she applied for the po. It was officially est on May 3, 1927, and closed in 1957. 1139.

Twin Meeting House PO (Owen). See *New Liberty*

Two Mile Town (Jefferson). See *Buechel*

Tyewhoppety (Todd): teye/*whah*/pə/tee (Rosewood). (Also spelled Tywoppity, Tiwappiti, etc.) This rural settlement is on KY 181, 14½ mi n of Elkton. The name is of uncertain origin and is believed to have been applied by Buchan Rager less than 100 years ago, for reasons unknown. The community has no po. It has been suggested that the name refers to an "unkempt, ill-appearing person," but George R. Stewart believes it to be Shawnee for "place of no return," transferred from a nearby stream, and implying a "place from which it is as easy to go forward as to return." 204, 929, 1295.

Tygarts Creek PO (Greenup). See *Lynn*

Tyner (Jackson): *tahn*/ər (Tyner). This village with po is centered at the jct of KY 30 and 1431, 7½ mi se of McKee. The po was est on Feb 10, 1880, by Robert D. Gibson. According to one tradition, none of the names Gibson submitted to the Post Office Department was acceptable so a postal official suggested his own name, Tyner. Others believe that Tyner was one of the original names submitted but they do not know why, nor why it was accepted. 1418, 1425.

Tyrone (Anderson): *teye*/*rohn* (Tyrone). Until Prohibition, Tyrone was a major distilling and trade center on the Kentucky R, at a point ¾ mi se of US 62, and 2½ mi e of Lawrenceburg. At or near the site of an earlier wharfhouse and landing called Streamville, James Ripy in 1869 opened a distillery, which he named Tyrone for his native co in Ireland. Under this name the town that grew up in the nearby bottoms was inc in 1879. The local po, est on Apr 7, 1882 as Coke for its pm, John T. Coke, was renamed Tyrone on Aug 9, 1893. Little remains of the town; the po and stores are gone and the buildings of the Ripy Bros. Distillery on the hill below the town are now occupied by the Austin-Nichols Distillery. Another example of folk etymology has been encountered here: "A man rode a roan mare to the river and tied her to a tree on the bank. Then he got in a skiff to row across the river. He looked around and saw that the horse was loose and he yelled to a man on the bank to 'tie er roan.'" 293, 1255, 1387.

Ula (Pulaski): *yū*/lə (Dykes). This extinct po on KY 1003, ¼ mi e of Buck Creek and 8 mi e of Somerset, was est on May 6, 1925, by Robert L. Hail and named for his baby daughter, Eula Hail. Hail originally submitted the name Sears but when he learned it was already in use he replaced it with Eula. For some reason it was spelled Ula in the application and this spelling was officially recorded and never changed. The po was discontinued in 1964. 837.

Ulvah (Letcher): *uhl*/vee (Vicco). This hamlet with po lies on the North Fork of the Kentucky R, 11½ mi w of Whitesburg. It was est on Oct 1, 1897, by William T. Haney, who called it Gourd. In 1912 the L&N RR reached this point and, it is said, named its local station for a line from Thomas Campbell's poem, *Lord Ullin's Daughter:* "Oh, I'm the chief of Ulva's Isle. . . ." Two years later the po also assumed this name. Mr. Watts' local "egg factory" recently inspired the nickname Chicken City. 1265.

Ulysses (Lawrence): yū/*lihs*/əs (Richardson). This extended settlement is centered at its po on old US 23 and Georges Creek, 11½ mi ssw of Louisa. The po, est on Feb 13, 1888, with Jedediah F. Davis, pm, is said to have been named for Ulysses S. Grant (1822–85), Civil War general and 18th US president. 1131.

Union (Madison). See *Union City*

Union City (Madison): *yūn*/yən *sih*/tee (Union City). This crossroads hamlet with recently discontinued po on KY 1986, 5 mi ne of Richmond, was first called Breckville. At least its first po was est with this name on Aug 15, 1851, with Absolom B. Stivers, pm. This po was discontinued in 1855 and reest in 1857 as Union Meeting House, which closed in 1859. The Union City po was est in 1876 with William Powell, pm. Thenceforth both Union and Union City identified the community, with the latter name probably in use to distinguish it from the Union Meeting House which had given it its name. 1294.

Union County: *yūn*/yən. 341 sq mi. Pop 17, 821. Seat: Morganfield. Union Co was est in 1811 from part of Henderson Co and is alleged to have been named for the united desire of its residents to form a new co.

Union Meeting House PO (Madison). See *Union City*

Union Star (Breckinridge): *yūn*/yən Stahr (Lodiburg). This hamlet with po is centered at the jct of KY 144 and 86, 10 mi n of Hardinsburg. This site was settled around 1790 by the family of John Helm from Severns Valley (now Elizabethtown) and was first called Jackeysburg for reasons unknown. The po was est as Union Star on Mar 12, 1852, with Jacob S. White, pm. It was named for the Union Meetinghouse organized there in 1845 by Thomas D. Helm, local landowner and storekeeper, and the 5 rds extending from this point to neighboring towns, a configuration said to have given the place the appearance of a star. Under this name the town was inc in 1868. 21.

Uniontown (Union): *yūn*/yən/town (Uniontown). This 5th class city with po, a former shipping port, is on KY 130, 268 and 360 and the Ohio R, 5 mi n of Morganfield. The town and its name resulted from the unification in 1840 of the towns of Francisburg and Locust Port. The first had been laid off by Benjamin Berry on his land and chartered as Francesburg (*sic*) by the Kentucky General Assembly in 1819. It was possibly named for Francis Berry, Sr., who in 1811 is known to have sold to William Berry part of a tract that had originally been granted to Andrew Waggener by the Virginia legislature. It was again inc, but as Francisburg, in 1839, probably to correct the original spelling error. In this year the adjacent town of Locust Port was also chartered, having recently been est on land owned by Peter and Philander Berry. According to tradition, rivalry between the 2 towns was ended when they were united and then aptly inc as Uniontown. The first po to serve this vicinity was Locust Landing, est on May 13, 1834, by Philander Berry who renamed it Locust Port in 1836. In 1842 the po assumed the name of the newly inc town. 238.

Uno (Hart): *yū*/noh (Park). This hamlet with extinct po at the jct of US 31E and KY 571, 6 mi se of Munfordville, is said to have first been called Clear Point or Clear Pint. Local people will not admit to the latter, but can not explain the former. The traditional tale is that it was first named for what one could buy there, a very clear brand of corn whiskey, and that when the po was est it was called Clear Point as more seemly for a po. The po of Uno was est there on Oct 24, 1887, with John M. Perkins, pm, with the Clear Pointers suggesting that this is but the Spanish word *uno* meaning "number one," obviously applied to the po and community as a commendatory name. The Clear Pinters, however, recall that, whenever a resident was asked where he was going, he would reply "Oh, you know." Actually there were 2 Clear Point po at 2 different locations. One was est on May 22, 1843, with William H. L. Renfro, pm, and closed in 1856; the other was est on Feb 20, 1846, with John B. Cobb, pm, and discontinued in 1860. It is not known which was the forerunner of Uno. The Uno po closed in 1906. 863, 1331.

Upchurch (Clinton): *uhp*/cherch (Savage). This settlement with extinct po is on KY 2063, (old KY 90) 3 mi n of Albany. The po was est on Aug 8, 1908, with Perry L. Brown, pm. It was probably named for the area's first settler, Ahile Upchurch, whose son Abe co-owned the local store with Brown. The po closed in 1940. 1263.

Upper Kings Addition (Greenup). See *South Shore*

Upton (Hardin and LaRue): *uhp*/tən (Upton). This 6th class city with po is centered at the jct of US 31W and KY 224, just w of I 65, 13½ mi s of Elizabethtown 10½ mi sw of Hodgenville. The first po to serve this area was est as Leesville in Hart Co on Jan 1, 1841, with Silas Lee, pm. In 1856 George Washington Upton moved this po about 2 mi n, to a site his father Edward had purchased around 1812 and on which a store was already in operation, and renamed it Uptonville for himself. By 1859 the local L&N RR station had been est as Upton's, and as Upton the town was inc in 1866. The po assumed the shortened form of the name in 1892. 136, 789.

Uptonville (Hardin and LaRue). See *Upton*

Uttingertown (Fayette): *uht*/ən/djər/town (Clintonville). This all black settlement is just off Royster Rd and n of US 60, 4½ mi e of Lexington's New Circle Rd. In 1869 Samuel L. Uttinger divided his farm and sold it off in individual lots to freed slaves; then, it is said, he mysteriously disappeared and was never seen or heard from again. The residents of this community later named it for him. 33, 393.

Uz (Letcher): *yū*/*zee* (Roxana). This one-time L&N RR station and extinct po were on the North Fork of the Kentucky R, 2 mi w of Whitesburg. This was the scene of the early frustrations of W. S. Morton, Jr., the resident engineer responsible for laying the eastern Kentucky Division tracks through Letcher Co in 1911–12. From the very beginning, wrote Mr. Morton some years later, "the railroad encountered tough sledding at and around what is now Uz. Property owners forbid surveying parties to cross their land; then the right of way could not be bought at a reasonable price; ground for a depot was hard to obtain; the contractor was always behind in his work; bootleggers kept the construction camp in an uproar; and the contractor and the resident engineer were always squabbling." Finally one day, after J. E. Willoughby, the L&N's supervising engineer, "had listened to a recap of Mr. Morton's troubles," he suggested the analogy to the biblical Job's difficulties in the land of Uz. Morton asked if he could honor Job's homeland and name the station Uz. This was done and it has been Uz ever since, though always locally pronounced "yuzee." The local po was est as Field on Mar 2, 1906, on the North Fork of the Kentucky R, just above the mouth of Dry Fork. In 1914 the po was renamed Uz when it was moved down r to the station site. 740, 1265.

Vail PO (Bath). See *Salt Lick*

Valley Hill (Washington): *vael*/ee *hihl* (Maud). This station on the L&N RR's Bardstown Branch and extinct po are on KY 55, just e of Cartwright Creek and 4 mi nnw of Springfield. The po was est on Mar 1, 1888, with Thomas S. Grundy, pm, and named for the home built in 1822 by Charles Grundy, son of pioneer Samuel Grundy and nephew of US Sen. Felix Grundy. The po closed in 1906. 523, 1314.

Valley PO (Lewis). See *Charters*

Valley Station (Jefferson): *vael*/ee *stā*/shən (Valley Station, Kosmosdale, Louisville West). This unincorporated area of over a dozen suburban subdivisions spreads out from the jct of US 31W/60 and Valley Station Rd (KY 907), 12 mi ssw of downtown Louisville. The local po, est on June 22, 1874, with William T. Kennedy, pm, and the community that grew up around it were named for the station built that year on the present Valley Station Rd by the Elizabethtown & Paducah (now Illinois Central Gulf) RR. The area no longer has its own po. 728.

Valley View (Madison): *vael*/ee *vyū* (Valley View). This hamlet with extinct po extends for nearly a mi along KY 169 s from the Kentucky R, 9 mi nw of Richmond. Laid out as a town in 1891 by J. H. Powell and S. F. Rock to accommodate a thriving though relatively short-lived sawmill operation, it partly occupies the site of a community that may be traced back to 1785 when John Craig est a Kentucky R ferry there. The community's name is known to have preceded its est as a po, on Nov 27, 1891, and town, and is believed to have been inspired by the beautiful view seen from the hilltop across the river in Fayette Co. 57, 790, 1294.

Vanarsdell (Mercer): və/*nahrz*/dəl (McBrayer). This settlement with extinct po and former station on what is now the Southern Ry lies just e of the Salt R, 8 mi n of Harrodsburg. The community, station, and po est on Nov 2, 1889, with George W. Robinson, pm, were probably named for Jackson Van Arsdall (*sic*), a local farmer and distiller and member of one of the co's distinguished pioneer families. 40, 1264.

Van Buren (Anderson): *vaen byū*/rən (Chaplin). This extinct village was on the Salt R, 14 mi wsw of Lawrenceburg. It was laid out in 1835 by Edward Harris on his farm at the mouth of Crooked Creek and named for Martin Van Buren who was soon to become president of the US. The po was est on May 23, 1850, with Jacob W. Lindle, pm, and with many intermissions it operated until it closed in 1922. From 1886 the name was spelled Vanburen, though on all recent maps the 2-word spelling has been used. 140, 1387, 1453.

Vanceburg (Lewis): *vaens*/bergh (Vanceburg). This 4th class city and seat of Lewis Co lies on the Ohio R and KY 8, 10, and 59, 123 mi ene of downtown Louisville. It was founded in 1797 by Moses Baird and Joseph Calvin Vance on land acquired that year from Alexander Keith Marshall, brother to the future Supreme Court Justice John Marshall, and named for Vance. The Vanceburg po was est on July 3, 1815, with George Swingle, Jr., pm, and the town was chartered by the Kentucky legislature in 1827. In Dec 1863 the legislature authorized the removal of the co's seat from *Clarksburg;* this was effected the following year. Vanceburg is still referred to by oldtimers as Alum City for a large rock, surrounded by deposits of alum, which lies on a hill overlooking the town from the e. 769, 1103.

Vandyke Mill PO (Spencer). See *Rivals*

Vanfleet PO (Hart). See *Priceville*

Van Lear (Johnson): *vaen* leer, *vaen leer* (Paintsville). This village and former coal town with po extends for several miles along Miller Creek, a tributary of the Levisa Fork of the Big Sandy R, 1½ mi se of Paintsville's present city limits. In 1909 the Consolidation Coal Co. acquired John C. C. Mayo's large coal holdings here and est a town named for Van Lear Black, a member of their board of directors. Frederick H. King became the first pm on Nov 10, 1909. The town was disincorporated in 1963. 19, 89, 350.

Van Lear Junction PO (Johnson). See *West Van Lear*

Varilla (Bell): və/*rihl*/ə (Varilla). This coal town and station on the L&N RR's Cumberland Valley Division are 5 mi e of Pineville. T. J. Asher, wealthy landowner and developer of the region's timber and coal resources, est the town and named it for his wife Varilla (nee Howard) (1848–1935). A po was in operation here from 1912 to 1930. 79, 1416.

Varney (Pike): *vahr*/nee (Varney). This po on the Left Fork of Brushy Fork of Johns

Creek, 11 mi nne of Pikeville, was est on Apr 6, 1904, and named by and for its first pm, William Larkin Varney. 1108.

Vaughns Mill (Powell): *vahnz mihl* (Clay City). This hamlet extends at least 1½ mi along KY 1057 and Hardwicks Creek, some 3½ mi sw of Stanton. It was named for a mill on Hardwicks Creek, about a mi s of its confluence with Red R, that was built by Samuel J. Vaughn, a Virginian. The po was est in Isaac Mize's store by the mill on Jan 12, 1881, with Mize as pm. The mill closed around World War I. The po moved at least twice up the creek until, at the mouth of Little Hardwicks Creek, it closed in the late 1950s. 701, 1334.

Veazey (Hopkins): *vee*/zee (Slaughtersville). This settlement with extinct po on KY 630, 7½ mi nw of Madisonville, was founded before the Civil War by the 4 Veazey brothers and their 2 sisters from Granville Co, North Carolina. The po was est on Apr 13, 1888, in Louis N. Veazey's store and was discontinued in 1909. 159.

Venters (Pike): *vehn*/tərz (Hellier). This hamlet with extinct po is centered on KY 195, at the mouth of Lick Branch of Marrowbone Creek, a tributary of Russell Fork of the Levisa Fork of the Big Sandy R, 10 mi sse of Pikeville. The po was est on July 10, 1882, and named for its first pm, Adam Venters, who owned most of the area at that time. The po was discontinued in 1894 and reest on Apr 30, 1910, as Carmen by Willie Ratliff who named it for his daughter. 934, 1354.

Vera Cruz (Gallatin): *vehr*/ə *krūz* (Sanders). This extinct village on the present KY 35, near the head of the Vera Cruz Branch of Craigs Creek, 2½ mi s of Warsaw, grew up around an antebellum stage stop and inn. According to tradition, inn, village, and stream were named for the coincidence of a local fight and the Mexican War battle of Vera Cruz on Mar 9, 1847. The village never had its own po. 87.

Verda (Harlan): *vɜd*/ə (Evarts). This coal town and rr station are on Clover Fork of the Cumberland R, at the mouth of Jones Creek, 4½ mi e of Harlan. The town and its now extinct po, est on Apr 24, 1917, with Chad Middleton, pm, are said to have been named for Verda Middleton, pioneer settler. 335.

Versailles (Woodford): ver/*sālz* (Versailles, Tyrone). This 4th class city and seat of Woodford Co is on US 60 and 62, 52 mi ese of downtown Louisville. It was laid out and founded in 1792 on the site of a pioneer settlement called Falling Springs and named by trustee Gen. Marquis Calmes for the birthplace of Lafayette, on whose staff he had served in the Revolutionary War. The po has been in operation since 1802. 180, 374, 1269.

Vertrees (Hardin): ver/*trees* (Constantine). This po lies just w of the jct of KY 86 and Rough R and 13 mi w of Elizabethtown. It was est on July 6, 1881, as Vertrus, an obvious error that was corrected in 1895. Both the po and the nearby Vertrees Creek, a tributary of Rough R, were named for an early family whose progenitor, Joseph Vertrees, built a cabin between the creek and the river in 1810. 136.

Vertrus PO (Hardin). See *Vertrees*

Vest (Knott): vehst (Vest). This hamlet with po is on KY 1087 and Balls Fork of Troublesome Creek, 3½ mi n of Hindman. The po was est on Jan 31, 1886, with William Grigsby, pm, and named for the postal inspector who had been sent to validate the need for a po and who stayed to assist in its est. Nothing else is known about him. 1391.

Vianna (Clark): vee/*aen*/ə (Palmer). This virtually extinct village is on the Red R, 12½ mi se of Winchester. It may have grown up around a mill and ferry depot before 1860 and named, for reasons unknown, for the Austrian capital. The Vienna po was est on Mar 3, 1863, with John Rucker, pm, and discontinued in 1874. Though the name was spelled Vienna in postal records and on 19th cent maps, it is now locally almost exclusively spelled Vianna, probably reflecting its traditional pronunciation. In the 19th cent, Vienna or Vianna was not an uncommon feminine given name and this could possibly have been its origin. 328, 975.

Vicco (Perry and Knott): *vihk*/oh (Vicco). This 6th class city with po is on KY 15 and Carr Fork of the North Fork of the Kentucky R, 5½ mi ese of Hazard. Though there may have been a settlement here prior to the est of the Montgomery Creek Coal Co. mines in the vicinity, it was at this time that the town and its po were est as Montago, named for the co. and the creek, which joins Carr Fork at this point. The Montago po, which opened on Mar 1, 1921, with William McK. Stacy, pm, was renamed Vicco in 1923 for the Virginia Iron Coal and Coke Co. which then dominated coal production in the area. 1186, 1327.

Vienna PO (Clark). See *Vianna*

Villa Hills (Kenton): *vihl*/ə *hihlz* (Covington). This 4th class city is between Crescent Springs and the Ohio R, 8 mi n of the court house in Independence. The community is centered on the 86-acre tract on Bromley Heights that the Benedictine Sisters of Covington purchased in 1903 and named Villa Madonna at the suggestion of Father Rhabanus, OSB, then pastor of St. Joseph Church in Covington. It means "Country Seat of Our Lady." The city of Villa Hills was inc in 1962. It does not have its own po. 41.

Vine Grove (Hardin): *vahn ghrohv* (Vine Grove). This 4th class city with po, contiguous to the larger and newer city of Radcliffe, centers at the jct of KY 144 and the Illinois Central Gulf RR, 6 mi nw of Elizabethtown. It was first located 1½ mi w, where KY 144 crosses Otter Creek. Here in 1850 Mike Flaherty opened a blacksmith shop, and on Aug 26, 1856, the po was est with Anthony Swabentham, pm. It was named for the "profusion of wild grape vines which grew intertwined in the oak forest that covered a major portion of the land at the town's inception." In or shortly after 1865, in anticipation of the coming of the rr that was completed in 1873, the town moved to its present site. 249, 1420.

Vineyard (Jessamine): *vihn*/yərd (Little Hickman). This hamlet at the jct of US 27 and Hoover Pike, less than 1½ mi s of Nicholasville, was named for a long-abandoned commercial vineyard about a mi se. The age of the community, which never had its own po, is not known, but the vineyard itself dates back to the antebellum period when it was worked by slave labor. 1390.

Viney Fork PO (Madison). See *Waco*

Vinnie (Russell): *vihn*/ee (Eli, Faubush). This extinct po lay just off KY 196, 10 mi e of Jamestown. The po was est on Jan 5, 1898, by Green M. McKinley, local storekeeper, who named it for his girl friend, Vinnie McClendon. For years the po and local school were located just over the Pulaski Co line. In 1938 the po was moved to Russell Co and was discontinued in 1958. 1410.

Viola (Graves): vah/*yohl*/ə (Hickory). This village with extinct po now occupies 2 sites: the original, on the Illinois Central Gulf RR, which consists only of John W. Whittemore's store, and what is now called West Viola, about a mi w, at the jct of US 45 and KY 408, 7 mi n of Mayfield. The community and station may have been named for the wife of an early Whittemore who is said to have given the right-of-way and station site to the New Orleans & Ohio RR in the 1850s. The Viola po was in operation from 1884 to 1910. In the days when the Whittemore family owned most of the businesses in town it had the nickname of Whittemoreville. 346, 1228.

Viper (Perry): *vah*/pər (Hazard South). This hamlet with po extends along KY 7 from the mouth of Elk Branch, 3 mi sse of Hazard, for almost a mi up the North Fork of the Kentucky R. The first po to serve this area, from 1875 to 1879, was Hallsville, at the mouth of Wicks Branch of Maces (Masons) Creek. It was named by and for its first pm, Philip W. Hall, a Virginia-born surveyor and timber dealer. On May 26, 1886, Enoch C. Campbell, who had succeeded Hall as pm, had the po reest at the mouth of Maces Creek, a branch of the North Fork. According to local tradition a young man, Phillip Fields, suggested the name for a large snake some boys had just killed on the rd near Campbell's store. 55, 114.

Virgie (Pike): *vɜ*/djee (Dorton). This village with po is on US 23/119, 9 mi sse of Pikeville. The po, est as Clintwood on Apr 3, 1890, with James M. Damron, pm, shortly assumed the name of the 14-year-old daughter of W. O. B. Ratliff, a Pikeville lawyer and timber dealer. 947.

Visalia (Kenton): vihs/*āl*/yə (Alexandria). This village with extinct po between KY 177 and the Licking R, 5 mi ese of Independence, was settled sometime before 1807 by Nathaniel Vise, Jr. In 1818 he was authorized by the then Campbell Co Court to est the town later called Visalia for him. For a brief period, in 1827, it was the Campbell co seat. The first po to serve that area was est on Jan 2, 1855, as New Canton, probably across the Licking. In 1859 George Watson moved it a short distance upstream to Visalia and it was renamed. 94, 753.

Viva (Laurel): *vee*/və or *vih*/və (London). This extinct po, coal camp, and station were on the long-defunct Altamont & Manchester Branch of the L&N RR, 3 mi n of London. The site was first called Wild Cat, but the po in operation from 1900 to 1933 was named for Viva Thompson, an early resident. Little remains to bear the name but the Viva Church. 1282.

Volney PO (Logan). See *Olmstead*

Volney Station PO (Logan). See *Olmstead*

Wabd (Rockcastle): waeb (Maretburg). This hamlet with extinct po is on KY 461, 3 mi sw of Mount Vernon. The name was derived from the initials of its first pm, William A.B. Davis, when the po was est on June 17, 1886. 1243.

Waco (Madison): *wā*/koh (Moberly). This hamlet with po is centered at the jct of old KY 52 and 977, 7 mi e of Richmond. The first po to serve this area was Viney Fork, est on June 2, 1837, with David S. Goodloe, pm, and named for the branch of Muddy Creek, several mi sw of Waco, that is overrun with trees and wild vines. In 1846 the po was moved to the site of William Covington Ogg's Mill on Muddy Creek. In 1850 Thomas S. Ellis moved the po to a site on Muddy Creek ½ mi w of the present Waco and renamed it Elliston. It was moved to and renamed Waco in 1861 when Lucien T. Griggs became pm. In 1866 it returned to Elliston but was brought back to Waco in 1869. Waco is alleged to have been named for Waco, Texas, by Phil A. Huffman who arrived around 1847 to buy Matthew D. Grinstead's pottery business. The Texas community in turn was named for the Hueco Indians who had a village there earlier in the cent. 57, 1076, 1294.

Waddy (Shelby): *wah*/dee (Waddy). This village with po is centered at the jct of KY 395 and 637, 8½ mi se of Shelbyville. Once inc, it was named for Maj. W. L. Waddy who donated the land to the Southern Ry for their right-of-way and depot on the condition that the town to be est there be named for him. The rr was completed through in 1888, and on Aug 22 of that year the Waddy po was est with Thompson M. Waddy, pm. 337.

Wadesboro (Calloway): *wādz*/buhr/ə (Dexter). The extinct first seat of Calloway Co was on the West Fork of Clarks R, 7 mi n of Murray, 300 yards from the Marshall Co line. This site may have been settled in 1817–18 by Banester (Banister or Bannister) Wade (1777?–1838), from Halifax, Virginia, for whom the community he was to serve as merchant was named when it was est in 1821–22. It became the seat of the new co in 1822 and the po was est on Mar 12, 1824, with James W. Calloway, pm. The co's seat was removed to Murray in 1847 and the po was closed in 1904. 588, 626, 972.

Wagersville (Estill): *wādj*/ərz/vihl (Irvine). This extinct po was in the bottoms of Station Camp Creek, a tributary of the Kentucky R, 4½ mi ese of Irvine. Storekeeper Jonah Wagers est the po on May 14, 1891, and named it for himself. It closed in 1972. 865.

Waggoners Corner (Rowan). See *Wagners Store*

Wagner (Pike). See *Mossy Bottom*

Wagner PO (Rowan). See *Wagners Store*

Wagners Store (Rowan): *waegh*/nərz *stawr* (Haldeman). This jct of KY 32 and 173, 8 mi e of Morehead, though not identified on any maps, is known locally as Wagners Store or Waggoners Corner (the spellings are interchangeable), honoring Uncle Bill Waggoner, a local storekeeper in the 1920s and 30s. According to a 1935 topographic map, the place may then have also been called Mt. Tabor. There never was a po at this site, but a po called Wagner, of unknown derivation, was est in 1894 by Samuel B. Caudill on Craney Creek, some 3 mi sw. It was moved in 1911 to a site on the present KY 1167, some 2½ mi s of Wagners Store, where it closed in 1933. 1412.

Waitsboro (Pulaski): *wāts*/buhr/ə (Delmer). This extinct town was at the head of navigation on the Cumberland R (a site now covered by Lake Cumberland), about 3 mi s of the present Somerset city limits. In 1844 the town of Waitsborough (*sic*) was est by legislative act and named for Cyrenius Wait [seye/*reen*/əs] (1794–1868), who had arrived in Pulaski Co from Chester, Massachusetts in 1818 and become a prominent Somerset businessman and the co's largest landowner. The po was est as Waitsboro on Mar 2, 1846, with William L. Wait, Cyrenius's brother, as pm. In 1864 Joseph R. Newell moved the po some 2½ mi sw and renamed it Clio, under which name it operated until 1885. A Waitsboro po was reest at the original site in 1905 but it closed after only 3 years. 767, 1410.

Walbridge (Lawrence): *wâhl*/brihdj (Louisa). This extinct po and C&O RR station were on KY 644, at the confluence of Three Mile Creek and the Levisa Fork of the Big Sandy R, 2 mi s of Louisa. The po, in operation from 1881 to 1913, and station were named for W. Delancy Walbridge, a 19th cent coal and rr developer. (See also *Helechawa.*)

Walden (Whitley): *wâhl*/dən (Wofford). This extinct po on KY 511, 6 mi n of Williamsburg, was named for Benjamin Walden who had come from Elk Valley, Tennessee in 1882. Neighbors came to call the immediate vicinity of his home Walden's Place and the po, est there on May 14, 1902, with B. F. Harp, pm, was called Walden. 1267.

Walden's Place (Whitley). See *Walden*

Wales (Pike): wālz (Wheelwright). This hamlet with recently discontinued po is on KY 122 and Indian Creek, just above the mouth of Turkeypen Branch, 10½ mi ssw of Pikeville. The po was est on Dec 28, 1907, with Henry C. Akers, pm. At the suggestion of local resident Jim Anderson, it was named for a small community in Giles Co, Tennessee, which is said to have been named for the division of the United Kingdom. 1456.

Walker (Knox): *wâhk*/ər (Scalf). This hamlet with po lies on Stinking Creek and KY

223, 9 mi e of Barbourville. It was named for a local family, probably before the po was est as Walkers by Augustus Walker on Jan 10, 1890. The po was discontinued in 1895 and reest as Walker in 1899. Brice Walker, son of John, a Knox Co pioneer, had settled in this vicinity sometime in the 1830s. 1409.

Walker's Station (Hardin). See *Glendale*

Wallace Crossroads (Garrard). See *Lancaster*

Wallace PO (Woodford). See *Nugents Crossroads*

Wallace Station PO (Woodford). See *Nugents Crossroads*

Wallace's Warehouse (Henry). See *Lockport*

Wallins Creek (Harlan): *wahl*/ənz *kreek* (Wallins Creek). This 6th class city with L&N RR station and po is on the Cumberland R at the mouth of Wallins Creek, 4½ mi w of Harlan. The creek was early named for a pioneer Virginia surveyor who is said to have been killed by Indians in that vicinity. The Wallins Creek po was est on May 22, 1866, with John C. Howard, Jr., pm. 46, 1173.

Wallonia (Trigg): wâhl/*ohn*/yə (Cobb). This hamlet at the jct of KY 128 and 276, 5 mi nne of Cadiz, was settled around 1820 and named for Maj. Braxton Wall, a pioneer mill builder and its first storekeeper. The po was est on Dec 18, 1838, with Samuel McKinney, another local storekeeper, as pm. After an intermittent existence, the po closed in 1952. 98, 166.

Walltown (Casey): *wawl*/town (Eubank). This hamlet on KY 837, 9½ mi e of Liberty, is on part of a 700-acre tract acquired by Jake and Bob Wall in 1807 and inherited by the latter's son in 1863. The local po, in operation from 1886 to 1907, was called Douglas for another local family. 212, 220, 1397.

Walnut Grove (Pulaski): *wahl*/nət *ghrohv* (Maretburg). This hamlet with po lies just s of Bee Lick Creek, ½ mi n of KY 934, 13½ mi ne of Somerset. On Aug 9, 1888, John Riddle est a po here called Glades, the descriptive name by which the area was then known. On June 15, 1889, he had it changed to Walnut Grove for the local walnut trees. 1410.

Walnut Grove Community (Morgan). See *Caney*

Walnut Grove PO (Caldwell). See *Crider*

Walnut Hill (Casey). See *Priceton*

Waltersville (Powell). See *Clay City*

Walton (Boone): *wahl*/tən (Walton). This 5th class city with po is on US 25, just e of I 75, and 11½ mi sse of Burlington. The site is said to have been first settled in 1786 by a Virginia-born Revolutionary War veteran, Col. Abner Gaines, who, with the financial help of a ship's captain named Walton, est an important tavern and stage stop on the rd between Covington and Lexington (now US 25). The local po was est as Gaines on July 4, 1815, with James M. Gaines, pm, and the community was called Gaines' Cross Roads until, by an act of the Kentucky legislature in 1840, it was renamed, allegedly for the captain. Curiously no record of this person has ever been found. The po also assumed the Walton name in 1840 and the town was inc as such in 1854. 26, 250, 281, 1284.

Walton City (Hopkins). See *Barnsley*

Walton's Lick PO (Washington). See *Polin*

Waltz (Rowan): wâhlts (Cranston). This extinct po 4 mi up Rock Fork of the North Fork of Triplett Creek, a branch of the Licking R, and 6½ mi n of Morehead, was est on Dec 26, 1906, with Dawson M. Waltz, pm, and probably named for the family of Richard Waltz.

Wanamaker (Webster): *wahn*/ə/māk/ər (Dixon). This extinct po on KY 1191, 5½ mi n of Dixon, was est on May 2, 1890, and named for John Wanamaker (1838–1922) who was then postmaster general of the U.S. but is better known today as a Philadelphia merchant. It closed in 1907. Emma G. Sammons, the local storekeeper, was the only pm. 1174.

War Creek (Breathitt): *wâhr* kreek (Jackson). This recently discontinued po on KY 541, at the mouth of Trace Fork of War Creek, 6 mi wnw of Jackson, served the residents of this branch of the North Fork of the Kentucky R. The po was est on Oct 27, 1908, with Andrew J. Johnson, pm, and named for the stream, which according to tradition was named for one or more early fights there.

Ward City (Johnson). See *Offutt*

Wardsville (Anderson). See *Sparrow*

Warfield (Martin): *wawr*/feeld (Kermit). This village with po on Tug Fork of the Big Sandy R is centered at the jct of KY 40 and 292, 6 mi e of Inez. It grew up around a salt works est at the mouth of Collins Fork of Tug in the early 1850s by George Rogers Clark Floyd and John Warfield of Virginia, and was named for the latter when the po was est on Apr 15, 1856. Floyd, a brother to the Virginia governor, is also said to have opened the first coal mine in the future Martin Co and to have developed this town as a shipping point on the r. The co seat, located here in the largest town when the co was est in 1870, was transferred to *Inez* 3 years later. 194.

Warnock (Greenup): *wâhr*/nək (Oldtown). This hamlet is on KY 2 and 7 in the Tygarts Creek bottoms, 9 mi sw of Greenup. It was probably named for James Warnock (1781–1856), who owned a large tract of land in the vicinity. The po was est in John P. Warnock's store on Mar 5, 1891, with Warnock as pm, and was discontinued in 1958. According to local tradition, at a sawmill which may have been located where KY 2 and 7 separate, a new fireman "was censured his first day for failing to keep up enough steam to operate the sawmill, so the next day he kept piling wood on the fires. An explosion resulted and pieces of the boiler flew into the air. . . ." Ever since then the section below Warnock has been called Red Hot. 23, 1447, 1451.

Warren (Knox): *wahr*/ən (Artemus). This residential community and former coal camp is on KY 225 at the mouth of Chestnut Branch of Brush Creek and 7 mi s of Barbourville. It is said that a syndicate from Warren, Pennsylvania, had acquired a large section of undeveloped coal land there and, as the Cumberland Coal Co. and the Cumberland RR Co., completed 8 mi of track up Brush Creek from Artemus, opened some mines, and named their coal camp there for their hometown. On Apr 4, 1906, the Warren po was est with James W. Owens, pm. However, it is also believed that the place was named for J. C. Warren, a local mine owner, and one James M. Warren became pm on Jan 25, 1907. Perhaps the Warrens came from the Pennsylvania town of that name. The po has since closed. 208, 1206, 1409.

Warren County: *wahr*/ən. 548 sq mi. Pop 70,068. Seat: Bowling Green. This co was est in 1796 from part of Logan Co and named for Gen. Joseph Warren, the Massachusetts physician, who was killed in the Battle of Bunker Hill in 1775.

Warsaw (Gallatin): *wawr*/sâh (Florence). This 5th class city and seat of Gallatin Co on US 42, 54 mi ne of downtown Louisville, is said to have been settled around 1800 by several Virginia and Pennsylvania families and laid out as a town by Robert Johnson and Henry Yates around 1815. By this time it may have achieved some repute as the Ohio R port of Great Landing or Johnson's Landing. Johnson, a Scott Co resident and the father of later US Vice Pres. Richard M. Johnson, owned property in the area and may have suggested Fredericksburg, as the first official name of the town, for the city in Virginia whence he had come. Or, Fredericksburg may have been named for

Adolphus Frederick, a local boat builder, who arrived in that vicinity before 1809. In either case, Henry Yates est the po under this name on June 10, 1816. The town was inc as Fredericksburg by an act of the Kentucky legislature on Dec 7, 1831, but a mere 5 days later another act officially changed the name to Warsaw to avoid confusion with another Fredericksburg in Washington Co, and the po name was also changed about this time. The name Warsaw is said to have been suggested by either Benjamin Franklin Beall or a retired riverboat captain, John Blair Summons, either (or both) having apparently been impressed by *Thaddeus of Warsaw,* Jane Porter's fictional account of Thaddeus Kosciuszko, which had been published in 1803. 24, 87, 1185.

Washington (Mason): *wâh(r)*/shiŋ/tən (Mayslick). This 5th class city with po extends over 1 mi along old US 68, and is centered at its jct with US 62, some 3 mi sw of Maysville. In 1785 William Wood, a Baptist minister from New York State, and Arthur Fox, Sr., a Virginia surveyor, bought 700 acres from Simon Kenton and laid out this town which they named for Gen. George Washington. It was chartered by the Virginia legislature in 1787. The po was est as Washington Court House on Oct 1, 1794, with Thomas Sloe, pm, and was the distributing office for all mail to the Northwest Territory. The town was the first seat of Mason Co when the latter was est in 1788, but in 1848 it yielded the seat to *Maysville.* Washington was reinc in 1882 and again in 1962. 858, 1246.

Washington County: *wâhsh*/ihŋ/tən. 301 sq mi. Pop 10,721. Seat: Springfield. This co was est in 1792 from part of Nelson Co and the first co formed after Kentucky became a state. It was named for George Washington.

Washington Court House (Washington). See *Springfield*

Washington Court House PO (Mason). See *Washington*

Wasioto (Bell): wahs/ee/*oh*/tə (Middlesboro North). Little remains of a once prosperous sawmill and later coal town on US 119 and the Cumberland R opposite Pineville's present southern limits. In 1889 T. J. Asher built one of the largest sawmills in se Kentucky at this site and, on Nov 5, 1889, est a po to which he allegedly gave the old Cherokee name for the Cumberland Gap—Ouasioto or "mountain pass." (See also *Tejay.*) 79, 839.

Watauga PO (Clinton). See *Pine Grove*

Waterford (Spencer): *wâht*/er/fərd (Waterford). This hamlet with extinct po at the jct of KY 44 and 1060, 4½ mi w of Taylorsville, was aptly named. The old ford is where KY 44 now crosses Plum Creek, a tributary of Salt R. The po, est on Feb 4, 1847, with Milton McGrew, pm, closed in 1917. 1239.

Watergap (Floyd): *waht*/er/ghaep (Lancer). This hamlet and po are centered at the jct of US 23/460 and the n terminus of the new KY 80, 2 mi s of Prestonsburg. The po was est on July 20, 1905, with Benjamin W. Craft, pm, and named for a gap in a ridge through which Bull Creek flows to join the Levisa Fork of the Big Sandy R 2½ mi n.

Water Valley (Graves): *wâht*/ər *vael*/ee (Water Valley). This 6th class city with po is on US 45 and the Illinois Central Gulf RR, 13 mi sw of Mayfield. After the citizens of *Feliciana* refused to permit the New Orleans & Ohio (now ICG) RR to extend its line through their town, the route was moved some 2 mi w and a station was built, presumably on land owned by a Mr. Morse, called Morse Station. In 1869 or 1870 the po was moved from Feliciana to the station site and renamed Morse. By this time a town had been founded around the station. The po and town were renamed Water Valley in 1872, to avoid remembrance of some scandalous affair involving Morse, it is said, and to describe its setting in a low drainage basin of several creeks, an area subject to flooding. According to one account, the night before it was renamed, a cloudburst all but covered the valley. The town was inc as Water Valley in 1884. 466, 1228.

Waterview (Cumberland): *wâht*/ər/vyū (Waterview). This hamlet centers at its po just w of the jct of KY 90 and 100, 4 mi wnw of Burkesville. The po, est on Mar 6, 1888, with Reuben T. Alexander, pm, serves the farm families of Marrowbone Creek, a tributary of the Cumberland R, and was named for the attractive view of the creek at that site. 223.

Watson's Store (Fleming). See *Plummers Landing*

Watsons Store (Monroe). See *Tompkinsville*

Waverly (Union): *wā*/vər/lee (Waverly). This 6th class city with po on US 60/641 and the Illinois Central Gulf RR, 4½ mi ene of Morganfield, occupies a site first called The Cross Roads for its location at the jct of 2 pioneer western Kentucky rds. When Arthur and John Donnelly opened their store here around 1815 it became known as Donnellys Store and later, when they sold out to John Payne, it was called Paynesville. Sufficient settlement warranted the est of a town and one was laid out here around 1869–70 by Hugh McElroy who, apparently unsatisfied with the earlier names, suggested it be called Waverly, probably for his nephew, Waverly Greathouse, who lived in New Orleans. Under this name the po was est on June 16, 1876, with Daniel Brown, pm. 151, 157.

Wax (Grayson): waex (Cub Run, Nolin Reservoir). This settlement and po, now at the jct of KY 88 and 479, 12 mi se of Leitchfield, were originally centered on an early 19th cent Catholic church on the Nolin R, now Nolin Lake. The name Wax was not applied until the est of the po on Jan 15, 1891, by Charles A. Pierce. According to tradition, the name was given by a postal inspector after he observed the local storekeeper, in whose est the po was to be located, weighing beeswax. Less likely is the account of the practice of a postal carrier who announced the delivery of cartons of chewing gum to the local store by calling out ''one for Wax Town.'' For a Wax po in western Iowa, this account was once given: Residents frustrated by the Post Office Department's rejection of a number of suggested names finally took the advice of a postal inspector to ''give us a name that will stick,'' and submitted Wax. 363, 477, 828, 929, 1307.

Wayland (Floyd): *wā*/lən(d) (Wayland). This 6th class city with po, a booming coal town before World War II, is centered at the jct of KY 7 and 1086 and the confluence of Steele and the Right Fork of Beaver Creeks, 14 mi s of Prestonsburg. In 1913, on land acquired from Dan Martin, the Elk Horn Coal Co. opened a mine and est the town, which it named for then US Sen. Clarence Wayland Watson (1864–1940) of West Virginia, president of the Consolidation Coal Co. (1903–11 and 1919–28) and later president and chairman of the Elk Horn Coal Co. The po was est on May 18, 1914, with Lewis Martin, pm. Within Wayland's western city limits lies part of the coal town of Glo, named by and for the local Glogora Coal Co. [*ghloh*/*ghaw*/ree] whose name is said to have been coined from those of some of the female relatives of company officials. The Glo po operated between 1921 and 1955. 834, 1370.

Wayne County: wān. 446 sq mi. Pop 16,894. Seat: Monticello. Wayne Co was est in 1800 from parts of Pulaski and Cumberland cos and named for Gen. ''Mad Anthony'' Wayne (1745–96), an officer in the Revolutionary War and the subsequent Indian campaigns who negotiated the treaty in 1795 that ended Indian raids into Kentucky.

Waynesburg (Lincoln): *wāns*/bergh (Eubank). This village with po is centered at the jct of KY 328 and the Southern Ry, 12½ mi s of Stanford. It was founded in the early 19th cent as a stage stop on the present US 27 and was named for Gen. ''Mad Anthony'' Wayne (1745–96), Revolutionary War hero and victor over the Indians at the Fallen Timbers in 1794. The Waynesburg po was est in 1824, and the town was inc in 1857. It was moved to its present site with the coming of the rr in the mid 1870s. 1448.

Weaver City (Union). See *Cullen*

Weaverton PO (Wayne). See *Touristville*

Webbs Cross Roads (Russell): *wehbz kraws* rohdz (Russell Springs). This hamlet with po lies at the jct of US 127 and KY 76, 7½ mi n of Jamestown. The po was est on Apr 24, 1878, and named for John Webb, the local storekeeper and first pm. 1211.

Webbville (Lawrence): *wehb*/vihl (Webbville). This hamlet with po, a former rail shipping point and terminus of the long defunct E.K. RR, is centered at the jct of KY 1 and 201, 14 mi wnw of Louisa. It was probably named for the family of George W. Webb, large landowner and businessman, who est the local po on Jan 11, 1867, and served as its first pm. 451, 1249.

Webster County: *wehb*/stər. 336 sq mi. Pop 15,200. Seat: Dixon. This co was est in 1860 from parts of Hopkins, Henderson, and Union cos and named for Daniel Webster (1782–1852), US congressman (1813–17 and 1823–27), senator (1827–41 and 1845–50), and secretary of state (1841–43 and 1850–52).

Weed (Adair): weed (Gradyville). This hamlet with extinct po lies at the jct of KY 80 and 768, ¼ mi n of the Cumberland Parkway and 9 mi wsw of Columbia. Charles Weed Sparks, Sr., est the po on Oct 15, 1901, and gave it his middle name. He had earlier run the po at nearby *Sparksville,* also named for him. 797.

Weeksbury (Floyd): *weex*/behr/ee (Wheelwright). This coal town with po is centered at the mouth of Caleb Fork of the Left Fork of Beaver Creek, 22½ mi s of Prestonsburg. It is said to have been named for Messrs. Weeks and Woodbury, vice presidents of the Elkhorn Piney Coal Mining Co., which opened the first mines there before 1914. In that year, the po est on May 4, 1909, as Rail with Eli C. Johnson, pm, was moved to and/or renamed Weeksbury. This place later became the terminus of the Left Beaver Branch of the C&O RR. 330.

Weir (Muhlenberg): wɛ, weer (Kirkmansville). This hamlet with extinct po is on KY 171, 5 mi s of Greenville. Its po, in operation from 1894 to 1915, was probably named for Max Weir (1863–1905), a Greenville merchant and the grandson of pioneer James Weir. 1253.

Welchburg (Jackson): *wehlch*/bergh (Tyner). This recently discontinued po is on Pond Creek, a tributary of the South Fork of Rockcastle R, and 8 mi sse of McKee. First called Pond Fork for its location near one of the forks of Pond when it was est on Mar 15, 1875, the po was renamed in 1890 for its then pm, Samuel E. Welch. 1418.

Welchs Creek (Butler): *wehl*/chəz *kreek* (Welchs Creek). This hamlet with po on KY 79, 10 mi ne of Morgantown, may early have been called Kill Time, though few today remember this name. The po was est on June 10, 1856, with Mark T. Brown, pm, and named for the nearby stream which joins the Green R just above Morgantown. No one knows the origin of the creek's name and no Welch families are known to reside in the co. 414, 1341.

Weldon (Meade): *wehl*/dən (Guston). This defunct station on the Louisville St. Louis and Texas (now L&N) Ry ¾ mi n of the present Brandenburg Station, was the first to serve the city of Brandenburg, 2 mi nw. It was called Weldon for Messrs. Cromwell and Herndon, engineers who helped locate the rr line through the co. A Weldon po was in operation here from 1889 to 1914. Only the nearby Weldon Church preserves the name. 856.

Wellington (Menifee): *wehl*/ihŋ/tən (Scranton). This hamlet with po at the jct of US 460 and KY 1569, 6½ mi ese of Frenchburg, was named for Wellington Davis, a wealthy landowner in the area, in appreciation of his getting the po est on Jan 15, 1880. 980.

Wells Mill (Morgan). See *West Liberty*

Wells PO (Martin). See *Tomahawk*

Wendover (Leslie): *wihn*/doh/vər (Hyden East). The headquarters of the Frontier Nursing Service with po lies on the Middle Fork of the Kentucky R, below the mouth of Hurricane Creek, 2 mi s of Hyden. Mary Breckinridge, who arrived there in 1925 to found the famed health care service for rural mothers and children, is said to have named the place in the summer of 1926. She relates that her aunt Jane had been asked to suggest a "good old British name to match the mountain people with their British heritage. After some travelers have made the trip across the mountains, they insist it should be called Scrambleover. . . . Suddenly Aunt Jane's eyes lighted up. 'I have it. Wendover . . . there's the name for you.' " The po was thus named Wendover when est on Nov 15, 1926, with Martha R. E. Pruitt, pm. 224.

Wesleyville (Carter): *wehs*/lee/vihl (Wesleyville). This extinct po on KY 2, above the mouth of Jordan Fork of Buffalo Creek, 12 mi wnw of Grayson, was relocated from Estell Flat, just upstream, on Apr 24, 1882, and renamed Wesleyville for Wesley Fults, the local storekeeper. It may also have borne the nickname Jim's Town for Jim Fults, an Estell Flat pm in the 1870s and the owner of a combination grist- and sawmill in the vicinity. The po closed in 1951. 36.

West Buechel (Jefferson). See *Buechel*

Western (Fulton). See *Sassafras Ridge*

West Fork (Allen). See *Halfway*

West Liberty (Morgan): wehst *lihb*/ər/tee (West Liberty, Lenox). This 5th class city and seat of Morgan Co is on the Licking R and US 460 and KY 7, 128 mi ese of downtown Louisville. The town was founded on land first settled around 1804 by Daniel Williams, a North Carolina-born Baptist preacher, and Edmund Wells, a Virginia-born miller, and first called Wells Mill for the water mill said to have been built by Edmund on the Licking in 1816. The name was changed to West Liberty when the town became the seat of the newly est co in 1823. It was chartered in 1825, about the time Benjamin F. Wells became the first pm. According to tradition, while a delegation was petitioning the parent Floyd Co officials for a separate Morgan Co in 1822, a similar group had come from the opposite direction to request the est of Pike Co. As the latter said they were going to name their seat Liberty, the Morgan Co group decided to name theirs West Liberty, it being over 50 mi w and n of the proposed Liberty site. Liberty, however, was never est. 479, 707, 1346.

West Louisville (Daviess): wehst *lū*/ee/vihl, *lū*/ə/vəl (Curdsville). This village with po is centered at the jct of KY 56 and 815, 8 mi sw of Owensboro. It is said to have been named by James A. Sivers, who arrived at this site from Louisville in 1854 and built a log cabin and opened a store. The po was est on May 24, 1867, with Henry Rennart, pm. 654.

West Paducah PO (McCracken). See *Maxon*

West Point (Hardin): *wehst point* (Fort Knox, Kosmosdale). This 5th class city with po lies at the confluence of the Salt and Ohio rs, 18 mi n of Elizabethtown. It was est in 1796 on the petition of Samuel Pearman and James Young, the proprietors of the site, who laid it off as a town in 1801. On Mar 1, 1819, the po was est with James W. Hall, pm. It was reinc in 1848. Across Salt R in Jefferson Co was the frontier town of

Williamsville, founded in 1792 by, and probably named for, William Johnson, owner of the site. West Point and Williamsville soon became essentially one community and were collectively known by early settlers as the Mouth of Salt River. 297, 298, 1420.

Westport (Oldham): *wehst*/pawrt (LaGrange). This is now a hamlet with po on the Ohio R, 6½ mi nw of LaGrange. The town is said to have been founded in 1797 by Joseph Dupuy and Harmon Bowman and may first have been called Liberty. It was known as Westport by June 1797, a reference to its early aspirations as a port to the w, i.e., the then Northwest Territory. The po was est on Apr 1, 1816, with Hugh Luckie, pm. Westport was chosen as the seat of the new co in 1823. In July 1827 the seat was temporarily relocated at what became *LaGrange* but by Mar 1828 it had returned to Westport, where it remained until 1838 when it was finally removed to LaGrange. 82.

West Prestonsburg (Floyd): wehst *prehst*/ənz/bergh (Prestonsburg). This village, now part of Prestonsburg, with branch po, was aptly named for its location at the mouth of Middle Creek, w across the Levisa Fork of the Big Sandy R from Prestonsburg. Its po, est as Middle Creek on Dec 29, 1904, with Job L. Spurlock, pm, was renamed West Prestonsburg in 1918.

West Van Lear (Johnson): *wehst vaen leer* (Paintsville). This village with po is on the Levisa Fork of the Big Sandy R, 1 mi sse of Paintsville. The po was est on Apr 29, 1912, with James H. Price, pm, and named for its location nw of the coal town of *Van Lear*. It was called Van Lear Junction when the C&O RR provided passenger service at the local station. 89.

Westview (Breckinridge): *wehst*/vyū (Kingswood). This hamlet with po is on KY 79, just n of its jct with KY 690, and 4½ mi sse of Hardinsburg. The po was est as West View on June 2, 1879, at the site of Vic Drane's store, and Isaiah T. Butler was appointed pm. After 1894 the name was spelled Westview. It is not known why this name was applied except to suggest that one could look w to see the sun go down. 1398.

West Viola (Graves). See *Viola*

Westwood (Boyd): *wehst*/wo͞od (Ashland). This suburban community without po, adjacent to the western boundary of the city of Ashland and less than 1 mi from the Greenup Co line, may have been named by John Seaton, presumably for its location. 1311.

Wheatcroft (Webster): *weet*/krâhft (Providence). This 6th class city, a coal town with po, is on KY 109 and the Illinois Central Gulf RR, 8½ mi w of Dixon. It was probably named for Irving Horace Wheatcroft, an Englishman, who in 1899 laid out and founded the town on land acquired from Elijah Cullen, opened one or more area coal mines, and built the Kentucky Western Ry from nearby Blackford to Dixon. The Wheatcroft po was est on Sept 10, 1900, with A. S. Logsdon, pm, and the town was inc in 1902. 208, 1088.

Wheatley (Owen): *weet*/lee (New Liberty). This hamlet with po on KY 227, 8½ mi nw of Owenton, was first called Dallasburg, perhaps as early as 1825. A po was in operation with this name from 1850 to 1863 and the town was inc as such in 1850–51. The po, reest as Wheatley on Aug 5, 1886, was named for the pm, Rev. George Wesley Wheatley, a highly respected citizen. The name Dallasburg, whose origin remains unknown, is retained in the name of the local Baptist church. 102.

Wheel (Graves): weel (Fancy Farm). This exintct community and po were on KY 408, 10½ mi nw of Mayfield. The po, in operation from 1892 to 1909, was est by Elisha J. Willett and named for the then active populist farm movement, the Agricultural

Wheel, which had been organized in 1882 in Prairie Co, Arkansas, and whose symbol, the wagon wheel, rallied American farmers in their efforts to achieve better prices, lower taxes and interest rates, and rr regulation. 14, 1228.

Wheeler (Knox): *weel*/ər (Kayjay). This settlement with extinct po on KY 225, near the head of Brush Creek, a tributary of the Cumberland R, and 9 mi s of Barbourville, was named for the Wheeler brothers, Ross and Robert L., who operated the Brush Creek Mining Co. there from 1912 to the early 1930s. Robert L. became the first pm on Jan 22, 1912. 11, 1068.

Wheelersburg (Magoffin): *weel*/ərz/bergh (Salyersville North). This hamlet with po lies on Big Mine Fork of Little Paint Creek, at the mouth of Litteral Fork, at the jct of KY 1081 and 1437, and 5½ mi nne of Salyersville. The po was est as Nehemiah nee/ə/*mah*/yə on Aug 29, 1881, and probably named by and for its first pm, Nehemiah Crace. In 1910 Greenville P. Wheeler, who had become pm in 1895, succeeded in having it renamed Wheelersburg for his family. 1422.

Wheeler Town (Morgan). See *Crockett*

Wheelrim (Morgan): *weel*/rihm (Lee City). This settlement with extinct po was named for its location near the head of Wheelrim Fork of Johnson Creek, at the mouth of Elam Branch and 13 mi s of West Liberty. The stream was named when some early settlers spied the rim of an old wagon wheel that someone had thrown up in the branches of a tree on its banks. The local po was est as Burg on Oct 6, 1924, with Kelson H. Risner, pm. For years the community was also officially called Burg until a Board on Geographic Names decision in 1965 ruled in favor of the local preference for Wheelrim, by which name the school (now closed) was known. For some reason the Board saw fit to spell the name of both community and stream as Wheel Rim. 998, 1027.

Wheelwright (Floyd): *weel*/raht (Wheelwright). This 6th class city with po extends over 2 mi along the Right Fork of Otter Creek, a branch of the Left Fork of Beaver Creek of the Levisa Fork of the Big Sandy R, and up several hollows off Otter, 22 mi s of Prestonsburg. In 1916 the Elk Horn Coal Co. est a coal town here, which they named for Jere H. Wheelwright (died 1920), president of the Consolidation Coal Co., 1911–19. The po was est on Dec 23, 1916, with John W. McIntyre, pm. Despite the known origin of the name, a local tradition persists that Wheelwright owes its name to a comment made by an early town developer about the need to get the local "wheels to rollin' right." 19, 194, 424.

Wheelwright Junction (Floyd). See *Bypro*

Whickerville (Hart): *wihk*/ər/vihl (Center). This settlement is ½ mi from the Green Co line, 1¼ mi from the Metcalfe Co line, and 11½ mi ese of Munfordville. The name was first applied in 1900 to a small store, since gone, as a joke by local residents and referred to a strange bird called "Whickers" that lived in a nearby swamp. The community has never had its own po. 863.

Whippoorwill (Logan). See *Ferguson*

White City (LaRue): *weyet siht*/ee (Hodgenville). This hamlet lies at the jct of US 31E and KY 84 and 470, 3½ mi e of Hodgenville. Mr. Anderson, a local storekeeper, is said to have painted several of his buildings white, inspiring his neighbors to do the same and later prompting a visitor, a Mr. Morrison to suggest calling the place White City. It has never had a po. 68.

Whitehouse (Johnson): *waht*/hows (Richardson, Offutt). This is now a hamlet with po strung out for about a mi along the Levisa Fork of the Big Sandy R, 6 mi ne of Paintsville. It was first aptly called Mt. Carbon, a community housing the workers of 2 rival coal cos. When the C&O RR was completed to this point in late 1887, the station was called Whitehouse, for a large white building near the landing that served as a landmark for r craft. The po was est on Apr 23, 1887, by John S. Rittenhouse and first called Myrtle for either the wife of one of the local coal operators or the abundance of myrtle or periwinkle on a nearby hill. By 1901 both po and community had been renamed for the rr station. 194, 867, 945, 1353, 1392.

White House PO (Lewis). See *Tollesboro*

White Lilly PO (Laurel). See *Lily*

White Mills (Hardin): *weyet mihlz* (Summit). This hamlet with po is centered at the jct of KY 1866 and the Nolin R, just n of KY 84, and 11 mi sw of Elizabethtown. It grew up around 2 mills, the first a gristmill built around 1830 and later destroyed by a flood, and its replacement, built in 1855 and also gone. The po was est on Jan 19, 1866, with Granville S. Hastings, pm. It is not known if either mill was painted white or owned by someone named White. 825.

White Oak (McCreary). See *White Oak Junction*

White Oak (Morgan): *waht* ohk (White Oak). This hamlet with po lies where US 460 crosses White Oak Creek, 1¼ mi above its confluence with the Licking R and 4½ mi sse of West Liberty. The first settlers may have been John May's family on a 1000-acre government grant along the creek, which was undoubtedly named for the local trees. The po was est on Nov 17, 1874, with John H. Henry, pm. 112, 1346.

White Oak Junction (McCreary): *waht* ohk *djuhŋk*/shən (Barthell). This settlement with extinct po at the confluence of White Oak and Rock Creeks, 7 mi w of Whitley City, was once called White Oak, but was renamed White Oak Junction when a spur line was extended from the main route of the Kentucky and Tennessee RR to the mine at *Co-operative* just over 1 mi up White Oak Creek. The po was est as White Oak Junction on June 6, 1931, with Homer Hamlin, pm. 208.

White Plains (Hopkins): *waht plānz* (Nortonville). This 6th class city with po is on the Illinois Central Gulf RR, just s of US 62, and 10 mi sse of Madisonville. A po was est 1 mi se of town on Aug 13, 1853, and called Little Prairie for the almost treeless plain on which it was located. According to tradition, such open lands in much of central and western Kentucky were the result of the deliberate burning of forests by Indian hunters to increase the growth of grass for their buffalo. When the Elizabethtown & Paducah (now Illinois Central Gulf) RR arrived at the present White Plains site around 1872, the station located there to supply the nearby Christian Co community and po of White Plains was called White Plains Station and later New White Plains. The Little Prairie po was moved here in 1874 and renamed White Plains, for by then the Christian Co po of that name had been renamed for nearby *Fruit Hill*. The Hopkins Co White Plains was inc in 1888. 500, 540, 1320.

White Plains PO (Christian). See *Fruit Hill*

White Rock (Rockcastle). See *Mount Vernon*

Whitesburg (Letcher): *wahts*/bergh (Whitesburg). This 5th class city and seat of Letcher Co is on KY 15 and the North Fork of the Kentucky R, 166 mi ese of downtown Louisville. It was founded in 1842 as the seat of the newly est co on land offered for this purpose by Stephen Hiram Hogg. It was named for Daugherty White of Clay Co, who as a state legislator had succeeded in getting the co organized that year. The po was est as Whitesburgh Court House on Feb 10, 1843, with William Carole, pm. In 1892 the terminal "h" was dropped. The town was inc in 1876. A folk account of the name, now hardly taken seriously, refers to an early snowstorm that blanketed the site of the future town for days. 1265.

Whitesburgh Court House (Letcher). See *Whitesburg*

Whites Chapel (Crittenden). See *Irma*

Whites Chapel (Drake PO) (Warren): *weyets chaep*/əl, drāk (Drake). This hamlet with po on KY 622, 7½ mi s of Bowling Green, was named over a century ago for the local church, which honors a family of early settlers. The Drake po was est just above the forks of Drake Creek, 1 mi n, on Mar 28, 1892 with John W. Goodrum, pm. Shortly before World War II the po was moved to its present site but retained the Drake name. The creek was named for the long hunter Joseph Drake. 1312, 1363.

White Star PO (Harlan). See *Dayhoit*

White Sulphur (Scott): weyet *suhl*/fər (Midway). Little remains of a famed antebellum health resort centered at the jct of the present US 460 and the Ironworks Rd, 7 mi w of Georgetown. The site was first owned by Col. Richard M. Johnson, who est the resort in the early 1830s in the vicinity of several white sulphur springs. The local po, est as Tailton on June 23, 1837, with James Combs, pm, was moved to and/or renamed White Sulphur the following year. It was discontinued in 1902. 13, 914.

Whitesville (Daviess): *wahts*/vihl (Whitesville, Philpot). This 6th class city with po centers at the jct of KY 54 and 764, 11½ mi ese of Owensboro. First called Cross Roads for its location, it was renamed for an early sojourner, Dr. William Lee White, who, with Benjamin F. Ramsey, built the first local building, a dry goods store, in 1844. A mile and a half w on KY 54 is the hamlet of Boston where, in 1851, the po of Pleasant Green (est in 1848 just over the Ohio Co line) was relocated and given the name Burtonsville, possibly to honor one Basset Burton who had settled in the vicinity around 1810. In 1852 this po was moved to and renamed Whitesville but was returned to Boston, again as Burtonsville, in 1860, and finally reest at Whitesville, with that name, in 1865. Boston or Burtonsville is now considered part of greater Whitesville. 99, 533.

White Tower (Kenton): *weyet tow*/ər (Independence). This once discrete hamlet on KY 16 is now partly contained within the newly inc eastern boundary of Independence. It was named sometime in the late 19th cent for a tower built on land owned by a George White, and has also been called White's Tower and simply Towers. A po of the latter name was in operation from 1900 to 1907. 991.

Whitley City (McCreary): *wiht*/lee *siht*/ee (Whitley City). This unincorporated seat of McCreary Co is on US 27, 117 mi se of downtown Louisville. While the site was still in Pulaski Co, the community was founded at some undetermined date on land early patented by one George Smith and later sold at public auction to Thomas Z. Morrow and Middleton B. Holloway. The local po was est as Coolidge [*kūl*/ədj] on May 12, 1880, with Holloway as pm, and by 1886 the Cincinnati Southern Ry station there was known as Whitley (Depot). When McCreary Co was created in 1912, its seat was located here as Whitley City and the po also took this name. No one seems to know why the name Coolidge was first applied nor why the name was changed to Whitley City though, in retrospect, it honors the Kentucky pioneer and Indian fighter, Col. William Whitley (1749–1813). 174, 1163.

Whitley County: *wiht*/lee. 443 sq mi. Pop 32,647. Seat: Williamsburg. This co was est in 1818 from part of Knox Co and named for Col. William Whitley (1749–1813), pioneer and Indian fighter, who was killed at the Battle of the Thames, Canada, in the War of 1812.

Whitley Court House PO (Whitley). See *Williamsburg*

Whittemoreville (Graves). See *Viola*

Whittinghill (Butler). See *Jetson*

Whittle (Russell): *wiht*/əl (Eli). This extinct po on KY 1611, 5 mi ene of Jamestown, was est as Sunshine on Sept 25, 1905, with Edker M. Whittle, the local storekeeper, as pm. It was discontinued in 1914 but reest by Whittle on Nov 7, 1921, and given his name. It closed for good in 1950. 1233.

Whoopflarea (Owsley): hūp/fə/*lɛ*/ee/ə, hūp/flə/*lɛ*/ee/ə, wūp/fə/*lee*/ree (Mistletoe). This settlement with extinct po lies near the head of the Right Fork of Buffalo Creek, 14 mi sse of Booneville. This curious name was first applied to a range of hills, then to a pioneer settlement, and later to the po, est in 1931, that served this inaccessible area. The name was derived most likely from the whoop of owls and, perhaps, of Indians but has since inspired a host of explanatory accounts. Hunters camping there heard the hoot of an owl; frightened, they scattered in all directions. Over the years, the owl became "some animal making screaming noises" or even a "hant." One account describes a man named Larry or Larrie who got separated from his companions. They spent the better part of a night (or several days) looking for him and would literally "whoop for Larry." Joe Creason identifies Larry as a moonshiner whose customers "would come to the head of the hollow and 'whoop for Larry.' " Or, Larry was a man in his cups, who, seeking his way home in the dark, would shout his name and be guided by the echo of his voice against the hills. His ghost may still be heard "whooping for Larry." In another tale, little Laura liked to wander around the countryside. To get her home for meals, her father would send one of his other children to "whoop for Laura." The spellings of this name have been as varied as its pronunciations and the explanatory accounts: Whooplarea, Whopflaeria, Whoopflara, Whoopferlarrie, Whoopferlorrie, etc. 322, 359, 1287, 1372.

Whynot PO (Lee). See *Old Landing*

Wiborg (McCreary): *weye*/bergh (Wiborg). This coal camp and rail shipping point with po is centered at the jct of US 27 and KY 1045, 5½ mi n of Whitley City. It was named for a Mr. Wilborg from New York who arrived in the area just before 1900 and soon initiated coal and timber production there. The po was est on Feb 2, 1915, with Hurchel E. Thurman, pm. 174.

Wickliffe (Ballard): *wihk*/lihf (Wickliffe). This 5th class city and seat of Ballard Co is on US 51, 60, and 62 and the Mississippi R, 189 mi wsw of downtown Louisville. The town was laid out in 1880 on the site of a small settlement and named for Col. Charles A. Wickliffe, attorney, state legislator, Confederate officer, and nephew and namesake of Kentucky's 15th governor, who inherited the land that his pioneer grandfather, Col. Benjamin Logan, had received for Revolutionary War service. The po at *Fort Jefferson* 1 mi s, had been moved to this site the year before, and in 1882, when Wickliffe was inc as a town, the co's seat was transferred from *Blandville*, 6½ mi e. 38.

Wideawake PO (Carroll). See *Prestonsville*

Wild Cat (Clay): *wahl(d)* kaet (Barcreek). This po is on KY 11 at the mouth of Wildcat Creek for which it was named, 6½ mi nne of Manchester. The creek, a tributary of Goose Creek of the South Fork of the Kentucky R, was settled early in the 19th cent, and the name had been applied to it by 1815. According to tradition, the area was inhabited by many wildcats, a favorite target of early hunters. The po was est on Sept 13, 1930, with Mrs. Lillie B. Hacker, pm. 940, 1418.

Wilder (Campbell): *wahl*/dər (Newport). This 5th class industrial city without po lies mostly along a 4½-mile stretch of KY 9, 4½ mi nw of Alexandria, and is bounded on the n by Newport, on the ne and e by Southgate, on the s by Pooles Creek Rd, and on the w by the Licking R. The city was est as such in 1935 around the Andrews (now Interlake) Steel Co. plant, which had been located in the 1890s in a section along the r then called Finchtown. The city adopted the name of a local L&N RR station that had been named for William Hamlin Wilder (1860–1931), a Covington-born ophthalmologist. 813, 814.

Wild Goose (Russell). See *Rowena*

Wildie (Rockcastle): *wihl*/dee (Wildie). This hamlet with po is on KY 1786, 4½ mi nne of Mount Vernon. It may have been named by D. N. Williams for Will and Dee, the sons of a local farmer named Albright, or possibly for the 2 sons of a Mr. Lumm, one of the engineers on an early run of the old Kentucky Central (later L&N) RR, which est a station at this site around 1883. The po was est on Oct 20, 1884, with Andrew J. Henderson, pm. 1243.

Wilhoit PO (Harlan). See *Dayhoit*

Wilhoyte PO (Jefferson). See *Prospect*

Wilhurst (Breathitt): *wihl*/herst (Landsaw). This extinct po was on Boone Fork of Frozen Creek and KY 1812, 5 mi n of Jackson. The first po to serve this vicinity was est as Boxer on Aug 2, 1901, with John L. Sewell, pm. Hannibal Hurst, who became pm in 1906, had it moved and/or changed to Wilhurst the following year. It may have been named for Hurst and a man or family named Wilson. Hurst's successor as pm, in Dec 1907, was William K. Wilson.

Willailla (Rockcastle): wihl/*āl*/ə (Maretburg). This hamlet and recently closed po are on KY 70, 7 mi wsw of Mount Vernon. According to a local tradition, they were named for the fact that Will Owens, a resident, was always ailing. Yet it is more generally accepted that the po, est on Feb 24, 1916, was named for Owens and his wife Ailla. 1251, 1271.

Willard (Carter): *wihl*/ərd (Willard). This village, once a rail shipping point, now extends for nearly 1 mi along KY 1, 7½ mi s of Grayson. It was founded in 1873 by a Mr. Willard, the president of the Etna Iron Co., and named for him. The local po was est on Oct 19, 1874, with George H. Jacobs, pm, and the town was inc on Apr 22, 1890. 36, 508.

Williams (Ohio): *wihl*/yəmz (Hartford). This extinct coal town, now a part of the inc *McHenry*, w of US 62 and the Illinois Central Gulf RR and 4 mi s of Hartford, is now referred to, if at all, as Williams Mines. In 1860 J. S. Williams acquired a 410-acre farm, ½ mi n of McHenry, and in 1891 his son, E. F. Williams, began mining on the land. Soon the Williams Coal Co. est the town for its workers. It never had a po. 473, 598.

Williamsburg (Mason). See *Orangeburg*

Williamsburg (Owen). See *Monterey*

Williamsburg (Whitley): *wihl*/yəmz/bergh (Williamsburg, Wofford). This 4th class-city and seat of Whitley Co is on US 25W and I 75, on the Cumberland R, 127 mi se of downtown Louisville. In 1818 the new co's seat was est on land then owned by Samuel Cox and, like the co itself, was named for Col. William Whitley (1749–1813), Virginia-born Indian fighter and victim of the Battle of the Thames. The town was chartered in 1819 and the po est as Whitley Court House. In 1882 the name was officially changed to Williamsburgh; the final "h" was dropped in 1890. 1267.

Williams Mines (Ohio). See *Williams*

Williamson PO (Jefferson). See *O'Bannon*

Williamsport (Johnson): *wihl*/yəmz/pawrt (Offutt). This hamlet with po is strung out along KY 40 and Two Mile Creek, 3 mi e of Paintsville. The po was est on Jan 8, 1897, as Eliza for its first pm, Eliza J. Rittenhouse. John W. Butcher, who succeeded her in 1901, had the po renamed in 1902, either for his father, William, or for Jim Williams, an engineer for several narrow gauge rrs that hauled cannel coal out of the area. 1353, 1411.

Williams Store PO (Casey). See *Dunnville*

Williamstown (Grant): *wihl*/yəmz/town (Williamstown). This 5th class city and seat of Grant Co is on US 25, 64 mi ene of downtown Louisville. On June 12, 1820, the commissioners, having accepted William Arnold's generous offer of land for the new co's seat on the site of the pioneer Littell's Station, proposed the name Philadelphia in anticipation of a future to rival the great eastern city. However, when it was learned that this name was already in use in Kentucky, the town was renamed for Arnold, a New Jersey native and veteran of the Revolution and the Indian battles of the 1790s, who had brought his family to the site in 1795 and was a town trustee. The po was est as Williamstown Court House on Feb 2, 1822, with Wesley Tully, pm. 69, 109, 530.

Williamstown Court House PO (Grant). See *Williamstown*

Williamsville (Hardin). See *West Point*

Williba (Lee): *wihl*/ə/bee (Tallega). This hamlet is on Fraley Creek, less than ½ mi from its confluence with the North Fork of the Kentucky R, and 7½ mi ene of Beattyville. The recently closed po was est on Mar 29, 1904, and allegedly named for Willoughby, a town in England from which the ancestors of some of the area's pioneer settlers may have come. The name is said to have been corrupted to make it short enough to place on a rubber stamp that the first pm, Thomas Colwell, used to cancel the mail. 1372.

Willisburg (Washington): *wihl*/əs/bergh (Brush Grove, Cardwell). This 6th class city with po extends over 1 mi along KY 53, 8½ mi nne of Springfield. It may first have been called Paoli (Paeola), which was the name of a po in the area from Feb 13, 1838, to Dec 11, 1839, but it was chartered by the Kentucky legislature as Willisburg on Feb 1, 1838. The Willisburg po was est on Dec 3, 1844, with William W. Phelps, pm. No one seems to know how it received its name; people claim it was named "for its first postmaster." It was inc in 1965. 821.

Williston PO (Calloway). See *Murray*

Willisville PO (Calloway). See *Tobacco*

Willoughby (Montgomery): *wihl*/ə/bee (Means). This settlement on Willoughby Rd, which extends w from KY 213 and Jeffersonville, 8 mi sse of Mt. Sterling, is sometimes called Willoughby Town and even Willoughby Nation. The Willoughbys were a prolific and tight-knit family whose married children remained near their parents' homes. The name identifies that community on an 1879 map. 959, 1237.

Willoughby Nation (Montgomery). See *Willoughby*

Willoughby Town (Montgomery). See *Willoughby*

Willow Shade (Metcalfe): *wihl*/ə shād (Dubre). This hamlet with po lies on Marrowbone Creek and KY 90, 8 mi s of Edmonton. The first Willow Shade po, named for the trees on the creek, was est on Sept 18, 1866, with Robert D. Traw, pm, and discontinued in 1878. On Feb 28, 1881, Thomas D. Riggs est the Riggs po, which was renamed Willow Shade in 1889. 1315.

Wilmington (Boone). See *Burlington*

Wilmore (Jessamine): *wihl*/mawr (Wilmore). This 4th class city with po is on the Southern Ry and KY 29, 3½ mi wsw of Nicholasville. The po was est on Sept 17, 1877, with James A. Sparks, pm, and named for John R. Wilmore, a local landowner. In 1882 the then Cincinnati & Chattanooga RR located a flag stop here and called it Scott's Station for John D. Scott, the owner of that site. The station's name shortly changed to conform to that of the po and a community soon grew up around both. The town was inc in 1918. 421, 672.

Wilson (Henderson): *wihl*/sən (Wilson). This settlement with onetime Illinois Central Gulf RR station and extinct po is about a mi se of US 60/641 and 3 mi sw of Henderson. The then Ohio Valley RR named its station in 1885 for John Thomas Wilson, a state legislator and local businessman, who donated its right-of-way through his farm and influenced his neighbors to do so also. On June 18, 1886, George W. Anderson became the first pm of Wilsons Station, which in 1894 became simply Wilson. This po was discontinued in 1907. 12, 1221.

Wilsonberger Station (Harlan). See *Grays Knob*

Wilson County. See *Corbin*

Wilsons Station (Henderson). See *Wilson*

Wilstacy (Breathitt): *wihl*/*stā*/see (Quicksand). This po, now a rural branch of the Jackson po, is on KY 1098 and the South Fork of Quicksand Creek, 5 mi e of the co seat. It was est on June 21, 1927, and named for its first pm, William Stacy. The area it now serves is said to extend down South Fork for several mi and may include the recently closed Portsmouth po, 2 mi above the mouth of Quicksand. 1310.

Winchester (Clark): *wihn*/chehs/tər (Winchester, Austerlitz). This 3rd class industrial city and seat of Clark Co is on US 60 and I 64, at the w terminus of the Mountain Parkway, 81 mi e of downtown Louisville. The town was est on Dec 17, 1793, on 66 acres of John Baker's farm and named for his hometown in Virginia. By one vote, that of John Strode, it was chosen as the co seat over Strode's Station; it is said that Strode did not want to appear selfish by supporting his own station. The Winchester po opened on Jan 8, 1803, with Edmund Calloway, pm. 328, 1349.

Wind Cave (Jackson): *wihnd kāv* (Leighton). This settlement with po lies near the forks of Lick Branch of War Fork of Station Camp Creek, 6½ mi ne of McKee. The po, est by Godfrey P. Isaacs on Apr 14, 1902, was named for a local limestone cave whose entrance, 50 or 60 ft high, "is as impressive as anything you'd find in Mammoth Cave. A cool breeze comes out of there because warm air goes into the top of the thing and then cools as it comes out the bottom, down next to the ground." 1418.

Windy (Wayne): *wihn*/dee (Powersburg). This crossroads hamlet with po on KY 1009, 7½ mi sw of Monticello. By 1918 this section of the larger Gap Creek community, with its po 1½ mi w, had come to be called Windy City. On Sept 17, 1924, a po was est at the intersection 500 ft from its present location and called simply Windy, ostensibly to avoid the misdirection of mail to Chicago (also known as "the Windy City"). No one is sure how or why the Wayne Co community was called Windy City. The name may refer to the local Wynn family who still maintain the po. But it is more likely to refer to the windy location, or perhaps to a cyclone that may have swept through the area earlier in this cent. There is even a story that the community was named for some local fellows called "the Windy Bunch," who would gather at the store to swap tales. It is still locally called Windy City. 1242, 1303, 1323, 1377.

Windy City (Wayne). See *Windy*

Windyville (Edmonson): *wihn*/dee/vihl (Brownsville). This hamlet lies at the jct of KY 70 and 655, 2½ mi nw of Brownsville. At certain times of the year, writes Lancie Meredith, the wind blows extremely hard on the ridge on which this community is located. A traveling salesman passing through asked the storekeeper what the place was named, and when told it had no name he suggested they call it Windyville. It has never had a po. 942.

Wingo (Graves): *wihŋ*/oh, *wihn*/ghoh (Mayfield, Dublin). This 6th class city with po is on the Illinois Central Gulf RR and US 45, 6 mi sw of Mayfield. It was est as a station when the New Orleans & Ohio RR was built through in 1854 and named for wealthy land- and slaveowner Jerman J. Wingo, who granted the site for the depot and the right-of-way through his land. Wingo, born in North Carolina in 1807, arrived with his family around 1825 and soon opened a grocery and saloon. The po of Point Curve, est by Theophilus I. Wingo on Jan 22, 1861, was moved a short distance to Wingo's Station in June of the following year and was known by this name until it was shortened to Wingo in 1882. The town was inc in 1872. Point Curve was probably named for the sweeping curve made by the rr as it approaches the business section of the town. Of the 2 pronunciations given, the first is the original and still used by oldtimers, while the 2nd is the one now preferred by most residents. 288, 1228.

Wingo's Station PO (Graves). See *Wingo*

Winstead PO (Webster). See *Clay*

Winston (Estill): *wihn*/stən (Panola). This hamlet with po is strung out along old KY 52, 5½ mi w of Irvine. According to Mrs. Doris Hardy, the current pm, it may first have been called Newman Stand for the family of Samuel Newman, listed as a local resident in the 1850 Census. The po of Winston was est on June 19, 1865, with William C. Smith, pm, and allegedly named for a family who owned land there for a short time before moving further w in Kentucky. 865.

Winston Park (Kenton). See *Taylor Mill*

Wiscoal (Knott): *wihs*/kohl (Vicco). This coal town with extinct po and L&N RR station is on KY 1088 and Yellow Creek, 7 mi ssw of Hindman. It was named for the Wisconsin Coal Co., which had a mine and offices there. The Wiscoal po was est on May 22, 1929, with Edward H. Griffith, pm, and closed when the mines did. 1262.

Wisdom (Metcalfe): *wihz*/dəm (Sulphur Well). This hamlet with extinct po is centered at the jct of US 68 and KY 640, ¼ mi n of the Cumberland Parkway and 5 mi w of Edmonton. This community was called Randolph by Mar 31, 1846, when the po of that name was est there with Edward V. Cummins, pm. Less than 10 years later the po was moved to a site about 2½ mi s, which is presently called *Randolph*, leaving the old village site as Old Randolph. On Oct 2, 1894, Em Evans est another po there, which he called Wisdom for then Co School Supt. Henry Wisdom. 232.

Wisemantown (Estill): *wahz*/mən/town (Irvine, Panola). This hamlet with extinct po on KY 499, at the foot of Pea Ridge and 2 mi se of Irvine, was named for early landowners, the brothers Jake and Abner Wiseman. The po was est as Bluebanks on Oct 22, 1883, with John M. Walker, pm, and was likely named for the local slate banks. The po became Wisemantown on June 20, 1893, when John P. Miller assumed charge. It closed in 1957. 116, 865.

Wises Landing (Trimble): *weyez*/əz *laend*/ihŋ (Bethlehem). This hamlet on KY 1488 and Barebone Creek, in the Ohio R bottom, 4½ mi w of Bedford, was once a busy port and landing probably named for the descendants of William Wise, a Revolutionary War veteran. From 1830 or earlier until 1913 it was served by the Corn Creek po, named for the stream that joins the r about 1½ mi n. 652, 761, 913.

Withers PO (Rockcastle). See *Mullins Station*

Wittensville (Johnson): *wiht*/ən(z)/vihl (Paintsville). This hamlet with po is on US 23 and Rush Fork of Toms Creek, at the mouth of Williams Creek, 3 mi n of Paintsville. The po, est on Sept 18, 1930, with Cue Witten, pm, was named for a prominent Johnson Co family, the descendants of pioneer Dr. William Witten from Tazewell Co, Virginia, who settled at Buffalo before 1819. 128, 1353.

Witt PO (Estill). See *Witt Springs*

Witt Springs (Estill): *wiht sprihŋz* (Panola). This community with extinct po is on Sand Hill, 3 mi nw of Irvine. The residents had wanted to name their po Witt, but the prior est of another Witt po 2 mi w of Wisemantown led them to add "Springs" to the name. On Sept 2, 1904, the Witt Springs po was est in Eugene Witt's general store with William L. Witt, pm. It was named by the descendants of Elisha Witt, a Revolutionary War veteran, for their pioneer ancestor and a large sulphur spring in the vicinity. In 1805 Virginia-born Elisha purchased 3500 acres of bottom land on the Kentucky R. It is not known if or how the 2 Witt communities, 8 rd mi apart, are related. The po closed in 1956. 865.

Wofford (Whitley): *wahf*/ərd (Wofford). This hamlet with L&N RR station is on KY 26, 2 mi nne of Williamsburg. It was first called Mahan [*mā*/haen] for a local family, and was renamed for another family when the po, now a rural branch of the Williamsburg po, was est on Apr 27, 1900. 1267, 1380.

Wolf Coal (Breathitt): *wo͞olf*kohl (Canoe). This coal town with po and L&N RR station lies at the mouth of Wolf Creek, a branch of the North Fork of the Kentucky R, 10 mi s of Jackson. It was named for the coal produced in the Wolf Creek area. The po was est on June 10, 1915, with Emma B. Arnett, pm.

Wolf Creek (Meade): *wo͞olf kreek* (Alton). Little remains of this 19th cent Ohio R port and manufacturing town at the mouth of Wolf Creek, for which it was named, 13 mi nw of Brandenburg. According to tradition, wolves would come together here in the spring to feed on the young buffalo making their way along a buffalo trail to the r. The Wolf Creek po was in operation from 1862 to 1967. 856, 1260.

Wolfe County: wo͞olf. 223 sq mi. Pop 6,712. Seat: Campton. Wolfe Co was est in 1860 from parts of Breathitt, Morgan, Owsley, and Powell cos and named for Nathaniel Wolfe (1810–65), who represented Jefferson Co in the Kentucky legislature (1853–55 and 1859–63).

Wolfpit (Pike): *wo͞olf*/piht (Hellier). This hamlet and former coal town with extinct po is on KY 195, at the mouth of Wolfpit Branch of Marrowbone Creek, 9 mi sse of Pikeville. The stream for which it was named is said to have been named in turn for the pits dug there to trap the large number of wolves that used to prey on local livestock. The Wolfpit po was est on July 19, 1918, and Ernest R. Nestor was the first pm. 1354.

Wolverine (Breathitt): *wo͞ol*/vər/een (Jackson). This hamlet with po is on the North Fork of the Kentucky R and 1½ mi nnw of Jackson. Around 1900, 1 mi from the present Wolverine po, the O. B. Robinson Co. est a community for its local sawmill workers on land leased from George Hays. From 1908 to 1914 the local po was thus called Hays. In 1916 Robert T. Gunn arrived in the Wolverine vicinity and soon began mining coal on some 2000 acres leased from the K. U. Land Co. In 1920 he reest the po at the present site of Wolverine but called it Gunn. In 1926 Gunn was bought out by the Wolverine Coal Co., and 2 years later the po was renamed for the new proprietors. 1064, 1222.

Woodberry PO (Butler). See *Woodbury*

Woodbine (Whitley): *wo͞od*/bahn (Corbin). This village with po and L&N RR station, now a suburb of Corbin, is centered at the jct of KY 6 and 26, 10½ mi nne of Williamsburg. It was first called The Joe Field(s) for Joe Johnson, pioneer settler who was killed by Indians in his cabin there. The community and its po, est on Mar 13, 1844, were named for the woodbine or honeysuckle vines growing in the area. 882, 1267, 1380.

Woodburn (Warren): *wo͞od*/bern (Woodburn). This 6th class city with po is centered on

KY 240, just e of US 31W, 8 mi ssw of Bowling Green. On Jan 17, 1843, the po of Woodburn was est at a stage stop called Mason's Inn on the present US 31W and allegedly named for an early fire that had destroyed much of the nearby forest. When in 1859 the L&N RR completed its main line, ½ mi e, and built its depot on land donated by Ewing Robertson, the po was transferred there as New Woodburn. This became simply Woodburn in 1864. The town was laid off at the depot site in Dec 1865 and inc in Feb 1866. 853, 1285.

Woodbury (Butler): *wŏŏd*/behr/ee (Morgantown). Now but a hamlet with po, this recently disincorporated community lies on the Green R, 3½ mi se of Morgantown. The town grew up around the site of Lock & Dam No. 4 built in 1839. The po, est on Apr 5, 1847, as Lock No. 4 was soon known as Woodberry (*sic*); the town's name was spelled Woodbury when it was inc in 1854. It was named for either the first family to settle there or its location in a heavily forested area. 1153, 1341.

Woodford City (Woodford). See *Clifton*

Woodford County: *wŏŏd*/fərd. 192 sq mi. Pop 17,000. Seat: Versailles. This co, est in 1788 from part of Fayette Co, was the last co formed while Kentucky was still a part of Virginia. It was named for Gen. William Woodford from Virginia, an officer in the Continental Army who died a prisoner of the British in New York in 1780.

Woodlake (Franklin): *wŏŏd*/lāk (Frankfort East). This hamlet with extinct po lies at the jct of US 460 and KY 1262, 3½ mi e of Frankfort. The po, in operation from 1879 to 1910, was named for the lake on the farmstead of Mexican War veteran Maj. Russell Butler. 864.

Woodland Hills (Jefferson): *wŏŏd*/lənd *hihlz* (Jeffersontown). This 6th class city and residential suburb is 12½ mi e of downtown Louisville. The community was developed around 1955 and is said to have been named for its then geographic situation. It was inc in 1961. It does not have its own po. 1296.

Woodland PO (Barren). See *Cave City*

Woodlawn (Campbell): *wŏŏd*/lâhn (Newport). This 6th class city lies between Newport on the w, Bellevue on the n, and Ft. Thomas on the e, and is 9½ mi ne of Alexandria. In 1905 the Woodlawn Home Co. subdivided what had, until then, been called the Odd Fellows Grove and est the community of Woodlawn. It was inc in 1922. The community has never had its own po. 705.

Woodlawn Park (Jefferson): *wŏŏd*/lawn *pahrk* (Jeffersonville, Anchorage). This 5th class city and residential suburb without po is 6½ mi e of downtown Louisville. It was est in 1954 and may have been named for the Woodlawn Race Track that operated nearby from 1866 until it went bankrupt in 1871, and was considered for that brief time the "Saratoga of the West." The Woodlawn name had also been applied by 1870 to a station, 5 mi w of Anchorage, on the Louisville Cincinnati & Lexington RR line between Louisville and Covington. 725.

Woodrow (Breckinridge): *wŏŏd*/roh (Custer). This crossroads hamlet lies 6½ mi ese of Hardinsburg. Its now extinct po was est on May 21, 1914, with storekeeper Jefferson E. Bruner as pm, and named for Pres. Woodrow Wilson. 660.

Woodruff (Hopkins). See *Saint Charles*

Woodsbend (Morgan): *wŏŏdz*/behnd (West Liberty). This recently closed po was on KY 205 and the Licking R, 3 mi w of West Liberty. It is said to have been a reest of the older Henry po, in operation on nearby Straight Creek from 1880 to 1913 and named for its first pm [William] Powell Henry. J.B. May, a local storekeeper and farmer, is said to have est and named the Woodsbend po for its location in a woody area in a bend of the Licking R. Zona May became the first pm on Dec 14, 1920. 202, 1346.

Woodsonville (Hart): *wŏŏd*/sən/vihl (Munfordville). This residential suburb, once an inc town just w of US 31E and across the Green R from Munfordville, was the s end of what was known to the pioneers as the Big Buffalo Crossing. James Amos est a ferry and flatboat landing here and called it Amos Landing. Either he or Thomas Woodson, a large landowner and early magistrate, laid out the town in 1816 and named it for Woodson. The Woodsonville po was in operation from 1841 to 1906. 863, 1331.

Woods Station (Floyd). See *Emma*

Woodstock (Jefferson). See *Graymour*

Woodstock (Pulaski): *wo͞od*/stahk (Woodstock). This rural settlement with extinct po, once an inc town, lies at the jct of KY 39 and 934, 11 mi nne of Somerset. It may first have been settled about 1820 by a Mr. Griffin who, by the end of the decade, had sold his land to a Mr. Freancy of Lexington, the first local storekeeper. No one seems to know when the name Woodstock was first applied and there is little agreement about its origin. It has been said that the town was named for the city of Woodstock in England whence an early settler had come; or for Woodstock, Virginia, the former home of an early resident, which in turn had been named for the English city; or for a stone house in the vicinity, which may have been named for the city in England. It is less likely that it was named for a Mr. Woods and the early store that he stocked with all kinds of useful goods, or for the woods through which local people ran their livestock. Yet an early settler of that vicinity was a John F. Woods (1777–1857) from Virginia. The Woodstock po was est on Sept 21, 1853, with Reuben F. Elkins, pm, and after a noncontinuous existence it closed for good in 1940. 215, 870, 1170.

Woodville (Logan). See *Auburn*

Woodwards Creek PO (Estill). See *Hargett*

Woodwards Crossroads (Bracken). See *Brooksville*

Wooldridges Store PO (Christian). See *Crofton*

Woollum (Knox): *wo͞ol*/əm (Hima). This hamlet with po is on KY 11 and Collins Fork of Goose Creek, 10 mi nne of Barbourville. It was named by and probably for its first pm, Samuel J. Woollum, who est the po just over the Clay Co line on Mar 5, 1900. In 1924 Henry W. Cobb moved it to its present location. 1409.

Worthington (Greenup): *w3th*/ihŋ/tən (Ironton). One of a string of industrial and residential communities along the Ohio River between Ashland and Greenup, this 5th class city with po lies between the C&O RR tracks and the Ohio R, 4 mi ese of Greenup. The site was once a part of Abraham Buford's patent and was later owned by the Means and Russell Iron Co. which sold it to Col. William Worthington (1832–1914), a successful businessman, lawyer, co judge, and elected state official. After his death, the land passed to his daughters, was divided into town lots and named for him. The community includes the site of the Ashland-Boyd Co Airport, which at one time was called The Black Bottom District of Raceland and still is by some oldtimers. The Melrose section adjacent to the airport was once a separate community. The Worthington po was est on Nov 10, 1933, with Mrs. Lizzie Mary Oney, pm. 23, 1447, 1451.

Worthington PO (McLean). See *Island*

Worthington Station (Daviess). See *Newman*

Worthville (Carroll): *w3th*/vəl (Worthville). This 6th class city with po is on Eagle Creek, 1 mi above its confluence with the Kentucky R and 6 mi se of Carrollton. A settlement here predated the Civil War by at least a generation and was first known as Coonskin, for local merchants would willingly accept skins in place of scarce money as payment for merchandise. On Nov 18, 1847, a po was est with Lewis V. Fleming, pm, and named Worthville for Gen. William Worth, who had recently achieved some fame as a Mexican War hero. The community was laid out as a town around 1867 with the coming of the Louisville Cincinnati & Lexington Ry (the so-called ''Short Line,'' that later became a part of the L&N system), and was inc in 1878. 87, 143, 646, 781, 1330.

Wrigley (Morgan): *rihgh*/lee (Wrigley). This crossroads hamlet with po lies at the jct of KY 7 and 711, 6 mi n of West Liberty. The po and a station on the newly completed Morehead and North Fork RR were est in 1908 by John W. Wrigley and his Clearfield Lumber Co. of Pennsylvania. The station soon became the rail shipping point for an important coal and timber producing area. 933.

Wurtland (Greenup): *wɜt*/lən(d) (Greenup). This 6th class city with extinct po extends for about a mi between Uhlens Run and Chinns Branch on the Ohio R bottoms, n of new US 23 and 2 mi ese of Greenup. On a site earlier purchased by John C. McConnell from Peter Taylor's Virginia patent, pioneer settlers Alexander Fulton and his family est the Fulton Forge Works sometime after 1830, and the community soon became known as Fulton's Forge; the nearby r landing was called Fultons Forge Landing. Around 1823 William Shreve and his brothers built a steam furnace nearby on Old Steam Branch of East Fork of the Little Sandy R, and it became known simply as (the) Old Steam Furnace. Since neither Fultons Forge nor Steam Furnace was acceptable as the name for a po to serve the vicinity, another local industry—a factory that in the 1850s made kerosene from cannel coal mined nearby—gave its name to the po of Oil Works, est on Jan 14, 1864. This po was closed in 1871 but was reest on Feb 28, 1876, as Wurtland, for George and Samuel Grandin Wurts (1810–69 and 1812–80, respectively) of a family of German immigrants from Wurtemberg, Germany, who settled near Philadelphia and later moved to Greenup Co to engage in the iron furnace business. The po closed for good in 1959. 22, 1177, 1213, 1447, 1451.

Yamacraw (McCreary): *yaem*/ə/kraw (Barthell). Almost nothing remains of a coal town on the Big South Fork of the Cumberland R, just s of the present KY 92 and 3½ mi w of Whitley City. It was est in 1905 by the Stearns Coal and Lumber Co. of Stearns, Ky, and the local po was est on Sept 2, 1905, with James R. Sparks, pm. No one knows why the name was applied to the vicinity, probably before the opening of the local mine. The name, actually that of a tribe of renegade Creek Indians that lived in the area that later became the city of Savannah, Georgia, was also given to the settlement that preceded that city. There is nothing to support the popular contention that the McCreary Co community honored the chief of the alleged corn-cultivating Comargo tribe who had brought his people to this area after the Treaty of Sycamore Shoals in Mar 1775. 129, 208, 336, 1162.

Yancey (Harlan): *yaen*/see (Harlan). This coal town with extinct po on Slaters Fork of Catron Creek, 5 mi s of Harlan, was built up around the mine est in 1919–20 by Elbert O. Guthrie and named by him either for a racehorse or for Yancey Gross, a civil engineer. Guthrie also est the local po on Jan 12, 1924. 335, 1173.

Yeager (Knox). See *Bimble*

Yeaman (Grayson): *yā*/mən (Falls of Rough). This hamlet with po at the jct of KY 736 and 878, 15 mi w of Leitchfield, had been called Crossroads since its est in the early 19th cent. According to tradition, when this name was rejected by the Post Office Department as too common, that of Yeaman, storekeeper Frank Patterson's youngest son, was offered and accepted. The po began operation on Nov 27, 1893, with Frank Green, pm. 832.

Yellow Banks (Daviess). See *Owensboro*

Yellow Rock (Lee): *yael*/ə rahk (Heidelberg). This po on the Kentucky R, 4 mi w of

Beattyville, was named for the yellowish cast of the local limestone rock which is still being quarried. 1372.

Yelvington (Daviess): *yehl*/vihŋ/tən (Maceo). This hamlet with extinct po at the jct of KY 405 and 662, 8½ mi ne of Owensboro, started as a stagecoach stop at the jct of 2 Indian trails. The po was est on June 25, 1832, by Thomas H. Pointer, the local storekeeper, and named for Yelvington Overly (1800–52), pioneer settler and local blacksmith. After an intermittent existence, the po closed for good in 1913. 99, 930.

Yessie (Yesse) (Allen): *yehs*/ee (Scottsville). This settlement with extinct po is on KY 234, 6 mi n of Scottsville. The po was est as Yessie on Mar 2, 1906, with Thoughty Y. Oliver, pm, and probably named for Yessie or Yesse Oliver whose name is mentioned in John Durham's *Day Book* in 1854. It was discontinued in 1916. The Yesse spelling appears on current maps and seems to be preferred by historian Louise Horton for both place and person. 915, 1204, 1281.

Yocum (Morgan): *yoh*/kəm (West Liberty). This hamlet with po on Pleasant Run and KY 519, 4½ mi nw of West Liberty, is now also locally known as Pleasant Run [*plehz*/ənt *ruhn*] for this tributary of the Licking R. The po, est as Yocum on Aug 23, 1875, with William H. Lewis, pm, was first located at what is today called Blaze, 3 rd mi n, and may have been named for Billy Yocum, a respected local resident. It was moved to Pleasant Run in the late 1880s. 1133, 1346.

York (Greenup): yawrk (Brushart). This po lies at the mouth of Stockholm Creek, a tributary of Big White Oak Creek, over 6 mi w of the latter's confluence with Tygarts Creek, and 11 mi w of Greenup. Since its est on Mar 5, 1891, with Daniel J. Stephenson, pm, it has served the settlement of Kenton Furnace [*kihn*/(t)ən *f3n*/əs], named for an iron furnace built there in 1854 by John Waring, which was named in turn for famed pioneer Simon Kenton. No one is sure of Kenton's connection with the place though he is known to have owned property in Greenup Co. An earlier po in that vicinity was est as Kenton Furnace on Oct 15, 1869, with Charles W. Ehrlich, pm, but was discontinued after only 15 months. 188, 1092.

Yosemite (Casey): *yoh*/səm/eyet (Yosemite). This village with po lies at the jct of KY 70 and 198, on Knob Lick Creek, ½ mi s of its confluence with the Green R, and 4 mi ene of Liberty. The town was est in the late 1870s by Eugene Zimmerman, a Cincinnati-based businessman, as the center of his extensive timbering operations in the area. On Dec 26, 1883, a po was opened and named Yosemite at the suggestion of his young daughter, Helen, whose first view of the valley below the town site reminded her of the Yosemite Valley in California which she had recently visited. The odd pronunciation of the name has never been explained. 1452, 220, 1397.

Yost PO (Muhlenberg). See *Belton*

Youngs Creek (Whitley): *yuhŋz kreek* (Wofford). This extinct po was on Bark Camp Creek, 9 mi nnw of Williamsburg. It is probable that the po, est on July 14, 1864, with John Ryan, pm, was originally located on the creek that bears this name, a tributary of the Cumberland R. The creek was named for pioneering families of Youngs. 1380.

Young's Mill PO (Lincoln). See *Halls Gap*

Young Town (Hart). See *Monroe*

Yowell PO (Harlan). See *Benham*

Zachariah (Lee): zaek/ə/*reye*/ə (Zachariah). This hamlet with po lies at the jct of KY 11 and 1036, 8½ mi n of Beattyville. The po was est by and named for Zachariah C. Ponder on Mar 9, 1883, and was discontinued the following year. The name was applied to another po, 1.8 rd mi s, in 1902 and this was transferred to the original site in

1908 where it remained in operation until 1918. Meanwhile, a po called Zoe was est at the 2nd site in 1915 and the Zachariah po was reest in 1926. Both pos are still active. 132.

Zag (Morgan): zaegh (West Liberty). This hamlet with recently discontinued po is on KY 976, 6 mi nw of West Liberty. Pearl Cox had seen the word "Zig Zag" in an old newspaper used to paper a wall, so after all 18 names on a list submitted to the Post Office Department were rejected, she sent in "Zig" and "Zag." The 2nd of these was accepted and on Sept 23, 1915, her father, Jeff D. Cox, became the first pm of Zag. 112.

Zebulon (Pike): *zehb*/yəl/ən, *zehb*/ələn (Meta). This village with a rural branch of the Pikeville po extends over 2 mi along US 119 and Burning Fork of Raccoon Creek from the foot of Town Mountain, 1½ mi ne of Pikeville, to the mouth of Burning Fork. The po, est on June 9, 1880, with John L. Hubbard, pm, was for years located at the jct of US 119 and Burning Fork. It was named, as were the co and its seat, for Zebulon M. Pike (1779–1813), US Army officer-explorer and the discoverer of Pike's Peak. 1354.

Zilpah PO (Shelby). See *Jacksonville*

Zion (Henderson): *zah*/yən (Spottsville). This hamlet on KY 54, 3½ mi e of Henderson, may date to the organization of the Graves Creek Church in 1815 or the Zion Baptist Church in 1853 on land donated by Miles Cooksey, pioneer settler. Yet Zion as the name for the community has been traced back at least to 1848 and, thus, it may not have been named for the church as has been popularly assumed. The Zion po was est on June 29, 1857, with Theodore R. T. Fowlkes, pm, and closed in 1913. 12, 1358.

Zoe PO (Lee). See *Zachariah*

Zoneton (Bullitt): *zohn*/tən (Brooks). This Louisville suburb with extinct po is centered at the jct of Preston Highway (KY 61) and Zoneton Rd (KY 1116), less than 4 mi n of Shepherdsville. The community grew out of a late 19th cent rural trade center whose po was est on May 17, 1883, and named by its first pm, John R. Holsclaw, M.D. It is said that the "patterns on the ground made by moonlight shining through the trees reminded [him] of zones on a map." The po closed in 1902. 31.

Zula (Wayne): *zū*/lə (Parnell). This hamlet with extinct po is now on old KY 90, 6½ mi sw of Monticello. At the original site on Otter Creek, ½ mi n, Thomas and Ramey Jones are said to have built a mill and opened a store sometime after 1882. On Nov 16, 1901, Ramey est the po of Zula, said by some to have been named for Zula Frost, born 1891, the daughter of U. Grant Frost. When the federal government acquired Lower Otter Creek for its Lake Cumberland backfill in 1948, the mill closed and the store and po were relocated on top of the hill. The po closed in 1975. 1286, 1302, 1323.

References

Bibliographical information is incomplete for some sources not seen by the author. The citation of specific pages of a publication or manuscript indicates that this is the only portion of the source used in the entries. Where the location of a manuscript is not mentioned, it is in the possession of the author.

BOOKS, BOOKLETS, BROCHURES, PAMPHLETS, LEAFLETS, CHAPTERS OF BOOKS

1 *Acts of the Kentucky General Assembly,* 561ff. Frankfort, Ky., 1817–19.

2 Ibid., 302–4. 1817.

3 Ibid., 76–77. 1845.

4 Ibid., 87. 1845–46.

5 Ibid., 115. 1847–48.

6 Adams, Frazier B. *A Man From Jeremiah,* New York: Vantage Press, 1975.

7 A History of Ashland, Ky. 1786 to 1854. Ashland, Ky., 1954. (Centennial souvenir.)

8 *A History of Kentucky.* Vol. 3, 276. Chicago: S. T. Clark, 1928.

9 Allison, Vista Royse. *Methodist History of Adair Co., Ky., 1782–1969.* N.d.

10 *American College Dictionary.* New York: Random House, 1967.

11 *Annual Report of the Department of Mines of the State of Kentucky for the Year 1914.* 93. Frankfort, Ky.

12 Arnett, Maralea. *The Annals and Scandals of Henderson Co., Ky., 1775–1975.* Corydon, Ky.: Fremar, 1976.

13 *B. O. Gaines History of Scott Co.* Vol. 2. Georgetown, Ky., 1904.

14 Barkley, Alben W. *That Reminds Me.* Garden City, N.Y.: Doubleday, 1954.

15 *Bath County Memories, 1811–1974.* Owingsville, Ky., 1974. (Historical booklet.)

16 Baylor, Orval W. *Early Times in Washington Co.* Cynthiana, Ky.: Hobson Pr., 1942.

17 ______. *Pioneer History of Washington Co., Ky.* Edited by Michael L. and Bettie Ann Cook. Owensboro, Ky.: Cook-McDowell, 1980.

18 Beach, Mrs. James, and James Henry Snider. *Franklin and Simpson Co.—A Picture of Progress, 1819–1975.* 1976.

19 Beachley, Charles E. *History of the Consolidation Coal Co., 1864–1934.* 1934.

20 *Bell County Centennial: The Bell County Story, 1867–1967.* Pineville, Ky., 1967.

21 Bennett, Ora E. *History of Union Star.* N.d.

22 Biggs, Nina Mitchell. *A Supplementery Edition of a History of Greenup Co.* 1962.

23 Biggs, Nina Mitchell, and Mabel Lee Mackoy. *History of Greenup Co., Ky.* 1951.

24 Bogardus, Carl R. *The Early History of Gallatin Co., Ky.* 1948.

25 Bohn, D. L. *On the Texas: A Sketch of a Railroad Town: Irvington, Ky.* 1974.

26 *Boone County 175th Anniversary Historical Book, 1798–1973.* 1973.

27 Bracken County Homemakers. *Recollections: Yesterday, Today for Tomorrow, 1969: A History of Bracken Co.* 1969.

28 Bratcher, Bennett F. *History of Butler Co.* 1960.

29 Brewer, Mary T. *Rugged Trail to Appalachia: History of Leslie Co., Ky. and its People.* 1978.

30 *Brooksville Centennial, 1839–1939.* Brooksville, Ky., 1939.

31 Bullitt County Historical Commission. *A History of Bullitt Co.* 1974.

32 Burdette, Ruth Paull. *Early Columbia: The Beginnings of A Small Kentucky Town.* N.d.

33 Burrell, Donald, and Michael Putnam. *Rural Settlements Housing Study.* Part 2, 1971 Housing Report of the City–County Planning Commission. Lexington, Ky., 1971.

34 Bussell, Opp, Jr. *The Boone Way Man.* 1971.

35 Calico, Forrest. *History of Garrard Co., Ky. and its Churches.* New York: Hobson Book Pr., 1947.

36 Carter County Bicentennial Committee. *Carter Co. History 1838–1976.* Grayson, Ky., 1976.

37 Caudill, Harry. *Night Comes to the Cumberland,* Boston: Little, Brown, 1963.

38 *Chickasaw Country.* Wickliffe, Ky: Advance–Yeoman, 1974.

39 Chinn, George Morgan. *Kentucky: Settlement and Statehood, 1750–1800.* Frankfort, Ky.: Kentucky Hist. Soc., 1975.

40 ______. *Through Two Hundred Years.* Harrodsburg, Ky.: Mercer Co. Humane Soc., 1974.

41 *The City of Villa Hills: One Tenth Centennial.* N.d.

42 Coffman, Edward. *The Story of Logan Co.* Nashville: Parthenon Pr., 1962.

43 Coke, Ben H. *John May, Jr., of Virginia: His Descendants and Their Land.* Baltimore: Gateway Pr., 1975.

44 Collins, Richard. *History of Kentucky.* Vol. 2. Covington, Ky., 1874.

45 Combs, Josiah H. *The Combses Genealogy.* 1976.

46 Condon, Mabel Green. *A History of Harlan Co.* Nashville: Parthenon Pr., 1962.

47 Conley, Joan W., comp. and ed. *History of Nicholas Co.* Carlisle, Ky.: Nicholas Co. Hist. Soc., 1976.

48 Corliss, Carlton J. *Main Line of Mid-America.* 1950.

49 Cornett, Essie R. *The Cornett Family.* New York: Vantage Pr., 1971.

50 Craig, Will N. "Crab Orchard Springs." In *Early Lincoln Co. History,* Compiled and edited by Mrs. M. H. Dunn, 80–83. Stanford, Ky., 1975.

51 Daughters of the American Revolution. *Historical Sketch, Mason Co., Ky.* N.d.

52 Darnell, Emma Jett. *Filling the Chinks.* Frankfort, Ky., 1966.

53 Daviess, Marie Thompson. *History of Mercer and Boyle Counties.* Harrodsburg, Ky., Harrodsburg Herald, 1924.

54 Davis, D. Trabue. *Story of Mayfield Through a Century, 1823–1923.* 1923.

55 Dehart, Taylor, and Dora Dehart. *A History and Genealogy of Right Hand Fork, Masons Creek, Perry Co., Ky.* 1979.

56 Dorris, Jonathan T. *Old Cane Springs: A Story of the War Between the States in Madison Co., Ky.* 1937.

57 Dorris, Jonathan T., and Maud W. Dorris. *Glimpses of Historical Madison Co., Ky.* Nashville: Williams, 1955.

58 Douglass, Byrd. *Steamboatin' on the Cumberland.* Nashville: Tennessee Book, 1961.

59 Drane, Maud Johnston. *History of Henry Co., Ky.* Louisville, 1948.

60 Dunn, Shirley. *Historic Homes and Old Buildings of Lincoln Co., Ky.* N.d.

61 Duvall, Richard Todd. *The Buck Creek Settlement and Finchville, Ky., 1780–1976.* 1976.

62 *Earlington 1870–1970.* 1970.

63 Edmiston, Carroll Evan. *Our Families from the Atlantic Coast Colonies of 1665 to the California Pacific of 1974,* 140–44. 1974.

64 Edrington, William C. *Ticket from Turners Station.* N.d.

65 Edwards, B. G. *Glimpses of Historical Wayne Co., Ky.* 1970.

66 Edwards, Cyrus. *Stories of Early Days.* Edited by Florence Edwards Gardiner. Louisville, 1940.

67 *1860–1960 Centennial Celebration of Wolfe Co., Ky.* Campton, Ky., 1960. (Souvenir book.)

68 Elliott, Bessie Miller. *History of LaRue Co., Ky.* 1969.

69 Elliston, Robert. *History of Grant Co., State of Kentucky.* July 4, 1876. Reprint. Grant Co. News, Williamstown, Ky., 1951.

70 Fackler, Calvin M. *Early Days in Danville.* Louisville: Standard Printing, 1941.

71 Fern Creek Woman's Club. *Fern Creek Lore and Legacy 200 Years.* 1976.

72 Ferris, Robert G., ed. *Explorers and Settlers.* Washington: U.S. Dept. of Interior, National Survey of Historic Sites and Buildings, 1968.

73 Firestone, Clark B. *Bubbling Waters.* New York: Robert M. McBride, 1938.

74 *First Trip—Lexington to Fleming, Highway Post Office.* Whitesburg, Ky., 1949.

75 Fogle, McDowell A. *Fogle's Papers: A History of Ohio Co., Ky.* N.d.

76 Freeman, Leon Lewis, and Edward C. Olds. *The History of Marshall Co., Ky.* Benton, Ky.: Tribune-Democrat, 1933.

77 *From Cabin to College: A History of the Schools of Mason Co., Ky.* 1976.

78 Fulton Chamber of Commerce. *Fulton, Ky. Historical Project Booklet, July 19–25, 1959.* 1959.

79 Fuson, H. H. *History of Bell Co., Ky.* Vol. 1. New York: Hobson Book Pr., 1947.

80 Garrett, Peggy Cooper, and Joe Garrett. *Cooper From Then till Now.* 1973.

81 Geuther, W. *An Account of Bon Harbor. . . .* London, 1849.

82 Giltner, Helen Fairleigh. *Westport.* 1947.

83 Gorin, Franklin. *The Times of Long Ago: Barren Co., Ky.* Louisville: J.P. Morton, 1929.

84 *Grant Co. Sesquicentennial Program.* Williamstown, Ky., 1970.

85 Graves, Ralph Ed, ed. *History of Carlisle Co., Ky. for the Years 1820–1900.* 1976.

86 Graves, Ran. *History and Memories of Carlisle Co.* Wickliffe, Ky.: Advance–Yeoman, 1958.

87 Gray, Gypsy M. *History of Gallatin Co., Ky.* Covington, Ky., 1968.

88 *Greene's Kentucky Memorette.* Ashland, Ky., 1938.

89 Hall, C. Mitchell. *History of Johnson Co., Ky.* Louisville: Standard Pr., 1928.

90 ———. *Jenny Wiley Country.* 1979.

91 Hallenberg, Leone W. *Anchorage.* 1959.

92 Harmon, Geraldine Clair. *Chaplin Hills: History of Perryville, Ky.* Danville, Ky., 1971.

93 Hartman, Margaret S. *A Historic Walking Tour of the City of Newport, Ky.* N.d.
94 ______. "Campbell Co. History and Genealogy," *Falmouth Outlook*, Falmouth, Ky., Dec. 15, 1978.
95 Hayes, Myrtle. *This Was Yesterday: Stories of Kentucky's Pennyrile.* 1969.
96 Henry, J. Milton. *The Land Between the Rivers.* 1976.
97 Herr, Kincaid A. *Louisville and Nashville Railroad, 1850–1963.* Louisville: Louisville & Nashville RR, 1963.
98 *Historical Record Commemorating 150th Anniversary of the Founding of Trigg Co. 1820–1970.* 1970.
99 *History of Daviess Co., Ky.* Chicago: Inter-state, 1883.
100 *History of Ohio Falls Cities and their Counties.* Vol. 2. Cleveland: L. A. Williams, 1882.
101 Horton, Louise. *In The Hills of the Pennyroyal.* Austin, Texas: White Cross, 1975.
102 Houchens, Mariam S. *History of Owen Co.* Owenton, Ky.: Owen Co. Hist. Soc., 1976.
103 Hubbard, Freeman H. *Railroad Avenue: Great Stories and Legends of American Railroading.* New York: McGraw, 1945.
104 *Hugh O. Potter's History of Owensboro and Daviess Co., Ky.* Owensboro, Ky.: Daviess Co. Hist. Soc., 1974.
105 Hunnicutt, John M. *History of City of Ludlow.* N.d.
106 Huston, Ruth. *Observations of God's Timing in the Kentucky Mountains.* Salisbury, N.C.: Rowan Printing, 1962.
107 *Jeffersontown's Past 175 Years 1797–1972.* 1972.
108 Jillson, Willard Rouse. *Early Frankfort and Franklin Co.* Louisville, 1936.
109 ______. *Pioneer Kentucky.* Frankfort, Ky.: State Journal, 1934.
110 ______. *The Coal Industry in Kentucky.* Frankfort, Ky.: Kentucky Geological Survey, 1924.
111 Jobson, Robert C. *A History of Early Jeffersontown and Southeastern Jefferson Co., Ky.* Baltimore: Gateway Pr., 1977.
112 Johnson, Arthur C. *Early Morgan County.* 1974.
113 Johnson, Augusta Phillips. *A Century of Wayne Co.* Louisville: Standard Printing, 1939.
114 Johnson, Eunice Tolbert, ed. *Perry County, Ky.—A History.* 1953.
115 Johnson, L. F. *The History of Franklin Co., Ky.* Frankfort, Ky.: Roberts Printing, 1912.
116 Johnstone, Hallie Tipton. *History of Estill Co.* 1974.
117 Journalism Class of Livingston Central High School. *History, Legend and Lore of Livingston Co.* Smithland, Ky.: Livingston Ledger, 1974.
118 *Kenton County, Ky. Centennial.* 1940.
119 Kentucky Historical Society. *Guide to Kentucky Historical Highway Markers.* No. 1136 237. Frankfort, Ky., 1969.
120 Ibid. No. 1109, 227.
121 Ibid. No. 906, 153–54.
122 Ibid. No. 1055, 205.
123 Ibid. No. 896, 151.
124 Kentucky Historical Society. *Supplement to Guide to Kentucky Historical Highway Markers.* No. 1310, 17. Frankfort, Ky., 1973.
125 Kerr, Charles, ed. *History of Kentucky.* Vol. 2. Chicago: Am. Hist. Soc., 1922.

126 Kinnaird, Dr. J. B. *Looking Backward: Historical Sketches of Lancaster and Garrard Co. from Authentic Sources and Tradition.* 1924.

127 Knapp, Paul T. *Ft. Thomas, Ky. Its History . . . Its Heritage.* 1967.

128 Kozee, William C. *Pioneer Families of Eastern and Southeastern Kentucky.* Baltimore: Genealog. Pub., 1973.

129 Krakow, Kenneth. *Georgia Place Names.* 264. Macon, Ga.: Winship Pr., 1975.

130 Lancaster Woman's Club. *Patches of Garrard Co.* 1974.

131 Layne, Floyd Benjamin. *Layne-Lain-Lane Genealogy.* 1962.

132 Lee County Centennial Book Committee. *Lee County Centennial, 1870–1970.* Beattyville, Ky., 1970.

133 Lemon, James R. *Lemon's Hand Book of Marshall Co. . . .* 1894.

134 *Lexington and the Bluegrass Country: A Guide.* Lexington, Ky.: E. M. Glass, 1938.

135 McAllister, Annabella, and Edward N. McAllister. *Brasfield-Brassfield Genealogies.* 1959.

136 McClure, Daniel E., Jr. *Two Centuries in Elizabethtown and Hardin Co., Ky., 1776–1976.* Elizabethtown, Ky.: Hardin Co. Hist. Soc., 1979.

137 McCuiston, Charles A. "History of New Concord." In *History of Calloway Co., Ky.* Murray, Ky.: Ledger & Times, 1931.

138 McDonald, Leslie. *Echoes of Yesteryear.* Smithland, Ky.: Livingston Ledger, 1972.

139 McDowell, Robert. *Rediscovering Kentucky: A Guide for Modern Day Explorers.* Frankfort, Ky.: Kentucky Dept. of Parks, 1971

140 McKee, Maj. Lewis W., and Mrs. Lydia K. Bond. *A History of Anderson Co.*, Frankfort, Ky.: Roberts Printing, 1937.

141 Magee, M. Juliette. *Old Fort Jefferson.* Wickliffe, Ky.: Advance–Yeoman, 1975.

142 Martin, Joseph. *A Brief History of Metcalfe Co., 1860–1970.* Statesman Heritage Series. Edmonton, Ky., 1970.

143 Masterson, Mary, comp. *Historic Carroll County.* N.d.

144 Mather, O. M. *The Mather Papers.* Hodgenville, KY.: LaRue Co. Herald-News, 1968.

145 Meacham, Charles Mayfield. *A History of Christian Co., Ky. from Oxcart to Airplane.* Nashville: Marshall & Bruce, 1930.

146 *Memorial Record of Western Kentucky.* Chicago: Lewis, 1904.

147 Middleton, Elmon. *Harlan County, Ky.* 1934.

148 Montell, William Lynwood. *Monroe County History, 1820–1970.* Tompkinsville, Ky., 1970.

149 Moore, Albert K. *1860–1960—Magoffin's First Century.* Salyersville, Ky., 1960.

150 Morgan, Kelly. *Pioneer Families.* 2nd ed. 1970.

151 *Morganfield Sesquicentennial Historical Program.* 1951.

152 Morlock, James. *The Evansville Story.* Evansville, Ind., 1956.

153 Neuman, Fred G. *The Story of Paducah.* Paducah, Ky., 1927.

154 Newman, Mary. *As It Was Told to Me: The History of Elsmere, Ky.* 1976.

155 Okolona Woman's Club. *History of the Okolona Area.* 1956.

156 Oldham Co. Historical Soc. Historical Brochure. 1963. (Souvenir program for "LaGrange Day," Oct. 19, 1963 .)

157 O'Malley, Charles J. *History of Union County, Ky.* Evansville, Ky., 1886.

158 *One Hundred and Seventh-Fifth Anniversary of Harrison Co., 1794–1969.* Cynthiana, Ky., 1969.

159 *Original Atlas and Historical Data of Hopkins Co., Ky.* Madisonville, Ky.: Hopkins Co. Hist. Soc., 1974.

160 *Owen County Almanac and Historical Fact Book.* 1964–65 ed. Owenton, Ky.: Owen Co. Historical Soc., 1964.

161 Owings, Lucille Bryars. *Old Columbus, Ky., Belmont, Mo. Civil War Battlefield Areas: A Brief History and Old Pictures.* 1974.

162 ______. *150 Years—Hickman County Sesquicentennial: Historical Program Book.* Bardwell, Ky., 1971.

163 Peck, Elisabeth S. *Berea's First Century, 1855–1955.* Lexington, Ky.: U. Kentucky Pr., 1955.

164 Pell, Edna S. *The Descendants of William Pell, Sr. of Kent Co., Md.* 1968.

165 Perkins, E. C. *The Borning of a Town: Newport, Cantuckie.* 1963.

166 Perrin, William Henry. *Counties of Christian and Trigg.* Chicago: F. A. Battey, 1884.

167 ______. *History of Bourbon, Scott, Harrison and Nicholas Counties, Ky.* Chicago: O. L. Baskin, 1882.

168 Perrin, William Henry, and J. H. Battle. *Counties of Todd and Christian.* Chicago: F. A. Battey, 1884.

169 Perrin, William Henry, J. H. Battle, and G. C. Kniffen. *Kentucky: A History of the State.* 1st ed. Part II. Louisville: F. A. Battey, 1885.

170 Ibid., 2nd ed., 1885.

171 Ibid., 3rd ed., 1887.

172 Ibid., 4th ed., 1887.

173 Ibid., 8B ed., 1888.

174 Perry, L. E. *McCreary Conquest: A Narrative History.* 1979.

175 Peter, Robert. *History of Fayette County.* Chicago: O. L. Baskin, 1882.

176 Pineau, Mary. *Pioneer People—A Story of David.* 1977.

177 *Pippa Passes: A Poem and a Place.* Ca. 1970. (Brochure prepared and distributed by Alice Lloyd College.)

178 Powell, Burnett. *Remembering: Glen Dean School.* n.d.

179 Ragan, Rev. O. G. *History of Lewis County.* Cincinnati, 1912.

180 Railey, William E. *History of Woodford County.* Rev. ed. Frankfort, Ky., 1938.

181 Ramsay, Robert L. *Our Storehouse of Missouri Place Names.* Missouri Handbook no. 2. *University of Missouri Bulletin* 53, no. 34, Arts & Science Ser. (1952) no. 7.

182 Ranck, George W. *Boonesborough.* Louisville: John P. Morton, 1901.

183 Rankins, Walter. *Historic Augusta and Augusta College.* 1949.

184 Reid, Richard. *Historical Sketches of Montgomery Co.* 1882. Reprint. Womans Club of Mt. Sterling, Ky., 1926. (Paper read at 4th of July celebration, 1876).

185 *Report of the Inspector of Mines of Kentucky.* Frankfort, Ky., 1905.

186 Richards, J[ohn] A. *An Illustrated History of Bath Co., Ky.* 1961.

187 Ridenour, George L. *Early Times in Meade Co., Ky.* Louisville: Western Recorder, 1929.

188 Rist, Donald E. *Kentucky Iron Furnaces of the Hanging Rock Iron Region.* Ashland, Ky.: Hanging Rock Pr., 1974.

189 Rothert, Otto A. *A History of Muhlenberg County.* Louisville: John P. Morton, 1913.

190 Sargent, Clara, *et al. Fulton County 74–76 BiCentennial.* 1974. (Souvenir book.)

191 Savage, Jacob. *We Are the Savages.* 1974.

192 Savoyard [Eugene W. Newman]. *In the Pennyrile of Old Kentucky and Men, Things, and Events*. Washington, D.C.: Sudwarth, 1911.
193 Scalf, Henry P. "Daniel Boone in Eastern Kentucky." In *150 Years Pike County, Kentucky, 1822–1972*, 9–14. Pikeville, Ky.: Pike Co. Hist. Soc., 1972.
194 ———. *Kentucky's Last Frontier*. 1966.
195 *Sesquicentennial Souvenir Program, 1815–1965*. Covington, Ky., 1965.
196 Shannon, Roy Lee. *Moorefield, Ky., 1796–1976*. 1976.
197 Smalling, Landon H. *Middlesboro and Before Middlesboro Was*. ca1924.
198 Smith, Katie S. *The Land of the Little Colonel: Pewee Valley*. 1975.
199 Smith, Sarah B. *Historic Nelson County*. Louisville: Gateway Pr., 1971.
200 *Souvenir Program—Brownsboro Day, Oct. 13, 1962*.
201 *Souvenir Supplement. The Marion Falcon*. Lebanon, Ky., Sept. 1, 1905.
202 Stacy, Helen Price, and William Lynn Nickell. *Selections from Morgan County History*. 1973.
203 Staples, Charles R. *History of Pioneer Lexington, Ky. 1779–1806*. Lexington, Ky., 1939.
204 Stewart, George R. *American Place-Names*. New York: Oxford U. Pr., 1970.
205 ———. *Names on the Land*. Boston: Houghton Mifflin, 1967.
206 Stratton, Margaret Barnes. *Place-Names of Logan County and Oft-Told Tales*. 2nd ed. 1947.
207 Suell, Robert M. *History of Freemasonry in Jessamine County, Ky*. 1974.
208 Sulzer, Elmer G. *Ghost Railroads of Kentucky*. Indianapolis, 1967.
209 Sumpter, Irene Moss. *An Album of Early Warren County Landmarks*. 1976.
210 Taylor, Harrison D. *Ohio County, Ky. in the Olden Days*. Louisville: John P. Morton, 1926.
211 *Tennessee: A Guide to the State*, 332–34. New York: Hastings 1939.
212 Thomas, Gladys Cothan, comp. and ed. *Casey County, Ky. 1806–1977: A Folk History*. Liberty, Ky.: BiCentennial Heritage Corp. of Casey Co., Ky., 1978.
213 Thomas, W. R. *Life Among the Hills and Mountains of Kentucky*, Allen, Ky.: Sandy Valley, 1926.
214 Thompson, Bill. *History and Legend of Breckenridge County, Kentucky* N.d.
215 Tibbals, Alma Owens. *A History of Pulaski County, Ky*. 1952.
216 Tinsley, Harry D. *History of No Creek, Ohio County, Ky*. Frankfort, Ky.: Roberts Printing, 1953.
217 Tipton, J. C. *The Cumberland Coal Field and its Creators*. Middlesboro, Ky., 1905.
218 Vaughn, Howard Willis. *The History of Rochester*. 1976.
219 Verhoeff, Mary. *The Kentucky River Navigation*, Filson Club Publications, No. 28. Louisville: Filson Club, 1917.
220 Watkins, W. M. *The Men, Women, Events. Institutions and Lore of Casey County*. Louisville: Standard Printing, 1939.
221 Weis, Capt. Daniel K. *Reminiscences of Eastern Kentucky*. (From feature articles in an area newspaper, 1905–7.)
222 Wells, J. K. *A Short History of Paintsville and Johnson County*. Paintsville, Ky.: Paintsville Herald, 1962.
223 Wells, J. W. *The History of Cumberland County*. Louisville: Standard Printing, 1947.
224 Wilkie, Katharine E., and Elizabeth R. Moseley. *Frontier Nurse: Mary Breckinridge*. New York: Messner, 1969.

225 Williams, Marion. *The Story of Todd County, Kentucky,* Nashville: Parthenon Pr., 1972.

226 Williams, W. T. *History of Ravenna, Ky.* Irving Times, 1956. (Published in installments; bound as a pamphlet by Kentucky Dept. of Libraries.)

227 Williamson, Gay Bolt, and Pauline Ross Yakley, *Descendants of Isaac and Elizabeth Bolt.* N.d.

228 Willis, George L. *History of Shelby County, Ky.* Louisville: C. T. Dearing Printing, 1929.

229 Wilson, Joyce. *This Was Yesterday.* Booneville, Ky., 1977.

230 Wiseman, Malvena, comp. and ed. *One Century of Lyon County History.* 1964. Based on interviews by Lyon Co. High School students.

231 *Within This Valley.* Morehead, Ky.: Rowan Co. Centennial Publication, 1956.

232 Wolf Creek Dam Homemakers District. *History of Metcalfe County.* c1949.

233 Wolfe County Woman's Club. *Early and Modern History of Wolfe County.* Campton, Ky., 1952.

234 Wolfford, George. *Lawrence County, A Pictorial History.* 1972.

235 Woman's Club of Stamping Ground. *Echoes of the Past.* 1975.

236 Works Projects Administration. Kentucky Writers Project. *In the Land of Breathitt.* Northport, N.Y.: Bacon, Percy & Daggett, 1941.

237 ______. *Lexington and the Bluegrass Country: A Guide.* Lexington: E. M. Glass, 1938.

238 ______. *Union County Past and Present.* Louisville: Schumann Printing, 1941.

239 Yealey, A. M. *History of Boone County, Ky.* 1960.

240 Young, Bennett H. *A History of Jessamine County, Ky.* Louisville, 1898.

NEWSPAPER, MAGAZINE, AND JOURNAL ARTICLES

241 Adams, James Taylor. "Red Bird Settlement School Serves Pupils Drawn from All Parts of Mountain Area." *Middlesboro Daily News,* May 27, 1954, 19.

242 "A Kentucky Town's Tradition." *Louisvlle Courier-Journal,* Nov. 24, 1926.

243 Alexander, Mrs. Woodrow. "Meredith." *Leitchfield Gazette,* BiCentennial Ed., 1976, Communities section, 8.

244 Allen, C. Hall. "Old Airdrie, Wealthy in Coal and History." *Louisville Courier-Journal,* Jan. 2, 1927.

245 Allen, Randy. "Lot of Working People, Lot of Senior Citizens." *Cincinnati Enquirer,* July 30, 1979.

246 Allen, Wendell. "Rosine Post Office 103 Years Old Today." *Ohio County News,* Jan. 16, 1975, 9.

247 *Allen County News,* May 17, 1939.

248 Ibid., May 24, 1939.

249 Alley, Terry M. "Vine Grove Residents Look Back at History with Pride." *Elizabethtown News,* BiCentennial ed., May 21, 1974.

250 Alter, Dave. "Your Town: Walton, Kentucky—Just Plain American." *Cincinnati Times-Star,* Apr. 25, 1956.

251 Ammons, Mrs. DuEthel, and Mrs. Maye Wall. "Cayce People Are Proud of Those Who Helped Make It What It Is." *Mayfield Messenger,* Purchase ed., Dec. 27, 1969, pp. 9–10.

252 Angel, Gladys. "Once Bustling Heidelberg. Barely a Whistle Stop Today." *Beattyville Enterprise,* Mar. 19, 1970, 2.

253 *ANS Bulletin Number 27*. May 1972, 14.

254 Ardery, Mrs. William B. "Historical Sketch of Paris, Kentucky." *Bourbon News*, Oct. 1, 1935.

255 Arnold, Loreca. "How Horse Branch was Named." *Ohio County Messenger*, Oct. 20, 1967.

256 *Ashland Daily Independent*, Centennial Issue, Sept. 29, 1954, Industrial and Business section, 9.

257 Ashley, Frank. " 'Spy' Scare at Majestic." *Louisville Courier-Journal*, Nov. 3, 1971, B1.

258 Atchey, Lowell. *Benton Tribune-Courier*, July 22, 1977, Leisure Scene Magazine section, 14.

259 Baker, Flossie J. "London–Laurel Story." *Corbin Daily Tribune*, 75th Anniversary Ed., Feb. 23, 1967, Laurel Co section, 2.

260 ______. "The Swiss Who Migrated to Laurel Became Highly Productive Citizens." *Corbin Daily Tribune*, 75th Anniversary ed., Feb. 23, 1967, Laurel Co section, 15.

261 Barclay, Dick. "Porter Family Was Probably the First to Settle Arlington in 1831." *Mayfield Messenger*, Purchase ed. Dec. 27, 1969, J4.

262 Barlow, E. H. "Pellville History—A Blend of Folklore and Fact." *Hancock Clarion*, 75th Anniversary ed., July 1968.

263 Barnett, Mrs. Mildred. "History of Atchinson—Part One." *Central Kentucky News*, June 28, 1973, B6.

264 Barton, Lon C. "Young South Carolinian and Wife Were First Settlers of Mayfield." *Mayfield Messenger*, Purchase ed., Dec. 27, 1969, I8.

265 "Beautiful Old Berry Homes." *Cynthiana Democrat*, Harrison Heritage Historical Houses ed., Aug. 21, 1975, 23.

266 "Beaver Dam." *Ohio County News*, July 19, 1973, sec. 1, p. 2.

267 Beckner, Lucien. "Eskippakithiki: The Last Indian Town in Kentucky." *Filson Club History Quarterly* 6 (1932): 355–82.

268 "Beechy." *Russell Times*, Sept. 25, 1942, sec. 3, p. 7.

269 Beeler, Mary Lou. "Spring Lick." *Leitchfield Gazette*, BiCentennial ed., 1976, communities section, 3.

270 Bennett, Edith. "Livermore." *McLean County News*, Bicentennial issue, July 1, 1976, 8.

271 Benton, Hilda L. "A History of Caney, Kentucky." *Recollections: A Journal of the Appalachian Oral History Project at Lees Junior College* 1, no. 2 (Spring 1973).

272 Bergstrom, Bill. Associated Press, Nov. 2, 1976. (Release on Democrat, Letcher Co., Ky.)

273 Berry, E. W. "What Ever Happened to White Plains?" *Madisonville Messenger*, July 31, 1971.

274 Bevins, Ann. "Turkeyfoot Was the Place Where 3 Forks Intersected." *Lexington Leader*, Apr. 8, 1966.

275 "Big Eagle Country Remembered as Enchanted Hillsides, Winding Paths." *Owenton News-Herald*, Bicentennial ed., July 4, 1974, 6.

276 Billiter, Bill. "Smoke at Fancy Farm Signals That Something's Cooking." *Louisville Courier-Journal*, Aug. 7, 1971, B1.

277 "Bill Powell's Symsonia, Kentucky." *Louisville Courier-Journal*, Bi-Centennial Monthly, May 1976, 3.

278 Blackburn, Mrs. Mac. "Fredonia: In the Beginning." *Princeton Leader,* Aug. 19, 1971.

279 Blakely, John R. "The Early History of Development of Fort Mitchell." *Papers of the Christopher Gist Historical Society* 6 (1954–5): 58–64.

280 ______. "The Old Latonia Race Track." Papers of the Christopher Gist Historical Society, 53 (1951–52): 94–100.

281 Blincoe, Caden. "Normally Quiet, City Alive with Auction This Month." *Cincinnati Enquirer,* Sept. 3, 1979.

282 ______. "Who Runs Elsmere." *Cincinnati Enquirer,* Jan. 5, 1979.

283 "Board Sought New Name for Mt. Pleasant in 1912." *Harlan Daily Enterprise,* 50th Anniversary ed., Sept. 23, 1962, 1.

284 Bolser, Harry. "Fancy Farm." *Louisville Courier-Journal,* Mar. 8, 1965.

285 ______. "La Center." *Louisville Courier-Journal,* Sept. 13, 1964.

286 ______. "Riverboats Churned Smithland's Colorful History." *Louisville Courier-Journal,* July 5, 1965.

287 ______. "Time Is Running Out for Paradise." *Louisville Courier-Journal and Times,* Mar. 12, 1967, B6.

288 ______. "Wingo." *Louisville Courier-Journal,* Nov. 1, 1964.

289 Booth, Mrs. Taylor. "Railroad Spanned Era of Industry in Wolfe." *Lexington Leader,* Mar. 20, 1965, 9.

290 Bowling, Lin. "History of Breckinridge County Postoffices." *Breckinridge County Herald-News,* Feb. 24, 1975.

291 "Bowling Green: A Town Erected with New Hope." *The Free Lance-Star: Town and Country,* July 16, 1966, A3.

292 Bowmar, Dan M. "Fayette Had 20 Post Offices 75 Years Ago." *Lexington Leader,* Oct. 2, 1970.

293 ______. "Tyrone: The River Town That Used to Be." *Lexington Leader,* Oct. 19, 1970.

294 Boyd, S. G. "Grahamton, Ky. and the History of the Company." *Louisville Courier-Journal,* Mar. 27, 1927.

295 "Bridgeport as Written in Spectator in 1800's." *Edmonton Herald-News,* Special Bicentennial ed., June 30, 1974, 3.

296 Briggs, Richard. "West Point History: Pitts Point." *Radcliff Sentinel,* Feb. 16, 1978.

297 ______. "West Point History: Williamsville." *Radcliff Sentinel,* Mar. 24, 1977, 5.

298 ______. "West Point: Isolated but Rich in History." *Elizabethtown News,* Bicentennial ed., May 21, 1974, E10.

299 Brooks, Rev. J. H., and H. H. Wilson, "Pioneer History of the Hammonsville Area of Hart County." *Hart County Historical Society Quarterly* 4 (1972): 3–5.

300 Brooks, Patricia. "A Night at Shakertown, Ky. Is a Journey into the Past." *New York Times,* May 11, 1969, sec. 10, p. 16.

301 Brown, Ann. "Hanson 100 Years Old This Year." *Madisonville Messenger,* Sept. 19, 1969, 1.

302 Brown, Annie Burnside. "Old Paint Lick: An Eighteenth Century Church and Cemetery." *Kentucky Progress Magazine,* Apr. 1931, 42.

303 Brown, Mike. "Bullitt Community Is Trying to Catch up with Its Growth." *Louisville Courier-Journal,* Mar. 17, 1977, 1.

304 ______. "It's Just Another Plum Day." *Louisville Courier-Journal,* Nov. 8, 1972, B1.

305 Bryant, Elsa. *Columbia Spectator,* Mar. 19, 1970. (Article on Crocus.)

306 *The Bulletin of the Kentucky Historical Society* 4, no. 2 (Apr. 1978): 1.

307 "The Burkesville Story." *Cumberland County News,* Sesquicentennial ed., Aug. 18, 1960, A1.

308 Burress, Susan. "Railroad History of Taylor County Recalled." *News-Journal Bicentennial Edition,* July 25, 1974, sec. 2, p. 7.

309 Burt, Jesse C. "Mortons Gap, Kentucky." *Ford Times,* Mar. 1959, 28–31.

310 Butcher, Nadene. "Johnson Communities Earned Colorful Names." *Ashland Daily Independent,* Dec. 14, 1969, 23.

311 Callahan, Dave. "One Man's Spite Annoys Both Residents of Poverty." *Owensboro Messenger and Inquirer,* June 23, 1972.

312 Campbell, Lois. "Bybee Pottery: Shapes in Clay for Five Generations." *Guide to Madison County,* Spring–Summer 1971, 10–11. (Published by *Madison County Newsweek.*)

313 "Caneyville in the Days Gone By." *Grayson County News,* July 22, 1955.

314 Cannon, Jean Ward. "Halfway Store and K. E. Pruitt Go Together." *Allen County News,* Mar. 16, 1972, 7.

315 Carter, B. N. "Sketch of a Kentucky Town—Petersburg." *Covington Journal,* Jan. 25, 1873, 1.

316 "Carter County's Heritage: Willard." *Grayson Journal-Enquirer,* Mar. 22, 1976, 1.

317 "Carter Early Tourist Center of County." *Carter County Historical Edition of the Grayson Journal-Enquirer,* Aug. 28, 1969, sec. 3, p. 1.

318 Carter, Tom. "Fayette Addresses Show History-Related Names." *Lexington Herald-Leader,* Apr. 12, 1970, 5.

319 Carver, Gayle R. *Greenville Leader,* Mar. 5, 1937.

320 Cather, Alexander R. "Origins of Muhlenberg County Place Names." *Central City Times-Argus,* Aug. 2, 1972, 3.

321 Caudill, Harry M. "Oral Traditions Behind Some Kentucky Mountain Place Names." *Register of the Kentucky Historical Society* 78 (Summer 1980): 197–207.

322 Celliers, Peter J. "Golden Hills of the Pioneers." *Redbook,* Sept. 1957, 54.

323 *Central Kentucky News-Journal,* July 16, 1931, 6.

324 "Centrally Located Owenton: Hub of Commercial and Government Activity Since 1850's." *Owenton News-Herald,* Bicentennial ed., July 4, 1974, 4.

325 Christie, Margaret Sue. "County Was Settled by English People." *Columbia Statesman.* Bicentennial ed., June 15, 1974, 18.

326 *Cincinnati Daily Enquirer,* Apr. 26, 1866, 1, July 4, 1866, 1.

327 *Cincinnati Daily Enquirer,* Apr. 28, 1866, 4.

328 "Clark County Chronicles." *Winchester Sun,* Dec. 14, 1922.

329 Cleaver, Leota. "Hawesville Began as Homesteads in 1820's." *Hancock Clarion,* 75th anniversary ed., July 1968.

330 "Coal Camp Names." *Mountain Memories* No. 13 (Summer–Fall 1979): 3.

331 "Coal Is Gone and Nearly All of the Town." *Henderson Gleaner,* Sept. 22, 1940.

332 Coleman, J. Winston. "Old Kentucky Watering Places." *Filson Club History Quarterly* 16 (1942); 1–26.

333 ______. "Historic Kentucky." *Lexington Leader,* Oct. 8, 1961. (Photo story on Burnt Tavern.)

334 ______. "Historic Kentucky." *Lexington Leader,* Sept. 24, 1961. (Photo story on Hazel Patch.)

335 Collins, Mabel. "Town Names Given by Railroads, Companies, Settlers." (Unidentified and undated newspaper article.)

336 Collins, Robert F. "Daniel Boone National Forest Historic Sites." *Filson Club History Quarterly* 42 (1968): 26–48.

337 "Coming of the Southern Railroad Places Waddy on the Map." *Shelbyville Sentinel,* 1940(?), 2.

338 Conn, Joseph. *Wayne County Outlook,* Dec. 25, 1975; Feb. 19, 1976. (Articles on Alpha.)

339 Conover, Rebecca, and Alma Ray S. Ison. "Captain Abraham Chaplin—One of Harrod's Men." *Harrodsburg Herald,* July 13, 1972, 3.

340 "Coon." *Hart County News,* Feb. 6, 1902. (Cited in the *Hart County Historical Society Quarterly* 5, no. 4 (Oct 1973): 8.)

341 "Cornwell Founded by English to Escape Crowded Conditions." *Menifee County Journal,* Heritage ed. Apr. 10, 1974, 14.

342 *Covington Journal,* Feb. 4, 1871, 2.

343 Cox, Bill. "Grass-Roots Voices. . . ." *Louisville Courier-Journal,* Nov. 8, 1972, 1.

344 Cox, Elizabeth Smith. "Beech Grove." *McLean County News,* Bicentennial issue, July 1, 1976, 13.

345 Cracraft, James O. "Most Came—Some Meet Them." *Robertson Review Centennial Edition,* July 1971, 19.

346 Craig, Berry. "Whittemore Is Viola: Old General Store a Depression Days Leftover." *Paducah Sun-Democrat,* Feb. 27, 1977, C1.

347 Crawford, Mrs. Mary E. "Millwood." *Leitchfield Gazette,* Bicentennial ed., 1976, Communities section, 10.

348 Creal, E. W. "Otter Creek and Malt Post Offices." *LaRue County Herald-News,* Aug. 29, 1974, D10.

349 Creason, Joe. "A Water Wonderland." *Louisville Courier-Journal Magazine,* Aug. 26, 1962, 40.

350 ______. "The Captive City That Was Set Free." *Louisville Courier-Journal Magazine.* Apr. 3, 1949, 5.

351 ______. "DeKoven, Once Coal Capital and Now a Ghost, Hopes to Make a Comeback." *Louisville Courier-Journal,* Oct. 17, 1954, sec. 3, p. 3.

352 ______. "4th Class Post Office Going, Going. . . ." *Louisville Courier-Journal,* June 29, 1958, sec. 4, p. 11.

353 ______. "Ghost Town's Day in the Sun." *Louisville Courier-Journal,* May 30, 1967, A11.

354 ______. *Louisville Courier-Journal,* Aug. 15, 1954.

355 ______. *Louisville Courier-Journal,* Mar. 4, 1964, A7.

356 ______. *Louisville Courier-Journal,* Apr. 7, 1971, B17.

357 ______. *Louisville Courier-Journal,* June 22, 1972, C1.

358 ______. *Louisville Courier-Journal Magazine,* Nov. 20, 1955, 8.

359 ______. "Some Place Names Just Can't Be Accounted For." *Louisville Courier-Journal,* Sept. 30, 1970, B13.

360 ______. "Tasteful Urban Renewal, the Rural Way." *Louisville Courier-Journal,* July 15, 1974, B1.
361 ______. "There's an Inferno Where Paradise Used to Be." *Louisville Courier-Journal,* Jan. 4, 1973, B1.
362 ______. "This, Then, is Tolu." *Louisville Courier-Journal Magazine,* Feb. 15, 1948.
363 ______. "Village Names that Just Come Naturally." *Louisville Courier-Journal,* Sept. 11, 1970.
364 Culbertson, Ben. "The Ghost of Blue Heron." *Louisville Courier-Journal and Times Magazine,* Jan. 9, 1972, 22.
365 Cummins, Squire. "Steam Mill at Milledgeville." *Interior Journal, Lincoln County Bicentennial, 1775–1975* ed., 1975.
366 Cunningham, J. W. *Leitchfield Sunbeam,* July 18, 1884. (Reprinted in *Leitchfield Gazette,* Mar. 1, 1929.) (Report of trip to Grayson Springs.)
367 Dahringer, John F. "History of Lebanon." *Lebanon Enterprise,* Aug. 12, 1965.
368 "Danleyton." *Russell Times,* Sept. 25, 1942, sec. 3, p. 7.
369 Darnell, Mrs. M. C. "Church Family Prominent in Early Days at Stedmantown." *State Journal,* May 12, 1960, 9.
370 ______. "Hockensmiths Were Early Settlers Here." *State Journal,* July 21, 1961.
371 ______. "Railroad Devised to Furnish Transportation When Navigation Proves Impossible." *State Journal,* July 29, 1962, 2.
372 ______. "Records Show Peaks Mill Built in 1819." *State Journal,* Oct. 4, 1959.
373 Davis, A. B. "Attorney at Richmond Relates Interesting History of Southeastern Madison County." *Lexington Leader,* Feb. 8, 1954.
374 Davis, Lucile S. "Historical Tidbits." *Woodford Sun,* June 1, 1978, 3.
375 "Death of Its Namesake an Irony for Okolona." *Louisville Times,* Nov. 27, 1972, B1.
376 Decker, Elmer. *The Barbourville Advocate,* ca. 1937.
377 Deitz, Robert E. "Martin County, Ky.: A Portrait of Poverty." *Louisville Courier-Journal Magazine,* Jan. 31, 1965, 7.
378 Dickey, Earle. "Cave City: Gateway to Kentucky's Cave Region." *L&N Employees' Magazine,* Nov. 1931, 13–15.
379 Dickey, Rev. J. J. *Fleming Gazette,* Aug. 19, 1930; Aug. 25, 1930. (History of Fleming Co.)
380 ______. *Fleming Gazette,* Sept. 9, 1930; Sept. 16, 1930.
381 ______. *Fleming Gazette,* May 3, 1932.
382 Dillingham, James E. *Dawson Springs Progress,* Special Centennial ed., July 25, 1974, passim. (History of Dawson Springs.)
383 "Distillery at Athertonville Since 1780." *LaRue County Herald-News,* Aug. 29, 1974, B7.
384 Dodson, Donald. "Brief History of Stephensport from 1803 to the Present." *Breckinridge County Herald-News,* Anniversary ed., July 4, 1976.
385 "Down by the Rough River, an Old Mill Stream" *Louisville Courier-Journal and Times,* Nov. 5, 1972, B1.
386 Dorris, Joe. "How It Started." *Kentucky New Era,* May 22, 1972, 4.
387 Downs, Barry W. "Anneta." *Leitchfield Gazette,* BiCentennial ed., 1976, Communities section, 8.

388 Dudgeon, Lester W. "Valley's First Settler Came in 1791." *Columbia Statesman,* Feb. 5, 1975, 2.

389 Duncan, Andrew W. "Graham and Luzerne Histories Are Traced." *Central City Times-Argus,* July 27, 1977, 10. (Originally presented in 1937.)

390 "Dundee Named." *Ohio County News,* Centennial ed., Dec. 26, 1974, sec. 2, p. 17.

391 Dundon, Robert E. "Wilson County May be Democratic Haven for Mountains Near Corbin." *Louisville Herald,* Jan. 9, 1924.

392 Dunn, C. Frank. "Fayette County Has Its 'Ghost Town' in Sandersville." *Lexington Herald-Leader,* Feb. 1, 1953, 54.

393 ——. "Slickaway and Donerail—Why Those Names?" *Lexington Herald-Leader,* Jan. 15, 1950, 90–91.

394 Durrett, Col. R. T. "Drennon Springs." *Register of the Kentucky Historical Society* 5 (1907): 87–90.

395 Dyche, Russell. "Sublimity Forest Community of 66 Model Homes and Small Farms in Laurel County, Ky." Laurel Co. Information Services No. 7. *Sentinel Echo,* Nov. 26, 1942.

396 *Earlington Bee,* Nov. 23, 1905.

397 "Early History of Butler, Pendleton County, Ky." *Butler Enterprise,* n.d. (Typescript in Special Collections, U. Kentucky Library.)

398 "Early Settler of County Furnished Necessary Land for Town of Barbourville." *Corbin Tribune,* 75th anniversary ed., Feb. 23, 1967, Barbourville–Knox Co. section, 2.

399 "Early Times in Woodford County." *Woodford Sun,* July 15, 1943.

400 Eckler, Ann. "History of Dry Ridge." *Grant County News,* Aug. 12, 1976, C9.

401 "Echols." *Ohio County News,* Apr. 13, 1978.

402 Edstrom, Ed. "Confusing 'Praise' Address to Be 'Elkhorn City' Sept. 1." *Louisville Courier-Journal,* Aug. 15, 1952, sec. 2, p. 1.

403 ——. "Poetic Justice Wins Victory at Pippapass." *Louisville Courier-Journal,* June 11, 1955.

404 Edwards, Don. "Building of Girl Scout Camp Puts Life into Dead Old Town." *Louisville Times,* Mar. 25, 1965.

405 Edwards, Richard A. "How It All Began for Trimble County." *Trimble Banner Bi-Centennial, Apr. 1974, 4.*

406 Ehrenstrom, Art. "Pins Economic Hopes on River Diversion Project." *Louisville Courier-Journal,* Aug. 21, 1974, 1.

407 ——. "Roads, Army Post Aid Hardin Town's Growth." *Louisville Courier-Journal and Times,* Mar. 23, 1975, D1.

408 "Elkhorn Lands Esteemed by Settlers." *State Journal,* July 16, 1961.

409 *Elizabethtown News,* Oct. 27, 1964.

410 "Elliott County Created in 1869." *Carter Caves/Greenbo Lake State Resort Parks,* Fall–Winter 1972, 36.

411 "Elliottville Used to Be Hogtown and Then Bristo." *Rowan County News,* Bicentennial ed., May 10, 1956, 76.

412 Ellis, James Tandy. "Carroll . . . Named for Wealthiest Signer. . . ." *Cincinnati Times-Star,* Centennial ed., Apr. 25, 1940, 2.

413 Elswick, Jeanette. "Pages of the Past." *Elkhorn City Enterprise,* May 11, 1972.

414 Embry, W. C. "Historical Sketches: Towns and Villages: Welchs Creek, Kentucky." *Green River Republican,* Apr. 12, 1951.

415 Engle, Fred Allen. "Some Old Places." *Richmond Daily Register,* Aug. 8, 1974.

416 Evans, Lucille, "C&O Railroad Crew Named Midland City." *Bath County News-Outlook,* Aug. 24, 1961, sec. 3, p. 3.

417 "Eveleigh Community." *Leitchfield Gazette,* BiCentennial ed., 1976, A8.

418 "Experts Say Florence Could Be Largest Northern Kentucky City." Associated Press, Jan. 10, 1979.

419 "Famed Springs Result in Formation of Russell Springs, Ky. in 1899." Russell Springs *Times-Journal,* BiCentennial issue, July 4, 1974, 8.

420 Feather, John D. "A History of Corbin." *Corbin Tribune,* 75th anniversary ed., Feb. 23, 1967, Corbin section, 2.

421 "Fence Fight Caused Scott's Station to Become Wilmore." *Lexington Leader,* June 30, 1938, sec. 3, p. 2.

422 Fields, Austin. "Early History—Carter County Was Named for State Senator William G. Carter." *Sandy Valley Enquirer,* Dec. 10, 1942.

423 Firestone, Clark B. "Adventure in the Wild Land of Callaboose." *Cincinnati Star,* Oct. 18, 1929.

424 Fleming, Kathy. "Place Names." *Mountain Memories* 1 (June 1972).

425 *Fleming Gazette,* July 16, 1972, 3.

426 "Flippin Community Now Enjoys Modern Highways." *Tompkinsville News,* 50th anniversary ed. Oct. 28, 1954, X1.

427 Foley, Sonja. "Stop, Kentucky." *Sprite and Bugle,* June 25, 1972, 9.

428 Ford, Stephen. "The Headquarters Name Still Untraced." *Louisville Courier-Journal,* May 30, 1973, A6.

429 ______. "Something Special at Flemingsburg—City Celebrates its 175th Birthday." *Louisville Courier-Journal,* July 18, 1972, B1.

430 "Fordsville Has Witnessed Steady Growth Since Establishment in 1833." *Ohio County News,* Feb. 3, 1966, 7.

431 "Forgotten Towns." *Louisville Courier-Journal,* Jan. 22, 1933.

432 Fowler, Ila Earle. "The Tavern of Free Charles." In *Original Atlas and Historical Data of Hopkins County, Ky.,* 1974. 74.

433 Fox, Frank. "St. Regis Park to Become 4th Class City on July 1." *Louisville Times,* Mar. 22, 1974.

434 "Fredericktown Was Once Shipping Port." *Springfield Sun,* BiCentennial ed., Jan. 31, 1974, 8.

435 Freels, Mrs. Wesson. "Island." *McLean County News,* Bicentennial issue, July 1, 1976, 12.

436 Freeman, Edward. "Brandon's Mill, Pottertown, and Peter Hamlin Enrichen Glamour of Calloway." *Murray Ledger and Times,* Apr. 28, 1938, 1.

437 ______. "Dog Furnishes Menu for Famous Feast." *Murray Ledger and Times,* Sept. 8, 1938. Reprinted in Ibid., Dec. 3, 1971, 2.

438 Fuller, R. C. "A Link with the Land." *Louisville Courier-Journal and Times Magazine,* Oct. 18, 1970, 30.

439 Gaines, J. W. *Anderson News,* June 1906, Souvenir Supplement, 19. Reprinted in Ibid., Jan. 31, 1974, sec. 3, p. 6.

440 Garrott, M. C. "Mrs Florence Holland Hale Set to Observe Her 100th Birthday." *Murray Times and Ledger,* Oct. 26, 1978.

441 Geaslen, Chester F. "Now They Know: Ft. Wright, Ky., Named After Area Defender, Engineer." *Cincinnati Enquirer,* Feb. 16, 1967.

442 "General Burnside—State Park on an Island." *Call of Kentucky,* Spring–Summer 1973, 43–44.

443 "Gen'l. William Clark Founded City of Paducah on May 26, 1827." *Mayfield Messenger,* Purchase ed., Dec. 27, 1969, J6.

444 Geveden, Charles R. "Mound-Building Indians Were First in Ballard County Section." *Mayfield Messenger,* Purchase ed., Dec. 27, 1969, D4.

445 ———. "Profiles of Ballard County Communities." *Mayfield Messenger,* Purchase Ed., Dec. 27, 1969, D4.

446 "Ghent First Settled in About 1795." *Carrollton News-Democrat,* Bicentennial issue, Feb. 21, 1974, 1.

447 Gibson, Greta. "Heyday of Green Farm Fades into Memory." *Breckinridge County Herald-News,* Aug. 26, 1971, B1.

448 *Glasgow Times,* 1937. (Otherwise unidentified article found in the E. B. Terry Scrapbooks, Glasgow Public Library, Book No. 17, p. 78.)

449 Gottbrath, Paul. "Early Days of Pewee Valley." *The Oldham Era,* Oct. 14, 1976, C2.

450 "Grahn History." *Carter County Historical Edition of the Grayson Journal-Enquirer,* Aug. 28, 1969, 4.

451 Grahn, K. G. *Greenup Independent,* Supplement, May 7, 1875. Reprinted in Helen Price Stacy and William Lynn Nickell, *Selections from Morgan County History,* 1973, 85. (Report of trip through eastern Kentucky.)

452 "Graymoor is County's 40th Sixth-Class City." *Louisville Times,* Nov. 29, 1959.

453 Greene, Alice, and Joyce Riggs. "History of Russell." *Russell Times,* Souvenir ed., Sept. 15, 1974, B2.

454 Greene, David. "History of Richmond, Kentucky." *Guide to Madison County,* Spring–Summer, 1971, 9. (Published by *Madison County Newsweek.*)

455 "Gregoryville History." *Carter County Historical Edition of the Grayson Journal-Enquirer,* Aug. 28, 1969, 2.

456 Griffin, Gerald. "A County's Birth." *Louisville Courier-Journal Magazine,* Dec. 1, 1957, 70.

457 ———. "Shakertown." *Louisville Courier-Journal and Times Magazine,* Aug. 13, 1961, 26.

458 Griffin, Ralph. "Brief History of Rockcastle County." *Mount Vernon Signal,* Nov. 30, 1939.

459 Grise, Robert N. "Big Hill and Mallory Springs." *Richmond Daily Register,* Apr. 14, 1971.

460 ———. "College Hill Receives Name." *Richmond Daily Register,* Apr. 19, 1978.

461 Groom, Littleton. *Princeton Times,* May 27, 1971; June 17, 1971; July 22, 1971. (Series of articles on Dulaney.)

462 Guthrie, Clyde. "Early Settlement of Cumberland Ford." *Pineville Sun,* Aug. 26, 1954.

463 Gutsell, Jeff. "Second Fastest Growing City in Area Right Now." *Cincinnati Enquirer,* June 4, 1979.

464 ———. "'Town Was Classified as Prettiest Along River' Before Closing." *Cincinnati Enquirer,* Apr. 30, 1979, A2.

465 Hall, David H. "Old Nelson Notebook." (Bardstown) *Kentucky Standard,* Sept. 16, 1976.

466 Halpert, Violetta Maloney. ''Place Name Stories about West Kentucky Towns.'' *Kentucky Folklore Record* 7, no. 3 (July–Sept. 1961): 103–16.
467 Hamlin, Charles Gatlin. *Murray Ledger and Times,* n.d. (Letter to the editor, found in Manning Stewart papers, Special Collections, Murray State U. Library. Gatlin was son of the first postmaster, Hamlin, Ky.)
468 Hammon, Neal. ''Historic Lawsuits of the 18th Century Locating 'the Stamping Ground.' '' *Register of the Kentucky Historical Society* 69 (July 1971): 197–215.
469 Hamon, Welcome. ''Seventy-Six Falls.'' *Columbia Statesman,* Feb. 26, 1970, 7.
470 Hancock, Greg L. ''Ottenheim—A Planned Community.'' *Interior Journal, Lincoln County Bicentennial, 1775–1975* ed., 1975.
471 Hardin, Thomas G., and Gladys Sale. ''The Naming of Lee County.'' *The Bulletin of the Kentucky Historical Society* 4, no. 6 (Dec. 1978): 8.
472 *Cynthiana Democrat,* Harrison Heritage Historical Houses ed., Aug. 21, 1975.
473 *Hartford Republican,* Sept. 22, 1911, 9.
474 Hartman, Margaret S. ''Covington and the Covington Company.'' *Register of the Kentucky Historical Society* 69 (Apr. 1971): 128–39.
475 Haviland, Sidney R. ''Interesting Bit of Kentucky History.'' *Louisville Times,* Nov. 24, 1931.
476 Hawpe, David. ''Bert's Namesake Town Offered Him Some Support.'' *Louisville Courier-Journal,* May 26, 1971, B3.
477 Haycraft, Marguerite. ''Wax.'' *Leitchfield Gazette,* BiCentennial ed., 1976, Communities section, 3.
478 Hayes, David W. ''History of Railroads in Breckinridge County.'' *Breckinridge County Herald-News,* Bicentennial ed., July 4, 1976.
479 Hazelrigg, Col. John T. *Licking Valley Courier, Feb. 7, 1952.* (Address at West Liberty, Ky., on July 4, 1876.)
480 Hedger, Mrs. Mary. *Anderson News,* June 1906, Souvenir Supplement, 19.
481 Henderson, Rose Pell. *Hancock Clarion,* 75th anniversary ed., July 1968. (History of Lewisport for its centennial, 1939.)
482 Higgins, Betty. ''Aberdeen.'' *Park City Daily News,* Dec. 17, 1975, 1.
483 Hill, Albert H. *Allen County News,* Dec. 24, 1965, 5A. (Letter.)
484 Hill, Bob. ''Bringing It All Home: Last Male Barlow Tells Some Tales Out-of-School.'' *Louisville Courier-Journal,* July 16, 1978, B1.
485 ''Hines Mill Burns.'' *Ohio County News,* Centennial ed., Dec. 26, 1974, sec. 2, p. 13.
486 ''Historical Sketches: Towns and Villages: Dexterville, Kentucky.'' *Green River Republican,* Apr. 5, 1951.
487 ''Historical Tour Features Interesting Sites.'' *Glasgow Times,* June 28, 1974, sec. 2, p. 7.
488 ''History Given of Adolphus Community.'' *Scottsville Citizen-Times,* Jan. 28, 1965.
489 ''History of Clarkson.'' *Leitchfield Gazette,* BiCentennial ed., 1976, Communities section, 15.
490 ''History of Dundee.'' *Ohio County Messenger,* Mar. 13, 1936.
491 ''History of Elizaville.'' *Fleming Gazette,* July 11, 1974, sec. 2, p. 19.
492 ''History of Hillsboro.'' *Fleming Gazette,* July 11, 1974, 4.
493 ''History of Mount Carmel.'' *Fleming Gazette,* July 11, 1974, sec. 2, p. 11.
494 ''Hitchins, Major Brick Maker.'' *Carter County Historical Edition of the Grayson Journal-Enquirer,* Aug. 14, 1969, sec. 1, p. 1.

495 Hodges, Carrie. "Fredonia Portrait. . . ." (Unidentified and undated newspaper article in the Coons Library, Princeton, Ky.)
496 Holbrook, Mrs. Olive. "A History of Ewing." *Fleming Gazette,* July 11, 1974, sec. 2, p. 18.
497 Holder, R. D. "Akersville Church Has Had Three Names." *Tompkinsville News,* 50th anniversary ed., Oct. 28, 1954, sec. 5, p. 4.
498 *Hopkins County Times,* Oct. 28, 1949.
499 Hornsby, Henry H. "Sourwood Is More Than a Song." *Lexington Leader,* Oct. 21, 1941.
500 "How White Plains Was Settled Told by Early Settlers." *Madisonville Messenger,* 50th anniversary issue, June 24, 1967, sec. 11, p. 13.
501 Hudgions, Jack. "Webster Town at One Time Called Savageville, Kentucky." *Henderson Gleaner,* June 14, 1940.
502 "Hysteam Corporation Mines Kentucky Beauty Coal." *Martin Mercury,* July 1970, 12.
503 Ingram, Sarah Wills. "Maytown As It Once Was and As it Now Is." *Mt. Sterling Advocate,* Nov. 4, 1954.
504 "Interesting Facts About Columbus." *Mayfield Messenger,* Purchase ed., Dec. 27, 1969, G10.
505 "In the Early 1900s City of Norton Changed Name." *Madisonville Messenger,* July 14, 1972.
506 Ison, Justine, and Joretta Davis. "The Rise and Decline of Cannel City." *Recollections: A Journal of the Appalachian Oral History Project at Lees Junior College* 1, no. 3 (Feb. 1973): 35–46.
507 "It's Hope, But the First Name Suggested was 'Magowan.'" *Mt. Sterling Advocate,* Aug. 25, 1971.
508 Jackson, Evelyn Scyphers. "Bicentennial Scrapbook." *Boyd County Post-Observer,* Oct. 30, 1975, 2.
509 ______. "Boyd County Ancestors." *Boyd County Press-Observer,* Oct. 10, 1974, 1.
510 *The Jackson Hustler,* June 17, 1892.
511 Jay Jay. "Four Bits." *Lexington Leader,* Apr. 26, 1940, 1.
512 Jenkins, Judy. "Slaughters." *Henderson Gleaner,* May 15, 1977, Tri-County Forward . . . Together section, 6.
513 Jerger, Lee. "Falls of Rough Village Steeped in Kentucky History." *Owensboro Messenger-Inquirer,* May 7, 1972, D1.
514 Jillson, Willard Rouse. "Old Bridgeport and Its Environs." *Register of the Kentucky Historical Society* 54 (Jan. 1956): 5–108.
515 Johnson, Charles. "Perry Park Prominent in History of Owen County." *Owenton News-Herald,* Dec. 5, 1957.
516 Johnson, J. B. *Corbin Daily Tribune,* 75th anniversary ed., Feb. 23, 1967, Whitley Co. section, 2. (History of Whitley Co.)
517 Jones, Camille. "Bagdad. . . ." *Shelby Sentinel,* Centennial ed., ca. 1940.
518 Jones, Clifton. "Bluff Boom—Where Did the Boom Originate?" *Greensburg Record-Herald,* Oct. 9, 1975, 2.
519 ______. "Exie, Kentucky Was Reportedly Named after Exie Dowdy." *Greensburg Record-Herald,* Oct. 23, 1975, 16.
520 ______. *Greensburg Record-Herald,* Dec. 18, 1975, 3.

521 Kaltenbacker, W. S. "Tourists Impressed by Pioneer Homes in State." *Louisville Courier-Journal,* June 23, 1929, sec. 5, p. 2.
522 Kane, Douglas. "Lake Site Lies Empty in Adair County." *Louisville Courier-Journal,* May 2, 1967.
523 Kelly, Marithelma D. *Springfield Sun,* Bicentennial ed., Jan. 31, 1974, passim.
524 "Kentucky Coal Town Blossoms Forth Where Few Years Ago Lone Cabin Stood." *Louisville Herald,* Aug. 19, 1923, 4.
525 "Kentucky's Ghost City." *Louisville Post,* Jan. 29, 1925.
526 Kitchens, Mrs. Edgar. "Factory: Historical Record of Towns and Villages in Butler County." *Green River Republican,* Aug. 28, 1952.
527 "Kuttawa—Founded in 1870, Still an Enjoyable Place to Live." *Eddyville Herald-Ledger,* Apr. 24, 1974.
528 LaGore, Joe. "Monkey's Eyebrow Rides the A-Boom. . . ." *Louisville Courier-Journal,* Sept. 28, 1952.
529 Lair, John. "History of Mount Vernon and Rockcastle County." *Mt. Vernon Signal,* Nov. 28, 1968, 14.
530 Lanter, Isabel. "Early Grant County Settlers a Hardy Lot by Necessity." *Grant County News,* Aug. 12, 1976, B3.
531 ______. "Southern Railroad Completion in 1876 Big Aid to Commerce." *Grant County News,* Aug. 12, 1976, B11.
532 Lawrence, Jay. "Breckinridge Town Will Be Spared Plant for Recycling Chemical Waste." *Louisville Courier-Journal,* Aug. 30, 1978, B4.
533 Lawrence, Keith. "Some Small Towns All but Gone . . . Sometimes Forgotten." *Owensboro Messenger-Inquirer,* Oct. 4, 1976, B1.
534 *Lebanon Enterprise,* Dec. 31, 1937.
535 Ledbetter, Harold G. "Alfred Townes, the Forgotten Pioneer." *Yearbook of the Historical Society of Hopkins County,* July 1977, 14–16.
536 "Lewisport: A Small City Moving Ahead." *Owensboro Messenger-Inquirer,* Mar. 14, 1971, sec. 3, p. 1.
537 "Liberty Station or Sanders Was Sizeable Town Back in 1883." *Carrollton News-Democrat,* May 16, 1963.
538 Lilleston, Blanche. "Place Names of Bourbon County." *Kentuckian-Citizen,* Jan. 2, 1924.
539 "Little Bit of Switzerland Came to Southeastern Kentucky in Late 1800's." *Tri-State Trader,* May 1969.
540 "Little White Plains Has Had Many Names throughout History." *Madisonville Messenger,* Aug. 18, 1973.
541 Loftus, Tom. "Indy's Growing Pains." *Kentucky Post,* April 9, 1977.
542 "The Logan Ewell Stories." *Sentinel Echo,* May 19, 1966.
543 "The Logan Ewell Stories." *Sentinel Echo,* Jan. 26, 1967.
544 "The Logan Ewell Stories." *Sentinel Echo,* Feb. 16, 1967.
545 "The Logan Ewell Stories." *Sentinel Echo,* Sept. 28, 1967.
546 Logsdon, Dollie, and Prisilla Stith. "Cub Run, Hart County, Kentucky." *Hart County Historical Society Quarterly* 4 (July 1972): 8–10.
547 Longest, Amy. "Powderly: Past and Present." *Greenville Record,* Mar. 1911.
548 *Louisville Courier-Journal,* Mar. 2, 1924.
549 *Louisville Courier-Journal,* Mar. 24, 1938.
550 *Louisville Courier-Journal,* July 21, 1953.

551 *Louisville Courier-Journal,* Oct. 12, 1973, B1.
552 *Louisville Courier-Journal,* Mar. 14, 1976.
553 *Louisville Courier-Journal and Times,* Sept. 10, 1972, B4.
554 *Louisville Herald,* Mar. 21, 1923.
555 *Louisville Times,* Mar. 3, 1922.
556 Lowe, Sue. ''Reasons for Haldeman Deterioration Unknown.'' *Morehead News,* Mar. 2, 1977, A3.
557 Luigart, Fred. ''Athens: Growing Pains May Wake a Sleepy Village.'' *Louisville Courier-Journal Magazine,* Jan. 10, 1965.
558 Lyons, Grace Whitler. ''McQuady.'' *Breckinridge County Herald-News,* Bicentennial ed., July 4, 1976.
559 ''Lyons Station Was Lumber Center.'' *LaRue County Herald-News,* Aug. 29, 1974, D9.
560 ''M. L. Evans Recollects about Arnold-Havens.'' *Ohio County News,* Centennial ed., Dec. 26, 1974, sec. 3, p. 9.
561 McCullough, R. A. ''History of Catlettsburg Site Traced from Military Grant of 1792.'' *Ashland Daily Independent,* Catlettsburg centennial ed., July 24, 1949, sec. 3, p. 1.
562 McDowell, Robert E. ''Bullitt's Lick, the Related Saltworks and Settlements.'' *Filson Club History Quarterly* 30 (July 1956): 241–69.
563 McGowon, Mary Margaret. *Kentucky Ancestors* 13, (Oct. 1977): 59–70. (Interview with Col. George M. Chinn.)
564 McIntyre, W. O. ''Blows the Bugle.'' *Louisville Courier-Journal,* May 5, 1929.
565 ______. ''Mark Twain's Mother Reared in Columbia, Ky.'' *Louisville Courier-Journal,* June 5, 1929.
566 Mackey, Eula G. *Clinton County News,* May 6, 1954.
567 ''McLean County Was Settled by 1784.'' *McLean County News,* Bicentennial issue, July 1, 1976, 1.
568 McMurtry, R. Gerald. ''Elizabethtown, Kentucky 1779–1879: The First Century of Its Existence.'' *Filson Club History Quarterly* 12 (Apr. 1938): 79–94.
569 McNeely, Lucile. *Caldwell County Times,* Feb. 25, 1926, 1.
570 McNeil, John C. ''Pittsburg Developed by Coal Operators and Central Kentucky Capitalists.'' *Sentinel Echo,* Diamond Jubilee ed., 1954, 176. Reprinted.
571 McReynolds, Dr. S. S. *Green River Republican,* Sept. 4, 1947. (Letter to Judge Otis White, Morgantown, Ky., June 12, 1947.)
572 Majors, Peggy. ''Caneyville—A Thriving Community.'' *Leitchfield Gazette,* Bi-Centennial ed., 1976, Communities section, 4.
573 ''The Man in the Big Hat Was Founder of Livermore.'' *McLean County News,* Oct. 9, 1958.
574 Manley, Edward. ''Historical Sketch: Towns and Villages: Huntsville, Kentucky.'' *Green River Republican,* [late winter], 1951.
575 ______. ''Rochester.'' *Green River Republican,* Jan. 4, 1951, 1.
576 Mansfield, Virginia. ''Famed Tavern That Never Was.'' *Glasgow Times,* June 28, 1974, sec. 3, p. 9.
577 Martin, Nancy Carlisle. ''The Founding of Ashbyburg.'' *Yearbook of the Historical Society of Hopkins County, Ky.,* July 1977, 41–43.
578 Martin, Sallie, and Jess Wilson. *Green River Republican,* Mar. 27. 1952. (Manuscript on Logansport.)

579 Marsh, Al. "Residents Reviving Their New-Bought Town." *Lexington Herald-Leader,* July 13, 1975, 1.

580 Matlock, Bill. "Only Old Store, Graves Memories Remain of Lyon's Confederate." *Paducah Sun-Democrat,* June 24, 1977.

581 Matera, Ann. "Frenchman's Knob—A Hart County Tragedy." *Hart County News, A Cave Country Salute to Kentucky's 1974 BiCentennial,* Mar. 1974, 4.

582 ———. "A Partial History of Horse Cave." *Hart County News, A Cave Country Salute to Kentucky's 1974 BiCentennial,* Mar. 1974, 6.

583 Maupin, Judith A. "Birmingham." *Murray Ledger and Times,* June 11, 1977.

584 ———. "The Grand River's Land Company." *Murray Ledger and Times,* Oct. 16, 1976.

585 ———. "New Concord." *Murray Ledger and Times,* Apr. 29, 1978.

586 ———. "Pottertown." *Murray Ledger and Times,* Sept. 17, 1977.

587 ———. "Spoon Grove." *Murray Ledger and Times,* July 30, 1977.

588 ———. "Wadesboro." *Murray Ledger and Times,* Jan. 8, 1977.

589 Merrell, Hazel Mattingly. "Sadler." *Leitchfield Gazette,* BiCentennial ed., 1976, Communities section, 14.

590 "Metcalfe County's Past: Our Early Years." *Edmonton Herald-News,* Special Bicentennial ed., June 30, 1974, 2.

591 "Midway Will Celebrate Construction of Railroad and Her Own Hundredth Birthday." *Lexington Leader,* May 7, 1933.

592 Miller, Johnny. "Bardwell Continues to Fight for Freedom." *Paducah Sun-Democrat,* Mar. 30, 1978, 1.

593 ———. "Hamlin Post Office Survives." *Paducah Sun-Democrat,* Oct. 21, 1977, 2.

594 Miller, Rebecca P. "Havilandsville, Once Prosperous, Thriving, Is Now Ghost Town of Only Seven Families." *Lexington Herald-News,* Jan. 13, 1957, B2.

595 "Milltown Mill Was Owned by Townsends." *Columbia Statesman,* Bicentennial ed., June 15, 1975, 16.

596 Minnix, Vicki. *Allen County News,* Mar. 3, 1965, 2A.

597 "Minor Lane Heights: A Blue Collar City Born out of a Need for Sewers." *Louisville Times,* Apr. 10, 1972.

598 Minton, Glendon. "A Salute to Coal Mining in Ohio County—Past and Present." *Ohio County News,* Centennial ed., Dec. 26, 1974, sec. 3, p. 14.

599 Mitchell, Albert Vaughan. *Greensburg Record-Herald,* Nov. 20, 1975, 4. (Letter to the editor.)

600 "Monterey, in Southern Owen County, Has a Colorful History." *Owenton News-Herald,* May 2, 1957, 6.

601 Moon, Mrs. Otis. "South." *Leitchfield Gazette,* BiCentennial ed., 1976, Communities section, 3.

602 Moore, W. D. *Anderson News,* June 1906, Souvenir Supplement, 45.

603 "Morgan County Rich in Cannel Coal." *Licking Valley Courier,* Morgan County Centennial ed., Dec. 27, 1923.

604 Morgan, W. H. *Anderson News,* June 1906, Souvenir Supplement, 19.

605 "Morehead Officially Became a Town with Incorporation Jan. 26, 1860." *Rowan County News,* Centennial ed., May 10, 1956, 48.

606 Morgret, C. O. "History of Southern Railway in Burgin." *Harrodsburg Herald,* Burgin Centennial ed., Aug. 1978, A6.

607 Morrison, Duvall. "Grayson Becomes a County in Jan. 1810." *Leitchfield Gazette,* BiCentennial ed., 1976, Tourism section, 14.

608 ______. "Millerstown One of Oldest Settlements in Grayson." *Leitchfield Gazette,* BiCentennial ed., 1976, Communities section, 5.

609 ______. "Settlers Moved into Pine Knob around 1835, Built School 1864." *Leitchfield Gazette,* BiCentennial ed., 1976, Communities section 14.

610 ______. "Short Creek." *Leitchfield Gazette,* BiCentennial ed., 1976, Communities section, 10.

611 ______. "Shrewsbury." *Leitchfield Gazette,* BiCentennial ed., 1976, Communities section, 5.

612 ______. "South First Called Bethel." *Leitchfield Gazette,* BiCentennial ed., 1976, Communities section, 14.

613 ______. "Spring Lick." *Leitchfield Gazette,* BiCentennial ed., 1976, Communities section, 12.

614 "Moscow Contended for County Seat." *Hickman County Gazette,* Sept. 30, 1971, B6.

615 *Mountain Eagle,* May 28, 1931.

616 "Muldraugh's Growth Impeded Due to Surrounding Installation." *Inside the Turf,* Aug. 18, 1977, supplement. (Fort Knox publication.)

617 "Munfordville—Its Founding and Settling." *Hart County News, A Cave Country Salute to Kentucky's 1974 BiCentennial,* Mar. 1974, 3.

618 Myers, Mrs. Carrie. "How Peeled Oak Got Its Name." *Bath County News-Outlook,* Aug. 24, 1961, sec. 3, p. 7.

619 Nevils, Mark E. "Grayson Springs Ever Popular Resort." *Leitchfield Gazette,* BiCentennial ed., 1976, Communities section, 1.

620 "Nicholasville: It's Been a Place to Grow." *Louisville Courier-Journal and Times,* May 19, 1974, D11.

621 Nichols, Edna B. "Magnolia Was on Early Coach Route." *LaRue County Herald News,* Aug. 29, 1974, C18.

622 Niles, Rena. "Salt of the Earth." *Louisville Courier-Journal Magazine,* Aug. 15, 1954, 28.

623 Nolan, Irene. "The Begleys Care for the Mountains and Their People." *Louisville Courier-Journal and Times,* Aug. 11, 1974, G1.

624 Norton, Zack. "Burnside Native Remembers Legends." *Commonwealth Journal,* Mar. 7, 1978, 1.

625 "Nostalgia of Smaller Communities Brought Back with Recollections." *Owenton News-Herald,* Bicentennial ed., July 4, 1974, 10.

626 "Notebooks of John Waters Tell of Calloway Lore." *Mayfield Messenger,* Purchase ed., Dec. 27, 1969, J9.

627 Nugent, Richard. "O Little Town of Bethlehem." *Louisville Courier-Journal and Times Magazine,* Dec. 19, 1976, 6.

628 Ochs, Marion. "History of Shively." *Shively Newsweek* 1 no. 1 (Sept. 24, 1964).

629 "Offutt-Cole Tavern Accepted for National Register Listing" *Woodford Sun,* n.d.

630 *Ohio County Messenger,* Mar. 13, 1936.

631 *Ohio County News,* Sept. 29, 1966, 3.

632 *Ohio County News,* Centennial ed., Dec. 26, 1974, sec. 2, p. 15.

633 "Old Eddyville—A Study in Contrasts." *Eddyville Herald-Ledger,* Apr. 24, 1974.

634 "Old Indian Believed Gold at Water Mark of Green at Ceralvo." *Ohio County News,* Sept. 8, 1977, 13.
635 "Old Timer." *Todd County Standard,* Jan. 19, 1950.
636 "Oldtown." *Rural Kentuckian* 19 (Sept. 1966): 14.
637 Ole Reliable [pseud]. "Our Place Names are Personalized." *L&N Employees' Magazine,* Feb. 1956, 20.
638 "Olive Hill's Century of Progress Began 1861." *Carter County Historical Edition of the Grayson Journal-Enquirer,* Sept. 4, 1969, 6.
639 "Origins of Names of Streams." *The Jackson Hustler,* Apr. 4, 1890.
640 Orrahood, M. David. "History of Coal in Ohio County, Ky. 1870–1953." *Ohio County News,* Dec. 26, 1974, 10.
641 Osinski, Bill. "Digging Up History." *Louisville Courier-Journal,* May 27, 1979, B1.
642 Pace Society of America. *Bulletin* No. 12, (June 1970).
643 Pardue, Leonard. "Goose Creek: Its Cleanliness and Its Life Are in Jeopardy." *Louisville Courier-Journal and Times,* Sept. 10, 1972, A1.
644 *Park City Daily News,* Dec. 3, 1944.
645 *Park City Daily News,* July 15, 1951.
646 Parker, Anna V. "A Short History of Carroll County." *Register of the Kentucky Historical Society* 57 (Jan. 1959): 35–48.
647 "Peaceful Hesler Community Once Blossomed with Trade as First County Seat in 1819." *Owenton News-Herald,* Bicentennial ed., July 4, 1974, 12.
648 Pearce, John Ed. "Daviess County." *Louisville Courier-Journal Magazine,* Nov. 6, 1977, 10.
649 ______. "Mason County." *Louisville Courier-Journal Magazine,* Sept. 24, 1978, 12.
650 ______. "Meade County." *Louisville Courier-Journal Magazine,* Mar. 25, 1979, 10.
651 ______. "Spencer County." *Louisville Courier-Journal Magazine,* Apr. 16, 1978, 10.
652 ______. "Trimble County." *Louisville Courier-Journal Magazine,* June 3, 1979, 10.
653 Pedigo, Martin. "Big Spring's Attraction: Just That." *Louisville Courier-Journal,* Apr. 26, 1965.
654 ______. "West Louisville." *Louisville Courier-Journal* Nov. 15, 1964.
655 Perry, Doug. "Cave City is Smallest of 22 All-Kentucky Cities." *Louisville Courier-Journal,* Feb. 3, 1974, B1.
656 Perry, Kathleen. "Scranton, Kentucky, and its Heritage." *Menifee County Journal,* Heritage ed., Apr. 10, 1974, 5.
657 Phillips, Mrs. Loucetta Whitaker. "Historical Sketch of Bethel and South Hill." *Green River Republican,* May 24, 1951, 1.
658 Piatt, G. Sam. "Just an Ordinary Christmas." *Ashland Daily Independent,* Dec. 24, 1976.
659 ______. "Yes, South Shore Really Is in Greenup County." *Ashland Daily Independent,* Aug. 17, 1980, 47.
660 Pile, Ora. "Woodrow." *Breckinridge County Herald-News,* Bicentennial ed., July 4, 1976.
661 "Pioneer Industry in Hart County." *Hart County Historical Society Quarterly* 3 (Jan. 1971): 10–13.

662 ''Pioneer Residents Staged Contest.'' *Lexington Leader,* June 30, 1938, sec. 2, p. 36.

663 Poehlein, Chuck. ''Holt House at Cloverport.'' *Owensboro Messenger-Inquirer,* Nov. 17, 1968.

664 Porter, W. L. ''Old Water Mills.'' *Glasgow Times,* Mar. 7, 1935, 1.

665 Powell, Bill. ''Columbus Cuts the Railroad Ties That Bound It to Another Era.'' *Louisville Courier-Journal,* July 16, 1978, B1.

666 ______. ''Floods, Rains Beat out Politics as Topic at Poll in Marshall County.'' *Louisville Courier-Journal,* May 30, 1973.

667 ______. ''Sale Ends 131 Years of Lowes Store.'' *Paducah Sun-Democrat,* Sept. 8, 1968, D9.

668 ______. ''Sassafras Ridge Turnout Helped by Bad Weather.'' *Louisville Courier-Journal,* Nov. 8, 1972, B1.

669 ______. ''Some Won't Leave Neatsville. . . .'' *Louisville Courier-Journal,* Sept. 5, 1976, A1.

670 ''Prestonville Was Once Larger Than Old Port William.'' *Carrollton News-Democrat,* Bicentennial issue, Feb. 21, 1974, 1.

671 ''Pretty Mining Village Nestles in Letcher Hills. . . .'' *Louisville Herald,* Jan. 20, 1924.

672 Pryor, Larry. ''Wilmore.'' *Louisville Courier-Journal,* Oct. 18, 1964.

673 Pryor, Lawrence. ''Tranquility Is its Magnet.'' *Louisville Courier-Journal,* ca. 1964.

674 Pulliam, Lillie. ''Patesville: Once a Way Station. . . .'' *Hancock Clarion,* 75th anniversary ed., July 1968.

675 ______. ''Patesville Post Office Was One of State's Oldest.'' *Hancock Clarion* 75th anniversary ed., July 1968.

676 Rambling Dick. ''Warren County Scenes, Natural and Historic. *Louisville Courier-Journal,* Apr. 20, 1924.

677 Rankin, Pat. ''Stanford Was Established by Logan. . . .'' *Lexington Leader,* June 30, 1938, sec. 3, p. 30.

678 Ratliff, G. C. ''Big Sandy—Past and Present.'' *Ashland Daily Independent,* July 6, 1952.

679 Ratliff, Paul E. ''Hellier.'' *Louisville Courier-Journal and Times Magazine,* Dec. 18, 1977, 17.

680 Reed, Billy. ''Fulton Plays Top Banana.'' *Louisville Courier-Journal,* Aug. 17, 1975, B1.

681 ______. ''Jabez People Seek Link to End Isolation.'' *Louisville Courier-Journal,* Apr. 11, 1976, B1.

682 Reed, David. ''27,000 Saw Bob Tail Win Raceland Derby.'' *Ashland Daily Independent,* Bicentennial ed., July 4, 1976, 35.

683 Remlinger, Connie. '' 'I Wrote the Mayor . . . We Arranged to Meet.' '' *Kentucky Post,* Oct. 5, 1970.

684 Richards, Mary Jolly, et al. ''The Southern Part of Hancock County.'' *Hancock Clarion,* 75th anniversary ed., July 1968.

685 Riley, Jean H. ''History of La Center.'' *Mayfield Messenger,* Purchase ed., Dec. 27, 1969, G5.

686 Robbins, A. ''Hickman Is a River Town.'' *Kentucky Progress Magazine,* Winter 1936, 1–4.

687 Robertson, Cary. ''Pewee Comes of Age.'' *Louisville Courier-Journal and Times Magazine,* Mar. 15, 1970, 25.

688 "Rockville, Farmers, Eadston . . . Had Saw Mills." *Morehead Advance.* Reprinted in *Rowan County News.* Centennial Ed., May 10, 1956, 38.
689 Russell, Charles Mead. "The Story of John Russell." *Russell Times,* Souvenir ed., Sept. 15, 1974, B6.
690 Russell, James R. "Monkey's Eyebrow 'Bloc' Vote Cast." *Louisville Courier-Journal,* Nov. 3, 1973.
691 ______. "What's in a Name?" *Louisville Courier-Journal* May 26, 1971, B1.
692 Ryce, Clay. "The South: Will It Ever Rise?" *Louisville Times,* June 7, 1974, 1.
693 St. Clair, Burl. "Rough River Country." *Leitchfield Gazette,* BiCentennial ed., 1976, Business and Industrial section, 1.
694 Sams, Parker. "Daviess County's Almost Forgotten Green River Towns." *Owensboro Messenger-Inquirer,* Aug. 22, 1971, sec. 3, p. 1.
695 "Sanders Was Summer Resort During Early 1900s." *Carrollton News-Democrat,* Bicentennial issue, Feb. 21, 1974, 1.
696 "Sandy Hook Owes Its Existence to Little Sandy River." *Carter Caves–Grayson Lake–Greenbo State Park,* Summer 1978, 14.
697 Sargent, Ed. "White Settlers First Visited Rowan County in Year 1773." *Rowan County News,* Centennial ed., May 10, 1956, 62.
698 Saunders, J. W. *Louisville Courier-Journal,* 1935 or 1937. (Cited by Cyrus Edwards, *Stories of Early Days,* 1940, 303.)
699 Scalf, Henry P. "Early Settlements of the Big Sandy Valley." Part IV. *Boyd County Press-Observer,* Jan. 29, 1976, 10.
700 Schiffer, Diane. "Research and Oral History: The Case of Quicksand, Kentucky." *Recollections: A Journal of the Appalachian Oral History Project at Lees Junior College* 1 (Dec. 1972).
701 Schimfessel, W. J. B. "Owner of Grist Mill Gives Community Its Name." *Clay County Times,* Oct. 9, 1975.
702 Schneider, Ellen. "Sense of Community. . . ." *Louisville Courier-Journal and Times,* Aug. 25, 1974, 20.
703 Schroader, Nina. "Horse Branch—Stage Coach and Railroad Played Initial Parts in Its Beginning." *Ohio County News,* Centennial ed., Dec. 26, 1974, sec. 3, p. 3.
704 ______. "One Hundred Years of Rosine Relived." *Ohio County News,* Sept. 13, 1973, 8.
705 Schroeder, Cindy. "Living up on the Hill . . . Like Being in Country." *Cincinnati Enquirer,* Feb. 19, 1979.
706 ______. "People Know One Another, Do Things Together" *Cincinnati Enquirer,* Sept. 24, 1979.
707 *Licking Valley Courier, 1822–1972,* Oct. 12, 1972, Sesquicentennial supplement, 16.
708 Shackelford, Nevyle. "Large Acreage of White Pine Timber in Wolfe County." *Lexington Leader,* Dec. 11, 1964.
709 ______. "Unusual Incidents Account for Many Odd Names of Kentucky Areas." *Lexington Leader,* May 29, 1962, 5.
710 Shely, Wyatt. "Glensboro 130 Years Ago." *Anderson News,* Jan. 31, 1974, sec. 3, p. 10.
711 ______. "Our Heritage." *Anderson News,* Sept. 16, 1971, 12.
712 ______. "Our Heritage." *Anderson News,* Oct. 21, 1971.
713 Simmons, Clayton C. "An Historical Journey through Barren County, Kentucky." *Glasgow Times,* Apr. 8, 1943.

714 Sinclair, Ward, and Harold Browning. ''Buechel's Rich Past Adorns What's New.'' *Louisville Times,* Oct. 5, 1965.
715 ______. ''The Dark and Bloody Ground.'' *Louisville Times,* Oct. 15, 1965, A8.
716 ______. ''Fern Creek Has a Past: Home-Cooked Meals and Vast Orchards.'' *Louisville Times,* Oct. 19, 1965, A14.
717 ______. ''For Lyndon, Incorporation as a City Was Better Than Being Annexed.'' *Louisville Times,* Nov. 16, 1965.
718 ______. ''From Salt to Moonshine, Fairdale's Colorful History Has a Flavor All Its Own.'' *Louisville Times* Oct. 12, 1965.
719 ______. ''Harrods Creek—A Stream, a Village, a Luxury Area.'' *Louisville Times,* Nov. 19, 1965.
720 ______. ''King Potato Ruled O'Bannon, Worthington at Peak of Their Heyday.'' *Louisville Times,* Nov. 12, 1965.
721 ______. ''Middletown—To Change or Not to Change.'' *Louisville Times,* Oct. 29, 1965, A16.
722 ______. ''Once Sleepy Jeffersontown Is Growing Up.'' *Louisville Times,* Nov. 5, 1965, A10.
723 ______. ''Pleasure Ridge Park Kindles Memory of Day When It was Dance Hall.'' *Louisville Times,* Nov. 9, 1965.
724 ______. ''Prospect Is Where Millionaires Meet with Commoners.'' *Louisville Times,* Nov. 30, 1965, A14.
725 ______. ''Rush to Suburbia Made St. Matthews.'' *Louisville Times,* Oct. 22, 1965.
726 ______. ''Serene, Elegant Glenview Imitated, Not Duplicated.'' *Louisville Times,* Nov. 23, 1965, A10.
727 ______. ''Shively Was Shaped by the Example 2 Vigorous Priests Set.'' *Louisville Times,* Oct. 9, 1965.
728 ______. ''Valley Station—An Endless Sea of Subdivisions and the Dixie.'' *Louisville Times,* Oct. 26, 1965.
729 Singletary, Donald. ''Hickman County History.'' Nov. ?, 1925, (Unidentified area newspaper in Hickman Co. files, Kentucky Hist. Soc. Library.)
730 Slack, Deborah. *Glasgow Times,* May 30, 1935.
731 Smith, Beulah Morgan. ''Pryorsburg Founder Friend of Andrew Jackson.'' *Mayfield Messenger,* Purchase ed., Dec. 27, 1969, I10.
732 Smith, Mrs. J. B. ''History of Grant's Lick, Campbell County Kentucky.'' *Falmouth Outlook,* Nov. 22, 1963, 3.
733 Snoddy, Virginia. ''The Merry Oaks of Long Ago.'' *Glasgow Times,* ca. June 8, 1936.
734 ''Soldier Prospered with the Coming of the Railroad.'' *Carter County Historical Edition of the Grayson Journal-Enquirer,* Aug. 21, 1969, 12.
735 ''South America.'' *Lexington Herald,* Oct. 1, 1933.
736 South, R. R. [pseud]. ''Our Station Names.'' *L&N Employees' Magazine,* June 1949, 37.
737 Ibid., July 1949, 20–21.
738 Ibid., Aug. 1949, 14.
739 Ibid., Sept. 1949, 14–15.
740 Ibid., Oct. 1949, 14–15.
741 Ibid., Nov. 1949, 14.
742 Ibid., Dec. 1949, 16–17.

743 Ibid., Jan. 1950, 16.
744 Ibid., Mar. 1950, 34–35.
745 Ibid., July 1950, 23.
746 Spaid, Ora. ''Wonder How Two Towns Named.'' *Louisville Courier-Journal,* July 3, 1961, A12.
747 Spalding, V. L. *Uniontown Telegram.* Reprinted in *Louisville Times,* Mar. 1, 1941.
748 Spires, Nancy. ''Knifley Was Part of Green County in Early 1880s.'' *Green River Sprite,* nd.
749 Stacy, Helen Price. ''Kentucky Place Names Sources of Endless Speculation.'' *Lexington Leader,* June 25, 1971.
750 ''Standing Rock.'' *Lexington Leader,* May 11, 1961. (Caption for a photo.)
751 ''State's First Mass Immigration.'' Reprinted in *Sentinel Echo,* Diamond Jubilee Ed., 1954, 182.
752 ''Stearns Builds Empire of Coal and Lumber. . . .'' *McCreary County Record,* July 3, 1962, 1.
753 Stevens, John W. ''Alexandria.'' *Newport Local,* Dec. 12, 1878, 1.
754 ______. *Newport Local,* Dec. 19, 1878, 1. (Letter to the editor.)
755 Stewart, Irene. ''Pebble Named for Rocky Creek That Flows There.'' *Bath County News Outlook,* Aug. 24, 1961, sec. 2, p. 4.
756 Stice, Sally Graham. *Louisville Courier-Journal,* Nov. 13, 1927.
757 Stiles, Mary Ellen. ''Cecilia Was Settled before Kentucky Was a State.'' *Elizabethtown News,* Bicentennial ed., May 21, 1974, 4D.
758 Stone, J. B. *Jamestown Record,* July 16, 1891. Reprinted in Russell Springs *Times-Journal,* Nov. 23, 1927. (History of Jamestown, Ky.)
759 ''Store in Same Family Since It Began in 1885;'' ''Old Creelsboro Ferry Was Area Lifeline.'' *The Sprite and Bugle,* Dec. 3, 1972, 5.
760 ''Streams in Allen County Named for Tragedy and Perseverance.'' *Allen County News,* Aug. 25, 1965.
761 Strother, John C. ''Trimble County Legacy.'' Feb. 2, 1920. Reprinted in *Trimble Banner Bicentennial, 1974,* Apr. 1974, 51.
762 Stuart, Jesse. ''Lynn: The Village That Disappeared.'' *Louisville Courier-Journal Magazine,* Apr. 10, 1949, 8.
763 ''Stubborn Town Just Keeps Bouncing Back.'' *Lexington Herald-Leader,* Apr. 8, 1979, J1.
764 ''Sugar Grove.'' *Green River Republican,* Aug. 31, 1950, 1.
765 ''Sulphur Lick History Told by Women of the Community.'' *Tompkinsville News,* 50th anniversary ed., Oct. 28, 1954, sec. 7, p. 8.
766 Sutton, Clay. *Lexington Herald,* n.d. Reprinted in *Louisville Times,* June 14, 1927.
767 Swain, Enos. ''Building of Southern Railroad Brought Boom to Somerset.'' *Lexington Leader,* June 30, 1938, sec. 3, p. 44.
768 Swem, Gregg. ''Big Bone Lick Park is Steeped in History.'' *Louisville Courier-Journal,* May 21, 1978, D8.
769 Talley, William M. ''Salt Lick Creek and Its Salt Works.'' *Register of the Kentucky Historical Society* 64 (Apr. 1966): 85–109.
770 ______. ''A Trip Down Kinniconick.'' *Lewis County Herald,* Nov. 16, 1972.
771 Tate, Robert S. ''The Grass Roots of Kenton County.'' *Register of the Kentucky Historical Society* 53 (Apr. 1955): 138–49.

772 Taylor, Hewitt. "Prospect." *Louisville Herald-Post,* Oct. 21, 1936.

773 "They Are Prominent Representatives of the Coal Industry in Western Kentucky." *Louisville Herald,* Mar. 21, 1923.

774 Thomas, Mrs. Brownie. "Higgasons and Sandiges Came from Virginia to Donansburg." *Greensburg Record-Herald,* Dec. 7, 1972.

775 Thomas, Edison. "The 20-Mile-Long Orphan." *L&N Employees' Magazine,* Oct. 1957, 13.

776 Thomasson, Wayman. "Moonshine Famed the Country Over." *Louisville Courier-Journal,* Jan. 29, 1939.

777 "Three Versions of London's Name." *Sentinel Echo,* Diamond Jubilee ed., 1954, 176. Reprinted.

778 Tilford, Ray R. *Ohio County Messenger,* Aug. 25, 1933.

779 *Tompkinsville News,* 50th anniversary ed., Oct. 28, 1954.

780 "Town Named after A.B. 'Bige' Combs." *The Combs Informer,* Aug. 17, 1969, 3.

781 "Town of Worthville Once Known as Coonskin." *Carrollton News-Democrat,* Bicentennial issue, Feb. 21, 1974, 1.

782 Treadway, C. M. "City of Irvine Was Named for Brothers." *Lexington Leader,* Apr. 4, 1957, 3.

783 Trout, Allan M. "Greetings." *Louisville Courier-Journal,* Mar. 2, 1950, 14.

784 ______. "Greetings." *Louisville Courier-Journal,* Apr. 16, 1951.

785 ______. "Greetings." *Louisville Courier-Journal,* Aug. 8, 1967; Sept. 22, 1967.

786 ______. "Pleasureville." *Louisville Courier-Journal,* Nov. 22, 1964, 4.

787 Tucker, Brown C. "Sounds of Calloway Land." *Journal of the Jackson Purchase Historical Society* 1 (June 1973): 14–23.

788 Turner, Carlie. "Historical Sketches: Towns and Villages: Turnertown, Kentucky." *Green River Republican,* Mar. 15, 1951, 1.

789 "Upton History." *LaRue County Herald News,* Aug. 29, 1974, D11.

790 "Valley View Ferry: Kentucky's Oldest Continuous Business." *Guide to Madison County,* Spring–Summer 1971, 7. (Published by *Madison County Newsweek.*)

791 Vance, Mrs. J. Wood. "Barren Towns: What's in a Name?" *Glasgow Times,* Anniversary ed., Mar. 10, 1968.

792 Vance, Kyle. "Minister and Wife Helped to Make 'Hells Corner' a Bit More Heavenly." *Louisville Courier-Journal,* Nov. 1, 1969, A11.

793 Van Curon, S. S. "Jett Post Office to Be Closed." *State Journal,* Mar. 21, 1971, 1.

794 Vansant, Mary. "Elliott County Formed in 1869. . . " *Morehead Independent,* Historical and Progress ed., Oct. 1934.

795 Varble, C. N. "Early Days in Sparta." *Owenton News-Herald,* Sesquicentennial ed., June 27–July 6, 1969.

796 Wagers, Myrtle. *Manchester Enterprise,* Oct. 5, 1972, B5.

797 Walker, Mrs. D. L. "How Sparksville, Weed Were Named." *Edmonton Herald-News,* May 18, 1967.

798 Ward, Kenny. "Sacramento." *McLean County News,* Bicentennial issue, July 1, 1976, 11.

799 Waters, John. "City of Murray Was Established in 1843." *Mayfield Messenger,* Purchase ed., Dec. 27, 1969, J5.

800 Watkins, Bob. *Elizabethtown News,* Aug. 6, 1970.

801 Watkins, Rayburn. "Marshall County Will Celebrate Centennial. . . ." *Paducah Sun-Democrat,* May 31, 1942.

802 Wehner, Jane. "Hikes Made Buechel Bustle." *Jefferson Reporter*, Jan. 30, 1974, A11.

803 Weis, Marybelle C. "The Pollit Record." *Maysville Ledger-Independent*, Bicentennial ed., July 2, 1976, 12.

804 Wells, Palmer. "Harlan County's Newest Town Will Begin Operation with No Bonded Indebtedness." *Lexington Herald-Leader*, Aug. 13, 1961, 15.

805 "What's in a Name? Plenty—in Lyon County!" (Unidentified clipping in the Kentucky Library, Western Kentucky U.)

806 Wheeler, Robert M. "History of Marion." *Crittenden Press*, Dec. 7, 1972, supplement.

807 "Wheelwright, Kentucky is Ultra-Modern." *In Kentucky* 12, no. 4 (Winter 1949): 38–39.

808 "Whitakers Settled Oddville Community." *Cynthiana Democrat*, Celebration ed., Aug. 7, 1969.

809 White, Roy R. "Y Hollow Was Location of Organization of Clay County Held in 1807." *Manchester Enterprise*, Aug. 28, 1952, 1.

810 White, Wordney. "Port Oliver Salt Works—Trading Post in Wilderness." *Allen County News*, Oct. 12, 1938.

811 Whitehead, Don. "Lots of Moonshine, But Not in Parson's Hills." *Milwaukee Journal*, Dec. 6, 1953, 3.

812 Whittle, Charles E. "Sketches in Edmonson County History—Flashlights in Folklore." Chap. 9. *Edmonson County News*, Oct. 6, 1955.

813 Wiegand, Rolf. "Growing Community Wants to Retain Its Identity." *Cincinnati Enquirer*, Feb. 26, 1979.

814 "Wilder History." *Campbell County Citizen*, Sept. 17, 1975.

815 Williams, Cratis. "History of the Blaine Community." *Big Sandy News*, July 6, 1972, 4.

816 Williams, Mrs. Hal. "Old Tavern Occupied Site of Nugent's Cross Roads." *Lexington Leader*, Apr. 10, 1964.

817 ______. "Railroad Bypassed Keene, Spelling Doom as Gay Watering Place for Blue Grass." *Lexington Leader*, Mar. 24, 1962, 6.

818 Williamson, Ruth R. "Felice and Anna Form Names of City with Interesting History." *Mayfield Messenger*, Purchase ed., Dec. 27, 1969, E11.

819 ______. "State Line Community of Jordan Was Once a Center of Industrial Activity." *Mayfield Messenger*, Purchase ed., Dec. 27, 1969, J2.

820 Williamson, Wallace J. "Old Economic Patterns Still Seen." *Ashland Daily Independent*, Bicentennial ed., July 4, 1976, 2.

821 "Willisburg Was Originally Named Paeola." *Springfield Sun*, June 22, 1967, 175th anniversary supplement, 8.

822 Wilson, Katherine. "This Old House." 1957. Reprinted in *Cynthiana Democrat* Celebration ed., Aug. 7, 1969.

823 Winstead, Mrs. T. D. "Much History Surrounds 'Howes Valley.'" *Elizabethtown Examiner*, Nov. 8, 1976, A1.

824 ______. "Railroad Responsible for Rineyville Progress." *Elizabethtown News*, Bicentennial ed., May 21, 1974, D8.

825 ______. "White Mills: Resort Hotels Brought Prosperity in Early 1900s." *Elizabethtown Examiner*, June 18, 1975, A4.

826 Winternitz, Helen. "Memories of Old McHenry." *Owensboro Messenger-Inquirer*, Apr. 20, 1976, C1.

827 Wolfford, George. "What's in a Name?" *Ashland Daily Independent,* Apr. 30, 1972, 29.

828 Woods, Grace. *The American Magazine,* Nov. 1947, 82.

829 Wrather, Logan. *Murray Ledger and Times,* 1940. Reprinted in *Murray Ledger and Times,* Apr. 28, 1967. (Letter to the editor.)

830 Yeager, Lyn Allison. "Swedish Immigrants Pleased in Rugged Ky. Hill Country." *Tri-State Trader,* June 30, 1973, 18.

831 Yealey, A. M. "Florence 138 Years Ago—Florence Today." Sept. 17, 1954. (Unidentified newspaper article.)

832 Young, Victor D. "Yeaman, from Backwoods to Modern Rural Living." *Leitchfield Gazette,* Bicentennial ed., 1976, Communities section, 10.

MANUSCRIPT SOURCES

833 Aaron, Phil R. Student paper, Campbellsville College, 1964. Folklore Archives, Western Kentucky U. Library.

834 Akers, Deborah Susan. Student paper, Prestonsburg Community College, 1970.

835 Allebaugh, Terry. "Disputanta: A Front Porch Chronicle," 1980. Appalachian Collection, Special Collections, U. Kentucky Library.

836 Allen, Nathan Perry. Manuscript history of the Smiths Grove area of Warren Co., n.d. Kentucky Library, Western Kentucky, U.

837 Allen, Mrs. Woodrow. Manuscript history of the Ula post office, n.d.

838 Anderson, Annie S. "St. Matthews, Its Beginnings and the Beargrass Settlements, 1938. Louisville Free Public Library.

839 Armstrong, Mrs. Marianne C. Paper presented to the Kentucky Path Chapter, DAR, Middlesboro, Ky., Jan. 1, 1942.

840 Arnett, Nina. "The Origin of Magoffin County Place Names." Student paper, Georgetown College, 1962.

841 Baird, Nancy. Manuscript history of the Hummel Company of Cincinnati, 1978. In Mrs. Baird's possession.

842 Baker, Mrs. J. M. "Historical Webster County," Paper prepared for the Henderson Co. Hist. Soc., n.d. Library, Kentucky Hist. Soc.

843 Baker, Dr. W. Leroy. Notes on Caldwell Co. place names. George A. Coon Library, Princeton, Ky.

844 Bank letter. Issued by the First National Bank of Wilmore, Ky., n.d., unsigned.

845 Barton, E. E. Manuscript on Pendleton Co. communities, 1968.

846 ———. "Railroad History of Pendleton County," 1968. Kentucky Hist. Soc.

847 Barton, E. E., and Mary Louise Barton. "Place Names of Pendleton County." DAR manuscript, n.d. Kentucky Hist. Soc.

848 Baylor, O. W. WPA manuscript on Adair Co. Kentucky Archives, Frankfort, Ky.

849 ———. WPA manuscript on Marion Co. Kentucky Archives, Frankfort, Ky.

850 Bernard H. Pollitte (Pollit?). Papers, as researched by Mrs. William Weis.

851 Birchfield, Bessie M. "Towns and Villages of Rowan County." WPA manuscript. Kentucky Archives, Frankfort, Ky.

852 Bishop, Margaret. WPA manuscript on Breathitt Co. Kentucky Archives, Frankfort, Ky.

853 Blackburn, Mrs. H. M. Manuscript history of Woodburn. Kentucky Library, Western Kentucky U.

854 Blair, Gary E. Student paper, Prestonsburg Community College, 1972.

855 Bowling, Viola. "Folk Customs." WPA manuscript, ca. 1936. Kentucky Archives, Frankfort, Ky.

856 Bowling, William Miller. "Rambling Remarks of William Miller Bowling." Manuscript compiled by Rita Adkisson Thompson, 1972, from his columns in the *Meade County Messenger,* 1938. Meade Co. Library.

857 Bradshaw, Mrs. Lou. "Some of the Historical Spots of Bath County and its Early History." Kentucky Hist. Soc.

858 Brand, L. Alberta. "Place Names of Mason County." DAR manuscript, 1941. Kentucky Hist. Soc.

859 Brannock, J. W. Manuscript history of Kelat, Ky., 1976. Harrison Co. Public Library.

860 Braun, Lorraine Funk. Student paper on history of Bullitt Co., 1960. Kentucky Hist. Soc.

861 Burgess, Deborah June. "History of the Cooper Community." Student paper, Wayne Co. High School, 1973.

862 Burris, Ray. "Mills and Stills, in Local Historical Research." Collection of student papers for Somerset Community College, prepared and edited by Edgar Spitzke, Jr., 1966.

863 Cann, Roy A. Manuscript history of Hart Co., 1971.

864 Cannon, J. L. "Place Names in Franklin County, Ky." DAR manuscript, 1940. Kentucky Hist. Soc.

865 Carter, Kathryn. "Place Name Survey of Estill County." Prepared for Kentucky Place Name Survey, 1978.

866 Cather, Alexander. Report on Muhlenberg County place names, for Kentucky Place Name Survey, 1972.

867 Chapman, Mary Lucile. "The Influence of Coal in the Big Sandy Valley." Ph.D. Diss., U. Kentucky, 1945.

868 Chipman, Lenore Patrick. Papers in the possession of Mrs. Connie Wireman, Fredville, Ky.

869 "Christmas Lives in Bethlehem, Kentucky." News release from Kentucky Dep. of Public Information, Nov. 28, 1967.

870 Clift, G. Glenn. "Kentucky Villages, Towns, and Cities, 1779–1893." Kentucky Hist. Soc. Research Contributions No. 4 1956. Kentucky Hist. Soc.

871 Clinton, Charles A. Manuscript history of Hancock Co., Ky., n.d. Owensboro Public Library.

872 Cole, Jennie B. "Some Place Names of Warren County, Ky." Kentucky Library, Western Kentucky U.

873 Conkwright, Bessie Taul. Manuscript on Indian Old Fields. Special Collections, U. Kentucky Library.

874 Manuscript of Corydon Centennial issue of Cardinal "Ancestral" Notes, n.d.

875 Coy, Mrs. J. Mack, and Miss Mary Q. Covington. "Place Names of Madison County." DAR manuscript, 1941. Townsend Collection, Eastern Kentucky U. Library.

876 Craig, Will N. "The Wilderness Road in Lincoln County." DAR manuscript, 1941. Kentucky Hist. Soc.

877 Crigler, John E. Paper on the Hebron community presented to the Boone Co. Hist. Soc., May 19, 1950. Kentucky Hist. Soc.

878 Cundiff, Mrs. Horace. "Adair County Place Names." DAR manuscript, 1941. Kentucky Hist. Soc.

879 Cunningham, Mike. "The Crescent-Villa Community, Bicentennial Celebration, 1776–1976," 1976. Kenton Co. Public Library.

880 Cusick, Betty. Student paper, Union College, 1956.

881 Daily, Janis K. "Place Names of McCracken County." Student paper, Western Kentucky U., 1971. Folklore Archives, Western Kentucky U. Library.

882 Decker, Elmer. Manuscript history of Knox Co. and Eastern Kentucky. Union College Library.

883 Doyle, George F. "Chronicles of Clark Co." (on Clark Co. waterways). U. Kentucky Library.

884 "Early Bloomfield." Typescript copy of article in *Bardstown Standard,* n.d. Kentucky Hist. Soc.

885 Edgeworth, Michael J. Manuscript on Daviess Co. place names, for Kentucky Place Name Survey, 1973.

886 Eller, David Barry. "The Brethren Settlement Along Hinkston Creek and the Ministry of Peter Hon: A Study in Kentucky Church History." Master's thesis, Bethany Theological Seminary of Oak Brook, Ill., 1971.

887 Ellis, Mike. Student paper, Grant Co. High School, 1964. Collection of papers compiled by Mrs. Hazel Ogden, May 1965. Grant Co. Library.

888 Elswick, Madeline. Student paper, Pikeville College, 1970.

889 Farmer, Lizzie. WPA manuscript on Harlan Co., 1938. Kentucky Archives, Frankfort, Ky.

890 ———. WPA manuscript on Harlan Co., 1939. Kentucky Archives, Frankfort, Ky.

891 Fitzgerald, William. "Origin of Place Names in Boone County," 1962. In possession of Mrs. Anna Fitzgerald, Florence, Ky.

892 Forsee, John S. WPA manuscript history of Owen Co., 1936. Kentucky Archives, Frankfort, Ky.

893 Fryman, Mrs. Virgil T. Manuscript history of Lewisburg and Mill Creek, based on a paper presented to the Washington Study Club, Feb. 24, 1961.

894 Gaines, Miriam, and B. M. Henry, WPA manuscript on Middlesboro, Ky. Kentucky Archives, Frankfort, Ky.

895 Gardner, Mrs. H. W. "Barren County Towns, Streams, Highways, and Origin of the Names." DAR manuscript, 1941. Library, Kentucky Hist. Soc.

896 Gentry, Aileen Pierce. "Old Port William's Founders and Foundations," 1961. Kentucky Hist. Soc.

897 Gibson, Golda. WPA manuscript on Cumberland Co. Kentucky Archives, Frankfort, Ky.

898 Goodson, Mary Allen. "Hardin's Fort and Its Founder," ca. 1924. Kentucky Hist. Soc.

899 Greene, Mary T. Student paper, Union College, ca. 1955.

900 Hamilton, Lamar. WPA manuscript on Cumberland Co. Kentucky Archives, Frankfort, Ky.

901 Hancock, Claudia. Manuscript report of interview at Campbellsville College. Folklore Archives, Western Kentucky U. Library.

902 Harbison, Martha S. DAR manuscript on Shelby Co. place names, 1941. Kentucky Hist. Soc.

903 Hart, Mae. Student paper, Union College, 1957.

904 Hayden, Francis L. Manuscript on the Parish of St. Francis of Assisi, St. Francis, Ky., cited by Gerald Thompson, St. Mary, Ky., in a letter to author, Dec. 6, 1980.

905 Heavrin, Musker L. ''Place Names of Ohio County.'' Manuscript sent to William G. Steel, Mar. 20, 1925. U.S. Board on Geographic Names, Reston, Va.
906 Hibbard, Patsy. Student paper, Union College, 1955.
907 Hickey, Nora. WPA manuscript on Robertson Co. Kentucky Archives, Frankfort, Ky.
908 Hieatt, Mrs. Allen. ''Boyle County Names.'' DAR manuscript, 194O. Library, Kentucky Hist. Soc.
909 ''History of Baskett Station, Ky.,'' 1926. Ms.
910 ''History of Dry Ridge.'' Manuscript prepared for the Rural Community Conference at Dry Ridge, n.d. Kentucky Hist. Soc.
911 History of Jackson. WPA manuscript. Kentucky Archives, Frankfort, Ky.
912 Hodges, Elizabeth. Manuscript history of Green Co. Green County Public Library.
913 Hollowell, C. A. ''History of the Post Offices . . . of Trimble County, Ky.,'' for Kentucky Place Name Survey, 1980.
914 Homemakers Club. Manuscript on Scott Co. history, 1950. Kentucky Hist. Soc.
915 Horton, Louise. ''Place Names of Allen County, Ky.'' Manuscript for the Kentucky Place Name Survey, 1974.
916 Hoskins, Harry P. Towns in Jefferson County . . . Outside the Limits of Louisville. WPA manuscript. Kentucky Archives, Frankfort, Ky.
917 Hughes, Hugh J. WPA manuscript on Louisville, 1937. Kentucky Archives, Frankfort, Ky.
918 Ison, Eliza. WPA manuscript on Garrard Co. place names. Kentucky Archives, Frankfort, Ky.
919 Johnson, D. ''Definition and Origin of Names in Hickman County, Ky.'' Manuscript sent to William G. Steel, Sept. 17, 1923. U.S. Board on Geographic Names, Reston, Va.
920 Johnson, Janet. ''Barren County Place Names,'' 1970. Notes in Folklore Archives, Western Kentucky U. Library.
921 Johnson, Lynn Tilford. Student paper, Pikeville College, n.d.
922 Joiner, Carolyn. ''The Boom Town That Failed to Boom.'' Student paper, Livingston Central High School, 1964. Special Collections, Murray State U. Library.
923 Jones, Lenneth. WPA manuscript on Monroe Co. Kentucky Archives, Frankfort, Ky.
924 Jones, Milford. WPA manuscript on Limestone, Carter Co. Kentucky Archives, Frankfort, Ky.
925 Jones, Mrs. W. B. ''Place Names of Pulaski County, Ky.'' DAR manuscript, 1941. Kentucky Hist. Soc.
926 Keck, Ruth [late postmaster of Sandy Hook, Ky.]. Student paper, Morehead State U., 1960.
927 Knott, W. T. ''History of Marion County, Ky.'' Typescript derived from article in *Lebanon Enterprise*. Kentucky Hist. Soc.
928 Kranz, Ida Lacy. Manuscript history of Allegree, 1971.
929 Ladd, M. WPA manuscript on Kentucky place names, 1941. Kentucky Archives, Frankfort, Ky.
930 Laswell, Cecilia M. ''Towns and Villages of Daviess County,'' WPA manuscript, June 19, 1936. Kentucky Archives, Frankfort, Ky.
931 Lavielle, L. WPA manuscript on Ft. Thomas. Kentucky Archives, Frankfort, Ky.

932 Leachman, Katharyn. Manuscript on McLean Co. place names, for Kentucky Place Name Survey, 1972.
933 Lewis, Bonnie R. Student paper, Morehead State U., 1959.
934 Long, Arthur. Student paper, Pikeville College, 1970.
935 Lyons, Fr. John A. Manuscript history of St. Theresa's Church, 1950. Meade Co. Public Library.
936 McDaniel, Alice Cheaney. Manuscript history of Spottsville, Ky., ca. 1928. Kentucky Hist. Soc.
937 McKnought, Mary. "Cloverport: A Bit of History," ca. 1932. Kentucky Hist. Soc.
938 McLemore, Mrs. WPA manuscript on Midway. Kentucky Archives, Frankfort, Ky.
939 Manuscript history of Hancock Co. Hancock Co. Public Library.
940 Martin, Marion. Manuscript on Clay Co. place names. Clay Co. Public Library.
941 Mendenhall, W. L. Manuscript on Kenton Co. Kenton Co. Public Library.
942 Meredith, Lancie. Manuscript on Edmonson Co. place names, for Kentucky Place Name Survey, 1972.
943 Montgomery, Glennora. "A Study of the Community of Auxier, Ky." Student paper, Prestonsburg Community College, 1971.
944 Morgan, Wilma. "The Creation and Partition of Knott Co.," 1946. Kentucky Hist. Soc.
945 Murray, Willard Roger. Student paper, Prestonsburg Community College, 1970.
946 Nelson, Mary S. Student paper, Morehead State, U., 1959.
947 Newsome, Sylvia. Student paper, Virgie, Ky., high school, Feb. 28, 1969.
948 Owens, Augusta. "Historical Homes in Henry County." WPA manuscript. Kentucky Archives, Frankfort, Ky.
949 Partin, Mrs. Angie. Student paper, Union College, 1957.
950 Pearce, Mrs. Maude Johnston. "Low Dutch Colony of Henry and Shelby Counties, Ky." DAR manuscript. Kentucky Hist. Soc.
951 "Pioneer Mortonsville." WPA manuscript, ca. 1938. Kentucky Archives, Frankfort, Ky.
952 Powers, J. H. Manuscript history of Rowan Co. Kentucky Collection, Morehead State U. Library.
953 Powers, L. S. WPA manuscript on Hancock Co. Kentucky Archives, Frankfort, Ky.
954 Profitt, Herbert G. WPA manuscript on Powell Co. Kentucky Archives, Frankfort, Ky.
955 Ramey, Clarice Payne. "History of Pulaski County." Master's thesis, U. Kentucky, 1935.
956 Randolph, Helen F. WPA manuscript on Clay Co. Kentucky Archives, Frankfort, Ky.
957 Reynolds, Nannie G. "History of DeKoven." WPA manuscript, 1940–41. Kentucky Archives, Frankfort, Ky.
958 Roberts, Mildred. WPA manuscript on Anderson Co. towns. Kentucky Archives, Frankfort, Ky.
959 Robertson, Gladys. WPA manuscript on the Willoughby Nation. Kentucky Archives, Frankfort, Ky.
960 Robertson, John E. L. "West to the Iron Banks." Master's thesis, U. Louisville, 1961.

961 Rodes, John B. "Early History of Bowling Green," 1927. Kentucky Library, Western Kentucky, U.
962 Rucker, Oscar. "A Geographic Study of Rural Settlement Clusters in Madison County, Ky." Master's thesis, U. Kentucky, 1967.
963 Rule, Lucien V. "The Towns and Villages of Oldham County." Part 3, Chap. 27 of his "Oldham County History," ca. 1922.
964 Shely, J. B. Manuscript history of Kirkwood. In the possession of Mrs. Rebecca Conover, Harrodsburg, Ky.
965 Shepherd, Sarah. Student paper, Morehead State U., 1958.
966 Smith, Opal. WPA manuscript on Clinton Co. Kentucky Archives, Frankfort, Ky.
967 Snyder, Ted. WPA manuscript on Limestone Springs. Kentucky Archives, Frankfort, Ky.
968 Sorrell, Mrs. Charlotte W. Student paper, Morehead State U., 1960.
969 Specht, Cliff. "History of the City of Southgate," 1939. Kenton Co. Public Library.
970 Steele, Willie. Student paper, Morehead State U., 1959.
971 Stevens, C. W. Manuscript on Grahn, Ky. In the possession of Christine McGlone, Grayson, Ky.
972 Stewart, Manning. Papers. Special Collections, Murray State U. Library.
973 Stewart, Thelma. Student paper, Morehead State U., ca. 1960.
974 Stone, May. "Origin of Names of Places and Streams in Some Eastern Kentucky Counties." DAR manuscript, 1941. Kentucky Hist. Soc.
975 Stuart, Col. T. G. Manuscript on Clark Co., Ky., place names, originally included in a letter to William G. Steel by E. G. Kingsbury, Sept. 21, 1923.
976 Sturgill, John I. WPA manuscript on Floyd Co. places. Kentucky Archives, Frankfort, Ky.
977 Sumpter, Mrs. W. C. Manuscript on Warren Co. and Bowling Green, Ky. Kentucky Library, Western Kentucky U.
978 Tarter, James L. "Name Places, in Local Historical Research." Collection of term papers, Somerset Community College, prepared and edited by Edgar Spitzke, Jr., 1966.
979 Thompson, Mrs. Dudley. Manuscript history of Mackville, 1940. Kentucky Hist. Soc.
980 Thompson, Mrs. Geneva. Student paper, Morehead State U., 1965.
981 Thornsberry, Terry L. Student paper, Prestonsburg Community College, 1972.
982 Tipton, French. "Chronology of Madison County." Townsend Collection, Eastern Kentucky U.
983 Towles, Susan Starling. Manuscript history of Henderson, Ky. ca. 1920s.
984 "Towns and Villages." WPA manuscript on Kenton Co. place names. Kentucky Archives, Frankfort, Ky.
985 Truesdell, C. B. Manuscript on Campbell Co. place names, 1949. Kenton Co. Public Library.
986 Turner, William. Student paper, Prestonsburg Community College, 1972.
987 United States Board on Geographic Names. Appeal to the Board from W. S. Massa of the Tennessee Valley Authority, for a name change from Calvert to Calvert City, Apr. 29, 1954.
988 ______. Correspondence between McCracken Co. officials and the Executive Secretary, B.G.N., May 1938.
989 ______. Controversial Names Report. Submitted to B.G.N., Mar. 1960.

990 ______. Mar. 1961.
991 ______. ca. 1964.
992 ______. Decision List, No. 5701, May 1957, 5.
993 ______. No. 6602, (1966), p. 11.
994 ______. No. 7803 (July–Sept. 1978), p. 14.
995 ______. Domestic Case Brief. Prepared for B.G.N., Feb. 8, 1950.
996 ______. Sept. 25, 1959.
997 ______. Domestic Geographic Name Proposal. Submitted to B.G.N., Feb. 23, 1965.
998 ______. Aug. 18, 1965.
999 ______. June 22, 1967.
1000 ______. Sept. 26, 1967.
1001 ______. June 12, 1968.
1002 ______. Domestic Geographic Name Report. Submitted to B.G.N., Dec. 1966.
1003 ______. Jan. 23, 1969.
1004 ______. Feb. 26, 1970.
1005 Walker, Garnet. "Weaverton—Circa 1897," 1976.
1006 Walters, Glenda. Student paper, Prestonsburg Community College, 1970.
1007 Webb, Hazel C. "An Interesting Story About Maud," 1969.
1008 Wheeldon, Jeffrey. Student paper, Campbellsville College, 1967. Folklore Archives, Western Kentucky U.
1009 Wigginton, Seth. Manuscript on Centerville, Ky.
1010 Wilhoit, Rupert. Manuscript. In the possession of Mrs. Christine McGlone, Grayson, Ky.
1011 Wilkerson, James Ralph. WPA manuscript on Ft. Jefferson, Ky. Kentucky Archives, Frankfort, Ky.
1012 ______. WPA manuscript on Monkeys Eyebrow. Kentucky Archives, Frankfort, Ky.
1013 Williamson, Edna. Student paper, Pikeville College, 1974.
1014 WPA manuscript on McCracken Co. Kentucky Archives, Frankfort, Ky.
1015 Yarbrough, Ronald Edward. "A Geographic Study of a Micro Region in Appalachia—The Clover Fork River Valley of Harlan County, Ky." Ph.D. Diss., University of Tennessee, 1972, 43–45.

LETTERS TO THE AUTHOR

1016 Allen, Eugene. Ruth Ky., Mar. 20, 1969, Feb. 9, 1970.
1017 Allen, Golden. Baptist, Ky., Mar. 3, 1980.
1018 Anderson, Thomas. Mt. Sterling, Ky., Sept. 30, 1980.
1019 Annis, Wendell. Logansport, Ky., Apr. 25, 1980.
1020 Ashley, L. E. N. Brooklyn, N.Y., Aug. 29, 1980.
1021 Banks, J. H. Viper, Ky., Feb. 4, 1980, Sept. 22, 1980.
1022 Barnes, Arnold, Fryer, Ky., Aug. 9, 1979.
1023 Bartley, Linda (postmaster). Jonancy, Ky., Nov. 21, 1980.
1024 Beach, Mrs. James. Franklin, Ky., Sept. 8, 1978.
1025 Beck, Nancy S. Princeton, Ky., Jan. 20, 1979.
1026 Benge, Elizabeth L. Coalgood, Ky., May 17, 1980.
1027 Benton, Raymond. Caney, Ky., June 11, 1979.

1028 Boling, Gladys (postmaster). Lackey, Ky., May 21, 1969, June 12, 1969.
1029 Boone, Sr. Regina. Maple Mount, Ky., Aug. 7, 1979.
1030 Bowling, Mrs. James. Essie, Ky., Mar. 5, 1969.
1031 Boyd, Ben P. Boaz, Ky., Sept. 6, 1979.
1032 Boyd, Hazel. Mt. Sterling, Ky., Aug. 25, 1977.
1033 Branham, Blanche. Millard, Ky., Feb. 20, 1981.
1034 Branscum, Zelma. Kidder, Ky., Sept. 17, 1976.
1035 Brantley, Bonnie. Dunbar, Ky., May 10, 1980.
1036 Brown, Mary Frances. Taylorsville, Ky., Dec. 1, 1980.
1037 Brown, Roberta. Louisville, Ky., Aug. 25, 1977.
1038 Bryant, Elizabeth (postmaster). Rogers, Ky., July 9, 1980, Nov. 8, 1980.
1039 Bullock, Jessie M. Science Hill, Ky., Jan. 21, 1980.
1040 Burkhart, Fred. Liberty, Ky., Feb. 1, 1971, Feb. 17, 1971.
1041 Calico, Forrest. Lancaster, Ky., May 21, 1969.
1042 Campbell, Bernice Treadway. Fall Rock, Ky., May 3, 1969.
1043 Cann, Roy A. Munfordville, Ky., June 29, 1971.
1044 Cawood, Edward. Harlan, Ky., Apr. 20, 1979.
1045 Childers, Dorothy, M. H. Thelma, Ky., Jan. 12, 1970.
1046 Chism, Robert W. Ekron, Ky., Apr. 14, 1980.
1047 Clark, Charles F. Hueysville, Ky., June 11, 1980.
1048 Clark, Sallye L. Prestonsburg, Ky., June 4, 1980.
1049 Clay, Mary E. (postmaster). Saldee, Ky., Mar. 11, 1981.
1050 Conrard, Charles A., Jr. Holmes Beach, Fla., Jan. 30, 1980.
1051 Cowen, Olen (postmaster). Cubage, Ky., Apr. 7, 1980.
1052 Creech, Vicki R. (postmaster). Dizney, Ky., May 27, 1980.
1053 Curnutte, Georgia Lee. Louisa, Ky., May 11, 1969.
1054 De Jong, Betty. Gray Hawk, Ky., Apr. 10, 1969.
1055 Dunn, D. Y. Murray, Ky., Mar. 5, 1980, Apr. 2, 1980, Apr. 9, 1980.
1056 Dunn, Mrs. Lonnie. Stella, Ky., Jan. 23, 1969.
1057 Easterling, Joan. Oldtown, Ky., July 14, 1971.
1058 Eldridge, Mrs. Donnie. Pineville, Ky., Apr. 22, 1980.
1059 Epperson, Robert. Kaliopi, Ky., Apr. 12, 1980.
1060 Evans, George. Lexington, Ky., Feb. 18, 1981.
1061 Fannin, Mabel A. Little Sandy, Ky., June 10, 1969.
1062 First, Janis R. Alexandria, Ky., Aug. 27, 1980.
1063 Flanary, Ron. Big Stone Gap, Va., June 26, 1980.
1064 Fletcher, Olan. Wolverine, Ky., Apr. 24, 1980, May 9, 1980.
1065 Floyd, Wilma E. Portsmouth, Ohio, Feb. 5, 1981.
1066 Former Postmaster. Relief, Ky., Aug. 22, 1980.
1067 Foster, Mary E. Chattanooga, Tenn., Jan. 3, 1979.
1068 Fox, Philip, Sr. Barbourville, Ky., June 27, 1978.
1069 Francis, Robert K. Yalesville, Ct., Mar. 19, 1969.
1070 Frymire, Margaret. Ekron, Ky., Apr. 10, 1980.
1071 Garland, Beckham, Bimble, Ky., Oct. 18, 1979.
1072 Gilbert, Russell (postmaster). Irvine, Ky., Jan. 23, 1970.
1073 Gilliam, Claud. Lamero, Ky., Jan. 22, 1980.
1074 Good, Alma. Melber, Ky., Aug. 11, 1980.
1075 Good, Otto B. (mayor). Melbourne, Ky., Nov. 2, 1980.
1076 Grise, Robert N. Richmond, Ky., Nov. 14, 1979.

1077 Hackney, Bernice. Fedscreek, Ky., Oct. 20, 1980.
1078 Hall, David H. Bardstown, Ky., Aug. 5, 1980.
1079 Hall, W. R. Hazard, Ky., Jan. 12, 1980.
1080 Hamer, Pauline. Livingston, Ky., Jan. 5, 1981.
1081 Hamilton, Ethel (postmaster). Grethel, Ky., Feb. 18, 1970.
1082 Hatmaker, Bertha. Lexington, Ky., July 8, 1980.
1083 Hibbs, Clifford L. Fairdale, Ky., Oct. 23, 1980.
1084 Higgins, J. W. Salyersville, Ky., Mar. 24, 1980.
1085 Hobbs, Dorcas M. Pikeville, Ky., Jan. 7, 1981.
1086 Hockenberry, Mabel Bowen. Echols, Ky., Dec. 29, 1979, Jan. 21, 1980, Feb. 6, 1980.
1087 Holman, James R. (postmaster). Provo, Ky., May 9, 1980.
1088 Holt, Elvis. Clay, Ky., Feb. 26, 1980.
1089 Hood, Keith H. Bedford, Ky., July 18, 1979, Aug. 1, 1979.
1090 Hood, Wallace T. Prospect, Ky., July 8, 1980.
1091 Jackson, Evelyn. Ashland, Ky., Sept. 19, 1972.
1092 ______. Oct. 7, 1973.
1093 Johnstone, Mrs. J. J. Irvine, Ky., Jan. 23, 1970.
1094 Kingsmore, Louise. Louisa, Ky., Mar. 27, 1969.
1095 ______. Feb. 27, 1979.
1096 ______. Mar. 26, 1979.
1097 ______. Apr. 6, 1979.
1098 ______. Apr. 8, 1979.
1099 Klinefelter, Gerald R. Brightshade, Ky., Mar. 16, 1969, May 20, 1980.
1100 Lacy, W. E. Jamestown, Ky., Mar. 7, 1969.
1101 Lott, Will. Owensboro, Ky., Jan. 11, 1980.
1102 Lucas, Ann (officer-in-charge, post office). Jetson, Ky., May 6, 1980.
1103 Lykins, Beulah Faye. Vanceburg, Ky., Feb. 3, 1973.
1104 McGann, Sr. Agnes Geraldine. Nazareth, Ky., Dec. 21, 1979.
1105 Manning, Iva J. Morehead, Ky., June 5, 1969, Sept. 1, 1969.
1106 Martin, Sandra. Dunbar, Ky., Apr. 30, 1980.
1107 Mason, C. R. Bristol, Va., July 19, 1979.
1108 Maynard, R. B. McCombs, Ky., July 4, 1979.
1109 Meadows, Larry. Clay City, Ky., Feb. 7, 1980.
1110 Meece, S. V. Russell Springs, Ky., Oct. 16, 1969.
1111 Messer, Lucille. Arjay, Ky., Mar. 31, 1980.
1112 Miller, Alice Meade. Kite, Ky., Apr. 8, 1971.
1113 Mills, Delta. Burnside, Ky., Jan. 9, 1980, Jan. 15, 1980, Jan. 25, 1980.
1114 Moore, Allen. Butterfly, Ky., May 30, 1969.
1115 Murphy, Dorothy. West Liberty, Ky., Feb. 2, 1970.
1116 Nicholson, Dorothy (postmaster). Grace, Ky., Aug. 5, 1966.
1117 O'Brien, Robert W. (director of Corporate Relations, Illinois Central Gulf Railroad). Chicago, Ill., Jan. 31, 1980.
1118 Owings, Lucille Bryars. Columbus, Ky., Mar. 16, 1979.
1119 Pelphry, Dr. Charles. Olive Hill, Ky., Dec. 22, 1980.
1120 Pennington, John. Webbville, Ky., Dec. 30, 1969, Mar. 7, 1970.
1121 Perkins, J. B. (postmaster). Nevisdale, Ky., Mar. 4, 1980.
1122 Porter, Mrs. Paul. Summersville, W. Va., Jan. 7, 1981.
1123 Postmaster. Argo, Ky., Dec. 1, 1980.
1124 Postmaster. Benham, Ky., May 15, 1980.

1125 Postmaster. Blairs Mills, Ky., Aug. 28, 1980.
1126 Postmaster. Crutchfield, Ky., Sept. 26, 1980.
1127 Postmaster. Elk Horn, Ky., Oct. 29, 1980.
1128 Postmaster. Riverside, Ky., Nov. 18, 1980.
1129 Postmaster. Rousseau, Ky., May 7, 1980.
1130 Postmaster. Sassafras, Ky., Oct. 6, 1980.
1131 Postmaster. Ulysses, Ky., Sept. 19, 1980.
1132 Postmaster. West Paducah, Ky., Aug. 5, 1980.
1133 Postmaster. Yocum, Ky., Aug. 22, 1980.
1134 Preston, Clell. Tutor Key, Ky., Dec. 4, 1971.
1135 Reed, B. F. Drift, Ky., Nov. 6, 1980.
1136 Reed, Rev. and Mrs. Grant. Lily, Ky., Feb. 13, 1970.
1137 Reynolds, Ervel. Culver City, Cal., June 4, 1969, July 18, 1969.
1138 Roberts, Leonard. Pikeville, Ky., Nov. 12, 1980.
1139 Rowland, Bertha. West Liberty, Ky., Sept. 6, 1980.
1140 Royal, Elva Payton. Louisville, Ky., Dec. 26, 1978, Jan. 7, 1979.
1141 Rudder, Julie Lee (postmaster). Marydell, Ky., Mar. 18, 1970.
1142 Runyon, Clyde. Belfry, Ky., Dec. 3, 1979.
1143 ______. Dec. 13, 1979.
1144 Russell, Sue T. Windsor, Ky., Mar. 12, 1969.
1145 Scalf, Henry P. Stanville, Ky., Jan. 22, 1974.
1146 Scott, Mrs. Albert (former postmaster). Pinsonfork, Ky., Feb. 4, 1970.
1147 Sebastian, Lillie. Sebastians Branch, Ky., Apr. 13, 1980.
1148 Shakertown Revisited, Inc. Harrodsburg, Ky., ca. 1972.
1149 Sharp, Ann R. Grays Knob, Ky., Apr. 28, 1969.
1150 Skaggs, Bertha. Brownsville, Ky., May 13, 1979.
1151 Slayden, Hodge. Salem, Ky., Sept. 25, 1979.
1152 Smith, Dorothy E. Louisville, Ky., July 9, 1969.
1153 Smith, Paul T. Woodbury, Ky., Apr. 24, 1980, Apr. 30, 1980.
1154 Sorrell, Clint. Mariba, Ky., Dec. 12, 1979.
1155 Stanley, Oma (postmaster). Laura, Ky., Jan. 17, 1981.
1156 Story, R. P. Rowena, Ky., June 11, 1969.
1157 Suell, Robert M. Nicholasville, Ky., Mar. 24, 1978.
1158 Sumpter, Irene. Bowling Green, Ky., Sept. 17, 1978.
1159 Suter, Aileen (postmaster). Perry Park, Ky., Jan. 9, 1980.
1160 Tanner, Douglas. Charlottesville, Va., Apr. 26, 1979.
1161 Taylor, Mabel H. Henderson Settlement, Frakes, Ky., Feb. 24, 1969.
1162 Thomas, Dr. Frank C. Stearns, Ky., Jan. 29, 1979.
1163 ______. Jan. 29, 1979, Aug. 7, 1980.
1164 Turner, Woodrow. Altro, Ky., Apr. 28, 1980.
1165 Walker, Garnet. Monticello, Ky., Aug. 13, 1975, Feb. 23, 1976.
1166 Walser, John A. Louisville, Ky., Dec. 1, 1980.
1167 ______. Jan. 9, 1981.
1168 ______. Jan. 9, 1981, Jan. 26, 1981.
1169 Ward, Millard (postmaster). Hode, Ky., July 9, 1980.
1170 Weaver, Mary. Somerset, Ky., Sept. 1, 1979.
1171 Weddington, Bertha. Emma, Ky., Aug. 15, 1966.
1172 Wells, J. K. Paintsville, Ky., Mar. 2, 1981.
1173 Whitfield, B. W., Jr. Ages-Brookside, Ky., June 28, 1980, May 11, 1979.
1174 Williams, Betty. Dixon, Ky., May 1, 1979.

1175 Williams, Cratis D. Boone, N.C., Jan. 24, 1972.
1176 Williams, Mrs. Oscar. Versailles, Ky., Apr. 9, 1980.
1177 Williamson, Wallace J. Ashland, Ky., Oct. 28, 1970, Mar. 8, 1971.
1178 Wilson, Nila. Russell Springs, Ky., Feb. 9, 1981.
1179 Wireman, Austin. Fredville, Ky., Mar. 6, 1969.
1180 Wireman, Connie A. Fredville, Ky., June 3, 1979.
1181 ______. Mar. 20, 1980.
1182 Wood, Kathy. Paducah, Ky., Sept. 5, 1978.
1183 Woolum, Edna (former postmaster). Jenson, Ky., Apr. 2, 1980.
1184 Wright, John C. N. Redington Beach, Fla., Oct. 31, 1978.
1185 Wright, John G. Warsaw, Ky., Sept. 9, 1971.

OTHER UNPUBLISHED CORRESPONDENCE

1186 Baker, W. E. Hazard, Ky. To William G. Steel, Apr. 21, 1922. U.S. Board of Geographic Names, Reston, Va.
1187 Burrill, Meredith, U.S. Board on Geographic Names. To the Kentucky secretary of state, Jan. 13, 1950. Kentucky Archives, Frankfort, Ky.
1188 Catron, John M. (postmaster). Ault, Ky. To William G. Steel, Apr. 20, 1925. U.S. Board on Geographic Names, Reston, Va.
1189 Champion, H. B. Hampton, Ky. To William G. Steel, Sept. 21, 1923. U.S. Board on Geographic Names, Reston, Va.
1190 Crank, Raymond D. Folsom, Calif. To Kentucky Hist. Soc., July 19, 1977. Kentucky Hist. Soc.
1191 Crump, Malcolm H. Bowling Green, Ky. To William G. Steel, Apr. 20, 1922. U.S. Board on Geographic Names, Reston, Va.
1192 Farmer, Stephen (postmaster). Herd, Ky. To William G. Steel, Oct. 13, 1923. U.S. Board on Geographic Names, Reston, Va.
1193 Gill, Thomas L. (postmaster). Knob Creek, Ky. To William G. Steel, Apr. 20, 1925. U.S. Board on Geographic Names, Reston, Va.
1194 Hammond, James W. Ashland, Ky. To Louise Kingsmore, Louisa, Ky., Mar. 22, 1979.
1195 Hardin, Bayless. Kentucky Hist. Soc. To C. Stewart Peterson, Baltimore, Md., Aug. 18, 1937.
1196 Howard, Mrs. Katie G. Cobb, Ky. To William G. Steel, May 18, 1925. U.S. Board on Geographic Names, Reston, Va.
1197 Hull, Fred (postmaster). Galveston, Ky. To William G. Steel, Oct. 10, 1923. U.S. Board on Geographic Names, Reston, Va.
1198 Kiddle, T. M. (assistant postmaster). Pikeville, Ky. To William G. Steel, Apr. 19, 1930. U.S. Board on Geographic Names, Reston, Va.
1199 Mathis, E. C. (Nashville Chattanooga and St. Louis Railroad agent). Murray, Ky. To C. B. Trevathan, Nashville, Tenn., Sept. 13, 1941 (from information supplied to him by Kit Redden, an early Dexter, Ky., druggist, 1914). Manning Stewart papers, Special Collections, Murray State U. Library.
1200 Mavity, John. Vanceburg, Ky. To William G. Steel, May 19, 1922. U.S. Board on Geographic Names, Reston, Va.
1201 Mellekan, E. W. (assistant postmaster). Aflex, Ky. To William G. Steel, Sept. 21, 1923. U.S. Board on Geographic Names, Reston, Va.
1202 Mobley, Harve. Washington, D.C. To Wallace J. Williamson, Feb. 20, 1973.

1203 Personnel Director, Blue Diamond Coal Co. To Rep. Carl Perkins (Dem., Ky.), Feb. 2, 1949.
1204 Postmaster. Adolphus, Ky. To William G. Steel, Oct. 2, 1923. U.S. Board on Geographic Names, Reston, Va.
1205 Postmaster. Ballot, Ky. To William G. Steel, Nov. 30, 1925. U.S. Board on Geographic Names, Reston, Va.
1206 Postmaster. Barbourville, Ky. To William G. Steel, May 31, 1922. U.S. Board on Geographic Names, Reston, Va.
1207 Postmaster. Mary Alice, Ky. To Robert K. Francis, Yalesville, Ct., n.d.
1208 Postmaster. Williamsburg, Ky. To William G. Steel, May 16, 1922. U.S. Board on Geographic Names, Reston, Va.
1209 Pryor, Helen R. Detroit, Mich. To Thomas P. Field, U. Kentucky, Jan. 27, 1970.
1210 Smallwood, Robert S. (editor of the Beattyville, Ky., *Enterprise*). To L. C. Turner (district supervisor, *The American Guide,* WPA), London, Ky., Apr. 1936. Kentucky Archives, Frankfort, Ky.
1211 Smith, H. M. (postmaster). Fonthill, Ky. To William G. Steel, Mar. 15, 1930. U.S. Board on Geographic Names, Reston, Va.
1212 Smith, Molly Hunter. To Alexander Cather, Drakesboro, Ky., Apr. 20, 1972.
1213 Stevens, M. M. Greenup, Ky. To William G. Steel, Apr. 20, 1922. U.S. Board on Geographic Names, Reston, Va.
1214 Thatcher, A. Morgantown, Ky. To William G. Steel, May 10, 1922. U.S. Board on Geographic Names, Reston, Va.
1215 Tilford, N. C. L. Leitchfield, Ky. To William G. Steel, Apr. 24, 1922. U.S. Board on Geographic Names, Reston, Va.
1216 Trafton, Spalding. Henderson, Ky. To William G. Steel, Apr. 20, 1922. U.S. Board on Geographic Names, Reston, Va.
1217 Trosper, J. S..Allais, Ky. To William G. Steel, Feb. 27, 1930. U.S. Board on Geographic Names, Reston, Va.
1218 Webb, N. M. Whitesburg, Ky. To William G. Steel, Apr. 22, 1922. U.S. Board on Geographic Names, Reston, Va.
1219 Wilson, Dr. R. W. Lebanon, Ky. To William G. Steel, June 19, 1930. U.S. Board on Geographic Names, Reston, Va.

PERSONAL INTERVIEWS BY THE AUTHOR

1220 Allen, Beatrice. Russell Springs, Ky. Nov. 26, 1971.
1221 Arnett, Maralea. Corydon, Ky. Oct. 19, 1978.
1222 Bach, J. Everett. Jackson, Ky. June 30, 1978.
1223 Baker, Floyd. Winchester, Ky. Apr. 23, 1973.
1224 Balden, Mrs. William. Danville, Ky. Aug. 23, 1978.
1225 Ballard, Pat. Lancaster, Ky. Apr. 21, 1978.
1226 Banks, J. H. Viper, Ky. Feb. 11, 1980.
1227 Barnes, Mrs. Floyd. Cynthiana, Ky. Nov. 12, 1977.
1228 Barton, Lon Carter. Mayfield, Ky. Aug. 5, 1977.
1229 Bell, Earl. Morganfield, Ky. Aug. 27, 1978.
1230 Bell, Ethel. Falmouth, Ky. Oct. 17, 1978.
1231 Bertram, Robert, and Flora Bertram. Sunnybrook, Ky. Aug. 11, 1975.
1232 Blackburn, E. J. Williamstown, Ky. Apr. 30, 1978.
1233 Blair, Richard. Jamestown, Ky. Nov. 27, 1971.

1234 Boone, George. Elkton, Ky. July 23, 1971.
1235 ______. July 20, 1972.
1236 Booth, Hazel. Campton, Ky. Aug. 11, 1978.
1237 Boyd, Hazel. Mt. Sterling, Ky. June 23, 1977.
1238 Bradley, Hiram. Vest, Ky. June 18, 1979.
1239 Brown, Mary Frances. Little Mount, Ky. July 15, 1978.
1240 Brumley, Edith. Brooksville, Ky. Apr. 15, 1978.
1241 Burgin, Welby. Stanford, Ky. Apr. 29, 1978.
1242 Burris, Claude. Monticello, Ky. Aug. 27, 1973.
1243 Bussell, Opp, Jr. Lawrenceburg, Ky. Apr. 29, 1978.
1244 Buster, W. E. Monticello, Ky. Nov. 4, 1974.
1245 Calloway, James. Bowling Green, Ky. Nov. 5, 1977.
1246 Calvert, Jean. Maysville, Ky. June 25, 1977.
1247 Campbell, Odell. Monticello, Ky. July 21, 1973, Dec. 5, 1976.
1248 Campbell, R. B. Hyden, Ky. May 27, 1978.
1249 Carey, Marie. Louisa, Ky. Oct. 14, 1977.
1250 Cargo, Faye. Grayson, Ky. Nov. 18, 1977.
1251 Carter, Charles. Mt. Vernon, Ky. Apr. 29, 1978.
1252 Castner, Charles. Louisville, Ky. Mar. 21, 1972.
1253 Cather, Alexander. Drakesboro, Ky. Apr. 21, 1978.
1254 Caudill, Harry M. Whitesburg, Ky. July 26, 1971.
1255 Chambers, Col. Robert G. Nicholasville, Ky. Jan. 11, 1972.
1256 Chilton, Ashley. Pleasureville, Ky. Mar. 26, 1979.
1257 Chitwood, J. C. Danville, Ky. June 22, 1978.
1258 Chriswell, Lyle. Monticello, Ky. Aug. 6, 1974.
1259 Cobb, Glada. Manchester, Ky. June 29, 1977.
1260 Coleman, Marie. Brandenburg, Ky. Aug. 23, 1978.
1261 Coleman, Zach. Center, Ky. July 20, 1978.
1262 Combs, Lucille. Mallie, Ky. Mar. 9, 1979.
1263 Conner, Eva. Albany, Ky. Mar. 22, 1979.
1264 Conover, Rebecca. Harrodsburg, Ky. Apr. 21, 1978.
1265 Cornett, William T. Whitesburg, Ky. Dec. 24, 1977.
1266 Cottongim, Mrs. Lewis. Shelbyville, Ky. Oct. 28, 1977.
1267 Crawford, John L. Corbin, Ky. June 22, 1978.
1268 Cruse, Susan. Hodgenville, Ky. Oct. 18, 1978.
1269 Davis, Lucile S. Lexington, Ky. July 15, 1978.
1270 Davis, Newton. Lexington, Ky. July 15, 1978.
1271 Davis, Mrs. Philip. Mt. Vernon, Ky. Apr. 29, 1978.
1272 Davis, Roscoe. Hazard, Ky. July 29, 1978.
1273 Dean, Lloyd. Morehead, Ky. Oct. 3, 1977.
1274 Denney, Schuyler, and Clarence Denney. Monticello, Ky. Aug. 11, 1975.
1275 Duff, Lionel. Decoy, Ky. Dec. 5, 1960.
1276 Dunn, Shirley. Stanford, Ky. Apr. 29, 1978.
1277 Easterling, Joan. Oldtown, Ky. July 14, 1971.
1278 Eldred, Olive, and Nancy Beck. Princeton, Ky. Oct. 1, 1977.
1279 Edmiston, Mr. & Mrs. C. Evan. Danville, Ky. Aug. 5, 1978.
1280 Elliott, Joan. Hunter, Ky. Fall 1970.
1281 Eubank, Mildred, and Jewell Eubank. Franklin, Ky. July 22, 1978.

1282 Ewell, Logan. London, Ky Apr. 29, 1972.
1283 Fig, Don. Stanton, Ky. June 17, 1978.
1284 Fitzgerald, Anna. Florence, Ky. May 21, 1979.
1285 Fletcher, Bill. Bowling Green, Ky. Sept. 1, 1978.
1286 Frost, John. Susie, Ky. Nov. 3, 1974.
1287 Gabbard, Fred. Booneville, Ky. July 8, 1977.
1288 Gayhart, Wilma. Emmalena, Ky. Nov. 25, 1978.
1289 Giles, Henry. Knifley, Ky. Mar. 22, 1979.
1290 Goin, Kenneth. Frankfort, Ky. July 14, 1978.
1291 Gorin, Betty Jane. Campbellsville, Ky. Oct. 18, 1978.
1292 Greene, Alma. Owenton, Ky. May 20, 1978.
1293 Griffith, Mattie. Georgetown, Ky. Apr. 8, 1978.
1294 Grise, Robert N. Richmond, Ky. Apr. 28, 1978.
1295 Grove, Jimmy. Elkton, Ky. July 21, 1972.
1296 Guthrie, Blaine. Louisville, Ky. Apr. 4, 1978.
1297 Hagan, Pat. Tompkinsville, Ky. June 29, 1972.
1298 Hardwick, Mrs. Wendell. Betsey, Ky. July 24, 1973.
1299 Harp, Kenneth. Manchester, Ky. Mar. 24, 1979.
1300 Hartman, Margaret S. Alexandria, Ky. May 22, 1979.
1301 Hensley, Bige. Manchester, Ky. Sept. 26, 1969.
1302 Hicks, Mollie. Monticello, Ky. Nov. 3, 1974.
1303 Hicks, O. M. Monticello, Ky. Nov. 3, 1974.
1304 Hightower, W. Claude. Claymour, Ky. July 24, 1972.
1305 Hobson, Cora. Ligon, Ky. Apr. 29, 1971.
1306 Howell, Carl. Hodgenville, Ky. Oct. 18, 1978.
1307 Hughes, William. Leitchfield, Ky. Sept. 28, 1977.
1308 Hume, Mrs. Hattie C. Stearns, Ky. Oct. 16, 1971.
1309 Hurt, Larry. Powersburg, Ky. May 4, 1975.
1310 Jackson, Clara. Jackson, Ky. June 30, 1978.
1311 Jackson, Evelyn Scyphers. Ashland, Ky. May 6, 1977.
1312 Jackson, Harry. Bowling Green, Ky. Aug. 31, 1978.
1313 Jones, Earl. Hodgenville, Ky. Oct. 18, 1978.
1314 Kelly, Mary D. Springfield, Ky. Aug. 10, 1977.
1315 Kidd, Leon. Center, Ky. July 20, 1978.
1316 Klein, Theodore. Crestwood, Ky. Apr. 7, 1978.
1317 Lair, John. Renfro Valley, Ky. Aug. 13, 1971.
1318 Lannom, Lester. Guthrie, Ky. July 20, 1972.
1319 LaRue, Jim. Hodgenville, Ky. Oct. 18, 1978.
1320 Ledbetter, Harold. Madisonville, Ky. Oct. 1, 1977.
1321 Lewis, Mr. and Mrs. Robert. Owingsville, Ky. June 24, 1977.
1322 Lusby, J. Lowell. Grayson, Ky. Sept. 23, 1977.
1323 Lyons, W. P., and Gladys Lyons. Monticello, Ky. May 4, 1975.
1324 McDonald, Braxton. Marion, Ky. Aug. 28, 1978.
1325 McDonald, Roy. Cadiz, Ky. Aug. 29, 1978.
1326 McGlone, Christine. Grayson, Ky. Nov. 18, 1977.
1327 McIntyre, Estill. Hazard, Ky. July 7, 1977.
1328 Marsh, Nell. Monticello, Ky. Aug. 5, 1974.
1329 Martin, Marion. Manchester, Ky. June 29, 1977.

1330 Masterson, Mary, and Ruth Adkinson. Carrollton, Ky. May 20, 1978.
1331 Matera, Ann. Horse Cave, Ky. July 21, 1978.
1332 Mayfield, C. D. Hawesville, Ky. Aug. 24, 1978.
1333 Maynard, Lucille. Wurtland, Ky. Aug. 18, 1977.
1334 Meadows, Larry. Clay City, Ky. Nov. 30, 1977.
1335 Milward, Burton. Lexington, Ky. Apr. 27, 1978.
1336 Minner, Niles. Tolu, Ky. Aug. 28, 1978.
1337 Mofield, Ray. Benton, Ky. Aug. 4, 1977, Aug. 28, 1978.
1338 Moore, Jack. Tyner, Ky. July 9, 1977.
1339 Moore, Sam. Greensburg, Ky. July 20, 1978.
1340 Morgan, Kelly. Manchester, Ky. Mar. 24, 1979.
1341 Morgan, Nyla. Morgantown, Ky. Oct. 19, 1978.
1342 Morgan, Ona. Williamstown, Ky. Apr. 30, 1978.
1343 Morningstar, Jane. Bowling Green, Ky. Sept. 1, 1978.
1344 Morton, May Belle. Russellville, Ky. Nov. 6, 1977.
1345 Murray, Winnie P. Meta, Ky. May 16, 1971.
1346 Nickell, Lynn. West Liberty, Ky. Dec. 1, 1978.
1347 O'Quinn, John S. Prestonsburg, Ky. Mar. 8, 1971.
1348 Orrahood, David, and Joyce Orrahood. Owensboro, Ky. Sept. 30, 1977.
1349 Owen, Kathryn. Winchester, Ky. June 1, 1977.
1350 Oxendine, Sherman. Barbourville, Ky. June 23, 1978.
1351 Pettit, Mary Grace. Princeton, Ky. Aug. 2, 1977.
1352 Pike, Burlyn. Louisville, Ky. Oct. 2, 1977.
1353 Pope, Arthur. Williamsport, Ky. Mar. 28, 1971.
1354 Powell, Eva. Elkhorn City, Ky. Aug. 16, 1977.
1355 Ragan, Charley. Susie, Ky. Nov. 3, 1974.
1356 Ramsey, Obie. Stop, Ky. July 12, 1975.
1357 Rankin, Sophronia. Monticello, Ky. Aug. 4, 1974.
1358 Ray, Jean. Henderson, Ky. Oct. 19, 1978.
1359 Rayburn, Helen. Vanceburg, Ky. June 20, 1977.
1360 Reed, Rufus. Lovely, Ky. July 4, 1971.
1361 ______. July 18, 1971.
1362 ______. Aug. 1, 1971.
1363 Richards, Frances, and Mary Ellen Richards. Franklin, Ky. May 17, 1972.
1364 Roberts, Edith. Pikeville, Ky. Apr. 3, 1969.
1365 Robinson, Lucien. Piqua, Ky. Apr. 22, 1972, Apr. 16, 1978.
1366 Roe, Thelma. Olive Hill, Ky. Nov. 18, 1977.
1367 Ross, Smith. Pine Knot, Ky. June 22, 1978.
1368 Rousseau, Vivian. Glasgow, Ky. Aug. 11, 1971.
1369 Royse, Martha. Poplar Plains, Ky. Sept. 26, 1977.
1370 Scalf, Henry P. Stanville, Ky. May 16, 1971.
1371 ______. May 28, 1971.
1372 Shackelford, Nevyle. Beattyville, Ky. July 8, 1978.
1373 Shannon, James. Richmond, Ky. Dec. 27, 1977.
1374 Shannon, Roy L. Lexington, Ky. Jan. 18, 1979.
1375 Shearer, Guy. Louisville, Ky. Jan. 19, 1974.
1376 Shearer, Ladonna. Hidalgo, Ky. Aug. 6, 1976.
1377 Shearer, Lynn. Hidalgo, Ky. Aug. 6, 1976.

1378 Members of the Shelby County Historical Society (at a picnic). Oct. 28, 1977.
1379 Shonert, Genevieve. Falmouth, Ky. Oct. 17, 1978.
1380 Siler, Eugene, Sr. Williamsburg, Ky. June 23, 1978.
1381 Simpson, Elizabeth. Monticello, Ky. Aug. 11, 1976.
1382 Singleton, Mary. Marion, Ky. Aug. 28, 1978.
1383 Slagle, Moah. Slickford, Ky. Aug. 11, 1975.
1384 Smith, Burris. Pine Knot, Ky. June 22, 1978.
1385 Smith, R. N. Burkesville, Ky. Sept. 22, 1978.
1386 Smith, Sarah B. Bardstown, Ky. Nov. 4, 1978.
1387 Spencer, Philip. Lawrenceburg, Ky. Aug. 4, 1978.
1388 Spradlin, Charles. Paintsville, Ky. Nov. 29, 1971.
1389 Stearns, Ina. Slickford, Ky. July 15, 1975.
1390 Suell, Robert M. Nicholasville, Ky. June 14, 1978.
1391 Sutton, Tom. Vest, Ky. June 18, 1979.
1392 Swain, Golda. Paintsville, Ky. May 21, 1971.
1393 ______. Mar. 24, 1973.
1394 Tackett, Lois. Amba, Ky. Apr. 19, 1971, Apr. 28, 1971.
1395 Taylor, Mae Carter. Tompkinsville, Ky. June 29, 1972.
1396 Taylor, Stanton. Tompkinsville, Ky. June 29, 1972.
1397 Thomas, Gladys, and Otis Thomas. Liberty, Ky. Sept. 21, 1978.
1398 Thompson, Bill. McDaniels, Ky. Sept. 28, 1977.
1399 Thompson, Gerald. St. Mary, Ky. Sept. 22, 1978.
14O0 Tinsley, Harry D. No Creek, Ky. Aug. 25, 1978.
1401 Tucker, Brown C. Kirksey, Ky. Aug. 4, 1977.
1402 Turner, Leonard. Monticello, Ky. Aug. 9, 1976.
1403 Turner, William T. Hopkinsville, Ky. Aug. 7, 1977.
1404 Unidentified informant. Eddyville, Ky. 1978.
1405 Walker, Garnet. Monticello, Ky. July 16, 1972.
1406 ______. July 23, 1973.
1407 ______. Aug. 9, 1974.
1408 ______. May 13, 1976.
1409 Warren, K. Sol. Barbourville, Ky. June 23, 1978.
1410 Weaver, Mary. Somerset, Ky. Mar. 23, 1979.
1411 Wells, J. K. Paintsville, Ky. Aug. 30, 1980.
1412 White, Bert, and Lucy White. Sandy Hook, Ky. July 28, 1978.
1413 White, Lynnie A. Monticello, Ky. Aug. 6, 1974.
1414 Whitley, Edna. Paris, Ky. Apr. 6, 1977.
1415 Williamson, Wallace J. Ashland, Ky. Mar. 6, 1971.
1416 Wilson, Dr. Edward S. Pineville, Ky. Nov. 27, 1978.
1417 Wilson, Gypsy. Pineville, Ky. Dec. 31, 1972.
1418 Wilson, Jess. McKee, Ky. July 9, 1977.
1419 Wilson, Vernon, and Maud Wilson. Peoples, Ky. July 9, 1977.
1420 Winstead, Mrs. T. D. Elizabethtown, Ky. Aug. 23, 1978.
1421 Wireman, Austin. Fredville, Ky. Apr. 20, 1979.
1422 Wireman, Connie A. Fredville, Ky. Apr. 20, 1979.
1423 Wiseman, Malvena. Eddyville, Ky. Aug. 29, 1978.
1424 Wright, Malvina, and Alfred Wright. Touristville, Ky. Aug. 10, 1976.
1425 York, Delbert. Annville, Ky. July 9, 1977.

OTHER INTERVIEWS

1426 Berley, Nancy. Columbia Ky. By Henry Giles, July 1979.

1427 Cheek, Mrs. Frank E. Lexington, Ky. By Thomas P. Field, May 1979.

1428 Clark, Helen. Lancaster, Ky. By Pat Ballard (for the Garrard County Oral History Project).

1429 Hall, Ermine. By Patti Rose (for the Alice Lloyd College Oral History Project), June 16, 1971.

1430 Kinder, Alice. Pikeville, Ky. By Leonard Roberts, Nov. 1980.

1431 Newman, Charlie. Hi Hat, Ky. By Luther Frazier (for the Alice Lloyd Oral History Project).

1432 Spurlock, Curt. Haddix, Ky. By Sandy Miller and Wanda Turner (for the Lees College Oral History Project).

1433 Sturgill, Alpha. Larkslane, Ky. By Judy Mullins and Sandra Richter (for the Alice Lloyd College Oral History Project), Aug. 9, 1972.

1434 Tharpe Everett. Christopher, Ky. By Mike Mullins (for the Alice Lloyd College Oral History Project), Jan. 21, 1972.

1435 Wampler, Walter. Mayking, Ky. By Kenny Garrett, Pikeville College (for Leonard Roberts).

1436 Nichols, Edna. Hodgenville, Ky. By the author, Oct. 18, 1978.

ADDENDA

1437 "Brief Outline of the Formation of Pike County and Pikeville, Ky." In *150 Years Pike County Kentucky, 1822–1972*, 7–8. Pikeville, Ky.: Pike Co. Hist. Soc., 1972.

1438 Burke, Faye Helvey. "Genealogical Information about the John Justice Family." In *150 Years Pike County* (see 1437), 81–83.

1439 "Carrsville Was Once Seat of Learning." In *Steamboat Days on the Cumberland.* Smithland, Ky.: Livingston Ledger, July 3, 1974.

1440 "Hampton Was Home of Academy." In ibid.

1441 Hart, Lochie B. "Origin of Names of the Towns in Calloway." *History of Calloway County*. Murray Ledger and Times, 1931.

1442 Henderson, K. H. "From Panhandle to Ledbetter." In *Steamboat Days* (see 1439).

1443 ______. "Smithland, Brawling River Town." In *Steamboat Days* (see 1439).

1444 Horne, Mrs. Jesse. "First Settlers on Robinson Creek." In *150 Years Pike County* (see 1437), 17–20.

1445 Ransom, Delmina. "Memories of Iuka." In *Steamboat Days* (see 1439).

1446 Wallace, James Sharon. Chap. 12 of *A Collection of Green County History,* 66. Compiled by Kate Powell Evans, Green Co. Library, 1976.

1447 *Russell Times,* Sept. 25, 1942.

1448 *Lincoln County Bicentennial, 1775–1975*. Stanford, Ky.: Interior Journal, 1975.

1449 "River Towns' Heyday Saw Steamboats and Shipping Surge in Prosperity along Owen's Western Border." *Owenton News-Herald,* Bicentennial ed., July 4, 1974, 7.

1450 Creason, Joe. *Louisville Courier-Journal,* June 23, 1971, B1.

1451 Savage, Bertha, and Jake Savage. Wurtland, Ky. Interview by the author. Aug. 18, 1977.

1452 *Casey County News,* Bicentennial ed., Aug. 29, 1974, sec. 2, p. 14.
1453 *Anderson News,* June, 1906, Souvenir supplement.
1454 *Rowan County News,* Centennial ed., May 10, 1956, 75.
1455 Burchell, Jimmy. Manchester, Ky. Interview by the author, Mar. 24, 1979.
1456 Roberts, Leonard. Notes on Pike County place names from material collected in the 1960s and 1970s. Pikeville College.
1457 Field, Willis W. "Clifton Was Once Known as Woodford City." *Woodford Sun,* Dec. 17, 1880.
1458 Nelson, Jackie. "Clifton: River Town Has Seen Many Wondrous Times." *Lexington Herald-Leader,* Sept. 12, 1976, Woodford section, 4.
1459 Chandler, Ben. "Happy Times." *Woodford Sun,* Dec. 1, 1972.
1460 Board on geographic names, Washington, D.C., Domestic geographic names report on Munk, Ky., n.d.
1461 William Littell, *The Statute Law of Kentucky,* 5 vols. (Frankfort, 1809–1819), 1:329–30.